Iowa Columbian Commission

**Report of the Iowa Columbian Commission**

Containing a full Statement of it Proceedings

Iowa Columbian Commission

**Report of the Iowa Columbian Commission**
*Containing a full Statement of it Proceedings*

ISBN/EAN: 9783337185589

Printed in Europe, USA, Canada, Australia, Japan

Cover: Foto ©ninafisch / pixelio.de

More available books at **www.hansebooks.com**

IOWA STATE BUILDING FROM THE SOUTH-EAST, FLAGS AT HALF MAST FOR THE DEATH OF MAYOR HARRISON.

# Iowa Columbian

# Commission,

CONTAINING A FULL STATEMENT OF ITS PROCEEDINGS,
INCLUDING A LIST OF ALL DISBURSEMENTS,
ACCOMPANIED BY COMPLETE VOUCHERS
THEREFOR.

## CHICAGO, A. D., 1893.

PUBLISHED BY THE COMMISSION.

CEDAR RAPIDS, IOWA.
REPUBLICAN PRINTING COMPANY, PRINTERS AND BINDERS,
1895.

## TABLE OF CONTENTS.

|  | PAGE |
|---|---|
| Letter of Transmission, | 7 |
| Report of the Commission, | 9 |
| Report of the Executive Committee, | 21 |
| Report of the Committee on Ceremonies, | 35 |
| Report of the Committee on Music, | 88 |
| Report of the Department of Live Stock, | 95 |
| Report of the Department of Agriculture, Dairy and Apiary, | 125 |
| Report of the Department of Horticulture, | 165 |
| Report of the Department of Minerals and Geology, | 177 |
| Report of the Department of the Press, | |
| Report of the Department of Woman's Work, | 188 |
| Report of the Department of Manufactures and Machinery, | 197 |
| Report of the Department of Education and Fine Arts, | 199 |
| Report of the Department of Forestry, Photography and Corn Food, | 214 |
| Report of the Committee on Archæological, Historical and Statistical Information, including discovery, settlement, boundaries geography and topography of Iowa, | 220 |
| Geology of the State, | 243 |
| Climatology, | 257 |
| Natural Resources, | 271 |
| Commercial Facilities, | 280 |
| Banking, Insurance and Taxation, | 286 |
| Legends of the Origin of Maize, | 297 |
| Live Stock, | 304 |
| Dairying, | 307 |
| Horticulture, | 309 |
| Native Flora, Forests and Artificial Groves | 314 |
| Manufacturing, | 318 |
| Work of the Fish Commisson, | 323 |
| Education, | 324 |
| Libraries, | 333 |
| Churches and Church Work, | 333 |
| Corn and and other Palaces, | 343 |
| Iowa Books and Authors, | 346 |
| Iowa at Expositions, | 358 |
| Iowa Population Tabulated, | 365 |
| State Government and Institutions, | 367 |
| Report of the Auditing Committee, | 378 |

## UNITED STATES COMMISSIONERS FOR IOWA.

PROF. W. F. KING.    COL. JOSEPH EIBOECK.

## ALTERNATE U. S. COMMISSIONERS FOR IOWA.

ANSWERING A REQUEST FOR HIS PHOTOGRAPH SAYS:

"I never have had, have not now and never expect to have the article you wish. Besides I have not the least desire 'to go rattling or thundering down the ages' posing as an alternate commissioner of the World's Fair."

JOHN HAYES.    C. E. WHITING.

To His Excellency Frank D. Jackson, Governor of Iowa:

SIR,—Chapter 116 of the laws of the 23d General Assembly, entitled "An act to provide for a creditable exhibit of the resources of the State of Iowa, in the Columbian Exposition, or the World's Fair, to be held in Chicago," approved April 15th, 1890, provides that "At the close of its services the Commission shall make to the Governor a statement of its proceedings, which shall include a list of all disbursements, with complete vouchers therefor attached."

In fulfillment of the statutory requirement, we have the honor to submit to your Excellency the following report, accompanied by the reports of all the Standing Committees and Commissioners in charge of departments, which show the plans of promotion and preparation, and the prosecution of the work committed to us by the Executive Council of the State, and are designed to be a complete history of Iowa at the World's Columbian Exposition of 1893, together with a full list of all disbursements and vouchers therefor.

Respectfully submitted,

JAMES O. CROSBY, President.
JOHN F. DUNCOMBE, Vice-President.
F. N. CHASE, Secretary.
WILLIAM HAMILTON DENT, Treasurer.
S. H. MALLORY,
S. B. PACKARD,    } Executive Com.
H. W. SEAMAN,
HENRY STIVERS,
CHARLES ASHTON,
J. W. JARNAGIN,
A. C. ROBERTS,

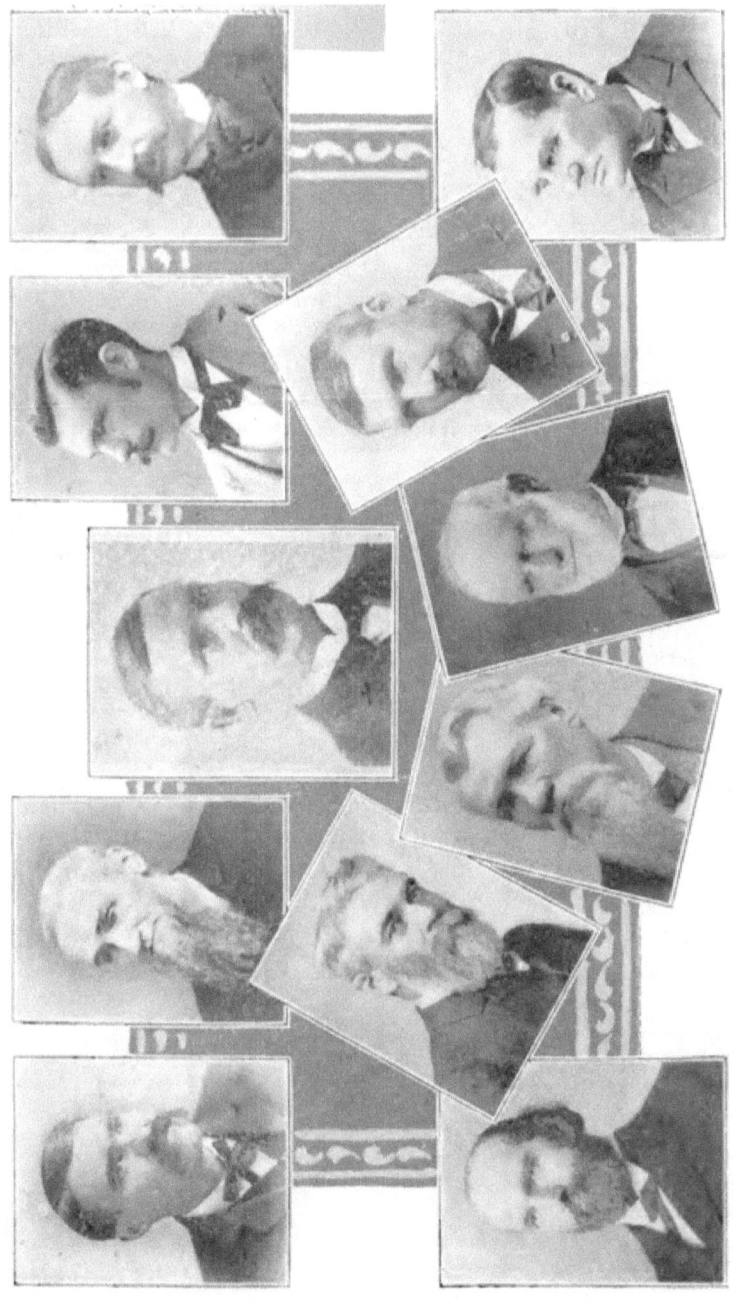

# Report of the Iowa Columbian Commission.

BY JAMES O. CROSBY.

*To his Excellency Frank D. Jackson, Governor of the State of Iowa:*

During the Exposition, pursuant to a resolution of the Commission, the committee on Archæological, Historical and Statistical information published "A Hand Book of Iowa," for general distribution from the Iowa State Building. A first edition of 20,000 copies was soon exhausted and a second edition of 5,000 was printed, and that too has been exhausted. The report of that committee is accompanied by a copy of the book and is herewith re-published. It contains the laws of the 23d and 24th General Assembly creating the Commission and making appropriations for its work, with a full account of the organization of the Commission, its officers, committees, and classification of departments of its work, to which reference is made without repetition here.

The second session of the Commission was held at Des Moines on the 15th day of October, 1890, when a set of rules was adopted that was published in pamphlet form, with the act of the 23d General Assembly and the act of Congress providing for the Exposition. The rules provided for regular sessions of the Commission to be held at the Capitol in Des Moines, on the first Wednesday of February, June and October. A committee was appointed to publish an address to the people of the state, in order to awaken an interest in preparing for a creditable representation of Iowa at the Exposition. Soon after President Harrison issued his proclamation setting forth that Chicago had complied with the requirements of the act of Congress, the committee issued the following address which was generally published in the newspapers of the state:

## The Iowa Columbian Commission,

*To the People of the State of Iowa:*

As it is fit and appropriate that the four hundredth anniversary of the discovery of America should be commemorated by an Exhibition of the resources of the United States of America, their development, and of the progress of civilization in the New World, the Congress of the United States has enacted "that an Exhibition of arts, industries, manufactures, and products of the soil, mine and sea, shall be inaugurated in the year 1892, in the city of Chicago, in the state of Illinois."

The President of the United States, in pursuance of said enactment, through the Department of State, has made Proclamation of the same, setting forth the time the Exposition will open and close, and in behalf of the Government and people has invited Foreign Nations to take part in said Exposition and appoint representatives thereto.

The buildings will be dedicated on the 12th day of October, 1892, with ceremonies appropriate to the four hundredth anniversary of the discovery of America by Christopher Columbus, and the Exposition will be open to visitors not later than the first day of May, 1893, and close not later than the 30th day of October thereafter.

The act of Congress provides that the Secretary of the Treasury shall cause to be erected, at a cost not exceeding $400,000, a suitable building in which there shall be exhibited from the Executive Departments, the Smithsonian Institution, the United States Fish Commission, and the National Museum, such articles and materials as illustrate the function and administrative faculty of the Government in time of peace, and its resources as a war power, tending to demonstrate the nature of our institutions and their adaptation to the wants of the people.

The Secretary of the Treasury is also directed to place on exhibition one of the Life Saving Stations authorized by existing laws to be constructed, and to cause the same to be fully equipped with all apparatus, furniture and appliances now in use in all life saving stations in the United States.

It is expected that Europe, Asia, Africa, Australia, Central, South and British America, the Islands of the Sea, and every State and Territory in our Union, will be represented with their finest productions of "arts, manufactures, and of the soil, mine and sea." The whole world "competing in generous rivalry for the palm of superior excellence."

In the things that make Nations great and prosperous and happy, Iowa stands in the front rank of States, and is situated so near the location of the Exposition, that she should avail herself of this opportunity to make such an exhibit as will fully show her real condition and thus augment our national exhibit, and add to the grandeur of the whole as a comprehensive display of the industrial, intellectual and moral development of the World.

International Expositions have grown to such immense proportions, and are prepared at such great cost, it is not probable that the present generation will be called upon to assist in the preparation of another within the United States.

The Commission will take pleasure in communicating all needed information and in furnishing all facilities within its power; yet with the people must rest the responsibility of the success or failure of our State to be properly represented; and we invoke the aid of every true citizen to do all within his power, in her exhibit to place Iowa before the assembled Nations, in the position to which she is justly entitled; that we may thus be enabled to compare with other States our condition and capabilities, and our Nation with other Nations of the World.

Ample buildings will be constructed to supply all the needs of the Exposition, and sufficient space will be secured for all exhibits from our State; and we earnestly urge all Agricultural and Horticultural Societies and Farmers' Alliances and Clubs, all Stock Breeders' Associations and Stock Breeders; Manufacturers of every description; all Miners, Mechanics, Farmers, Nurserymen, Quarrymen; all persons in control of State Institutions; all Institutions of Learning, Teachers and School Boards; Artists, Musicians, Photographers, Printers, Publishers, Bankers, State Officers, Managers of Rail Ways, Insurance Companies, and Producers of every kind, to begin now to plan for the best contribution you can make to the World's Columbian Exposition.

This Exposition will be a school of observation to the farmer, of technical education to every artisan, a school of design to every manufacturer; it will stimulate progress in the sciences, arts and industries that benefit mankind; it will advance knowledge, dispel conceit and prejudice; cultivate friendship between individuals, States and Nations.

There is no other means of diffusing knowledge in so short a time, so wide and varied in its scope, to an extent so great and far reaching in its refining and elevating influence.

It is desirable that the greatest possible number of our people should attend the Exposition, and devote as much time as they can give to the study of its mammoth collection of object lessons, for it will be an opportunity the value of which is beyond computation.

Address all communications to F. N. CHASE, Secretary, Cedar Falls, Iowa.

Signed by the Members of the Commission.

At the regular meeting in February, 1891, a committee was appointed to visit Chicago and make application for a site for an Iowa State Building. Being the first state with an organized World's Fair Commission, and the first to apply for a location, before the plan for laying off the grounds had been fully matured, an acre and a half was assigned to Iowa, and formally accepted, which was afterwards given to France and Ceylon, upon which their buildings were erected.

When Jackson Park was surveyed and plat completed, the ground assigned to our state was found to be within the location desired for foreign countries and a favorable exchange was made, by which we received the beautiful site, including the "Shelter," on the shore of Lake Michigan, with a finely constructed sea wall in front, and permission was given to make such use of the building as we desired, conditioned that at the close of the Fair we return it as it came to us.

A large expense was thus saved in the cost of a sufficient building for the needs of the state during the Exposition. There is a tradition that the architect employed, some years before the Fair, by the South Park Commissioners, to design a structure for that place as "A shelter in the time of storm" for visitors and pic-nic parties, and for romantic worshipers at the shrine of Terpsichore, had in his possession plans of the French Chateau de Josselyn, and took a section of it for the design, and called it "The

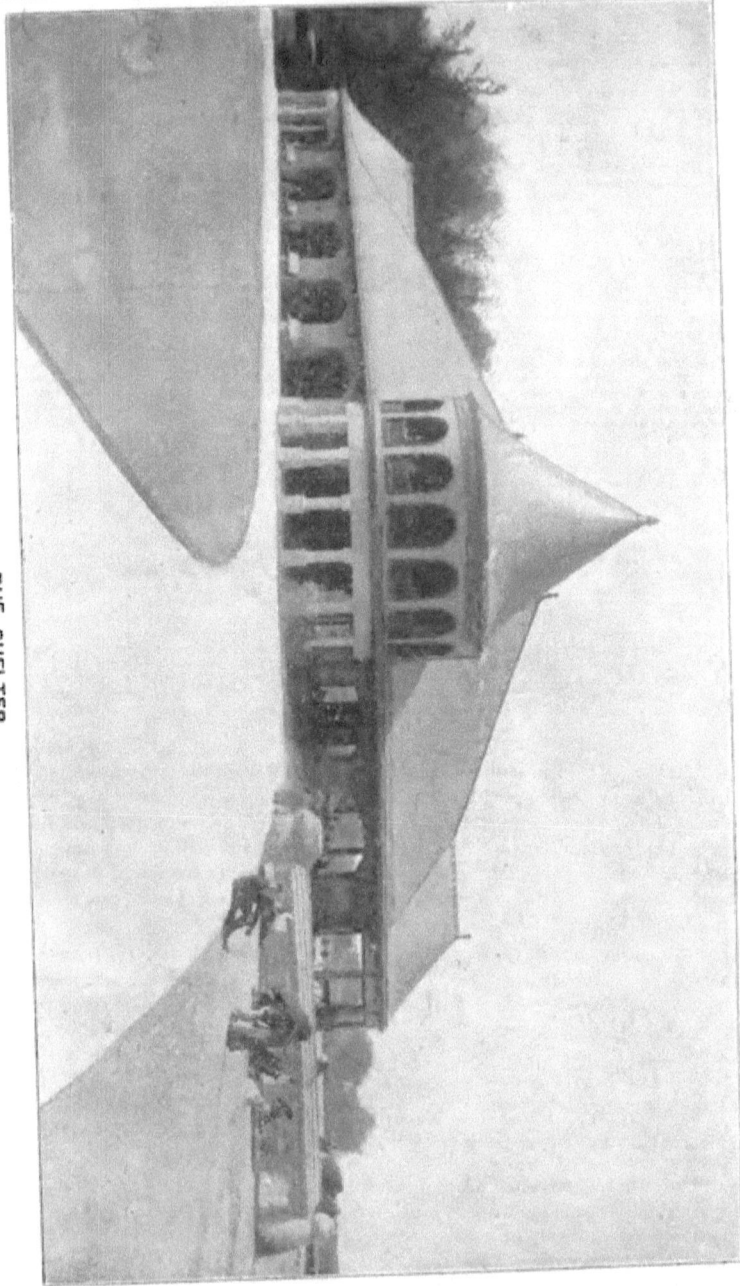

THE SHELTER.

Shelter." After Messrs. Josselyn & Taylor of Cedar Rapids were chosen architects for the Commission, and we had come in possession of the Shelter, Mr. Josselyn made a visit to the grounds for the purpose of studying the situation, when he recognized a section of his ancestral chateau, of which he also possessed the plans. The additions made took another section, nearly reproducing the chateau, with only such changes as were necessary to adapt it to its use as the Iowa State Building.

The following preliminary plan of promotion and preparation was adopted:

1. Requiring each Commissioner to ascertain and report at the next meeting, the agricultural, industrial, mineral, mechanical, educational, and other resources and advantages of the congressional district of his residence worthy of being represented at the Columbian Exposition.

2. That all individual exhibitors in this state be assisted in the transportation of their exhibits to the Exposition and return; that a competent person shall be in attendance at Chicago to give full information and assist in properly locating such exhibits according to classification and space allotted.

3. That there be procured an educational exhibit of the State University, State Agricultural College, all Colleges and Academies, all High Schools, all Normal Schools and common schools, and the State Teachers' Association.

4. That statistical charts be prepared of all state institutions, showing their history and extent, with full statements of their management.

5. That Ottumwa be requested to furnish a model of its Coal Palace, Creston of its Bluegrass Palace, Sioux City of its Corn Palace, and Forest City of its Flax Palace.

6. That an exhibit of soils to the depth of five or six feet, as it is in place, be made in glass tubes six inches in diameter, samples of soil to be taken from different localities so as to show the general character of the soil throughout the state.

7. That a large geological map be constructed after the model at p. 33 of White's Geological Report of Iowa, and a collection of specimens of the different formations as they occur in place from the lowest exposures in the state to the highest, to be exhibited in cases with glass fronts 12 inches wide and 6 feet high.

8. That all proprietors operating quarries of building stone be requested to furnish samples of stone in 12-inch cubes with different dress for each face, but one left to show cleavage.

9. That a collection be made of all varieties of grasses growing in the state, both wild and cultivated, and artistically arranged for an exhibit.

10. That the State Horticultural Society and State Agricultural Society be invited to make exhibits to worthily represent their respective departments, and the Fish Commission to make such representation as will show the growth of pisciculture in the state.

11. That a suitable building be erected on the State Agricultural Fair grounds for the Commission to hold open headquarters during the fairs of 1891 and 1892. A committee was appointed to procure from the department of promotion and publicity such suitable World's Fair literature as

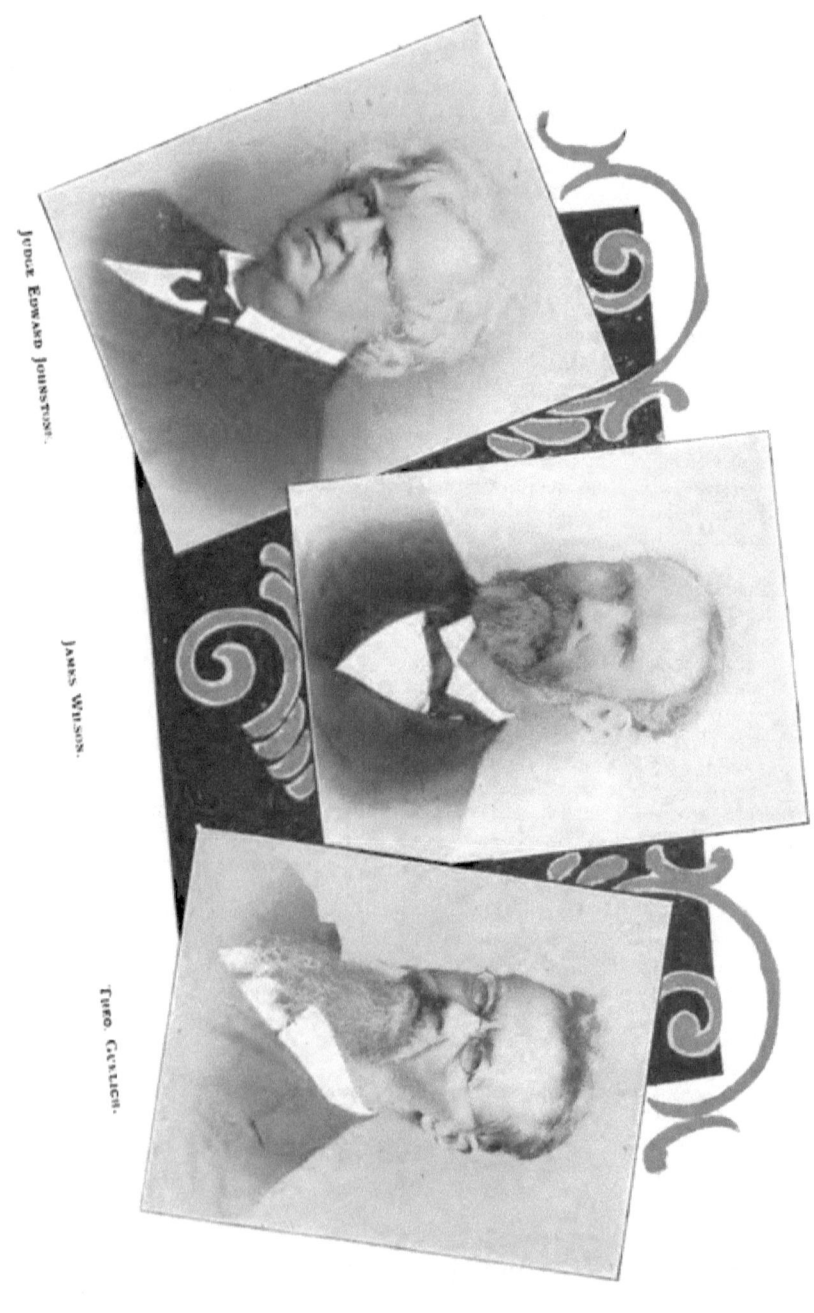

was obtainable, and to prepare such printed matter as was necessary to place before Iowa people the work and the needs of the Commission in relation to it, to be for free distribution at the headquarters, which was placed in charge of the executive committee and the secretary.

12. That the executive committee prepare a detailed statement of the amount necessary to enable the Commission to make such an exhibit as will worthily represent the state.

13. A committee was appointed to prepare a list of all the periodical publications in the state, their characteristics and circulation.

Also a committee to prepare a list of the religious denominations in the State, the number of church buildings, parsonages, schools and their endowments and number of students; number of ministers and church members, Sabbath Schools with their officers, teachers, scholars and libraries.

The Secretary visited many cities of the state for the purpose of securing the co-operation of the Press, Boards of Trade, and industrial organizations. He also issued the following circular letter:

"CEDAR FALLS, IOWA, April, 1891.

*To the Farmers of Iowa:*

"MY DEAR SIR: The Iowa Columbian Commission for the World's Columbian Exposition, to be held in Chicago, is now organized and is perfecting plans which will, if carried out, insure an exhibit of all the resources and all the varied industries of our great State which will be to our credit, and also add greatly to the future growth and prosperity of our commonwealth.

The Board of Management at Chicago is preparing immense buildings on Jackson Park in which the competitive exhibits, by individuals and firms from all the states and territories in the United States, and all the Foreign Nations will be exhibited in their proper departments according to their classification, but each state is asked to erect a suitable building for their headquarters, in which will be shown the collective state exhibit, representing the advantages, resources and possibilities of their respective states.

A circular will be issued later on that will more fully explain the scope and variety of the exhibits in the different departments of this state collection.

The Iowa Commission realize that the extent magnitude and success of the Iowa State Exhibit in this department, depends largely upon the farmers We therefore respectfully ask your hearty co-operation and invite correspondence. We believe that at the proper time the state will grant all the financial aid that is needed to make the Exhibit a credit to the state We desire especially at this time to call your attention to the importance of securing, during this season, the best possible specimens of corn, of the many different varieties; of all the grasses, also of grain, wheat, rye, oats, barley, flax, millet, broom corn and any other cereals that can be preserved in good form till 1893. We ask you to take special care to select and save any unusually large ears of corn, and extra heavy heads of grain with very long straw. All the small grains should be preserved in the straw with the roots attached.

Our object in asking your co-operation at this time is, to procure the best possible samples during the two seasons intervening between now and the opening of the Exposition, May 1st, 1893, to prevent a failure in case the season of 1892 should, by unfavorable weather render it impossible to obtain the best that our soil could produce under favorable circumstances. If the season of 1891 should prove to be bad, we would still have next year's crop to draw from, and Iowa which now takes the lead as an agricultural state, must show her best soil, and her best products, and she will then stand first in all the states with her State Exhibit at the Great Exposition.

For the Iowa Columbian Commmission

F. N. CHASE, Secretary."

The Populist, Republican and Democratic parties at their State Conventions in 1891, all adopted resolutions in their platforms favoring a liberal appropriation by the Legislature to convene the following winter, to enable the Commission to make a creditable Exhibit.

In response to a request from Chief Buchanan, to furnish three columns, of three pieces each, of Iowa tree trunks for the colonnade of the Forestry building, a committee was appointed that procured and forwarded the number desired.

Large quantities of World's Fair literature were distributed in the fall of 1891, from the headquarters of the State Fair, and at the Coal Palace, the Blue Grass Palace, the Corn Palace, the Flax Palace, and generally at the county fairs.

In December of that year, the Executive Committee, after consultation with many organizations and individual stock breeders and agriculturists, made the following report, which was adopted, and printed copies placed in the hands of all the members of the 24th General Assembly which convened on the second Monday of January, 1892:

*To the Iowa Columbian Commission:*

"The Executive Committee present the following estimate of money required to prepare, install and maintain an exhibit of the products of Iowa at the World's Fair at Chicago in 1893. In making these estimates, your committee realizes the fact that a large amount of money must be expended in making preparations. The success of our representation all lies in getting ready. Our stock raisers and farmers are not able to work a year to get ready, and then devote the next season, when they shall be planting and harvesting, to making an exhibit to the world for the benefit of the state of Iowa at large. The Commissioners must offer sufficient encouragement to induce the people to get ready whatever they can, that is worthy and creditable to the state. No Iowan will begrudge the money necessary for a state building equal to our sister states. We undertake this enterprise for the purpose of making known to the world the resources of Iowa, and if it is worth doing at all it is worth doing well.

In making these estimates we have added the cost of transportation and also provided for renewals of perishable articles. We estimate:

For state building and equipment for same ----------------------- $ 75,000

Live Stock This to include domestic animals of all varieties, kinds and classes of Iowa breeding, rearing and ownership; including a poultry exhibit; also including all premiums, medals and prizes for the entire live stock industry of the state ------------------ 50,000

Agriculture—This to include all grains, grasses, field seeds, root and vine products, including the sugar beet and other sugar producing plants; also all manufactured articles from the above products, such as flour, meal, starch, glucose, sugar, sorghum and products of the canning factory and packing house; especial attention being given to corn as an article of food.................. 25,000

Horticulture—All orchard fruits, products of the vineyards, garden fruits, nursery stock and orchard appliances, all processes for preserving, evaporating or drying fruits; floriculture and forestry; specimens of native woods.................................... 10,000

Manufactures—Machinery of Iowa invention or manufacture, used in mechanical, agricultural, mining or artistic operation; manufactured products from wood, leather, cotton, wool, hemp, flax, paper and all metals; the object being to present the variety, magnitude and excellence of the manufacturing industry of the state, giving special attention to the abundance of raw material and the cheapness of fuel........................................... 15,000

Dairy Products—Cheese and butter made by the factory or creamery, or of domestic manufacture, all dairy appliances of Iowa invention or manufacture.............................................. 10,000

Education and Liberal Arts—This to embrace the work of the common school system; the academy, college, university, art institutes, technical and professional schools, the educational, reformatory and charitable state institutions; the plastic, pictorial and decorative arts, including photography and a photographic exhibit of the state; school appliances and furnishings, music, drawing, engraving and kindergarten appliances, and public libraries ........................................................................... 20,000

Bee Culture—Bees and their products, bee management, apiarian appliances of Iowa invention, manufacture or use................. 3,000

Woman's Work—embracing all departments of female industry, such as needle work, embroidery, fancy work for home use, comfort or ornamentation, painting, special designs in wood, leather and other materials and fabrics; pantry stores, cookery, woman's inventions and woman's work in Iowa literature history and development........................................................................... 20,000

Fish Exhibit—Native fishes, embracing the work of the fish commission, state hatchery, fish hatching and fish production in Iowa streams, lakes and ponds.................................................. 2,000

Mineral and Geological—Mineral ores, products of mines, embracing coal, lead, iron, aluminum and other metals; gypsum, marble, granite, limestone and other building stone; mineral paints, fire and potter's clay and other valuable clay and sands and articles manufactured from them, including brick and tile; specimens of soil, a geological exhibit, fully illustrating the geology of Iowa, properly classified and arranged.......................... 6,000

Sanitary—Work of the state board of health; hospital accommodations for the use of Iowa visitors at the Exposition, who may be taken down by sickness or injured by accident, and other sanitary requirements during the Exposition................................. 4,000

Decorations—Artistic designs in Iowa corn and other Iowa grains and grasses used in decorating the interior of the Iowa building; the purpose being to make an artistic and beautiful display of the field products of Iowa; a display of all Iowa birds, properly mounted, will be used for the double purpose of exhibiting such specimens and beautifying the building.................................. 6,000

Promoting, Printing and Publication—A statistical exhibit of the resources, productiveness and other interests essential to a complete exhibit of the material progress and social, civil and moral life of Iowa; also the supplying of literature for free distribution, advertising the advantages and excellencies of the state; also maintaining a bureau of information for the benefit of the Iowa visitors to the exposition; an illustrative exhibit of the climatology of Iowa and the weather and crop reporting service of the state; this department embraces all the clerical and mail service essential to the advertising of an Iowa exhibit at Chicago in 1893 ............................................................................ 25,000

Press Department—Embracing Iowa press headquarters at the exposition with complete files of all the periodical publications of the state properly displayed; also the literature of Iowa, including all works of Iowa authorship in law, history, science, poetry, travel, etc., and their proper classification and display............ 5,000

Administration and Installation—All clerical hire, furniture for secretary and other officers, secretary's salary, expense of stationery, postage, express charges, insurance, telegraphing blanks and blank books for secretary, treasurer, superintendent and other officers; expense of commission and all others essential to the installation of an Iowa exhibit........................................ 30,000

Salaries of superintendents, assistants and helpers.................. 23,000

Incidental and contingent expenses ................................... 10,000

Total ....................................................... $339,000

This seems a large amount to any one who has not figured up the cost and detail and considered that it will require about two years time of the promoters and operators engaged in making a showing of the wonderful resources of our great state, an opportunity that we will not again have during this generation. Respectfully submitted,     S. H. MALLORY,
J. W. JARNAGIN,
J. F. DUNCOMBE,
Executive Committe."

At the regular meeting of the Commission in February the General Assembly was in session and bills alike providing for an appropriation of $300,000 had been introduced in the Senate and House and referred to special committees. Each committee had a meeting with the Commission at which a general conference and free discussion was held. Both committees reported favorably on the bills and recommended their passage; but when final action was taken the amount was reduced to $125,000.

From the time of the passage of the act of Congress authorizing the World's Columbian Exposition its plans grew broader to the day of its opening. Minute histories of all preceding World's Fairs had been published and they showed how great must be the effort to excel them, and energy never before equalled was put forth and each month stimulated to higher and grander achievements.

To any person familiar with the exhibits of that great Exposition, who will carefully peruse the above detailed estimate prepared by the executive committee, it will be easy to see how far short the exhibit came of what was contemplated, and necessarily so by limiting the appropriation to an amount insufficient for the plans adopted; and they were revised and cut down in every department.

Immediately after the passage of the act appropriating $125,000 for the use of the Commission, a session was held and the Commission re-organized, standing committees re-arranged, the work of collecting exhibits classified into nine departments, each placed under the special charge of one Commissioner.

From that time till the opening of the Exposition, the work of preparation was actively and energetically carried forward; the details of which will fully appear from the accompanying reports of each standing committee and department.

A record of the proceedings of every meeting of the Commission was kept by the secretary, and printed copies made for the use of its members, which record and some printed copies are to be deposited in the state archives for the benefit of the Commission which shall be charged with the preparation of Iowa's exhibit at the next quadri-centennial exposition in celebration of the discovery of America.

The report of the auditing committee complies with the statute requiring a list of all disbursements, and complete vouchers thereof will accompany it. In November last the sum of $3,000 was covered back into the state treasury from the unexpended funds in the treasury of the Commission, which included salvage, retaining sufficient for the publication of an edition of 5,000 copies of this report and final expenses of closing the work of the Commission.

The Commission was unwilling to incur risks that could by any possibility exhaust the appropriations and leave an empty treasury before its work was fully completed. Several states, by reason of the extremely high price of labor in building and decorating and in unexpected necessary expenditures, found their appropriations exhausted in mid-summer. Experience admonished us that a small surplus is easier to turn over to the state at the close than a deficiency, and much pleasanter to account for. The full sum estimated might all have been used in a more thorough exhibit of the substantial resources of our state, and been like seed sown in good Iowa soil that brings forth fruit abundantly.

The Commission aimed to make the best showing possible with the means placed at their disposal; and already the expenditure has borne more than one hundred fold increase, in the great number of good citizens that have since made their homes in our state through its influence. And still they come and will continue to come. Our own citizens learned from it to appreciate the excellence of Iowa as they never had before; and now it is believed that there is not on this earth another 55,000 square miles of land in one body so productive with so small a percentage of waste.

On the 19th day of October, 1892, at Chicago a "National organization of state executive officers" was formed that held weekly meetings during the continuance of the Exposition. Its object was to gain the strength of union in promoting the best interests of the Exposition, and to secure the rights and privileges to which the states were justly entitled. In preparing the program for the closing day exercises the national committee on ceremonies invited that organization to select a person to represent the states on that occasion, and Iowa was honored by the selection of the president of her Commission as such representative. By reason of the assassination of Mayor Harrison which cast a cloud of sadness over all, the program was not carried out; but the committee requested all who had parts assigned them to forward to the secretary of the National Commission the papers prepared by them, to be published as a part of the Exposition's final report.

The following poem was written by John Brayshaw Kaye, Esq., of Calmar, Iowa, and given as a tribute to the closing scene of the World's Columbian Exposition, October 30, 1893:

    City of Nations! thou white builded dream,
        Sprung like a mirage margined on this plain
        Of inland waters, and so soon again
    To sink in wreck on Time's engulphing stream;
    Thy fame as Sardis' fame shall be enduring,
    Thy fetes than Shushan's, ever more alluring.

    Oh, City of Good Will and Human Love,
        Millennium glimmers from thy domes and towers;
        Thy Colonnades lead from this life of ours
    To visions of the broader life above,
    And back through coming vistas where we scan
    The free and perfect Brotherhood of Man.

    City of Wonders! here hath blessed Peace
        Builded her altar and set up her shrine.
        High human purpose nearing the Divine
    Found here in Colon's Land the Golden Fleece,
    And here the fearless argonauts of Spain
    Behold their ships and meet their Chief again.

    Great anti-Babel! out from Shinar's plain
        After four thousand years drifting apart
        The peoples of the earth, in heart and art,
    Within thy fanes and courts have met again,
    And shown in many ways whence all are sprung,
    Speaking the simples of a common tongue.

    What though to-morrow thou shalt disappear,
        The memory of thy presence like a dream
        Of Childhood's light half slumber, still shall seem
    So more than real, well defined and clear,
    Fixed in perspective ever to remain
    Where will, to being calls thee forth again.

    Oh, offer praise and prayers and prayers and praise
        Alternate with sweet interludes of song;
        Let glad Hosannas from the mighty throng
    Well up to Heaven in these closing days
    Of thy World triumph! Nations here have met
    And now the parting only brings regret.

S. H. MALLORY.

# REPORT OF EXECUTIVE COMMITTEE.

#### BY S. H. MALLORY, CHAIRMAN.

The Executive Committee of the Iowa Columbian Commission respectfully submit the following report, regarding the work done under their direction, before and during the World's Exposition at Chicago.

## PRELIMINARY WORK.

From September second, 1890, when the Committee was appointed, up to April seventh, 1892, its work was chiefly assisting the Commission in procuring information for its future guidance, preparing estimates of the outlay desirable to occur, and debating methods and plans for a State Exhibit.

In compliance with instructions given us by resolutions passed on June fourth, 1891, we secured from the State Board of Agriculture a very desirable building site, on the State Fair Grounds, and erected on it a neat wooden cottage, 16x20 feet, at a total cost of $196.60, which was used as headquarters for the Commission during the holding of the State Fairs of 1891 and 1892.

In April, 1892, the state having appropriated $125,000 instead of the much larger sum asked for, the Executive Committee at the request of the Commission, prepared the following estimate of how said appropriation should be expended to attain the most satisfactory results, and presented it to the Commission on June 23d, 1892, viz:

| | |
|---|---:|
| For Pavilion alteration and restoration | $ 5,500 |
| For New Building, structure complete | 27,000 |
| For Decorations | 3,000 |
| For Furniture and Furnishings | 5,000 |
| For Attendants, Helpers, etc., during six months of Fair | 15,500 |
| For Administration, Commissioners, per diem and Railway | 12,500 |
| For expressage, P. O. stamps and stationery | 4,000 |
| For contingent expenses | 7,500 |
| | $80,000 |

| | | |
|---|---:|---:|
| For Collective Exhibit | $8,000 | |
| For Literary Bureau | 8,000 | |
| For Live Stock | 5,000 | |
| For Agriculture and Dairy | 8,000 | |
| For Horticulture | 2,000 | |
| For Minerals and Geology | 2,000 | |
| For Press | 1,500 | |
| For Woman's Work | 1,500 | |
| For Manufacturing and Machinery | 2,000 | |
| For Education and Liberal Arts | 5,000 | |
| For Forestry and Sanitary Work | 2,000 | $ 45,000 |
| | | $125,000 |

IOWA STATE BUILDING FROM THE SOUTHWEST.

On the 7th and 8th of April, 1892, resolutions were passed by the Commission greatly enlarging and defining the powers of our Committee, delegating to them all the powers of the Commission, to execute all plans then or thereafter to be devised or ordered by the Commission, with full power to act in the premises at all times, when the Commission was not in session.

## LOCATION AT WORLD'S EXPOSITION GROUNDS.

In deference to the wishes of the Directors of the World's Exposition, the site for our State Building which had been selected and granted, (lot Y) was resigned, and Lot 11 taken instead; the change was confirmed by letter on April 23, 1892, and the contract between the Exposition Officials and the Iowa Commission for the new site, executed on the 23d of June following. Your Committee thought the change an advantageous one for Iowa, as the new location was on the Lake Front and Grand Boulevard, sufficiently conspicuous, easy of access, open to the cool lake breezes, and with a commodious, handsome pavilion on it, which the Exposition permitted the State to use as part of their State Building, with the sole proviso, that it should be left as found, at the close of the Exposition.

## STATE BUILDING.

On April 13th, 1892, Architect Josselyn was instructed to prepare two or three studies for the State Building, to be erected upon the site as selected, and on May 5th, he was advised to proceed to prepare plans and specifications for the same in accordance with his sketch, that day approved by Chief of Construction Burnham.

The Committee next proceeded to advertise for proposals from contractors for furnishing all material and labor and constructing the building, in accordance with said plans and specifications, work to be awarded about June first.

On June eighth the plans and specifications as presented by the Josselyn & Taylor Co., architects, were approved.

On June 23d, seven propositions were received from three different contractors, to construct the building as advertised, the bids ranging from $38,500 (the highest) to $23,700 (the lowest). On July seventh, John G Coder, the lowest bidder, having satisfied the Committee as to his responsibility, was awarded the contract. On the same day, it was agreed with the architects, Josselyn & Taylor Co., to pay them five per cent of the cost of the building, as full compensation for preparing the plans and specifications, and superintending its construction.

A brief description of the architectural features of the building is as follows:

The pavilion (lettered "A" on the plans) is a building 80 ft. x 120 ft. one story in height, and was utilized as an Exhibition Hall. To the west, with a south frontage, was the addition, 60 ft. x 112 ft. This portion was arranged for and devoted to, the accommodation of the public and officials. It contained a Reception Hall, about 16x50, Ladies' Parlors about 20x40, Gentlemen's Parlor, about 24x32, Governor's and Commission's rooms, Postoffice,

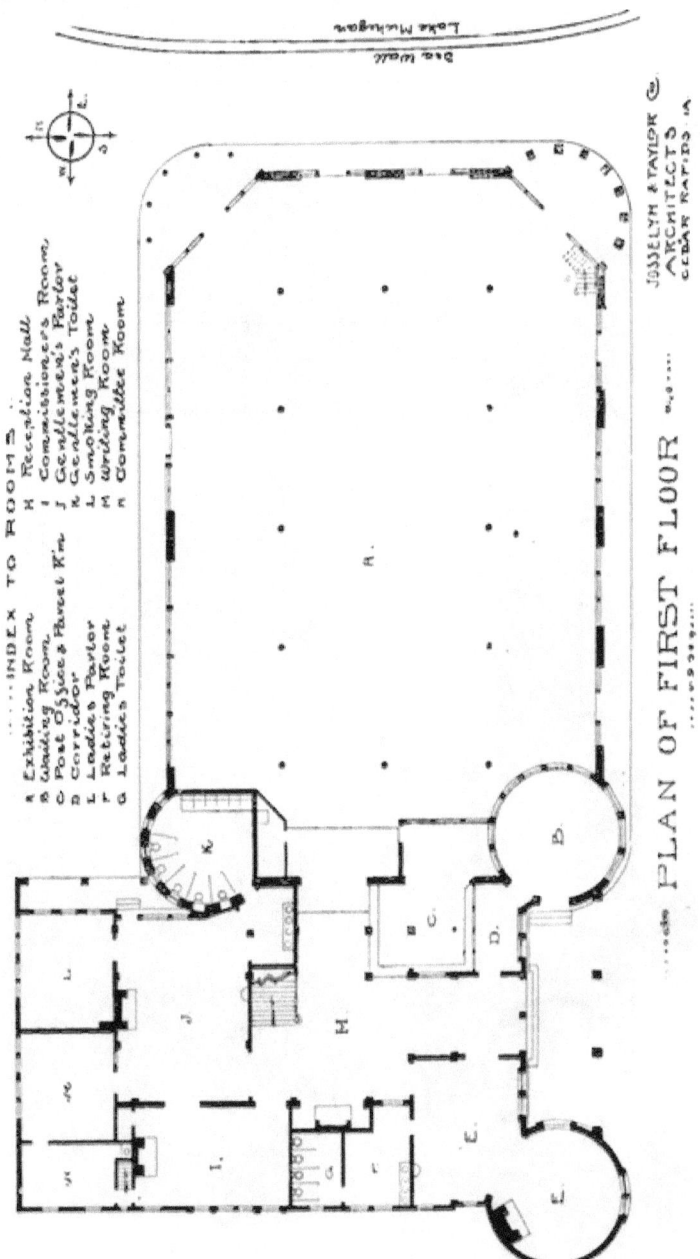

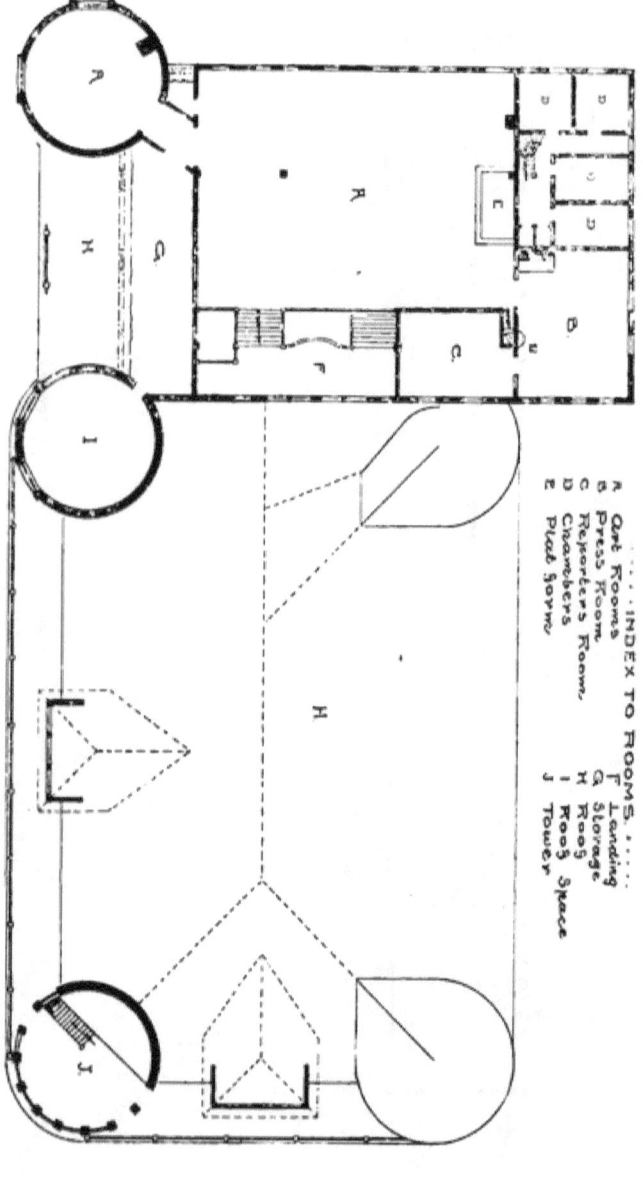

Writing rooms and Toilets. On the second floor was a large Assembly Hall, utilized for Exhibition purposes, rooms for the accommodation of the Press, sleeping rooms for Officers, with rooms in the third story for janitors. The exterior of the Pavilion was slightly modified in its outline, to bring it into harmony with the addition, and give the whole building as much as possible the appearance of one structure. The whole length of the old and new parts gave a frontage towards the south of nearly two hundred feet.

The principal entrance was toward the western end of the building, between two large circular towers. The two western towers had friezes with decorated panels. In the panels of the one to the left of the entrance were the names of thirteen of the principal cities of the State, arranged alphabetically, and selected from the census list of 1890: Burlington, Cedar Rapids, Clinton, Council Bluffs, Davenport, Des Moines, Dubuque, Fort Madison, Keokuk, Marshalltown, Muscatine, Ottumwa and Sioux City.

In the panels of the other were the names of the following historical events in Iowa: Settled by Dubuque in 1788. Louisiana Purchase, 1803. Territory of Michigan, 1834. Territory of Wisconsin, 1836. Territory of Iowa, 1838. State of Iowa, 1846. There were other panels filled with decorations illustrative of Iowa's progress and industries, with portrait heads in high relief of the Indian Chiefs, Keokuk and Blackhawk, modeled from authentic engravings lent by the State Masonic library at Cedar Rapids. The Park Pavilion gave the key to the style of architecture adopted which was that of the French Manoirs, with decorations and enrichments after the style of the Chateaux of France.

Inside were some handsome mantels, modeled and decorated in the latter style.

The following inscription was placed over the fire-place in the main hall, "Iowa; the affections of her people, like the rivers of her borders, flow to an inseparable union."

## INTERIOR DECORATIONS.

Milward and Clark of Sioux City, were employed in the fall of 1892, to design and superintend the decorations of the Exhibition Hall with the principal products of the State.

The charming and novel effects they produced by covering the ceilings, walls and columns with grains, seeds, grasses, corn, etc., all products of the State, wrought into pictures and fanciful decorative designs of form and color, gave a unique and unusually attractive interior, making one of the most novel features of the Exposition. The most favorable comments were made by the throngs of visitors, of all nationalities, whom it attracted.

The views here shown, give but a faint idea of the beauty of the work. The remainder of the mural decorations in the building, with the exception of the Press room, were designed and executed by the fresco artists, Andrews and Noel, of Clinton Iowa, and received much favorable comment.

Mrs. John F. Duncombe, of Fort Dodge, requested permission to decorate the two Press rooms at her own expense, which was granted. She employed Mr. Colwell, who furnished the design and executed the work, using only materials manufactured and produced in the State. The walls and

IOWA STATE BUILDING, MAIN ENTRANCE.

ceilings were decorated with a finish called cementico, made at Fort Dodge; it commenced in the center of the ceiling with a greenish blue tint, blending the field as it approached the Style, to a warm buff. The Style was pale sage-green, done in a heavy stipple, representing icicles tipped with gold. The corners of the ceiling were in scroll with a running vine in which was interwoven a fac-simile of the leading newspapers of the State. The walls were stippled in light, warm buff, to the chair rail, above which was an extensive border, composed of ink and quills, or pens and ink, so arranged as to appear ready for use. Below the chair rail, the tint was a light terra cotta. The frieze was blended and done in rosette stipple, lined in gold and copper. The mantel was finished in harmonious colors, and the fire breast filled with a large painting, representing the Printing Press of the day, or the Iowa Cultivator. The wood work was painted to match and striped with gold.

The mantel shelf in the Ladies' Parlor contained a clock furnished by the ladies of Iowa City. The case was modeled after the old Capitol Building at Iowa City, and made of Iowa City marble.

The Committee received a proposition from C. S. Young & Co., of Chicago, to place in the center of the Pavilion a miniature reproduction of the State Capitol Building at Des Moines, to be made entirely of glass and the grains of the State. They proposed to pay the Commission $5,000 for the privilege, and expected to reimburse themselves from the sale of the surplus samples of grain, received from the farmers, and the sale of photographs of the exhibit. Their proposition being accepted by the Committee, they appointed solicitors in every county in the state, to canvass and secure samples of all kinds of grain, so that every farmer might have an exhibit at the Exposition. Their names were to be listed and published in a book, describing the same. The scheme was not a financial success, as the contributions were too few. The miniature Capitol was constructed by Mr. Schuman, of the Wells Glass Co. Chicago, under the direction G. P. Bell, architect for the contractor. It attracted much attention and received great praise. At the close of the Exposition it was presented to the Agricultural College at Ames, which assumed all expense, of removal and installation.

The Flax Palace and flax exhibit was sent by the Flax Palace Association of Forest City; it was prepared under the direction of Jasper Thompson, ex-President of the Flax Palace Co., and the entire expense, except transportation, was borne by the citizens of Forest City.

## FURNITURE AND FURNISHINGS.

The necessary furnishings for a Postoffice, Parcel room and Registry room were purchased of John McLane, of Milford, N. H., and erected in the building. They proved of the greatest convenience to the Public and the Commission.

L. S. Merchant, of Cedar Rapids, generously furnished free of charge, a large and elegantly bound Register, with an adjustable stand, to be used as an official register at the Building. At the close of the Exposition, they were placed in the Aldrich Collection in the State Capitol.

The office furniture was kindly loaned to the Commission by the Rand & Leopold Desk Co., of Burlington, Iowa.

IOWA STATE BUILDING, CEREAL DECORATIONS IN PAVILION.

George P. Bent, of Chicago, loaned a fine Crown Cabinet Organ and an elegant Upright Crown Piano, and at the close of the Exposition put the latter in first-class condition and presented it to the Commission, who shipped it to Des Moines, and had it placed in the Governor's room in the Capitol, as the property of the State. The furniture in the parlors and reception rooms was purchased of the Haywood & Morrill Manufacturing Co. of Chicago.

The ladies of Vinton loaned a table and two chairs for use in the parlor. They were elegant specimens of carving done by the Vinton ladies.

The ladies of Dunlap contributed a magnificent great carved chair, upholstered in leather, as an example of their handiwork. At their request, it was afterward sent as a gift from them to the Governor and is now in the historical rooms at the Capitol.

## SALVAGE.

On September fifteenth, 1893, the disposition of the property of the State on the Exposition Grounds, was delegated by the Commission to the Executive Committee.

Sales were accordingly made and the sum of twenty-five hundred seventy-seven dollars nineteen cents realized; in more detail as follows:

| | |
|---|---:|
| Sale of building | $ 235 00 |
| Sale of postoffice fixtures | 185 00 |
| Sale of furniture and fixtures | 900 24 |
| Sale of dairy products | 828 67 |
| Sale of electric fixtures | 100 00 |
| Sale of grain and lumber | 143 67 |
| Sale of wool | 50 80 |
| Rebate on safe | 50 00 |
| Rebate on gas | 50 00 |
| Miscellaneous articles | 33 81 |
| Total | $2,577 19 |

SCHEDULE OF EXHIBITS AND OTHER ARTICLES TURNED OVER BY THE IOWA COLUMBIAN COMMISSION TO THE GOVERNOR AND EXECUTIVE COUNCIL FOR THE USE OF THE STATE.

1 Geo. P. Bent "Crown" Piano (cover and stool.)
1 water color painting, framed, "Interior Iowa State Building."
1 long mirror.
8 cases inverted glass show bottles and exhibition bottles.
1 lot glass soil cylinders.
3 gas logs.
1 box Rosier fire extinguishers.
1 lot Hardin hand grenade fire extinguishers.
1 lot cuspidors.
3 step ladders.
4 paper racks and fixtures.
And the following list was deposited in the State Library:
1 water color painting, framed, "Iowa State Building."

IOWA STATE BUILDING, SECTION IN PAVILION.

IOWA STATE BUILDING, WEST END OF PAVILION.

BOOKS—
    1 copy Illinois hand book.
    1 copy Manitoba hand book.
    1 copy New South Wales hand book.
    1 copy Canadian Educational hand book.
    1 copy Black Hills hand book.
    1 copy Costa Rica Publication.
    1 copy Canadian Agricultural Report.
    1 copy Philadelphia hand book.
    1 copy Classification World's Columbian Exposition.
    1 copy Wisconsin hand book.
    1 copy Minnesota hand book.
    1 copy Louisiana hand book.
    1 copy Kansas hand book.
    1 copy Minneapolis hand book.
    1 copy Spanish hand book.
    1 copy British hand book.
    1 copy Iowa hand book.
    1 copy Iowa Dedication Souvenir.
    1 copy Iowa State Day Souvenir.
    2 large volumes Statutes of New South Wales.
    List of articles placed with Historical Department:
    3 large registry books and stand, used at Iowa State Building, and containing lists of names of visitors to the Exposition.
    250 volumes Iowa hand book, for distribution.
    Specimens of Iowa stone and marble were placed with the Geological Department.
    Also 1 large glass cabinet, sent to college for blind at Vinton.
    1 large glass cabinet, sent to school for deaf at Council Bluffs.
    1 " " " " institution for feeble minded at Glenwood.
    1 " " " " State Normal Shool, Cedar Falls.
    3 large glass show cases to State Agricultural Society.
    8 Iowa caps to State Agricultural Society.
    1 step ladder to State Agricultural Society.
    Large model of Iowa State Capitol building to Agricultural Hall.
    The World's Fair Cottage, on Iowa State Fair Grounds, was given to Director J. R. Sage and his successors, for headquarters for weather and crop service.

F. N. CHASE.

# Report of the Committee on Ceremonies.

BY F. N. CHASE, CHAIRMAN.

The committee named by this Commission to act as committee on ceremonies was appointed with special reference to the dedication ceremonies of the Iowa State Building, October 22, 1892. After the ceremonies above referred to, this committee reported to the Commission, the report was accepted and the committee discharged.

At a subsequent meeting of the Commission the same committee was re-appointed to act until the close of the Exposition, and now beg to submit the following as their report:

While the Iowa State Building was not so large and imposing as some of the state buildings, and was not built with special reference to giving public entertainments, but more especially adapted to the comfort and convenience of those who daily visited the building for rest and comfort, to see the various exhibits representing the resources and products of the state and the refinement and culture of its citizens, to listen to the grand concerts given daily by the justly celebrated Iowa State Band, and to view the wonderful decorations of natural products in the pavilion; still, with the large reception rooms and parlors on the first floor and the assembly room on the second floor, it made it possible on special occasions to accommodate large crowds of people. Yet it was impossible to entertain all the Iowa visitors, their friends and the multitude of visitors from other states, territories and foreign nations.

The following is a list of the more public and official meetings under the direction of the Iowa Commission. The three most important of these ceremonies were the dedicatory ceremony at the Iowa State Building, October 22, 1892; the formal opening and presentation of the Iowa State Exhibit to Director General Davis and the Board of Management of the World's Columbian Exposition, May 1, 1893; and the Iowa State Celebration Days, September 20 and 21, 1893.

In addition to these was the reception to Miss Clara Barton, president of the American Red Cross Association; reception to West Point cadets; the public exercises and reception to the Iowa Press Association, August 3, 1893; the reception to Hon. Horace Boies, Governor of Iowa, Director General Davis and Board of Management of the Exposition, United States and Foreign Commissioners, United States Board of Lady Managers, and the Commissioners and Lady Managers of the states and territories, from 2 to 5 o'clock p. m., September 20; also the Corn Food Banquet given in October, to which were invited the foreign and state commissioners and ladies. This last occasion, however, was in charge of a special committee.

In addition to these ceremonies at the Iowa State Building, there were many occasions where ceremonies more or less public were held in the assembly room under the auspices of the various societies and organizations of the state of Iowa.

RECEPTION ROOM.

The presence of the Iowa State Band during the entire period of the Exposition made it possible to give these entertainments and make them successes.

### DEDICATION OF THE IOWA STATE BUILDING.

On October 22, 1892, the day following the general dedication of the Exposition buildings and grounds, the Iowa State Building—then nearly completed—was presented to the Governor by President Crosby, and by the Governor dedicated and tendered to the Board of Management of the Exposition.

Governor Boies and staff, members of the Executive Council, the Iowa State Band, several regiments of the Iowa National Guard, and a large number of citizens of Iowa and other visitors, more than could be accommodated, were present and the program was successfully carried out. The proceedings were published in an Edition de Luxe of 2,500 copies, entitled "Souvenir of the Dedicatory Ceremonies of the Iowa State Building at Jackson Park, Illinois, October 22, A. D., 1892," which is here reproduced entire.

### PROGRAM OF CEREMONIES OF DEDICATION.

Overture—Barber of Seville—Rossini, - - Iowa State Band
Invocation, - - - - - Rev. T. E. Green, D. D
Presentation of the building to the Governor of Iowa,
        James O Crosby, Pres. Iowa Col. Commission
Dedication and tender to the World's Exposition, Governor Horace Boies
Response (in the program only), - Director-General Geo. R. Davis
Music—Reminiscences of all Nations, - - Iowa State Band
Poem—The Ballad of Columbus—Maj. S. H. M. Byers,
        Mrs. Lucia Gale Barber
Song—Star Spangled Banner, - - Mrs. Ida Norton, accompanied by
    Iowa State Band, with Audience joining in the Chorus.
Oration, - - - - - - Hon. E. P. Seeds
Doxology, - - Audience, accompanied by Iowa State Band
Benediction, - - - - - Rev. T. E. Green, D. D
Music—Iowa Columbian March—Prof. Phinney, - Iowa State Band
F. N. CHASE, S. B. PACKARD, HENRY STIVERS, Committee on Ceremonies

## IOWA OFFICIALS OF THE WORLD'S COLUMBIAN COMMISSION.

*Chief of the Bureau of Agriculture.*—W. I. Buchanan, Sioux City.
*U. S. Commissioners for Iowa*—W. F. King, Mt. Vernon; Joseph Eiboeck, Des Moines.
  *Alternates.*—John Hayes, Red Oak; Charles E. Whiting, Whiting.
*Members of Woman's Board of U. S. Commissioners for Iowa.*—Mrs. Whiting S. Clark, Des Moines; Miss Ora E. Miller, Cedar Rapids.
  *Alternates.*—Mrs. Ira F. Hendricks, Council Bluffs; Miss Mary B. Hancock, Dubuque.

### IOWA COLUMBIAN COMMISSION.

Pres.—J. O. Crosby, Garnavillo; V-Pres.—J. F. Duncombe, Ft. Dodge; Secy.—F. N. Chase, Cedar Falls; Treas.—Wm. H. Dent, LeMars.
*Executive Committee.*—S H. Mallory, Chariton; H. W. Seaman, Clinton; S B. Packard, Marshalltown.

IOWA STATE BUILDING, LADIES' PARLORS.

***Auditing Committee.***—Theo. Guelich, Burlington; S. B. Packard, Marshalltown; Henry Stivers, Des Moines.
*On Compilation of Archæological, Historical and Statistical Information.*—Chas. Ashton, Guthrie Center; J. O. Crosby, Garnavillo; J. W. Jarnagin, Montezuma.

### DEPARTMENTS.

"A" Live Stock—S. B. Packard; "B" Agricultural, Dairy and Apiary—F. N. Chase; "C" Horticultural—Wm. H. Dent; "D" Mineral and Geology—J. F. Duncombe; "E" Press—Henry Stivers; "F" Woman's Work—J. O. Crosby; "G" Manufactures and Machinery—H. W. Seaman; "H" Education and Fine Arts—J. W. Jarnagin; "I" Forestry—Theo. Guelich.

### IOWA BOARD OF LADY MANAGERS.

Pres.—Miss Ora E. Miller, Cedar Rapids; V-Pres.—Mrs. N. C. Deering, Osage; Secy.—Mrs. Eliza G. Rhodes, Mt. Pleasant; Treas.—Miss Mary B. Hancock, Dubuque; Mrs. Flora J. McAchran, Bloomfield; Mrs. Whiting S. Clark, Des Moines; Mrs. Orry H. Salts, Corning; Mrs. L. O. Ferson, Council Bluffs; Mrs. John F. Duncombe, Ft. Dodge; Miss Jennie E. Rogers, Sioux City; Mrs. Ellen K. Cook, Davenport.

## PRAYER BY REV. THOS. E. GREEN, D. D.,
### CHAPLAIN OF THE FIRST REGIMENT, IOWA NATIONAL GUARD.

We praise Thee O Lord: We acknowledge Thee to be the Lord. Thou art the ruler of the nations and the King of Kings. By Thy sovereign will have the bounds of the earth been set, and out of the counsels of Thy wisdom have the nations been established.

We praise Thee for all Thy manifold mercies, and especially at this time for the Providence that called into being this our western world, and has made and preserved for us our beloved nation.

And as we give Thee thanks so we supplicate Thy continued blessing. We pray for our land and nation. Preserve it from peril, establish it in righteousness, and fill it with Thy fear and obedience to Thy law.

Bless we beseech Thee the President of the United States; in this his hour of sore distress, manifest to him the comforts of Thy grace. We pray for the Governor of our state, and for all who are over us in authority. May they be men of clean hands and pure hearts, whose strength is in Thee and in Thy righteousness.

Bless our Commonwealth. Save us from sin and iniquity and establish us in prosperity and peace.

Accept we beseech Thee the work which we now dedicate to humanity, and therefore to Thee. May it serve its purpose in the advancement of Christian civilization, in the building up of the brotherhood of humanity and the proclamation of the Fatherhood of our God. And so may Thy blessing be upon us, and Thy mercy upon our children—and to Thee, Father, Son and Holy Ghost, shall be glory and honor, now and evermore. Amen.

IOWA STATE BUILDING, GENTLEMEN'S PARLORS.

## ADDRESS OF JAMES O. CROSBY,

### PRESIDENT OF THE IOWA COLUMBIAN COMMISSION.

National celebrations in great measure show forth the character of the people constituting the nation.

In early ages the conquests of arms were made the greatest occasions for long continued and enthusiastic celebrations, and the order of exercises indicated what the people deemed best calculated to express their joy and admiration and to afford them their highest pleasure and gratification.

The savage chieftain celebrated his success upon the war path by midnight orgies with the weird war-dance and superstitious sacrifices.

In A. D. 70, a Roman army occupied Palestine menacing Jerusalem, because the Jews failed to pay to Rome the stipulated tribute money. The presence of the army alone was not enough to bring the tribute, and Titus destroyed the city, razing its walls to the ground.

He returned to Rome with 60,000 prisoners, and by the Senate was accorded a thiumphal procession. The prisoners built the Coliseum, with a seating capacity of 87,000, and upon its completion in A. D. 80, one hundred days were spent in celebrating with games and shows, gladiatorial combats to the finish, and contests with wild beasts. The triumphal arch of Titus and the Coliseum still stand to perpetuate the fame and glory achieved in the destruction of Jerusalem.

A few years later, when the emperor Trajan returned from the Danube, after his conquest of the Dacians, again the Coliseum was thrown open to celebrate his victory, and for 120 days, for the entertainment of the people, the Dacian prisoners were compelled to fight with wild beasts and to butcher one another to make Roman holiday. The statue of the Dying Gladiator perpetuates the memory of that butchery, and the column of Trajan and the Forum in ruins, bearing his name, are reminders of the history of the close of the first and the beginning of the second centuries of the Christian Era.

The destructive wars of Napoleon Bonaparte are commemorated in Paris by triumphal arches in Place du Carousel and Place de l'Etoile; and in Place Vendome rises a column modeled after the column of Trajan. The galleries of France glare with highly imaginative representations of the Napoleonic wars. A turn of the kaleidoscope, and standing on the field of Waterloo we see a mound of earth 150 feet high, on the summit of which the British Lion triumphantly looks defiance over the site of Napoleon's headquarters at Belle Alliance.

Pomp and glitter with the excitement and victories of war, have educated men to hero worship of the military chieftain who through blood and carnage attains signal victory; and the sculptor's and the painter's art are exhausted to cultivate admiration for military achievements; and they are commemorated in song and story.

4

In the progress of the world's civilization, the cultivation of the arts of peace is resulting in victories, which if not so glittering are more beneficial to mankind, lifting them to a higher and better plane of life.

Friendly contests among the nations in the arts, sciences and industries which benefit mankind are celebrations that stimulate the world to the building up of all the nations in those things that make a people great and prosperous and happy. Such are the conquests of peace. No ruined cities or devastated fields follow in the path of such victories. From them some noble structures are left as monuments to perpetuate their memory, like the beautiful crystal palace of Sydenham, the palaces of Industry and Trocadero in Paris, and the Horticultural and Memorial Halls in Fairmount Park at Philadelphia.

When in 1876 our nation celebrated the centennial anniversary of its birth by such an exhibition, the different sections of our Union were drawn into closer relations of amity, and our nation with the other nations of the world; while the central thought of Republican Liberty, that "MANKIND IS CAPABLE OF SELF-GOVERNMENT" was sown like the seed of the sower that, in the parable, went forth to sow.

Acts that are truly great and far-reaching in their influence, in human estimation grow with the lapse of centuries.

Four hundred years ago, Christopher Columbus discovered America. which in effect was the discovery of a new world and joining it to the old. For a brief period following his heroic discovery he was treated with marked favor, but afterward there were few to do him honor, and neglected, he died in poverty. After four centuries his courage, skill, daring adventure and grand achievement have come to be appreciated in the new world which he discovered, and popular sentiment decreed that its fourth centennial must be celebrated with a world's fair.

The Congress of the United States recognized this decree in the following words: "Whereas, it is fit and appropriate that the four hundredth anniversary of the discovery of America be commemorated by an exhibition of the resources of the United States of America, their development, and of the progress of civilization in the new world," and enacted that this commemoration shall be a World's Columbian Exposition to be inaugurated in the year 1892, in the city of Chicago, in the state of Illinois.

The location was most happy, for its citizens, in leading characteristics, are like Columbus, energetic, courageous, daring and persevering. As the storm spirit was unable to deter the great navigator from pressing on in his voyage of discovery, so the fire fiend spreading devastation through the heart of this city, sweeping away its noblest structures like chaff before the wind, could not deter its citizens from pressing forward in the building of the finest and greatest city that was ever constructed in so short a time, since the creation of the world, and it has been truly said that one of the greatest exhibits of the exhibition, will be the city of Chicago itself.

With characteristic energy and boldness they entered upon the herculean task of preparing for the reception of the world upon a scale of grandeur and magnificence never before equalled, and the result of their labors is to-day before us.

While the bill was pending before Congress providing for the Columbian Exposition, the 23d General Assembly of the state of Iowa, passed an act approved April 15th, 1890, making an appropriation and providing for an Iowa Columbian Commission charged with the duty of devising and executing plans to creditably represent at such Exposition, the agricultural, mineral, mechanical, industrial, educational and other resources and advantages of the state.

When the President of the United States in pursuance of the act of Congress had issued his proclamation, our Commission issued an address to the people of the state, invoking their aid to place Iowa in her exhibit before the world in the position to which she is justly entitled, that we might be enabled to compare with other states our condition and capabilities, and our Nation, with other Nations, and setting forth that this Exposition "will be a school of observation to the farmer, of technical education to the artisan, of design to the manufacturer; it will stimulate progress in the sciences, arts and industries that benefit mankind; it will advance knowledge, dispel conceit and prejudice, and cultivate friendship between individuals, States and Nations."

"There is no other means of diffusing knowledge in so short a time, so wide and varied in its scope, to an extent so great and far reaching in its refining and elevating influence."

"It is desirable that the greatest possible number of our people should attend the Exposition, and devote as much time as they can give to the study of its mammoth collection of object lessons, for it will be an opportunity the value of which is beyond computation."

It was deemed of first importance that a commodious building should be erected as a headquarters for the numerous visitors from our state that would avail themselves of the advantages here to be gained, and an early application for a site on which to build, resulted finally in the acquisition of this delightful location on the shore washed by the waves of Michigan, the head of the great chain of American lakes.

It is a fitting locality to serve as a headquarters for our beloved state that lies within the embrace of the two great rivers of the West, the Missouri and Mississippi, within that temperate zone that gives health and vigor to its people—and with a soil of great fertility, irrigated by nature, seed time and harvest never fail. Providence has spread its gifts with bountiful hand throughout its borders.

In 1854 when it became my home, there was not a mile of railway within its limits, and the population numbered 326,000. Now, it is enveloped in a network of 10,000 miles, extending into all of its ninety-nine counties, affording railway facilities for its 2,000,000 inhabitants and its $474,000,000 worth of annual products. This marks the progress of Iowa.

Designed by Iowa Architects, Josselyn & Taylor of Cedar Rapids, under the supervision of the Executive Committee, Commissioners Mallory, Packard and Seaman, this structure has been prepared in which to install a collective exhibit of Iowa products, not for competition, but to show the wealth of the resources of our state.

Spacious apartments are provided, attractively decorated, in part by the skill and labors of the ladies of our state generously contributed, for the accommodation of Iowa visitors, where kindly attention will be cheerfully bestowed to minister to their comfort and make their stay pleasant; a place to welcome friends, to greet the stranger, to write and to receive letters, to read the home papers, to gain information in general about the Exposition; a place where weary ones can rest and be thankful that they are citizens of the Hawkeye State; in short, as complete a home as we can make it, and from its highest pinnacle floats our National Banner;

> "As it floated long before us,
> Be it ever floating o'er us,
>   O'er our land from shore to shore;
> There are freemen yet to wave it,
> Millions who would die to save it,
>   Wave it, save it evermore."

In its constellation of states there will be no star that in patriotism shall shine brighter than Iowa.

And now in behalf of the Iowa Columbian Commission, to you Governor Boies, as the chief Executive Officer of the State of Iowa, I present this structure, to be by you dedicated to the uses and purposes for which it is designed.

## DEDICATION BY HIS EXCELLENCY, HORACE BOIES, GOVERNOR OF IOWA.

*Mr President of the Iowa Columbian Commission:*

I am assured by those who have perfected the arrangements for this occasion that the duty assigned me is a purely formal one.

Before discharging this, permit me in behalf of the people of our state to express to you and those associated with you their gratitude for the faithful and efficient manner in which you have discharged your duties as members of that Commission, and the pride we all feel in the work you have thus far accomplished.

And now, Mr. President, as the representative of the citizens of Iowa, I accept from your hands this beautiful edifice and in their name dedicate it to the noble purposes for which it was constructed, hoping it will largely assist in bringing to the attention of the world the many advantages of the state whose munificent bounty has produced it. And to the President of the World's Columbian Exposition, for and in behalf of my people, I tender this building a contribution from their hands to the great work over which he has been called to preside, believing it worthy of those who present it, and hoping it will prove of substantial assistance in the accomplishment of that grand success which we earnestly pray may crown his efforts and make this the greatest and the best of all the World's Expositions.

IOWA STATE BUILDING, GOVERNOR'S ROOM.

## THE BALLAD OF COLUMBUS.

### BY MAJ. S. H. M. BYERS.

### READ BY MRS. LUCIA GALE BARBER.

Copyrighted).

It was fourteen hundred and ninety-two,
    The close of the New Year's day,
When the armies of Catholic Ferdinand,
The flower of all the Spanish land,
    At the siege of Granada lay.

Ten thousand foot and ten thousand horse
    And ten thousand men with bows
Were on the left, and as many more
Had stormed close up to the city's door,
    Where the Darrow River flows.

And the king held levee, for on that day
    Great news had come to court—
How on the morrow the town would yield,
And the flag of Spain, with the yellow field,
    Would float from the Moorish fort.

There were princely nobles and high grandees
    That night in the royal tent;
And the beautiful queen with the golden hair
And shining armor and sword was there—
    On the king's right arm she leant.

It was nine, and the old Alhambra bells
    Tolled out on the moonlit air;
And over the battlements far there came
The murmuring sound of Allah's name,
    And the Moorish troops at prayer.

"Hark!" said the king, as he heard the sound,
    "Hark! hark! to yon bells refrain—
Five hundred years it has called the Moor;
This night, and 'twill call him nevermore—
    To-morrow 'twill ring for Spain."

Then spake a guest at the king's right hand :
    "To-morrow the end will be;
Hast thou not said, when the war is done
And the Christ flag floats o'er the Moslem one,
    Thou would'st keep thy promise to me?

"Thou wouldst give me ships, and wouldst give me men
    Who would dare to follow me?
Help thou this night with thy royal hand,
And I'll make thee king of a new-found land
    And king of a new-found sea.

"For the world is round, and a ship may sail
    Straight on with the setting Sun,
Beyond Atlantis a thousand miles,
Beyond the peaks of the golden isles,
    To the Ophir of Solomon.

"So I'll find new roads to the golden isles,
    To the gardens that bloom alway,
To the treasure-quarries of Ispahan,
The sunlit hills of the mighty Khan,
    And the wonders of far Cathay.

"And gold I'll bring from the islands fair,
    And riches of palm and fir
Thou shalt have, my king; and the lords of Spain
Shall march with the Christ flag once again,
    And rescue the Sepulchre."

But the nobles smiled and the prelates sneered,
    With many a scornful fling;
"Had not the wisest already said
It was but the scheme of an empty head,
    And no fit thing for a king?

"And were it true that the world is round,
    And not like an endless plain,
Were our good king's vessels the seas to ride
Adown the slope of the world's great side,
    How would they get up again?

"And the land of the fabled antipodes
    Was a wonderful land to see,
Where people stand with their heads on the ground,
And their feet in the air, while the world spins round"—
    And they all laughed merrily.

But the king laughed not, though he scarce believed
    The things that his ears had heard;
And he thought full long of the promise fair,
And he knew that the day and the hour were there,
    If a king were to keep his word.

So he said, "For a while, for a little while,
    Let it bide, for the cost is great;"
But the guest replied: "Nay, seven years
I have waited on with my hopes and fears;
    And soon it will be too late."

Then spake the queen, "Be it done for me.
    Here are jewels for woe or weal;"
And she took the gems from her shining hair,
And the priceless pearls she was wont to wear,
    And she said, "For my own Castile."

  \*      \*      \*      \*      \*      \*

There were three ships sailing from Palos town,
    Ere the noon of a summer's day,
And the people looked at the ships and said,
"God pity their souls, for they all are dead;"
    But the ships went down the bay.

And an east wind blew and the convent bells
    Rang out in sweet accord,
And the master stood on the deck and cried,
"We sail in the name of the Crucified,
    With the flag of Christ our Lord."

They were ten days out when a storm wind blew—
    Ten days from the coast of Spain
And the sailors shrived each other and said,
"God help us now, or we all are dead!
    We shall never see land again."

They were twelve days out when an ocean rock
    Burst forth in a sea of fire.
As if each peak and each lava cliff
Of the red-hot sides of Teneriffe,
    Were a sea-king's funeral pyre.

And the sailors crossed themselves and said,
    "Alas, for the day we swore
To follow a reckless adventurer—
Though it be at last to the Sepulchre
    In search of an unknown shore."

And they spoke of the terror that lay between,
    Of the hurricanes born of hell,
Of the sunless seas that forever roar,
Where the moon had perished long years before,
    When an evil spirit fell.

And ever the winds blew west, blew west,
    And the ships blew over the main.
"They are cursed winds," the mariners said,
"That blow us forever ahead—ahead;
    They will never blow back to Spain."

But the master cited the Holy Writ;
    And he told of a vision fair,
How a shining angel would show the way
To the Indus Isles and the sweet Cathay,
    And he "knew they were almost there."

But a sea-calm came, and the ships stood still,
    And the sails drooped idle and low,
And a seaweed covered the vasty deep
As darkness covers a world in sleep,
    And they feared for the rocks below.

It was twelve that night when a breeze sprang fresh,
    As from a land close by,
And the sailors whispered each other and said,
"God only knows what next is ahead—
    Or if to-morrow we die."

It was two by the clock on the ship next morn,
    And breathless the sailors stand,
With eyes strained into the starless night,
When, lo! there's a cry of "A light, a light!"
    And a shout of "The land, the land!"

There were weeping eyes, there were pressing hands,
    Till the dawn of that blessed day;
When the admiral, followed by all his train,
With the flag of Christ and the flag of Spain,
    Rode proudly up the bay.

In robes of scarlet and princely gold,
    On the New World's land they kneel;
In the name of Christ, whom all adore,
They christened the island San Salvador,
    For the crown of their own Castile.

And the simple islanders gazed in awe
    On the "gods from another sphere;"
And they brought them gifts of the Yuca bread,
And golden trinkets, and parrots red,
    And showed them the islands near.

They told of the lords of a golden house,
    Of the mountains of Cibao,
The cavern where once the moon was born,
The hills that waken the sun at morn,
    And the isles where the spices grow.

From isle to island the ships flew on,
    Like white birds on the main,
Till the master said, "With my flags unfurled,
I have opened the gates of another world
    I will carry the news to Spain."

It was seven months since at Palos town,
    Ere the noon of that summer's day,
The good ships sailed, with their flags unfurled,
In search of another and far-off world—
    And again they are in the bay.

Twelve months have passed, and the king again
    Holds levee with all his train,
And Columbus sits at the king's right hand,
And, whether on sea or upon the land,
    Is the greatest man in Spain.

IOWA STATE BUILDING, ASSEMBLY ROOM, SECOND STORY.

And the queen has honored him most of all—
    She has taken him by the hand:
"Don Christopher thou shalt be called alway;"
And a golden cross on his heart there lay,
    And over his breast a band.

And ships she gave, and a thousand men,
    With nobles and knights in train;
And again the convent bells they rung,
And the praise of his name was on every tongue,
    And he sailed for the west again—

To the hundred islands and far away
    In the heats of the torrid zone,
To gardens as fair as Hesperides,
To spice-grown forests, and scented seas
    Where no sails had ever blown.

And up and down by the New World's coast,
    And over the western main,
With but the arms of his own true word,
He lifted the flag of the blessed Lord
    And the flag of the land of Spain.

And he gave them all to the king and queen,
    And riches of things untold;
And never a ship that crossed the sea
But brought them tokens from fruit and tree,
    And gems from the land of gold.

Three times he had sailed to his new-found world,
    Five times he had crossed the main,
When, walking once by the sea, he heard,
By secret letter or secret word,
    Of a murderous plot in Spain

How that envious persons about the court
    Had poisoned the mind of the king
By many a letter of false report,
By base suspicion of evil sort,
    And words with a traitorous sting.

And the king, half eager to hear the worst,
    For he never had been a friend,
Believed it all, and he rued the hour
He gave to the master rank and power,
    And resolved it should have an end.

So with cold pretence of the truth to hear,
    And with heart that was false as base,
A ship was hurried across the main,
With Bobadilla, false knight of Spain,
    To take the admiral's place.

O that kings should ever unkingly be!
    O that men should ever forget!
For that fatal hour the false knight came,
To the king's disgrace and the great world's shame
    The star of Columbus set.

They took the queen's cross from off his breast,
    And chains they gave him instead;
And iron gyves on his wrists they put,
Vile fetters framed for each hand and foot –
    " 'Twere better they left him dead."

For he who was first of the new-found world,
    And bravest upon the main,
Who had found the isles of the fabled gold,
And the far-off lands that his faith foretold,
    Was dragged like a felon to Spain.

But the whole world heard the clank of his chains,
    When he landed in Cadiz bay;
And fearing the taunt and the curse and scoff,
The false king hurried to take them off,
    At the pier where the old ship lay.

But little it helped, or the king's false smile,
    As he sat in his robes of state;
For wrong is wrong, if in hut or hall,
And the right were as well not done at all,
    If done, alas! too late.

And little it helped if, here and there,
    The mantle of favor stole
Across his shoulders, to hide the stain
Of a broken heart or a broken chain—
    They had burned too deep in his soul.

So the years crept by, and the cold neglect
    Of kings that will come the while;
Forever and ever 'tis still the same –
Short-lived's the glory of him whose fame,
    Depends upon a prince's smile.

And long he thought, could he see the queen,
    Could he speak with her face to face,
She would know the truth and would be again
What once she was, ere his hopes were slain;
    And he sighed in his lonely place.

And on a day when he seemed forgot,
    And darker the fates, and grim,
A letter came, 'twas the queen's command,
"Come straight to court," in her own fair hand,
    And she would be true to him.

But alas for man, and alas for queen,
    And alas for hopes so sped!
He had only come to the castle gate,
    When the warder said, "It is late—too late,
For the queen, she is lying dead."

And the king forgot what the fair, good queen
    With her dying lips had said;
And he who had given a world to Spain
Had never a roof for himself again,
    And he wished that he, too, were dead.

Slow tolled the bells of old Seville town,
    At noon of a summer's day;
For up in a chamber in yonder inn,
Close by the street with its noise and din,
    The heart of the New World lay.

Perhaps the king, on his throne close by,
    No thought to the tolling gave;
But over a world, far up and down,
They heard the bells of Seville town,
    And they stood by an open grave.

And the Seville bells, they are ringing still,
    Through the centuries far and dim;
And though it is but the common lot
Of men to die, and to be forgot,
    They will ring forever for him.

## ORATION BY JUDGE EDWARD P. SEEDS.

As citizens of the Commonwealth of Iowa, we have gathered here upon the shores of the ever-throbbing lake, whose waves kiss a landscape spreading away to the west in one long vista of grassy, cultivated beauty; here in this wonderful city of Chicago,—the most marvelous evolution of municipal growth, business energy and unconquerable faith known in history, for the purpose of dedicating this building to the services of the Columbian Exposition, in exhibiting in material form the growth of our noble state. The purpose, the place the time are filled with inspiration, and, let us hope, prophetic of splendid victory for good government and individual character. The States of our Union are here in no jealous rivalry. Each glories in the garnered results of all the others. They were born into the life of our Republic at different times and sprang from variovs and dissimilar causes. They have not alike the same number of talents, but none, upon this occasion, brings her talents without usury, or tarnished with the dirt of burial. Each commonwealth pours into the lap of this wonderful city the richest productions of her farms, the surprising creations of her workshops, the varied product of her roaring furnaces and busy manufactories, the noblest and best results of her intellectual efforts: in fact all that is truest and best in her history. And this, that the citizenship of the world may see and realize that our people have been blest, materially and intellectually, and we hope spiritually, as no other people upon the earth; that other nations as they study this wide-spread and far-reaching expansion of life may take therefrom inspiration to utilize and adopt all that is truly good and wise in our growth. Each state, necessarily, from its geographical position, its climatic conditions, and other physical environments, together with its historical developments, has an individuality peculiarly its own. Upon such occasions as these, when for months the state will stand forth in the full light of day, "to be seen and read of all men," that individuality becomes dynamic in its expression; it prompts the state to spread a wide canvass, and to paint her picture in grand relief; to lay the colors on with a heavy brush, yet with the touch of a skilled artist; to so arrange the background as to catch the light of history at every coigne of vantage. The artist who paints this picture for Iowa must not only be a master in technique, an adept in coloring, and skilled with the brush, but beyond and above all, he must have the inspiration of the poet, and the vision of the prophet in order that the grace and charm which cling to such a subject, like the perfume to the rose, may be caught and made to live. The speaker is aware that he is not the artist which such a work of art demands; but he trusts that he may gather into a general outline the prominent facts of Iowa's short and luminous history, and so present them that your loyal and loving imaginations may fill up the outline with beauty, and so be held in proud remembrance until the artist shall come to paint our picture in elegant and charming prose for the delight of the future. That such an artist will come admits not of a doubt. A great occasion demands and will produce its interpreter.

Geographically Iowa is centrally located in relation to the territory of our nation, and is located in fruitful embrace by two of the mightiest rivers of the earth—the Mississippi and the Missouri, while upon the north and south it is bounded by the two powerful and growing states of Minnesota and Missouri respectively. Within the area so circumscribed lies 55,000 square miles of the most productive, well watered, undulating and beautiful land that the sun enriches with its wealth of heat and light in all its yearly journey. There is probably less waste land to the amount of arable land than in any equal area of soil in the wide world. Its position too, as to climatic conditions could not well be improved; in the winters the cold is of that bracing, invigorating character, which locks and conserves the productive elements of the soil, and at the same time makes vigorous and vitally active the powers of the human body; while the warmth of our summers brings into lavish activity all of the productive forces of our protean soil. Our springs and autumns are nature's poems; filled with the music of purling streams, the anthems of rustling leaves and soughing branches, the melody of the sweet-voiced meadow-lark; made beauteous with the profusion of prairie flower—the butter-cup, the daisy, the violet and golden rod; and glory crowned with the yellow, russet, brown and red of autumnal fruitage. A beautiful land indeed! The seat of no fabled Hesperides, but a present and visible paradise full of unnumbered beauties. Historically our commonwealth has but recently become a product of articulate Time. For three centuries after the discovery of this continent our land slept in the bosom of the great unknown, with only an occasional whisper that there was a land "of pure delight" far beyond the towering heights of the Alleghenies. When

IOWA STATE BUILDING, LOOKING SOUTH FROM EAST END.

the cruel and senseless edicts of kings and the fierce oppression of bigotry in the old world was driving the brave and true-hearted into the rugged wilderness of our Atlantic coast, the land now known as Iowa was the home of the buffalo and the Indian. The population upon our eastern shores had become quite numerous; the first stirrings of National life were being felt; the prophecies of a New Nation were being uttered, when in 1673, Joliet and Marquette, two French missionaries, floating upon the placid waters of the Mississippi, first gazed upon the flower-decked prairies of our Iowa. The white man was now looking upon a far-reaching picture of Nature's loveliness, and we may well believe that visions of future greatness, as to the occupants of the land before him, began to take shape in his historical consciousness; a vision not unfolded in words, but handed down from generation to generation, with the potency of unuttered thought, until it burst into a reality in this century. The two missionaries must pass away, and a century sift its dust upon their tombs, ere that vision begins to assume form and fashion; a century of struggle and storm; a century in which freedom, emerging from the pit of slavery, grapples in deadly strife with monarchical pretension and aristocratic greed and triumphs. A century without which the history of Iowa might have been one of darkness and sorrow, instead of joy and gladness. During these years, slow going, the population upon the Atlantic coast increased greatly, and pushed, amid multitudinous difficulties, over the mountain wall, and obtained a footing upon the eastern edge of the Mississippi valley. Not until 1788 did any white man look again upon the soil of Iowa. Then it was that Julien Dubuque, a French Canadian, staked a claim upon the picturesque site of the present prosperous, wealthy and enlightened city named for himself. The vision of the Frenchmen of a century before had begun to take form — Iowa was to be. Beginnings are proverbially slow. The inertia of great masses is not easily overcome. The wider the room in which any given expansive force is to act, the less effective the force; so it was only when the energy, hope and practical business activity of the people in the eastern portion of our country became so confined as to need an outlet, that the population rolled through and over the magnificent states of Ohio, Indiana and Illinois and entered into the Promised Land. It was about the year 1833 that this onward moving tide of civilization first made permanent settlement upon the eastern borders of our state. A year or so on either side of that date is immaterial to the general fact. The places upon which they pitched their tents were pleasant to look upon, but there was nothing about them to suggest that in a few short years those sites would be occupied by the energetic, progressive and handsome cities of Keokuk, Ft. Madison, Burlington, Davenport, Muscatine and Dubuque. Gathered at nightfall around their camp-fires, these pilgrims of the prairies, tired, lonely and no doubt homesick, their eyes may have been rested and their souls exalted, by gazing upon a scene more enchanting than any of the marvelous creations of a Michael Angelo; a scene to them of passing beauty simply, but in truth a scene fresh from the brush of the great Creator and carrying in it a prophecy of the future. At their feet moving in majestic grandeur were the blue waters of the Mississippi; its waves, faintly breaking on the grassy banks, seemed to the homeless pilgrims, to be chanting a requiem over their happy past, and yet its music entered into their unuttered musings with that gentle touch of nature which soothes and at the same time engenders courage. The wide, rolling, grass-covered prairies stretched in unbroken loveliness, except where broken by the rippling waters of the merry stream, far into the west; there the great luminary of day was just sinking from sight, bathing the earth and sky in one transcendent flood of golden light; just before it sinks behind the golden-tipped line of our western boundary, there might have been seen athwart its red disk the rushing, plunging shadow of the buffalo, and closely following the dark, savage silhouette of a red warrior, his form erect and defiant, his visage stern with wrath yet over it all the shadowed fear of final defeat; for one moment he stands in haughty defiance, and then the warrior and buffalo plunge into the Sun and are gone. As the myriad stars, in their silvery splendor, swing out their lights in the dark vault of heaven, the lonely pioneers on the margin of the river might have guessed the prophecy in the scene the dawn had risen upon Iowa, and its ancient denizens must depart.

Let us, for a moment consider who these pioneers were, and what their character, as they stand upon our soil for the first time in 1833. This is an initial point in our history—in truth, here and with these men and women our history begins. Previous to this time Iowa is mentioned only in connection with other large areas of land; its existence had been but a whispered one; it had no civilization, it had no promise. But now we are in the presence of the genesis of a commonwealth—and what it shall *be* depends upon what those homeless wanderers *were*. They were to be the fathers and mothers of a people who now and here proudly and confidently challenge the admiration of the world. Is our challenge justified? Who were the pioneers of 1833? They were the commonality from the states of New England, New York, Ohio and Indiana; men and women who thought that they could make more of life and its opportunity in the far west. They had descended from a yeoman stock that had upon innumerable battle fields in this and the old world defended the rights of man. Were they a people blessed with an abundance of material wealth? Far from it. They may have had the bare necessities of life, but that was all. But in their characters they had the wealth of the ages; their souls were filled with that indomitable courage which knows no moral fear; their minds were stored with that wholesome knowledge which teaches one to grasp at Nature's resources and transmute them into agencies for man's benefaction; they possessed a faith that surmounted the things of time and sense, and saw the completion of man's nature in the radiant beauty of a higher life. They were not educated in the learned institutions of the east; but they had studied deeply in the Unversity of Nature and had treasured up and made a part of themselves her lessons of manhood and womanhood. They knew the value of education though, and sacrificed much that those who came after them might drink deep and long at the fountains of knowledge. They never had rested in the lap of luxury, but they had learned well that lesson, first taught by the Almighty, that labor is honorable in all men; and that the sun-browned face and the calloused hand is the best diploma man can possess. In the presence of such evidences of graduation from God's University the dilettanteism of the 400, the sensualism of the court, and the aristocracy of slavery alike shrink away. Those women may not have graced the salons of the rich and cultured; their forms may never have been robed with the silks and satins of the orient; their days were probably spent in the hard cares of household drudgery; but in nobility of soul, in sweetness of disposition, earnestness of character and true courage they never had superiors. Their kisses were inspirations, their smiles were benedictions, while their words of love and instruction wrought miracles in the human soul. Motherhood never found more lovely caskets than in those lonely, unknown, immortal women who watched by the river brink in 1833. From such women are born noble sons and lovely daughters; sons and daughters who rear monuments more durable than stone or brass to their memory as they build a commonwealth founded in courage, love and truth. Those men and women have gone to their reward, but the soil of Iowa is sanctified by the presence therein of their dust. May we hold them in sweet and lasting remembrance!

From this time forward our history becomes more marked and important. In 1846, after various efforts, Iowa took her place in the sisterhood of states. There she has taken an important place. In every effort for the amelioration of the condition of humanity she has been in the foremost ranks. She determinedly set her face like a flint against the crime of slavery; and when that crime had brought upon this Nation the mad passion of war, she sent to the front 75,000 of her sons to emphasize her protest against the wickedness of that system; to aid in maintaining the integrity of the Union; to uphold the nobility of manual labor. Into the varied character of our history, since we became a state, other than it is developed in our industrial, intellectual and moral growth, we can not enter to-day. Industrially, our progress has been phenomenal; and its direction and amount is the necessary outgrowth of our conditions and personal characteristics. It is no easy undertaking to present in a compact form, and yet vividly, the many factors which go to make up the industrial life of a people; to bring before your imagination the thousands and thousands of acres of grain, waving in the summer's breeze; to present to you the equal or greater acreage of maize, which stands like great banks of swaying emerald, until by the alchemy of the Sun's rays it is transmuted into fields of gold; to lead before you the countless herds of meek-eyed kine, and recite to you the tales of their production of milk and butter—tales which sound like stories of the Arabian Knights, but are true as Holy Writ itself; to ask you to listen to the rolling thunder as it tells of the approach of an army of horses which equal in speed, beauty and power the far famed steeds of Araby the Blest; to summon from a hundred thousand farms the innumerable concourse of Chicago jewels, and to hush their unmelodious voices in your presence; to take you into our myriad workshops, and into the darkness of our mines of coal and there show you our intelligent artisans turning the crude material into articles of use and beauty; to take you along our handsome streets, and broad highways and with conscious pride point you to our palatial stores, our humming factories, our noble public buildings, and tell you how they are all developed from the crude, inartistic buildings of 1846-in a word to hang before you a word-painting, even in faint outline, that would do justice to Iowa's present grandeur is for me impossible. I can only submit to you a column of figures—the driest of facts—the indices simply of the possible, for they can not, in truth, unfold to you the fact. Nor can I give you the figures for a series of years, for it would be too voluminous, and make of this faint effort of an oration a catalogue of names and figures, instead of an inspiration, as it ought to be. I have chosen as years for comparison 1849-50 and the year 1891. In so doing I have chosen the earlier year somewhat arbitrarily, and with no idea of picking out one of less relative prosperity than those immediately preceding it, but mainly because I have had access to the statistics of that year and not to those preceding it. The time which has elapsed from 1850 to last year is indeed short, it is but a span, and yet what a marvelous growth is exhibited by this small array of figures! To understand how incomprehensible these figures are, you have but to ascertain the ratio of increase for any given number of years, say five, and apply that to the half century of our existence as a state, and the result will surprise you by its vastness. In 1850 our population was 192,124, or about one-sixth as many as now inhabit this one city; at the present time our population is at least 2,000,000. This represents the unity of our present brain power.

In 1849-50 our industrial condition stood about as follows:

| | |
|---|---|
| Wheat, bushels | 1,530,581 |
| Oats, " | 1,524,345 |
| Corn, " | 8,656,799 |
| Potatoes, " | 282,368 |
| Butter, pounds | 2,171,188 |
| Cheese, " | 209,840 |
| Horses | 38,536 |
| Cows | 45,704 |
| Swine | 323,247 |
| Other cattle | 91,000 |
| Sheep | 149,960 |
| Value of live stock on farms | $3,689,275 |

At the first glance these figures may seem large, and to the average citizen, who has no occasion to hunt about in musty records or to burden his mind with figures, it may seem that any enlargement of them to any great extent will be an attempt to impose upon one's credulity. When we strike the million figure we have about reached the limit of average computations, and anything above it has the air of oriental exaggeration. However that may be, the following statement of production is substantially correct, and indicates what Iowa citizens accomplished along one channel of their activity in 1891:

| | |
|---|---|
| Corn, bushels | 335,031,598 |
| Wheat, " | 27,586,000 |
| Oats " | 115,810,800 |
| Rye " | 2,051,400 |
| Barley " | 4,528,660 |
| Potatoes," | 25,828,250 |
| Hay, tons | 5,882,800 |
| Butter, pounds | 168,690,715 |
| Cheese, " | 5,000,000 |
| Horses | 1,095,300 |
| Mules | 42,739 |
| Sheep | 452,000 |
| Hogs | 5,921,100 |
| Milch cows | 1,278,612 |
| Other cattle | 2,680,247 |

These amounts, together with various smaller items, which belong to the part of our industry known as agricultural, aggregate in money value the enormous sum of $474,097,710. Are you able to comprehend it? But this is not all there is of our industrial life. Take our coal. Nearly one-half of our state is underlaid with this heat producer. It is produced in twenty-six counties. During the year 1889 there were mined 4,061.704 tons, valued at $5,392,220; and there was distributed in wages among 9,198 employees $2,903,291.

It must not be forgotten that in 1850 the production of coal was of little consequence; and at the same time our manufactories amounted to nothing. It is true that we are principally an agricultural state, but that does not preclude the possibility of our having a large capital in manufactories. The truth is that we have over $100,000,000 invested in those institutions, and there is hardly a town of three thousand inhabitants in our state, from which may not be seen daily the smoke from a factory. This accumulation of ever changing forms of wealth is carried from place to place, from farm to market by means of over 8,440 miles of railways, the total earnings of which in 1890 was $43,102,399; and the number of employees was 27,580.

A fair index of the industrial standing of a people may readily be gained by consulting the bank accounts. Last year in the savings banks (and they usually represent the common laborer,) the deposits aggregated $20,821,495, while in the state banks the deposits were $12,060,211. It is hardly possible that any citizen of this proud Nation, whether his home be in Maine or Texas, or in our own loved state, can be other than greatly pleased by such a showing of the industrial forces of one of the commonwealths of our land. But if this was all that we had to bring to this exhibition, if we only had the material to call the world's attention to, I question if we would have much worthy a noble people's consideration. Thank God that our material is but the pedestal upon which is reared a character for true manhood and womanhood unsurpassed, as I believe, in the whole world! And that character has for its inner motive the intellectual and moral life of our people. Our intellectual life is represented principally by two factors; the common school system, together with its cognate system of higher education, and the public press. In 1850 the number of schools were few indeed; the accommodations poor and the system of education crude and mechanical in the extreme. In 1891 the statistics of the common schools were as follows:

| | |
|---|---|
| Children of school age | 668,541 |
| Enrolled in public schools | 503,755 |
| Number of teachers | 26,769 |
| Number of school houses | 13,129 |
| Value of school houses | $13,184,914 |

The total expenditure for school purposes is now over $6,000,000 annually. We have over twenty institutions entirely given to higher education. The character of our instruction in these schools is of the highest. Our teachers are in the front ranks as educators, and are ready and anxious to adopt all improved methods whereby our children may obtain the requisite knowledge for life's work in the most scientific manner. That our educational system is doing good work, and is entitled to our most earnest praise and acknowledgment is shown in the fact, that in 1880 and 1890 the census showed that our people had the least amount of illiteracy among them of any state in the Union, and of a consequence of any people on the earth. The greatest power to-day for all purposes is the Press. Find the general character of that instrument of progress and you can at once tell the general character of the people.

The press takes up the ideas, the thoughts, the aspirations of a people and spreads them broad cast. It makes possible the permanent good accomplished by the schools, though, unfortunately, it may be the active means of turning the rational product of the school to bad ends. In our state in 1850 the press was of that crude make that characterized all the instruments of progress of that day. There were but a dozen or so of papers published in our wide domain, and they were principally given to the spreading of local news. The telegraph and railroad had not at that time made it possible to bring daily to the editor's table the facts of the world, and hence he did not see or feel the necessity of writing leaders, which should present the good or bad principles behind the daily facts for the consideration of the people. Now that is all changed; not alone do the papers come to our homes laden with a multiplicity of fact, but there is with them the editorial, from which the newspaper takes a large part of its character. In 1890 there were published in our state 756 newspapers. Of these 47 were daily and 646 were weekly, the balance being tri-weekly, monthly and fortnightly. Our daily press is exceptionally free from the vice of some of the metropolitan dailies, which find their greatest force in spreading, with great particularity, the latest social scandal, the brutal action of *things*, masquerading as men, in their efforts to eclipse the dogs in fighting, or in retailing fully the rascality of the previous day. Our dailies seem to appreciate the the fact that they enter pure homes, they are read by noble boys and lovely girls, and that they are responsible for their growing characters. The weekly press is unquestionably the bulwark of our homes and of our morals. With hardly an exception they are ably edited, carefully sifted that nothing impure enters their columns, and filled with the character of general literature which aids in moulding good lives. Our state is too new to have developed any great strength in the line of pure literature; though a number of our citizens have become authors of very creditable works. In the line of art our state has produced some paintings and statuary, which conclusively demonstrate that the artistic faculty is present with our people. But art in its highest form can not be produced while a people are given over principally to the accumulation of material wealth; and yet, that is necessarily our present condition. Not that we choose the latter in preference to the former, but because the conditions are such as to compel us to take the direction which we do. But our intellectual development, our moral growth are both in the direction which will, if not turned aside by the lack of faith or religious aspirations, ultimately lead to an artistic expression. Our moral life is shown in our homes and our religious institutions. And I believe that the power of our state is found in this department of our life. Iowa is great and prosperous; Iowa has taken a foremost position in this Nation, not because she has a broad and fruitful soil, not because she has the material elements which enter into the activities of our modern life, not because she has splendid schools and wide-awake newspapers, but because she has pure and God fearing homes, and the institutions in every hamlet and town and upon her wide prairies, which stand for a higher and a better power than is found in man alone. Iowa has never forgotten that there is a God.

Thus imperfectly, but in truthful effort, have I endeavored to present to you in words, the political, material, intellectual and moral history of one of the foremost Commonwealths of this Nation; a Commonwealth of which we are all proud to be citizens. In a more substantial, in a more concrete manner will the evidences of these great elements of our prosperity be presented to the admiring gaze of the peoples of the earth in the months which are to follow at this Exposition. No true citizen of Iowa can feel insensible to the splendid opportunity thus afforded his state, and duty and pleasure alike, should move him to do all in his power to so present the evidences of our marvelous growth, as to leave a lasting impression for good upon every individual who attends this Fair, and to advance to a higher plane the already enviable reputation which we possess as a people. But, my fellow-citizens, we will fail, and sadly fail of seizing the supreme opportunity of this occasion, if we are simply satisfied with a magnificent display of our farm products, of our herds and flocks, of the workmanship of our shops and manufactories, of our mines and railroads, of our school system, and the various evidences of our intellectual productiveness. This must constitute the basis, but it ought not to be the glory and truth of the impression which is to be the permanent impression made by our state. Who now puts his knowledge-seeking interrogation, as to Greece or Rome in this form: "What did Greece do, or what did Rome do?" Who cares for the simple fact, *solely*, that Greece conquered at Salamis, or that three hundred patriots died at Thermopylae in defense of their country? Such facts have been repeated many times since, in their essence. Why waste time reading of the victories of Cæsar, or of the stern, and oft-times barbarous rule of the City by the Tiber? Who cares whether those ancient people had few or many cattle, good roads or bad ones, one lyceum or a dozen, homes of luxury or of poverty? Not that all these things are not of interest and importance to the historian or the sociologist, but they are of little importance to the world at large. But our interrogation becomes instinct with life, it is of importance to all men when put in this fashion: "What was *the Greek*, or what was *the Roman?*" "I am a Roman citizen," meant much, not of herds, and houses and schools, but as to character. That character stood for the supremacy of law, justice and order; and that character is Rome's gift to the world. Rome's influence on earth to-day is through the power of that gift. The Roman citizen, the man, the woman, were the authors of that gift. To be a Greek meant, not to be identified with great battles, with goat-raising, and with money-getting, but to be a lover of the beautiful—whether in form, thought, or deed; and it is this character of the Greek, not of Greece, which has saved that Nation from being buried beneath the waters of oblivion. Out of the things which are called material, out of the acts which make history, is evolved that which characterizes a people and the individual; and that character is the crowning gift of the people to posterity. In a few months all this wonderful aggregation of wealth will have been dissipated to the four quarters of the globe. The multitudes of the world's citizens will have returned to their respective homes with generalized impressions of this Exposition. No brain is large enough, no memory is strong enough, no imagination is vivid enough to take into itself, call up and illumine the myriad facts which will be here presented. Only general impressions, which the individual is forming in his mind as he passes about among the exhibits, can become permanent and of future importance to him. What is to be the general impression that Iowa is to make as its permanent addition to the stock of the World's good? Shall it not be that her men are honest, intelligent and noble; her women lovely, true and queenly? Each of our citizens while here, whatever be your avocation in life, should endeavor to impress upon all with whom you come in contact that Iowa has none but gentlemen and ladies, none but loyal and intelligent persons in all her broad domain, none but men and women of broad culture, high thought and noble aspiration. You should remember constantly that here you are the walking, living epitome of all our history. Iowa has made you what you are; show the world that her production is almost an ideal one.

And, in conclusion, let us hope that when the world has given its final verdict upon this wonderful Exposition, when it has formed its supreme impression of the peoples represented here; that that verdict, and that impression as to Iowa will be, her citizenship is the true flower of righteous self-government, and then may we feel that our history is justified by her supreme production—a CITIZEN.

### BENEDICTION.

The Blessing of God, the Father, the Son and the Holy Ghost, be upon you and remain with you always. Amen.

### THE FORMAL OPENING CEREMONIES, MAY 1ST, 1893.

The next public ceremony at the Iowa State Building was May 1st, 1893, the opening day of the great Exposition. The attendance was larger on that day than for many weeks following. Not only was Iowa among the few states and nations that were prepared to open their buildings to visitors on the first day of the Exposition, but she was also able to show to the many thousands that visited her headquarters on that day and entered her neat and comfortable home, listened to the exercises in the assembly room and heard the pleasing concerts of her great band, the installation of her exhibits complete and wonderfully attractive, the wonderful designs and decorations in the pavilion and the superb exhibition of her natural products. People went away singing their praises of Iowa and telling all to visit "Iowa's Home" at the Exposition and they would be made welcome.

This occasion brought Iowa to the front and was the key note that gave her State Building and Exhibit the prominent place maintained throughout the entire period of the Exposition.

The exercises were held in the Assembly Room according to the following program.

## PROGRAM OF EXERCISES AT 1:30 P. M.

### ASSEMBLY ROOM, IOWA STATE BUILDING.

| | |
|---|---|
| Overture, "William Tell," | Iowa State Band |
| Invocation, | Rev. Charles Ashton |
| Introductory Address, | President James O. Crosby |
| Music, "American Airs," | Iowa State Band |
| Address, | Hon. W. M. McFarland |
| Musical Benediction, | Iowa State Band |

## INTRODUCTORY ADDRESS BY THE PRESIDENT.

*Fellow Citizens:*

The world with eager anticipation has awaited the arrival of this opening day of the World's Columbian Exposition.

International exhibitions were originally designed as competitive displays of products, for the encouragement of arts and manufactures and the promotion of commerce. Gradually they have enlarged their scope, and education and the liberal arts have been coming to the front, until the world's progress in the sciences, arts and industries that benefit mankind can be seen in them as in a mirror, and they are powerful influences in the advancement of civilization.

This Iowa State Building, on the 22d day of October, A. D., 1892, by the Iowa Columbian Commission, was presented to Gov. Boies as the Chief Executive Officer of the State of Iowa, by whom it was dedicated "to the noble purposes for which it was constructed."

Since that time it has been suitably furnished and decorated to minister to the comfort, convenience and pleasure of the citizens of our state, and there has been installed herein an exhibit of its bountiful resources now ready for the inspection of all people.

On this day, in this magic White City, all nations are assembled by their representatives, presenting the exhibits which they believe will best evidence their advancement in the world's march of progress.

And now to you Mr. McFarland, as Secretary of the State of Iowa, and member of its Executive Council, in behalf of the Iowa Columbian Commission, I present this building, with its furnishings, its decorations and its collective exhibit of art and handiwork and the product of her soil and mines, that you may officially, in the name of the state we dearly love to call our home, "Sweet Home," authoritatively declare the same to be open as a headquarters to our citizens, and open to the inspection of all the world.

The Governor, Hon. Horace Boies, not being able to be present, the State was represented by Hon. W. M. McFarland, Secretary of State, who delivered the following address:

*Mr. President, Members of the Iowa Board of Commissioners, Ladies and Gentlemen:*

In receiving this beautiful building and its magnificent exhibits, at the hands of your President, for the purpose of formally throwing it open to the inspection of the people of the world, I do so fully realizing the importance of the act as affecting the great state of Iowa. It is by this building and its exhibits that we are to be judged. So far as the world is concerned, we are now about to unveil the evidences of our material resources; of our material growth and prosperity. More than this: We are now about to present the evidence by which our civilization will be estimated, and measured by the people of the world. Thanks to the intelligence, energy, and untiring labor of our Iowa Board of Commissioners, the evidence we are about to submit will not dishonor Iowa. I need not enlarge upon what you see before you. Iowa will be justly proud of her building and its exhibits. We have here a great object lesson. An object lesson that will impress upon the minds of the people of this country and all nations, that, beyond the Mississippi river exists a commonwealth rich in all the elements of material greatness, that that commonwealth is the home of two and one-half millions of happy, prosperous people, rich in the sentiments, attainments and culture that constitute the highest civilization of the race.

But exhibits at best are but partial. Samples necessarily illustrate but a few important facts. To represent the full measure of Iowa's greatness by these exhibits here, would be paralleled by an attempt to illustrate a great piece of masonry by a sample stone. The Commissioners have collected here sample products of Iowa farms, unexcelled in this or any other Nation; but this does not tell you that Iowa has thirty-five million acres of land, as rich in soil as was ever fertilized by God's sunlight and rain, and that eight million acres of that land is virgin soil untouched by the hand of husbandry.

It does not tell you that in 1892, Iowa farms gave to the wealth of the world over four hundred million dollars in value. It does not tell you in express language at least, that the Iowa farmer is annually adding to his store of gains; annually adding to the pleasures and comforts of his home; annually surrounding that home by all the higher tokens of civilized life. Neither does it tell you that seventy-five million dollars of the surplus deposits in the nine hundred Iowa banks are there as a guarantee that the homes of the Iowa farmer are not to be destitute.

The Commission has also collected here samples of the Educational work of our public schools; but these do not tell you that the ninety-nine counties of Iowa are decorated by fourteen thousand school buildings, in which twenty-two thousand teachers are presiding over nearly six hundred thousand children. And this does not include the vast army of pupils under instruction at our Universities, Colleges, Academies, Normal, Parochial and other private schools.

Neither do these exhibits tell you that Iowa stands first among the Commonwealths and Nations of the world in point of average intelligence, our per cent of illiteracy being but a little more than one per cent. of our entire population! Neither do you learn from these exhibits that any five pupils of school age anywhere in the State, who may be inconveniently located as to schools, by application properly made, may have a school building erected and a teacher furnished for their education. And yet our school fund is in excess of the demands of this most munificent system of our State Government, which expends more than seven million dollars annually upon our public schools

Our State does not pretend to compete with the older states in bulk of manufactured goods, and yet, we have millions of dollars profitably invested in the various industries other than husbandry, which employs in the aggregate over one hundred and thirty thousand laborers at an annual average wage in excess of that paid in this or any other country. Our mines in 1892 yielded an output valued at over ten million dollars, the valuation being based upon one dollar and forty cents per ton at the mine, over eight millions of this amount being paid direct to labor. Our water power is vastly superior to that of many of our great manufacturing states, and our fuel is not only easy of access and cheap, but almost inexhaustible, while the raw material for the mill, the loom, the shop, and canning establishment is abundant in every county, thus offering conditions to the manufacturer that will inevitably make of Iowa a busy manufacturing center at no distant date.

Our transportation facilities are represented by a little less than nine thousand miles of railroad, safely ballasted and admirably equipped to meet the highest demands of that kind of transportation. This enormous mileage is so dispersed over the State as to form a complete net-work of lines touching every town and village that makes any pretense of being a market. The management of this vast system is under intelligent and honest control, giving a rate of transportation that in the main is fair and just, and that enables every industry within the borders of the State to successfully compete with like industries elsewhere. This has inaugurated a spirit of good feeling and good understanding between the people and the transportation companies that now promises to be lasting and mutually beneficial to all interests.

It is proper to say here, that thirty thousand of the best paid laborers in our State are in the employ of these railroad lines.

The great Mississippi river on our East border, and the Missouri on the West, add greatly to our transportation facilities and open a cheap roadway to the Atlantic ocean, to the value of which each year adds unmistakable evidence, and which roadway is accessible to every section of our state.

Iowa is located between the fortieth and the forty-fourth degrees of north latitude and will profitably produce all of the products common to the temperate zone. It is the native home of all the valuable tame grasses, such as blue grass, timothy, and the various clovers, which are universally produced with great profit both as hay and pasture. We have the natural soil and climate for that great cereal, Indian Corn, which gives a yield unexcelled elsewhere, and responds to intelligent husbandry with wonderfully gratifying profits. The same is substantially true of oats, rye, barley, and in the North, wheat and flax, the latter being enormously profitable, but, I need not go into further details. Our dairy interest employs more cows than that of any state in the Union, save New York; but in the production of cattle in general, we excelled New York by one million head in 1892, and was excelled by only one state, Texas, in point of numbers, but not in value, while we excelled all other states in both number produced and value of product. We excelled in 1892, the combined cattle product of Illinois and Indiana as to both numbers and value. We also the same year equaled in numbers and value, the combined product of Ohio, Missouri and North Dakota; also the combined product of Wisconsin, Minnesota, Michigan, New

Mexico and South Dakota; also nearly equaled the combined product of Kansas and Nebraska.

During the same year we excelled all other states in the production of horses save Illinois, which excelled us but by a few thousand. We excelled the combined product of Ohio and New York; also Missouri and Minnesota; also Nebraska and North and South Dakota; also nearly equaled the combined product of Wisconsin, Michigan and Kentucky.

We raised more swine in 1892, than any state in the Union, our nearest rival, Illinois, falling behind fifteen million head, while we exceeded the combined product of New York, Ohio, Indiana, Michigan and Minnesota by three million head.

The same year we produced more Indian Corn than any state in the Union. Ninety-seven million bushels more than Indiana; twenty million more than Illinois; over forty million more than either Kansas, Nebraska, or Missouri; and an amount equal to the combined product of Wisconsin, Minnesota, Michigan, Ohio, Pennsylvania and New York.

In the production of oats we are able to make as favorable a showing as in corn. Comparing with the oats producing states, in 1892, we find that we produced twenty million bushels more than Illinois, sixty-six millions more than Indiana, forty-one millions more than Kansas, fifty-two millions more than Nebraska, seventy-one millions more than Missouri, fifty-two millions more than Minnesota, forty-five millions more than Wisconsin, sixty-eight millions more than Michigan, and two millions more than the combined yield of New York, Ohio and Pennsylvania.

In the production of barley, rye, wheat, and flax, we can make a comparative showing, that will almost equal the foregoing, while our hay crop is comparatively as good as any crop we produce. With the exception of a very few kinds adapted to the latitudes south of us, our whole line of vegetable products is unexcelled by any state in the Union.

The comparisons above made, are with states the most closely rivaling us in the products under consideration, many of which greatly exceed us in extent of territory and number of population. Figures are generally dry and uninspiring, but to an Iowan these figures are not only full of interest, but charged with eloquence, demonstrating as they do, that our thirty-five million acres of land are unexcelled, for the general purposes of agriculture, by any other equal body of land in the world.

The vital statistics of 1892 give us second place as to health, and, we have less criminals per capita than any other state.

Our winter climate, we must confess is a little rigorous, but being dry and invigorating, is for that reason more favorable to support the animal life at a minimum expenditure of vitalizing food than the damper but milder climate of latitudes south, while our springs, summers and autumns, are unrivaled for pleasant temperature and healthfulness.

We live also within the zone of greatest human activity. Removed to any considerable distance either north or south, life becomes less active and vigorous and human powers, mental and physical, suffer degeneration.

In short, Iowa loved and honored by its citizens, is a commonwealth in which the sturdier virtues of manhood are developed and in which enterprise and honest toil meet a full measure of reward. It is not a haven for the sluggard, and our broad prairies are not congenial homes for the criminal classes.

Our people are earnestly attached to republican institutions and are loyal supporters of law, and we guarantee to the honest and industrious citizen, who seeks a home with us, the rights and blessings of a republican form of government, in its purest and simplest form, and unparalleled returns for thrift, enterprise and toil. Only upon this basis, do we invite citizenship. Upon this basis, we know no nation, no race, no color, no condition, believing as we do in the eternal fatherhood of God, and its corollary the universal brotherhood of man.

With it all, we must not forget that less than fifty years ago Iowa that now occupies such a proud position in the galaxy of states, was carved from a practically unknown country. We can easily imagine that the gentle poet may have stood on the banks of the Mississippi river at that time, and, with his ear bent to catch the faint rumbling of the oncoming tide of immigration, was inspired to write:

"I hear the tread of pioneers of Nations yet to be,
The first low plash of waves that soon shall roll a human sea."

We have heard the tread of pioneers; the first low plash of waves, and we have seen it roll a human sea of immigration till the very miracle of transformation has been wrought before our eyes. During this transformation period, we have been a practical, busy people. Five hundred thousand homes have been carved from the wild prairies and nearly fifteen hundred cities and towns have been built of the raw material of the wilderness. Very little time has been spared for aught save empire building, and yet, we have built up an Iowa literature of which we may well be proud, and art and music, with their softening charms, have spread a halo over our home life and character that brings out into overshadowing distinctness, the gentler and more refined attributes of the world's best civilization. Much of this has already found expression in some of the highest works of art, many of which are to be seen in our collection here to-day. And who that have heard the thrilling strains from our State Band can doubt that music has found a permanent lodgment in our midst.

And now, for the Board of Commissioners, permit me to say that this beautiful structure by the lake was built as a haven for Iowa people visiting this, the greatest of International Expositions. Here is your Chicago home. Here you will find your home literature. Here you will meet a hearty welcome from the Board. Here also you will meet your Iowa friends. This is to be the social and intellectual center of Iowa in Chicago, for the next six months. It is yours, come and possess it.

And now, Mr. President and members of this Commission, in the name of the people of Iowa, whom by your courtesy I temporarily represent to-day, permit me to thank you for the zeal, enterprise and labor which you have so wisely expended in the interests of our beloved state. I know that every Iowa citizen will be proud of this, the completed product of your toil and diligence, and will be grateful for your distinguished services. Laboring as you have under the embarrassment of an inadequate appropriation, with consummate skill and loyal patriotism you have marshaled here every farthing of that appropriation into substantial form, endowing it with greater eloquence than the tongue of oratory, where during the next six months it will tell to the people of all nations the simple story of Iowa's greatness. In honoring Iowa you have honored our common country, reflected credit upon the American name and added new luster to the stars and stripes, the honored and revered emblem of the World's greatest Republic.

And now, gentlemen, thanking you for the distinguished privilege I have enjoyed at your hands to-day, at your request and in the name of the people of the State of Iowa, I declare this building and its exhibits formally opened as Iowa's contribution to the International Exposition of 1893.

## RECEPTION IN HONOR OF MISS CLARA BARTON.

About the middle of July, word was received from Mr. B. F. Tillinghast of Davenport, saying that Miss Clara Barton, President of the American Red Cross Association, would soon visit the Exposition and had expressed a desire to meet some of the Iowa people; Iowa had done so much and so willingly to relieve the suffering of the famine stricken people of Russia. We begged Mr. Tillinghast, in behalf of the Iowa Columbian Commission and the members of the Iowa Board of Lady Managers, then present, to extend to Miss Barton a most cordial invitation to visit Iowa's headquarters at the Exposition.

When Miss Barton arrived, an informal reception was given in her honor. She was accompanied by Mr. Tillinghast, Dr. and Mrs. Joseph Gardner, of Bedford, Indiana, and Dr. Hubbell, General Field Agent of the Red Cross Association.

President Crosby extended greetings in the following words:

*Ladies and Gentlemen:*

We are to-day favored by the presence of one whom the people of Iowa delight to honor, and who is honored wherever active sympathy is manifested for multitudes of human beings suffering from fire, plague, famine, flood or earthquake; and many are they who regard her with feelings of love and abiding gratitude.

I now introduce to you Mr. B. F. Tillinghast, who will tell you why Miss Clara Barton, President of the Iowa Red Cross Association, is so worthily loved and honored.

MR. TILLINGHAST.

*Mr. President, Ladies and Gentlemen:*

Out on the prairies of Iowa, almost under the shadow of our magnificent capitol building, there is now being erected a soldiers monument. This monument was designed by an Iowa woman, Mrs Harriet N. Ketcham, who was awarded the prize after a severe competitive contest with the world's artists. On the floor above this is a piece of statuary, the handiwork of this noble woman, and Iowa is proud of the name of Mrs. Ketcham and what she has done to perpetuate the memory of the brave deeds of Iowa soldiers.

To-day we have with us another woman, perhaps not an Iowa woman, but a woman who has attended Iowa soldiers on the field of battle; a woman who worked for the Russian famine sufferers, who was at Jacksonville during the fever, at Charleston during the earthquake, and at Johnstown during the recent flood.  There are other Iowa women, a few of whom I will mention: Mrs. A. W. Swalm of Oskaloosa, Miss Alice French of Davenport, Mrs. E. S. Schaeffer, wife of the President of the Iowa State University, Mrs. Governor Larrabee, Mrs. Matt Parrott of Waterloo, Mrs. F. N. Chase of Cedar Falls, Mrs. John F. Duncombe of Fort Dodge, Miss Jessie Boies, Mrs. Ella H. Durley of Des Moines, Mrs. Ketcham of Mt. Pleasant, and others, who were associated with Miss Barton in the splendid Iowa gift which went to Russia.

"Hundreds of thousands of our fellow beings are famishing in portions of the Russian Empire."

These were the first words of a proclamation issued by Gov. Boies to the people of Iowa, December 22d, 1891.  The work of organization was then officially begun and the relief movement continued until April, 1892.

May 2d, the steamship Tynehead—length 278 feet, beam 39 feet—sailed from New York to Riga, bearing Iowa's gift of grain to the starving peasants.  The vessel's charter was $12,651.62, and this amount was paid by Miss Clara Barton, President of the American National Red Cross Society, for the city of Washington, whose people claimed the privilege of transporting Iowa's cargo to Russia.  The Tynehead's cargo aggregated 6,830,652 pounds, or more than 224 carloads, itemized in the manifest as follows:

    2 boxes hospital stores.
    1 box canned goods.
    10 bags wheat.
    9 bags grain.
    1 box drugs.
    95,656 bushels corn in bulk.
    1 barrel bacon.
    731 sacks flour.
    2 bags meal.
    1 barrel grain.
    400 sacks meal
    21,201 bushels corn in bags.

In addition to the ship's cargo more than $5,000, received too late to be converted into grain was remitted to Miss Clara Barton from Iowa, and by her cabled to her representatives in Russia.

The Tynehead arrived at Riga, May 27th, Dr. J. B. Hubbell, General Field Agent of the American Red Cross, had preceded the ship more than a month, and all arrangements had been made for the prompt distribution of the grain.  The reception given the Iowa ship was royal and Capt. Carr was the recipient of a rich silver tea service.  An eye witness, an American, writes: "Every facility was offered by every official and person to help the unloading."  Two hundred of the common peasants of Riga were in waiting for the Tynehead's arrival, a full day, and insisted upon bearing the bags of grain to the cars without pay; twelve women sewed the rents in the sacks  While the Tynehead lay at her dock the American

THE IOWA RELIEF STEAMSHIP "TYNEHEAD," AFTER UNLOADING AT RIGA.

flag was displayed from the ships and from the custom house. The American above quoted says: "In the shop windows are displayed title pages of sheet music bearing the American flag in colors, 'Hail Columbia,' 'Yankee Doodle,' and 'The Star Spangled Banner.' Children carried the American flag in the streets. I saw a boy carrying the flag in the streets on one side of which was the stars and stripes and on the other side the Russian National colors."

The Russian government anticipated the coming of the Iowa ship and had in waiting 310 freight cars, which were given the right of way over all imperial trains, both passenger and express. As fast as the cars were loaded they were sealed, weighed, made up into trains and forwarded to consignees. The assignment of cars was made after conference with Dr Hubbell, by the committee of the British and American church of St. Petersburg A complete list is on file and it shows that the 310 cars of grain were consigned to 75 persons of the highest character at quite as many centers of distribution in 16 different provinces.

The General Field Agent of the Red Cross, Dr. Hubbell, who is a native of Iowa, personally visited many of the famine districts, and but recently returned to his duties at Washington. He holds the gratifying and conclusive evidence that every bushel of corn and every dollar in money served its intended purpose, and that the generosity shown on this side of the ocean in gathering and transporting to the seaboard, Iowa's cargo, was more than equaled in Russia by the gratitude of its recipients.

Dr. Joseph Gardner, of Bedford, Indiana, has just presented to the Red Cross eight hundred acres of choice land in Indiana, which is to become the home of that organization. With him are Mrs. Gardner, and Dr. J. B. Hubbell, General Field Agent of the Red Cross, who received and distributed Iowa's food stuff in Russia. I have great p'easure in presenting each and all of them.

MISS MILLER, presenting to Miss Barton a bouquet of La France roses, said:

In behalf of the ladies of Iowa, I wish to say that we are pleased with the opportunity of presenting these to you in token of our appreciation of your life efforts, and to show you how dearly they love to honor you.

MISS BARTON:

I do not know that this calls for remarks from me. 'If so, I fear I shall greatly fail in making them. It is only just to myself and those present who have accompanied me, to say we are here without any thought of having a reception like this. We are not only unexpectedly recognized but pleased by this meeting. Last night we left Bedford, Indiana, by night train, simply because we knew that our friend, your friend and worker, Mr. Tillinghast, was here. I had not seen him since he turned over that cargo of grain from Iowa into my hands to send to Russia. Dr. Hubbell who distributed the grain in Russia, had not seen him at all. It was a'so proper for Dr. Hubbell, Dr. Gardner and myself, whose guests we are, to come to see Mr. Tillinghast and the friends who participated in that grand work, and personally return our thanks and recognition. We had no thought that Iowa was going to open her doors. We expected perhaps we might meet them under this roof, but we had no thought that the state of Iowa would greet us with her beautiful music, open her ears and doors to us. Our hearts are full of love and gratitude for the grand work that you as a state have always done in deeds of humanity. It is not many years since Iowa was one of the first to recognize and aid in the work the Red Cross has opened to the world. This brings to my mind a little incident which it may not be out of the way to relate here.

When we first stood on the fields of Johnstown with homes swept away, trees carried down the river, mud, suffering humanity everywhere about us, almost the first thing, and it was difficult to reach us by dispatch, express, and certainly by letter, almost the first thing that came to me was from the lumbermen of Davenport who said that if the Red Cross—Miss Barton—is there, she is without shelter and needs lumber. I do not now remember how many car loads of lumber there were, but lumber came—the first lumber at all events, and so early was it that out of the lumber were made the first buildings, which received the Governor of Pennsylvania when he came to make his first visit. He was sheltered by the lumber sent from Iowa by Iowa lumbermen.

Iowa is known to be one of the first states in the Union to recognize the suffering and do good in whatever capacity she is able. In this last work that called us together, this great relief of Russia, I did my best to dispose of the corn, this unparalleled gift. There is nothing on record like it. And the person into whose hands it was placed and whom I pledged to your state would see that it was properly delivered to Russia, is here and is the suitable person to take it up where I left it. I received it from Mr. Tillinghast at the port of New York, and Dr. Hubbell received it abroad for distribution.

I trust you will bear with me for the poor remarks that I have made, for they were so unexpected that it has almost taken the words from me.

DR. HUBBELL:

*Mr. President, Ladies and Gentlemen:*—This is taking one by surprise. Referring to the gift from Iowa that was sent to the Russian people, I will say that with great reluctance the charge of that gift to take to Russia was accepted, for the reason that at that time we knew Russia so much poorer than we do now, it was doubtful how they might receive our gifts. We knew they went with the right spirit, but we did not know that they might be received with the same spirit. But the Russian people in receiving it, received it in such a beautiful way that instead of being a difficult task, it was most delightful, most pleasant in its memories and in the way received that it will be remembered not only by our people, but by the Russian people, and it has cemented the friendship of Russia and the Russian people and the people of America, and I believe that friendship can never be broken. It was the general expression among the Russian people that they wanted to see America, and all the traveling elements of Russia expressed their determination to visit the World's Exposition, and if it is within their power they will be here. This wish was also expressed by Count Tolstoi, with whom I was personally acquainted, that he wished to come and live with the American farmers and see how they live, and compare them with the peasants who are the farmers of Russia. The good done by the gifts from Iowa I cannot express. It not only relieved the suffering and hunger, but those actively engaged in the work said it came just at the right time—when it was most needed. Came just as if the Lord had sent it, at just the time it was needed most.

PRESIDENT CROSBY:

*Ladies and Gentlemen:*—All hearts go out to those who feel for suffering humanity, who come forward to aid in its relief, and we are doubly blessed to-day by the presence of those who have put forth such exertions, and who have made such a magnificent gift in behalf of suffering; I present to you Dr. Gardner, who has made such a valued gift to the Red Cross, and I take pleasure in introducing him.

DR. GARDNER:

*Mr. President, Ladies and Gentlemen:*—I must confess to being embarrassed. You might not think it, but I am bashful and I feel so much embarrassed that I hardly know how to commence to address you. I will not say much—I will promise to be brief. In putting me forward as one of the benefactors, I think you have taken the intent for the act. For years I have been in tolerably close touch with the workings of the Red Cross. My wife, before I married her, was one of Miss Barton's lieutenants in the Mississippi river overflow, in the Mount Vernon cyclone and later she was called to her aid in the Johnstown trouble. I saw the merits of organized relief under the superintendence of Miss Barton, under the American National Red Cross, and it seemed to me that if Providence ever blessed me to be in a position where I could be of benefit, I would do so. In looking over the field I did not see anything that would do a great deal of good with so little as was promised under the auspices of Miss Barton. Then I took steps to ascertain if the gift I was to make would be acceptable, and I took an early date to present my views of the matter to Miss Barton, and she was so kind as to say that she would take charge of the only neutral ground, so far as we knew, in the United States. We now have in Indiana such a piece of ground. Nature has dealt very liberally with that piece of ground, primeval forests stand there, cultivated lands are also there, hills and fertile river bottoms. Miss Barton has just paid a visit there, and will return there from Chicago, and we will wait to say at a later date what noble results for the relief of suffering humanity shall come out of that piece of neutral ground.

Introductions followed, light refreshments were served, after which Miss Barton and the distinguished guests accompanying her, were shown through the building, where they greatly admired the display, the decorations and the wonderful exhibitions of corn and other Iowa grains.

The Assembly room was assigned to the non-Partisan W. C. T. U. of Iowa for the 27th day of June, "Amendment Day," at which time it was filled to its utmost capacity. President Crosby made a short address of welcome, and addresses were made by Mrs. J. Ellen Foster, Mrs. Burrington, of Maine, and Dr. E. R. Hutchins. The Iowa State Band furnished the music.

Two meetings were also held in the Assembly room by the students and alumni of Cornell College, at which many sparkling brief speeches were made, interspersed with vocal and instrumental music by the students.

At a meeting of the Iowa Columbian Commission, July 19th, Commissioner Stivers stated that Hon. Lafayette Young, President of the Iowa Press Association, had called a meeting of the Iowa editors to take place August 3d, 1893, and moved that the freedom of the Iowa Building and the hospitalities of the same be extended to the Iowa editors, and that the services of the Iowa State Band be tendered them on that day. The motion was adopted and a committee of three gentlemen and three ladies was appointed by the President as preparation and reception committee, with authority to prepare program and provide refreshments. President Crosby named the following persons as members of the committee: Commissioner J. W. Jarnagin, chairman; Commissoners Ashton and Stivers, and Mrs. Duncombe, Mrs. Stivers and Mrs. Young.

## PROGRAM.

### IOWA PRESS ASSOCIATION.

The editors arrived at Mount Vernon station (near the Iowa State Building) *via* Intramural Railway, at 11 o'clock a. m., and were received by the Reception Committee and the Iowa State Band.

After reaching the Assembly room, the following program took place:
Music, - - - By the Iowa State Band
Address of Welcome, - by Commissioner J. W. Jarnagin,
　　　　　　　　　　　　　　Chairman Reception Committee
Response, - - by Hon. Lafayette Young,
　　　　　　　　　　　　　　Pres. Press Association
Music, - - - by the Iowa State Band
Whistling Solo, - - by Miss Floy Brundage, Des Moines, Iowa
Short Addresses, - - - by Editors present

At 12:30 p. m., the officers of the Intramural Railway tendered a free trip to the Iowa State Band and the members of the Press Association from Mount Vernon station to the North Loop, from North Loop back the entire trip to the South Loop, then back to the Administration Building where the editors disembarked and paid their respects to the United States Commissioners in session at the Administration Building.

From three to five o'clock p. m., a reception was given by the Iowa Columbian Commission and the Iowa Board of Lady Managers to the members of the Press Association and members of the United States Board of Lady Managers, in the parlors of the Iowa State Building.

In the latter part of September, the evening before the departure of the West Point Cadets, who had been in camp at the Exposition for several weeks, the Iowa Columbian Commission, assisted by the Iowa young people who were in the city at that time, opened the Iowa Building to receive and entertain them. This reception was given as a mark of respect to the young soldiers of the United States.

## IOWA STATE DAYS.

From the opening of the Exposition the Iowa Columbian Commission had given much careful thought to the matter of celebrating the day or days that might be assigned to Iowa by the Director General and Board of Management of the Exposition, at which time Iowa would be given the opportunity in a special manner and in her own way to advertise and bring her interests and industries prominently before the world.

It was the unanimous opinion of the officers and members of the Commission that such a demonstration should be made at such time as would attract the attention of the illustrious representatives of all the foreign nations and provinces, and the thousands of visitors from our sister states and territories to *Iowa*, and that the Committee on Ceremonies appointed by this Commission should be authorized and empowered to make the necessary arrangements, and that a sum sufficient to defray the necessary expenses of such a celebration should be set aside from the funds in the hands of the Commission.

The twenty-first day of September had been agreed upon by the Commission as "Iowa Day," and when your committee conferred with Colonel E. C. Culp, secretary of Committee on Ceremonies for the Exposition, we made application for that day, also September twentieth, and the two days September twentieth and twenty-first were formally assigned to us and set apart as "Iowa Days."

These state and national days were planned from the beginning of the Exposition by the Board of Management, and they proved to be very attractive features.

Your committee, in studying plans and making arrangements for Iowa's celebration, did not forget that Iowa had taken a prominent part in the Exposition from the first and realized that much would be expected of her on this occasion. We now have the satisfaction of knowing that the vast concourse of people present on that occasion were not disappointed.

The occasion had been well advertised by the Iowa press and we had secured from all railway lines running through the state a rate of one fare for the round trip, and in some instances even a lower rate. The attendance from Iowa was estimated at from forty to sixty thousand. Twenty-five thousand people wore the Iowa badge.

It would be impossible to give details of Iowa's celebration without making this report much too lengthy, so we simply embody as a part of this report a few of the preliminary notices and an outline, as indicated by the programs for the various features, including the parades, civil and military, the public exercises in the Iowa Building and in Festival Hall, addresses, illuminations, fire-works and receptions.

Ten thousand programs of each day's exercises were printed and distributed. Twenty-five thousand Iowa pins and badges were given away and were worn and kept as souvenirs of the occasion. In addition to these, your committee published and distributed an edition of five thousand copies of a souvenir program of Iowa State Days, a little pamphlet bound in neat covers and containing thirty-two pages. In addition to the title page was an outline program for each day and a number of views representing different sections of the Iowa State exhibit. Quite a number of these, together with the souvenir of the October dedication, have been sent by mail to parties in many of the foreign countries at the request of the commissioners representing those nations at the Exposition.

Referring to pending arrangements for the celebration of Iowa Days at the World's Fair, the Iowa Columbian Commission made the following announcement: The necessary expenses for transportation of the Governor, his staff, and the executive council, based upon one fare for round trip—including sleeping car fare—will be paid by the Iowa Commission. Headquarters for the Governor and his party were provided in Chicago and they were entertained during their stay in the city as guests of the Commission.

## PROGRAM IOWA STATE DAYS.

### SEPTEMBER 20, 1893.

At 10 o'clock a. m., the Committee on Ceremonies met the Governor and his party at their hotel and escorted them to the 57th Street entrance to Jackson Park, where they were met by the Iowa Columbian Commission, Iowa State Band, military escort, speakers, Iowa Board of Lady Managers, prominent Iowa citizens, invited guests and ladies, and paraded south past the Woman's Building and Horticultural Building, thence east to Wooded Island, north to Illinois State Building, east to British Building on Lake Front, and north on Esplanade to Iowa State Building. There was an ovation to Iowa by the immense crowds along the entire route of the procession.

After reaching the Iowa Building, the cadets from Iowa State Agricultural College, under command of General J. Rush Lincoln, gave an exhibition drill, which was followed by spear drill by a brigade of young ladies from the same college.

At 1:30 p. m., the C. L. Root Drill Corps, under command of C. L. Root, of Clinton, gave a fancy drill on the Esplanade in front of the Iowa State Building.

At 2 p. m., a grand concert was given by the Iowa State Band.

The following letter of invitation had been sent out in numbers equalling the capacity of the Iowa State Building to accommodate:

"The Iowa Columbian Commission requests the pleasure of your company at a reception to be given in honor of His Excellency, Governor Horace Boies, and Staff, Members of the Executive Council of Iowa, Director General Davis and Board of Management of the Exposition, U. S. and Foreign Commissioners, National Board of Lady Managers, and the Commissioners and Lady Managers of the States and Territories on Wednesday afternoon, September 20, 1893, from two to five o'clock, at the Iowa State Building, Jackson Park.            JAMES O. CROSBY, President."

F. N. CHASE, Secretary."

Each invitation was accompanied by a card as follows:

"Iowa's Reception to Gov. Horace Boies and others. Present this card at the door."

During the three hours designated for the reception, the house was filled with happy guests, representative of all nations, who came to pay their respects to Iowa's Governor and chief officials and to the others in whose honor the reception was given. Light refreshments were served, and at intervals the Iowa State Band discoursed its choicest music.

The day's program closed with a magnificent display of fire works prepared especially for this Iowa occasion, and among the beautiful set pieces was one representing the Iowa State Capitol and another showing a fine large portrait of Governor Boies.

SEPTEMBER 21, 1893.

At 10:30 a. m., the Committee on Ceremonies conducted the Governor and his party to the Cottage Grove entrance to Midway Plaisance, where they were met by the Iowa Commission, the Iowa State Band, Agricultural College Band, cadets and spear brigade, officers of the day and invited guests and ladies, and a grand procession formed and paraded east through Midway to Transportation Building, thence south to Administration Building, east past south end of Liberal Arts Building to lake front, thence north on Esplanade past the building of the United States Government to the Iowa State Building where the military escort, under command of Col. C. L. Root, gave an exhibition drill, followed by Gatling gun drill and drill by battalion of Agricultural College Cadets, under command of Gen. J. Rush Lincoln.

At 2 p. m., the Governor and staff, military escort, Iowa Commission and invited guests, headed by the Iowa State Band, marched to Festival Hall, where the following program took place:

Overture, "Semiramidi" Rossini, - - - Iowa State Band
Organ Solo, - - - - - Prof. Frederick Self
Introduction, - - Hon. James O. Crosby, Pres. Iowa Col. Com
Selection, - - - - - - Male Quartet
Invocation, - - - - - Rev. J. H. Palmer
Solo, selected, - - - - - Miss Genevieve Shaffer
Address, - - - Hon. Horace Boies, Governor of Iowa
Address, Hon. W. I. Buchanan, Chief Dept. of Agriculture—Representing Board of Management of the Exposition.
Selection, Fantasia on "My Old Kentucky Home"—Dalby, Iowa State Band
Oration, - - - Hon. W. M. McFarland, Secretary of State
Solo, selected, - - - - - Miss Marie Chambers
Selection, "American Patrol"—Meacham, - - Iowa State Band
Reading, a. "Blessing the Cornfields"—from Longfellow's "Hiawatha."
b. "A Dream of Woman"—Olive Schreiner. —Mrs. Lucia Gale Barber
Solo, "When the Heart is Young" Buck, - Miss Jennie Madge Sugg
America. (Audience requested to join), - - Iowa State Band

## INTRODUCTION—BY PRES. JAMES O. CROSBY.

In Jackson Park we stand to-day in the presence of the largest representation of the peoples of the earth, and of its resources and the products of human industry and invention, that has ever been gathered together. It is wonderful in magnitude and excellence, and the co-operation of the whole world was needed to produce it. Much labor and study are required to comprehend it, and it will pass into history as the Exposition beyond which no city, state or nation will ever attempt to go.

It has been a distinctive feature, to arrange with the joint Committee on Ceremonies, for special days to be set apart to each nation, province and state, to be called their own, and *to-day is Iowa's day*, and thousands of our citizens have come to make it memorable. Among all the assembled thousands there can not be one who is not proud to call our noble state his home.

In behalf of the Iowa Columbian Commission, representing the state of Iowa, I bid you a cordial, hearty welcome.

To-day the World's Columbian Exposition is ours, and we have the freedom of the White City.

Let us realize the wealth of this opportunity, for when it is passed it will never return.

All states and nations join with us in our jubilee, and we extend to them our kindly greetings, and so we are drawn into closer fellowship with all mankind.

The extent of the influence of this Exposition in advancing the progress of the world's civilization is beyond our estimation; yet, we may rest assured that it will be a powerful influence in hastening the time when "Nation shall not lift up sword against nation, neither shall they learn war any more, for He hath made of one blood all nations for to dwell on the face of the earth."

## ADDRESS BY GOVERNOR HORACE BOIES.

*Mr. President, Ladies and Gentlemen:*

I should fail to express the wishes of the people of my state if I did not at this time, and in this public way, extend to the Iowa Columbian Commission, and its faithful employes, the gratitude we all feel for the manner in which they have discharged the laborious duties their positions impose.

In behalf of the same people it is a pleasure to me to publicly express the obligations they are under to the National Commission for its generous treatment of Iowa interests, and for the uniform justice and courtesy of its members, individually and collectively, in all their dealings with the representatives of our state.

I should be false to my own feelings, and to those of my people as well, if I should strive to conceal the pride we feel in the exhibit here presented by our youthful commonwealth, and the proud position it has gained for us in the estimation of those who are permitted to view this, the greatest of the world's expositions.

I am justified in speaking of Iowa as a youthful state, for it is scarcely more than a quarter of a century since the era of rapid development began which has crowded her so far towards the front when compared with sister states.

It was not until 1867 that the first trunk line of railway to cross the state reached its western boundary, spanning as it did at that time an almost unbroken wilderness of raw prairie for more than half its length of 355 miles. Now every one of its ninety-nine counties is penetrated by one or more of these great highways that stretch across her plains in every direction, until their total legth exceeds 8,500 miles, employing in their operation an army of more than 30,000 men, and moving annually from place to place within her borders 12,000,000 tons of freight.

She has in round numbers 35,000,000 acres of land, of which 95 per cent is susceptible of the highest degree of cultivation.

Although her annual rainfall is less than that of most of the eastern states, it is so distributed that during the spring and summer months it is

GOV. HORACE BOIES.

greater than theirs, assuring thus far in her history never failing and abundant crops.

The sixteenth in number of the states admitted to the Union, Iowa already leads her sisters, both old and young, in the total value of her grain productions and her live stock, two of the most important of all the staples produced on the American continent.

For many years she has held her place at the head of the column of states in the production of that greatest of staples of the great northwest—Indian corn—of which, in a single season, she has harvested more than three hundred and thirty millions of bushels. In all other products of the farm grown in this latitude in any part of our country her soil has always been most liberal in its returns for the labor of the husbandman.

In 1892 she was second to Illinois only in the number and value of her horses; to New York only in the number and value of her milch cows; to Texas only in the number and value of other cattle, and the first of all the states in the number and value of her swine, and also in the total value of all live stock upon her farms.

The fame of her dairy products is already as wide as the markets of the world. In the year ending September 30, 1892, we shipped to eastern and foreign markets almost seventy-two million pounds of butter and consumed at home, as estimated by our dairy commissioner, one hundred millions more.

A few counties in the southern and southwestern parts of the state have already become famous as a fruit bearing section, producing as they do apples of the best quality in great abundance as well as large quantities of other useful fruit. There is, I believe, no part of the state in which sufficient for the wants of our people cannot be produced, but with the exception of the southern and southwestern counties it cannot be said to be a fruit bearing state.

Nor is it in the products of her farms alone that Iowa is rich.

She has within her boundaries not less than ten thousand square miles of most valuable coal lands, besides large areas which produce lead, zinc, iron and other valuable minerals.

She has now in operation nearly five hundred coal mines that give constant employment to an aveaage of twelve thousand men, and produce an annual output of more than three million tons, of the value of five million dollars.

In nearly all her cities manufacturing enterprises of many kinds are permanently established and these are being largely increased as the fact of her boundless supply of cheap fuel for motive power becomes more generally understood.

It is not, however, to her agricultural or mineral wealth, boundless as it is, that Iowans point with greatest pride when speaking of their state, for it is not in these alone that she ranks so high.

Gleaned as our population has been from every state in the Union and almost every country of the globe, she has a less per cent of illiterate persons than any of her sister commonwealths. More than one-fourth of all her inhabitants are enrolled as pupils in her common schools, in which an army of 27,000 devoted teachers are employed, and $7,500,000 are annually expended by her people, in their support.

She has too, a state university, an agricultural college, a normal school, a school for the deaf and dumb and a school for the blind—all supported at public expense, and all ranking high among institutions of their class in any part of the world. All over the state are sectarian colleges of almost every denomination, and non-sectarian schools of a high order so that every want of those who are in pursuit of an advanced education is easily supplied in her own schools.

Outside of as well as in her school buildings her state institutions have been constructed upon a lavish, if not an extravagant scale.

She has three insane asylums, costing an average of nearly a million dollars each; two penitentiaries, two reform schools, a school for the feeble minded, a home for the adult blind, a soldiers' home and an orphans' home, all supported at public expense.

Her annual expenditure of money for the support of all her public institutions is in round numbers $2,000,000, or about two-thirds of the entire revenues of the state.

There are few, if any, of the religious denominations known to the western hemisphere that are not represented among her church-going people, and all of the principal sects are abundantly supplied with church edifices and liberally supported by her citizens.

Her climate, though cold in winter and warm in summer, varying on rare occasions from 30 degrees below zero in the coldest of winter days to nearly 100 above in the hottest of summer days, is largely tempered by the fact that her atmosphere as a general rule is comparatively free from moisture which adds so much to discomfort on chilly days in much warmer latitudes.

Many of our friends, in the east, especially, have formed most exaggerated opinions of the dangers we are in from death dealing storms. In the whole history of the state three only have been known that are worthy of note. These have often been spoken of as cyclones. This is a misnomer, for cyclones usually cover large areas of the earth's surface, both in length and breadth, the recent one on the Atlantic coast reaching, it is said, three thousand miles in length and covering a space on land and sea from three to five hundred miles in width.

The three storms from which Iowa has suffered were tornadoes that appeared in the form of funnel-shaped clouds with the larger portion upward and reaching almost to a point were they touched the earth. Their destructive force was exerted by a rotary or whirling motion that never, I believe, covered a space to exceed half a mile in width (usually much less) and but a short distance in length. Their tracks, devastated as they were, were mere dots on our great prairies. These storms were not as destructive to life or property as the aggregate casualties of ordinary thunder storms that sweep over most of our states in the same number of years.

It must be remembered, too, that Iowa is no more subject to such storms than many of the other states, and but little, if any, more so than the most of the country east of the Rocky mountains. Those who fear our storms so much should remember that the one cyclone that swept the Atlantic coast a few weeks since caused more destruction to life and property than all the storms known to Iowa since its discovery.

For the information of those who are strangers to our state, and whom I have the honor to address, I have tried to portray her advantages and disadvantages with equal truthfulness and without prejudice because of its being my own home.

I want now to speak of Iowa as she appears to her own people and call attention to her present advantages as they see them.

There are still within the state thousands upon thousands of acres of land, richer than the valleys of the Nile and fresh as it came from the hands of the creator, for it has never felt the plowshear's touch or ministered to the wants of the children of men.

Down deep beneath the surface of her great plains and far out under the bluffs of her winding streams are stores of nature's wealth that no man has fathomed; that no time can exhaust.

In her cities and towns are numberless opportunities for the profitable employment of millions upon millions of capital in various kinds of manufacturing enterprises, and in their constantly widening fields of trade.

Everywhere, on every hand, along her crowded railways, in the fields of her great farms, in the lengthening drifts of her mines, in the hum of her busy shops, in her varied forms of undeveloped natural wealth is a never satiated want for the toilers of the world, for men like those whose brawny arms and steady nerves have made her what she is, and enabled her each year from field and mine and shop to pour into the great streams of commerce that flow across her plains the tribute of her own productions and help to swell the mighty torrent of trade that has built the city in which we meet, a city that for its years has not now and never had a peer in any age.

From the abundance of her resources such as they represent we have necessarily brought to this Mecca of the world's best treasures but limited specimens of the products of our state, and yet in the glare of this babel of priceless and indescribable things we are proud of our exhibit and proud of the men and the women whose deft hands and untiring zeal have made it so conspicuous a feature in such a marvelous show.

For twenty-six years, more than half her existence as an independent commonwealth, Iowa has been my home, and long before I knew her well, I have seen most of her great enterprises grow from infantile proportions to their present proud positions.

From a few short pieces of railway at different points on the eastern border I have witnessed her present magnificent system of more than eight thousand miles of road grow to completion and its operation improved until its present state of usefulness has been attained, and along the lines I have seen cities and towns by hundreds, by thousands, by more than this, spring like magic from these limited years; and out upon her trackless prairies, as I knew them first, I have seen fields of waving grain and pastures filled with grazing herds usurp the places of the wild flowers and timid game of these great meadows, planted by the hand of the Omnipotent and reserved for the use of man in this "the best of ages."

With all her magnificent resources for the accumulation of wealth, with social, educational and religious advantages that should satisfy the most exacting, with her busy, bustling throng of 2,000,000 of human beings, Iowa is not yet half peopled. To the good and the brave of every land her arms are open, and with all her heart she bids them come.

## ADDRESS—CHIEF W. I. BUCHANAN.

*Governor Boies and Members of the Commission:*

I have been requested by the Director General to extend to you, Governor Boies, and through you to the people of your state, the thanks and congratulations of the Exposition for the splendid work they have accomplished and the prominent part taken by them in this magnificent Exposition. This duty is the more gratifying because I can do so, not only as an official of the Exposition, but as an Iowa man. The compliment paid the people of Iowa by the officers of the Exposition in thus attesting their enterprise, zeal, public spirit and skill, is most sincere and just. No state has been more loyal to the Exposition from its inception than Iowa, none more ready to grasp the opportunities of showing the progress made by its people, and as all of you can testify who have followed the work of the State Commission, from our beautiful and unique State Building through the different great department buildings, none more successful in doing so, and none that contributes daily to the hosts of visitors in this enchanted city more of her people than the state of Iowa. It is, for these reasons, especially gratifying to me to extend the compliments of the officers of the Exposition to yourself personally, and as the chief executive of the people who have from the first taken so much interest in their state's success and the greater success of this enormous undertaking. No state had a more intelligent idea of the herculean work Chicago undertook, in agreeing to build this gigantic wonderland, than did Iowa; and by reason of her close commercial ties with this metropolis of the greater west, certainly no state had more interest in seeing the Exposition such a glorious success as would immortalize the west, than the state of Iowa. For these reasons every Iowa man and woman is to-day glad that their wishes are being realized. And why not, as good citizens, be proud of what the great west has accomplished? Picture the energy, intellect, labor and sacrifice it has taken since that September day one hundred years ago last Monday on which Washington laid the corner stone of our national capitol, to evolve, out of the unending and almost unknown wilderness west of the city of Washington, the millions of homes; establish in what was then a wilderness the granary of the world; build mighty cities; establish the greatest universities in our country; cement friendships and commercial interests in one common bond with lace work of railroads and telegraph wires, and, as a climax, on which the white lime lights of the future historian will be forever thrown, build this magnificent White City, and, as an unanswerable conclusion, support it with an attendance of over one million a week during a time of one of the greatest financial troubles the country has ever known. In making the history of our country's development during this marvelous century, Iowa has stood well to the front, and it is but natural that we, as citzens of the state, should rejoice over our own and the Exposition's success.

I am glad of this opportunity to express my own thanks to yourself and

W. I. BUCHANAN,
CHIEF OF THE AGRICULTURAL DEPARTMENT.

to the State Commission for the splendid support you have given me in making a success of that part of the Exposition work that has fallen to my hands. The members of your State Commission have been faithful, have worked diligently, and are entitled to the thanks of the people of our state for what they have done to uphold Iowa's position in the greatest Exposition ever organized.

We can congratulate the Commission upon the success of Iowa's Day, and we can rest assured that our state will long be remembered by the people of Chicago for the confidence expressed by them in the final success of this work and the assistance given them at all times, and we sincerely hope that the participation of our good state in this Exposition may be an added bond of friendship between our people and the citizens of this great metropolis and our sister state Illinois.

At the close of the exercises at Festival Hall, the procession re-formed and marched to the plaza on west front of the Administration Building, where the great Columbian Liberty and Peace Bell was located. The Governor and people were received at the bell by President Thomas W. Palmer of the World's Columbian Commission, where the liberty bell was rung in honor of the admission of Iowa into the Union. The ceremonies were opened by the Iowa State Band playing "America." The bell was then rung by Governor Boies, three quick strokes to call attention, followed by thirteen strokes given slowly—representing the thirteen original states—this being the regular celebration ring for a liberty event of the bell.

Speeches were then made by President Thomas W. Palmer, of the World's Columbian Commission, and by Hon. Horace Boies, Governor of Iowa.

Following the speeches the Iowa State Band played "The Star Spangled Banner," each line being emphasized by a stroke of the bell.

As an appropriate closing for Iowa's Celebration Days, an open reception with refreshments and musical program at the Iowa State Building from 7:30 to 10:00 o'clock p. m. was tendered by the Iowa Columbian Commission to all Iowa visitors and their friends.

At the close of these celebration days, it was the universal expression that no state had surpassed Iowa in her celebration, the program having been a complete success from beginning to end.

The duties of your committee in devising plans and perfecting the arrangements for so great an occasion as the proper and appropriate celebration of Iowa Days at the Exposition, in a manner that would be satisfactory to the Commission, and also be such a representation as would honor the name of the great state our Commission represented, were many; and the difficulties that had to be met in arranging the many details were numerous and hard to overcome.

The attendance of so many thousands of the intelligent citizenship of Iowa was a marked feature of the celebration. This was a great satisfaction to your committee, and I have no doubt was equally well pleasing to all the members of this Commission; and the impression made upon the mass of visitors representing all the nations of the world, was such that Iowa and her celebration will be long and favorably remembered.

## CHICAGO DAY.

The only other public occoasion that we desire to mention in which Iowa took a prominent part, is the great demonstration made on October 9th, "Chicago Day," which called together a greater number of people than were ever before assembled in this nation.

In the procession which marched on that day and in the impressive exercises, Iowa was assigned a prominent place. At the request of the General Committee having the program in charge, Iowa appeared in the parade with designs representing her as a "Corn State." This was an honor to Iowa and it proved that by her exhibit at the Exposition she made prominent her principal industry and won the position as the chief corn growing state of the Nation.

# Report of the Committee on Music.

BY F. N. CHASE.

The Music Committee beg to submit the following report:

The importance of having the musical talent of Iowa represented at the Exposition led to the discussion of plans by the Commission by which music might be used to attract attention to Iowa and her exhibit, and if the necessary funds could be spared, to procure the best, and make it a part of the State Exhibit.

At a meeting of the Commission held January 12, 1893, Commissioner Stivers, who had been previously appointed to make investigation in regard to securing music for Iowa at the Exposition, offered a resolution which was adopted, requesting the President to appoint a committee of three members of the Commission as Music Committee with power to act, and especially to confer with the Executive Council of the State and ask their aid and co-operation. The following members were appointed as such committee: Henry Stivers, S. B. Packard and F. N. Chase. Various plans for presenting vocal and instrumental music were submitted to the committee. Some of these contemplated organizing a large chorus, bringing to the Exposition Iowa's best artists; others contemplated erecting and furnishing a large music hall, and bringing the best talent from all the counties in the State to the Fair and giving concerts at intervals during the entire period of the Exposition. But this would have made it necessary to employ a musical director to visit the different counties to perfect organization and for general preparation, and would require a vast outlay of money. Your committee could not entertain any of these propositions; they were not feasible on account of their great expense.

Band concerts daily at the Iowa State Building during the entire period of the Exposition by the best artists that Iowa could furnish, was the ambition of this committee, and we believed that to be the sentiment of the entire Commission. Proposals were received from a number of Iowa's best bands. After giving the matter careful consideration, it was determined to secure the *Iowa State Band*, then under the leadership of Band-master Frederick Phinney.

The legislature had recognized this band, giving it its name, and to some extent had placed it under the direction of the Executive Council.

Your committee had an interview with Mr. Phinney and heard from him the condition of the band and obtained from him an estimate of the cost of suitable preparation and maintenance of such a band. Band-master Phinney's faith in the accomplishment of so magnificent a project as the maintaining of a band of fifty pieces, equal in ability and excellence to any in the United States, at the Iowa headquarters during the Exposition, was unbounded. We felt we must secure this band, if possible. We then had a conference with the State Executive Council and submitted our plans to them, and finally secured from them the promise of aid to the extent of $2,000 per month and $500 for transportation on the following conditions, to-wit: The Iowa State Band to consist of not less than fifty pieces should be secured and maintained during the whole period of the Exposition; it should play two concerts daily at the Iowa State Building, and it should at all times be under the direction of the Iowa Columbian Commission; the above must be paid in monthly installments through the Iowa Commission as follows: $500 for transportation and $2,000 at the end of each month, commencing May 1st, 1893; payments to cease if for any reason the Iowa Commission failed to maintain said band, and they should leave the Exposition. These terms were accepted by your committee, subject to the approval of this Commission.

Negotiations were then completed with Band-master Phinney, he agreeing to fully equip a band of fifty members and have in the band a representative from as many counties in Iowa as possible, to be ready at the opening of the Exposition, and to assume the responsibility of earning a large per cent of the cost of maintaining the band during the Exposition, with the understanding that the Iowa Commission should supplement the earnings of the band and the amount appropriated by the Executive Council when necessary. The total expense of maintaining the band, the equipment, instrumentation, transportation, and paying the salaries of the men were estimated at $5,000 per month, or a total of $30,000.

Band-master Phinney visited a number of counties for the purpose of securing additional members for the band; quite a number of good musicians were selected, a few counties made donations to aid in equipping the band. The Iowa Commission also gave financial aid, but great credit is due to Band-master Phinney for it was through his untiring and persistent efforts that the difficult task of reorganizing and equipment was accomplished.

The band commenced its services on May 1st, the opening day of the Exposition, and from that time on it was one of the leading attractions at the Iowa State Building. Their excellent music, and their general appearance and deportment attracted the attention of all the states and foreign nations as well as the Board of Management of the Exposition.

Iowa was the only state that had its own band to give daily concerts at their state building, and the Iowa State Band was the only one that was engaged and gave concerts daily during the whole period from the opening day until the close of the Exposition. Their excellence soon became known, and their services were often in demand for state occasions by the leading states and nations represented at the Exposition, and later their services were often requested by the Board of Management to take part in public parades on special occasions, and during the months of September and October they were employed by the United States Commission and the Board of Management at a liberal salary to play regularly for them at the principal band-stands in front of the Administration Building, and in the Agricultural and Manufactures Buildings. They also built for the special use of the Iowa State Band a pavilion on the north front of the Art Palace in which they gave concerts evenings until the close of the Exposition.

The following is a complete roster of the band as furnished by Bandmaster Phinney:

## MEMBERSHIP OF IOWA STATE BAND
### AT
### WORLD'S COLUMBIAN EXPOSITION, 1893.

1. Band Master and Manager—Frederick Phinney, Des Moines, Ia.
2. Oboe, 1st—Leo Morley, New York.
3. Oboe, 2d—L. H. Woolworth, Ottumwa, Iowa.
4. Flute, 1st—Dewey Heywood, Chicago
5. Flute, 2d—George Davis, Newton, Iowa.
6. Piccolo—L. H. Davis, Des Moines, Iowa.
7. E♭ Clarinet, 1st—Joseph S. Ulch, Solon, Iowa.
8. E♭ Clarinet, 2d—L. A. Matthews, Sioux City, Iowa.
9. B♭ Clarinet, Solo—A. C. Davis, Des Moines, Iowa.
10. B♭ Clarinet, Solo—Arthur S. Phinney, Des Moines, Iowa.
11. B♭ Clarinet, Solo—F. Nelson, Burlington, Iowa.
12. B♭ Clarinet, 1st—S. T. Carter, Sioux City, Iowa.
13. B♭ Clarinet, 1st—Rufus Phinney, Lynn, Massachusetts.
14. B♭ Clarinet, 1st—J. W. Doyle, Salem, Massachusetts.
15. B♭ Clarinet, 2d—F. Wittich, Keokuk, Iowa.
16. B♭ Clarinet, 2d—A. Cox, Des Moines, Iowa.
17. B♭ Clarinet, 2d—C. Newerf, Winterset, Iowa.
18. B♭ Clarinet, 2d—H. Scoukup, Decorah, Iowa.
19. B♭ Clarinet, 3d and 4th—Geo. Beebe, Ackley, Iowa.
20. B♭ Clarinet, 3d and 4th—I. P. Cox, Scranton, Iowa.
21. B♭ Clarinet, 3d and 4th—J. R. Parker, Parkersburg, Iowa
22. Soprano Saxiphone—J. E. Agnew, Creston, Iowa.
23. Alto Saxiphone—F. E. Redhead, Des Moines, Iowa.
24. Tenor Saxiphone—F. Nixon, Chicago.
25. Bass Saxiphone—J. R. Scott, Sheldon, Iowa.
26. Alto Clarinet—Chas. D. Bushby, Brooklyn, Iowa.
27. Bass Clarinet—Geo. Redhead, Des Moines, Iowa
28. Bassoon, 1st—L. H. Jones, New York.
29. Bassoon, 2d—J. Baldwin, Sioux City, Iowa.
30. Cornet, Solo—W. Merrill, Boston, Massachusetts.
31. Cornet, Solo—V. W. Kenney, Pella, Iowa.
32. Cornet, 1st—C. Johnson, Des Moines, Iowa.
33. Cornet, 1st—Horace Shadel, Oskaloosa, Iowa.
34. Cornet, 2d—F. Jones, Breeda, Iowa.
35. Flugle Horn, 1st—T. B. Boyer, Keokuk, Iowa.
36. Flugle Horn, 2d—C. Keeler, Mason City, Iowa.
37. Trumpet, 1st—Scott Heywood, Chicago.
38. Trumpet, 2d—V. Russell, Adel, Iowa.
39. Trombone, Solo—H. Carlson, Des Moines, Iowa.
40. Trombone, 1st—A. Hiltwein, Chicago.
41. Trombone, 2d—D. Platt, Sanborn, Iowa.
42. Trombone, Bass—F. E. Mills, Peoria, Illinois.

43. French Horn, 1st — H. Rohrs, Council Bluffs, Iowa.
44. French Horn, 2d — A. Johnson, Des Moines, Iowa.
45. French Horn, 3d — W. L. Burchard, Des Moines, Iowa.
46. French Horn, 4th — O. L. Waldenville, Rockwell City, Iowa.
47. Euphonium, 1st — F. C. Kendall, Grinnell, Iowa.
48. Euphonium 2d — C. Hardy, Manchester, N. H.
49. Baritone — Winslow Phinney, Lynn, Mass.
50. E♭ Bass — Geo Rohrs, Council Bluffs, Iowa.
51. E♭ Bass, C. Sucher, Ogden, Iowa
52. BB♭ Bass — J. Mundhauk, Toledo, Iowa.
53. BB♭ Helicon Bass — F. Whalen, Washington, D. C.
54. Helicon Bass — L. F. Andrews, Mashalltown, Iowa.
55. Snare Drum — J. L. Obertop, Des Moines, Iowa.
56. Snare Drum — P. Boesch, Burlington, Iowa.
57. Bass Drum — Wm. Launsbery, Des Moines Iowa.
58. Tympani — C. Prater, Des Moines, Iowa.
59. Librarian — C. W. Dalby, Council Bluffs, Iowa.
60. Asst. Librarian and Saxhorn — C. Eadie, Manson, Iowa
61. Master of Effects — C. W. Phinney.
62. Custodian — F. S. Phinney.

A few of the above-named members only remained with the band a short time.

In addition to the daily concerts at the Iowa State Building, we mention some of the more important engagements of the Iowa State Band at the World's Exposition:

Dedication of the New York State Building
Dedication of the Massachusetts State Building.
Dedication of the New Hampshire State Building.
Dedication of the Maine State Building.
Dedication of the Connecticut State Building
Dedication of the Pennsylvania State Building.
Dedication of the Maryland State Building.
Dedication of the Virginia State Building.
Dedication of the West Virginia State Building.
Dedication of the Louisiana State Building.
Dedication of the Ohio State Building.
Dedication of the Indiana State Building.
Dedication of the Kentucky State Building.
Dedication of the Texas State Building.
Dedication of the California State Building.

### FOREIGN COUNTRIES.

Dedication of the French Building and Exhibits.
Dedication of the Denmark Building and Exhibits.
Dedication of the Russia Building and Exhibits.
Dedication of the Hayti Building and Exhibits.
Dedication of the Guatamala Building and Exhibits.
Dedication of the Costa Rica Building and Exhibits.
Dedication of the Venezuela Building and Exhibits.
Dedication of the Ceylon Court

Among the other engagements was the celebration of the Krupp Gun Exhibit and reception at the Naval Battle Ship.

The New York State Commissioners were enthusiastic in praise of Iowa's great band and engaged them on several state occasions after the dedication of their state building. Their Executive Commissioner, Col. McNaughton, was a warm friend of Band-Master Phinney, and the members of his band, and he was planning an engagement for them when taken with a serious illness which caused his death after a few days of intense suffering, during which he expressed a desire that Iowa's band should play at his funeral, which they did, and rendered two appropriate selections which added greatly to the solemnity of the occasion.

These engagements were all arranged so as not to interfere with their contract with the state of Iowa, and was the means of bringing in a revenue which made it possible for the Commission to carry out the arrangement and maintain the band until the close of the Exposition. From the following statement it will be seen that Professor Phinney's effort to secure engagements was quite successful and compensation liberal, amounting to more than one-half the entire cost of maintenance of the band at the Exposition.

The Iowa Commission received from the Executive Council and
  paid over to the band in monthly installments ............... $12,500
From Board of Management of the World's Columbian Exposition  13,200
From special engagements (approximate) .................. 4,000
From Iowa Columbian Commission ...... ............. 4,000

  Total. ... .... ...... .... ... ..... ... .................. $33,700

The amount given by the Iowa Commission was paid in insta'lments as needed, and it was used in part for new uniforms and for the better equipment of the band not provided for in Mr. Phinney's previous estimate of the cost of maintenance. The band was thus enabled to return to Iowa at the close of the Exposition free from debt, and with great honor for themselves and credit to our state.

The Board of Management allowed the band free admission to the grounds at all times. Their services were solicited often for special parades and when it did not interfere with other engagements the request was granted by the Iowa Columbian Commission, and given free of charge to lead some of the most noted processions and parades that were given during the Exposition.

Among them was a banquet given in honor of Princess Eulalia Infanta Spain, the parade in honor of the "King of Kings" of India, the Congress of all Nations, the grand parade of premium live stock of the world. At the opening of the celebrated Ferris Wheel, the Iowa State Band was invited to play, and made the first trip that was made by the Ferris Wheel on that opening day.

They played the celebrated "Sacred Concert" for the benefit of the cold storage fire heroes. The Commission also tendered the services of the Iowa Band to the city of Chicago at the funeral of Mayor Harrison, where they were accorded the position of honor in heading that memorable military and civic funeral procession. At the close of the Exposition the Iowa Band was chosen from all the bands to play a week's engagement for the World's Chrysanthemum Exposition given under the auspices of Mrs. Potter Palmer,

President of the Woman's Board of United States Commissioners, and Harlow N. Higinbotham, President of the Board of Management of the Exposition. They were then engaged for thirteen weeks at the Mid-winter Exposition at San Francisco. In fact, their reputation became not only national, but world wide. They have since played many engagements and made tours to the principal cities and towns from the Atlantic to the Pacific, and everywhere they have carried the splendid banner presented them by the Iowa Columbian Commission, bearing the name of "Iowa" and "Iowa State Band" to all parts of our country, and your committee believe that no part of Iowa's splendid exhibit has done more to advertise and honor the name of our grand and glorious commonwealth than the Iowa State Band, and its record at the World's Columbian Exposition at Chicago in 1893.

After the meeting of the Commission in October, 1894, a gold medal was presented to Band Master Phinney, as shown by the annexed letter which accompanied the medal when delivered.

"PROF. FREDERICK PHINNEY, Des Moines, Iowa:

Dear Sir: At the 24th session of the Iowa Columbian Commission held at Des Moines on the 13th day of December, A. D., 1893, Vice-President Duncombe offered the following resolution, which was unanimously adopted:

Resolved that a gold medal of the value of at least $50 be furnished to Prof. Phinney of the Iowa State Band, in consideration of the high appreciation of this Commission of his services rendered in behalf of the state of Iowa during the World's Columbian Exposition, and that the thanks of this Commission be tendered to him and to the members of the Iowa State Band for their diligent, faithful and artistic performances; and that the secretary of this Commission prepare a design and inscription for said medal and that he be authorized to procure and deliver the same on behalf of this Commission.'

At the regular session of the Commission convened at Des Moines on the 3d day of October, A. D., 1894, the Secretary reported that he had procured the medal and it was ready for delivery. Whereupon Commissioner Seaman moved, 'That the Secretary deliver the medal to Prof. Phinney, accompanied by a written testimonial to be signed by the President and Secretary of this Commission,' which motion was unanimously carried.

Pursuant to the foregoing resolutions, the accompanying medal is presented to you by the Iowa Columbian Commission for the State of Iowa, in whose behalf you labored so earnestly and successfully in organizing the Iowa State Band and bringing it to such a high degree of excellence, that for the entire duration of the World's Columbian Exposition it was a leading attraction at the Iowa Home, drawing forth the admiration of our citizens and the vast concourse of representatives from all the nations of the earth; and joined with the exhibit of the products of her soil and wealth of resources you contributed to the store of pleasant memories the World has of Iowa.

Accept this testimonial with the thanks of this Commission, between whose members and yourself most pleasant relations have existed, and convey to the members of your Band the thanks of this Commission and its high appreciation of their artistic and faithful services.

"In testimony whereof we hereunto subscribe our names and affix the official seal of the Commission at Des Moines, the 8th day of October, A. D., 1894.       JAMES O. CROSBY,
F. N. CHASE, Secretary.                                President."

STEPHEN B. PACKARD.

# Report of the Department of Live Stock.

### BY S. B. PACKARD.

I have the honor to report the results achieved by the Iowa Live Stock Exhibit at the Exposition. The proceedings of this department were reported to the Commission from the time the work was assigned to me and have been recorded in the minutes of the Commission's meetings. That work was one of preparation and may therefore be omitted in this report, which will deal only with the record of the exhibit at Chicago. The exhibit of breeding cattle and horses began August 21st and closed September 9, 1893. The Exposition rules provided classes for Short Horn, Aberdeen Angus, Galloways, Devons, Jerseys, Holstein-Friesians, Ayrshires, Guernseys, Sussex, Red Polled, Polled Durham, Dutch Belt and Brown Swiss. Iowa exhibited one herd each of Herefords, Aberdeen Angus, Galloways, Red Polled and Jerseys. The Holstein and Short Horn breeds were notably absent, though the most prominent breeds of cattle of the state. No consideration should have kept these breeds from participating, but it is believed that the inadequate amount of money in the hands of the Commission with which to encourage a reflective and creditable Iowa exhibit will account for their absence.

The entries of cattle in full were as follows:

### HEREFORDS.

GEO. S. REDHEAD, Des Moines:

Bull 3 years old or over, Captain Grove 41219.
Cow 3 years old or over, Sunol 44663.
Heifer 2 years old or under 3, Cherry Duchess 49178.
Heifer 1 year old and under 2, Wall Flower 54355.
Heifer under 1 year, Dora 53368.

### ABERDEEN-ANGUS

W. A. McHENRY, Denison.

Bull 3 years old or over, Prince of the Realm 8250; bred by J. J. Rodgers, Abingdon, Ill.
Bull 2 years old and under 3, Keillor McHenry 13225; bred by exhibitor.
Bull 1 year old and under 2, Jeans Abactor 2d, 15403; bred by exhibitor.
Bull under 1 year old, Abactor's Barbary 17481; bred by exhibitor.
Cow 3 years old or over, Progress of Turlington 7116; bred by J. W. Harvey, Turlington, Neb.
Heifer 2 years old and under 3, Nell Gwynne 3d 17497; bred by Leslie & Burwell, Cottage Grove, Wis.
Heifer 2 years old and under 3, Blackbird McHenry 2d 13744; bred by exhibitor.
Heifer 1 year old and under 2, Queen McHenry 2d 15407; bred by exhibitor.
Heifer under 1 year, Blackbird McHenry 3d 17479; bred by exhibitor.
Heifer under 1 year, Blackbird McHenry 4th 17480; bred by exhibitor.

## GALLOWAY.

WM. McTURK & SONS, Crystal, Tama County, Iowa.
Bull 3 years old and over, Hunter 2d of Dyke's Creek.
Bull 2 years old and under 3, Marco of Wolf Creek.
Bull 2 years old and under 3, Sir Charles of Wolf Creek.
Bull under 1 year, Sulwood 10344, of Wolf Creek.
Cow 3 years old or over, Alice of Cornwall.
Cow 3 years old or over, Auricula 1st.
Heifer 2 years old or under 3, Maria of Wolf Creek.
Heifer 1 year old and under 2, Flora of Wolf Creek.
Heifer 1 year old and under 2, Queen of Wolf Creek.
Heifer under 1 year old, Matilda of Wolf Creek 10342.
Heifer under 1 year old, June Bug of Wolf Creek 10343.

## JERSEY.

RICHARDSON BROS., Davenport, Iowa.
Bull 3 years old or over, Chromo 26113.
Cow 4 years old or over, Comanca 19381.
Cow 4 years old or over, Alexa 64929.
Cow 4 years old or over, Lorita 33750.
Heifer 2 years old and under 3, Campania 88475.
Heifer 2 years old and under 3, Elturia 80701.

D. J. HEINSHEIMER, Glenwood, Iowa.
Cow 4 years old and over, Hugo Countess 68304.

## RED POLLED.

J. H. GILFILLAN, Maquoketa, Iowa.
Bull 3 years and over, Davyson 18th.
Bull 3 years and over, Iowa Davyson 14th 2769.
Bull 2 years and under 3, Iowa Davyson 20th 2773.
Bull 1 year and under 2, Iowa Davyson 22d 3151.
Bull 1 year and under 2, Columbus 30492.
Bull under 1 year, Iowa Davyson 23d.
Bull under 1 year, Iowa Davyson 25th.
Cow 4 years and over, Priscilla.
Cow 4 years and over, Eulalie 2d.
Cow 3 years and under 4, Eulalie 3d 7086.
Cow 3 years and under 4, Iowa Davy 9th.
Heifer 2 years and under 3, Iowa Davy 12th 7193.
Heifer 2 years and under 3, Iowa Davy 13th 7194.
Heifer 1 year and under 2, Iowa Davy 14th 7195.
Heifer 1 year and under 2, Iowa Davy 15th 7936.
Heifer under 1 year, Munnis.
Heifer under 1 year, Gladys.

HUGO COUNTESS 68394.

NORA.

The herd of Aberdeen-Angus, Galloway and Red Polled were shown for herd prizes and sweepstakes, and most successfully, as will appear hereinafter.

## FAT STOCK—POLLED-ANGUS.

### STEERS.

W. J. NILES, Wyoming.

Two years and under 3, Earl of Sunny Slope.
One year old, Knight of Sunny Slope.
Calf, Prince of Sunny Slope.

A brief description of the breeds of cattle comprised in the Iowa Contingent may interest some, at least those less familiar than with the Short Horns, which are found in such perfection in this state.

The Hereford, Aberdeen-Angus and Galloways are classed in this country as beef breeds, though in England where the Herefords have been bred to milk strains they have been found superior in the dairy. This breed originated in Herefordshire, England, and in adjoining counties, where they are principally bred. They are red with a white face, breast, abdomen, and mane usually white, with white on the legs, and white switch to the tail. They are very docile cattle, early maturing, excel in grazing and are easily fattened. Their herd book dates from 1845.

The Aberdeen-Angus are black without horns, and belong to Aberdeenshire and Forfarshire, Scotland, those shires being the chief centers. They mature rapidly, are easily fattened and growing greatly in favor in this country. The first herd book dates from 1862.

The Galloways are also natives of Scotland, as their name implies, from the southwestern portion, Galloway and Dumfrieshire. They are hornless and have a long soft coat of black hair. They are a very old established breed, were improved in the last century, as claimed by the society, without a cross with other breeds, are good feeders, kill well, and their meat classes with the Aberdeen and West Highland cattle on the Smithfield market as "Prime Scots," realizing the highest current price.

## RED POLLED.

The Red Polled cattle come from the counties of Norfolk and Suffolk England. Formerly there were two varieties, known as the Norfolk Polled and Suffolk Polled, but they have been amalgamated since 1846, and are now known simply as Red Polled. The herd book was first issued in 1874. These cattle lay on flesh rapidly even on indifferent pasture. Their average weight at maturity is something less than the breeds mentioned before, but they are esteemed as choice cattle both for beef and milk.

## JERSEYS.

The Jerseys are distinctively a dairy breed, standing unquestioned at the head of all dairy breeds, yielding a quality of milk so rich that no other compares with it. Their specialty is butter, but their record in cheese at the Exposition was a great surprise to the general public; but this branch of the subject will be treated in another place in this report. These cattle have been bred pure for five centuries and are so well known that a description is unnecessary. The Jersey Island, twelve miles long and six broad, commonly exports 2,000 cattle annually. It has more cattle to the square mile than any other place. On this island wherever there is a green spot a Jersey cow may be seen tethered. Now for the record of our exhibit.

## HEREFORD HERD.

The competitors of the Iowa herd were as follows:

One herd from Ohio, composed largely of recent and carefully selected importations; one each from Missouri, Kansas and Minnesota, two each from Indiana, Nebraska and Canada, and three from Illinois. Many of the herds showed two animals of the same age in each class. The total reached 140 head. Unquestionably there was no stronger ring of cattle exhibited than the Herefords. Mr. Redhead of Des Moines, exhibited the Iowa white faces, and obtained above an average rating. His Captain Grove in the aged bull c'ass, was placed 7th in a class of 13.

Sunol, aged cow, was 16th in a class of 18.

The 2-year-old heifer Cherry Duchess was 7th in a class of 16.

The yearling heifer Wall Flower was 9th in a class of 21.

The heifer calf Dora was 11th in a class of 16. None of this herd was shown for sweepstakes. The Aberdeen-Angus ring was about half as large as the Hereford, and was equally choice.

## ABERDEEN-ANGUS HERD.

Mr. McHenry, of Denison, exhibited the Iowa Polled Angus herd. His competitors were a herd each from Canada, Missouri and New York, and three herds from Illinois. The winnings of the Iowa herd were in part as follows: Four prizes in the grand sweepstakes beef breeds, consisting of a first, two seconds and a third; also three prizes in class sweepstakes, consisting of a first, second and third. The winnings in all classes number four first prizes, ten second prizes, four third prizes and three fourth prizes, which will be found in detail in the list of awards in another part of this report. Mr. McHenry was not content with the championship on his 2-year-old cow, but purchased, at a long price, the cow Abbess of Turlington in the aged class, which was awarded grand sweepstakes as the best cow in the world, beef breeds, to which he already stood second with his Progress of Turlington. Mr. McHenry exhibited his cattle in rare fettle and fully deserved the honors he won.

## GALLOWAYS.

The Galloway herd shown from this state by Messrs. Wm. McTurk & Sons, Crystal, Tama county, met a Canadian herd, also one each from Indiana, Minnesota and Illinois, and took several prizes as appears in the table of Iowa winners.

## RED POLLED.

A battle royal was fought between a herd from Missouri, one from Nebraska, one from Ohio, and our Mr. Gilfillan's herd from Maquoketa, Iowa. These four herds were reputed as the four crack herds in the four states named, and Iowa could have been well contented with a "drawn" fight, since the reputation of the contesting herds stood so high. Iowa distanced all others, however, as the eleven first cash prizes, three seconds, three thirds, and four fourth prizes awarded Mr. Gilfillan, amply demonstrate. The reader is invited to examine the lists of awards elsewhere in this report for the details of the phenomenal winning of this herd. Too much credit cannot be given this enterprising breeder for the thorough manner in which he fitted his cattle for the ring.

## JERSEYS.

The Iowa Jerseys were sent to Chicago to enter in the dairy contest proper, and their exhibition in the ring was incidental rather than the main purpose, to show the kind and quality of cows that were making such famous records in the butter and cheese tests that had already taken place during the summer months, having been led into the ring more to satisfy the desires of cattle men than as competitive exhibits. These cattle were taken to Chicago the winter previous, to acclimate and test them for the dairy contest, and were never fitted for ring contests. Mr Heinsheimer's, of Glenwood, cow Hugo Countess took fourth in the aged cattle class, and Richardson Bros, of Davenport, were fifth in the two-year-old heifer class, and same in the aged bull class

## FAT STOCK SHOW.

The exhibition of fat stock began October 16, and continued until the 28th. The small number of entries prepared the public mind for the limited number of animals displayed in each branch of the show, but the exhibit was on the whole a good one, as the animals exhibited showed to what a high standard the art of feeding stock has reached. Next in importance to knowing how to breed good ones is to know how to feed them for a fat stock ring.

Mr. Niles of Wyoming with his herd of doddies rounded out and completed the splendid success of Iowa in the cattle exhibit. Mr. Niles' Earl of Sunny Slope easily landed the first in his class of two-year-olds; the Knight of Sunny Slope took first in the yearling ring; and Prince of Sunny Slope won first in the calf ring, and then in sweepstakes for all ages easily beat the Shorthorn, Hereford, Galloway, and Devon calves, and stood as the best fat calf in the world.

In closing this review of the Columbian Cattle Exhibit I submit that our breeders made a grand step when they undertook an exhibit of their herds; that the honors won have been proportionately greater than any other state, for it must not be forgotten that the breeds which have won these honors have done so without the aid of the Shorthorns, the leading breed to be found everywhere across the state, in such perfection. In the last state census, 1885, the pure bred Shorthorns were returned as numbering 28,336, the Herefords 2,802, the Jerseys 1,264, the Black Polled, which is supposed to mean the Aberdeen-Angus and Galloways together 394, the Red Polled 65 head. From this small beginning, Iowa at the Columbian Exposition has the grand sweepstakes, Aberdeen-Angus cow of two years old, over all beef breeds in the world; while in the Red Polled herd there is also a grand sweepstakes two-year-old winner over all general purpose breeds, and in both herds several winners of firsts over all others of their breeds respectively in the world. Ancient Britton, the best Columbian Hereford bull, and second only to the young Abbotsburn for the championship of beef breed bulls of all ages competing, has been added to the Iowa World's Fair Hereford herd, by Mr. Redhead. And as stated in another place Mr. McHenry added to his herd the champion cow of the world's beef breeds, Abbess of Turlington, Aberdeen-Angus. Verily the cattle industry is pushing on.

The total number of cattle entered for exhibition was officially stated at 1,205; the number of exhibitors and number of cattle entered from each state was said to be as follows:

| State | No Ex | Cattle | State | No Ex | Cattle |
|---|---|---|---|---|---|
| Canada | 29 | 234 | Iowa | 5 | 54 |
| Illinois | 17 | 172 | Kansas | 3 | 42 |
| Minnesota | 10 | 152 | Nebraska | 4 | 40 |
| Ohio | 6 | 99 | Kentucky | 2 | 33 |
| Missouri | 7 | 83 | Michigan | 2 | 17 |
| Indiana | 7 | 78 | Maine | 1 | 13 |
| New York | 9 | 67 | North Dakota | 1 | 10 |
| Pennsylvania | 3 | 50 | Massachusetts | 1 | 1 |

The total amount of cash premiums, general and special, exclusive of medals and cups won by Iowa cattle at the Exposition, was $2,362, in the breeding and fat stock rings.

## HORSES.

The Exposition established classes for the following breeds of horses: Standard trotters; Thoroughbred, French Coach; Oldenburg Holstein, Hanoverian and Trakehnen to compete together, commonly called in this country German Coach; Cleveland Bay, Percheron, Clydesdale, Shire. French Draft, Belgian, Suffolk Punch, Hackney, Morgan. Arab, Americo-Arab, French Trotters, Saddle Horses, Shetland Ponies, Jacks, Jennets, and Mules. The Iowa Horse Exhibit was comprised in the following entries:

### GERMAN COACH.

#### FIVE-YEAR-OLD STALLIONS.

Greeley Horse Imp. Co., A. B. Holbert, agent, Greeley—Moltke
Holbert & Lewis, Greeley—Musikant.
E. Knott & Co., Waverly—Young Reyenhold.
Verband of Holstein Marshes, Ger., A. B. Holbert, agt, Greeley—Amandus.

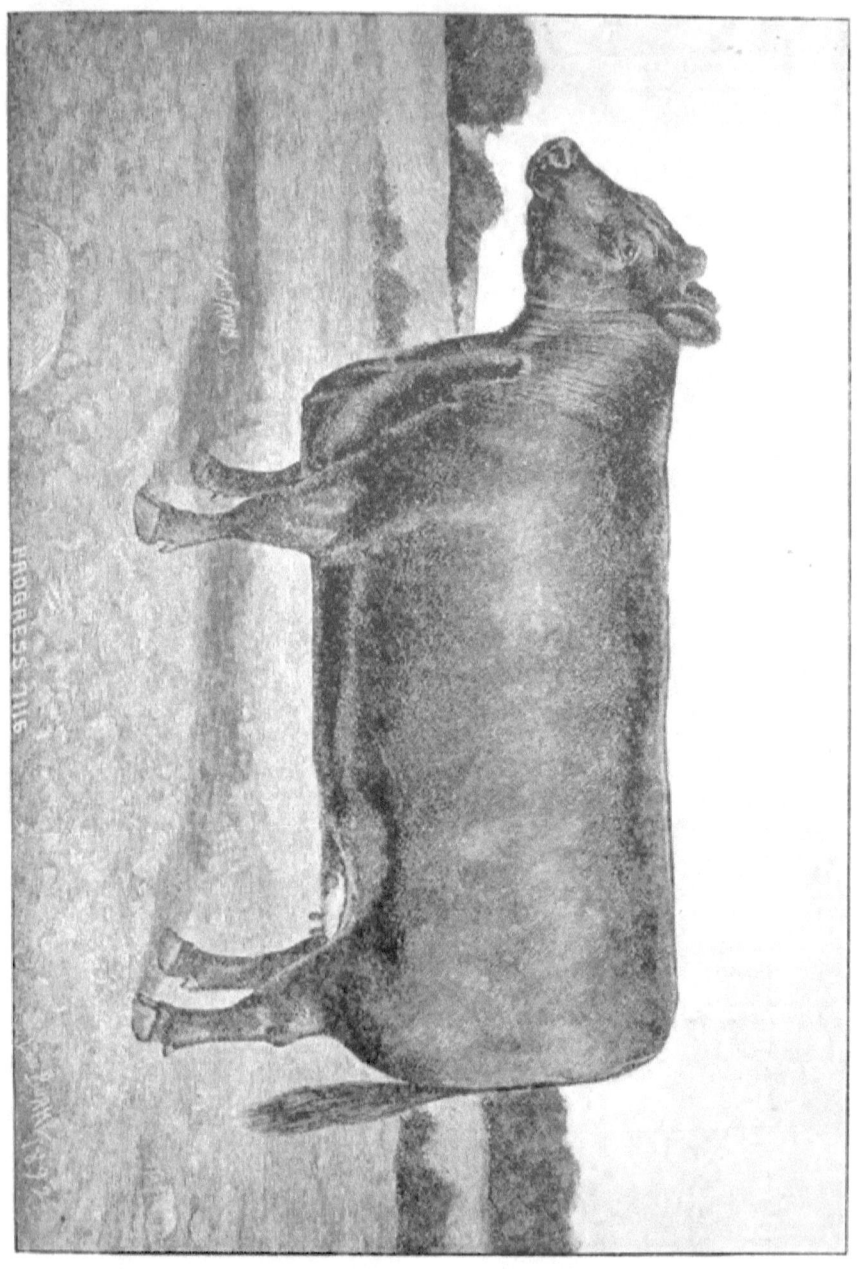

#### FOUR-YEAR-OLD STALLIONS.

A. B. Holbert, Greeley—Mikado and Figaro.
E. Knott & Co., Waverly—Diocletian and Erzfiend.
Verband of Holstein Marshes, Ger., A. B. Holbert, agent, Greeley—Kaiser Frederick.

#### THREE-YEAR-OLD STALLIONS.

A. B. Holbert, Greeley—Affect and Von Moltke.
E. Knott & Co., Waverly—Totalisator and Sperber.
Verband of Holstein Marshes, Ger., A. B. Holbert, agent, Greeley—Weissfuss.

#### TWO-YEAR-OLD STALLIONS.

Verband of Holstein Marshes, Ger., A. B. Holbert, agent, Greeley—Bodo and Blondel.
E. Knott & Co., Waverly—Minister and Danillo.

#### ONE-YEAR-OLD STALLIONS.

E. Knott & Co., Waverly—Goldsucker and Rothbart.

### MARES.

#### THREE YEARS AND UNDER.

Verband of Holstein Marshes, Ger., A. B. Holbert, agent, Greeley—Lillie and Dora.

### SUFFOLK PUNCH.

#### STALLIONS FIVE YEARS OR OVER.

Peter Hopley & Co., Lewis—Blazer and Connaught.
B. Ramsay, Hancock—Nonpareil.

#### ONE YEAR OLD AND UNDER TWO.

Peter Hopley & Co., Lewis—General Bragg and Golden Bow.

#### UNDER ONE YEAR

Peter Hopley, Lewis—Prince of May.
B. Ramsay, Hancock—Cupbearer.

#### STALLION AND THREE OF HIS COLTS, UNDER ONE YEAR OLD, EITHER SEX

Peter Hopley & Co., Lewis—Connaught, General Bragg, Maud Riverside, and Golden Bow.
B. Ramsay, Hancock—Nonpareil, Beauty, Cupbearer, and Alice

#### MARE, FIVE YEARS OR OVER.

Peter Hopley & Co., Lewis—Daffodil and Chorus.
B. Ramsay, Hancock—Saxstead Sal.

#### MARE, FOUR YEARS AND UNDER FIVE.

B. Ramsay, Hancock—Jessie and Mirth.

### MARE, TWO YEARS AND UNDER THREE.

Peter Hopley & Co., Lewis—Maud Riverside.

### MARE, ONE YEAR AND UNDER TWO.

B. Ramsay, Hancock—Beauty.

### MARE, UNDER ONE YEAR.

Peter Hopley & Co., Lewis—Dora and Cora
B. Ramsay, Hancock—Alice.

### SWEEPSTAKE STALLIONS, ANY AGE.

Peter Hopley & Co., Lewis—Blazor and Connaught.
B. Ramsay, Hancock—Nonpareil.

## BELGIAN.

### STALLION, FIVE YEARS AND OVER.

Van Valsom Bros., A. B. Holbert, Agt., Greeley—Hercules and Bismark 2d.

### STALLION, FOUR YEARS AND UNDER FIVE.

Van Valsom Bros., A. B. Holbert, Agt., Greeley—Vingtmars and Fox.
A. B. Holbert, Greeley—Eiffel and Glorieux.
Petersburg Horse Breeding Co., Greeley—Robert II.

### STALLION, THREE YEARS AND UNDER FOUR.

Van Valsom Bros., A. B. Holbert, Agt., Greeley—Richelieu.
A. B. Holbert, Greeley—Bidel.

### STALLION, TWO AND UNDER THREE.

Van Valsom Bros., A. B. Holbert, Agt., Greeley—Royal Corbias.
A. B. Holbert, Greeley—Fox.

### STALLION, ONE YEAR AND UNDER TWO.

Van Valsom Bros., A. B. Holbert, Agt., Greeley—Florentine.

### MARE, FIVE YEARS OR OVER.

A. B. Holbert, Greeley—Jeannette.

### MARE, TWO AND UNDER THREE.

Lefebure & Sons, Fairfax—Rosette and Cocotte.

### MARE, UNDER ONE YEAR.

A. B. Holbert, Greeley—Antoinette.

## CLYDESDALE.

L. B. GOODRICH. State Center.
Stallion five years or over, MacClaskie 6542.
Stallion three and under four, MacNaught 7174.
Stallion two and under three, McCloskie 6820.
Stallion one year and under two, MacRadnor 6927, and Radnor Brown 6928.
Stallion under one year, MacCraskie.
Mare five years and over, Lizzie Findlay, Queen of Scots 6801.
Mare two and under three, Lady McJess.
Mare one and under two, Ambrose 6924.
Mare under one year. Fidelas, Lilly Radnor.

## HACKNEY.

L. B. GOODRICH, State Center.
Five years or over, Dorrington.

## PERCHERON.

E. F. KLEINMEYER, Wilton Junction.
Stallion two years and under three, Prince Model 14364.
Stallion under one year, Model.
Mare one year and under two, Princess of Wilton 17744.

## FRENCH DRAFT.

E. F. KLEINMEYER, Wilton Junction.
Stallion five years or over, Colored Gentleman 1168, Iowa King 8646.
Stallion one year and under two, Perche Duke 8747, Wilton King 8646.
Mare five years or over, Marie.
Mare one year and under two, Pride of Pleasant Hill 8651, Queen of Pleasant Hill 8646.

## SHIRES.

A. B. HOLBERT, Greeley.
Stallion three years and under four, Echo Chief.

## CLEVELAND BAY.

A. B. HOLBERT, Greeley.
Stallion three years and under four, Almoner.

## SHETLAND PONIES.

J. MURRAY HOAG, Maquoketa.
    Stallion four years or over, Howard B and Good Boy.
    Stallion three years and under four, Jed and January.
    Stallion two and under three, Knapsack.
    Mare four years or over, Cora and Dora.
    Mare three and under four, Jessie and Julia B.
    Mare two and under three, Knickerbocker Lass and Kena.
    Sweepstakes Stallion, any age, Sparkle and Moir Jr.
    Mare any age, Belle and Dot.
    Double team, Sparkle and Joker; Good Boy and Felix.
    Tandem team, Howard B, Eureka, Jay and Colorado.
    Team three abreast, Good Boy, Garibaldi and Felix.

## STANDARD TROTTERS.

JOHN JACOBS, Langworthy.
    Mares five years and over, Kitty Creek Bird and Langworthy Lady.

## COACH HORSES.

    The Iowa horse exhibit was substantially as the foregoing entries indicate. The exhibition of horses at the Exposition commenced August 21st and closed September 9th. The Oldenburg, Holstein and other German breeds of coachers were to the front in the Iowa string, A. B. Holbert, of Greeley, leading, with E. Knott & Co., Waverly, as second in the number shown. The ring was a strong one, with two good stables present from Illinois and one from Indiana, and consignments from the Oldenburg Agricultural and other German societies. The judging was done by two gentlemen from Germany with a Wisconsin gentleman as consulting judge. The awards in the aged stallion class brought the first, fourth and sixth prizes to Iowa. In the four-year-old stallion class, the judges sent the first, second, third and seventh to Iowa, Waverly taking its turn, with Greeley for the first. In the three-year-old stallion class the second and third came to Iowa. Waverly again standing above Greeley, the judges taking the first for the Oldenburger's Society. In the two-year-old stallion class, Iowa took the first and third for Greeley, and the fifth and sixth for Waverly. In the yearling class for stallions, the first and second went to Waverly, no other Iowa yearlings having been entered. Two Iowa German coach mares were entered; these were in the three-year-old class and took the second and third prizes for the Greeley string. In sweepstakes best stallion, any age, the first, sixth and seventh awarded to Greeley, the second and fourth to Waverly, seemed to literally scoop the Illinois, Indiana and the other stables, and laid these great trophies about equally at the feet of the enterprising competitors from Greeley and Waverly. Sweepstakes mares, any age, Greeley was third and fifth.

    It will be noted that Iowa won three of the six prizes awarded in the aged stallion class for German coachers and four of the six prizes in the four-year old class of stallions. In the sweepstakes stallion, any age, sixteen of the best stood as the representatives of the stallions exhibited, Iowa winning the medal and first on Moltke and having five horses in the first seven places. There were special prizes given to the German breeds of horses by the German Government, which were awarded publicly in the pavilion by Dr. Richter, the Imperial German Commissioner, an event attracting great attention at the time. In a neat speech, after having been introduced by Chief Buchanan, Dr. Richter said that the exhibit of horses of German breeding was in keeping with the prominent place held by his country in all departments of the Exposition, that he had nine prizes to award for the excellence of the collection of horses, a first each to the Holstein, the Hanovarian, and the Oldenburg collections; second to the breeders of the champion stallion Moltke; to the best and second best Hanovarian mares; to the breeders of Lerche, the best Holstein mare, and to the President of the Verband of Holstein Marshes, as breeder of Blondell. Thus the Greeley string had a first for the Verband of Holstein Marshes collection, and an award for the championship of Moltke; also an award to the breeders of Blondel and Lerche. Special prizes were also given by the Oldenburg Stud Book Society to the best stallion and mare, gold medal, and second best silver medal. E. Knott & Co. took first on Sperber, and second on Diocletian. The Verband of Holstein Marshes gave special prizes to the Holstein horses on exhibit in classes and sweepstakes, all of which were won by the Iowa string from Greeley.

Quite a deal of rivalry developed among the German Coach horse exhibitors. The Oldenburg, Holstein, Hanovarian and Trakehnen horses have considerable resemblance in style and action, and yet, in size and stoutness, and it may be said in use, are somewhat dissimilar. In the old country the first named is generally regarded as the correct heavy Coach Horse and has great utility as a draft horse. The Holsteins are a similar type to the Oldenburgs, not so large as a rule, standing between the Hanovarian and Oldenburgs, the three having less thoroughbred blood than the East Prussian horse known as Trakehnen. The Trakehnen is the lightest type of the four breeds, a saddler and carriage horse, having good bottom and is a favorite for its beautiful carriage. It is the horse of the German cavalry and artillery, which likely accounts for the flourishing condition of the horse breeding industry in that province, together with the fact that the Imperial Stud is located at Trakehnen. The East Prussian horse record is known as the "Book of Pedigrees of Fine Half-Thoroughbreds." The Greeley string of German Coachers were Holsteins and the Waverly string were Oldenburgs; thus it will be seen that the honors were so evenly divided that the owners of either breed have reason to support their claims for the general excellence of their especial breeds. With a Hanovarian mare as sweepstakes, that breed is not without strong backing for the supporters of that favorite branch of the German coach horse family. There was an interesting struggle over the blue ribbon in the three-year-old stallion class between two Oldenburgs. While the judges gave the first to the Oldenburg Society's horse "Athling," the bystanders and best German Coach Horse judges of this country present there, justly claimed the blue ribbon for Messrs. E. Knott & Co.'s grandly made horse Sperber, which for some unknown reason was placed second. In this controversy the crowd placed the Iowa horse first, and the record should set the facts right, so that history may place the horses as they merited.

The horses entered in the name of Verband of Holstein Marshes were fitted by Mr. Holbert at his breeding stud at Greeley and all were purchased by him to be delivered at the close of the Exposition. The horses were all returned to Iowa with his string after the Exposition closed. Mr. Holbert's colors were everywhere greeted with admiration when his horses were paraded in public.

## DRAFT HORSES.

In point of number, the prizes won by the Iowa draft horses, the Suffolk Punch horses led. The string of the Silvertailed Chestnuts brought into the ring by Messrs. Peter Hopley & Co., of Lewis, and B. Ramsay, of Hancock, marked a new epoch in horse breeding in this country. As an agricultural and draft horse these easy keeping and fairly strong boned and well muscled horses are bound to have a place among American draft horses. They should not be forgotten by the farmers when looking for hard workers and easy keepers on the farm. A good stable of Suffolk Punches was exhibited from New York and two from Ontario, but the Iowa Suffolks were with hardly an exception, decorated with the ribbons of winners as they were led back to their barns after the judging, as shown in detail elsewhere. They were the largest winners from Iowa, Mr. Hopley alone winning $1,010 cash, besides cups and medals.

## THE CLYDESDALE.

The battle was fierce in the extreme in the aged stallion class between the sixteen best Clydesdale stallions in the world. McGregor was again on his native heath in the blood of the "Macs." MacQueen, American Horse Show winner; Rosewood, a son of McFarlane; MacClaskie, winner of the Toronto stallion show; and Macara, winner of the Royal, were placed by the judge in the order named. This is another instance where the judge and the crowd differed, for in the opinion of most horsemen, themselves acute judges, MacClaskie was entitled to the blue ribbon, or at least his colors should have been lowered to none other than MacQueen. Other prizes were taken by the young ones, and considering the company the Marshall county string was in, the record was excellent. Old Scotland and the rest of the Clydesdale world was canvassed, and the best horses obtained at extravagantly long prices to meet those descendants of the great sires, Prince of Wales, Darnley and McGregor, in honor of Auld Lang Syne.

## BELGIANS.

An Indiana exhibitor alone joined issue with the Iowa contingent of Belgians, with the result that all the first prizes came to Iowa, and Indiana drew a second premium in the three-year-old stallion class, but the rest of the prizes went deservedly to the following Iowa gentlemen:

Van Valsom Bros. and A. B. Holbert, of Greeley, and Lefebure & Son, of Fairfax, all taking their proportion as shown in another part of this report. The string of Belgians from Iowa was an attractive adjunct to the horse exhibit, and merited as it received, the heartiest approval of the pavilion visitors at the Exposition.

## FRENCH DRAFT.

The Iowa string of French Draft horses was exhibited by Mr. E. F. Kleinmeyer, of Wilton Junction, who showed stallions only in aged and yearling classes. Two exhibitors besides the invincible Oak Lawn stud of M. W. Dunham, of Illinois, and one Canada stable, made it a stout fight for Mr. Kleinmeyer's horses. The draft horses of Oak Lawn are known as Percherons, but being of French breed are eligible to entry in the French Draft Stud Book. The Oak Lawn horses were too numerous for the Percheron classes alone, being limited to two of same age, so to the dismay of the other French Draft Horse exhibitors, a number of the Oak Lawn Percherons were at the last moment recorded in the French Draft Stud Book, apparently for the express purpose of competing in the French Draft classes.

In the two stallion classes in which Iowa stood, this maneuver of Oak Lawn beat Iowa out of the first prizes, but the Wilton Junction string easily beat off the other stables, and stood second in both classes. In all other classes where competing, Mr. Kleinmeyer's horses were placed, and in the yearling mare class, with Pride of Pleasant Hill, he easily won the first over the Oak Lawn filly, which was certainly "glory enough for one day."

In the Percheron class it will be observed that the Wilton Junction stable exhibited a two-year-old and colt in the stallion classes, and one yearling in the mare class. Two of these were fourth, and the other was placed.

## SHIRES AND CLEVELAND BAYS.

Mr. Holbert showed a stallion in the Shire and one in the Cleveland Bay class, both being placed by the judge, one second, and the other fifth.

## STANDARD TROTTERS.

Two standard trotters entered by John Jacobs, of Langworthy, Iowa, in the aged mare class, were placed by the judges as follows: Kitty Creek Bird third, and Langworthy Lady sixth; Kitty Creek Bird, shown as single driver in sweepstakes, any age, to harness, won second premium, and the two together in double harness, third premium. The ring was a good one.

## SHETLAND PONIES.

The exhibit of Shetland Ponies from Maquoketa was a strong feature of the Iowa Exhibit. There were three stables from Wisconsin and two each from New York and Michigan, which made a very attractive exhibit, and gave Mr. Hoag healthy competition. The ponies were shown in stallion and mare classes according to age, and in sweepstakes as usual; then in harness, single and double teams; team four abreast, and team of eight, with four abreast; in tandem, and under the saddle. In all the teams, and under the saddle, geldings were allowed to compete. The display will long be remembered, especially by the children, as one of the most fascinating of the Exhibition. The aged stallion and mare classes, as well as in the sweepstakes and team of eight, the Iowa ponies brought home the blue ribbon. Indeed, I believe that about every entry of Mr. Hoag's was placed for some of the prizes offered in each class, and the number of prizes won must have been sufficient to decorate the ponies in blue, red and white.

The Maquoketa stable of Shetlands, at all events, is easily at the head of all similar breeding studs in the country.

Were this review of the Iowa Horse Exhibit not already too lengthy, an interesting comparison of winners from Iowa to those from other parts of the world could be made, and would demonstrate that nearly every Iowa horse exhibited won prizes in class, and many in sweepstakes, showing the great superiority of the Iowa breeding horses over those met and vanquished during the great contest. The reader is invited to look once at the table of winners for the mathematical side of this report, for the verification of this statement.

## SWINE.

The swine exhibit from Iowa maintained the high standing of the breeding stock of the state. While the numbers shown were but an atom compared with the number annually exhibited at our state fair, yet the showing was representative of the two breeds participating. Poland-China and Duroc Jersey. The entries of the Poland-China were as follows:

MESSRS. TAFT & CO., Humboldt,
 6 Hogs, 8 Pigs.

PETER MOUW, Orange City,
 Yearling boar, Grand Chief 20177. 2 year old sow, Miss Jumbo 57666, Jno. K. 57678, yearling sows, Perfect Lady 66860, Esther 66862.

A. J. LYTLE, Oskaloosa,
 Yearling boar, Tecumseh 20499, 18 months.

W. G. MARSHALL, Iowa City,
 Yearling boar, Free Trade Chip 19225.

JOHN JOHNSTON & SONS, Humboldt,
 Aged boar, Oxford Duke.

STONE & STONE, Le Claire,
 6 months, under 12. Rival Wilkes.

M. DUNN, Van Meter,
 Fancy Golddust.

J. F. BONNER, Morning Sun,
 Miss Allerton 55342.

T. R. WILSON, Morning Sun,
 Renick Rose 68140.

## DUROC JERSEYS.

Wm. Roberts & Son, Paton,
  11 Hogs, 11 Pigs.

J. H. Lathrop, Oxford Junction,
  4 Sows, seven months old, Minnie 812, Winnie 802, Iowa Queen 3d. 806, and Iowa Queen 4th 808.

There were forty-five exhibitors of Poland-China swine, of which number Iowa furnished nine, Nebraska thirteen, Illinois five, Ohio five, Missouri five, Kansas three, Indiana three and Minnesota one.

The aged boar class opened the fight with twenty candidates for honors, representing every type of the Poland-China, the fine and chubby sort, the medium, and lastly the heavy boned style with length and scale, the sort the trade demands in this state. Messrs. Johnston & Sons of Humboldt were to the front with Oxford Duke, the Iowa Champion of last year; Messrs. Taft & Son of the same town had a good one in Black Wilkes. Ohio was there also with two good ones, and they caught the judge's eye for first and second, and Oxford Duke brought the third honor to Iowa. The yearling boar class was no less a battle royal, since eighteen of the best that the eight states mentioned above had to show, were in competition. Mr. Lytle's L. Tecumseh, the Iowa and Nebraska yearling boar champion of last year, rightly claimed first honors, while Mr. Marshall of Iowa City with Free Trade Chip (second to L. Tecumseh at Des Moines) asserted his right to be thereabouts when Mr. Lytle's should receive the blue ribbon. Indiana appeared, however, with one having the style and type suited to Ohio and Indiana taste, and as the judge was from Indiana, and had more authority in distributing ribbons than the crowd standing for Iowa's champion, the end came with Indiana taking first, and Iowa second and third, with the Oskaloosa and Iowa City yearlings. Messrs. Stone & Stone, of Le Clair, Peter Mouw and T. R. Wilson, of Morning Sun, also had yearlings in this ring.

## AGED SOWS.

The ring was strong, and Iowa had good ones. Peter Mouw's was fourth with Miss Jumbo. Taft & Son's showed Rosalind. M. Dunn showed Fancy Golddust. J. F. Bonner showed Miss Allerton, and they were all toward the best end of the string.

## YEARLING SOWS.

The yearling sow ring was one of the best of the Poland China Exhibit. It had no exciting incidents outside of the sending of the blue ribbon, as with the other yearling ring, to Indiana, which award was generally criticised. Iowa was in the ring, but not among the first six placed.

The boar and sow pig rings over six months were interesting displays, especially the latter. Among the competitors was Mr. Wilson's Renick Rose, the only Iowa representative.

In the aged herd ring, Iowa stood with only one herd, Mr. Peter Mouw's. It was awarded fifth place.

## DUROC JERSEYS.

The show of the red hogs had two exhibitors from Iowa, Messrs. Wm. Roberts & Son, of Paton, and J. H. Lathrop, of Oxford Junction. The former had the largest exhibit made of either breed of hogs, twenty-two including the pigs. Illinois exhibited three herds, Ohio two, Nebraska two, and Wisconsin one. Mr. Lathrop's pigs were seven months old, too young to win in the over six months class, but won as the get of one sire, bred by exhibitor, of any age. It was about a drawn fight between the Duroc Jersey exhibitors from Illinois, Ohio, Nebraska and Wisconsin, Iowa taking with the Roberts herd, one first with Alice, one second with Jack R., one third with Columbian, three fourths with Lugura B., Motor Jr. and Charity. The same proportion of prizes was won in the herd classes, the details of which will be found in another place.

## POULTRY.

The Iowa Exhibit of Poultry was very small in numbers, but choice in quality. The consignments of this Exhibit were as follows:

G. W. STOUT, Rose Hill,
  6 birds.
JOHN WILSON, What Cheer,
  9 birds, White-faced, Black Spanish 8 to 18 months old.
G. H. STROHMEIER, Independence,
  1 bird, Indian Game Cock.
W. H. GARLAND, Aurora,
  5 birds, B. G. Polish Breed.

The entries from all quarters at the Columbian Poultry Show numbered between five and six thousand birds, and upwards of four thousand were on exhibition. Canada was present with about one-third of the entire exhibit.

Iowa brought home a first premium on breeding pen, also first on cockerel, and third on pullet, on Mr. Wilson's white-faced Black Spanish birds. Mr. Strohmeier's Indian Game Cock won second prize. Mr. Garland took second on his breeding pen of B. G. Polish breed consisting of one cockerel, and four pullets.

## AWARDS TO IOWA STOCK.

The following list comprises the awards made to exhibitors of Cattle, amount of the premiums paid to the same by the Exposition company, names of the animals winning, also the special premiums that were given by certain herd book societies, and the prizes paid by this Commission to the owners of cows competing in the dairy test.

## BREEDING CATTLE.

### ABERDEEN-ANGUS—CLASS THREE.

Exhibitor—W. A. McHenry, Denison, Iowa.

| Animal. | Age. | Prem. | Amount |
|---|---|---|---|
| Prince of the Realm | Aged | 4th | $ 15 00 |
| Keiller McHenry | 2 years | 2d | 35 00 |
| Jeans Abactor 2d | 1 year | 1st | 50 00 |
| Abactor's Barbara 1st | calf | 4th | 15 00 |
| Progress | Aged | 2d | 35 00 |
| Nell Gwynne 3d | 2 years | 1st | 50 00 |
| Black Bird McHenry 2d | 2 years | 2d | 30 00 |
| Minnie McHenry 5th | 1 year | 1st | 40 00 |
| Black Bird McHenry 3d | Heifer c'lf | 4th | 20 00 |
| Herd | | 2d | 75 00 |
| Young Herd, bred by exhibitor | | 2d | 75 00 |
| Four animals, get of one sire | | 2d | 75 00 |
| 4 animals, either sex, get of 1 sire | | 4th | 25 00 |
| Two animals, produce of one cow | | 3d | 20 00 |

### SWEEPSTAKES.

| | | | |
|---|---|---|---|
| Jeans Abactor 2d | | 2d | |
| Progress | Aged | 2d | |
| Nell Gwynne 3d | 2 years | 1st | |

### SWEEPSTAKES BY AGES—BEEF BREEDS.

| | | | |
|---|---|---|---|
| Nell Gwynne 3d | 2 years | 1st | Medal and $25.00 |
| Progress of Turlington | Aged | 2d | |
| Jeans Abactor 2d | 1 year | 2d | |
| Minnie McHenry 5th | 1 year | 3d | |
| Total awards to W. A. McHenry | | | $585 00 |

Special awards by Aberdeen-Angus Society ..... $791 00

Grand total .......................................... $1,376 00

### RED POLES—CLASS XI.

Exhibitor—J. H. Gilfillan, Maquoketa, Iowa.

| Animal. | Age. | Premium. | Amount |
|---|---|---|---|
| Iowa Davyson 14th 2769 | Aged | 2d | $ 25 00 |
| Iowa Davyson 20th 2773 | 2 years | 1st | 35 00 |
| Columbus 30404 | 1 year | 1st | 35 00 |
| Iowa Davyson 22d 3151 | 1 year | 4th | 10 00 |
| Iowa Davyson 23d | calf | 1st | 25 00 |
| Iowa Davyson 25th | calf | 5th | highly commended |
| Eulalie 2d 5453 | Aged | 3d | 15 00 |
| Priscilla | Aged | 5th | highly commended |
| Eulalie 3d 7086 | 3 years | 1st | 35 00 |
| Iowa Davy 18th 7194 | 2 years | 1st | 35 00 |
| Iowa Davy 12th 7193 | 2 years | 3d | 15 00 |
| Iowa Davy 14th 7195 | 1 year | 1st | 25 00 |
| Iowa Davy 15th 7936 | 1 year | 3d | 15 00 |
| Munnis | calf | 2d | 20 00 |
| Gladys | calf | 4th | 10 00 |

### HERD PREMIUMS.

| | | | |
|---|---|---|---|
| Aged, five animals.............. | ........... | 1st .. | 80 00 |
| Aged, five animals............... | ........... | 4th... | 25 00 |
| Young, 5 animals, bred by exhibit'r | ........... | 1st ... | 75 00 |
| Get of one sire, four animals...... | ........... | 1st ... | 75 00 |
| Get of one sire, four animals...... | ........... | 4th .. | 20 00 |
| Produce of one cow, two animals.. | ........... | 1st ... | 40 00 |
| Produce of one cow, two animals.. | ........... | 2d ... | 30 00 |

### SWEEPSTAKES.

| | | | |
|---|---|---|---|
| Iowa Davy 13th ............... | 2 years... | 1st .. | $ 25 00 and medal |
| Total awards to J. H. Gilfillan | ........... | ........ | $ 670 00 |

### GALLOWAYS—CLASS IV.

EXHIBITOR—WM. MCTURK & SON, Crystal, Iowa.

| | | | |
|---|---|---|---|
| Hunter 2d, Dykes Creek........ | 5 years | 5th .. | highly commended |
| Columbus of Wolf Creek........ | 1 year | 4th ... | $ 15 00 |
| Sulwood of Wolf Creek......... | calf..... | 3d ... | 20 00 |

### YOUNG HERD.

| | | | |
|---|---|---|---|
| Columbus, Matilda ............. | ........... | 4th... | 25 00 |
| June Bug, Sulwood ............. | ........... | 4th... | 25 00 |

The Galloway Herd Book Society duplicated above premiums.

### FAT STOCK.

#### ABERDEEN ANGUS STEERS.

EXHIBITOR— W. S. NILES, Wyoming, Iowa.

| | | | |
|---|---|---|---|
| Earl of Sunny Slope ............ | 2 years ... | 1st ... | 35 00 |
| Knight of Sunny Slope.......... | 1 year .... | 1st ... | 35 00 |
| Prince of Sunny Slope .......... | calf....... | 1st ... | 35 00 |

### HERD SWEEPSTAKES.

| | | | |
|---|---|---|---|
| Above named steers............ | ........... | 1st ... | 50 00 |

### SWEEPSTAKES.

| | | | |
|---|---|---|---|
| Prince of Sunny Slope ........ | ........... | 1st ... | 50 00 |

### GRAND SWEEPSTAKES, ALL BREEDS.

| | | | |
|---|---|---|---|
| Prince of Sunny Slope ........ | ........... | 1st ... | 50 00 |
| | | | $255 00 |

## DAIRY COWS.

WHEREAS, This Commission at the meeting held September 1, 1892, adopted the following resolution:

RESOLVED, That the Iowa Columbian Commission, to aid the breeders of dairy cattle in their efforts to further the dairy interest of Iowa at the World's Exposition, will pay the sum of three hundred dollars, pro rata, to the resident owner of Iowa dairy cattle that may be accepted by the Department of Agriculture at the World's Columbian Exposition for any of the tests in the dairy school, provided that no more than one hundred dollars shall be paid for each cow accepted, and in addition that this Commission will pay the further sum of three hundred dollars to the resident owner of Iowa cows that are members of herds winning the medals or awards in the aforementioned dairy tests, provided that no more than one hundred and fifty dollars shall be given to the owner for each cow, and

WHEREAS, The number of cows accepted from Iowa exceeded the number expected to participate at the time of the adoption of above resolution, therefore,

BE IT RESOLVED, That the limit of the amount of money authorized in that resolution be increased to thirteen hundred dollars to pay the owners of the cows accepted in the dairy tests, as follows:

Messrs. Richardson Bros., Davenport, for cows Lorita, Campania and Elturia, $300.

Messrs. Dan'l Sheehan & Son, Osage, for cows Nora and Belle Price, $200.

D. J. Heinsheimer, Glenwood, for cow Hugo Countess, $100.

William Miller, Storm Lake, for cow Imported Bashful 2d., $100.

John M. Sterr, New Hampton, on cow Christata, $50. (Cow accepted but disqualified through sickness after two weeks.)

RESOLVED, That the owners of the following named cows belonging to the Jersey herds which won all the tests, be entitled to receive as follows:

D. J. Heinsheimer, cow Hugo Countess, $150.

Richardson Bros., cows Campania and Elturia, $300.

BE IT FURTHER RESOLVED, That Daniel Sheehan & Son, Osage, the owners of Short Horn cow Nora, be awarded $100; that cow having stood first in the Short Horn Herd in the dairy tests, making a record in the cheese and ninety day butter tests beyond any Short Horn cow on exhibition.

BE IT FURTHER RESOLVED, That the thanks of this Commission are extended to the owners who so generously permitted the use of their cows to compete in that great dairy test of the world, the result of which has brought great credit to the state and vast benefit to the dairy interests of this commonwealth. Adopted December 14th, 1893.

Awards made to Iowa exhibitors of horses and ponies by the Exposition, showing amount of premiums won, and names of animals winning.

Exhibitors to whom awards were made:

## HORSES.

#### SUFFOLK PUNCH. CLASS 31.

#### EXHIBITOR—PETER HOPLEY, Lewis, Iowa.

| Animal. | Age. | Prem. | Amount. |
|---|---|---|---|
| Blazor | Aged | 1st | $110.00 |
| Connaught | Aged | 3rd | 35.00 |
| General Bragg | 1 yr | 1st | 110.00 |
| Golden Bow | 1 yr | 2d | 70 00 |
| Prince of May | Foal | 1st | 60.00 |
| Connaught with three | colts | 1st | 150.00 |
| Bragg | Aged | 1st | 110.00 |
| Daffodil | Aged | 2d | 70.00 |
| Maud of Riverside | 2 yrs | 1st | 110 00 |
| Dora | Foal | 2d | 35.00 |
| Total amount | | | $1010 00 |

#### SWEEPSTAKES.

| | | |
|---|---|---|
| Stallion | Blazor | Medal |
| Mare | Bragg | Medal |

### SPECIAL PREMIUMS.

#### AWARDED BY AMERICAN SUFFOLK HORSE ASSOCIATION.

Best Three Suffolk Colts—General Bragg, Golden Bow and Maud of Riverside.

Best Suffolk Mare with two of her colts—Smart and colts, Golden Bow and Maud of Riverside.

Best Suffolk Stallion and two mares—Stallion Blazor and Mares Bragg and Smart.

#### SUFFOLK PUNCH—CLASS XXXI.

#### EXHIBITOR—ROBERT RAMSAY, Hancock, Iowa.

| | | | |
|---|---|---|---|
| Nonpareil | Aged | 2d | 70 00 |
| Cupbearer | Foal | 2d | 35 00 |
| Nonpareil with three colts | | 2d | 100 00 |
| Saxstead Sal | Aged | 4th | 25 00 |
| Bessie | 4 years | 1st | 110 00 |
| Mirth | 4 years | 2d | 70 00 |
| Beauty | 1 year | 1st | 110 00 |
| Alice | Foal | 1st | 60 00 |
| Saxstead Sal with two colts | | 2d | 100 00 |
| Total awards to Robert Ramsay | | | $680 00 |

### GERMAN COACH,—CLASS 24.

#### STALLIONS, 5 YEARS AND OVER.

Greeley Horse Improvement Company, A. B. Holbert, Agent.
    Moltke, 13 (70), 5 years, 1st; $150.
Verband of Holstein Marshes, Germany, A. B. Holbert, Agent.
    Amandas, 689 (571). 5 years, 4th; $25.

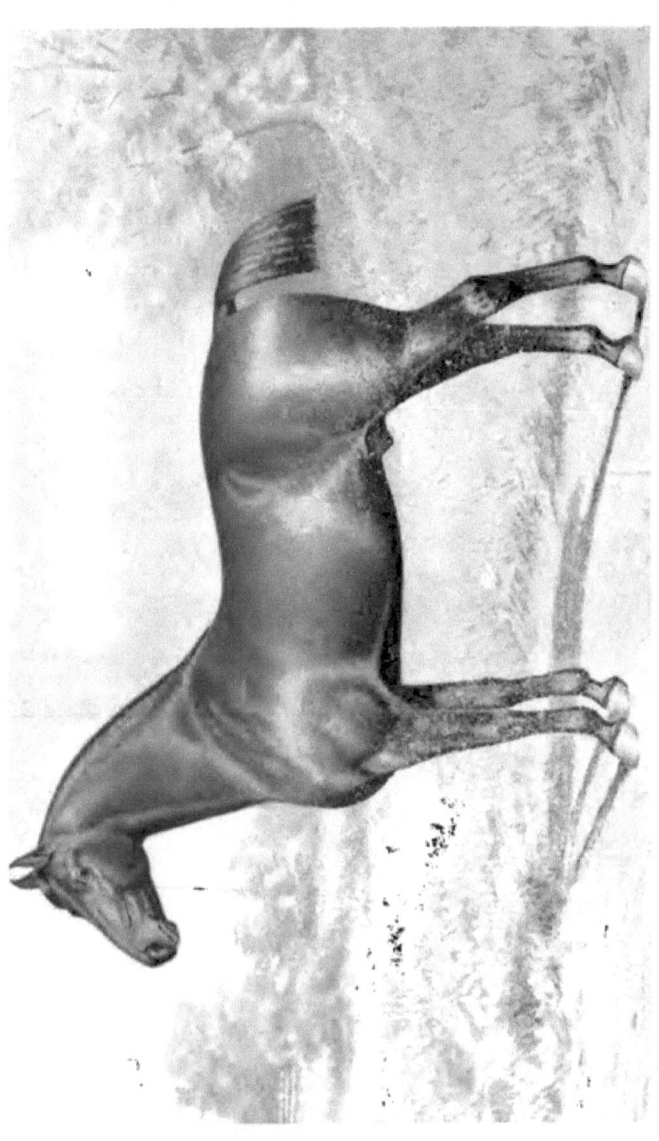

Holbert & Lewis, Greeley, Iowa.
  Musikant, 563 (1228). 5 years, 6th; Commended.
E. Knott & Co., Waverly, Iowa.
  Diocletian, 117, 4 years, 1st.; $150.
Verband of Holstein Marshes, Germany, A. B. Holbert, Agent.
  Kaiser Frederick, 495, 4 years, 2nd.; $100.
A. B. Holbert, Greeley, Iowa.
  Mikado, 4 years, 3d; $50.
A. B. Holbert, Greeley.
  Figaro, 655 (578), 4 years. 6th; Commended.
E. Knott & Co., Waverly
  Sperber, 61, 3 years, 2d; $100.
Verband of Holstein Marshes, Germany, A. B. Holbert, Agent.
  Weissfuss, 677 (621), 3 years, 3d; $50. Bodo, 683 (588), 2 years, 1st; $150.
  Blondel, 685 (587), 2 years, 3d; $50.
E. Knott & Co., Waverly, Iowa.
  Danilo, 156, 2 years, 5th; Highly Commended. Minister, 160, 2 years, 6th; Commended. Rothbart, 158, 1 year, 1st; $150. Goldsucker, 157, 1 year, 2d; $100.

## MARES.

Verband of Holstein Marshes, Germany, A. B. Holbert, Agent.
  Lillie, 679 (787), 3 years, 2d; $100.
Verband of Holstein Marshes, A. B. Holbert, Agent.
  Dora, 681 (4140), 3 years, 3d; $50.

## SWEEPSTAKES STALLION, ANY AGE.

Greeley Horse Improvement Co., A. B. Holbert, Agent.
  Moltke, 13 (70), 1st; Medal.
E. Knott & Co., Waverly, Iowa.
  Diocletian, 117, 2d. Sperber, 161, 4th.
A. B. Holbert, Greeley, Iowa.
  Kaiser Frederick, 495, 6th.
A. B. Holbert, Greeley, Iowa
  Bodo, 683 (588), 7th.

## SWEEPSTAKES MARE, ANY AGE.

Verband of Holstein Marshes, Germany, A. B. Holbert, Agent.
  Lerche, 675 (786), Any age, 3d. Lillie, 679 (787), Any age, 5th.

## HORSES, BELGIANS, - CLASS 30.

Van Valsom Bros., A. B. Holbert, Agent.
  Bismark II, 529, 5 years, 1st; $110. Hercules, 5 years, 2d; $70.

Petersburg Horse Co., A. B. Holbert, agent—Robert II 1858. 4 years, 1st; $110.
Van Valsom Bros., A. B. Holbert, agent—Fox Vol. II 4 years, 2d; $70.
A. B. Holbert, Greeley—Glorieux 1802, 4 years, 3d; $35.
Van Valsom Bros., A. B. Holbert, agent—Vingt Mars, 4 years, 4th; $25.
A. B. Holbert, Greeley—Eiffel Vol. 2. 4 years, 5th; highly commended.
A. B. Holbert, Greeley—Bidel 3668, 3 years, 1st; $110.
Van Valsom Bros., A. B. Holbert, agent—Richelieu 340, 3 years, 3d; $35.
A. B. Holbert, Greeley—Fox 120, 2 years, 1st; $110.
Van Valsom Bros., A. B. Holbert, agent—Royal Carbias 228, 2 years, 2d; $70.

### MARES.

A. B. Holbert, Greeley—Jeanette 4380, 5 years, 1st; $110.
Lefebure & Son, Fairfax—Cocotte 2 years, 1st; $110. Rosette 2 years, 2d; $90.
A. B. Holbert, Greeley—Antoinette 99, under 1 year, 1st; $60.

### SWEEPSTAKES.

#### MARE, ANY AGE.

A. B. Holbert, Greeley—Jeanette 4380, 1st; medal.
Lefebure & Son, Fairfax—Cocotte 2d; Rosette 3d.
A. B. Holbert, Greeley—Antoinette 99, 4th.

#### STALLION, ANY AGE.

A. B. Holbert, Greeley—Bidel 3668, 1st; medal.
Petersburg Horse Co., A. B. Holbert, agent—Robert II 1858, 2d.
Van Valsom Bros., A. B. Holbert, agent—Bismark 529, 3d.
A. B. Holbert, Greeley—Glorieux 1802, 4th.
Van Valsom Bros., A. B. Holbert, agent—Hercules, 5th.

### SHIRES—Class XXVIII.

A. B. Holbert, Greeley—Echo Chief 13026, 3 years, 2d; $100.

### SWEEPSTAKES.

#### SHIRE STALLION, ANY AGE.

A. B. Holbert, Greeley—Echo Chief 13026, 4th.

### CLEVELAND BAY—Class XXV.

A. B Holbert, Greeley—Almoner 1012, 3 years, 5th; highly commended.

## SPECIAL PREMIUMS.

### GERMAN COACH—Class XXIV.

Special prizes given by the Verband of the Holstein Marshes, Germany, to horses recorded in Holstein Stud Book.

#### STALLION, FOUR YEARS OLD AND OVER.

Verband Holstein Marshes, Germany, A. B. Holbert, agent—Kaiser Frederick 496, 4 years, 1st; $60. Amandus 689 (571) 4 years, 2d; $40.
A. B. Holbert, Greeley—Figaro 655 (578) 4 years, 3d; $25. Mikado 635 (579) 4 years, 4th; $10.
Verband Holstein Marshes, Germany, A. B. Holbert, agent—Diplomat 691 (577) 4 years, 5th; highly commended.

#### STALLION, THREE YEARS OLD AND UNDER FOUR.

Verband Holstein Marshes, Germany, A. B. Holbert, agent—Weissfuss 677 (601), 3 years, 1st; $60.
A. B. Holbert, Greeley—Von Moltke 669 (600) 3 years, 2d; $40. Affect 659 (583), 3 years, 3d; $25.
Verband Holstein Marshes, Germany, A. B. Holbert, agent—Antone 3 years, 4th; $10.

#### STALLION, TWO YEARS OLD AND UNDER THREE.

Verband Holstein Marshes, Germany, A. B. Holbert, agent—Bodo 683 (588) 2 years, 1st; $60. Blondel 685 (587), 2 years, 2d; $40.

#### MARE, THREE YEARS OLD OR OVER.

Verband of Holstein Marshes, Germany, A. B. Holbert, agent—Lerche 675 (786), 3 years, 1st; $60. Lillie 679 (787), 3 years, 2d; $40.
A. B. Holbert, Greeley—Dora 681 (4140), 3 years, 3d; $25.

#### SWEEPSTAKES—MARE, ANY AGE—RECORDED IN HOLSTEIN STUD BOOK.

Verband of Holstein Marshes, Germany, A. B. Holbert, Agent—Lerche 1st; statue.

#### STALLION, ANY AGE—RECORDED IN HOLSTEIN STUD BOOK.

Verband of Holstein Marshes, Germany, A. B. Holbert, Agent—Kaiser Frederick 496, 1st; statue.

### GERMAN COACH—Class XXIV.

Gold and silver medal by the Oldenburg Coach Horse Association for best Oldenburg stallion two years old or over, registered in the Oldenburg Book.
E. Knott & Co., Waverly—Sperber 161, 1st; gold medal. Diocletian 117, 2d; silver medal.

Special complimentary and honorary prizes given by the German Government and awarded by Herr Richter, the Imperial German Commissioner to the Columbian Exposition.

Greeley Horse Improvement Company, A. B. Holbert, Agent—Moltke 13 (70), 5 years, 1st; diploma.

### YOUNG STALLION.

Verband of Holstein Marshes, A. B. Holbert, Agent—Blondel 685 (587), 2 years, 1st; diploma.

### BEST HOLSTEIN COACH MARE.

Verband of Holstein Marshes, A. B. Holbert, Agent—Lerche 675 (786) 1st; diploma. Collection of stallions and mares, 1st; diploma.

### FRENCH DRAFT—CLASS XXIX.

E. F. Kleinmeyer, Wilton Junction, Iowa—Iowa King, aged, 2d; $100. Wilton King, 1 year, 2d; $70. Colored Gentleman and three colts under 4 years, 2d; $100. Marie, aged, 4th; $25. Pride of Pleasant Hill, 1 year, 1st; $150. Marie, with two colts, 2d; $100.

### SWEEPSTAKES.

Iowa King, any age, 3d. Marie, any age, 4th. Collection, two stallions and three mares—Perch Duke, Iowa King, Queen of Pleasant Hill, Pride of Pleasant Hill and Princess of Wilton 3d.

### PERCHERON.

Princess of Wilton, 1 year, 4th; $25. Model, foal, 4th; $25. Prince Model, 2 years; commended. Total awards to E. F. Kleinmeyer, $595.

#### SPECIAL PREMIUMS BY FRENCH DRAFT HORSE ASSOCIATION.

#### FOR BEST STALLION, ANY AGE.

Iowa King, 3d; Colored Gentleman, 5th; Perch Duke, 7th.

### CLYDESDALE—CLASS XXVII.

L. B. Goodrich, State Center, Iowa—MacClaskie, aged, 3d; $50. MacCaskie, 2 years; commended. McCroskie, foal; commended. MacClaskie and three colts, highly commended. Lizzie Finley, aged; commended. Lilly Radnor, foal, 3d; $30.

#### SPECIAL PREMIUMS AWARDED BY AMERICAN CLYDESDALE ASSOCIATION.

MacNaught, stallion, 3 years, 3d; $75. Lilly Radnor, mare under 1 year 2d; $100. Fidelas, mare under 1 year, 4th; $40.

Total awards to L. B. Goodrich, $295.

## SHETLAND PONIES—Class XXXVIII.

J. Murray Hoag, Maquoketa—Howard B, aged, 1st; $100. Jed 832, 3 years, 2d; $65. Knapsack 1343, 2 years, 2d; $65. Cora 19, aged. 1st; $100. Dot 29, aged, 2d; $65. Julia B 844, 3 years, 3d $35. Jesse 874, 3 years, 4th; $20. Kena 1344, 2 years, 3d; $35. Knickerbocker Lass 1345, 2 years, 4th; $20. Total, $505.

### SWEEPSTAKES.

Cora, mare any age, 1st; medal. Team of 8, 4 abreast, 1st; medal.

### SPECIAL PREMIUMS AWARDED TO J. MURRAY HOAG BY AMERICAN SHETLAND PONY CLUB.

Silver cup awarded for best show of Shetland Ponies consisting of one tallion and four Mares.

First premium, for best pair ponies in harness, Jay 835, and Colorado 843, and

First premium to Bella 17. best single pony in harness.

The two awards last named were at October classes.

## STANDARD BRED TROTTERS Class XXI.

John Jacobs, Langworthy—Kittie Creek Bird, aged, 3d; $75. Langworthy Lady, 6th; commended.

### SWEEPSTAKES.

Single driver, Kittie Creek Bird, 2d; diploma. Team to harness, Kittie Creek Bird and Langworthy, 3d; diploma.

## AWARDS TO SWINE.

### POLAND-CHINA—Class LVI.

A. J. Lytle, Oskaloosa—L's Tecumseh 2049ç, 1 year, 2d; $40

#### SWEEPSTAKES.

L's Tecumseh, 2d.
Wm. G. Marshall, Iowa City—Free Trade Chip (A) 19225, 1 year, 3d; $30.
John Johnston & Sons, Humboldt—Oxford Duke (O) 27663, aged, 3d; $30

### DUROC JERSEY—Class LVIII.

J. H. Lathrop, Oxford Junction—Four swine, get of one boar, bred by exhibitor, 4th; $55. Winnie 812, Winnie 802, Iowa Queen 3d 806, Iowa Queen 4th 808.

Total awards to J. H. Lathrop, $55.

Wm. Roberts & Son, Paton—Motor, aged, 6th; commended. Charity, 2 years, 4th; $20. Lugura B, 2 years, 4th; $20. Columbian Duke, 1 year, 3d; $30. Motor Jr, over 6 months, 4th; $20. Alice R, under 6 months, 1st; $40. Jack R, under 6 months, 2d; $35. Zeek, under 6 months, highly commended. Boar and three sows over 1 year, Motor, Sugura B, Miss Christopher and Charity, 4th; $30. Boar and three sows bred by exhibitor, Motor, Sugura B, Charity and Miss Christopher, 4th; $40. Boar and three sows under 1 year, bred by exhibitor, Jack R, Penrose, Roberts Pride, Alice R, 2d; $40. Four pigs under 6 months, product of same sow, same pigs as above, 2d; $75. Total, $350.

Official awards were not made on the poultry show but the score of each exhibit was given the exhibitor.

The official sheet of awards to Iowa gives the following to live stock:

Number of first premiums............................ 41
Number of second premiums......................... 37
Number of third premiums........................... 22
Number of fourth premiums.......................... 25
Number of special premiums......................... 5
Number of medals for sweepstakes................. 15
Number of diplomas..................................... 3
Number of cash prizes.................................125

## DAIRY TEST.

The Dairy Test, sometimes called the Dairy School of the Exposition, became one of the most interesting features. It was established mainly to test the merits of the dairy breeds of cattle of the world, and incidentally to illustrate and educate the people interested in this leading industry as to the proper methods of handling milk and cream, and the value of machinery and appliances in the economic production of butter and cheese.

The breed tests were four in number, the first one commencing May 11th and continuing fifteen days, known as the cheese test, in which all commercial products—cheese, whey, gain or loss in weight of the cow—were considered in making the award.

The second test began May 31st, continuing till August 28th, and was known as the ninety-day butter test. In this test all commercial products—butter, butter milk, skimmed milk, increase or decrease in weight, and the cost of color, if used—were considered in making the award.

Breed Test No. 3, from August 29th to September 27th, was known as the thirty-day butter test. In this test no product except butter was considered in making the award.

Breed Test No. 4, from September 28th to October 27th, for young herds, heifers to be under three years old on September 1, 1893, was on the same plan and under the same rules as Test No 2. This was known as the heifer test

Tests Nos. 1 and 2 were conducted under uniform methods of handling the milk and the cream and the manufacture of the cheese and butter. In Test No. 3 the committee of each breed was allowed to decide the method of handling the milk and cream and the manner in which the same should be manufactured into butter. In the first two tests each breed was represented by twenty-five registered cows, in the third test by fifteen cows. These three tests were participated in by the Jerseys, Guernseys and Short Horns. In the Heifer test the Jerseys and Short Horns fought it out without the Guernseys. A record was kept of the weight of milk from each cow, weight of milk from each breed, the percentage of butter fat in the milk from each cow, the percentage of solids other than butter fat, the same for each breed, amount of butter in pounds produced by each breed, per cent of butter fat in such butter. Similar regulations were adopted respecting the cheese tests, and an accurate record was kept of the feed consumed by each cow, and likewise the product was credited showing the net profit of each cow and each breed.

In the first three tests awards were made for the best cow of each breed; the best cow of any breed; the best five cows of each breed; the best five cows of any breed; and for the best breed.

These are the leading points governing the tests, though those interested should obtain the complete rules governing, which are too long to include in this report.

Iowa had representatives in the herd of Jerseys and Short Horns as follows:

### JERSEY COWS.

Richardson Bros., Davenport—Lorita, Campania, Elturia
D. J. Heinsheimer, Glenwood—Hugo Countess.

### SHORT HORN COWS.

Daniel Sheehan & Son, Osage—Nora and Belle Price.
William Miller, Storm Lake—Imported Bashful 2d.
John M. Sterr, New Hampton—Christata.

In the Cheese test the record of the breeds was as follows:

| HERD | Milk, lbs | Cheese, lbs. | Total Value Products | Cost of Feed | Net Profit |
|---|---|---|---|---|---|
| Jerseys | 13,296.4 | 1,451.76 | $217.96 | $98.14 | $119.82 |
| Guernseys | 10,938.6 | 1,130.62 | 164.55 | 76.25 | 88.30 |
| Short Horns | 12,186 | 1,077.6 | 180.70 | 99.36 | 81.34 |

In the Jersey herd the Iowa cows, Hugo Countess and Lorita, competed, and in the Short Horn herd Nora, Imported Bashful 2d, Belle Price and Christata competed. On the basis of the net profit Nora's standing was 5th in the 75 cows competing, four Jerseys leading. The first, Ida Marigold, showed a profit of $6.97, and Nora gave a profit of $6.27, the two Jerseys immediately above her giving a profit of $6.34 each, beating her by 7c. Hugo Countess followed in the 8th place among the 75, with a profit $5.96. The value of the live weight gain of Nora was $2.52, having gained 56 lbs. at 4½c per lb; while Hugo Countess gained but 16 lbs., valued at 72c. Hugo Countess produced 66.96 lbs. of cheese, and Nora 60.56 lbs. in the fifteen days.

The other Iowa cows stood: Imported Bashful 2d, 27th; Lorita, 44th; Belle Price, 63d; and Christata, 74th; but the latter, being incapacitated at the close of the test by illness, was sent home. It should be stated in justice to the cow Christata that the value of her cheese, $5.35, if not drawn against for the loss of 17 lbs of flesh through illness, would have placed her much higher in the list.

In the Ninety-day Butter Test, all commercial products being considered, the record of the breeds was as follows:

| HERD | Milk, lbs. | Butter, lbs. | Value of Product | Net Profits |
|---|---|---|---|---|
| Jersey | 73,488.8 | 4,274.010 | $1,876.671 | $1,323.812 |
| Guernsey | 61,781.7 | 3,360.431 | 1,465.464 | 907.639 |
| Short Horn | 66,263.2 | 2,890.869 | 1,286.789 | 910.117 |

The Iowa cows were Hugo Countess and Lorita in the Jersey herd; Nora, Imported Bashful 2d and Belle Price in the Short Horn herd. Hugo Countess gave 3,542 9 lbs of milk, made 191.894 lbs. of butter at a net profit of $60.72 3. Lorita gave 2,320.3 lbs of milk, made 146.619 lbs. of butter at a net profit of $39.49 8. Nora gave 3,679.8 lbs. of milk, made 160.579 lbs. of butter at a net profit of $52.63 4. Imported Bashful 2d gave 3.341 lbs. of milk, made 162.095 lbs. of butter at a net profit of $47.19 6. Belle Price gave 3,249.4 lbs. of milk, made 151.93 lbs. of butter at a net profit of $41.12 8. Hugo Countess was 5th of the 24 cows competing, with a net profit of $60.72 3, thus was one of the best five cows in the award.

THIRTY-DAY BUTTER TEST, AUG. 28TH TO SEPT. 27TH INCLUSIVE.

In the Thirty-day Butter Test the records of the breeds, 15 cows of each breed participating, was as follows:

| HERD | Milk, lbs | Butter, lbs. | Value of Butter | Cost of Food | Net Profit |
|---|---|---|---|---|---|
| Jersey | 13,921.9 | 837.21 | $385.59 2 | $111.21 3 | $274.34 9 |
| Guernsey | 13,518.4 | 724.17 | 329.76 8 | 92.76 6 | 237.00 2 |
| Short Horn | 15,618.3 | 662.66 | 303.68 5 | 104.55 1 | 119.13 4 |

Hugo Countess was the only Iowa cow in the Jersey herd in this test, with Bashful 2d, Nora and Belle Price competing in the Short Horn herd, and taking rank in the order named. Hugo Countess encountered an accident early in this test. The stall companion of Hugo Countess, while the Countess was lying down, stepped on one of her teats and nipped off the end. The milk had to be drawn with a tube from the sore teat and her feed reduced. The result was that the Countess presumably lost considerably in the flow of milk, inasmuch as she lost 120 lbs. in her weight. It will be remembered that in this test the butter was the only product considered, and the loss of flesh, while not charged, showed the result of short feeding, which fact is supported by the small sum charged against her, $5.20 9, a sum less than anyone of the 45 cows is charged with, the average being between $8.57 4, the highest, a Jersey, and the lowest, $5.45 8, a Guernsey.

The individual record of the best cow in the test, a Jersey, was a net profit of $24.69 7 on the 72.235 lbs. of butter credited. The Iowa cows stood as follows:

| Name | Breed | Butter, lbs. | Net Profit |
|---|---|---|---|
| Hugo Countess | Jersey | 48.712 | $16.96 0 |
| Bashful 2d | Short Horn | 47.474 | 15.49 5 |
| Nora | Short Horn | 47.197 | 14.30 5 |
| Belle Price | Short Horn | 42.168 | 12.14 3 |

The best Short Horn cow in this test was a fresh one, July 19th, not competing in the former tests. It made a record of the third best in the test with its 62.243 lbs. of butter, and a net profit of $20.03 5. The best Guernsey, also not in former test and fresh August 12th, was fifth in the rank, producing 60.268 lbs. of butter with a net profit of $19.37 7. Of the five leading cows in the test, three (one Jersey, one Guernsey and one Short Horn) were not in former test; the other two were Jerseys that had been in former tests. The Iowa cows at the close of this test had been in milk as follows:

Hugo Countess, last calf was dropped March 7th.
Imported Bashful 2d, calf was dropped March 17th.
Nora, last calf was dropped April 13th.
Belle Price, last calf was dropped March 3d.

The standing of the Iowa cows in the test was: Hugo Countess, 20th; Bashful 2d, 24th; Nora, 30th; Belle Price 40th, with 45 cows competing. The best five cows of any breed in this test were three Jerseys, a Short Horn and a Guernsey. The best five Jerseys would have included the Hugo Countess but for her accident. The best five Short Horns included the Iowa cows, Bashful 2d and Nora. The winning breed of cows in the test was Jersey, and the winning cow a Jersey whose last calf was dropped April 21st and had been in the former tests.

### THE HEIFER TEST—21 DAYS, OCTOBER 1ST TO 21ST INCLUSIVE.

It will be noticed that this contest was between the Jerseys and Short Horns, the Guernseys not competing; Jerseys having seven heifers and the Short Horns six. In this test we had two heifers, Campania and Elturia, in the Jersey herd, but no Short Horns competed. The amount of butter given is on the basis of 80 per cent butter fat by the Babcock test, and solids not butter fat credited at 2c per lb., and gain in live weight at 4½c per lb.

| HERD | Milk, lbs. | Butter, lbs | Value of Products | Cost of Feed | Net Profits |
|---|---|---|---|---|---|
| Jersey | 3,356.6 | 194.226 | $90.71 7 | $34.43 9 | $56.27 8 |
| Short Horn | 2,581.0 | 122.362 | 70.94 9 | 23.52 8 | 47.42 1 |

The number of animals in each herd being averaged, the total net profits was ascertained to have been for the Jerseys $56.27 8, or an average of $8.03 9, and the Short Horns showed an aggregate net profit of $47.42 1 or $7.90 3 each. The best heifer of either breed was a Jersey, followed by two Short Horns as second and third, and the fourth and fifth were Jerseys. The best five Jersey heifers included the Iowa heifers, Campania and Elturia, which stood 7th and 9th in the list of 15, with a credit of net profit of $7.90 1 and $7.20 9 respectively, the highest cow having a credit of $11.22 and the lowest $5.39 1. Excluding the live weight gains, and dairymen generally consider such a proper test, Campania would be advanced to second place.

Returning to the first three tests it will be observed that special awards were made for the first 15 days of each of the three tests, namely, the 15-day cheese test, the 90-day butter test, and the 30-day butter test. The net profits of each cow in the first 15 days of each test was the basis of the awards. The award was made to the Jerseys as the best breed; the best cow was a Jersey; the best Short Horn cow was Daniel Sheehan & Sons' Nora. The best five Jerseys included D. L. Heinsheimer's Hugo Countess. The best five Short Horns included Nora, and Wm. Miller's Imported Bashful 2d as fourth best. The rank of the Iowa cows in the list of 26 cows that competed in all of the three first tests was as follows: Hugo Countess, 5th; Nora, 11th; Bashful 2d, 19th; and Belle Price, 24th. Ten of these 26 cows were Jerseys, seven were Guernseys, and the nine were Short Horns. The net profit of the sweepstake cow, a Jersey, for the first fifteen days of each test was $31.65. The net profit of Hugo Countess was $25.92; Nora $23.76 3; Imported Bashful 2d $20.41 3; and Belle Price $13.52 7. The lowest cow, or the 26th on the list, gave a profit of $12.91 8. The record of all the cows competing was remarkable, in that the surroundings were so uncomfortable, the barn so hot, and the feed so indifferent, and much not at all wholesome. So it is not surprising that in some cases the home records were not equalled, though in most cases they were fairly well maintained. In the 90-day test it took 17.2 lbs. of Jersey milk to one lb. of butter, Guernseys 18.4 lbs., and Short Horns 22.9 lbs. of milk to one of butter. The cost of feed per lb. of butter produced was Jersey 13.75c., Guernseys 14.41c., and Short Horns 17.76c.

## FINANCIAL STATEMENT.

The amount awarded the Department of Live Stock for cost of preparation and exhibit was $10,000.

Under the regulations of the Commission, there has been paid to each exhibitor of live stock the actual cost of railway or express transportation on their stock, including the terminal charges in and out of the Exposition, the cost of forage not exceeding 40c per diem for horses, 30c for cattle, and 12c for swine; also $2 per day for each care taker necessary, covering substantially the actual cost of the exhibit. The disbursements were, under this resolution, as follows:

### HORSES.

| EXHIBITOR AND RESIDENCE. | AMOUNT. |
|---|---|
| Peter Hopely, Lewis, Robert Ramsay, Hancock | $ 551 70 |
| J. Murray Hoag, Maquoketa | 419 80 |
| E. F. Kleinmeyer, Wilton Junction | 321 10 |
| L. B. Goodrich, State Center | 433 58 |
| A. B. Holbert, Greeley | 467 80 |
| E. Knott & Co , Waverly | 373 00 |
| Lefebure & Son, Fairfax | 99 75 |
| John Jacobs, Langworthy | 73 05—$ 2,739 78 |

## CATTLE.

| | | |
|---|---:|---:|
| W. A. McHenry, Denison | $ 252 45 | |
| J. H. Gilfillan, Maquoketa | 310 70 | |
| Wm. McTurk & Son, Crystal | 232 30 | |
| Geo. S. Redhead, Des Moines | 184 60 | |
| Richardson Bros., Davenport | 217 50 | $ 1,197 55 |

### COWS IN DAIRY TEST.

| | No. | |
|---|---:|---:|
| Richardson Bros., Davenport | 3 | $ 300 00 |
| Daniel Sheehan & Son, Osage | 2 | 200 00 |
| D. J. Heinsheimer, Glenwood | 1 | 100 00 |
| Wm. Miller, Storm Lake | 1 | 100 00 |
| John M. Sterr, New Hampton | 1 | 50 00 |

### PRIZES TO JERSEY WINNERS.

| | | |
|---|---:|---:|
| Richardson Bros, Davenport | 2 | 300 00 |
| D. J. Heinsheimer, Glenwood | 1 | 150 00 |

### PRIZE FOR BEST SHORT HORN.

| | | |
|---|---:|---:|
| Daniel Sheehan & Son, Osage | 100 00 | $ 1,300 00 |

### FAT CATTLE EXHIBIT.

| | |
|---|---:|
| W. S. Niles, Wyoming | $ 106 93 |
| D. M. Monniger, Supt. Cattle and Horses | 83 20 |

### SWINE.

| | | |
|---|---:|---:|
| Stone & Stone, LeClaire | $ 56 40 | |
| John Johnston & Son, Humboldt | 42 40 | |
| M. Dunn, Van Meter | 42 40 | |
| Wm. Roberts & Son, Paton | 212 60 | |
| Taft & Co., Humboldt | 187 00 | |
| Peter Mouw, Orange City | 166 55 | |
| J. F. Bonner, Morning Sun | 61 20 | |
| T. R. Wilson, Morning Sun | 52 90 | |
| J. H. Lathrop, Oxford Junction | 80 10 | |
| A. J. Lytle, Oskaloosa | 67 90 | |
| W. G. Marshall, Iowa City | 66 40 | |
| W. W. McClung, Waterloo, Supt Swine Exhibit | 73 85 | $ 1,109 00 |

## POULTRY.

| | | |
|---|---:|---:|
| G. W. Scott, Rose Hill | $ 3 50 | |
| John Wilson, What Cheer | 4 25 | |
| E. W. Strohmeier, Independence | 1 85 | |
| W. H. Garland, Aurora | 1 25 | |
| W. W. Wyant, Waterloo, Assistant Expenses | 3 03 | |
| C. S. Gabrilson, New Hampton, Supt. Sheep & Poultry | 29 28 —$ | 43 16 |
| Per diem of Commissioner in charge | $ | 398 80 |

    Total expense of Live Stock Department .......... $ 6,959 32

    Amount in the Treasurers fund not drawn ........ $3,040 68

In the preparatory work of the live stock exhibit, your commissioner in charge of the Live Stock Department has received loyal support from the Breeders Committee, consisting of J. J. Richardson, Chairman, Davenport, and D. P. Stubbs, Fairfield, P. S. Kell, Des Moines, W. A McHenry, Denison, C. W. Norton, Wilton Junction, W. B. Barney, Hampton, W. W. McClung, Waterloo, Daniel Sheehan, Osage, and C. S. Barclay, West Liberty. The immediate management of the Iowa cattle and horse exhibit at the Exposition was entrusted to the expert hands of D M. Monniger, and the swine exhibit to W. W. McClung, and to all these gentlemen my cordial thanks are extended.

IOWA EXHIBIT IN AGRICULTURAL HALL.

# Report of the Department of Agriculture.

BY F. N. CHASE.

In submitting this report I desire to call attention to a few of the rules adopted by the Board of Management of the World's Columbian Exposition.

## DEPARTMENT OF AGRICULTURE.

### SPECIAL RULES AND INFORMATION.

1. Articles intended for exhibition will be admitted to the Agricultural Building on and after November 1st, 1892.
2. All exhibits, except those of a perishable character, must be in position on or before April 20th, 1893. Vegetables and other perishable products will be admitted during their season, and may be replaced by fresh specimens when found necessary, by obtaining a special permit from the Chief of the Department.
5. A special display of potatoes and other tubers will be made during the two weeks beginning Monday, Sept 11, 1893.
7. The space granted an exhibitor will be indicated on the permit, in feet and inches, together with its location. It may be utilized in such a manner as the exhibitor may think best in arranging his exhibit, under the direction of the Chief of the Department, subject to the approval of the Director-General, in accordance with the following specific regulations:

All platforms must be of uniform height, namely, eight inches. All railings and counters must be of uniform height, namely, thirty-six inches above the floor. No partition will be permitted exceeding six feet in height above the floor. Space will be computed to an aisle or to some definite point, and all railings and ornamentations are to be included therein. No distinct form or design is prescribed for the construction of counters, railings, etc., or for the arrangement of an exhibit (columns, pyramids, cones, etc.), except that a drawing to a scale of one-quarter of an inch to the foot must be submitted by each exhibitor to the Chief of the Department, showing elevations, construction, material to be used, and the arrangement of the exhibit, so far as possible. This design must be approved by the Chief of the Department before such exhibitor will be permitted to proceed with the installation of his exhibit.

10. Exhibits of cereals, and other farm products, must be accompanied with the following data and information:
    a. Name of object.
    b. Name of producer.
    c. Place where grown.
    d. Character of soil.
    e. Date of planting.

f. Quantity of seed planted per acre.
g. Method of cultivation.
h. Date of harvesting.
i. Yield per acre.
j. Weight.
k. Price of product at nearest home market.
l. Average temperature by months for the time intervening between planting and harvesting.
m. Average rain or snow-fall by months for the time intervening between planting and harvesting.
n. Was exhibit produced by irrigation?

Rule 13. If exhibits are intended for competition it must be so stated by the exhibitor, or they will be excluded from examination for award.

Rule 14. The Chief of each Department will provide cards of uniform size and character, which may be affixed to the exhibits, and on which will be stated only the exhibitor's name and address, the name of the object or article exhibited, and its catalogue number.

In the general classification of exhibits by the Board of Management of the World's Columbian Exposition, the Agricultural Department or Division "A" contained nineteen groups and one hundred and eighteen classes, including Agriculture, Food and its accessories, Forestry and Forest Products, Agricultural Machinery and Appliances.

The State of Iowa was honored by the selection of one of her citizens (Hon. W. I. Buchanan of Sioux City) as Chief of this—the largest and most far-reaching of any department of the Great Exposition. We deem this an acknowledgement of Iowa's supremacy as an agricultural state.

In outlining the department of the Iowa State Exhibit by the Iowa Columbian Commission, three divisions of the Agricultural Department were placed in my charge, namely, the divisions of Farm and Garden Products, the Dairy and the Apiary, and to defray the expense of collecting, preparing and installing a creditable exhibit in the divisions named, the Commission set aside the sum of eight thousand dollars ($8,000).

It seemed almost impossible to make an exhibit of these, the most important and valuable industries of this great commonwealth, with the sum placed at my disposal. The following letter had previously been sent to the Press and Farmers of the State:

CEDAR FALLS, IOWA, April, 1891.

*To the Farmers of Iowa:*

MY DEAR SIR:—The Columbian Commission for the World's Columbian Exposition, to be held in Chicago, is now organized and is perfecting plans which will, if carried out, insure an exhibit of all the resources and all the varied industries of our great State, which will be to our credit, and also add greatly to the future growth and prosperity of our commonwealth.

The Board of Management at Chicago is preparing immense buildings on Jackson Park in which the competitive exhibits, by individuals and firms from all the states and territories in the United States, and all the foreign nations, will be exhibited in their proper departments according to their classification, but each state is asked to erect a suitable building for their headquarters, in which will be shown the collective state exhibit, representing the advantages, resources and possibilities of their respective states.

A circular will be issued later that will more fully explain the scope and variety of the exhibits in the different departments of this state collection.

The Iowa Commission realize that the extent, magnitude and success of the Iowa State Exhibit in this department depends largely upon the farmers. We therefore respectfully ask your hearty co-operation and invite correspondence. We believe that at the proper time the State will grant all the financial aid that is needed to make the exhibit a credit to the State. We desire especially at this time to call your attention to the importance of securing, during this season, the best possible specimens of corn, of the many different varieties; of all the grasses, also of grain, wheat, rye, oats, barley, flax, millet, broom corn, and any other cereals that can be preserved in good form until 1893. We ask you to take special care to select and save any unusually large ears of corn, and extra heavy heads of grain with very long straw. All the small grains should be preserved in the straw with the roots attached.

Our object in asking your co-operation at this time is to procure the best possible samples during the two seasons intervening between now and the opening of the Exposition, May 1st, 1893, to prevent a failure in case the season of 1892 should, by unfavorable weather, render it impossible to obtain the best that our soil could produce under favorable circumstances. If the season of 1891 should prove to be bad, we would still have next year's crop to draw from, and Iowa, which now takes the lead as an agricultural state, must show her best soil, and her best products, and she will then stand first of all the states with her exhibit at the great Exposition.

For the Iowa Columbian Commission,

F. N. CHASE, Secretary,

As no cash prizes were offered by the Exposition except in the Live Stock Department, I was obliged to depend wholly upon the generosity and state pride of the Farmers, Dairymen and Bee-keepers of Iowa to assist in making a creditable showing of the resources of the State. They responded, and I take this opportunity to thank all those whose aid made it possible for me to make an exhibit worthy of our State.

To further increase an interest in an exhibit of our cereals, and other products, at a meeting of the Commission, the following resolution was introduced by Commissioner Packard, and adopted:

"The following action was taken by the Iowa Columbian Commission in session at Des Moines, June 9th, 1892:

'Commissioner Packard spoke of the importance of offering prizes and recommended to the Commissioner of Agriculture of this Commission that he offer cash prizes for grains, seeds and grasses, to be competed for at the Iowa State Fair in 1892. The Committee was empowered to offer such prizes.'"

SPECIAL PREMIUMS.

HEADQUARTERS IOWA COLUMBIAN COMMISSION,
OFFICE OF SECRETARY, CEDAR FALLS, IA , June 15th, 1892.

*To the Farmers of Iowa:*

GENTLEMEN:—At a regular meeting of the Iowa Columbian Commission held at the Capitol, Des Moines, Iowa, June 8, 1892, the Commissioner in charge of the Department of Agriculture of said Iowa Commission, (F. N. Chase, Cedar Falls, Iowa) was authorized to offer special premiums on grain in the straw and grasses to be competed for at the Iowa State Fair, August 26th to September 2d, 1892.

Your attention is called to the following premiums together with instructions and rules governing the contest.

### PREMIUMS ON GRAIN IN STRAW.

|  | 1st. | 2d. |
|---|---|---|
| Best fall rye, any variety | $10 00 | $ 5 00 |
| Best spring rye, any variety | 10 00 | 5 00 |
| Best fall wheat, any variety | 10 00 | 5 00 |
| Best spring wheat, any variety | 10 00 | 5 00 |
| Best fall barley, any variety | 10 00 | 5 00 |
| Best spring barley, any variety | 10 00 | 5 00 |
| Best white oats, any variety | 10 00 | 5 00 |
| Best black oats, any variety | 10 00 | 5 00 |
| Best flax | 10 00 | 5 00 |
| Best and largest collection of grain in straw by one individual | 25 00 | 10 00 |

Specimens for this collection must be in addition to all exhibits competing for other premiums. Each exhibit to be accompanied by a statement showing date of seeding, date of harvesting, mode of cultivation, kind of soil and yield per acre. No entry fee required.

### PREMIUMS ON GRASSES.

|  | 1st | 2d |
|---|---|---|
| Best specimen of timothy | $10 00 | $ 5 00 |
| Best specimen of blue grass | 10 00 | 5 00 |
| Best specimen of red clover | 10 00 | 5 00 |
| Best specimen of white clover | 10 00 | 5 00 |
| Best specimen of millet, any variety | 10 00 | 5 00 |
| Best specimen of alfalfa | 10 00 | 5 00 |
| Best and largest number of named varieties of grasses grown in Iowa | 15 00 | 10 00 |

Additional samples must be brought to compete for premium on collection of grasses.

Articles competing for these special premiums will not be allowed to compete in the regular classes of the State Agricultural Society. The following rules and conditions must be strictly adhered to:

Rule 1. All entries must be made through John R. Shaffer, Secretary State Agricultural Society, on or before the 27th day of August, 1892.

Rule 2. Exhibitors competing for these special premiums on Grain in Straw and Grasses must have their exhibits in place in the Agricultural Hall by Saturday night, August 27th, 1892.

Rule 3. Exhibitors must have two (2) specimens of each variety, one with full length straw with roots, and one with full length straw without roots. These specimens to be neatly tied and protected in bundles of one and one-half (1½) inches in diameter and each specimen must be accompanied by two ordinary size field bundles of the same quality as specimens exhibited.

Rule 4. All exhibits of grains and grasses to become the property of the Iowa Columbian Commission, to be exhibited (at the discretion of said Commission) at the World's Fair, and, if practicable, said grain and grasses may be placarded, giving name of grower and his county.

Rule 5. Competition limited to Iowa. No entry fee required.

Note. Three expert judges, consisting of one from the Agricultural Society, one from the State Horticultural Society, and one from the State Agricultural College, will be selected. These judges may decide the scale of points by which the awards will be made.

Note. The premium list of the State Agricultural Society, having been printed and distributed, this special list will be mailed direct to probable exhibitors and given an extremely wide circulation throughout the State.

Note. Your attention is called to the special premium offered on farm products by the Hon. W. I. Buchanan, Chief of Department of Agriculture, World's Columbian Exposition, on page 148, Premium List of the Iowa State Fair for 1892.

Note. Also note carefully on pages 138, 139, 149 and 150 of Premium List, the premiums offered for corn, grain and seed specials, at the winter meeting of the State Agricultural Society.

Note. All exhibits must be grown in Iowa and must be the product of 1891 or 1892, but exhibitors must be able to furnish the required amount specified in Rule 3, of each year's growth, or no premium will be awarded for that year.

F. N. CHASE,
Commissioner in Charge.

Additional premiums were offered by State Agricultural Society, and by W. I. Buchanan.

The following premiums were also offered and paid by the Iowa Commission and State Agricultural Society at the winter meeting of the State Agricultural Society held in Des Moines, in January, 1893.

The premiums in classes Nos. 1 and 2 were offered and paid by State Agricultural Society to aid the Iowa Commission in making the Agricultural exhibit at the World's Columbian Exposition. The offerings in classes 3 and 5 were made and paid by this Commission.

CLASS NO. 1.—CORN.

(Competition limited to the State).

Entries in all these classes must be made on or before January 9th, 1893. Address John R. Shaffer, Secretary, Des Moines.

No premiums will be paid unless the following conditions are fully complied with—no entry fee required in any of the following classes. Exhibits to be grown by exhibitor and to be the growth of 1892.

Statements as to kind of soil, mode of saving, preparing seed, and time of planting, mode of culture and period of maturity to accompany each entry. The exhibit to be made at Capitol.

Premium corn to become the property of the Board.

In each exhibit made in this list, each 20 ears must be accompanied with one-half peck shelled corn of same kind as ears exhibited, except in collective exhibit. The collective exhibit must be separate and distinct from individual exhibits. Parties making the collective exhibit can enter and compete for the minor premiums with the same varieties of corn, but not with the same specimens.

In collective exhibit the greatest number of varieties shown will not be the only test. Quality and display (quality especially) will both be taken into consideration. All varieties must be named. Not more nor less than eight ears of each variety will be exhibited.

|  | 1st. | 2d. |
|---|---|---|
| Best twenty ears large yellow dent | $10 00 | $5 00 |
| Best twenty ears small yellow dent | 10 00 | 5 00 |
| Best twenty ears large white dent | 10 00 | 5 00 |
| Best twenty ears small white dent | 10 00 | 5 00 |
| Best twenty ears mixed dent | 10 00 | 5 00 |
| Best twenty ears bloody butcher dent | 10 00 | 5 00 |
| Best twenty ears hackberry dent | 10 00 | 5 00 |
| Best twenty ears yellow flint | 10 00 | 5 00 |
| Best twenty ears white flint | 10 00 | 5 00 |
| Best twenty ears sugar corn | 10 00 | 5 00 |
| Best twenty ears pop corn | 10 00 | 5 00 |
| Best twenty largest ears, any variety | 10 00 | 5 00 |
| Largest number of varieties, best, and best displayed collective exhibit by any one individual | 30 00 | 20 00 |
| Third | 10 00 | |

### SCORE OF POINTS FOR EAR CORN.

Length of ear, 10; circumference of ear, 10; evenness of ear, 10; per cent of net grain to cob, 30; color and uniformity of grain 20; quality and ripeness of grain, 20.

The standard for large varieties of Dent are length of ear. 10 inches; circumference of ear. 7 inches; length of kernel, 3-5 inches.

Small Dent: Length of ear. 8 inches; circumference of ear, 6½ inches; length of kernel, 3-5 inches.

All ears should be cylindrical, tapering slightly to the tip; well filled out, both butt and tip.

Scale of points for sugar corn: Shape of ear, 20; evenness of ear. 20; length of kernel, 10; quality, 10; ripeness of grain, 20; sweetness, 20, sweetness to be decided by taste.

Shelled corn will be submitted to the ordinary commercial test, and the foregoing scale.

Ear exhibits to be shelled and tested by the scale of points given, the object being to obtain the greatest per cent yield of weight, clear corn with the least yield possible of weight and dimensions of cob. Any number of ears to be subject to test the committee may decide upon.

NOTE—We hope, for the pride of our people, and to aid the World's Fair Commission. that our growers of corn will make this exhibit worthy of the great name and State of Iowa. No grander opportunity will ever come to us to show up our vast resources than is given us now at the World's Columbian Exposition. Let us accept the invitation and add fame and wealth to the garden spot of the nation.

## CLASS NO. II.—SYRUP AND SUGAR.

Parties making entries for the premiums on sugar and syrup must file with the Secretary at time of entry, on or before January 9th, 1893, a written statement, giving variety of seed planted, kind of soil, mode of culture and manufacture, cost and yield per acre. The sugar and syrup receiving the first premium to be left with the Secretary for the Museum of the Society.

|  | 1st. | 2d. |
|---|---|---|
| Gallon of syrup made from northern cane grown in Iowa, product of 1891 | $20 00 | $10 00 |
| Gallon of syrup made from northern cane grown in Iowa, product of 1892 | 10 00 | 5 00 |
| Ten pounds of sugar made from northern cane grown in Iowa, product of 1892 | 10 00 | 5 00 |

## SPECIAL PREMIUMS.

### CLASS NO. III.—CORN.

Offered by the Iowa Columbian Commission.

|  | 1st. | 2d. | 3d. |
|---|---|---|---|
| For the largest and best display of corn in the ear by any individual or county in the State of Iowa | $50 00 | $25 00 | $15 00 |

The exhibit must be the product of the years of 1891 or 1892, or both, and must contain at least forty (40) varieties.

Not more or less than ten ears of each variety to be shown, independent of that which may be suspended with the husks on.

A part of the exhibit must be shown with a few husks on.

The corn exhibited to become the property of the Commission, for Exhibition at the World's Fair.

### CLASS NO. V.—GRAIN AND SEED.

Offered by the Iowa Columbian Commission.

|  | 1st. | 2d. |
|---|---|---|
| Best peck spring wheat, any variety | $10 00 | $5 00 |
| Best peck fall wheat, any variety | 10 00 | 5 00 |
| Best peck spring rye, any variety | 10 00 | 5 00 |
| Best peck fall rye, any variety | 10 00 | 5 00 |
| Best peck spring barley, any variety | 10 00 | 5 00 |
| Best peck oats, any variety | 10 00 | 5 00 |
| Best peck buckwheat | 10 00 | 5 00 |
| Best peck flax seed | 10 00 | 5 00 |
| Best peck timothy seed | 10 00 | 5 00 |
| Best peck clover seed | 10 00 | 5 00 |
| Best peck blue grass seed | 10 00 | 5 00 |
| Best peck millet seed | 10 00 | 5 00 |
| Best peck amber cane seed | 10 00 | 5 00 |

The grain and seed exhibited to become the property of the Commission, for exhibition at the World's Fair.

Exhibits can be the product of the years 1891 or 1892, or both.

A little later the following letter referring to exhibits in Agricultural, Dairy and Apiary Departments was sent to the Press, the State Farmers Alliance, State Dairy Association, Beekkeeper's Association, Secretaries of County and District Fairs, and Farmers and Dairymen generally:

## IOWA COLUMBIAN COMMISSION.

### DEPARTMENT OF AGRICULTURE, DAIRY AND APIARY.

CEDAR FALLS, IOWA. 1892.

DEAR SIR:—Having been appointed by the Iowa Columbian Commission to take charge of the work of collecting and installing an exhibit of such products and articles as are embraced in the Department of Agriculture, including the Dairy industry, the Apiary, and Agricultural Machinery, I beg to call your attention to the great prominence Iowa has already attained as an agricultural state, and the importance of our having an exhibition of our soil and the very best of the products of our soil, the finest specimens that can be produced from our creameries and the dairy, and an exhibit of the honey we produce, at the World's Fair, and thereby attract the attention of the millions of visitors to that great Exposition to Iowa and to her wonderful resources and possibilities in the line of Agriculture.

The question is sometimes asked, have the farmers and producers any interest in making this kind of an exhibit? Most certainly, yes. All classes will be benefitted, but I believe the farmer more than any other. Iowa is now only in its infancy. We know our soil and its producing qualities. We now stand first as a corn producing state, and, without doubt, will always grow more corn than any other state in the Union (to say nothing of our $150,000,000 worth of other farm products grown annually in Iowa), but the greater the production the worse off we are unless we can find more consumers.

The World's Fair is the great opportunity of our generation to show to the world what we produce, and to induce the peoples of the world to use it. The increased consumption in this and other countries, making a greater demand for export, will surely give the farmer what he so much needs, and most earnestly desires, a good price for his corn and other farm products. In 1891, Iowa produced 335,000,000 bushels of corn. If we increase the price only 5c per bushel, by this exhibit it would add to the Iowa farmers' pocket money nearly $17,000,000 annually. We ask your hearty co-operation.

First: To aid in making a creditable collective exhibit of our products in the Iowa State Building now being erected on the World's Fair Grounds.

Second: To aid in making an exhibit in the various classes in the competitive departments in the Agricultural and Dairy Buildings.

For an exhibit of farm and garden products in the Iowa State Building we must have the very best samples that Iowa can produce We are all alike interested in this, and we solicit specimens of any of the following products:

1. Shelled corn, any kind, 2 qts of each variety.
2. Corn in the ear, any kind, not less than six ears of each variety.
3. Corn in the ear with a few husks attached.

4. Grains, all kinds, threshed, 2 qts. of each variety.
5 Farm, garden and flower seeds, from ½ pt. to 1 qt. each.
6. Grains of all kinds in straw, full length, part with roots attached. tied in bundles about 1½ inches in diameter.
7. Grasses of all kinds put up same as grains in straw.
8. Flax and flax seed, flax fiber, millet, broom corn with seed and in the brush
9. Specimens of anything in the bee industry, and apiary supplies.
10. Honey in the comb and extracted.
11. Amber cane, and sugar and syrup manufactured from the same. One gallon of syrup and not less than five pounds of sugar.
12. Beet sugar not less than five pounds.

Any of the samples contributed can, if desired, have the name of the individual or county placed upon the exhibit.

Small cotton sacks for grain and seeds, also tags, will be furnished upon application to me

When samples or anything for exhibition are ready for shipment, write for full shipping directions—(make no shipment without first writing for shipping directions)—and full information will be sent. Freight will be paid by this Department on all samples furnished as part of the State Exhibit.

It is hoped that the secretaries and other officers of county and district agricultural societies will secure from exhibitors at their respective fairs as many samples as possible, bearing in mind that it is the best quality and and not quantity that is wanted. Such exhibits as are secured in this way will be taken in charge by the Secretary and any expense for storing and draying will be paid by this Department.

The exhibit in the State Building is to advertise the resources of the state and will not be classified.

Articles for competition in the various Exposition buildings in the several departments will be classified and shown under the rules of the Exposition management.

Further information in regard to exhibits in the Agricultural, Dairy and Apiary Departments, also the general rules issued by the Exposition management governing the competitive exhibits in the different departments and classes, will be sent on application.

F. N. CHASE,
Commissioner in Charge of Dept. of Agriculture,
Cedar Falls, Iowa.

Later the following letter was sent:

DEPARTMENT OF AGRICULTURE, DAIRY AND APIARY.
CEDAR FALLS, IOWA, February, 1893.

DEAR SIR:—Since issuing my last bulletin the Board of Management of the World's Columbian Exposition have decided to publish the names of all exhibitors in the competitive classes of the various departments in the "Official Catalogue of the Exposition," and no separate state catalogue of these exhibitors will be permitted. As this catalogue must be completed by May 1st. it is imperative that you send your names immediately, as the printing must be done at once.

We therefore request that you act promptly; send your name, with county and town, immediately, to F. N. Chase, Cedar Falls, Iowa. Do not put this off even for a day.

The State Agricultural Exhibit will be made up of these individual exhibits, and when the awards are made a Certificate, Diploma or Medal will be awarded to the individual exhibitors that receive an award.

The exhibitor will be at no expense whatever in the departments named in this bulletin, except for the samples furnished. Do not send any inferior samples. Iowa must show her best if she wins.

Yours respectfully,<br>
F. N. CHASE,<br>
Cedar Falls, Iowa.

Commissioner in charge of Department of Agriculture, Dairy and Apiary.

The first important step was to secure a good location in the Agricultural Building, with sufficient amount of space on which we could install the cereals and other products of the farm and garden.

Iowa was the first state to make an appropriation for an exhibit, and among the first that made application to the Chief of the Agricultural Department of the Exposition for space in the Agricultural Building, and was assigned what was known as Section 1, and containing two thousand one hundred and five square feet of space on the main floor. The location was very desirable, in the center of the building, being one of the four corners facing on the grand avenues running through the building east and west and north and south.

Iowa having been assigned a very prominent location, the installation and the exhibit must be worthy of the location, and a credit to our great and growing state, which now ranks as the leading agricultural state in the Union.

## THE PAVILION.

The plans for the pavilion to be erected for this department of the Iowa exhibit were made by the Josselyn & Taylor Co., Architects, of Cedar Rapids. It was Moorish in design, and the decorations were all done in natural products, and wrought in beautiful designs and figures, made up of staple and fancy colored corn, small grain, seeds, grasses, golden rod, sumach, sorghum stalks and seed, cat-tails, corn tassels, wild sage, and many other seeds, plants and flowers, all together making a marvelous picture.

When completed it was a thing of beauty and greatly admired by the many millions that visited the great Exposition.

Nearly all the displays, both domestic and foreign, made in the Agricultural Building, were a revelation to every one, but none were more highly commended or praised than Iowa's artistic pavilion, and the unique exhibition of its natural products.

The decorations on this pavilion and on the pagodas were all done by Messrs. Milward & Clark, Decorators, of Sioux City, who had just completed the natural products decorations in the pavilion of the Iowa State Building, which was a leading, if not the greatest attraction of the whole Exposition.

## THE EXHIBIT.

The assistants in charge of the division of Farm and Garden Products were Ben S. Packard and L. G. Clute.

Six ornamental pagodas were built in this pavilion, on which were installed the exhibits. These pagodas were decorated in same style as the pavilion itself. The exhibits installed were the best specimens and samples of all the cereals grown in the state. Corn was very properly made a prominent feature of the exhibit—one hundred and thirty different varieties being shown—and very many samples were the finest ever shown at any Exposition Many of the exhibits were donated by individual farmers of the state. These were exhibited in the name of the grower and many of them were awarded a medal or diploma or both. The list of names of exhibitors and those that received awards is hereto attached and made part of this report. A beautiful large silk banner and fourteen smaller banners with the word "Iowa" wrought in golden grain told everyone that this was the Iowa Agricultural Exhibit.

As evidence that the exhibit was creditable and the installation artistic and attractive, the Jury of Awards gave Iowa both Medal and Diploma for the best and most artistically arranged collection of farm and garden products.

## SOIL.

The samples of Iowa soil were exhibited in white glass cylinders six (6) feet long, and six (6) inches in diameter, placed in cylinder showing the natural strata from the sod or surface down to the subsoil. Each of these cylinders had a fine white enameled label with border and letters in gold "Iowa Soil." A number of these were shown in the Iowa Exhibit in Agricultural Building; also in the Iowa State Building, and attracted much attention and favorable comment.

It was the design of the Commissioner in charge to show samples of soil obtained from different localities, not from every county, but representing all parts of the state.

Galvanized iron tubes of the same size of the glass exhibition tubes were made for transporting the soil, and sent to the different parts of the State, and were filled gratuitously by the following named persons:

Hon. James O. Crosby, Garnavillo, Clayton Co.; Hon. Jasper Thompson, Forest City, Winnebago Co.; J. J. Madden, Le Mars, Plymouth Co ; Hon. S. B. Packard, Marshalltown, Marshall Co.; Hon. Chas. Ashton, Guthrie Center, Guthrie Co.; Hon. B. F. Clayton, Macedonia, Pottawattamie Co.; Dr. A. C. Roberts, Ft. Madison, Lee Co ; Prof. Jas. Wilson, Experimental Station, Ames, Story Co.; L. G. Clute, Greeley, Delaware Co.; J. F. Record, Glenwood, Mills Co.; F. N. Chase, Cedar Falls, Black Hawk Co.

Other samples of soil were offered, but these were deemed sufficient to show the world the character, depth and richness of Iowa soil.

## IOWA FARM PRODUCTS. 1891.

| CROPS. | BUSHELS. | VALUE. |
|---|---|---|
| Corn | 335,031,598 | $100,509,479 |
| Oats | 115,810,800 | 26,636,484 |
| Wheat | 27,586,000 | 31,517,080 |
| Rye | 2,051,400 | 1,333,410 |
| Barley | 4,528,669 | 1,811,467 |
| Flax | 3,154,016 | 2,523,212 |
| Buckweat | 414,000 | 276,000 |
| Timothy, clover and millet seed, estimated value | | 1,750,000 |
| Irish potatoes, 25,620,350 bushels | | 5,380,273 |
| Sweet potatoes, 207,000 bushels | | 207,000 |
| Broom corn | | 270,570 |
| Hay—Timothy and clover, tons, 5,582,890 | | 33,479,340 |
| Prairie hay and other forage crops, estimated | | 6,800,000 |
| Sorghum | | 904,718 |

The government estimate of corn in Iowa in 1891 was 350,580,000 bushels, based on an overestimate of acreage, but we take the State Official Report as correct, although not as large as the government estimate

Butter and cheese 173,690,715 lbs., value, $34,188,148.
This does not include milk consumed in cities and families.

Mr. Secretary Shaffer, of the Agricultural Society, estimates total soil products of Iowa, including fruits, for 1891, $314,968,284.

## CLIMATE.

Average temperature and rainfall in the six crop months.

| TEMPERATURE. | | RAINFALL. | |
|---|---|---|---|
| April | 45 degrees | April | 2.60 inches |
| May | 60 " | May | 4.10 " |
| June | 69 " | June | 4.94 " |
| July | 74 " | July | 4.30 " |
| August | 71 " | August | 3.60 " |
| September | 62 " | September | 3.70 " |

Average per month.. 63.8 degrees  Total for crop months ...23.24 inches
Average temperature in summer months ..................71.3 deg.
Total rainfall of summer months...........................12.84 inches

GEO. M. CHAPEL, M. D.,                            J. R. SAGE,
  U. S. Bureau, Ass't Director.        Iowa Weather Service Director.

## WOOL.

The Iowa wool exhibit was shown in the North Gallery of the Agricultural Building. This exhibit numbered about fifty fleeces, and Iowa captured two awards in this division, namely:

    Iowa Agricultural College, Ames.
    W. H. Edgerton, Nassau.

## FLAX.

This industry, now in its infancy in our State, gives evidence of wonderful results in the near future. In Winnebago and other counties in the northwestern part of the State the industry is already quite large, and very remunerative.

Some very fine samples of flax seed, and flax spinning fiber were exhibited, but not entered for competition.

The citizens of Forest City, under the direction of Hon. Jasper Thompson, reproduced a model of the "Flax Palace," which was placed in the Iowa Building. It was a great attraction, and Mr. Thompson and the members of the Flax Palace Association deserve the thanks of the Iowa Columbian Commission, and of every Iowa citizen for this valuable contribution to the Iowa Exhibit.

Some very fine samples of flax seed and flax spinning fiber were exhibited, but not entered for competition.

## NAMES OF EXHIBITORS IN AGRICULTURAL BUILDING.

### GROUPS 1, 4, 5, SOIL, FARM AND GARDEN PRODUCTS

J. B. Rutherford, Manchester, fall rye.
J. J. Wilson, Norwark, fall rye.
Lee Hudler, Audubon, fall rye and timothy seed.
E. H. Smith, Dubuque, corn and other cereals and grasses.
L. G. Clute, Greeley, 94 varieties of corn and a large variety of cereals and grasses.
James Hethershaw, Des Moines, 15 varieties of potatoes.
Nims Bros., Emerson, 16 varieties of grain and grasses.
Harvey Graves, Des Moines, millet seed.
John Price, Des Moines, cereals.
E. B. Clark, Red Oak, fall wheat
F. S. White, Des Moines, grain, field, garden and flower seeds.
E. P. Wright, Summerset, corn and small grain, many varieties
L. Rundell, Iowa City, Egyptian barley and spring wheat.
Chas. Ashton, Guthrie Center, fall wheat.
S. B. Packard, Marshalltown, fall wheat, (Turkey Red).
John Cownie, South Amana, timothy seed.
F. R. Eral, Rolfe, corn and German millet.
Wm. Thompson, Humboldt, corn and timothy seed.
Henry Herrold, Ridgedale, sorghum syrup and corn.
J. P. Wherry, Guernsey, sorghum syrup.
J. S. Crawford, Atlantic, corn.
W. A. Wilson, Waterloo, wild and tame grasses.
Isaac Bird, Sheffield, corn.
Alex Kelly, Creston, corn.
H. C. Brown, Dumont, corn.
W. M. Lovett, East Elkport, corn and seeds.
Fred McCullock, Hartwick, corn, grasses and grain.

S. A. McCandless, Belle Plaine, corn.
W. J. McCammon, Perry, corn.
Andrew Preston, Battle Creek, corn.
Jasper Thompson Forest City, flax fiber.
Abraham Smith, Grand Mound, corn.
W. J. McClimon, Villonova, corn.
A. L. Plummer, Ivy, seeds and corn.
J. C. Ellis, Truro, corn.
A. F. Collman, Corning, corn, grain and grasses.
J. E. Doolittle, Cresco, corn and oats.
E. W. Kregel, Garnavillo, corn, oats and timothy seed.
F. L. Morgan, Perry, corn.
E. H. Knickerbocker, Fairfax, corn, wheat and rye.
G. W. Bingham, Jesup, corn and soil.
M. H. Connell, Guernsey, grain and seeds.
John H. Alberts, Jefferson, corn and German millet.
C. V. Surfus, Bristow, corn, grain and seed.
C. Rockville & Sons, Conrad Grove, corn, grain and seed.
Elmer Reeves Waverly, grain and corn.
Wm. M Husted, Des Moines, corn.
C. L. Gabrilson, New Hampton, Snow Flake potatoes.
M. Crail, Mason City, corn.
J. J. Russell, Mason City, corn.
Joseph Elliott, Polen, corn and wheat.
W. F. Steigerwalt, Carroll, oats, rye and timothy seed.
Henry Spintig, Perry, corn.
Henry Bills, Perry, corn.
Moses James, Perry, corn.
Clyde Bice, Perry, corn.
Guy Roger, Perry, corn.
Jacob Snyder, Marshalltown, corn and oats.
Wm. Angus, Strahan, corn.
S. V. Swearingen, Sidney, corn.
A. H. Beecher, Ida Grove, wheat and oats.
Hugo Buyer, New London, 40 varieties vegetables.
Geo. W. Franklin, Atlantic, wheat.
Joseph Holmes, German millet.
Fred Werges, National, corn, wheat and oats.
P. F. Meighan, Garnavillo, corn and Red clover seed.
Wm. Krueger, Garnavillo, large white corn.
E. Dougal, Panama, corn.
C. L. Gabrilson, New Hampton, barley and oats.
Plymouth Co. World's Fair Ass'n, Le Mars, wheat, flour and mill feed
Fred Murrah, Red Oak, potatoes.

Many others whose names do not appear in this list sent very fine samples of corn and other cereals, but as they were not accompanied by the necessary data for the competitive exhibit, were placed on exhibition with the collective exhibit in the Iowa State building.

## IOWA AWARDS IN THE AGRICULTURAL DEPARTMENT.

### FARM PRODUCTS.

#### CORN.

James B. Wise, Sabula.
J. O. Stephens, Shelby.
A. Doty, Shelby.
Martin Nelson, Shelby.
Chas. Haldoof, Shelby.
Hyram Kastor, Manchester
B. Wragg, Creston.
C. T. Lambert, Mills County.
John Lawrence, Emerson.
S A. McCandless, Belle Plaine.
John H. Alberts, Jefferson.
A. L. Plummer, Ivy.
H. S. Brown & Son, Emerson.
Ed. Connell, Greeley.
Jas. Fitzpatrick, Greeley,
F. S. White, Des Moines.
J. S. Crawford, Atlantic.
C R Taylor, Hamburg.
Nathan Drake, Decorah.
E. P. Cooper, Shelby.

Hugh Linn, Shelby.
H. N. Frum, Shelby.
J. Q. Rathburn, Stinnett.
John and Roy Brown, Shelby.
M. Wilcox, Shelby.
J. R. Turner, Wiota.
S. D. Brothers, Emerson.
Nims Bros., Emerson.
Fred McCullock, Hartwick.
P. F. Meighan, Clayton.
J. C. Ellis, Truro.
A. F. Collman, Corning.
John Cruise, Jr., Earlville.
Samuel Way, Greeley.
J. W. Rector, Oneida.
M. C. Davis, Creston.
L. S. Rockwell, Rockwell.
J. E. Branch, Elkader.
J. W. Miles, Miles.
Fred Werges, National.

Wm. Krueger, Garnavillo.

#### WHEAT.

Chas. Ashton, Guthrie Center.     B. B. Clark, Red Oak.

#### OATS.

E. H. Smith, Dubuque.     C L. Gabrilson, New Hampton.

#### BARLEY.

A. H. Cane, Corinne.

#### BUCKWHEAT.

L. Hudler, Audubon.

#### TIMOTHY SEED.

John Cownie, South Amana.     S. S. Patterson, Cresco.

#### MILLET SEED.

John H. Alberts, Jefferson.     William Angus, Strahan.

#### TIMOTHY, RED TOP AND SEEDS.

H. H. Connell, Guernsey.

RED CLOVER SEED.

A. L. Plummer, Ivy.

POTATOES.

Fred Murrah, Red Oak.

 BEANS.

J. W. Rector, Oneida.   L. G. Clute, Greeley, twenty-one awards on corn, wheat, oats, barley, buckwheat, rye, potatoes, clover and grasses. State of Iowa. Artistic Display of Farm and Garden Products.

Forty Iowa Exhibitors received awards on corn, and this does not include the collection of corn, or the prize awarded to the State of Iowa.

## IOWA DAIRY EXHIBIT.

### DEPARTMENT OF AGRICULTURE.

Believing that this was Iowa's opportunity to show her strength as a Dairy State, and not only maintain, but surpass, her grand record made at previous World's Fairs and expositions as a prize winner in the Dairy Department, I determined, if possible, to make the Iowa Butter Exhibit at the World's Columbian Exposition the best that could possibly be made, and to this end I visited the Dairymen in the different counties, and also attended the State Convention of the Iowa State Dairy Association, and found them ready to co-operate in such a way as to enlist a large per cent of the more than 800 Creameries of the State, as well as the Dairymen, large and small, throughout Iowa.   On their recommendation, I appointed the Secretary of their Association, Mr. C. L. Gabrilson, of New Hampton, as Superintendent of this department, and placed the work of selecting and installing the exhibit in his hands.   He immediately commenced to correspond with the managers of this great industry, and personally visited many of the leading Creameries of the State, and it is simply justice for me to state that the grand success of the Iowa Butter Exhibit was largely due to his experience and faithful services.

The dairy industry, particularly the butter making in our numerous creameries and dairies, is now one of the most important and profitable of any industry in our commonwealth, and it was determined to expend the small amount of money at our disposal for use in this division of the Agricultural Department in making the best possible exhibit of butter, and for this reason, although there is a large number of cheese factories in our State, and cheese of excellent quality is made, no effort was made to put Iowa cheese on exhibition.

The rapid growth of the dairy industry in Iowa has been made since 1876, when at the Centennial at Philadelphia, a citizen of Iowa surprised the world by securing premiums on butter.  There was no great showing of butter at the Philadelphia Exposition, but the premiums received were on absolute merit.   At the World's Industrial and Cotton Centennial in New Orleans in 1885, Iowa was awarded a gold medal on sweepstakes, and about twenty (20) first premiums.   At the World's Columbian Exposition in 1893, as later shown in this report, Iowa exhibitors in this department received one hundred and twenty (120) awards, and will bring to the State seventy-eight (78) medals and diplomas stating the degree of excellence of each exhibit. This shows that at each Exposition we have made great improvement, and in this last competitive exhibit against the world, there was no butter that excelled that shown by the Iowa exhibitors.

The Iowa Exhibit of Butter occupied fifty lineal feet of glass refrigerating cases, installed in the center of the Dairy Building on the west side. These cases were built at a cost of about $500, including the refrigeration.

The following letter was mailed to the managers of over 800 creameries, and to a large number of dairymen in the State.

## IOWA COLUMBIAN COMMISSION.

### DEPARTMENT OF AGRICULTURE.

### F. N. CHASE, COMMISSIONER.

### C. L. GABRILSON, Superintendent in Charge.

*To the Butter Makers of Iowa:*

Secretary Chase, of the Iowa Columbian Commission, has secured fifty lineal feet of glass exhibition cases in the Dairy Building at the World's Fair for the display of Iowa's dairy product. No other state, or country, has more space.

There is room in the cases, which are to be refrigerated, for ten tubs of butter in each five feet five inches of space. This would provide place for 100 tubs of creamery butter, if no space were used for butter in fancy forms. Below the show case proper there is place for the smaller packages of dairy butter.

There is to be a new exhibit of butter from the 1st to the 10th of each of the following months: June, July, September and October. Seventy-five tubs of creamery butter is about all that can be used at each exhibit. Applications for space from the creameries and private dairies are now called for.

The honor of having butter on exhibit at the World's Fair is an opportunity which does not come in the lifetime of many. To be enrolled in the Exposition catalogue, and have the privilege of competing for the prizes offered, is a mark of distinction in which high merit only can expect to participate. Iowa must sustain its world wide reputation as the banner dairy state, when it comes to winning universal honors.

Although the value of Iowa's dairy products exceeds that of any other state, we are far behind in means for making such a display as the importance of our leading industry demands. The cost of installation will be one thousand dollars. Illinois is asking its legislature, now in session, to vote $20,000 to defray the expense of its dairy exhibit. New York has $10,000 set aside for this purpose, while Iowa has less than half the latter sum. And the Commission feels that the dairymen of Iowa must come forward and sustain its position by contributing samples of their best product. Wherever this has been broached there is an entire willingness to thus help in making a creditable display.

Tubs of uniform size, quality and make will be used to contain the butter. These will be sent to the creameries and dairies selected to supply the butter required.

The packages must be carefully protected from injury by being covered with canvass (salt sacks will answer) so that they will arrive at their destination in the pink of condition.

Nominations for the privilege of exhibition are requested at once, since the names of exhibitors are wanted for publication in the general catalogue which is to be issued before the Exposition opens.

For further particulars apply to C. L. GABRILSON, In Charge of Dairy Department of Iowa State Exhibit, Secretary Iowa State Dairy Association, New Hampton, Iowa.

Instead of writing at length, giving the plans and methods of making the four separate exhibits of butter, I copy here extracts from the General Rules of the Board of Management of the Columbian Exposition, which fully explain the conditions under which all exhibits have to be made:

## RULES GOVERNING THE EXHIBIT IN GROUP 7.

Which included all the exhibits of butter and cheese.

11. Dairy products will be received for exhibition only between the 1st and 10th of the following months: June, July, September and October, 1893.

12. The arrangement of all dairy exhibits will be under the control of this Department.

13. Exhibits of butter will be classified and limited as follows:

Class 1—*Dairy*—Butter made by exhibitor on the farm from a mixed herd. Exhibit to consist of not more than one package, weight to be not less than 10 nor more than 20 pounds.

Class 2—*Dairy*—Butter made by exhibitor on the farm from a herd of one breed. Exhibit to consist of not more than one package, weight to be not less than 10 nor more than 20 pounds.

Class 3—*Prints and Fancy Packages*—Butter must be manufactured by exhibitor. Exhibit to occupy space not exceeding 18 inches square. Total weight of exhibit not to exceed 20 pounds.

Class 4—*Creamery*—butter made by the exhibitor from the milk of mixed herds from cream separated from the milk in the creamery where the butter is made. Exhibit to consist of one commercial package to weigh not less than 55 pounds.

Class 5—*Creamery*—Butter made by exhibitor from gathered cream. Exhibit to consist of one commercial package, to weigh not less than 55 pounds.

Butter will be judged on the following points, the figures set opposite indicating the maximum per cent, the total of all such maximums being 100:

| | |
|---|---|
| Flavor | 45 |
| Grain | 25 |
| Color | 15 |
| Salting | 10 |
| Packing | 5 |
| Total | 100 |

The general standard of color for butter will be "June Grass Butter."

Iowa entered all the butter classes of the four distinct exhibits, viz.: June, July, September and October. The Bureau of Awards of the Columbian Exposition adopted a more rigid test than was ever made at any previous exposition, and yet under this severe test, Iowa scored a higher record than ever before, and the exhibit of creamery and dairy butter was one to be proud of, being alike an honor to the exhibitor and a credit to the state.

The butter of the first test or June exhibit was nearly all donated by the exhibitors, both in the creamery and dairy classes, which was, after the test and examination by the jury, sold and netted the Iowa Commission over $800, which was turned over to the Treasury of the Commission. All butter which made up the three following exhibits was sold at the close of each test for the benefit of the exhibitor.

I embody as a part of this report one of the letters sent out from this Department to the exhibitors by Superintendent Gabrilson. This letter was sent after the June and July tests had been made, and was intended to give such information as would enable the exhibitors to present butter at the following tests that would score even higher, if possible, than the two months previous.

DAIRY BUILDING, JACKSON PARK, August 14, 1893.

The time has come to make preparations for the September test in the World's Fair Dairy exhibits, although the judging does not take place until about the 10th of next month.

Preliminary work is called for because of the activity which is manifested in every section from whence butter has been entered for competition in the present international contest. It is not only necessary that creamery operators and butter makers should be very careful and nice in the manipulation of milk and cream in the churning room, but this same pains-taking care and watchfulness must be shared by all who deal with this product, either as feeders of cows whose milk enters into its composition or as milkers and milk haulers. In every step the same vigilance is called for, else the entire product suffers.

It is not only that these tests reflect the skill and high intelligence of those who provide the milk and manufacture its product—which is of importance to those directly interested—but there is yet the honor and credit of proud Iowa to be sustained, and everyone connected with these exhibits should feel that this duty rests upon himself or herself.

In many cases too much latitude was assumed in getting the exhibits to Jackson Park in time. The butter must all be here and entered by September 10th according to the rule; and this rule will probably be rigidly enforced hereafter. Now, in order to come within the limit, each exhibitor must closely calculate the time required to accomplish this, allowing 24 hours for transfer from the cold storage rooms in Chicago to Jackson Park. Better ship several days earlier than run risk of late arrival. Do not ship anything by express but by refrigerator car only, to A. H. Barber, as in July.

With perfect arrangements for holding the butter in Chicago, we suggest that the shipment be made by the refrigerator which leaves on the 5th or 6th of September rather than trust to the hope of getting through late in the week. Study this matter please.

Make special effort to cool the butter as quickly and thoroughly as possible after churning; and do not spare covering to keep it so while in transit. Avoid the risk of impure milk through the intervention of a rain storm at milking time, or from any other cause.

The score card is an unprejudiced umpire and the lessons taught should be heeded. Let us all try—for IOWA.

Enclosed find shipping tags.     Yours truly,

C. L. GABRILSON,
Superintendent Iowa Dairy Exhibit.

As a result of this, Iowa scored a higher scale of points on the four consecutive tests than any other state or nation.

The following is a list of names of exhibitors in the various butter classes and tests.

## NAMES OF EXHIBITORS IN DAIRY DEPARTMENT.

New Hampton Creamery, New Hampton.
Williamstown Creamery, Williamstown.
Little Turkey Creamery, Little Turkey.
North Iowa Creamery, Forest City.
North Iowa Creamery, Clarion.
Livermore Creamery, Livermore.
E. L. Bracy, Maynard.
Henderson & Babcock, Central City.
J. W. Darby, Greenfield.
Levi A. Jenkins, St. Ansgar.
W. S. Smarzo, Maynard.
Golden Star Creamery, Dyersville.
Manchester Co-operative Creamery Co., Manchester.
H. A. Miller, Oelwein.
W. H. Blunt, Fairbanks.
H. J. Neitert, Walker.
Devon Creamery, Devon.
H. D. Parsons, Newton.
Fayette Creamery Association, Fayette.
C. W. Adams, Breda.
W. H. Sanford, Amber.
S. K. Swenson, Story City.
Rock Creek Creamery, Osage.
Jefferson Creamery, Oelwein.
Spring Branch Creamery, Manchester.
Hampton Creamery, Hampton.
Lewis Forthum, Chapin.
E. E. Van Auken, Clear Lake.
Louis Brahe, Andover.
Riverton Creamery, Spencer.

E. M. Haven, Bristow.
J. F. Powers, Plainfield.
G. B. Strayer, Lawn Hill.
Postville Creamery, Postville.
Frankville Creamery, Decorah.
Union Creamery, West Union.
Bassett Creamery, Bassett
Ionia Creamery, Ionia.
North Washington Creamery, North Washington.
Castalia Creamery, Castalia.
Festina Creamery, Festina
Giard Creamery, Giard.
Highlandville Creamery, Hesper.
Hesper Creamery, Hesper.
Decorah Creamery, Decorah.
Ridgeway Creamery, Decorah
Elgin Creamery, Elgin.
Lime Springs Creamery, Lime Springs.
Ossian Creamery, Ossian.
Clermont Valley Creamery, Clermont.
G. B. Lawson, Grinnell.
Protovin Creamery, Protovin.
J. Waughtal, Clear Lake.
Diamond Creamery, Monticello.
W. W. Bennett, Churdan.
R. M. Fonda, Luana.
H. S. Waid, Charles City.
C. L. Gabrilson, New Hampton.
B. P. Norton, Cresco.
P. H. Young, Garden Grove.
L. L. Parker, Greeley.
Mrs George Tyler, Decorah.
J. D. Herrick, Fredericksburg.
Mrs S. D. Martin, Belmond.
C. Schruber, New Hampton.
G. W. Russell, Greene.
Mrs David Blake, Greene.
Mrs M. Putnam, Greene.
F. D. Pierce, Cedar Falls.
Mechanicsville Creamery Co., Mechanicsville.
B. W. Kenyon, Masonville.
Eden Valley Creamery, Low Moor.
Globe Creamery, Luxemburg.
Greeley Farmer's Creamery, Greeley.
A. R. Carrier, Garnavillo.
Ft. Atkinson Creamery, Ft. Atkinson.
Jerico Co-operative Creamery, Jerico.
J. Garber, Rockwell.
S. B. Mills, Elmont.

P. G. Henderson, Central City.
J. Varney, Dickens.
Cold Water Creamery Company.
W. I. Moody, Nashua
Iowa Butter and Cheese Co., Corning.
Grimes Butter and Cheese Co., Grimes.
C. W. Mead & Sons, Manchester.
Osage Co-operative Creamery, Osage.
West Hamlin Creamery, Exira.
H. L. Test, Ross.
Clelland Bros., Parkersburg.
E. D. Wilcox, Clarksville.
Nordness Creamery, Nordness.
Glenwood Creamery, Decorah.
Village Creek Creamery, Decorah.
Iowa Agricultural College, Ames.
Mason City Creamery, Mason City.
Harry A. Bates, What Cheer,
Minerva Valley Creamery.
F. L. Huxtable, Clear Lake.
Elma Creamery, Elma.
Charles Brown, Cresco.
Aaron Sheatz, Decorah.
Frank Dodson, Logan.
Mrs. C. H. Lyon, Dexter.
Mrs. D. Leach, Decorah.
J. K. Jorgenson, Fredsville.
M. N. Smith, Grundy Center.
Watson Child, Manchester.
S. C. Seaman, Clinton.
Jerry Sheehan, Osage.
Samuel Rowell, Osage.
P. L. Yonker, Belmond.
Dan Sheehan, Osage.
A. S. Brownell, Rudd.
Mrs. Wm. Crawford.
Mrs. E. F. Brockway, Washington.
E. W. Proctor, Williamstown.
Renner Bros., Grand Junction.

W. L. Passmore, West Branch, exhibited Cheese, but as this was the only exhibit of cheese, it was not entered for competition.

The list of winners given below, shows that a very large per cent of those entering the list as competitors were prize winners.

## AWARDS IN THE DAIRY DEPARTMENT.

### BUTTER EXHIBIT.

#### IOWA'S RECORD AS A DAIRY STATE.

The Columbian Board of Awards, at the suggestion of the judges who passed on the exhibits, adopted the following scale as the standard of excellence for butter:

For June exhibit, in all classes, 97 points.

For July exhibit, as follows:

    Separator class, 96 points
    Gathered cream class, 95 points.
    Dairy class, 94 points.

For September and October, the range was:

    Separator class, 95 points.
    Gathered cream class, 94 points, and
    Dairy class, 93 points.

On the basis of the above qualifications, Iowa secured awards as follows:

(The different classes are designated by numbers as follows:

Dairy (1) Separator (4) Gathered Cream (5.)

| NAME. | June | July | Sept. | Oct | Class |
|---|---|---|---|---|---|
| New Hampton Creamery, New Hampton | 98 | 97 | 94½ | 90½ | 4 |
| Williamstown Creamery, Williamstown | 96 | 94½ | 96½ | 93 | 4 |
| Little Turkey Creamery, Little Turkey | 98 | 96 | 89 | 89 | 4 |
| N. Iowa Creamery, Forest City | 97 | | | | 5 |
| N. Iowa Creamery, Garner | 97 | | | | 4 |
| Livermore Creamery, Livermore | 99 | 94 | | | 4 |
| E. L. Bracy, Maynard | 99 | 96 | 97½ | 88½ | 4 |
| Henderson & Babcock, Central City | 91 | 95 | 95 | 93¼ | 4 |
| J. W. Darby, Greenfield | 97 | 91 | 95 | 91 | 4 |
| Levi A. Jenkins, St. Ansgar | 97 | 91 | 88 | 88 | 5 |
| W. S. Smarzo, Maynard | 98 | 87 | 94½ | 94½ | 4 |
| Golden Star Creamery, Dyersville | 98 | 94½ | 97 | 96 | 4 |
| Manchester Co-operative Cr'y., Manchester | 92 | 96 | 95 | 95 | 4 |
| H. A. Miller, Oelwein | 93 | 97 | 94½ | 92½ | 4 |
| W. H. Blunt, Fairbank | 96 | 95 | 91½ | | 4 |
| H. J. Neitert, Walker | 98 | 94 | 94½ | 90 | 4 |
| Devon Creamery, Devon | 98 | 96 | 95 | 94½ | 4 |
| H. D. Parsons, Newton | 98 | 95½ | 96¼ | 95 | 4 |
| Fayette Creamery, Fayette | 97 | 97 | 95 | 92½ | 4 |
| C. W. Adams, Breda | 96 | 96 | 94 | 94 | 4 |
| W. H. Sanford, Amber | | | 95 | 95 | 5 |
| S. K. Swenson, Story City | 98 | 96 | 97 | 88 | 4 |
| Rock Creek Creamery, Rock Creek | 98 | | | | 5 |
| Jefferson Creamery, Oelwein | 96 | 94½ | 95 | 92 | 4 |
| Spring Branch, Manchester | 99 | 98 | 97 | 93 | 4 |
| Hampton Creamery, Hampton | 92 | 95 | 96½ | 93½ | 4 |
| Lewis Forthum, Chapin | 100 | 95 | 96 | 93 | 4 |
| E. E. Van Auken, Clear Lake | 97 | 93½ | 93 | | 4 |
| Louis Brahe, Andover | 98 | 95 | 96 | | 4 |
| Riverton Creamery, Spencer | 98 | 94½ | 97 | 95 | 5 |
| E. M. Haven, Bristow | 100 | 93 | 95 | 92½ | 5 |
| J. F. Powers, Plainfield | 94 | 96 | | | 5 |

| NAME | June | July | Sept. | Oct. | Class |
|---|---|---|---|---|---|
| G. B. Strayer, Lawn Hill | 89 | 94 | 89½ | | 5 |
| Postville, Postville | 99 | | | | 5 |
| Frankville Creamery, Decorah | 96 | 98 | 94½ | 94½ | 5 |
| Union Creamery, West Union | 95 | 89 | 94 | | 5 |
| Bassett Creamery, Bassett | 98 | 97 | 93½ | 94½ | 5 |
| Ionia Creamery, Ionia | 94 | 96 | 95 | 94 | 4 |
| N. Washington Creamery, N. Washington | 98 | 98 | 95 | 95 | 4 |
| Castalia Creamery, Castalia | 98 | 95½ | 95 | 95 | 4 |
| Festina Creamery, Festina | 93 | 96 | 94 | 93½ | 4 |
| Girard Creamery, Girard | 97 | | | | 4 |
| Highlandville Creamery, Hesper | 97 | 93 | 95 | | 5 |
| Hesper Creamery, Hesper | 96 | 96 | 94½ | 90 | 5 |
| Decorah Creamery, Decorah | 95 | 96 | 93 | 93½ | 5 |
| Ridgeway Creamery, Decorah | 99 | 95 | 91½ | | 5 |
| Elgin Creamery, Elgin | 97 | 96 | 92 | 92 | 5 |
| Lime Springs, Lime Springs | 97 | | 93 | 87 | 5 |
| Ossian Creamery, Ossian | 94 | 97 | 92 | 95 | 5 |
| Clermont Valley Creamery, Clermont | 96 | 96 | 94 | 94 | 4 |
| G. B. Lawson, Grinnell | 93 | 96½ | 97 | 89 | 4 |
| Protovin Creamery, Protovin | | | 94½ | | 5 |
| J. Waughtal, Clear Lake | 96 | | | | 4 |
| Diamond Creamery, Monticello | | | 97½ | 95 | 5 |
| W. W. Bennett, Churdan | 95 | 95 | 92½ | | 1 |
| R. M. Fonda, Luana | 95 | 94 | 94 | | 1 |
| H. S. Waid, Charles City | 94 | 95 | 94 | 93 | 1 |
| C. L. Gabrilson, New Hampton | 92 | 95 | 92 | 92½ | 1 |
| B. P. Norton, Cresco | 93 | 94 | 89½ | | 1 |
| P. H. Young, Garden Grove | 95 | 96 | 87 | 90 | 1 |
| L. L. Parker, Greeley | 93 | 96 | 86 | 93½ | 1 |
| Mrs. Geo. Tyler, Decorah | 93 | 96 | 91½ | 87 | 1 |
| J. D. Herrick, Fredericksburg | 95 | 93 | 91 | 94½ | 1 |
| Mrs. S. D. Martin, Belmond | 96 | 94 | 86½ | 85 | 1 |
| C. Schruber, New Hampton | 91 | 96 | 86 | 88½ | 1 |
| G. W. Russell, Greene | 93 | 97 | 89 | 95½ | 1 |
| Mrs. David Blake, Greene | 93 | 95½ | 87 | 90 | 1 |
| Mrs. M. Putnam, Greene | 93 | 95 | | | 1 |
| F. D. Pierce, Cedar Falls | 95 | 97 | 89 | 95½ | 1 |
| Mechanicsville Cr'y. Co., Mechanicsville | 93 | 95 | | | 4 |
| B. W. Kenyon, Masonville | 98 | 97 | 94½ | | 4 |
| Eden Valley Creamery, Low Moor | 99 | 95 | 93 | 86½ | 4 |
| Globe Creamery, Luxemburg | 96 | 96 | 95 | 95½ | 4 |
| Greeley Farmer's Creamery, Greeley | 98 | 94½ | 93 | 93½ | 4 |
| A. R. Carrier, Garnavillo | 97 | 91 | | | 4 |
| Ft. Atkinson Creamery, Ft. Atkinson | 90 | 91½ | 94½ | 93 | 5 |
| Diamond Creamery, Monticello | | 99 | 96 | 94 | 4 |
| W. L. Passmore, West Branch | cheese | | | | |

Taking the basis for awards as outlined at the beginning of this article, and accepting as final this last decision of the Board of Awards, the seventy-eight individuals will each receive one World's Fair medal, accompanied by a beautifully executed diploma which will recite the points of excellence in the exhibit. To these seventy-eight persons, or creameries, one hundred and twenty-eight awards are given.

It will be observed that, according to the latest decision of the Board of Awards, the individual, or creamery, which made one successful exhibit gets a medal of equal value with that of the person who made four successful entries. This last individual must derive his satisfaction from the record which the diploma gives to the world. The exhibitors of butter as well as exhibitors of pianos realize that neither get credit for super-excellence. There is no *best*.

## REPORT OF IOWA APIARY EXHIBIT.

AGRICULTURAL DEPARTMENT.

At the suggestion of the Hon. Eugene Secor, President of the Iowa Beekeepers' Association, Mr. E. Kretchmer, of Red Oak, a prominent member of the Iowa Beekeepers' Association, was appointed assistant, and placed in charge of the Iowa Apiary Exhibit.

This exhibit was installed in the center of the east gallery of the Agricultural Building, and was a part of group 3. In the various classes of this exhibit were shown both comb and extracted honey, honey plants, beeswax, and bee implements and appliances. The following general and special rules governed the installation, and established the character of the exhibit.

## WORLD'S COLUMBIAN EXPOSITION.

DEPARTMENT OF AGRICULTURE.

Special rules and information governing the exhibit of

### BEES, HONEY, BEESWAX AND BEE APPLIANCES.

1. Exhibits of honey will be classified as follows:
CLASS 1. Clover and basswood.
CLASS 2. White sage.
CLASS 3. Buckwheat.
CLASS 4. All light honey other than enumerated in Classes 1 and 2.
CLASS 5. All dark honey, other than enumerated in Class 3.

2. Exhibits of honey produced during 1892, or earlier, must be in place on or before April 20th, 1893.

3. Exhibits of honey in classes 1, 2, and 4, produced during 1893, will be received between July 15th and August 15th; and in classes 3 and 5, between August 15th and Sept. 1st, 1893.

4. The following information should accompany each exhibit:
(*a*). Kind of honey.
(*b*). Name of exhibitor.
(*c*). Place where produced.
(*d*). Character of soil in locality where produced.
(*e*). Variety of bee.
(*f*). Name of plant from which honey was produced.
(*g*). Yield per colony.
(*h*). Average price of product at nearest home market.

5. In order to secure a uniform, handsome and economical installation of honey and beeswax, the Exposition will erect suitable glass cases, of a uniform character, in which such exhibits will be made; the cost of these cases will be borne by the different State Commissions, Beekeepers Association, or by individual exhibitors, in proportion to the number of lineal feet occupied. These cases will become the property of such exhibitors at the close of the Exposition. The dimensions are as follows: Height of base,

18 inches, width of case 5 feet, height of case above base (inside measure) 6 feet, total height 8 feet. The case has sliding doors on both sides.

6. Individual exhibits of comb honey will be limited to 100 pounds and may be made in any manner the exhibitor may desire, subject to the approval of the Chief of the Department.

7. Individual exhibits of extracted honey must be made in glass, and must not exceed 50 pounds.

8. Individual exhibits of beeswax must not exceed 50 pounds, and should be prepared in such a manner as will add to the attractiveness of the exhibit.

9. Exhibits of primitive and modern appliances used in bee culture, both in this country and abroad, will be received, subject to the approval of the Chief of the Department.

10. Special arrangements will be made by the Chief of the Department for a limited exhibit of bees.

11. Collections of honey producing plants, suitably mounted and labeled, will be accepted if satisfactory to the Chief of the Department.

12. The right is reserved to add to, amend or interpret the above rules.

         Signed, W. I. BUCHANAN,
Approved, GEORGE R. DAVIS,  Chief Department of Agriculture.
  Director General.

Immediately after Mr. Kretchmer was appointed, he issued the following letter:

        IOWA COLUMBIAN COMMISSION.
          APIARY DEPARTMENT.
F. N. CHASE, Cedar Falls.
 Commissioner, Departments of Agriculture, Dairy and Apiary.
E. KRETCHMER, Red Oak,
 Asst. in Charge of Apiary Department

DEAR SIR:—Having been appointed on the recommendation of the President of the Iowa Beekeepers' Association to assist in collecting and installing an exhibit of the products of the Apiary Industry of Iowa, I take the liberty of addressing you as one of the prominent beekeepers of Iowa, to lend a helping hand in making this exhibit one that will not only increase the pride of every citizen of Iowa, but one that will also materially assist in filling the pockets of every beekeeper within our State; because next to the question, "How to obtain the greatest amount of honey," comes the question, "Where shall I find a remunerative market?"

No greater opportunity to advertise their products was ever offered to the beekeepers of Iowa than the present one of making an elaborate and attractive exhibit of the products of the Apiary Industry of Iowa, at the World's Columbian Exposition, drawing not only the attention of our neighbors to the attractiveness of Iowa honey, but the attention of the world at large, thereby inducing the people of the world to use it to a greater extent than ever before.

For this exhibit we must have the very best samples of comb and extracted honey, and the brightest specimens of beeswax that can now be obtained. We ask your hearty co-operation,

1st. To make an exhibit in the Iowa State Building erected on the World's Fair ground.

2d. To aid in making an exhibit in the various classes in the Competitive Department in the Agaicultural Building where we meet the competition of the world.

For the exhibit in the State Building, we desire cases of comb honey from white clover, basswood, goldenrod, buckwheat, heartsease, or other sources, but especially from white clover.

The special requirements are: White comb, even face, well capped section well filled, no holes,—comb not cracked by frost or marred in any way, sections white and well cleaned.

We desire specimens of the different varieties of extracted honey, and nice bright beeswax which should be prepared in such a manner as will add to the attractiveness of the exhibit. The necessary vessels for exhibiting extracted honey will be provided by the Commissioner in charge.

1st. Please advise us at once of what you can furnish now, or if you have none yourself, give the name and address of any beekeeper who you think may have some.

2d. Will you try to obtain some honey or wax to replenish the exhibit which, if white clover or basswood honey, should be in place between July 15th and August 15th; and if fall honey, should be in place between August 15th and September 15th, 1893.

Any of the samples contributed can, if desired, have the name of the contributor placed upon it; and such contributed parcels of honey, wax, etc., will be sold at the close of the Exposition, (or sooner if necessary to replenish it) for the benefit of the exhibitor, or disposed of as he may direct—thus reimbursing him.

The exhibit in the State Building is to advertise the resources of the State, and affords an excellent opportunity of advertising the contributor as being a prominent producer.

If you have any honey suitable for exhibition, write us at once, stating what kind of honey, whether comb or extracted. If comb honey, state in what size sections and how much you have of each kind. If you do not wish to make an individual exhibit with your name attached, please write me at what price per pound it can be purchased, as we want to purchase some for the state exhibit; make no shipments without first writing me for shipping directions. Beware of frost,—freezing cracks the comb.

Honey, wax, and "exhibits of Primitive and Modern Appliances used in Bee Culture," for competition in the Agricultural Building at the World's Fair, will be classified and shown under the rules of the Exposition Management. A copy of the rules for the Apiary Department is herewith enclosed. Further information in regard to exhibits in the Apiary Department will be furnisheed on application.

E. KRETCHMER, Red Oak, Ia.,

Asst. in Charge of Apiary Department.

Iowa made an exhibit of all the various kinds of honey, and also had a fine exhibit of honey plants, beeswax, bee implements and appliances. The installation was made in one of the standard cases provided by the Chief of the Apiary Department at the expense of the Iowa Commission. These cases were of glass on all sides, and contained over 800 cubic feet of space, inside measure. The exhibit of honey at the opening of the Exposition was from the crop of 1892, and made a good showing for old honey. Later the exhibit of new honey from the crop of 1893 was very large, and of excellent quality. The state exhibit was made up of individual exhibits, which were furnished by the beekeepers of the state, and at the close of the Exposition these samples were sold, and the proceeds returned to exhibitors. To increase the interest in the Apiary Department and to add to the exhibit, some of the finest samples that could be procured from the product of 1893, Superintendent Kretchmer sent the following letter to the beekeepers of the State:

IOWA COLUMBIAN COMMISSION,
APIARY DEPARTMENT, July 15, 1893.

F. N. CHASE, Cedar Falls,
Commissioner Departments of Agriculture, Dairy and Apiary.
E. KRETCHMER, Red Oak,
Ass't. in Charge of Apiary Department.

DEAR SIR: —The time is at hand to install the white honey of this year's crop (1893). We desire some comb and extracted honey as soon as it can be obtained.

There never was a grander opportunity for Iowa beekeepers to distinguish themselves; already we have had an inquiry from Austria for Iowa extracted honey, such as is shown now in the Iowa case.

Can you not ship us some nice honey? Would you not feel proud if a medal or diploma were awarded you by the largest World's Fair ever held?

Such contributed parcels of honey will be sold at the close of the Exposition (or sooner if necessary to replenish it) for the benefit of the person who furnished the honey, or otherwise disposed of as he may direct.

Please notice, the Iowa Columbian Commission takes your honey to the best market, furnishes shipping cases pays all the freight from your place to Chicago and the Fair ground, provides all the glass-ware for extracted honey, and honey from the World's Fair will certainly bring the *highest* price.

Please advise me at once, how much comb honey you can furnish; how much extracted honey; and we will at once ship you proper shipping cases for comb honey or cans for extracted honey, all charges prepaid.

E. KRETCHMER, Red Oak, Iowa,
Ass't. in Charge of Apiary Department.

In response to this letter a large assortment of both comb and extracted honey was received during July and August, and was very artistically arranged. The quality of honey was not excelled by any state or nation. The Iowa exhibitors in the Apiary Department received their full share of awards, and the exhibits showed that very many of Iowa's best citizens are engaged in this very pleasant and profitable industry.

The Iowa honey, the comb on account of its delicate color and complete comb, and especially the extracted honey with its clear color and dense consistency was a tempting exhibit, and was admitted even by our competitors to be superior to any on exhibition. We received in exchange for samples of our Iowa honey nineteen samples from foreign countries, and it was not strange that the foreign representatives after comparing the quality of the different samples eagerly asked for our price on such honey; and we learned that our extracted honey at present prices can be placed on the markets of Russia, Germany, Austria and Turkey for less money than they now pay for an inferior article. A large number of foreign visitors obtained samples of our honey with the name and address of the exhibitor, with a view of obtaining shipments from Iowa.

One order from Vienna and one from Saxony has already been filled, and no doubt others will follow; orders have also been received from California to cater to the taste for Iowa clover honey. Taken as a whole, the Iowa Apiary exhibit was a grand success, and the demand from abroad, and for home use will, undoubtedly, be largely increased by the exhibit made at Chicago.

The following is a list of names of exhibitors. Exhibited honey from crop of 1892.

L. G. Clute, Manchester.
E. Kretchmer, Red Oak.
F. Furst, Adair.
J. H. Stanford, Cherokee.

The following exhibited honey, crop of 1893:

R. B. Arnold, Foster.
E. J. Cronkleton, Dunlap.
T. C. DeClercq, De Soto.
Oliver Foster, Mt. Vernon.
Thomas Johnson, Coon Rapids.
William Kimble, De Witt.
J. L. Strong, Clarinda.
F. A. Beals, Salix.
L. G. Clute, Manchester.
A. J. Duncomb, Hartford.
Thomas O. Hines, Anamosa.
E. Kretchmer, Red Oak.
Noah Miller, North English.
J. H. Stephens, Riverton.
Mont. Wyrick, Cascade.

Iowa received six awards, two of which were by the same exhibitor, and as no other state or nation received the same number of awards on the crop of 1893 honey, Iowa heads the list, and for the two seasons, 1892 and 1893 combined, only one state exceeds Iowa by a single award. The following is a list of names of the winners to whom medals and diplomas will be issued:

E. Kretchmer, Red Oak—Extracted clover honey and alfalfa comb honey.

Oliver Foster, Mt. Vernon—Extracted basswood honey.
L. G. Clute, Greeley—Comb honey.
William Kimble, De Witt—Extracted honey

The glass case in which the Apiary Exhibit was made, was donated to the State Agricultural Society by vote of the Iowa Columbian Commission.

I cannot close this report without again referring to the assistants that were in charge of the several divisions of the Agricultural Department, and thank them for their faithful and efficient services, and congratulate them upon the success that crowned their efforts, and placed Iowa and her exhibits among the leading prize winners at the World's Columbian Exposition; and to the officers and members of the Iowa Columbian Commission, I desire to express my sincere regards and appreciation of their aid and encouragement, and I only regret that my duties as Secretary, and in other departments of the work of the Commission, made it impossible for me to devote as much time and thought to this great and important branch of Iowa's Industries as its extent and magnitude demanded.

All of which is most respectfully submitted.

F. N. CHASE,
Commissioner in charge of Department of Agriculture, Dairy and Apiary.

WM. HAMILTON DENT.

# Report of the Department of Horticulture.

BY WM. HAMILTON DENT AND CHARLES ASHTON.

At a meeting of the Commission, held April 7th, 1892, for the better performance of its duties, it arranged its work in departments, and to the charge of the Department of Horticulture named Commissioner W. H. Dent.

At a subsequent meeting of the Commission, held June 9th, 1892, C. L. Watrous, in behalf of the Iowa State Horticultural Society, presented to the Commission a communication proposing on behalf of the said society to collect, install and maintain in a proper and creditable manner an exhibit of the Horticultural productions of the State of Iowa in the World's Columbian Exposition. In its action upon said communication the Commission adopted the following resolution:

*Resolved*, That Commissioner Dent, being in charge of the Department of Horticulture be, and he is hereby authorized to enter into an agreement with the State Horticultural Society for the purpose of taking charge of the exhibit in that branch, and that he be allowed an amount not in excess of $2,000 as a contribution to that end.

Subsequently an agreement was entered into as follows:

"In the matter of making an exhibit at the World's Columbian Exposition of 1892-3, of the horticultural resources and progress of the State of Iowa, it is understood and agreed by and between the Columbian Commission of Iowa and the Iowa State Horticultural Society, in substance as follows: For the purpose of aiding such exhibit the Columbian Commission will assist officially in all proper ways within its power and will contribute of its funds the sum of two thousand dollars, to be paid from time to time as needed, to the representative of the State Horticultural Society upon the certificate of its President and Secretary that such sums are needed in the work of making the exhibit.

The Iowa State Horticultural Society, on its part, undertakes and agrees to make at such exposition the best exhibit of the horticultural resources of the State which its skill, knowledge and financial resources will allow, binding itself to contribute to the work out of its own funds, a sum at least equal to that contributed by the Columbian Commission and as much more as can be profitably used, to the extent of its ability.

It agrees to place the work in charge of one of its responsible members, as superintendent of the exhibit and to be responsible to the Commission and to the public for the creditable character and for the proper and honorable conduct of the exhibit from beginning to end.

The display is to be under the general auspices of the Iowa Columbian Commission, but the Iowa State Horticultural Society is to be responsible for and to direct all details of the work of gathering, forwarding and displaying such exhibit, hereby agreeing to hold the Iowa Columbian Commission financially harmless in all matters relating thereto, save and excepting the sum of two thousand dollars to be paid as before stated.

Signed July 11, 1892, on the part of the Iowa State Horticultural Society, by
A. F. COLLMAN, President.
J. L. BUDD, Secretary.
SILAS WILSON, Treasurer.

And on the part of the Iowa Columbian Commission, July 13th, by William Hamilton Dent, Chairman of the Horticultural Committee of said Committee, and by the President also of said Commission.

WILLIAM HAMILTON DENT,
Chairman.

Approved, subject to the condition that only sixty per cent shall be drawn upon during the year 1892.

JAMES O. CROSBY,
President Iowa Columbian Commission."

That the matter of making an exhibit of the horticultural products of the State of Iowa was thus placed in the hands of the Iowa State Horticultural Society and an appropriation of $600 made, and was duly paid to the said society, or its duly appointed agent, when the proper vouchers were presented for the same.

That at a meeting of the Commission held early in May, 1893, Commissioner Dent reported to the Commission that he was not satisfied with the exhibit then made by the Society, or its agent; whereupon the Commission by vote, requested its President to correspond at once with the officers of the Iowa State Horticultural Society, to call their attention to the obligations of their contract and urge upon them immediate action to make the necessary improvements in the exhibit, which was promptly done.

That the desired improvement not being made to the satisfaction of the Commission, August 2d, 1893, it rescinded its contract with the State Horticultural Society. Commissioner Dent being pressed with other duties, Commissioner Ashton was added to the Committee on Horticulture to assist in the oversight of the exhibit in that department. President Collman, duly authorized by the Executive Committee of the State Society, at once visited the exhibit, and met Commissioner Ashton. Their communication resulted in a renewal of arrangements with the said Society for its management of the exhibit, with Mr. Collman in charge. By this arrangement, harmony was at once restored with the Iowa State Horticultural Society, the Horticulturists of the State, the Iowa Columbian Commission and the officials in charge of the Horticultural Division of the World's Columbian Exposition.

On entering upon his work in this department Commissioner Ashton at once opened correspondence with leading fruit growers in different sections of Iowa to secure enlarged supplies of needed fruits. Mr. Collman earnestly seconded these efforts. On August 24th Mr. Collman was placed fully in charge of the exhibit. At once application was made in the name of the Commission for additional space in the Horticultural Building, and enlarged and contiguous space was at once awarded. The table formerly occupied with the Iowa exhibit was refitted and improved in arrangement and decorations The tables in the additional space secured were readjusted, all being harmoniously arranged and decorated. Large supplies of fruits were then received daily, and at once were neatly installed and the Iowa Exhibit being tastily arranged and tidily kept, at once became one of the most attractive exhibits in that important department of the great Exposition and to the close of the Fair won high and deserved encomiums from the thousands daily passing through the great Horticultural Hall.

By resolution of the Commission $1,400 in addition to the $630 previously paid the Horticultural Society was placed at the disposal of the Committee for use in this department. Expenditures were made with the greatest economy possible to the accomplishment of such an exhibit of the horticultural productions of the state as should win for it the greatest possible honor in the judgment of the multitudes of visitors from other states and countries, who should daily view it, and pass judgment upon it. The unusual sparseness and inferior quality of the fruit crop in Iowa in 1893, made the collection of fruits in the necessary quantities and of the proper qualities for the exhibit unexpectedly laborious and expensive. It is but deserved justice to report that in consequence of its larger crop, and better organization of the Fruit Growers of southwestern Iowa, and the efficient organization of the Mills County Horticultural Society, that portion of the state furnished the largest share of the apples placed in our State Exhibit. It affords us great pleasure, however, to report that many enterprising, liberal fruit growers in other portions of the state rendered generous and earnest assistance in the collection and shipment of the fruits needed to make and maintain the winning exhibit made under Mr. Collman's superintendence; an exhibit in which was displayed upon our tables upwards of 2,000 plates laden with the most inviting specimens of Iowa grown apples, pears, plums and other fruits, besides the large quantities of grapes and other fruits installed.

The Iowa Horticultural Exhibit was one of the few that opened in that department with the opening of the Exposition. Every species of fruits cultivated in our state had place in the Iowa display at some time during its continuance. Many specimens of our wild fruits were placed in the display and added to its interest. By being thus placed in contrast with the cultivated varieties, the qualities developed by cultivation were at once distinctly seen.

## THE COST OF THE EXHIBIT.

The cost of the Exhibit during the period in which Mr. Watrous had charge is shown in the following summary.

| | | |
|---|---:|---:|
| Per diem and expense, C. L. Watrous, per his bill rendered | $1,564 01 | |
| Paid for Mills County apples, Crop 1891 | 74 25 | |
| Incidental expenses paid by Commission | 22 48 | $1,660 74 |

### EXPENSES UNDER MR. COLLMAN'S ADMINISTRATION.

| | | |
|---|---:|---:|
| Paid for fruits, express charges on same, and labor and expense in collecting | $929 32 | |
| Paid for help in installing and maintaining exhibit, railroad fare, and other expenses therefor | 1,025 17 | |
| Paid for material and labor arranging and decorating tables | 65 00 | |
| Paid for telegrams | 7 94 | |
| Paid for printing | 12 00 | |
| Paid for postage, stationery, drafts and postal orders | 10 00 | |
| Paid for gate tickets for Collman | 3 00 | |
| Paid for railroad fare for Collman, and per diem attending meeting of Commission for Settlement | 17 20 | $2,069 63 |
| Gross cost of Exhibit | | 3,730 37 |

LESS AMOUNT SALVAGE RECEIVED.

| | | |
|---|---:|---:|
| For desk sold | $ 12 50 | |
| For fruit sold | 38 72—$ | 51 22 |
| Net cost Collman and Watrous administration | | $3,678 15 |
| Per diem Charles Ashton, 19 days service | | 95 00 |
| Add am't allowed Lotspeich by Commission Feb. 8, '94 | | 3 00 |
| Add am't allowed Carson by Commission Feb. 8, '94 | | 4 75 |
| Total cost of exhibit | | $ 3,780 90 |

The Competitive Horticultural exhibit made by the State of Iowa consisted in the display of fresh ripe fruits. Other garden products were shown in the Iowa Pavilion and in the Agricultural Building. No display of fruits in glass, dried or evaporated fruits or products from the juices of fruits was attempted, the only effort at an exhibit of preserved fruits being an exhibit of apples of the crop of 1891 and 1892 preserved in cold storage. We believe that Iowa was the only State that displayed apples of the crop of 1891, that were preserved by cold storage methods. Of the crop of 1892 but little effort was made to gather and preserve fruits for the exhibit in 1893.

## AWARDS.

The following awards to Iowa Horticulture were made by the Board of Judges of the Exposition:

### GROUP 21—CLASS 133.

Iowa State, Des Moines; Collection of apples, Crop 1892.
Iowa State Horticultural Society, Corning; Collection of stone fruits and apples.
Mills County Horticultural Society, Glenwood; Collection of apples.
A. F. Collman, Corning; Collection of apples.

### GROUP 20—CLASS 122.

Iowa State Horticultural Society; Collection of grapes.

### GROUP 21—CLASS 138.

G. B. Brackett, Denmark; Models of fruits.

### GROUP 22—CLASS 155.

I. N. Kramer, Cedar Rapids; Collection of Cannas.

The following awards were posted at the door of the room of the Committee of Awards in the Horticultural Department at the close of the Exposition.

### GROUP 133—CLASS 21.

State of Iowa; Collection of apples and pears.
J. L. Budd, Ames, Iowa; Collection of plums.
State of Iowa; Collection of plums.
M. E. Hinkley, Marquis, Iowa; Collection of Plums.

IOWA EXHIBIT, HORTICULTURAL HALL.

## GROUP 21  CLASS 136.

Iowa State Horticultural Society; Continuous collection of small fruits.

### LIST OF COUNTIES FURNISHING FRUITS.

We report the following as the counties furnishing fruits for the Iowa exhibit, and so far as we have information, the several species of fruits furnished by each.

| COUNTIES. | FRUITS. | COUNTIES. | FRUITS. |
|---|---|---|---|
| Audubon | grapes, apples | Adams | apples, pears, plums, grapes |
| Blackhawk | apples, pears, plums, grapes. | Benton | grapes |
|  |  | Clarke | grapes |
| Boone | apples, grapes | Bremer | apples, grapes, plums |
| Buchanan | apples, plums | Calhoun | grapes, plums |
| Butler | apples, grapes | Cherokee | plums, apples |
| Cerro Gordo | grapes, apples | Cass | grapes, apples |
| Cedar | apples, plums | Carroll | apples, grapes |
| Clayton | grapes, apples | Dallas | plums, grapes, apples, peaches |
| Clinton | grapes, apples | Floyd | apples, grapes |
| Fremont | apples, grapes | Emmet | apples, pears |
| Dubuque | apples, pears | Harrison | grapes, plums |
| Guthrie | apples, grapes, plums | Johnson | apples, pears, grapes |
| Hancock | plums, grapes, berries | Ida | apples, grapes, berries |
| Keokuk | apples, pears, plums | Linn | apples, plums |
| Jones | apples, grapes, plums | Mahaska | apples, grapes |
| Lucas | apples | Mills | apples, grapes, plums, crabs, peaches. |
| Marion | apples, grapes, plums |  |  |
| Monona | plums, apples, crabs | Mitchell | apples |
| Montgomery | apples | Muscatine | apples, grapes |
| Palo Alto | apples, grapes | Page | apples |
| Pottawattamie | apples, grapes, plums | Polk | apples, pears, plums, grapes, crabs, berries. |
| Poweshiek | apples, plums, grapes |  |  |
| Washington | apples | Scott | apples |
| Woodbury | apples, plums | Wayne | grapes, apples |
| O'Brien | apples | Howard | apples, grapes |

The list names fifty-one counties furnishing fruits for the state's exhibit

### OF THE FRUITS EXHIBITED.

#### SUMMER FRUITS.

The Pacific Coast states, the southwestern territories, the British Provinces, and many of the states of this central region of the country made large exhibits of fruits in glass, dried and evaporated fruits, canned fruits, jellies, preserves, and wines. The management entrusted by the Iowa State Horticultural Society with the preparation of the exhibit failed to make any display in these forms. Other states opening their exhibits shortly after the opening of the Exposition, placed our exhibit at that time at a serious disadvantage. When the summer fruits began to ripen supplies were gathered and forwarded for the exhibit, and were duly installed and the Iowa exhibit won some attention at that stage. An award was made for the continuous collection of small fruits. Of our summer fruits, strawberries, raspberries, gooseberries, currants, blackberries, and cherries were shown. In the construction of the Iowa table no provision was made for the use of ice or other refrigerating service and after the picking, transporting and the time necessarily elapsing from the time of their gathering to their installation in the heated season, it was found impossible to maintain such fruits long in presentable condition.

## PEARS AND PEACHES.

The display made of these fruits was not large, yet it was important. It was sufficient to show the possibilities of their production in our meteorological conditions and soil. So far north as the forty-second parallel, hardy varieties of the peach may be grown, with reasonable care. The pear may be grown in numerous varieties. Ten varieties of peaches were exhibited; of the pear twenty-five. We believe the exhibits of these varieties of delicious fruits, although small, were of great value in promoting increased interest in their cultivation. The following varieties of pears were shown, many of the specimens being very fine:

| | | |
|---|---|---|
| Bartlett, | Louise B De Jersey, | Vermont Beauty, |
| Howell, | Sickel, | Flemish Beauty, |
| Keifer, | Smith's Beauty, | Iowa Beauty, |
| Sand Pear, | Duchess, | Pride of New York, |
| Snow Flake, | Lincoln, | Smith's Golden, |
| Clapp's Favorite, | Russell. | White Doyenne, |
| Johnson's Best, | Sheldon, | |

and five un-named seedlings.

## PLUMS.

Of this desirable fruit, the Iowa exhibit was surprisingly large, fine and valuable. The fine form, size and rich color of many of the varieties shown made the exhibit peculiarly attractive and gave it great excellence. It speedily won large attention from prominent horticulturists of other states. The varieties developed from the native wild stock of the prairie states, or from crosses with foreign varieties, making our exhibit especially attractive to intelligent fruit growers. Many varieties of our wild plums, some of them large fine fruit, were placed in the exhibit and lent variety and attraction. A number of foreign varieties cultivated in Iowa were shown, the display embracing with others the following:

| | | |
|---|---|---|
| Wild Goose, | Blue Damson, | The Adams, |
| Ungarist Prune, | Egg, | Wolf, |
| Hummer, | Rockford, | Woldafskee, |
| Green Gage, | Lord Russell, | Pond's Seedling, |
| General Hand, | Spanish King, | Charter Downing, |
| Forest Garden, | Early Red, | Sloe, |
| Golden Drop, | Carson, | Pottawattamie, |
| Weaver, | De Soto, | Yellow Egg, |
| Miner, | Hawkeye, | Wyant. |
| German Prune, | Blue Gage, | |

## THE GRAPE.

The Iowa display of this common, easily cultivated and desirable species of fruit was large, and by its unique installment and the excellent quality of the fruit shown was especially attractive to visitors. Two shelves elevated one above the other, supported by light neatly turned columns, rose from the center of the main table, central in the Iowa space. Around the table and suspended from these elevated shelves were strung artificial vines, very perfect imitations of the grape vines both in form and color of leaf. On them numerous clusters of the fruit were placed so that at a glance, the hue, size and form as well as the perfectness of the bunches was at once seen. The total length of these vines used was about 150 feet. Their entire length was thickly hung with large and selected clusters of the numerous varieties shown, they being displayed in the most natural and attractive manner possible. It will be seen from a casual glance at the table given above of the counties furnishing fruits that the grape exhibit came from all parts of the State. Mr. John E. Corlett, of Farmersburg, Clayton county, furnished for the exhibit fifty-one varieties, many of them being fruit of very superior quality. These were grown in the extreme northeastern part of the State. Mr. Silas Wilson, of Cass county, in the southwestern portion, furnished 40 varieties, being a very fine addition to the exhibit. Unfortunately two shipments sent by Mr. Corlett were not received. Mr. Bomberger, of Shelby, furnished some very fine samples, especially of the Moore's Early varieties. The grape exhibit certainly demonstrated that if the people of Iowa may not sit under their own fig trees, they may rest under the shadow of their vines, and feast on the fruits of their bearings. We name the following 89 varieties that were placed in the exhibit:

Agawam, August Giant, Amber Queen, Amina, Brighton, Black Eagle, Bacchus, Barry, Berchmain, Brilliant, Boyer, Catawba, Clinton, Cottage, Centennial, Crevelling, Champion, Concord, Delaware, Duchess, Diana, Dracut, Defiance, Eaton, Empire State, Elvira, Eldorado, Early Ohio, Early Victor, Etta, Esther, Emmalan, Geneva, Green Mountain, Hartford, Hellen, Highland, Herbemont, Herbert, Iowa, Iona, Ives, Isabella, Jefferson, Janesville, Jessica, Lady, Lady Washington, Lindley No. 9, Lutie, Lenoir, Martha, Merrimack, Moore's Diamond, Moore's Early, Moyer, Morgan, Monroe, Miller, Mason, Niagara, Norfolk, Norton, Normal, Perkins, Pocklington, Prentice, Potter's Early, Poughkeepsie Red, Oriental, Salem, Roger's No. 1, Roger's No. 3, Roger's No. 5, Roger's No. 8, Roger's No. 30, Rockwood, Requa, Rebecca, Rag No. 2, Telegraph, Triumph, Victory, Ulster Prolific, Vergennes, Wilder, Wyoming Red, Worden, Woodruff Red.

## THE CRAB.

The exhibit of this useful but often slightly regarded fruit won commendation. It demonstrated the possibilities of its plentiful production, of the most desirable and beautiful varieties throughout Iowa. The twenty varieties named below, with several plates of the wild crab of the larger species, that grows so plentifully in all our prairie groves, were displayed.

The show of the specimens of wild fruits revealed clearly the transformations from the wild to the present cultivated condition:

General Grant, Hyslop, Hesper Blush, Hughes' Virginia, Large Native, Large Red, Lady, Little Red Siberian, Large Yellow, Martha, Minnesota, Montreal Beauty, Purple Siberian, Quaker Beauty, Ream's White, Red Siberian, Ressonant, Showy, Soulard, Striped Siberian, Silver Sweet, Sweet Crab, Vassils, Transcendent, Williams' Favorite, White, Waughs.

## THE APPLE.

By its display of the apple, the king of northern and pomological fruits, Iowa won most honorable awards, as well as highest commendation from the thousands who daily passed through the vast Horticultural halls and viewed our extensive and superb exhibit. Its magnitude and excellence was a surprise to thousands dwelling in other states and unacquainted with our capabilities for the production of this class of fruits, who imagined that Iowa was a borean, fruitless region. Iowa was not excelled by any other state in the neat and attractive manner in which its display of apples was installed and maintained. No exhibit of this most important fruit production in the vast pomological hall gave forth a richer fragrance, or bore a more beautiful hue. The solid marketable qualities of "Iowa's apples" won the regard of the numerous visitors who attended the Exposition to study that important feature in the qualities of the exhibits from the several states. No other state made so large an exhibit of its apple production as did Iowa. None other displayed so great a number of distinct varieties. Iowa showing 61 recognized summer sorts, 124 fall varieties and 166 known winter kinds, upwards of 30 unnamed seedlings, besides many foreign varieties of unknown name, being displayed. The thousands daily passing by it were astonished at the magnitude as well as the excellence of our exhibit. We present the following list of named varieties of apples placed in the Iowa exhibit:

Alexander, Allen's Choice, August Sweet, American Golden Pippin, August Pearmain, Autumn Favorite, American Golden Russett, Aunt Hannah, Antihonka, Autumn Strawberry, Autumn Striped, Aunties.Apple, Arabian, Aport Orient, Autumn Pearmain, Aport Fosci, Annissin, Armstrong, Arkansas Black, Adams, Autumn Swaar, Bailey Sweet, Baldwin, Ben Davis, Benoni, Blue Anis, Blushed Collville, Boiken, Borivinka, Burlington, Blue Pearmain, Babot, Black Twig, Briggs' Seedling, Baldwin Sweet, Bentley Sweet, Bethlehemite, Bergamot, Bishop's Russet, Black Gillflower, Black Annette, Buker, Boorsdorf, Babuscheno, Byromanti, Cannon Pearmain, Carmoni's June, Caleb Sweet, Chenango Strawberry, Collini, Charlemoff, Curt du Pendu Plat, Champonki, Cayuga Red Streak, Collman's Seedling No. 1, Carthouse, Carter, Collman's Seedling No. 3, Colvert, Cole's Quince, Collman's Seedling No. 10, Drap D'Or, Dennis Red, Duchess of Oldenburgh, Drops of Gold, Delaware Red, Dixon's Sweet, Early Harvest, Early Strawberry, Early Joe, Early Pennock, Early Market, Esopus Spitzenburgh, Early Red, Egg Top, Early Colton, Fulton, Early Sweet Pearmain, Early Summer Pearmain, English Golden Russet, Fall Orange, Fall Jeanetting, Fall Pippin, Fall Spitzenburgh, Fall Wine Sap, Frank, Fife's Choice, Flory's Bellflower,

Flory, Fall Wine, Fife's Seedling, Fameuse, Fall River, Fulton, Golden Reinette, Gravenstein, Golden Russet, Sops of Wine, Grimes' Golden,Green Aport, Gipsey Girl, Golden White, Great West, Glass Apple, Gideon No. 4, Glori Mundi, Grand Sultan, Gideon No 6, Grandmother, Good Peasant, Gideon No. 8, Golden Pippin, Grindstone, Gilpin, Haas, Hibernal, Hutchins Sweet, Harry Komp, Hagloe, Hanley, Hutchins, Illinois Russet, Isham's Sweet, Iowa Keeper, Iowa Beauty, Iowa Pippin, Jeffrey, Jersey Sweet, Jesse Homan, Jersey Red, Jonathan, June Market, Keswick Coddling, Kansas Blush, Koutchnovi, Kansas Red, King of Tompkins County, Kentucky, Kirkbridge White, Limber Twig, Longfield, London Pippin, Luland Raspberry, Lubsk Queen, Large Anis, Lead Apple, Little Hat, Leonard, Leonard Seedling, Longworth Russet, Large Romanite, Lufkin, Lufkin's Seedling, Lansingburgh, Ladies' Favorite, Little Romanite, Ladies' Choice, Lowell, Lyman's Sweet, Louvre, Lady Finger, London Sweet, Lady Sweet, Magog, Magog Red Streak, Marble, Milam, Mann, Malitt, Mason's Best, Montreal Beauty, Missouri Flat, Mammoth Black Twig, Mercer's Best, Missouri Pippin, Mohawk, Mercer, Micheal Henry, Minden, Mayner's Red, Minkler, McIntosh Red, Mother, Maiden Blush, Munson Sweet, Malinda, McMahon's White, Melon, New York Russet, Nitrone Erdbeer, Northern Spitzenburgh, Native Rishki, Noble Red Streak, New York Seek No Further, Newhall, New Burlington, Newton Pippin, New York Pippin, New York, Newton Spitzenburgh, Never Fail, Newport, Nollicoffer, Northern Greening, Northwest Greening, Nonesuch, Northern Spy, Nonpareil, Northwest, Osterkoff, Ortley, Old Gold, Ohio Beauty, Oxford, Ohio Pippin, Osceola, Pointed Pipka, Partonvonski,Pipka Champonski, Possatt Native, Pryor's Red, Pottawattamie Chief, Price's Sweet, Patton's Greening, Pearmain, Peck's Pleasant, Porter, Pewaukee, Perry Russet, Pound Sweet, Parker Earl, Quaker Beauty, Queen of the West, Red Ox, Red June, Red Reinette, Rosa Aport, Red Queen, Reinabourka, Ratinschana, Red Transparent, Red Astrachan, Repka Melinka, Ramsdell Sweet, Redfield, Red Streak, Raymond Gano, Red Romanite, Red Winter Pearmain, Rome Beauty, Rhode Island Greening, Rambo, Striped Gilliflower, Sweet June, Sweet Blush, St. Lawrence, Seedling No 3, Seek No Further, Swaar, Silken Leaf, Sandy Glass, Sklanka, Skush-apple, Scott's Winter, Switzer, Summer Pearmain, Summer Sweet Pearmain, Sheep Nose, Summer Sweet Paradie, Spotted Pearmain, Steele's Red, Sweet Sough, Stark, Saint Peter, Sutton Beauty, Stoner's Hardy, Striped Pippin, Stripped June, Seedling Duchess No. 1, Summer Sweet No. 166, Smiths' Cider, Seedling Duchess No. 5, Summer Queen, Sheriff, Seedling Duchess No. 6, Saxton Stripe, Summer Sport, Seedling Duchess No. 7, Tetofsky Tissenhausen, Twenty Oz. Pippin, Tallman's Sweet, Titonka, Terry's Best, Tulpehocken, True Cross, Tracy, Utter's Red, Varonica Red, Vandevere, Virginia Crab, Vermont Beauty, White Astrachan, Wine Apple, Winter Greening, Winter Sweet Paradise, Winter Sweet, White Belleflower, White Winter Pearmain, Whitney, Wolf River, Westfield, Winter Rambo, Walbridge, Wealthy Seedling, Wythe, Wealthy, Windsor Chief, Wayne, Winter Stripling, Winter Aport, Wine Sap, Wagner, Winter Pearmain, Winter Sweet Pearmain, Willow Twig, Winter Erdbeer, Warfield, Yellow Ingester, Yellow Callville, Yellow Anis, Yellow Transparent, York Imperial, Yellow Bellflower, Zuzoff.

The Iowa exhibit of its fruit productions in the Columbian Exposition was certainly of material value to the people of the state, demonstrating as it did the possibilities of abundant production in every part of the state of the most important fruits of the temperate zone. Many intelligent citizens of the state visiting the exposition were surprised at the magnitude and excellence of the attractive display. To every interested visitor it was a strong incentive to more patient and intelligent effort in the industries of the orchard and the garden. To visitors from other and distant states it was a communication of actual conviction, that the people of our beautiful state not only produce meats and cereals in vast abundance to feed multitudes beyond its own boundaries, but that luxurious as well as dainty fruits of their home growing, in great abundance to grace their homes and tables, may be produced and enjoyed by the citizens of the state honored by the fine exhibit.

The work of the committee in this department was to its members their first experience in the management of an exhibit of such great importance. Our state had never previously undertaken an exhibit of its products, and especially of its productions of fruits, on so large a scale as its interests and [...] alike demanded should be made in the World's Columbian Exposition. [...] searching through the records of the Centennial Exposition, no precedents were found to guide in the important duty of gathering and installing a proper exhibit of the resources of the state in this important branch of its industries. In concluding this report the committee would respectfully suggest the following line of preparation, should ever the people of our generous state again undertake the presenting of their productions and resources in another such magnificent exposition.

1. That the idea should at once be definitely accepted, that all other states and countries will exhibit their best, and only the best of their productions; that Iowa must show of its best and only the very best of its productions; that nothing second rate in quality, especially of its horticultural productions, should be allowed place in its exhibit.

2. That the work of preparation, so that the very finest quality possible should be produced for the exhibit, of every variety of horticultural production, especially in the line of fruits, should be commenced at least two years prior to the opening of the exposition. This should be done by the employment of active, intelligent, competent men in all portions of the state to carefully cultivate, produce and collect the most perfect specimens of all horticultural productions, especially of all kinds of fruits cultivated in the state. Such specimens of fruits should be gathered and preserved either in glass or by cold storage until time for their installation prior to the opening of the exposition. This action is urged as the year of the exposition may be a barren one in the production of summer or autumn fruits. Because of the adversities of the season of 1893 the great states of Indiana and Ohio made no exhibit of their fruits in the Columbian Exposition. Both Illinois and Iowa found themselves put to extraordinary expense and trouble to collect the exhibits they made.

3. The tables upon which the exhibits will be installed should be tastily designed, wisely planned and appropriately decorated before the open-

ing of the exposition. The expense in this line need not be extravagant, it should not be parsimonious. The portion of the space intended for the exhibition of tender summer fruits should be arranged for the use of refrigerating service, and they should be kept under glass.

This committee found itself handicapped by the meager amount that could be placed at its command by the commission for the great work it was appointed to do.

The following letter addressed to A. F. Collman, Esq., is an honorable commendation of the Iowa Horticultural Exhibit:

WORLD'S COLUMBIAN EXPOSITION, OFFICE OF THE DIRECTOR GENERAL OF THE EXPOSITION, Chicago, Ill., U. S. A., Jan. 29, 1894.

MR. A. F. COLLMAN, Corning, Iowa.

Dear Sir: Among the many fine exhibits of fruits at the Columbian Exposition, that of Iowa was one of the best. Under your supervision the tables were artistically arranged, every variety of fruit which could be obtained in your state was properly labelled, the different species conveniently grouped for comparison of their special characteristics, and the exhibit was always in a neat and orderly condition. There is no doubt that such an exhibition of fine fruit attracted much attention to your state, and as a result many persons from the east learned for the first time what Iowa's genial climate and soil could produce. You and the other gentlemen in charge of the exhibit deserve the gratitude of the state for the excellent display made and the courtesy and attention you gave to all inquiring visitors.

Yours Very Truly,    J. M. SAMUELS,
Chief Department of Horticulture.

JOHN F. DUNCOMBE.

# Report of Department of Minerals and Geology.

BY JOHN F. DUNCOMBE.

When I was appointed by your commission to take charge of the mines and mining department for Iowa, I informed you that it would be impossible for me to give a sufficient amount of time to properly and thoroughly do the work necessary to do justice to the mineral exhibit of the state. Therefore, in order to more thoroughly prepare an exhibit and to reduce the expenses in its preparation, in the spring of 1892 I employed with the consent of the commission, and which was afterwards ratified by the commission, Thomas W. Meers at a salary of $60 per month, his necessary expenses to be paid by the commission. Mr. Meers was recommended to me above all other persons for the place by many of the most prominent people of Iowa as one having had much experience in geology and mineralogy, and which was of much importance in his selection, a practical miner.

He immediately set to work with great zeal to accomplish the object of making the best possible display in this department.

As the work advanced plans were prepared for the exhibit and a place for the exhibition secured in the Mines and Mining Building. This was found to be an exceedingly difficult task on account of the fact that Iowa was looked upon as a strictly agricultural state, and unworthy of a display in the general exhibit of the mines and mining department.

The following is a list of the exhibits installed in this department:

### GROUP 42.

Caldwell, G. W., Keokuk—Geodes.
Dubuque World's Fair Association—Lead ore, zinc (dry bone).
Lansing Mining and Smelting Co.—Lead ore, lead from lower magnesian limestone.
Waukon World's Fair Association—Iron ore.

### GROUP 43.

Centerville Coal Co.—Bituminous Coal.
Chicago Coal Co., Seymour—Coal.
Crooked Creek Railroad Co., Lehigh—Coal.
Diagonal Coal Co., Dawson—Coal.
Diamond Coal Co., Centerville—Coal.
Eldora Improvement Association—Coal.
Ketchem, L. & Bro., Farmington—Coal.
Phillips Fuel Co., Ottumwa—Steam Coal.
Raven Coal Co., Mystic—Domestic Coal.
Standard Coal Co., Centerville—Coal.
Tudor Coal Co., Dawson—Coal.
Whitebreast Fuel Co., Ottumwa—Coal.

## GROUP 44.

Adams County Association, Corning—Marble.
Bishop & Treat, Charles City—Marble.
Cedar Valley Quarry Co., Cedar Valley—Bridge stone.
Chamberlain, W. H., Independence—Granite.
Crowley, Edward, Iowa City—Mottled stone.
Dubuque World's Fair Association—Specimens from caves.
Fairchild, H. W., Iowa City Coral specimens.
Faus, T. W., Cherokee Monumental design, artificial stone.
Green, J. A., Stone City Structural limestone, carved stone fruit and flowers.
Hutchinson, Frank, Iowa City Building stone.
Iowa River Stone Co., Eldora—Limestone.
Irish, Gill R., Iowa City Limestone.
Kemper, E. G., Burlington—Brown stone (Jasper County).
LeGrand Quarry Co., Marshalltown Building stone, fossil marble.
McGregor Improvement Co. Fossil marble.
Ft. Madison & Appanoose Stone Co., Ft. Madison—Building stone.
Moir, M. W., Eldora Blue limestone.
Polk, Jefferson S., Des Moines Red, buff and variegated sandstone.
State Quarry, Iowa City Building stone.
Sterns, W. W., Humboldt Oolitic limestone.
Thompson, J. K. P., Rock Rapids Red and purple jasper.
Treat, A. H., Charles City—Fossil marble and examples.
Waukon Association Limestone, marble and sandstone.
Williams, Wilkes, Postville Niagara dolomite building stone.

## GROUP 46.

Barnard, Charles, Waukon—Ornamental and moulding clays and sands.
Buhlman, J. H., Clayton—Silica and glass made from it.
Carter, Charles, Marengo Brick.
Centerville Association—Fire clay.
Clemens, Andrew, McGregor Ornamental sand work.
Clermont Brick & Tile Co. Brick and tile.
Close, W. H., Red Oak Pottery.
Crooked Creek Railroad Co., Lehigh Silica.
Fairchild, H. W., Iowa City Building and fire sand and fire stone.
Faus, T. W., Cherokee Artificial stone.
Granite Brick Co., Burlington—Vitrified brick.
Holman, C. J. & Bro., Sergeant's Bluff Clay, pottery and paving brick.
Indianola Brick & Tile Co. Brick and tile.
Iowa City Association Clay and Brick.
Iowa Pipe and Tile Co., Des Moines—Sewer pipe.
Johnson County, Iowa City Silica.
Keokuk Brick and Tile Co.—Vitrified brick.
Kettle, William, Tipton Tile.
McGregor Improvement Co.—Marl, clay and samples of silica.
Moir, M. W., Eldora Clays and examples, fire sand and silica.
Montpelier Tile Works—Tile and brick.

Muscatine Pressed Brick Co. Brick and clay.
Muscatine Terra Cotta Co. Brick.
Ottumwa Brick Co. Brick.
Pella Drain Tile Co. Tile.
Shattuck, A. L... What Cheer Fire clay.
Stone, W. B., Webster City—Artifical stone.
Waukon Association Brick, tile, potter's clay, and sands.

## GROUP 47.

Duncombe Stucco Co., Fort Dodge Plaster Paris, gypsum fertilizer.
Fairchild, H. W., Iowa City—Gravels.
Hurst, A., Maquoketa—Lime.
Iowa City Association—Lime.
Moir. M. W., Eldora—Limestone.
Steel, Wm. A., Des Moines Limestone.

## GROUP 48.

Waukon World's Fair Association—Iron oxides and examples.
Wilkison, L. A., Des Moines—Iron oxides and examples.

## GROUP 61.

Morgan, Kelly & Taneyhill, Waterloo—Well-drilling machinery.

## GROUP 63.

Ottumwa Iron Works—Tail rope haulage, engine and fixture; unchilled, self-acting mine car wheel.

## GROUP 65.

Sackett, H. B., Council Bluffs—Coal and barrel screens.

## GROUP 67.

Centerville Coal Co. Model of plant.

Every part of the State was thoroughly canvassed, either by carefully prepared letters and circulars or by Mr. Meers in person. This department was, however, very much embarrassed by the small sum of only $2,000 set apart by the Commission for this work, when immediately opposite to the mineral exhibits of Iowa, were exhibits from mineral states which cost hundreds of thousands of dollars. If a larger sum had been appropriated, say $5,000 or $6,000, the exhibit of Iowa could have been made to compare favorably with the exhibits of almost any of the states in coal, building stone and all the valuable clays for the making of potteryware, sewerage pipe, vitrified brick and building brick. Efforts were made to secure the best information from Prof. Calvin of the Iowa State University, and others versed in geology and mineralogy. Efforts were also made to secure from Dr. Hoffman, of Oskaloosa, a portion of his enormous collections. The doctor was an enthusiastic assistant in this work, but the value of his collection, the danger of loss and the lack of power to properly secure him, prevented us from having his exhibits. All he required was, that his name be placed as the owner of the exhibit and securities given that the same should be returned complete without any expense to himself. The danger of loss by theft and

IOWA EXHIBIT, MINES AND MINING.—PLATE I.

breakage was too great to take the risk of so valuable a collection, which is perhaps the largest and one of the most valuable in the State. Another very important collection was that of Mr. Meyer, of Fort Madison, Lee county, and valuable collections were offered from other sections of the State, which would have added very much to our general collection, and as a scientific exhibit of great value, and would have proved very attractive. They met, however, the same difficulty as to security as in the case of Dr. Hoffman.

The principal effort was, under the head of mines, mining and geology, to secure a mineral exhibit which would be a complete demonstration of the great mineral wealth of the State, from a practical standpoint, and show that Iowa is very rich in mineral resources as well as in agricultural products, and efforts were made to place this fact before the world. Every object promoting and developing to a greater extent commerce, manufacturing and other interests of the State were sought after, and coal, stone, clays and sands were made the foundation, principal or basis of the exhibits. The great coal fields of Iowa, covering nearly one half of the State, had been to some extent developed, and the purpose was, to make the development of this great mineral resource an inducement to the investing of capital in the State, and by means of the Iowa system of railroads, place it before the people of the country and before foreigners, that our coal fields were comparatively accessible from every section, and practically inexhaustible, and thus induce manufacturing, by showing the advantages offered in the abundance, good quality and cheapness of fuel for that purpose.

In relation to the stone in the State, the purpose was, to show the people of this State and other states and countries, that in Iowa we had building stone of the very best quality, thereby attracting wide spread attention to the capabilities of the country in material for building purposes. As to our marbles, while they are not of the highest grade, the purpose was to show, that they were susceptible of a very fine polish.

As to the gypsum beds in the neighborhood of Fort Dodge, the purpose was, to show that this valuable material for building purposes and ornaments was practically inexhaustible and the quality, for walls and other practical purposes, was equal, if not superior, to any yet discovered. As to lime stone, the purpose was to show, that the quality was unexcelled and that it was easy of access.

As to the clays, which are abundant in nearly every part of the State, the object was to show that these clays were of such a quality and character as to bring them into notice and make them exceedingly useful. Such clays as are fit for common brick are abundant in nearly every county in the state. White brick clay is also found in very abundant quantities in several parts of the state. Fire clays, potter's clay and clays that are used for paving brick were collected, the object being to show that these clays abound in different parts of Iowa. Also to show that the finer clays for the manufacture of pressed brick, terra cotta and fine pottery were abundant in the state, and clays for artificial stone, sewer pipe and drainage tile also are plenteous. Also to show that clays in large quantities essential for the manufacture of mineral paints are abundant, thereby showing, that the state of Iowa has a bountiful profusion of clays for the manufacturers by whom this article is used

The object in relation to the various kinds of sands, was to show that silica for the manufacture of glass, exists in large deposits within the borders of the state, which for fineness and superiority is not surpassed, and that not many years would pass before the manufacturing of glass would be an important industry in Iowa. Also to show that moulder's sand abounds in many localities, and building sand in almost every locality in the state; to show that cannel coal is abundant, and that lead, copper and iron ore abound to a considerable extent.

So far as we were able to do so with the small sum of money in our hands, it was also proposed to show, that Iowa is rich in geological exhibits; that fine and valuable specimens are continually being brought to light, which has attracted the attention of the scientific world. That vegetable fossils of many kinds and sizes, carboniferous and sub-carboniferous fossils and geodes, the finest yet seen, abound in Iowa. That in many parts of the state pre-historic remains and relics have been found in profusion.

The proposition was made, considered and carried out for the establishment of a model coal mine to represent, as nearly as possible, the methods of mining coal; also to represent the mining machinery and apparatus, including mining cars, tracks, etc., of some of the best mining works in the state.

Much work was performed in this direction, and a vast number of letters written, and Mr. Meers traveled over the state in various places to create an interest in this development upon the plan proposed; interviewed all those who were likely to furnish important information; saw the various mineral deposits; examined them in person; made arrangements with different operators of mines to send specimens and gained such information as would be necessary and best calculated to arrive at the result suggested and laid out to be done.

As rapidly as possible collections were made and placed for the accomplishment of the proposed purposes. Circulars and letters were sent out setting forth the plans named; giving the number of pieces and size of building stone and manufactured stone; the number of blocks and size of coal; the number of specimens requested from each county producing coal, and the size of each, with the number of tons of coal required for the purpose of the miniature mining operation.

Various samples of clays were procured from various sections of the state, and the amount to be furnished and directions given. Also samples of the manufactured product, burned and not burned, consisting of pottery, terra cotta ware, sewerage pipe, drainage tile and paving brick, together with the clays suitable for the manufacture of minerals, and as far as possible, examples of manufacturing produced with instructions relating to the samples of lime in bulk or otherwise, accompanied by samples from which the lime was manufactured, together with manufactured articles produced, when that was possible; together with samples of iron ore, copper, lead, zinc, mica, cannel coal, gypsum and other mineral deposits.

Circulars containing information necessary to accomplish these purposes were sent out everywhere in the state and a continuous effort was

IOWA EXHIBIT MINES AND MINING—PLATE II.

made to secure all of the specimens that were possible in each of the branches referred to.

Many of the persons seen promptly and enthusiastically responded to the request made of them; others seemed to take but little interest in the matter and to consider the mineral department of Iowa, a state which stands out so prominently, noted for its cattle, horses, hogs and corn, as of no great importance and not worthy of attention. I have to report, however, that nearly all the plans referred to were carried out and exhibits from nearly every line named were furnished, presented and put in place in the very crowded and limited space furnished by the Superintendent in charge of the Mines and Mining Building, which was not one-fourth the size demanded by Iowa.

It is not my purpose in making this report to state the various specimens that were presented and placed in this exhibit, and I have not sufficient space allotted me to do so if I desired; but I will mention one of the most attractive of all. The display of the coal mine, with a cast representing a man in the act of mining coal, with the entry rooms, track, pick, and miner's lamp, by every one who has ever seen a coal mine, was considered a remarkably fine display. Another that was well worthy of mention was that furnished by the ladies of Dubuque, showing a grotto with many beautiful specimens of lead ore, stalactites and stalagmites, fossils and numerous local specimens that were exceedingly attractive. Another very attractive display which also demanded attention was the collection of blocks of coal from twenty-seven coal producing counties in the state, built in a pyramidical form, on which was placed a fine miniature specimen of the works for operating a coal mine. Another very attractive specimen was a beautiful variegated marble mantel, which was admired by all who observed it.

For a fuller account of the Geology of Iowa reference is had to that part of the Hand-Book of Iowa prepared by the committee on Archæological, Historical and Statistical Information, Iowa Columbian Commission, published herewith.

Seven medals and seven diplomas were awarded to the mines and mining department of the World's Columbian Exhibition of Iowa exhibitors. A description of only six of these have been returned, as follows:

These were certified by the gentlemen of the Department of Mines and Mining February 17, 1894, as follows:

## AWARDS TO IOWA EXHIBITORS IN DEPARTMENT OF MINES AND MINING—WORLD'S COLUMBIAN EXPOSITION.

### GROUP 42.

Lansing Mining & Smelting Co., Lansing, Iowa—Lead ore from lower magnesian limestone.

### GROUP 43.

State of Iowa—Coal and Coke.

### GROUP 44.

State of Iowa—Marble and Building Stone.
Ft. Madison & Appanoose Stone Co., Ft. Madison—Building Stone.

GROUP 61.

Morgan, Kelly & Taneyhill, Waterloo—Well Drilling Machinery.

GROUP 65.

H. B. Sackett, Council Bluffs—**Sackett's Improved Coal Screen.**

GROUP 67.

Iowa World's Fair Board—Model of Coal Mine.

To mention names of all the exhibitors who were not awarded medals and diplomas, and to describe each of the localities and qualities of the rock, clays, sands, ores, etc., would take more space than can be spared for this report. In fact, it would require a book of itself, as these exhibits were very abundant and more than the space allotted to Iowa would permit.

In addition to the exhibit in the Mines and Mining Building, there were some fine exhibits, particularly of coal, in the Iowa building, which were well worthy of notice and description if space would permit.

I am satisfied that the Iowa exhibit in the Mineral department very greatly surprised people of the state and from all parts of the country who visited the exhibition and carefully examined Iowa's mineralogical and geological collection.

This state, situated between the two great rivers, in the very heart of the Mississippi valley and almost in the geographical center of the nation has a supply of useful minerals, with the exception of iron ore, far surpassing all but a very few of the states in the Union, and those who saw this exhibit, considering the very small sum allowed for the exhibit, expressed great satisfaction and astonishment.

JAMES O. CROSBY

# Report of the Department of Woman's Work.

BY JAMES O. CROSBY.

On the 4th day of May, 1892, the Commission resolved that there be created an Iowa Board of Lady Managers, to be composed of one member from each congressional district, and appointing the members and alternates of the National Board of Lady Managers as members of the Iowa Board for their respective districts; the others to be named by the Commissioners, each for his respective district, and Miss Ora E. Miller was elected by the Commission, President of the Board.

The Board was constituted of the following members: 1st district, Mrs. Eliza G. Rhodes, of Mt. Pleasant; 2d, Mrs. E. E. Cook, of Davenport; 3d, Miss Mary B. Hancock, of Dubuque; 4th, Mrs. N. C. Deering, of Osage; 5th, Miss Ora E. Miller, of Cedar Rapids; 6th, Mrs. Flora J. McAchran, of Bloomfield; 7th, Mrs. Whiting S. Clark, of Des Moines; 8th, Mrs. Orry H. Salts, of Corning; 9th, Mrs. Ira F. Hendricks, of Council Bluffs, who resigned shortly after her appointment, and Mrs. L. O. Ferson, of the same place, was appointed in her stead; 10th, Mrs. J. F. Duncombe, of Ft. Dodge, who was chosen by the Commission on failure of the Commissioner of that district to make selection; 11th, Miss Jennie E. Rogers, of Sioux City, who resigned in consequence of poor health and Mrs. A. M. Ainsworth of Onawa, was appointed to fill the vacancy.

At the same time that it was determined to create the Iowa Board of Lady Managers, a plan was adopted for raising additional funds through the Board by means of organizations of Township Clubs and County Societies, which were also designed for the preparation and collection of exhibits, and articles of association were framed for that purpose, as fol'ows:

## ARTICLES OF ASSOCIATION FOR IOWA WORLD'S FAIR COUNTY SOCIETIES.

### ARTICLE I.

This society shall be known as the..................County World's Fair Association.

### ARTICLE II.

SECTION 1. The object of this Association is to establish World's Fair Clubs in every city, town and village in the county where members can be obtained; to assist in providing funds for collecting and maintaining an exhibit from this county at the World's Columbian Exposition in 1893, in the Iowa State Building, under the control of the Iowa Columbian Commission, and in the general Exposition buildings. This association shall be auxiliary to the Iowa Columbian Commission, and execute its policy as far as possible,

SEC. 2. Any resident of this county is eligible to membership and may become a member thereof on payment of one dollar, and the secretary of the Iowa Columbian Commission shall issue to such person a certificate of membership, upon receipt of seventy cents thereof, the remaining thirty cents to be paid as hereinafter provided.

### ARTICLE III.

SECTION 1. The first meeting of this association shall be held at ........ ........on the .... day of ......, 1892, at ....o'clock .... M., at which time a majority of the members, when the number in the county equals 25, may elect by ballot a president, vice-president, secretary and treasurer, who shall hold their offices until the first day of January, 1893, and until their successors are elected and qualified.

SEC. 2. When a township or village club consists of fifteen members, and is organized by the election of a president, secretary and treasurer, the president thereof shall be a director in this association. The management of this association shall be vested in a Board of Directors, consisting of the president of such clubs within this county. A majority of the directors shall constitute a quorum for the transaction of business. They may choose an executive committee for the purpose of performing such duties as may be required by the board of directors.

SEC. 3. The regular meetings of the board of directors shall be held on ........day of each month.

### ARTICLE IV.

SECTION 1. It shall be the duty of the directors to secure as many members as possible in this association, and to organize World's Fair Clubs throughout the county, under such rules and local management as may be determined by the board of directors.

SEC. 2. The board of directors shall appoint a board of lady managers, consisting of one from each club of not less than 15 members, each of whom shall be a member of this association, and to provide such rules for their government and co-operation with this association, as they may deem best.

SEC. 3. The necessary expenses of this association and expenses attendant upon collecting and securing material for exhibition, shall be paid under the direction of this board, on the order of the president, attested by the secretary.

### ARTICLE V.

SECTION 1. The president shall preside over all meetings of the members and directors. He shall call a meeting of the board of directors whenever he deems it necessary, or when requested in writing by three directors. He shall sign all warrants on the treasurer for funds of the association, when authorized by a vote of the majority of the board of directors, or of the executive committee, if the authority shall be conferred on such committee by the board of directors.

The vice-president shall act in the absence or inability of the president. In the absence or inability of both to act, a temporary president may be chosen to perform the same duties.

SEC. 2. It shall be the duty of the secretary to keep a correct record of the proceedings of all meetings of the association, the board of directors and the executive committee. On the order of the president he shall issue calls for special meetings. He shall receive all moneys for the sale of certificates and contributions or otherwise and pay over the same as follows: 15 per cent to the treasurer of the club to which the member paying the same belongs; 15 per cent to the treasurer of this association, and 70 per cent to the secretary of the Iowa Columbian Commission. taking the receipts therefor, and entering, in a book kept for that purpose, the date and amount of such payments and receipts. He shall attest all warrants on the treasurer of this association duly authorized, that have been signed by the president. He shall distribute to the clubs all literature sent to him for that purpose by the Iowa Columbian Commission, and perform such other duties as may be required of him by the Board of Directors. At each monthly meeting of the board of directors he shall present a detailed statement of receipts and expenditures, and shall report each week to the secretary of the Iowa Columbian Commission the names and address of new members added, and remit to him the 70 per cent of membership fees, together with all matters of general interest connected with the work.

SEC. 3. The treasurer shall receive all moneys paid over to him by the secretary as above provided, giving his receipt therefor. He shall pay out the moneys only on the warrants of the president, attested by the secretary. He shall keep an accurate account of all receipts and disbursements, and preserve all vouchers for payments, and give such bond as shall be prescribed by the board of directors. He shall make a full and complete report at each monthly meeting of the board, and such other reports as may be required by such board.

SEC. 4. It shall be the duty of the executive committee to transact all business necessary to carry out the objects of this association, that may be required of them by the board of directors. They shall audit all bills and claims against the association.

### ARTICLE VI.

Robert's Rules of Order shall be the authority on all parliamentary questions not provided for in these articles.

### ARTICLE VII—AMENDMENTS.

These articles may be amended by a vote of the majority of the directors present at any regular meeting, provided specific notice, thereof, in writing, be given at the previous monthly meeting, except as to the apportionment of moneys received for certificates of membership.

### ARTICLE VIII.

SECTION 1. Any county association adopting the foregoing articles and forwarding a certified copy thereof to F. N. Chase, secretary of the Iowa Columbian Commission at Cedar Falls, Iowa, will become auxiliary to state organization, and entitled to all the privileges and benefits resulting therefrom, and upon payment of said 70 per cent of membership fees, will receive from him certificates of membership, enumerating special privileges to which the holder is entitled.

SEC. 2. We hereby certify that the foregoing articles were adopted at ............ in the county of ............ on the ......... day of .......... 1892.
................................., President
......... ............. ......, Secretary.

### ORDER OF BUSINESS.

The following is suggested as a convenient order of business:
1. Roll call.
2. Reading and approving minutes of previous meeting.
3. Reports of officers.
4. Reports of standing committees.
5. Reports of special committees.
6. Receiving communications.
7. Unfinished business.
8. New business.

### CERTIFICATE OF MEMBERSHIP.

"This is to certify that.................. has paid one dollar into the treasury of the World's Fair Association of .......... county, in the State of Iowa, and is a member thereof, and entitled to all the benefits and privileges appertaining thereto.   F. N. CHASE, Sec'y.
{ Seal of the }   Iowa Columbian Commission.
{ Commission. }

(Reverse Side.)

Companies of twenty, holding certificates of membership in this association, by arrangement to be previously made with the corresponding secretary at the Iowa headquarters in Jackson Park, Chicago, may have reliable boarding places engaged by an agent of the commission, be met by a guide at the railway station, on their arrival, and accompanied to their quarters so engaged; and, if desired, to be accompanied once from their quarters to the Iowa Building and through the Exposition grounds."

On the 29th day of June, 1892, the members of the Iowa Board of Lady Managers convened at Cedar Rapids and organized, the president, Miss Ora E. Miller, presiding. Mrs N. C. Deering was chosen vice-president; Mrs. E. G. Rhodes, secretary; Miss Mary B. Hancock, treasurer.

Executive Committee: Mrs. Ellen K. Cook, Miss Jennie E. Rogers and Mrs. J. F. Duncombe.

Auditing Committee: Mrs. Whiting S. Clark, Mrs. Flora J. McAchran and Mrs. Ira F. Hendricks.

Rules of order were adopted, and a resolution requiring the treasurer to keep separate accounts with each district of the proceeds of membership tickets, and that such funds be expended only for the use of the district in which the same were collected.

A committee was appointed who prepared and distributed the following circular "Address to the Women of Iowa by the Iowa Board of Lady Managers:"

## ADDRESS TO THE WOMEN OF IOWA BY THE IOWA BOARD OF LADY MANAGERS.

| | | |
|---|---|---|
| Miss Ora E. Miller, Cedar Rapids, | - - | President |
| Mrs. N. C. Deering, Osage, | - - | Vice-President |
| Mrs. Eliza G. Rhodes, Mt. Pleasant, | - - | Secretary |
| Miss Mary B. Hancock, Dubuque, | - - | Treasurer |

*To the Women of Iowa:*

The Iowa Board of Lady Managers desires to call your attention to our State Exhibition of women's work and through this circular to enlist your assistance and co-operation in securing for Iowa at the World's Columbian Exposition such a representation of woman's skill and industry as shall be second to none in America.

The Iowa Board of Lady Managers was created by a recent Act of the Iowa Columbian Commission, for the purpose of organizing throughout the State of Iowa, County World's Fair Associations and Clubs, and also for the purpose of securing a creditable exhibit of woman's work and achievements. The members of this Board are eleven in number, as follows:

Mrs. Eliza G. Rhodes, Mt. Pleasant, 1st Congressional District.
Mrs. Ellen K. Cook, Davenport, 2d Congressional District.
Miss Mary B. Hancock, Dubuque, 3d Congressional District.
Mrs. N. C. Deering, Osage, 4th Congressional District.
Miss Ora E. Miller, Cedar Rapids, 5th Congressional District.
Mrs. Flora J. McAchran, Bloomfield, 6th Congressional District.
Mrs. Whiting S. Clark, Des Moines, 7th Congressional District.
Mrs. Orry H. Salts, Corning, 8th Congressional District.
Mrs. L. O. Ferson, Council Bluffs, 9th Congressional District.
Mrs. John F. Duncombe, Ft. Dodge, 10th Congressional District.
Miss Jennie E. Rogers, Sioux City, 11th Congressional District.

To these members has been assigned the supervision of the woman's department in the congressional districts in which they respectively reside, and the organization of the above mentioned clubs.

It is their earnest desire that the exhibit of the Iowa Woman's Department shall compare favorably with the work of women of other states and shall reflect credit on the womanhood of Iowa. This board of eleven women can do very little toward effecting this great object unless they shall have the sympathy and active co-operation of all the intelligent women of our state.

They are the more in need of this co-operation because of the short time allotted them for this work and because of their hampered financial condition owing to the failure of the Iowa Legislature to appropriate any money for their use. We, therefore, earnestly appeal to the generous and public-spirited women of our state to come forward and help us. We can do nothing without your assistance; whereas, with it we can still hope to make the Iowa exhibit of woman's work such a one as will make every Iowa woman feel proud of the attainments of her sex.

Our desire is to exhibit at the World's Columbian Exposition of 1893 all articles which illustrate woman's share in the industrial, educational, artistic, religious and philanthropical activities of Iowa, especially to set forth said exhibit in such a manner as to indicate the progress which women have made in all these various departments during the comparatively few years of our state's existence.

It is a difficult task to enumerate all the lines of work in which women are engaged, and an attempt failing of completeness may possibly be misleading, but in order to point out some of the special representations of woman's industries and interests which the Iowa Board of Lady Managers desires to secure, we would especially ask your assistance in the following lines:

To secure for exhibition:

(a) Noticeably, fine specimens of every industry carried on by women in our state; this to embrace every department of woman's work.

(b) Copies of all books, pamphlets or newspapers now or heretofore written or edited by Iowa women.

(c) All books and papers illustrated by Iowa women.

(d) Scientific collections of every kind made by Iowa women, if of genuine scientific value.

(e) A list of all inventions made by Iowa women, and whenever possible small models of the same not exceeding twelve inches in any one dimension.

(f) Colonial relics owned by residents of Iowa.

(g) Statistical and graphic representations of the educational and charitable works of women; the graphic representations preferable, by means of maps so marked as to indicate the location of schools and charities operated in whole or in part by women.

(h) Representations for a historical exhibit of women's work, which will illustrate how Iowa women have grown with the state, beginning with the first achievements of women during Iowa's infancy, and illustrating her progress through the succeeding epochs of Iowa's growth.

Exhibitors in all departments of the exposition will be furnished blanks containing the question, "What per cent of labor was furnished by women?" The answer to this question will be used in the preparation of statistics that will entitle women to one or more members of the jury of award in each department.

The Iowa Board of Lady Managers also solicits the assistance of all Iowa women:

First. To encourage the organization of Iowa world's fair county associations in every county and world's fair clubs in every village and township in Iowa, the object of which is to provide state accommodation and protection for the benefit of the individual holding a certificate of membership in said associations or clubs; and also for the purpose of securing funds for collecting and maintaining an exhibit from each county in the Iowa State Building and in the general exposition buildings; and to place the people of the state in close communication with the state organizations engaged in world's fair work, and by means of club meetings to encourage the study of such subjects as will conduce to an intelligent and profitable understanding of the exposition.

Second. To urge upon the women of the state the advisability of entering the general competitive exhibits at the exposition.

Third. To secure works of superior merit for the gallery of honor in the Woman's Building.

The Iowa Board of Lady Managers will be pleased to receive suggestions and information relating to these subjects from the women of Iowa, and will esteem it a pleasure to render assistance in their power.

MARY B. HANCOCK, Chairman,<br>
MRS. WHITING S. CLARK,<br>
MRS. FLORA J. MCACHRAN,

Dubuque, July 25, 1892.   Committee on Circular Letter.

The following is a list of the congressional districts, the number of World's Fair organizations effected in each and the total membership therein:

First district: 10 societies, 308 members.
Second district: 4 societies, 170 members.
Third district: 7 societies, 366 members.
Fourth district: 7 societies, 194 members.
Fifth district: 1 society, 38 members.
Sixth district: None.
Seventh district: 1 society, 37 members.
Eighth district: 3 societies, 120 members.
Ninth district: 4 societies, 104 members.
Tenth district: 3 societies, 118 members.
Eleventh district: 2 societies, 103 members.
Making a total of 41 societies and 1558 members.

The total amount received for certificates of membership was $1558, of which 30 per cent was retained by the local societies. $545.30 was paid to the treasurer of the commission and expended in part payment of the sum of $1,291.41 expenses of the department of woman's work paid by the commission; and $545.30 was paid into the treasury of the Board of Lady Managers, who also received the additional sum of $25, a donation made from the first district. The whole amount $570.30 was expended in the respective districts from which it came.

Of the results accomplished by the Board of Lady Managers through these societies, Miss Ora E. Miller, the president, reports as follows:

"The women of these associations did a large amount of excellent work in making special exhibits, among which were the following:

Centerville, coke exhibit; Sioux City, splendid corn decorations; Iowa City, clock of Iowa marble, built in the form of the State University of Iowa; Vinton, carved table and chairs of native wood; Burlington, large birds-eye view of that city, done in oil, and framed in hand carved native wood frame; Ft. Dodge decorated two rooms in Iowa Building in cementico, a product of that vicinity; Dunlap, a massive carved chair; Decorah, a table of native marble; Mitchell County, a beautiful large banner; Dubuque, grotto of minerals; Maquoketa, exhibit of polished woods.

The school of corn cooking conducted by Iowa women was not only an attractive feature but very beneficial in promoting the interest in this great industry of the state.

In the Woman's Building, the Iowa women were well represented in the various congresses, musicales, arts and inventions, exhibits being in almost every department. Exceptionally fine was the exhibit in lace, receiving the award of first merit and competing successfully with a large amount of foreign competition. The exhibits of art, needle work, wood carving, ceramic, scientific taxidermy, inventions, designing, and literary work were well represented. The artistic corn decorations were excellent, as was attested by the fine awards received.

In the general departments throughout the fair the idea of sex was eliminated as far as possible, as in the educational, art, agricultural, and other departments, no distinction was made. The work of woman stood side by side with that of man, and was received and cared for without discrimination by the directors of the various departments. As there is no occupation which women are not engaged in, they were well represented, and have every reason to be proud of their united efforts."

There were additional exhibits made by societies, as follows:

Centerville, model of coal mine; Dubuque, lead ore, zinc and spar; Iowa City, clay and brick; Waukon, iron ore, limestone, marble, sandstone, sands, bricks, tile, potter's clay, and iron oxides.

Owing to the inefficiency of the commissioner in charge of this department, or his lack of adaptation to the work in hand, or from other causes, the plan of association organizations was not as thoroughly exploited and popularized throughout the state, and did not produce results as great, as he had anticipated.

H. W. SEAMAN.

# Report of the Department of Manufactures and Machinery.

BY HALLECK W. SEAMAN.

J. W. JARNAGIN.

# REPORT OF THE DEPARTMENT OF EDUCATION AND FINE ARTS.

### BY J. W. JARNAGIN.

When it was determined to make the Manufactures and Liberal Arts Building the most conspicuous on the ground, the plan contemplated that a large section of the first floor would be utilized for an exhibit of the schools and educational institutions of the world. It was afterwards discovered that the demand for space made by manufacturers was so much greater than contemplated in the original plans that it would be necessary to place the contemplated exhibits on the gallery floor. This brought forth a vigorous protest from the educators of the country and an attempt was made to induce the management to erect a separate building for the schools, colleges and various institutions of learning. The question was not decided for several months, and when a decision was reached but little change was made in the former plans. The fact that not half of the space was available that was demanded deprived those in charge of the educational exhibits of much enthusiastic support, and as a result the preparation of the work was encumbered with doubt and uncertainty which made progress both slow and expensive.

Under date of May 3, 1892, the following circular was issued:

*To the School Superintendents and Teachers of Iowa, Greeting:*

At the April meeting of the Iowa Columbian Commission, held in the city of Des Moines, the undersigned was appointed, on behalf of the Commission, to take charge of the work of arranging for the Iowa Educational Exhibit at the World's Fair.

The dedication of the buildings of the World's Columbian Exposition, to be held in Chicago will occur October 11, 12 and 13, 1892. The general reception of articles at the Exposition buildings will commence November 1, 1892, and no articles will be admitted after April 10, 1893.

It will thus be seen that less than a year remains for the preparation of an Educational exhibit that shall creditably represent the public school system of the state as well as other lines of educational work represented by the higher institutions of learning. All phases of intellectual development from the Kindergarten to the University are to be shown under the classification formulated by the World's Fair management and in harmony with the rules governing the same.

In addition to the exhibit made in the Department of Liberal Arts there will be a collective exhibit in the Iowa building which shall contain everything necessary to a full and complete exposition of the actual work done in the various grades of our public schools.

In all departments it is expected that the work exhibited will be specimens of the handiwork of the pupils themselves, free from any interference on the part of teachers and parents.

At the beginning of next school year this department will offer premiums for various lines of both individual and class work, for the purpose of enlisting the boys and girls of the Iowa schools in friendly rivalry in preparing the very best specimens of their work for the Columbian Exposition.

### SYSTEM OF CLASSIFICATION.

From the system of classification adopted by the World's Fair management the following under the head of Primary, Secondary and Superior Education will best indicate the scope and extent of the proposed educational exhibit:

Class 841. ELEMENTARY INSTRUCTION.—Infant schools and kindergartens. Descriptions of the methods of instruction, with statistics.

Class 842.—PRIMARY SCHOOLS, CITY AND COUNTRY.—School houses and furniture. Apparatus and fittings. Models and appliances for teaching, text-books, diagrams, examples. Specimens of work in elementary schools.

Class 843. DOMESTIC AND INDUSTRIAL TRAINING FOR GIRLS. Models and apparatus for the teaching of cookery, housework, washing and ironing, needle-work and embroidery, dressmaking, artificial flower-making, painting on silk, crockery, etc. Specimens of school work.

Class 844.—HANDICRAFT TEACHING IN SCHOOLS FOR BOYS. Apparatus and fittings for elementary trade teaching in schools. Specimens of school work.

Class 845. SCIENCE TEACHING.—Apparatus and models for elementary science instruction in schools. Apparatus for chemistry, physics, mechanics, etc.; diagrams, copies, text-books, etc.; specimens of the school work on these subjects.

Class 846.—ART TEACHING.—Apparatus, models and fittings for elementary art instruction in schools; diagrams, copies, text-books, etc.; specimens of art work, modeling etc., in schools.

Class 847.—TECHNICAL AND APPRENTICESHIP SCHOOLS.—Apparatus and examples used in primary and secondary schools for teaching handicraft; models, plans and designs for the fitting up of workshop and industrial schools; results of industrial work done in such schools

Class 848—Special schools for the elementary education of Indians.

Class 849. EDUCATION OF DEFECTIVE CLASSES.—Schools for the deaf, dumb, blind and feeble-minded; adult schools for the illiterate.

Class 850.—PUBLIC SCHOOLS.—Descriptions, illustrations, statistics, methods of instruction, etc.

Class 851.—HIGHER EDUCATION. Academies and high schools; descriptions and statistics. Colleges and universities; descriptions, illustrations of the buildings, libraries, museums, collections, courses of study, catalogues, statistics, etc.

Class 852.—PROFESSIONAL SCHOOLS. Theology, law, medicine and surgery, dentistry, pharmacy; mining, engineering, agriculture, mechanic arts; art and design; military, naval, normal, commercial; music.

The Iowa Columbian Commission will render all possible assistance in the furtherance of the work necessary to make a display that is in keeping with our advanced position in educational matters. The limited means at its disposal makes enthusiasm on the part of the educators of the state a prime necessity in the work.

I will at all times work in harmony with the State Teachers' Association and other educational organizations and I solicit the assistance of all who believe with me, that Iowa's educational exhibit should be second to none at that great gathering of the Nations of the World.

Very respectfully,

J. W. JARNAGIN.

The first move made by the Iowa Columbian Commission looking toward an exhibit of its public school work was the decision to offer three hundred dollars in premiums, to be given to the schools meeting the conditions imposed, at a preliminary contest to be held at Cedar Rapids during the meeting of the State Teachers' Association in December, 1892. A committee was appointed to draft a premium list that should conform as far as possible to the requirements imposed by the chief of the Department of Liberal Arts. Circulars were issued setting forth this feature of the State Teachers' Association and at the appointed time a suitable room was procured and the work of the school children of Iowa was placed on exhibition in friendly rivalry in the laudable effort to gain some of the premiums offered. The following is the report of the committee appointed to pass upon the work:

*To Hon. J. W. Jarnagin, Representative of the Iowa Columbian Commission:*

The committee appointed by you to examine the exhibits made by the schools of Iowa at Cedar Rapids in connection with the Iowa State Teachers' association December 29, 1892, and to make the awards as set forth in your premium list, a copy of which accompanies this report, begs leave to report as follows:

We have examined the exhibits as carefully as the magnitude of the work and the time at our disposal have allowed and wish to say, first, that those who have responded to your invitation and have presented work for inspection have manifested a degree of enterprise in this work that deserves high commendation. Second, the display is to be especially commended in that it makes decidedly a nearer approach to an exhibition of actual school work than is usual in exhibitions of this character. Much of the honor for this is due to the committee which prepared the classification under which the exhibits were prepared. Much honor in this regard is also due to those who prepared and presented work that wasn't called for in the classification; third, much credit is due to the county superintendents and teachers of rural schools who have presented work, some of which compares favorably with work from graded schools; fourth, the cities of Sioux City, Iowa City, Oskaloosa and Cedar Rapids presented excellent work which was not entered in competition for prizes, but simply as an exhibition of the work being done in the public schools of those cities. The displays from these cities were very full in all lines of work that can be properly presented.

A novel and valuable feature was the phonographic representation of class exercises by the schools of Sioux City. In the judgment of the committee this plan of presenting work might be extensively employed with much advantage.

In the exhibits under each number in the classification, three awards were made, when the number of exhibits was sufficient. The awards have been designated first, second and third respectively.

The accompanying schedule will indicate with sufficient clearness the judgment of the committee in the matter of awards:

### GENERAL EXHIBITS.

1. Best exhibit of country school work from any county, $15: Poweshiek county first, Greene county second, Buena Vista county third.

2. Best exhibit from any country school, $15: District No. 8, Nokomis township, Buena Vista county, first; second best, $10, District No. 2, Blue Grass township, Scott county; third best, District No. 5, Adams township, Greene county.

3. Best exhibit of school work from any town or city, $25: Cedar Falls first, Mason City second, Clinton third.

4. Best exhibit of school work of one pupil, $10: Minnie Shafer, Cedar Falls, first; Daisy Heath, Brooklyn, second; Emma Gulbrauson, District No. 8, Nokomis township, Buena Vista county, third.

5. Best display from a manual training school, $15: Davenport.

### CLASS A—WRITTEN WORK.

1. Best collection of examination papers in United States history, physiology, geography, and arithmetic, $15; Cedar Falls first, Marengo second, McGregor third.

2. Best collection of examination papers in any one branch, $10: Clinton first, McGregor second, Oskaloosa third.

3. Best collection of letters or composition from any one class, $15: Clinton first and second, Mason City third.

4. Best condensation of fifty-word exercise into a telegram, $5: Mason City.

### CLASS B—DRAWING.

1. Best set of illustrative drawings from any one class in any branch not to exceed four by same pupil, $10: Maquoketa first, Adair second, $5, Clinton third.

2. Best collection of free-hand drawing from any school, not to exceed one from each pupil, $10; second, $5: Maquoketa first, Waverly second, Mason City third.

3. Best collection of original designs from any school, not more than one from the same pupil. $10: Waverly first, Cresco second $5.

4. Best collective exhibit in drawing from any school, not more than one drawing from the same pupil, $20: Mason City first, Waverly second $10, Orange City third.

### CLASS C—APPARATUS.

1. Best collection of illustrative apparatus made by the pupils of any school, $10: Montezuma first, Cedar Falls second.

EDUCATIONAL EXHIBIT LIBERAL ARTS GALLERY. PLATE I.

2. Best chart of graphic presentation of schemes or methods of work used by any teacher, $10; Miss Elma R. Combs, Cedar Falls; second best, $5, Mason City; third, Clinton.

Same by superintendent. $10: S. W. Heath, County Superintendent Poweshiek.

3. Best graphic scheme of statistical information concerning any district, $10: Cedar Falls first, Buena Vista County second.

### CLASS D—PHOTOGRAPHY.

1. Best collection of photographs of schools in working order, $10: Clinton first, Cedar Falls second, Fairfield third.

2. Best collection of photographs of school buildings and grounds, $10: Fairfield first.

3. Best collection of photographs illustrating courses and methods, $10: Clinton first, Cedar Falls second.

Respectfully submitted,    J. J. McCONNELL,
J. A. BISHOP,
Committee.

The work thus passed upon was taken as a nucleus for Iowa's educational exhibit at the Columbian Exposition. The preliminary exhibit cost in premiums, rent for room, help, etc., something near $700.

No sooner had the enthusiasm kindled by this exhibit commenced to spread, than a renewed agitation began for a separate building for the school exhibits at the World's Fair; and so determined were educators to carry their point that many conventions, round tables and associations passed resolutions declaring it to be the purpose of the members thereof to refrain from taking any part in preparing exhibits unless the new building was guaranteed by the management of the Columbian Exposition. This determined effort counteracted about all the inspiration that came from the preliminary exhibit and made the question of a creditable educational exhibit from Iowa extremely problematical. About this time the colleges of Iowa were resolving not to take part in the work if the World's Fair was to be kept open on Sunday. The uncertainty surrounding the solution of that question was so great that the colleges maintained this determination and prepared nothing.

In the face of all this opposition the work of preparing the exhibit was prosecuted with all diligence. The determination for a new building was finally abandoned and two thousand feet of space was set aside as Iowa's territory in the gallery of the Liberal Arts Building. Afterwards Germany demanded more room for her educational exhibit and three hundred feet were taken from Iowa in order that this demand might be met.

When the Exposition was opened on May 1, 1893, the exhibit was practically ready for the inspection of the world. The following schools were represented:

Des Moines, West Side—Photographs of buildings, interior of buildings, pupils at work, kindergarten work; drawings from the first to the eighth grade, and from high school; manual training; model of cooking apparatus; cooking exhibits.

What Cheer—Five regular solids.

Iowa City—Drawing; twelve bound volumes representing paper folding, parquetry, manuscript, geography, language, essays, drawings, arithmetic; letter writing; seven relief maps.

Corning—One bound volume of penmanship.

State Center—Eight bound volumes representing primary work, geography, history, arithmetic, language numbers and physiology; clay modeling.

Three bound volumes representing arithmetic, geography and language.

Davenport—Manual training; mechanical drawings by pupils.

Orange City—Drawings from different grades.

Burlington—Drawings from the first to the eighth grade and high school; ten bound volumes, representing spelling, numbers, arithmetic, penmanship, language, grammar, word analysis, mathematics, United States history, civics, English literature, geography, physiology, science, Latin and German; paper folding. Photographs of buildings and interiors.

Fairfield—Three bound volumes of mathematics, language and science; photographs of buildings, exterior and interior.

McGregor—Six bound volumes of numbers, geography, geometry, physiology, language, United States history, algebra, German.

Cresco—Six volumes of penmanship.

Monmouth—One volume of geography.

Des Moines, East Side—Thirty volumes of history, geography, grammar, language, arithmetic, numbers, civics, algebra, rhetoric, chemistry; product map of Iowa; product map of the United States; product map of South America.

Waverly—Drawings; kindergarten work; product map of Iowa; photographs of buildings and interior; thirteen volumes of geography, language, algebra, physics, rhetoric, geometry, literature, arithmetic, reading, numbers, German, Latin, history, physiology and spelling.

Grinnell—Drawing from grades and high school; studies in biology.

Mason City—Drawings and color work; five volumes of arithmetic, physiology, history, penmanship, geography and language.

Brooklyn—Photographs of buildings, interiors and pupils at work; drawings from several grades; one volume of history, mathematics and geography.

Ottumwa—Photographs of buildings; drawings from the first to the eighth grade and high school; six volumes of penmanship and drawings.

Fort Madison—Kindergarten work; photographs of buildings.

Marengo—Four volumes arithmetic, algebra, physiology, literature, geography, history, political economy.

Montezuma—Eight volumes of history, physiology, astronomy, book-keeping, geography, geometry, physics, picture stories; photographs of buildings, interior and pupils at work; map showing number and location of school houses in the state.

Mount Pleasant—Color drawings; four volumes of primary work, botany and miscellaneous.

Maquoketa—Four volumes of botanical drawings.

Poweshiek County—Examination papers; one volume of rural school work drawings; photographs of country school houses and schools; glass model of country school house.

Clinton—Photographs of building, interior and pupils at work and charts of course of study; twenty-three volumes of composition, drawing, geometry, physics, algebra, arithmetic, botany, language, color, U. S. history, grammar, geography, physiology, German, Latin, English, geology, kindergarten; drawings from all grades.

Clinton County—Photographs of country schools and school houses.

Oskaloosa—Four globes; ten relief maps; twelve volumes of number work; geography, language, arithmetic, U. S. history, English, narcotics, rhetoric, Latin, music, physics, drawings, reports, records, diplomas, courses of study; drawings.

Cedar Falls—Statistical and comparative charts; photographs of different grades at work; photographs of calisthenic exercises; ten volumes of geography, penmanship, examination papers, physical culture; four geographical maps.

Marshall County—Three volumes of arithmetic, language, history, geography; drawings and photographs of country schools.

Boone County—Two volumes of botany, physical geography and miscellaneous drawings.

Ogden—One volume of miscellaneous.

Paulina—One volume of geography and language; one relief map of North America.

Newell—Drawings.

Malcom—Drawings.

Hardin County—Drawings.

Greene County—Drawings.

Erie Schools—Drawings.

State Department—Photographs of officers of State Teachers' Association; one volume of work from country schools, annual reports, blanks, school laws, photographs from state department; Iowa school system; Iowa school statistics; Iowa teacher's institute; comparative statistics; summary of finances; summary of statistics; enumeration, enrollment and attendance; school houses, number and value; teachers, sexes; bound volumes of official reports.

Sioux City—Clay modeling; phonographic records of public school work of different grades; photographs of school buildings and pupils; photographs of physical culture; drawings.

Creston—Photographs of buildings.

Marshalltown—Photographs of buildings.

Chariton—Photographs of buildings.

Normal School—Drawings; photographs of buildings, interior and faculty; military photographs; physical science apparatus from laboratory; bound volumes of exercises in geometry; thesis on zoology and elementary science; bound reports and catalogues; charts showing grounds of the school; Delsarte exercises.

The work shown attracted the favorable attention of the educators of this and foreign countries. The commissioners from France and Germany

EDUCATIONAL EXHIBIT LIBERAL ARTS GALLERY PLATE II.

solicited part of the exhibit to take home with them to be used in normal training, and the proposed Columbian Museum applied for part of it as did also the Philadelphia Educational Museum and the National Bureau at Washington.

It was an exhibit of actual public school work and as such made a most favorable impression upon those who were interested in studying our school system.

The following awards were made by the World's Fair authorities as shown by the official records:

Public schools Montezuma—high school work.
Public schools, Iowa City—drawing and history.
Public schools, Davenport—mechanical drawing.
West side public schools, Des Moines—photos of pupils at work, manual training, cooking school and kindergarten.
East side public schools, Des Moines—product maps, history, scientific papers, literature, geography, etc.
Public schools, Clinton—grammar and high school work.
Public schools, Waverly—school and kindergarten work.
State of Iowa, educational exhibit of public schools—charts of comparative statistics.
Public schools, Montezuma—map of Iowa showing location of schools.
Public schools, Maquoketa—botanical drawings.
Public schools, Sioux City—phonographic records of school work of all grades and clay modeling.
Public schools, Mt. Pleasant—primary work.
Public schools, Ottumwa—penmanship and drawing.
Public schools, Oskaloosa—primary, grammar and high schools.
Public schools, State Center—primary and grammar work.
Iowa State Normal school, Cedar Falls—physical science apparatus.
Public schools, Paulina—relief map of North America.
Country schools of Iowa—chart of comparative statistics.
Public schools, Burlington—school work of all grades.
Trustees Cornell college—courses of study, work and results.
Powshiek county—photographs of country schools.
Marshall county—photographs of country schools.
Clinton county—photographs of country schools.
S. W. Heath, Superintendent of Poweshiek county, glass model of country school house.

## FINE ARTS.

In the interest of the Fine Arts department the following circular letter was published:

"*To the Artists of Iowa, Greeting:*

There will be an exhibit of paintings by Iowa artists at Cedar Rapids, Tuesday, Wednesday and Thursday, December 27, 28 and 29, 1892.

The object of this exhibit is two-fold:

First. To give to those who desire to exhibit their work at the World's Fair an opportunity to have it passed upon by a jury of artists in order that the possibility of its rejection may not be so great when sent to Chicago, as everything intended for the Department of Fine Arts must pass under the scrutiny of a jury of art'sts in that city.

Second. For the advancement of art in Iowa, and the benefit of Iowa artists. This will be the only opportunity offered before the World's Fair to show what Iowa artists can do, and to create an interest in art throughout the state.

### RULES GOVERNING THE EXHIBIT.

All exhibits will be limited to original work.

Pictures must be packed, shipped and delivered at Cedar Rapids, Iowa, at the risk and expense of the exhibitor, not later than December 22.

All paintings will be taken in charge by reliable and competent persons and hung in a favorable light, with suitable colored back-ground.

The paintings will be insured against loss or damage by fire while on exhibition, without expense to the owner, and will be repacked and returned to the owner at the expense of this department.

If desired, and so stated by the exhibitor, the merits of the pictures will be considered by the Advisory State Board before formal application is made to the Columbian Exposition in Chicago.

Those selected for exhibition at the World's Fair will be carefully packed, safely stored away and kept well insured by this department unless the owner desires the same returned. In all cases definite instructions as to the above should accompany the work.

Paintings will be catalogued and numbered.

Attendants will be in charge who will attend to the sale of pictures, without expense to the exhibitor, in case the owner desires to part with them. The price at which pictures are offered for sale must be stated by the owner.

Pictures should be plainly marked on the back with the name and address of the owner.

The exhibit will be under the direction of Miss Ora E. Miller, President of the Iowa Board of Lady Managers, Cedar Rapids, to whom all pictures should be addressed and to whom all communications touching the exhibit should be sent.

### SPECIAL TO IOWA ARTISTS.

This exhibit is open only to Iowa artists. The time for preparation is short and immediate action is necessary. It will be an excellent opportunity to witness the work executed by both professionals and amateurs and you are cordially invited to not only exhibit your work but to visit Cedar Rapids and behold the handiwork of others

The exhibit being held during the meeting of the State Teachers' Association the railroads of the state will give a rate of one and one-third fare to all who desire to attend. Procure certificates at the place of purchasing tickets.                                  J. W. JARNAGIN,

In charge of Department of Fine Arts."

Montezuma, Iowa, December 5, 1892."

When the time came for collecting specimens of the handiwork of Iowa artists it was discovered that there was no organization through which to work, as no association of artists had ever been formed. It was determined to invite the artists of the state to send the best specimens of original work to Cedar Rapids and exhibit them there at the preliminary educational exhibit. Miss Ora E. Miller visited a number of places and succeeded in creating considerable interest in the undertaking. When the time came for the opening of the preliminary exhibit a large number of paintings were available and Hon. D. N. Richardson, of Davenport, and Hon. W. A. Lyons, of Iowa City, were appointed to pass upon them and indicate which ones were worthy a place in the Iowa collection at the World's Fair. At the same time an organization was formed whereby the artists of the state might become better acquainted and the interest in the proposed exhibit materially enhanced. This created considerable enthusiasm and the assembly room in the Iowa building bore witness to the result during the great Exposition. The following is a

LIST OF PAINTINGS IN THE IOWA STATE BUILDING.

Julia I. Leonard, Decorah—"Iowa Scenery."
Mrs. M. Van Cise, Clear Lake—"Shadows of the Past," "Sketch from Nature."
Mrs. E. A. Jarrett, Des Moines—"Still Life—Violin," "Portrait," "Dutch Subject."
Johannes Scheiwe, Ottumwa—"Cinderilla Guided by a Page to the King's Ball."
Oscar Coast, Iowa City—Two paintings.
Mrs. Gorham, Council Bluffs—"Iowa Cattle."
Portrait of the late Mrs. McKee, of Centerville; presented by the Traveling Men of Iowa.
Mrs. Alma Glasgow White, Washington—"An Old Elm Log," "The Wood-Choppers," "Stack Field," "The Last Shock," "Iowa Corn."
C. E. Baldwin, Des Moines—"The Bird Slayer," "Portrait of Mr. S."
F. Seimetz, Dubuque—"Peonies," "Portrait of Gen. Jones."
Miss Mattie A. Isherwood, Mt. Vernon—"After a Nap," "Still Life," "Fruit."
Geo. W. Carver, Ames—"Yucca and Cactus."
Bianca Wheeler, Davenport—"Iowa Corn," "Scene in France."
J. M. Huiskamp, Keokuk—"Squirrels and Powder Horn," "Ducks and Powder Flask."
May McClure, Mt. Pleasant—"Kentucky Beech Woods."
Mary E. Price, Sioux City—"Sleeping Cupid," "Ruins of Karnak, Egypt."
Mrs. W. A. Liston, Indianola—"Phyllocactus."
Roscoe L. Mark, Davenport—"A Grey Day."
Miss Laura George, Des Moines—"Fishing near Venice."
Mrs. I. M. Kimball, McIntyre—"Oil Sketch."
Mrs. Ella Lyon, Iowa City—"Grapes."
Luetta B. James, Des Moines—"Iowa Prairie," "Ossipee Mountains."
Frances Schaffer, Davenport—"Cattle."
Helen A. Snow, Keystone—"Horse."
Mrs. K. K. Starr, Algona—"Roses."
Miss E. M. Budd, Des Moines—"Roses."
Hattie J. Stimmel, Iowa City—"Landscape"—2; "Study of Head," "Corn."
Mrs. M. A. Adams, Mason City—"Golden Rod and Astors."
Viola Gardner Brown, Marengo—"Masquawott," "Portrait."
Gertrude Witmer, Des Moines—"Quaint Old Brick Yard," "Still Life."
Bertha S. Stacy, Indianola—"Still Life," "Rabbit."
Francis M. Bemis, Davenport—"Iowa Apples."
Mamie Macy, Des Moines—"Roses."

EDUCATIONAL EXHIBIT LIBERAL ARTS GALLERY PLATE III

Mrs. Gorham, Council Bluffs "Cows."
W. Ullmer, Des Moines—"Portrait."
Bessie M. H. Robert, Grinnell "Life Study."
Mrs. W. M. Price, Des Moines "Group of Old Books," "Bunch of Lilacs," "Group of Shells."
D. J. Gue, Ft. Dodge—"Stacking Oats," "Portrait of Mrs. Coffin."
Dr. A. C. Roberts, Ft. Madison—"Portrait of Black Hawk."

## MISCELLANEOUS.

The Home for the Feeble Minded at Glenwood made an excellent presentation of the work done by the inmates of that institution. The exhibit made was studied by representatives from similar institutions in other states and much favorable comment was heard touching the excellency of the work done. This institution also had an exhibit in the Liberal Arts building along with the work displayed by similar institutions from other states.

The School for the Deaf at Council Bluffs was represented by work done in the school room and also by specimens from the manual training departments, together with a full set of photographs of pupils at work, buildings, etc. The work shown was displayed in a handsome glass case and attracted the attention of visitors and the commendation of those specially interested in caring for the unfortunates who did the work.

The College for the Blind at Vinton was represented by a splendid exhibit of all work done in the school. There were bound volumes of manuscript work done by the pupils, showing the peculiar characters used; fancy work wrought by those who are deprived of sight, and articles of utility from the work shop. This exhibit was one of the most interesting in the building and the skill required in producing it was the subject for much discussion touching the acuteness of special senses when required to do double work.

While the Department of Liberal Arts and Fine Arts was not represented so lavishly as some others, it has been clearly proven that educational advancement in Iowa has kept pace with the great and growing industries of our commonwealth and oftentimes leads them, and that in the midst of our rapid strides in material advancement, æsthetical culture has not been wholly neglected. The part Iowa took at the World's Fair in the presentation of our culture and refinement was a revelation to many from the older states and an inspiration to our own people.

Respectfully submitted,
J. W. JARNAGIN,
In charge of Department of Liberal Arts and Fine Arts.
Montezuma, Iowa, June 7, 1894.

A. C. ROBERTS, M. D.

# Report of the Committee on Forestry, Photography and Corn Food.

### BY A. C. ROBERTS, M. D.

During the existence of the Exposition I was held responsible for the departments of Forestry and Photography, by the direction of our Commission; but as I came in so late as a member, I must beg indulgence for the paucity of the exhibits in these departments.

The Hon. Edward Johnstone, the first President of the Board, died before the departments for exhibits were assigned to individual members. He was succeeded by the Hon. Theo. Guelich, to whom was assigned these departments; but he also died before he was able to do much and before the Exposition was inaugurated. The First District of Iowa was most fortunate in securing the appointment of such able men and most unfortunate in their deaths.

I will attempt to give you what little was done in the departments of Forestry and Photography, for our great State of Iowa, in the Columbian Exposition, the greatest exposition of the world.

## FORESTRY.

Before I was a member of the State Board, as I learned by the kindness of Hon. J. W. Jarnagin, of Montezuma, the member from the Sixth District, "each state was asked to contribute specimens of its timber to be used as supports for the colonnade of the Forestry Building. This contemplated such varieties as would best represent the various native woods and those which were of the most commercial value. Ten pieces were sent from Iowa. The three long ones were twenty-five feet long, eighteen inches in diameter at the base and twelve inches at the smaller end. As far as possible they were to be free from knots and limbs and as straight as could be selected. The seven small ones were each twenty-five feet long and twelve inches in diameter at one end and eight at the other, also free from knots and crooks. The varieties sent were Walnut, Red Elm, White Oak, Red Oak, Linden, Shell-bark Hickory, Hackberry, Maple, Cottonwood and White Walnut. These pieces were all placed in position as columns in the colonnade of the Forestry Building and properly labeled. They were representative of our native trees and in variety and quality ranked with the specimens sent from states much more noted for forestry."

This is in accordance with the records and facts. Besides these, there was no opportunity to exhibit to the world, outside of the Iowa Building, any of the wonderful examples of the forestry of our great prairie state; as the Forestry Building was closed for exhibits before I was appointed to the duty, or at least before I had time to prepare specimens for exhibit there.

It was perhaps as well, as the naturally wooded states and nations would probably have greatly outdone us in the competitive exhibit of woods in the Forestry Building, however complete ours could have been made.

I contined my brief effort to an exhibit, in the Iowa Building, of as many and good specimens as I could procure in the short time of the second growth of timber of our state, so as to show to the world how quickly a prairie state can be sufficiently wooded, as our state has been, in the few short years of its existence. In this I believe we excelled all other states. I placed on exhibit there the following specimens of

### SECOND GROWTH WOODS:

Oak: genus quercus; varieties; q. alba, nigra and rubrum.
Ash: genus fraxinus; varieties; f. alba, nigra and excelsor.
Hickory: genus carya; varieties; c. alba, glabra, amara and nigra.
Elm: genus ulmus; varieties; u. Americana, alba and fulva.
Cottonwood: populis manifolia.
Maple: genus acer; varieties; a. sacharinum and a. rubrum.
Locust: genus robinia; varieties; r. pseudacacia; also honey locust, genus tricanthos.
Walnut: genus juglans; j. nigra and cinerea.
Buttonwood or plane tree: plantanus occidentalis.
Mulberry: genus morus; variety; alba.
Hackberry: Celtis Occidentalis.
Basswood: Tilia Americana.
Willow: genus salix; variety—
Paw Paw: genus asimina.
Cherry: genus prunus; variety; p. Virginiana
Birch: genus betula; variety; b. alba
Poplar: genus populus; varieties; p. alba and nigra, with a few other woods that have escaped my memory and also that of Mr. McMillen, who procured all these woods for me. (Unfortunately the copy, prepared carefully, from which the labels on the woods were printed is lost, and none of the printed labels were preserved, except such as may remain on the specimens now at Cornell College.)

These specimens of Iowa second growth trees were all prepared in the usual manner to exhibit their qualities as useful and ornamental woods, and especially so as to show their rapid growth. Though hastily selected and prepared, all from the green and growing trees, these specimens attracted much attention from the many thousands of people who visited the Iowa Building, acknowledged to have been the most interesting state building on the grounds of the whole number of state buildings there, so far as the exhibition of the principal resources of states were concerned. People from the naturarally wooded states and the thousands of people from foreign countries, who had always read of Iowa as a prairie state, were surprised at the exhibit that a new prairie state could make in forestry, even though the exhibit was scarcely half perfect. They wondered that a vast area, so short a time ago a sea of grass, could exhibit such specimens of cultured wood, and they were led readily to believe, what all Iowans told them, that now a person walking or riding across our state would not know from observation that Iowa was but a few short years ago a prairie state, a vast field of meadow, except on a narrow margin of our streams and on the adjacent bluff sides.

I was indebted to Mr. McMillen, of Van Buren county, for the selection of the specimens. Mr. McMillen is engaged, and has been for several years, in shipping woods from Iowa to Europe. He selects, prepares and ships annually 500,000 feet of black walnut and as much of other woods to Hamburg, Liverpool and other European ports, and his is not the only firm in Iowa engaged in the same business. He says: "The specimens I furnished you for the Exposition have all grown on the prairies within the last forty years; the specimen of osage orange was thirty-five years old only; and the specimen of solid and good tough white ash was only twenty-five years old and a foot in diameter." Mr. McMillen makes another remark in a letter to me as follows: "The large trees are fast disappearing from the borders of the streams of Iowa; but there is a fine growth of natural young timber coming on which I think ought to be preserved by the owners of the land. The older trees are mostly damaged by the prairie fires of an early day and are defective and dying out."

This brings us to remark that in the exhibit at the Iowa Building was a specimen of all the woods of Iowa, old and new growth, in small and carefully prepared and polished specimens, kindly furnished by the Ladies' Club of Monticello, Iowa. We had, therefore, on exhibition, a very fair representation of our Iowa Forestry, though it was confined to the Iowa Building and did not come in prize competition with the Forestry of other states.

At the earnest solicitation of the President of Cornell College, of this state, all the forestry exhibit, including that from Monticello, was given to it and was shipped at the close of the Exposition, at the expense of the College, to where it is now, no doubt, an exhibit for the benefit of its students and subject to the inspection of all our people.

About the matter of

## PHOTOGRAPHY.

I labored under the same difficulty that I did in the Forestry Department, of my duty. Mr. Guelich, however, had offered prizes to the photographers of the state for an exposition of their art. Comparatively few responded. The competitive photographs were placed in the Iowa Building. Three prizes were offered and were won by C. F. Bush, of Dubuque, first prize, $50; W. H. Morhizer, Dubuque, second prize, $30, and Grosheim Bro's., Muscatine, third prize, $20, in accordance with Mr. Guelich's offer.

Besides the photographs that competed, there were many others placed on exhibition in the Iowa Building, representing nearly all the various state buildings and several cities, all exhibiting the highest skill of the art.

Besides there were in the artistic line two large maps of Iowa cities on exhibit, one representing Burlington and one Fort Madison.

The finest specimens of the photographic art, not prize exhibits, and unique in themselves, were exhibited by Monfort and Hill of Burlington; their *genre* photographs, which drew much attention, their fine frames first attracting notice and then the excellent pictures themselves forcing a long study and great pleasure from many thousands of visitors.

## MAIZE AS A FOOD.

Having been deeply interested and therefore urgent in having the exhibition of Indian Corn, the principal production of grain in our state, on the walls of the Iowa Building, after the manner of the Sioux City corn palace, and also in having the use of Indian Corn, in all its food forms, practically exhibited to all the United States and to the whole world generally, a little before the last month of the Fair I was made chairman of a committee for the corn food exhibit in our proud Iowa Building. The decoration was done before the Exposition opened and was most beautifully done by Messrs. Milward & Clark, of Sioux City, exclusive and really artistic in that line, and it made the Iowa Building, more than any other state building, attractive to all the multitude that visited the grounds. This having been done it only remained to show that maize was good for something besides hog, cattle and horse feed.

Mrs Mary Scott, good wife of Hon. John Scott, of Story county, Iowa, came to our aid most nobly and persuaded Mrs. Emma P. Ewing, of New York, to volunteer her most valuable service to give the people of the world practical lessons in Indian Corn cooking for human food. Daily, from 11 a. m. to 12 for a month, Mrs. Ewing, ably assisted by Mrs. Scott, showed to the people what an appetizing and delicate as well as nourishing food could be made from Indian Corn. A corn banquet was served, at which many foreigners partook, some for the first time of that kind of food, and the universal opinion was that it was most excellent. During the daily lectures Mrs. Ewing and Mrs. Scott gave the products of their cooking of corn, as far as it would reach, to the multitude always assembled in the Iowa Building, and the universal regret was that this part of the program had not been started sooner, so as to have exhibited to more people that Indian Corn not only makes good bread and common food, but that it is capable of being made into many of the most delicate of nourishing and appetizing viands.

Mrs. Ewing and Mrs. Scott were unanimously voted by the Board of Commissioners hearty thanks and also a gold medal each, properly engraved, for their intelligent and arduous labors.

There is no doubt now that the grain exhibit in the Iowa Building, beautifying as it did the pavilion and chiefly filling its space, with the practical lectures on Indian Corn as human food, were the greatest attractions and were of the greatest benefit to Iowa of all the efforts to benefit the state by exhibits, of whatever kind, in the great Columbian Exposition.

I may be permitted here to give from our state statistics such advertisement and permanency as this report may have to the production of Indian Corn for last year, (1893):

The average yield of this crop was 35.7 bushels per acre. This is about three bushels above the average of the past fifteen years. The number of acres planted, as shown by the reports of assessors and correspondents, was 6,016,940, producing a total yield of 214,804,758 bushels, which was over 40,-000,000 bushels in excess of the product of 1892.

As I, as Commissioner, never drew from the fund any money on requisition, I have no account to render as required by the Board resolutions. All the expenses for the departments under my control were paid on vouchers, duly audited. The expense was very little, as will be seen in the final accounting.

CHARLES ASHTON.

# Report of Committee on Archæological, Historical and Statistical Information.

## BY CHARLES ASHTON.

This committee in accordance with the direction of the Commission has the honor to report that at a meeting of the Iowa Columbian Commission held April 7th, 1892, this committee was constituted for the collation and publication of Archæological, Historical and Statistical matter pertaining to the Agricultural, Mineral, Mechanical, Industrial, Educational and other resources and advantages of the State of Iowa, to be placed in the World's Columbian Exposition. In addition to his other important duties as President of the Commission, Mr. Crosby was placed in charge of Department F., Woman's Work. Mr. Jarnagin was assigned to the charge of Eucation and Fine Arts (Department H). These separate duties engaging the full time of these gentlemen, by mutual agreement of the Committee, its work was placed in charge of Mr. Ashton.

Upon considering the duty assigned it, the committee found that the record of its appointment did not clearly indicate the scope of work it was appointed to do. Consulting the Commission at a subsequent meeting, its work was more clearly defined. At the meeting of the Commission held June 22d, 1892, the sum of $8,000 was named for the use of "The Literary Bureau." Mr. Ashton then prepared in outline a plan for the work of the committee, submitting it to the committee for its approval. The committee approved the plan submitted, and instructed Mr. Ashton to prepare, in accordance therewith, "A Hand Book of Iowa," for general, gratuitous distribution at the World's Columbian Exposition as a part of the exhibit of the State of Iowa. In the preparation of the work, the committee held frequent consultations and the work progressed satisfactorily to its several members.

On account of the limited appropriation made by the General Assembly, it was found necessary to restrict the amount to be used by this committee to a sum greatly below the amount above named.

The committee planned for the publication of a book of about two hundred pages, the pages when trimmed to be six by nine inches, to be set in brevier type, to be suitably illustrated, the body of the book to be on special sized and super-calendered paper, to be bound in heavy paper covers, to contain a two-page colored map of the State, showing all railroads, railroad stations, principal streams and county seats. On submitting these plans of the committee to the commission they were approved.

In February, 1893, circular letters were sent to the leading publishing houses within the State, requesting bids for printing an edition of 20,000 copies of the book. In response to these letters many bids were received. The bid of the Dubuque Telegraph Printing Company was considered by the committee, as the most favorable, and the contract was awarded to it. A copy of the contract made with said Company is in the printed minutes of the Commission, at pages 299-301. Subsequently a change was made in said contract under which 5,000 copies of the book were bound in board. A subsequent contract was made for a second edition of 5,000 copies. The two editions, aggregating 25,000 copies, were distributed, mostly, during the continuance of the Exposition.

At a meeting of the Commission held April 30th, 1893, the committee reported a copy of the contract referred to above, also a title page for the book, with table of contents, and the larger part of the matter for the work in type written copy. This report was approved by the Commission.

The entire cost of the work (25,000 copies) including expense of its preparation, illustration, express charges, telegraphing, postage for near 2,000 copies distributed by mail, transportation of books from Dubuque to the Iowa Building in Jackson Park and all other expenses in its publication, aggregated $3,504.15, making an average of 14 cents per copy. The 1,995 copies distributed by mail, were sent to prominent citizens of our own and other states, commercial agencies, public libraries, educational institutions, editors, foreign and state commissions and to other parties requesting copies. Many copies of the work went into foreign countries, the postage on the book being six cents to any postoffice in our own, and in all European, American-Asiatic and African countries excepting a few colonies in South Africa. Upon its appearance the work was very favorably commended by the press and prominent citizens of the State.

A copy of the work is herewith submitted, as a part of this report.

IOWA STATE CAPITOL.

THE DISCOVERY, SETTLEMENT, GEOGRAPHICAL LOCATION,
TOPOGRAPHY, NATURAL RESOURCES, GEOLOGY, CLIMA-
TOLOGY, COMMERCIAL FACILITIES, AGRICULTURAL
PRODUCTIVENESS, MANUFACTURING ADVAN-
TAGES, EDUCATIONAL INTERESTS, HEALTH-
FULNESS, GOVERNMENT, AND THE
EXCELLENCE OF THE SOCIAL
AND MORAL LIFE

......OF......

# THE STATE OF IOWA.

Brightest Star in the American Constellation.

CHARLES ASHTON, JAMES O. CROSBY AND J. W. JARNAGIN,

Committee on Archæological, Historical and Statistical Information, Iowa
Columbian Commission.

PUBLISHED BY THE COMMISSION A. D. 1893.

# INTRODUCTORY...

Of Iowa we write. Our task is to set forth its discovery, settlement, geographical location, topographical features, geology, climate, soils, minerals, rivers, agricultural advantages and productiveness, its commercial opportunities, educational facilities, development, progress and the excellence of its intellectual, social and moral life. The subject is broad yet inviting, the duty is a pleasant one, yet in many respects one difficult of accomplishment. The artist who would attempt to present with the brush the grandeur of hue and majestic form of the bow of promise would find the task to lie beyond the reach of his culture or the grasp of his endowments. So the pen is inadequate to present in its bright and winsome reality this realm of topographical beauty, rich resources, gracious climate and excellent development which earth's millions now know as the State of Iowa.

## THE NAME, IOWA.

Prior to the settlement of the region a tribe of the aboriginal inhabitants were designated by a term from which we have the name of Iowa. An intelligent and early pioneer of the territory now forming the state, well acquainted with its native tribes and their languages, Mr. Antoine Le Claire, stated that this word, used by its original inhabitants to designate the portion of the country which they occupied, signified "This is the land." Pre-eminently among its sister states Iowa is "the land."

## DISCOVERY.

Iowa was first seen by white men in the summer of 1673, two hundred and twenty years ago. The French settlers then occupying Lower Canada, in exploring the great lakes and their connections, had reached Mackinaw, and the Catholic church had formed at that place a missionary settlement. In their association with the Indians its missionaries heard of a great river in the west that came out of the north and flowed into the far-away south, and a wonderful land along its shores. So enrapturing were the descriptions given of the "Father of Waters" and the beauties of the treeless land bordering it, that an educated missionary, then laboring at Mackinaw for the conversion of the Indians, became possessed of an intense desire to explore it.

Louis Joliet, a young man of Canadian birth, but of French descent, well educated, active and ambitious, traveling under the authority of the government of Quebec, reached Mackinaw in one of his adventurous voyages of exploration. There he met Jacques Marquette, an educated missionary priest. These two energetic men with five French-Canadian attendants, left Mackinaw on the thirteenth day of May, 1673, in two bark canoes to reach, if possible, the great river of which they had heard, and explore "the beautiful land." Father Marquette and his companion, Joliet, were both intent on enlarging the dominion of the French government, but the former was more directly concerned in propagating the Catholic faith among the native tribes in the then unknown interior region of this then unknown west. Leaving Mackinaw in their two canoes, frail vessels for such a voyage, with "some Indian corn and some dried meats as their stock of provisions," these intrepid Christian leaders coasted along the western shores of Lake Michigan into Green Bay. On reaching the mouth of the Fox River they entered it and ascended to the portage, where, being directed by Indian guides, they transferred their canoes and provisions to the Wisconsin river and descended the stream. On the seventeenth day of June when near its mouth they looked across a greater stream, the "Missi," great, and "Sepe", river, on the western shore of which rose the high bluff on which, in 1805, Lieut. Pike planted the United States flag. Then had they the first view ever enjoyed by white men of the strange land on the sunset side of the great river which their venturous voyage was made to discover.

Of the thoughts and emotions of those men, forming that day the vanguard of our present Christian civilization in this central west, we have no record. Something of the strange musings they indulged as they rode in their fragile vessels amidst their strange, weird surroundings, we are left to imagine. Gliding slowly down the great stream on that June day, the valley and the not far away hills that bound it were clothed in summer luxuriance. As they entered the Mississippi to their right, but little above them on the Wisconsin shore lay a beautiful prairie, reaching miles up the great stream and some three miles back from the river, but this they did not see. In front of them on the Iowa side of the larger river were the high bluffs, but turning down the stream they were soon in a delightful river archipelago. The first Iowa prairie they beheld was that on which the town of Guttenburg was built. In all this varying scenery they saw no sign of human form or habitation. It is said they rode on the river four days before the first sign of human inhabitant was seen. Then they beheld human footprints in the sand.

How profound the solitude in which they rode!

How wonderfully different that great valley now from its condition, then! Those men must have been conscious that they were in a vast inhabitable region, but had but slight conception of its present wonderful development and civilization, more beneficent than any which in their day shed blessings upon humanity; which in this celebrative year graces with its wealth of happiness the dwellers in the great central region which they then discovered, but now having world-wide fame alike for its beauty and its productiveness.

In this commemorative year which calls the millions of the nation to the shores of the great lake, from which those men began their voyage, should any of these millions traverse this interior region they will find on the shores of the great river then discovered, ten Christian commonwealths, all free, powerful states, yet parts of this one powerful Nationality. Those ten states have a population of nineteen millions of Christian people, and possess a wealth surpassing the riches of the wealthiest nation of as recent date as Iowa's discovery; while on that tree-clad, western shore, on which those men first looked with inquiring anxiety, there is now this beautiful state, the home of two millions of the most prosperous, intelligent, orderly and happy people of earth. In the intervening years, this region, then nameless to those adventurous voyagers, largely covering the fertile peninsula formed by the two largest rivers of the country, then an unexplored, herbage-covered land, inhabited only sparsely by an uncultured, savage race, has made a progress in civilized attainment that must ever be the marvel of the country's history. Here are now commercial facilities, manufacturing forces, educational advantages, and a Christian freedom and liberality unknown to the world when this beautiful portion of the country was discovered.

## THE SETTLEMENT OF IOWA.

The territory bordering the Mississippi river extending eastward of that stream to the Alleghanies and westward to the Rocky Mountains, and from the Gulf by which thrives the stately palm and fragrant orange, to the great lakes, was by right of discovery subject to the crown of France. In the course of human events that portion of this interior territory west of the Mississippi and reaching from Lake Superior to the Gulf of Mexico passed under the dominion of the Spanish crown. In 1800 Spain receded this great territory to the French government. That part of the original French possessions in this region lying north of the Ohio and east of the Mississippi had, by the conquest of Canada, become subject to the British crown, and by the fortunes of war in the American Revolution had subsequently become United States territory. In 1803, by the treaty arrangement known as the Louisiana Purchase, France ceded its possessions along the Mississippi river to the United States government. The wise action of the Jefferson administration in extending the western frontier of the country to the Rocky Mountains, secured to this fertile prairie-interior the advantages, forever, of free government and liberal laws.

When the Revolutionary war closed settlements soon began to extend west of the Alleghanies from New York, Pennsylvania, Virginia and the New England states. In 1802 Ohio was admitted into the Union. In 1730 the French had formed a settlement at Vincennes and in 1809 Indiana was given state government. Yet in 1810 its population numbered only 23,890 white persons. In 1720 the French had formed a settlement at Kaskaskia. In 1818, lacking but two years of a century thereafter, Illinois was given a place as a state in the Union. Yet in the centennial anniversary year of the founding of that settlement at Kaskaskia that state contained a population of only 53,788 white persons. A French settlement was formed at Detroit, Michigan, in 1701 but the census of 1830, taken 129 years thereafter, reported the population of the Michigan territory at only 31,346. Several more years passed before the American Congress gave it statehood.

At the close of the first third of the present century the population of the four states formed out of the old Northwestern Territory covering the region between the Ohio river, the Mississippi and the Great Lakes had a

THE MOUTH OF THE WISCONSIN RIVER AS SEEN FROM PIKE'S PEAK, TWO MILES BELOW McGREGOR.

population only a little in excess of one and a half millions of white persons. In 1870, forty-three years after the permanent settlement of Iowa began, it had a larger population than Michigan, the settlement of which was commenced a century and a half before the first settlement was founded in Iowa.

For 113 years after the discovery of Iowa by Joliet and Marquette it remained virtually an unknown land. In that cycle of slow transportation, limited reading, but numerous discoveries of new lands, the discovery of this interior portion of the North American continent had failed to attract public attention. No effort was made to effect any settlement within the borders of what is now the state of Iowa, until the fall of 1788. Julien Dubuque, an adventurous French trader, having secured from the Indians a grant of land extending southwardly from the Little Maquoketa river seven leagues along the Mississippi by three leagues inland, embracing about 121,000 acres, formed a settlement thereon. On it, it is said Dubuque "improved an extensive farm, built houses to dwell in, erected a horse mill, cultivated the farm and mined lead." He died in 1810 and his possessions were soon controlled by others. The Indians became dissatisfied with the lead mining and other conduct of their French and half breed neighbors, drove them from their mines and homes, and broke up the settlement.

In March 1799 Louis Honori obtained a grant of land from the government of Upper Louisiana in Lee county, where the town of Montrose now stands, near the head of the rapids in the Mississippi river. The tract was sold from him in 1803 and a settlement, founded by him, was abandoned.

Various venturesome parties of hunters, trappers and Indian traders made temporary settlement along the Mississippi, within the limits of Iowa, from 1820 to 1830, but did not permanently remain. In 1809 a military post had been established on the present site of Ft. Madison. The troops however did not long occupy the post, its establishment having been in violation of treaty stipulation made with the Indian occupants of the region it was abandoned by the government.

The city of St. Louis was founded in 1764. It soon had trade with the Indians. In 1804 that city, the river approaches of which were then navigated by only flat boats and Indian canoes, passed, by the Louisiana Purchase, under the dominion of the United States government. Three years later Robert Fulton made his successful trial trip on the Hudson with the "Clermont", and steam, as a motive power on American rivers, was demonstrated to be a practical force, and soon had large application. In 1817 the first steamboat reached St. Louis. That city then passed from its primal stage, as a mere trading post for Indians and hunters, to a growing and important commercial center. Steam navigation being applied on the Ohio and Mississippi brought settlers into southwestern Illinois and northeastern Missouri and prepared the way for the settlement of Iowa.

The western border of Iowa was first traced in 1805 by the Lewis and Clark expedition on its famous journey across the continent by way of the Missouri and Columbia rivers. Maj. Pike traced its eastern border as he ascended the Mississippi river to its source about the same time. The reports of these expeditions published by the government, with the reports of the journeys of hunters and Indian traders through the territory, spread knowledge of the remarkable beauty and natural excellence of this then far western region. When the Indians were finally subdued by the defeat of Black Hawk at the "Bad Axe" in 1832, and permanent safety was thereby assured to venturesome pioneers, settlements rapidly formed on the Iowa side of the Mississippi. No region, ever opened for settlement, offered more inviting advantages to home seekers, and they were rapidly embraced.

In 1833 the area now comprising the state of Iowa was a part of the territory of Michigan. Its legislature organized two counties within what is now Iowa, naming them Des Moines and Dubuque. Three years later, namely in 1836, Congress organized the territory of Wisconsin—Iowa constituting a part of that territory. In 1838 the territory of Iowa was constituted by act of Congress, and Robert Lucas of Ohio was appointed to the office of Governor. The first legislature of the Iowa territory assembled November 12th, 1838, at Burlington. Iowa, as a territory, embraced a considerable portion of what is now the state of Minnesota, and had almost unlimited expansion toward the setting sun.

On the opening of Iowa for settlement in 1833 settlers rushed into the lead mining regions surrounding Dubuque, and that city was founded. In 1836, three years after Iowa was opened for settlement, the population of the territory numbered 10,315. Two years later the population had increased to 22,850. In the census of 1840, taken but seven years after the territory was opened for settlement, the population numbered 43,112. Six years later a state enumeration found the population to be upward of 100,-000. The star of empire was taking its way westward, the people of the timber-clad east had heard of the beauty and richness of this prairie land where a farm could be made in a season with a yoke of oxen and a plow, and were coming in by thousands to enjoy the beauty of its broad landscapes, the glory of its sunshine, the purity of its waters and the fertility of its acres. In 1850, but seventeen years after the building of the first cabin in its permanent settlement, the second national enumeration therein reported a population of 192,214 free men and women. December 8, 1846, but thirteen years after its first permanent settlers entered upon its soil, Iowa was admitted into the Union. The fame of its wonderful natural meadows and the beauty and fertility of its prairies had spread, not only over this country, but had crossed the seas and the people of other countries, as well as the states in the east were crowding in to find homes in this richly inviting region of the prairie west.

## BOUNDARIES AND AREA.

The constitution under which Iowa was admitted into the Union fixed the boundaries of the state as follows "Beginning in the middle of the main channel of the Mississippi river at a point due east of the middle of the mouth of the main channel of the Des Moines river, thence up the middle of the main channel of the said Des Moines river, to a point on said river where the northern boundary line of the state of Missouri, as established by the constitution of that state, adopted June 12th, 1820—crosses the said middle of the main channel of the said Des Moines river, thence westwardly along the said northern boundary line of the state of Missouri

MISSISSIPPI RIVER, LOOKING UP FROM PIKE'S PEAK.

CITY OF McGREGOR, MAIN STREET.

as established at the time aforesaid, until the extension of said line intersects the middle of the main channel of the Missouri river; thence up the middle of the main channel of the said Missouri river to a point opposite the middle of the main channel of the Big Sioux river, according to Nicollet's map; thence up the main channel of the said Big Sioux river, according to the said map, until it is intersected by the parallel of forty-three degrees and thirty minutes north latitude; thence east along said parallel of forty-three degrees and thirty minutes, until said parallel intersects the middle of the main channel of the Mississippi river; thence down the middle of the main channel of the said Mississippi river to the place of beginning." A closer study of its boundaries, shows that this state lies between the parallels of forty degrees thirty minutes and forty-three degrees thirty minutes north latitude, (a range of latitude possessing a temperate climate most highly favorable for agricultural production.) The area of the state covers on the forty-second parallel six ranges of townships east of the fifth P. M., the fourteenth meridan west of Washington and the ninetieth west from Greenwich, and on the same parallel forty-five townships west of that meridan. Estimating each township at six miles the state has an extreme length east and west of 306 miles by a breadth of about 204 miles, including in its breadth thirty-four surveyed townships. According to a report made by the Secretary of the Treasury to the United States Senate in March, 1863, it embraces 55,044 square miles, or 35,220,200 acres—an area larger than Scotland, almost as large as England, four times the size of the kingdom of Denmark, five times as large as Belgium; three times as large as the kingdom of Greece, that made the world's pre-Christian history interesting by it glorious deeds and the splendor of its philosophy and architecture; and it is five times the area of the land of Judea, that gave to the world its noblest ethical code, and to the race its Redeemer.

## GEOGRAPHICAL LOCATION.

An artist once represented Columbus as standing and surveying the North American continent. When his eyes rested upon the brightest spot, central in the vast expanse, that spot was named Iowa. Geographically it is centrally located in this union of states. On the forty-second parallel its eastern boundary is upwards of one thousand miles from the Atlantic's tide by Plymouth Rock, while on the same parallel from its western border to the Pacific's surf-beaten shore, fifteen hundred miles intervene. From the northern line of the state to the British possessions by the Lake of the Woods, the distance is four hundred miles, while between the southern border of the state and the Gulf coast lie the states of Missouri, Arkansas and Louisiana, covering an expanse of 760 miles. A position so central in the richest, freest and most powerful nation of modern times, and central in the vast system of river navigation connected with the great streams that form its eastern and western boundaries, and so situated that the principal lines of railway binding ocean to ocean must cross its territory, must ever possess incalculable advantages in the security its location affords, the markets it assures, and the commercial advantages that must ever accrue to its citizens.

## TOPOGRAPHY.

Iowa is not only princely in its area and highly fortunate in its geographical location, but it is winsome in its topography. In the days of a geographical ignorance, which an intelligent world remembers now with smiles, Iowa may have been placed in school-book maps in "The Great American Desert." But if this beautiful and fertile state was ever a desert, then surely it was that one of which the Lord's prophet spoke when he declared "The wilderness and the solitary place shall be glad for them and the desert shall rejoice and blossom as the rose. * * * * * * The glory of Lebanon shall be given unto it and the excellency of Sharon." No grander cedars ever grew on Lebanon than now adorn Iowa homes, and no more beautiful or fragrant roses ever bloomed along the sunny slopes of Sharon than now grow in this realm of Edenic loveliness.

One of the more noticeable features of the topography of Iowa is the entire freedom of the state from barren, rocky elevations, or other waste lands. It has no Saharas, dismal swamps, nor fever-breeding everglades.

From railroad surveys and other sources of information we have definite knowledge of the elevation of the chief portions of the state. Low water in the Mississippi at the southeastern corner of the state, its lowest point, being 444 feet above sea level.

The point recognized as its highest elevation is on the summit divide near Spirit Lake, Dickinson county, it being estimated at 1250 feet above low water at Keokuk, giving the highest point in Iowa an elevation of only 1,694 feet; between these extremes in elevation lies all of Iowa. To show more clearly by comparison the moderate elevations of this area, we notice that its highest point is 165 feet lower than the Union Pacific railroad grade in the Platte valley at Grand Island, Nebraska, the grade at that station being 1,860 feet above tide.

The water in the Big Sioux river at the northwestern corner of the state is 1344 feet above the tide level. This is the descent from that point to the Gulf of Mexico via the Missouri and Mississippi rivers.

The crest of the state or the summit forming the water shed between the waters of the Mississippi and the Missouri lies diagonally across the state; its general trend being from the northwest to the southeast. Entering Iowa from Minnesota where it separates the waters of the Des Moines and Little Sioux rivers, it leaves the state entering Missouri near the southeast corner of Appanoose county, there separating the waters of the Chariton river from the Fabius creek, having crossed in its course through the state Dickinson, Clay, Buena Vista, Sac, Carroll, Audubon, Guthrie, Adair, Madison, Union, Clark, Lucas, Monroe and Appanoose counties.

The altitude of this important ridge is shown by the elevations at which it is crossed by the five chief railroad lines crossing the state from east to west. The most southern of these lines is the Chicago, Burlington and Quincy. It touches this great water-shed twice. First at Chariton Lucas county, at an elevation of 1,080 feet, and the second time at Murray, Clark county, thirty-seven miles west of Chariton at an altitude of 1,268 feet. This line of road reaches its highest altitude in the state at Creston, Union county, 1,355 feet, on the divide separating the Platte and Grand rivers, affluents of the Missouri. The Chicago, Rock Island and Pacific railroad, the next line north of the one first named, crosses this watershed in the northwestern part of Adair county, at the town of Adair, at an elevation of 1,389 feet. The summit of the divide at this point is fifty feet above the railroad grade. The Chicago and Northwestern railroad crosses this watershed at or near Arcadia, in Carroll county, at an elevation of 1,437 feet. The Dubuque and Sioux City (Illinois Central) crosses it at Alta. Buena Vista county, at an altitude of 1,521 feet. Thus the three roads named reach their highest elevations in the state at the crossing of this divide.

The Chicago, Milwaukee and St. Paul railway crosses it at or near Ruthven, Palo Alto county, at an elevation of 1,424 feet, but this road reaches its summit elevation at Sanborn, O'Brien county, 1,537 feet above tide, on the divide separating the east and west branches of the Floyd river.

The facts here stated show the evenness of the altitude of the summit of the state and that there is a very moderate and easy descent across the state from the northwest to the southeast. From Sanborn to Chariton the descent is 475 feet. The distance is two hundred miles in a direct line, the descent averaging 2.37 feet to the mile.

Any map of Iowa will show that the rivers in that part of the state which lies east of the great watershed, trend toward the southeast and flow into Mississippi, and that in the portion lying west of that summit all the rivers flow into the Missouri with a southwesternly trend. The traveler crossing Iowa soon discovers that, although a prairie state, and lying under the moderate elevations given, it is not a breadth of swampy levels, but a realm of beautiful undulations,—in some places rising from the streams somewhat abruptly but seldom precipitously. The divides separating the numerous streams generally rising to an altitude of 175 to 250 feet, afford a constant succession of changing scenery. No country affords more graceful landscapes, when clothed in summer's green or when its groves are dyed in their autumn robes of silver, scarlet, gold and purple. Iowa landscapes are grandly beautiful, and the traveler sees a breadth of farm homes beautiful in situation and surroundings. The great fields of growing grain, in their season, add beauty to the delighting panoramas by every shade of green, covering the broad and billowy areas over which the eye extends. In the summer season great herds and flocks feed amid blooming flowers and rich herbage, and add enchanting variety to the inviting picture. In that season the enriching, life-giving sunshine paints the floral gemmed-meadows with a brilliancy of hue that makes the broad landscapes over which the vision reaches, constantly discovering new charms, superbly winsome. Paraphrasing the language of inspiration we may truly say, "beautiful for situation, and the joy of her people" is beautiful, fertile Iowa.

## RIVERS.

Iowa is a realm of beautiful, perennial streams flowing in deep channels and with rapid current. Prof. White in the first volume of his report on the geology of the state, tabulates the descent of the principal rivers of the state according to railroad surveys and other sources of information which we here copy.

| NAME OF RIVER. | PART OF COURSE. | SLOPE PER MILE. FT. IN. | | AUTHORITY. |
|---|---|---|---|---|
| Mississippi | From Lansing to the Confluence of the Missouri | | 6 | J.E. Ainsworth. |
| Missouri | From Sioux City to Council Bluffs | 1 | | R. R. Surveys. |
| Des Moines | From Fort Dodge to Ottumwa | 2 | 4 | R. R. Surveys. |
| Des Moines | From Ottumwa to its mouth | 1 | 11 | R. R. Surveys. |
| Raccoon | From Forks near Van Meter to mouth | 2 | 11 | R. R. Surveys. |
| North Raccoon | From Jefferson to Forks near Van Meter | 4 | | R. R. Surveys. |
| Skunk | From Oakland to its mouth | 1 | 6 | R. R. Surveys. |
| Skunk | From Colfax Station to Oakland | 2 | 2 | R. R. Surveys. |
| Iowa | From Iowa Falls to Iowa City | 3 | 1 | R. R. Surveys. |
| Iowa | From Iowa City to its mouth | 2 | 4 | R. R. Surveys. |
| Cedar | From State boundary to Cedar Falls | 3 | 7 | R. R. Surveys. |
| Cedar | From Cedar Falls to Moscow | 2 | 5 | R. R. Surveys. |
| Wapsipinicon | From Independence to mouth | 2 | 10 | J.E. Ainsworth. |
| Maquoketa | From Manchester to the mouth | 3 | 4 | J.E. Ainsworth. |
| Turkey | From Crane Creek to the mouth | 5 | | R. R. Levels. |
| Upper Iowa | From Decorah to the mouth | 8 | 6 | R. R. Levels. |
| E. Nishnabotna | From C. R. I. & P. R. R. to mouth | 2 | 5 | R. R. Levels. |
| W Nishnabotna | From C. R. I. & P. R. R. to mouth | 2 | 8 | R. R. Levels. |
| Boyer | From Denison to its mouth | 3 | 3 | R. R. Levels. |
| Big Sioux | From Indian Creek to mouth | 1 | 4 | Estimated. |
| Big Sioux | From N. W. corner of State to Indian Creek | 3 | 2 | Estimated. |
| Little Sioux | From Cherokee to Smithland | 2 | 6 | R. R. Levels. |
| Little Sioux | From Smithland to its mouth | | 4 | R. R. Levels. |
| Floyd | From fork of Willow Creek to mouth | 3 | | J.E. Ainsworth. |

From this table it will be seen that the rivers of Iowa are not sluggish, stagnant streams. The Little Sioux has rapid fall from its source in the lakes in Dickinson county, on the summit divide, to Smithland. The stream furnishes many water powers in its course through Clay and other counties. Below Smithland it strikes the broad flood-plain of the Missouri, and so its small descent below that town is explained.

The Skunk is perhaps the flattest stream in the state, yet it flows with a strong current in its labyrinth of bends through the broad flood-plain in which its channel is cut. The traveler who had to cross this river in early days will never forget the "Skunk bottoms." But now with graded and bridged roads, its wide bottom lands are grand pastures and wealth producing properties.

Lying in the peninsula bounded by the rivers forming its eastern and western boundaries, Iowa is not situated to afford interior navigable streams. Its largest interior river, the Des Moines, has its source in Minnesota, and flows with a southeasterly trend east of the great watershed and empties its volume into the Mississippi at the southeast corner of the state. From Fort Dodge to Ottumwa, a distance in a direct line of 150 miles, its descent of two and a half feet per mile gives it a rapid current precluding any great value as a navigable stream but rendering it of great value for manufacturing purposes. At Bonaparte, Ottumwa, Des Moines and other places it is made to furnish important water power. Before the advent of railroads, steamboats plied on this river in the spring and early summer, an occasional small boat running up as far as Fort Dodge. Steam boats occasionally, in those days, plowed their way up the Iowa and

Cedar rivers, but the advent of railroad facilities rendered those streams unnecessary for navigation and they have been given up to manufacturing purposes. Many of the rivers of Iowa and their affluents furnish numerous and valuable water powers. Some are improved for grist and other mill purposes, but many of the most valuable yet invite improvement. The Cedar furnishes water power of great value at Cedar Falls where the river descends about twenty-two feet in three-quarters of a mile. At Waterloo and also Cedar Rapids it furnishes important hydraulic power. The Iowa and many other streams also furnish valuable water powers at numerous places.

The rivers of Iowa are classed in two systems. The one embracing the streams east of the watershed, the other the streams west of that ridge. The principal streams in the eastern system are the Upper Iowa, Turkey, Maquoketa, Wapsipinicon, Cedar, Iowa, Skunk and the Des Moines and its affluents, the principal of which are South, Middle and North rivers, the Raccoon with its branches and the Boone. In the western system we name the Floyd, Rock River, Little Sioux, Maple, Boyer, Nishnabotna, Nodaway, Platte, Grand and the Chariton. These are mostly perennial, many of them serviceable in the milling and manufacturing power afforded. Along their course were many fine native groves that attracted early settlers. All flow in fertile valleys bordered by sloping uplands and are sources of pleasure as well as utility and add beauty by giving variety to the luxuriant landscapes through their course.

## LAKES.

The people of Iowa do not boast of the magnitude of their lakes nor the surrounding grandeur of their "unsalted seas." Yet there are numbers of lakes with charming surroundings, several of which are becoming famous as places of resort for rest and pleasure. Iowa's lakes all lie in the central third of the northern half of the state, and its most elevated portion, where the watersheds are developed into broad table lands. None of her lakes are of value in aiding commerce by furnishing important water transportation. In the sporting season they are inviting to sportsmen, as they are visited by immense numbers of migrating waterfowls, as geese, ducks, brants, swans, pelicans, cranes, etc., and furnish large quantities of fine fish; it being true of them in this particular that "The waters brought forth abundantly." The lakes are mostly bodies of clear, pure water. On the shores of many of them are beautiful groves of native timber, located in breadths of charming scenery and are specially inviting to rest seekers and those desiring health-giving recreation. Clear Lake, in Cerro Gordo county, is about five miles in length by two in breadth. Rice Lake, Silver Lake and Bright's Lake in Worth county are small bodies of water from one to two miles long, Rice Lake lying partly in Winnebago county. Crystal Lake, Eagle Lake, Wood Lake, Lake Edwards and Twin Lakes are in Hancock county, Eagle Lake being the largest of the three. Lake Gertrude, Elm Lake, and Wall Lake beautiful bodies of water, lie in Wright county, the largest of the three, Wall Lake, being about three miles long by two broad Twin Lakes in Calhoun county are becoming a noted resort for fishing and pleasure parties; the Des Moines and Northwestern R. R. making them easi'y accessible. The two cover a length of about four miles. They are separated by

A PRAIRIE FARM NEAR GARNAVILLO, HOME OF WM. M. ALLYN.

a narrow belt of land through which is cut a narrow stream. Some twenty-five miles from these Twin Lakes lies Wall Lake in Sac county, which is becoming a famous health and pleasure resort.

The maps of Iowa show three separate lakes within the state denominated Wall Lake, one lying in Sac county, one (the largest of the three) in Wright county, and one (the smallest of the three) in Hamilton county. The idea has been entertained that at some time in the ante-historic period some strange people built veritable stone walls along portions of the shores of these lakes; but that idea is a myth. Over that region in which those lakes lie, when vast icebergs or ponderous glaciers were exerting their mighty forces in forming the wonderful drift coverings of the region, great numbers of boulders were borne by these forces from the north country and deposited about these fresh water bodies. The forces of winter frosts and ice have lifted these boulders in the shallow portions of these lakes and have piled them by their shores. Fancy has conjured them into walls and so they have their name, and thus the stories of the "Walled lakes of Iowa" had their origin.

In addition to the above named lakes we notice Swan Lake in Emmet county, which is one of the largest of Iowa lakes. It lies in the central portion of that county and is readily accessible from Estherville, the county seat. It is a beautiful pleasure resort. Storm Lake, one of the most beautiful lakes of Iowa, lies in Buena Vista county, on the line of the Illinois Central railroad and by it is the beautiful town of Storm Lake. The largest lakes in Iowa are Spirit Lake and the Okoboji, in Dickinson county. These lie on the great watershed and near the Minnesota line and being accessible by the B., C. R. & N. and the C., M. & St. P. railways have become very popular summer resorts.

In the winter of 1857 a band of Sioux Indians passed southwardly through northwestern Iowa, and on their return passed through Sac, Cherokee and Dickinson counties. The winter was a severe one and in the first week of March the ground was covered with deep snow. The Indians had trouble with the few white settlers then dwelling in Sac and Cherokee counties, stealing and destroying the settlers' property. Reaching the Okoboji Lakes they perpetrated a fearful massacre of white settlers who were then dwelling in the surrounding groves.

The few families settled in those groves, on account of the inclement weather and the deep snow covering the wide unsettled prairies of northern Iowa, were unable to seek protection from the distant settlements, there being no possibility of relief nearer than Fort Dodge, a hundred miles distant. Upwards of forty persons were killed outright by those savages. The settlers' cabins were burned and their property destroyed, and some three or four females were carried off as prisoners. When the news of the massacre reached Fort Dodge a force was immediately raised to go to the relief of these settlements. The sufferings of that brave band of civilian soldiers were terribly severe. Two of them were frozen to death. The Indians immediately after the massacre fled into Minnesota and could not be overtaken by the pioneer force.

Perhaps the only battle ever fought on Iowa soil between United States troops and Indian warriors took place some thirty miles east of Spirit Lake.

A company of United States dragoons under command of Captain N. Boone, about 1842, while crossing the state had a skirmish with an Indian band. Iowa has but a brief history of the heroic in Indian wars, or the sorrowful in the massacre of its early settlers by Indian foes.

## PRAIRIE.

Iowa was early known as a prairie state. Its broad, treeless areas were its glory. Its prairies were not in their natural condition vast marshes, or great breadths of sterile sand, barren of productive power, nor were they regions of cold barren clay. They soon became known as of the finest land, awaiting the plow to turn them into productive farms. On the fourth day after Monsieurs Marquette and Joliet entered the Mississippi they had their first view of an Iowa prairie in its summer dress of green and bloom. This great, central region of the country was largely treeless then. How long it had existed thus is only known to Him who created it. Why, how, or when these breadths of fertile acres and beautiful landscapes became treeless, would be useless for us to inquire.

Iowa's being so largely prairie favored its rapid settlement. Its first settlers had known something of the toilsome, slow process of making farms with a mattock and an axe in a heavily wooded country. In 1845 a man went into northwestern Ohio, bought an axe and commenced on a piece of timbered land to make a farm. He found it slow work. He afterwards came to Iowa, bought a half section of "raw prairie," went upon it with a breaking plow and team and broke the first furrow made on the tract a mile in length without a rock, grub, tree or stumb to hinder the plow. That was a speedier, saying nothing about its being an easier, way to make a farm. Then there was the continuous advantage of a stumpless field. When he settled in the Ohio woods he could not have cut a ton of hay on a hundred acres of his land; when he came to Iowa he could go out on the prairie with a mowing machine, cut the finest of blue-joint and make all the hay he wanted; as fine as was ever fed a horse. He visited a neighbor, an old settler, and going into his hay-yard he asked: "How much hay have you there Mr. S———?" "I guess about 800 tons," was the reply. Every stem of it made from wild grass. The settler in Iowa soon saw there was a distinction with a difference between making a farm on eastern wooded lands and the prairies of Iowa. Infinite wisdom contrived seven-eights of Iowa's surface to be prairie that Iowa might the more speedily and easily be turned into a paradise. The prairies of Iowa did not invite settlers merely by the ease by which they were turned into fine farm homes, but the beauty of the views they afforded, the breadth and grandeur of the great natural meadows and pastures they offered, and the ease of communication they provided between neighbors and neighborhoods were potent influences in inducing settlers from the heavily wooded east.

The facility of intercourse offered by the Iowa prairie was no mean factor in inviting their rapid settlement. In driving across them there was no climbing over stumps and logs. A few trips indicated a road which was soon worn, if not into a straight, at least into a fine smooth, traveled way. The Iowa farmer had use for a carriage from his first settlement on the prairie. The writer knows something from experience of opening and traveling new roads in the east. Talk about the settler there having use for a carriage from its first settlement, he scarcely had use for such a vehicle in the first generation of its settlement.

It has been objected that there are terrible blizzards and awful cyclones on these Iowa prairies. We admit that there are storms in Iowa, but are there no tornadoes, no terrible storms and blizzards in timber covered countries? We know there are tumults in nature's domain in all regions. Men are helpless before nature's forces in all places, but destructive tornadoes in Iowa, like destructive earthquakes in California, are of but rare occurrence.

There have been severe winters in Iowa but they have been few in its history. There may have been danger for pioneer settlers in journeying across Iowa prairies from winter blizzards in the past, but those dangers are now matters of history. Iowa winters on Iowa prairies are desirable now for the benefits and pleasures which they afford.

The prairies, yet beautiful, are not now as they were when the pioneer chased over them the agile deer and the fleeing elk. Their great breadths were then open commons with sloughs and streams unbridged. Fire, in the fall, swept off their summer vegetation and left naught to hold in place the falling snow. The settlers' cabins, built in grove or sheltered nook, were far apart. The great breadths of open prairie were houseless and many of the pioneer settlers were poor and thinly clad. Then there was nothing to mark the traveled road in the winter's snow storm, and the traveler seeking to cross the broad prairie may have been in danger when such a storm overtook him, distant from his home or a shelter. But terrible, life-destroying blizzards have been of rare occurrence in our history, while mild, beautiful, healthful winters, giving months of delightful sunshine and the smoothest, possible roads for winter travel, have been common.

Our broad prairies, originally beautiful, have been made more grandly so by human handi-work, directed by cultured mind. Terrible prairie fires may be read about in our history, but they will never more be seen. Our great prairies now are broad realms of finely improved, or improving, productive and enclosed farms. Good roads are common and the farms distinctly mark them. Streams and sloughs are bridged. Thrifty villages and thriving towns and cities are multiplied while the whole breadth of the country is flecked by beautiful artificial groves. Now, every where over Iowa prairies there are human habitations and the danger to a traveler in a winter blizzard is passed forever.

But with all of this improvement and change made by human intelligence and industry there are some things pertaining to the prairies of Iowa which are unchanged. The depth, the richness, the porousness of the soil, qualities which give it superior excellence for agricultural productiveness, are yet unchanged. Proper culture never diminishes but increases its productive power. The perennial streams coursing through these broad prairies, yet flow in the same channels cut deep into the earth, with the same, ever continuing, rapid current, yielding untold advantages in their surroundings. The prairies of Iowa, no longer grand in their wild luxuriance, have been made more truly beautiful by the art and industry inspired by our Christian civilization, and will ever be renowned for their agricultural superiority. Beautiful, fertile and exuberantly productive, their possessors are truly a fortunate people.

## GEOLOGICAL SURVEYS.

The first geological explorations in Iowa were made by Dr. D. D. Owen, under United States authority. His field of work embraced parts of Wisconsin, Minnesota and Iowa. His report was published, a large quarto-volume

The first geological survey in the state was made under the direction of Professor James Hall, State Geologist, in parts of the years 1855, 1856 and 1857, with J. D. Whitney as chemist and mineralogist. Their reports were published in two illustrated volumes by authority of the General Assembly of 1858.

In the years 1866, 1867, 1868 and 1869 a second and more extensive geological survey of the state was made by Dr. Charles A. White, State Geologist, Orestes H. St. John, assistant; and Rush Emery, chemist. Their work is reported in two volumes printed by F. M. Mills, state printer, in 1870.

The twenty-fourth General Assembly, deeming a new geological survey of Iowa desirable, made an appropriation for the work and appointed a commission to select a suitable geologist to make the survey. This commission selected Professor Samuel Calvin of the State University to take charge of the work, Dr. Charles R. Keyes, Assistant State Geologist and Professor G. E. Patrick, chemist. It is believed that this survey will lead to an enlarged development of the mineral interests of Iowa, and a fuller knowledge of the extent and value of its coal fields.

## A SKETCH OF THE GEOLOGY OF IOWA.

### By Charles R. Keyes, A. M., Ph. D., Assistant State Geologist.

Iowa is so pre-eminently an agricultural state that usually her mineral resources are almost entirely overlooked. Yet her geological features are none the less interesting scientifically, none the less important from an economic standpoint.

The mineral wealth of a community can only be developed through a liberal appreciation of its proper functions. Geology ranking first among the useful sciences, has for one of its leading objects the investigation of the natural resources of a region. It considers the characters of the different soils and their capabilities for agricultural purposes; the extent and value of the different deposits of coal and lead, iron and other ores; the distribution, properties and uses of the exhaustless beds of valuable clays; the accurate determination of the areas for artesian waters; the analysis of the mineral, well and river waters; the relative value and durability of the numerous kinds of building stones; and all kindred subjects which are of the utmost importance to the great body of citizens.

Agriculture and geology are daily becoming more intimate in their relations. Nowhere has their inter-dependence been more clearly understood and nowhere have the benefits been more apparent than in certain

European countries. Some of the older states of the Union, especially those along the Atlantic border, have followed the same line of work with the most happy results. To-day it is almost universally conceded that a good geological map of a region is practically a soil map also. The proper comprehension of the close relations of the two sciences cannot fail, therefore, to impress the truth of the statement.

In pointing out the various mineral deposits a knowledge of the distribution of the geological formations is of prime importance. Iowa possesses a measureably complete sequence of strata. The Paleozoic beds, from the Cambrian to the Upper Carboniferous, are very fully represented. The Mesozoic deposits, of Cretaceous age chiefly, are found in considerable thickness. Over all spreads a thick mantle of drift or glacial debris.

Below the soft, uncousolidated drift material the indurated sediments are everywhere exposed through erosion. The complete vertical section of the rocks in the state shows a thickness of about five thousand feet.

### ALGONKIAN ROCKS.

*Sioux Quartzite.* The rocks exposed within the limits of the state which are usually regarded as the oldest geologically are those, called the Sioux quartzite or Sioux "granite," which form outcrops of considerable extent in the extreme northwestern corner of the state. While there is no doubt that all the stratified sediments of Iowa rest at no very great depth upon the fundamental complex of crystallines which probably support all the sedimentary rocks of the globe, the Sioux quartzite and its associated masses are the only truly metamorphosed or massive crystalline rocks having a surface exposure in the state. The common phase of the rock under consideration is a completely vitreous type not unlike red jasper in general appearance and properties. Other parts of the mass are less indurated; and still others are simply loose sand. In places the formation is distinctly conglomeratic. Although the quartzite has been rendered in places so thoroughly crystalline since its original deposition, no igneous rocks have been noted in the vicinity until very recently.

A few months ago Professor G. E. Culver found in the midst of the Sioux quartzite of southeastern Dakota, within a few miles of the Iowa boundary, a large exposure of black trap rock, which extends for more than a mile along one of the minor streams flowing into the Big Sioux river. Dr. W. H. Hobbs, who has made careful microscopical examinations of the rock, finds it to be a coarse-grained olivine diabase—a massive basic rock unquestionably igneous in origin. It seems not improbable that further search will reveal other masses of the same rock or even other types of eruptives very similar.

In quarrying, the quartzite presents numerous difficulties; but the labor in getting out the material is greatly reduced by the fact that it is everywhere jointed and cracked in such a manner as to enable it to be removed readily in convenient sizes for handling. It is one of the most compact and durable building stones in the northwest. For architectural purposes it forms a very beautiful stone and is used for all kinds of construction throughout the region. Some of the leading churches and office buildings in Sioux City, Omaha, Council Bluffs, Des Moines, Burlington, and other places have been erected from this rock, with very pleasing effects.

It has also been used with good results as a paving material both in blocks and macadam. The chief quarries in Iowa are near Rock Rapids, in Lyon county, where the development of the quarry industry, though not so great as a few miles northward and westward, is capable of great expansion, since the stone may be obtained in practicaly inexhaustible quantities.

Reference has been made to the occurrence of igneous rocks near the state boundary. It may be of considerable interest therefore to mention the fact that in sinking a number of deep wells in different parts of northwestern Iowa the drills have passed completely through sedimentary rocks into the crystalline basement below, penetrating the latter in some cases to the extent of several hundred feet. At one of the latest borings, at Hull, in Sioux county, several thick beds of flint-like rocks were passed through, the different layers being separated by sands and gravels. These flint-like layers were found to be typical quartz-porphyry, a truly igneous rock, or lava, very acid in nature and essentially identical with granite, but cooling under somewhat different physical conditions.

The presence of these massive crystalline rocks is very suggestive of agencies that may have been involved to some extent in metamorphosing the old Sioux sandstone.

## CAMBRIAN.

*Saint Croix Sandstone.* In the extreme northeastern corner of Iowa, at the base of the high bluffs along the Mississippi river and its tributaries there is exposed a thick unconsolidated sand bed, which has been called by Minnesota geologists the Saint Croix sandstone. Its greatest thickness shown in Iowa is about two-hundred and fifty feet; but it is known to have a thickness of not less than one thousand feet, as has been disclosed by borings. While for the most part it is a soft sandstone wearing away rapidly under atmospheric influences there are in places clay seams and thin layers of lime-rock frequently developed. In the neighboring states the calcareous and argillaceous beds assume a much greater importance and form shales and shaley limestones which are charged with the remains of trilobites. This sandstone has been called by most writers on the geology of the Upper Mississippi Valley the "Potsdam," and has been regarded as the western extension of the formation known by that name in New York. There is but little doubt, however, that the Saint Croix is very distinct from the Potsdam sandstone of the Appalachian region, though the fauna is possibly equivalent to the similiar one of the New York horizon.

Although the formation has such a thickness in Iowa no subdivision of it into minor beds has been attempted. It does not have so great an importance in this state as in the neighboring regions of Wisconsin and Minnesota.

As a whole the Saint Croix sandstone of Iowa is of little economic value. At Lansing and some other localities there are thin beds of this formation which are sufficiently compact to furnish building stones of inferior quality. These layers are as yet only used for rough masonry. As most of the sandstone is very incoherent, it will furnish unlimited quantities of coarse and fine building sand; while certain light colored layers could be used for the manufacture of glass.

## SILURIAN.

*Oneota Limestone.* The name of this formation is that proposed by

McGee for the rock usually known as the Lower Magnesian limestone. Though attaining a thickness of between two and three hundred feet it is exposed only over a small area in the northeastern portion of the state. Along the borders of the Mississippi it rises above the soft Saint Croix sandstone in bold escarpments and castellated walls. For the most part the rock is a rather impure dolomite with occasional thin sandstone layers in the upper part. In color it is buff to brown. It is often vesicular and cavernous. In Wisconsin and Minnesota the lower Magnesian limestone embraces other layers than those represented in Iowa. The principal beds thus referred to are called the Willow river limestone and New Richmond sandstone in Wisconsin and the Shakopee limestone and white sandstone in Minnesota.

The Oneota limestone is quarried at Lansing, Waukon, McGregor and other places in Clayton and Allamakee counties. For all ordinary masonry it supplies unlimited quantities of good material. Lime of a very good quality is also manufactured from this rock at a number of places. In certain localities considerable amounts of lead ore are found, but as yet this mineral has not been mined to any great extent in the lower Magnesian limestone.

*Saint Peter Sandstone.* Overlying the Oneota limestone is a heavy bed of pure silicious sandstone, very friable and with few lines of stratification. It is sometimes somewhat indurated, but as a rule incoherent. This is the formation that has long been known in the Upper Mississippi region under the name of the "pictured" rocks, best exposed perhaps in the vicinity of McGregor. Along the boundary of the state northward thin limestone layers are often intercalated. In places this sand formation graduates downward by a rapid increase of calcareous matter into the Oneota limestone. Economically it is of considerable importance in Iowa. Many of the layers are very pure and form excellent material for the manufacture of glass.

*Trenton Limestone.* Contrasting sharply with the other Silurian limerocks of Iowa the Trenton is an ordinary blue limestone instead of a dolomite. For the most part it is a very compact rock, and often fossiliferous. Owing to its difference in lithological characters as compared with the other Silurian limestones it is honeycombed in places by cavities and caverns of greater or less extent. "It constitutes a conspicuous feature of the Mississippi river bluffs from above McGregor to near Eagle Point, Dubuque, and occurs as the surface rock over all or part of the counties of Allamakee, Howard, Winnesheik Fayette and Clayton. The Trenton limestone is interesting to the scientist on account of the number and beauty of the fossil remains inclosed in some of the strata. Here occur the oldest types of life that have been preserved in any degree of perfection within the limits of the state. The old Potsdam trilobites are few and fragmentary, and their structural characters are very obscure. In the Trenton are found countless multitudes of organic remains literally crowded together, and retaining in absolute perfection every structural feature even to the minutest detail. Owing to the slight southerly or southwesterly dip the strata pass successively below the level of the Mississippi river, and so just above Dubuque the Trenton limestone disappears from view." (Calvin.)

The Trenton limestone is quarried in numerous places throughout the counties mentioned. Lime of very good quality is made of this stone. Certain of the clay shales afford good material for the manufacture of light colored brick.

*Galena Limestone.* Overlying the Trenton limestone in northeastern Iowa is a heavily bedded brown dolomite which attains a maximum thickness of between two and three hundred feet in the vicinity of Dubuque. In many places it is very coarse, vesicular and unevenly textured. It frequently contains some cherty matter. The entire bluffs at Dubuque are formed of this limestone. Some sandy material is present in different portions of the formation. The partings are usually argillaceous and are more massive and important toward the top where the formation gradually passes into the overlying shales. As shown by Chamberlain, the conditions of the deposition, in southwestern Wisconsin and vicinity were changed somewhat from those which had existed during the Trenton.

One of the most characteristic features of the Galena limestone is the surface fissures which everywhere traverse this formation. Sometimes they are mere vertical cracks or horizontal partings of the strata, but often widen out into broad cavities. In these openings are found the lead and zinc ores of the region. The metallic ores taken from this limestone form perhaps one of the most important economic characters. It was in the Dubuque region that the lead ore of the upper Mississippi valley was first mined in a systematic way.

The Galena limestone furnishes a considerable quantity of good material for heavy masonry. The chief quarries are located at Dubuque, though everywhere throughout its geological range the rocks are adapted and used for ordinary building purposes. A superior quality of lime is also manufactured from this rock.

*Maquoketa Shales.* Along the entire western slope of Turkey river and below the mouth of that stream on the Mississippi as far as Clinton county, there is exposed between the Galena limestone and the Niagara an extensive bed of bluish or greenish clay-shale. Disintegrating readily under the influence of weathering, these shales allow the massive overlying dolomites to form a bold, mural escarpment which extends the entire length of the river mentioned. The shales have not been reported north of the Iowa boundary. Beginning at a point in Winneshiek county about twenty miles from the Minnesota line the Maquoketa shales have a thickness of over a dozen feet or more. This thickness rapidly increases till at its southernmost exposure it attains a vertical measurement of more than one hundred and twenty-five feet. At Dubuque a few feet of these shales are seen in isolated patches in the summits of the bluffs. For the most part these shales form alternating bands of dark and light colored clays with occasional thin seams of impure limestone. On the upper Maquoketa where the typical locality is situated, the shales are highly charged with many species of fossils. This formation is of small economic importance, unless the clays can be utilized in the manufacture of brick and pottery.

*Upper Silurian.* The "Niagara" escarpment which rises in great prominence on the western slope of Turkey river and continues southward along the Mississippi nearly to Davenport is one of the most important topographical features in northeastern Iowa. The upper Silurian limestones which form this elevation in Iowa are massive dolomities yellowish or brown in color, having a very considerable thickness. Although presenting great uniformity in texture there are locally large amounts of cherty material in bands or irregular nodules. Silicious material is also often disseminated in fine particles throughout the rocks, but as a rule it is concentrated into the masses already referred to.

Chemical analysis of the limestone itself shows that most of the formation is a very pure magnesian limerock or dolomite with scarcely any foreign material. In different layers the percentage of lime and magnesia vary somewhat. In a few cases the latter is almost entirely wanting and the beds assume the condition of a normal limestone.

From its southern exposure where it is thought to attain a thickness of more than five hundred feet it rapidly thins out northward until just beyond the Iowa-Minnesota line its vertical measurement is very insignificant. At the southern end it is heavily bedded. In many places the inclination of the beds is very considerable, sometimes as high as sixty degrees. Lying directly upon the inclined strata are often seen perfectly horizontal beds. At first sight it appears as if there was a marked unconformity. But from a careful examination of some of the exposures it seems probable that the apparent dip is in some cases due to false-bedding on a large scale. In other instances it may be that very decided disturbances have occurred in the strata.

The exact subdivisions of the upper Silurian rocks in Iowa is yet somewhat undetermined. Hall in 1858 regarded the limestone as made up of an upper member which he termed the Le Claire limestone and a lower portion which was regarded as the same formation to which in New York the name Niagara had been applied. With the exception of White, all geologists who have examined the upper Silurian strata in Iowa regard these rocks as made up of at least two distinct formations. These subdivisions greatly differ not only faunally but in a less marked degree in stratigraphical and lithological characters. For the reason set forth above, Hall's Le Claire appears to be a desirable name for the upper member as now understood; while Niagara, for the present, will be retained for the lower member. For the latter term some other name will probably have to be substituted after a further investigation of these rocks has been made.

Perhaps no other geological formation in the state furnishes a better quality of building stone for general purposes than the upper Silurian strata. The great extension of these rocks both in thickness and surface area make the supply inexhaustible. They form also the best lime in the world. This industry has already begun to assume very considerable proportions in this state.

### DEVONIAN.

The broad belt of Devonian rocks in Iowa is traversed medially its entire length by the Cedar river, the beds of this age extending from fifteen to twenty-five miles on each side of the stream. The formation is made up chiefly of massive limestones with magnesian layers. These rocks form one of the most important geological horizons in the state. Although widely known in a general way their details are as yet little understood, as the various minor subdivisions recognized by different writers readily show. Until much additional information has been obtained it seems desirable to recognize now only four sections of the Devonian in Iowa. Some of these formations will probably require further breaking up as the rocks become better understood. Regarding the equivalents of the Iowa Devonian beds with the more eastern formations much has been written, but as yet no satisfactory results have been obtained.

*Independence Shales.* For a long time the Devonian beds of Iowa were regarded as made up almost entirely of limestones. Hall and others found clay beds in the northern part of the state; while still more recently Calvin has discovered important shales layers at the base of the Devonian, in Buchanan county. The latter beds are made up of dark carbonaceous clays with thin bands of impure concretionary limerock. In places the shales are so highly charged with bituminous matter that considerable excitement has been caused at different times, on account of their supposed nearness to coal deposits. Remains of plants have been found scattered through these clays; and they have also accumulated so abundantly locally as to form thin veins of true coal. The shales also yield a very considerable number of animal remains.

*Cedar Valley Limestones.* As already remarked the greater portion of the Devonian in Iowa is made up of limestones, for which it seems desirable to revive Owen's old name of Cedar Valley. These limerocks present very considerable differences in lithological characters. Although for the most part they are ordinary limestones they pass rapidly into argillaceous, dolomitic or even bituminous phases. Many of the beds are very massive though others are somewhat shaley. Everywhere the rocks of this age are highly charged with fossils of many kinds.

Some of the most valuable building and ornamental stones occurring in Iowa are of Devonian age. Perhaps the best limestones for heavy masonry found anywhere in the state are those quarried on the Iowa river north of Iowa City. The old state house at the place just mentioned, and the basement of the new Capitol building at Des Moines were both constructed of this rock. Unlimited quantities of good building stone are accessible in the Devonian throughout the exposed area. Abundant supplies for the manufacture of quick-lime are present everywhere but the quality of lime is not as good as that furnished by the upper Silurian strata.

*Montpelier Sandstone.* This name is applied to certain arenaceous beds that are well exposed in Muscatine county, and which have been recently differentiated by Calvin from the lower Carboniferous sand-rocks found farther to the southward. They are Devonian in age, but were formerly regarded as being identical with the Kinderhook sandstone exposed in the vicinity of Burlington. The Montpelier sandstone lies immediately above the Devonian limestone. The chief exposures of this rock are near the mouth of Pine Creek in the county mentioned. It is composed of yellowish or brownish material, somewhat friable, but in places indurated sufficiently to afford blocks for common masonry. Large quantities of this rock have been quarried and used for the rip-rap which extends for many miles along the Mississippi above Muscatine as a protection for the railroads from the waters of the river.

*Lime Creek Shales.* These beds have long been supposed to form the uppermost member of the Devonian in Iowa. They are well exposed in many places in Floyd county especially. Some of the most important outcrops being at Rockford and along Lime Creek. At the latter place there is exposed a vertical thickness of about one hundred feet of dark argillaceous shales which are highly fossilferous. They disintegrate rapidly under the influences of the weather, forming a plastic clay which will probably prove quite valuable for the manufacture of brick. The geographic extent of these shales is not known at present; nor is their stratigraphic position fully understood.

## CARBONIFEROUS.

### Lower Carboniferous or Mississippian Series.

At the base of the Carboniferous rocks as represented in Iowa and forming one of the most important geological formations exposed within the limits of the state is the great series of limestones which have commonly been termed the "Subcarboniferous." These rocks in Iowa form a sinuous belt twenty-five to forty miles in width midway between the Cedar and Des Moines rivers. The zone mentioned thus extends from the southeastern corner of the state northwestward as far as the Minnesota line.

In southeastern Iowa the lower Carboniferous rocks form percipitous bluffs along the Mississippi and Des Moines rivers and their tributaries. The Mississippian series as represented in the continental interior is made up of four distinct formations. Only three of these however are exposed in Iowa. They are the Kinderhook, Augusta and St. Louis formations.

*Kinderhook Beds.* In the southeastern part of the state the Kinderhook beds are largely hard clay-shales with occasional bands of limestone. At Burlington these shales attain a thickness of over two hundred feet, not all of which, however, are exposed above the water level of the Mississippi river.

Lithologically this formation as exposed at Burlington is a massive clay-shale, often highly calcareous and in the upper part contain silicious matter in the form of fine yellow sand which occasionally assumes the character of a soft sandstone. Below the sandy portion these shales have long been supposed to be destitute of fossils, but recent exposures have disclosed faunas of a most interesting and instructive character. A short distance below Burlington near the mouth of the Skunk river these shales disappear below the water-level. At Keokuk, as has been shown by recent borings, they are in the neighborhood of one hundred and fifty feet below the water-level in the Mississippi. At Burlington immediately beneath the Burlington limestone are several beds a few feet in thickness of limestone and oolite. These are separated by clay shales. The exact relation of these beds to the rocks farther southward in Missouri is not known at present. Beyond the immediate vicinity of the Mississippi river the shales in question are not exposed at the surface in Iowa; but they apparently have a considerable geographical extent and are thought to be recognizable in a number of deep well sections in different portions of the southeastern part of the state.

A hundred miles northwest of Burlington, in Tama and Marshall counties, rocks which have been referred to the Kinderhook are well exposed along the Iowa river and some of its tributaries. The exact correlation of these beds with those of southeastern Iowa has not as yet been fully made out. As shown in the LeGrand quarries the formation is chiefly a rather soft, somewhat irregularly bedded, buff limestone, probably containing a considerable percentage of magnesia. It seems from an examination of the fossils contained in the Le Grand beds that a part of them at least correspond to the limestone at Burlington.

In southeastern Iowa no good quarry rocks have been found in the Kinderhook formation. Occasionally the oolitic beds are used, but they withstand weathering only a short time. The clay-shales at Burlington have recently been brought into prominence in the manufacture of paving brick.

Toward the northern limit in Iowa the Kinderhook assumes a calcerous facies. It is extensively quarried at numerous places in Humboldt, Hardin, Grundy, Tama and Marshall counties. In the latter localities the rock is a fine-grained limestone and forms a very durable building stone. It has been used largely for bridge piers and architectural purposes. Portions of it contain ferric-oxide in narrow veinings. It takes a fairly good polish and is extensively used for interior work in place of ordinary marble. The lower part of the Le Grand section is made up of very compact oolitic rock which withstands very well all weathering influences, as is shown in the court house at Marshalltown which is constructed almost entirely of this stone.

*Augusta Limestone.* The two formations commonly known as the Burlington and Keokuk limestones have recently been found to form properly but a single sequence of rocks. The Burlington and the Keokuk groups are called after the cities of the same name in southeastern Iowa. At these localities the rocks have been regarded as typical developments. A careful examination of the fossils contained and of the relations of the different beds indicate that the limestones under consideration which were formerly considered as two distinct formations should be included under a single term. The lower portion of the formation commonly known as the Burlington limestone is a coarse-grained, encrinital rock, usually white and very pure in certain layers. It often contains considerable ferric-oxide and consequently a reddish hue is imparted to it upon exposure. The lithological characters of this rock are remarkably constant over broad areas. There are also in certain places silicious beds, the lowermost of which have thickness of twenty-five feet or more. They are made up largely of nodular masses and irregular bands of chert with some calcareous matter. There are other layers of flint of equal if not greater importance in the Augusta beds than those just mentioned. The so-called Keokuk limestones are essentially the same as the Burlington rocks. They are usually more compact, less fossiliferous and have a bluish cast instead of the pure white color. The upper portion of the formation also contains beds of clay-shales.

The Augusta Limestones are quarried rather extensively; the chief localities being at Columbus Junction, Burlington and vicinity, Ft. Madison, Keokuk, Bonaparte, and Bentonsport. The rocks at Burlington are used for ordinary masonry; some of the layers, the more massive ones, forming fairly good material for building. Large quantities of good lime could be manufactured, but at the present time only a few small kilns are in operation. Farther southward in Missouri, the Burlington limestone is quarried largely for the manufacture of lime as well as for ordinary masonry. The lower layers at Keokuk have been used for bridge work and all kinds of common masonry. A good quality of lime is burned at various points in the vicinities of the places just mentioned. The sandy magnesian layers at the top of the Keokuk limestone have been extensively used for building and a number of churches and other structures are composed of this material. Along the Des Moines river the rocks of this formation were formerly used in the construction of dams at the time when slack-water navigation was proposed for the Des Moines river.

*St. Louis Limestone.* The rocks of this stage have commonly passed under the name of Concretionary limestone. But they are the same as those developed at the mouth of the Missouri river which Shumard called after the city of St. Louis. The northern limit of these rocks is one hundred miles beyond any known exposure of Augusta rocks. From this northern border nearly to the mouth of the Missouri river the limestone is comparatively thin; but southward from the latter point it thickens rapidly until it attains a measurement of more than two hundred feet. Everywhere over the northern area of the St. Louis, characteristic brecciated rocks are seen. In Iowa this formation has probably a surface exposure much greater than any other member of the Lower Carboniferous. It is usually a fine-grained, compact, bluish rock breaking with conchoidal fracture. The upper portion of the formation is often covered by a white, highly fossiliferous marl.

The St. Louis limestone is made up largely of pure calcium carbonate. Quick-lime is manufactured at numerous places everywhere throughout the range of the formation. At Tracey, and elsewhere in Marion, Wapello and Van Buren counties certain of the St. Louis rocks furnish excellent material for heavy constructional purposes, bridge piers and foundations

### COAL MEASURES.

From an economic standpoint the most important geological formation in the state is that yielding coal. The strata of Iowa furnishing this valuable product form the northernmost extension of the great interior coal field of the American continent. The beds occupy the southern third of the state and are distributed more or less extensively through one-half of the entire number of counties. The area covered by the Carboniferous strata is therefore not far from twenty thousand square miles. It must not be inferred, however, that the coal is equally distributed over all this district, for such is not the case. The broad belt running southeast and northwest and traversed its entire length by the Des Moines river from Ft. Dodge to Keokuk has heretofore been found to be much more productive of coal than other parts of the region. Lately in many places outside of the belt named, coal has been discovered in abundance, often where its presence was unsuspected before.

Taken as a whole there are two kinds of beds, sharply contrasted, which go to make up the Coal Measures of the state. The first is marked by a great predominance of clay shales and sandstones, often to the total exclusion of the limestone. The individual beds have usually a very limited extent and replace one another in rapid succession. On the other hand, the second class of sediments above mentioned is made up chiefly of calcareous shales with heavy beds of limestone. The layers are evenly bedded and extend over very considerable areas.

As the conditions of deposition were evidently those of a slowly sinking shore the marginal deposits as a whole practically underlie the open sea formations, the former being regarded as the "Lower" Coal Measures and the latter as the "Upper" Coal Measures. At the same time it must be remembered that this does not necessarily imply that the "Lower" measures are to be considered much older than the "Upper;" but rather that along the great and successive planes of sedimentation different beds of the upper and lower divisions were laid down contemporaneously. The limits of the two formations in Iowa thus assume somewhat different lines from those that have commonly been recognized.

It has been proposed, therefore, to divide the Coal Measures, or Upper Carboniferous, into:

(2) The "Upper" Coal Measures, or Missouri Stage.
(1) The "Lower" Coal Measures, or Des Moines Stage.

The Des Moines formation represents the Lower Coal Measures or marginal deposits of the upper Carboniferous. It takes its name from the Des Moines river which flows for more than two hundred miles directly through the beds of this terrane. It extends into Missouri forming the northern and western boundaries of the Ozark mountains and extends still farther southward into Kansas and Indian Territory.

The Missouri formation corresponds essentially to the upper Coal Measures, representing the more strictly marine deposits. It is the formation typically developed in the northwestern part of Missouri. The Missouri river also winds its way for more than four hundred miles through the beds of this stage, exposing numerous fine sections on both sides of the stream throughout the entire distance.

In the order of their abundance the rocks of the Coal Measures are clay-shales, sandstones, limestones and coals. The secondary part that the calcareous beds play in the Coal Measures of the state, especially in the lower division, contrasts this formation with the other paleozoic rocks. Below, the Coal Measures rest on a great basement of massive limestones with but few clayey or sandy beds of separation. Not less striking is the relative thinness, as a rule, of the individual layers which replace one another upwards and laterally in rapid succession. If the upper and lower divisions of the Coal Measures in Iowa were to be contrasted upon lithological characters alone it would be found that the former is prevailingly lime bearing; the latter largely clayey.

Little need be said here concerning the quality of the coals of the state. They are all of the bituminous variety and are fully described in another place. The carbonaceous seams vary from a few inches to seven or eight or even ten feet in thickness; the average of the veins at present worked is between four and five feet. These beds are deposited not in two or three continuous layers over the entire area, as has been commonly supposed, but in more or less lenticular masses varying from a few feet to several miles in extent.

The stratigraphical importance of the coal seams is not so great as has been generally supposed, since the bituminous beds are, with very few exceptions rather limited. Only a single case is at present known in which the geographic extent of a coal stratum is more than a few miles, and for a part of this distance the coal is but two or three feet in thickness. On the other hand, the amount of coal in the state, is probably very much greater than has been commonly supposed.

For reasons which need not be stated in detail here, considerable difficulty has been encountered in working out the structural features of the Coal Measures of Iowa. The general inclination of the beds is to the southwestward. Careful estimates indicate that the greatest thickness of the Lower Coal Measures in the state is probably in the neighborhood of four hundred feet; and that the maximum vertical measurement of the upper division is thrice that figure. Erosion has removed much of the coal bearing strata of this district and the original thickness of these rocks is not now represented at any one place.

The basal coal seams of the Lower Coal Measures of Iowa appear to be much more extensive than those toward the top, where they are only a few inches in vertical measurement and perhaps a hundred yards in extent. The coal may therefore be regarded as disposed in numerous basins of greater or less area, thickened centrally, but gradually becoming attenuated toward the margins. These are arranged in various horizons interlocking with one another, but separated by varying thicknesses of sandstone and shale. Thus at any one point a dozen or more seams may be passed through in sinking a shaft, several perhaps being workable.

The disposition of the coal in numerous limited lenticular basins instead of a few layers extending over broad areas is of the utmost importance from a purely economical standpoint. In all mining operations and in all prospecting it is very essential that this fact be kept constantly in mind. With methods of boring more modern than those commonly in vogue throughout the western states there is every reason to believe that in the Lower Coal Measures especially the large majority of good coal seams twelve inches in thickness and over encountered in prospecting may be traced readily and easily to localities where they are thick enough for profitable working.

In Iowa the restrictions upon the distribution of the individual seams are not numerous as compared with other regions. Yet there are disturbances of various kinds which break the continuity of the coal strata, locally interfering slightly with mining operations. They are referable to the three general agencies of deposition, erosion and dislocation.

From careful estimates made from reliable sources the production of coal for the past year amounted to more than 5,340,000 tons, valued at $7,750,000. By comparisons it will be seen that Iowa as a coal producer ranks first among the states west of the Mississippi river and fifth among the states of the Union.

Throughout all of the Coal Measures in Iowa occur unlimited quantities of clay of excellent quality for the manufacture of paving, pressed, fire and other kinds of brick. An excellent quality of potter's clay and material for tiling, terra-cotta, and in fact nearly all other kinds of clay products, are plentiful.

## CRETACEOUS.

Although formerly known to be exposed only over a small area near Sioux City, the Cretaceous rocks of Iowa have recently been found to occupy a very considerable district in the northwestern portion of the state. On account of a thick mantle of drift over all this portion of the state there is considerable difficulty in locating the exact boundary along the eastern margin of the deposits. From numerous borings, however, the Cretaceous beds have been recognized over more than a dozen counties, showing that the approximate eastern boundary is a somewhat sinuous line running through a point midway between Sioux City and Council Bluffs nearly to Fort Dodge and thence bending northward. Beyond the limits of this line numerous outliers have been recognized, some appearing more than fifty miles beyond the boundary mentioned.

There are four formations in Iowa which are probably referable to the Cretaceous, though the exact stratigraphical equivalents of two of these, the Fort Dodge gypsum deposits and the Nishnabotna sandstone are at present somewhat doubtful.

*Nishnabotna Sandstone.* Although the beds under consideration have usually been referred to the Cretaceous they have never been directly traced to the outcrops of the Woodbury shales. The geographical distance between the nearest exposures of the two formations as at present known is very considerable. If the Nishnabotna is Cretaceous it may be the equivalent either of the Woodbury shales or of the Niobrara chalk; which one it is cannot now be stated. In regard to the gypsum beds their formation indicates a saline lake deposit such as might be left by a retreating ocean. This fact taken in connection with the probable great eastern extension of the Niobrara suggests that the Fort Dodge beds were formed during the retreat of the Niobrara waters through Iowa. At the present time it seems best not to attempt a specific correlation of the gypsum deposits, nor of the Nishnabotna sandstone, but merely to regard them as Cretaceous in age. The sandstones and loose sands that have been called Nishnabotna are to be regarded as shore deposits; along with numerous other beds of similar character which occasionally are found as outliers through central and northern Iowa.

The Nishnabotna as reported by White has a thickness of fifty to seventy-five feet; and is seen exposed in the southeastern part of Guthrie county, southern Montgomery county, and elsewhere in the western part of central Iowa.

Quarries have been opened in these rocks at Lewis, in Cass county. In its lithological characters the formation is a coarse-grained, ferruginous sandstone, dark brown in color and usually quite friable. Occasionally thin clay seams are intercalated.

*Fort Dodge Beds.* This name is applied to the gypsum deposits and certain associated beds which are well exposed in the neighborhood of Fort Dodge. The gypsum attains a vertical measurement of from two to thirty feet, its average thickness being perhaps about fifteen to sixteen feet. It occupies an area, in the central part of Webster county, of about twenty-five square miles. It is traversed north and south its entire length by the Des Moines river and is cut through by many of this stream's smaller tributaries.

Probably more than one-half of the entire deposit has been removed through erosion by the chief water course. The most extensive exposures now open are about six miles below Fort Dodge.

To some extent the massive gypsum of Fort Dodge has been quarried for building purposes. A number of buildings and foundations have been constructed of this material. It has also been used quite extensively for heavy masonry. Its most important use, however, is its manufacture into stucco and land-plaster. During the past year more than fifty thousand tons of these materials were prepared in the vicinity of Fort Dodge.

*Woodbury Shales.* As already intimated, the typical outcrops of this formation are to be seen in Woodbury county along the Big Sioux river. The formation corresponds essentially with the Dakota and Fort Benton groups of Hayden. The beds represent shore deposits and it seems desirable to retain the name in preference to the two proposed by Hayden. "Woodbury" as defined by White expresses more accurately than any other name yet proposed the lithological features of the rocks as represented in Iowa.

The Woodbury shales are made up in certain places largely of the sandstone, which sometimes form hard concretionary masses not unlike quartzite. In some localities these masses are so near together that they may be quarried to advantage for building stone. The most important of these openings is in the vicinity of Sioux City and is now known as the Rees' Granite quarry. The rock has apparently all the qualities of the regular crystalline massive rocks. The greater portion of the Woodbury shales is argillaceous and afford inexhaustible quantities of good clay for the manufacture of pottery, fire and paving brick.

*Niobrara Chalk.* These beds in their chalky facies have been observed in Iowa in the vicinity of the Big Sioux river. They are probably represented further eastward by more strictly shore deposits. They consist of fine soft calcareous layers appearing not unlike clay at first glance. These chalky layers in connection with the clays form excellent material for the manufacture of Portland cement. This industry has already begun under favorable circumstances on the Missouri above Sioux City.

## PLEISTOCENE, OR SURFACE DEPOSITS.

Over all Iowa, covering the indurated rocks to a depth of from a few inches to two or three hundred feet, is a mantle of loose incoherent material. This material is chiefly of three kinds; known as the drift, loess, and alluvium. The latter may be regarded as the deposits of the modern rivers, the two former as glacial debris.

*Alluvium.* Little need be said here in regard to the alluviul deposits. They are the fine sediments laid down in the river valleys making up what is commonly known as the flood plain. Many of the river terraces are also alluvial. These materials will be treated at length in another place in connection with an account of the soils of the state.

*Drift.* To the heterogeneous mixture of clay, sand, gravel and boulders which is seen everywhere throughout the state there has been applied the name of drift. Everwhere the proportions of these drift constitutents vary. It changes rapidly from place to place passing from one kind into another. The clays form by far the largest portion of the mixture and is usually mingled with more or less fine sand. In color it has a characteristic brown or buff tint. When excavated the surface exposed quickly breaks up into small cubic or angular fragments commonly known as joint-clay. The sand and gravel often form considerable beds yet they are usually quite limited in extent. The boulders are chiefly of crystalline rocks of northern origin. They represent a great variety of eruptive and metamorphic types.

The drift is largely of glacial origin. It has been shown in Iowa to be made up of two sheets. The lowest or earliest drift forms a part of the great drift mantle extending over northern United States. In the Mississippi valley it has its southern boundary along the line of the Ohio and Missouri rivers. The upper till belongs to a later glacial epoch and is included within the area bounded by what is known as the moraine of the Des Moines lobe of the second great ice invasion. This forms a narrow triangle in Iowa with its apex reaching to the city of Des Moines.

*Loess.* This deposit is well displayed along the Missouri and Mississippi rivers and at numerous places throughout the interior of Iowa. It is a fine homogeneous clay-like material which seldom shows any tendency toward stratification. It is friable enough to be impressed with the finger but resists weathering in a remarkable way.

The surface deposits of the state belong chiefly to the Quaternary age of geology. Over a great part of Iowa the soils are formed directly through these deposits. The purer clays afford good material for the manufacture of brick; while certain portions afford sand which can be utilized in glass making.

## CLIMATOLOGY OF IOWA.

### By John R. Sage, Director Iowa Weather and Crop Service.

The prime factors of agricultural prosperity are a fertile soil and a favorable climate, the latter being the more important. There are in this country millions of acres of soil, which, though abundantly supplied with the elements of fertility are comparatively worthless, because of unfavorable climatic conditions. Nothing can fully compensate for the lack of rainfall in the growing season, for only a small portion of any arid region can be made productive by irrigation.

The claim may be made in behalf of Iowa that in respect to these two essentials, soil and climate, it stands foremost among the agricultural states of the Union. There is no question as to the exceeding richness and depth of its soil, for it has maintained a large measure of its original fertility under a system of continual cropping which would have reduced to barrenness the thinner soils of less favored sections. And its climate has served as a fit complement of its soil in the production of those vast crops which have figured so conspicuously in the agricultural statistics of the country.

The establishment of the National and State weather bureaus has incited public interest in questions relating to the climate of the different sections of our greatly diversified country. And the census reports have revealed the fact that the settlement of the country and increase of population bear a very definite ratio to the average yearly precipitation, mean temperature and the general climatic conditions affecting crop production and the public health. People who are about to emigrate, to better their condition in life, are largely influenced in their choice of a new home by such facts as they are able to obtain relative to climate. With the larger number this is very properly a consideration of chief importance.

### WEATHER REPORTS.

Fortunately we have at hand ample meteorological records to illustrate the constants of temperature, humidity, wind movement and the general characteristics of the climate of Iowa. Weather observations were begun at the military posts in the territory as early as the year 1820, and records were made with some degree of regularity under military auspices until 1849, when the Smithsonian Institution, aided by the general government, took up the work of systematic observation, establishing stations wherever intelligent observers could be secured. Since 1871 this work has been done under the auspices of the National and State weather services. There is, therefore, no lack of material, in the form of official records, from which we may obtain a knowledge of the more important features of Iowa's climate. A careful study of the voluminous data will convince any one interested in the subject that for all-the-year-round residence, for the promotion of health, physical vigor and agricultural prosperity there is no more favorable climate in America than in this favored section of the great Mississippi valley.

### GENERAL CLIMATIC FEATURES.

Situated near the geographical center of the United States, the climate is strictly continental. This term being used in contradistinction to marine climate implies that it has winters of considerable severity, and summers of unusual warmth, with large seasonal and daily temperature ranges, a generally dry and salubrious atmosphere, small percentage of cloudiness and large percentage of sunshine. The altitude of the State ranges from 444 feet above sea-level at the confluence the Des Moines and Mississippi rivers, to 1,650 feet at a point near Spirit Lake; and as there are no mountain ranges nor extensive forests the physical conditions give to the State a homogeneous climate, with only such variations of temperature, rainfall and other meteorological elements as result from latitude and elevation.

Despite its remoteness from the sea its climatic characteristics are remarkably constant; in fact, no section of the country enjoys a greater degree of uniformity of the conditions favorable to the production of the staple crops. In attestation of this it may be stated that, while there have been seasons of variable productiveness, there has never been a total failure of the principal crops in this State since the virgin soil was first broken by the plow-shares of the white settlers.

The climate of this section is affected by the general topography of the continent, the great mountain ranges, and the oceanic and atmospheric currents, all of which must be duly considered in a thorough study of the subject. A glance at the map of the continent will show a great central depression extending from the Gulf of Mexico to the Arctic sea, formed by the vast mountain ranges at the west and the lesser uplift skirting the Atlantic coast. This interior valley is much wider and somewhat lower at the north than at the south, and two-thirds of the drainage of the continent flows northward. The upper Mississippi valley, of which Iowa is a part, forms the water-shed about midway between the Gulf and Hudson Bay. It has been stated that in time of high water a canoe can be rowed from the Mississippi up the Minnesota to its source in Big Stone Lake, and thence across a slough to Traverse Lake, the source of the Red River of the North. The altitude at this point where the waters of the Gulf and the Arctic ocean are in touch is less than one thousand feet above sea level.

Through this vast channel in ancient geologic periods the glaciers pushed their way, forming the drift deposits, and laying the foundation of soil of the most productive empire on the surface of the globe. And now, in these latter years, this mid-continent depression gives free passage to the boreal breezes from the north and the humid winds from the south, which here meet and commingle to refresh the earth with copious showers in the season when they are most needed. It is easy to see what an important part is borne in the climate of the interior by the great physical feature herein described. If the mountain ranges crossed the continent east and west, instead of north and south, this central valley would be a veritable desert, instead of the garden and granary of the western hemisphere. The cool waves from the north and the vapor-laden winds from the south are equally important factors in making this a habitable, productive and prosperous region.

### PRECIPITATION.

The moisture precipitated over Iowa and contiguous portions of the Mississippi and Missouri valleys comes almost entirely, either directly or indirectly, from the Gulf of Mexico. The warm southerly winds, heavily laden with humidity from that source, drawn hither by the passage of low area storms from the west, deposit a portion of their moisture in advance of the storm centers as they move toward the Atlantic. Following in the rear of these depressions the cold and dry air from the northward condenses the remaining moisture in the rear quadrants of departing storms. These alternating currents flowing northward and southward through the valley, with their sharp contrasts of temperature, brought thus into action by the passage of low areas across the continent, form the warp and woof of the fabric of the weather of this section. And as the Gulf, which is the great fountain of humidity whence our annual supply of moisture is drawn, is permanent, and the atmospheric waves of high or low pressure are constantly passing, there is no danger that this region will become arid and unproductive. The people may safely bank upon the permanence of their climate and an ample supply of moisture.

Various early historic publications placed the average yearly precipitation of Iowa at forty-four to forty-seven inches. These figures are too high, being obtained from insufficient data. The correct mean obtained from all available records, covering a considerable number of years in all sections of the state is about thirty-five inches.

Blodget's rain chart for the continent shows the average annual precipitation in the eastern and southeastern counties to be forty-two inches; through the central belt from southwest to northeast it is thirty, and in the extreme northwestern section twenty-five inches. In the United States

Army Meteorological Register, published in 1855, Mr. Blodget, referring to the precipitation in the Mississippi Valley, says:

"There is an exceptional district in eastern Iowa having a great rainfall, which requires some explanation, especially in its contrast with the small quantities at Lake Michigan. The exception is due apparently to the elevation of central Missouri in comparison with lower Iowa, causing an atmospheric eddy similar to that of the lower Mississippi."

A careful study of meteorological data covering the period since the above was published does not show so wide a difference between the average annual precipitation of the eastern, central and western districts of the State. For example, the average at Keokuk, from 1872 to 1892, is 35.87 inches; at Muscatine, 1845 to 1892, 39.21 inches; at Davenport, 1872 to 1892, 34.70 inches; at Dubuque, 1874 to 1892, 37.00 inches; at McGregor, 16 years record, 34.97 inches. These stations are all in the eastern part of the State, and it will be seen the average is below the figures of Blodget's rain chart. In the central and western sections of the State, the following averages are obtained: Des Moines, 35.06 inches; Sioux City, 25.58 inches; Council Bluffs, 33.36 inches; Logan, 35.50 inches; Sac City, 30.82 inches; Glenwood, 31.70 inches. These figures indicate that there is a more equable distribution of rainfall than the earlier charts and tables showed. And it may be stated further that in the western half of the State the precipitation in the winter months is considerably less than in the eastern half, while the rainfall in the summer months is greater in the western than in the eastern districts.

## COMPARISON WITH EASTERN STATES.

The annual precipitation in Iowa is equal to the averages in the northern, central and western portions of New York, northern Vermont and New Hampshire, northwestern counties of Pennsylvania, northern Ohio and the larger part of Michigan. In fact it compares favorably with all the Atlantic and Middle States on the same latitude, except points along or near the sea coast, or in the mountainous districts. The following yearly averages are from the United States Weather Bureau tables of recent date:

| STATIONS. | INCHES. | STATIONS. | INCHES. |
|---|---|---|---|
| Charlotte, Vt | 33.79 | Fort Niagara, N. Y | 25.52 |
| Hanover, N. H | 30.94 | Buffalo, N. Y. | 38.55 |
| Portland, Me | 41.55 | Pittsburgh, Pa | 38.29 |
| Fitchburg, Mass. | 38.07 | Cleveland, Ohio | 37.90 |
| Woodstock, Vt | 37.90 | Toledo, Ohio | 32.94 |
| Albany, N. Y | 38.83 | Detroit, Mich | 33.83 |
| Cooperstown, N. Y | 35.60 | Alpena, Mich | 36.00 |
| Madison Barracks, N Y. | 27.07 | Escanaba, Mich | 33.93 |
| Rochester, N. Y | 35.52 | Marquette, Mich | 33.93 |
| Ithaca, N. Y | 31.73 | Lansing, Mich | 33.75 |

Comparison of these yearly averages with the accompanying tables of annual precipitation at a large number of Iowa stations will show that the eastern states on this parallel have no advantage over Iowa in respect to the yearly supply of moisture.

And it will be seen that these figures do not sustain the theory that the annual precipitation of a locality is affected by contiguity to the lakes or extensive forests. In fact, local evaporation, whether from marshes, lakes or forests does not materially affect the rainfall of the interior of the continent. The following from the United States Army Meteorological Register is to the point:

"The lake district presents a somewhat anomalous result, in comparison with the interior portions, as it has less rainfall than the valley of the Mississippi in their latitudes. The effect of these bodies of water is clearly to diminish the quantity of rain for the whole period of the warm season. This deficiency appears very clearly in the mean for the spring, and it is conclusive proof that local evaporation adds little or none to the quantity of rain of these interior districts. The valley of the Mississippi, and its extension in the Ohio valley, strikingly contrast with the rainfall in the lake districts.

### DISTRIBUTION BY SEASONS.

A peculiar feature of the climate of the trans-Mississippi region is that it has its minimum of precipitation in the winter, and its maximum in the spring and summer, or in the crop growing season. This characteristic of the climate is of great economic importance, since it insures an abundance of food products even in years of the greatest variability in the distribution of moisture. In this respect Iowa has a most decided advantage over the eastern states which have a much heavier annual rainfall, for in this State two-thirds of the yearly moisture comes in the six crop growing months, when it is most needed. Professor Blodget, in his American Climatology, refers to this feature as follows:

"For the whole period of the warm months, in which May and September should be included, the quantity of rain distributed over the Mississippi valley is comparatively very great, and there is no great area so far in the interior which presents a similar result. The quantities are absolutely as well as relatively large, and they considerably exceed those of the plains of the Atlantic coast in the same latitude. The line of fifteen inches for the three (summer) months goes only to 38 of latitude on the Atlantic coast, yet it rises nearly to 44 in the Mississippi valley, and occupies a very wide area below the fortieth parallel. The measure of twelve inches is equally more extensive in the interior, though neither of these stretches upon the plains beyond 100 west longitude."

The fact here stated is undoubtedly due to the prevalence during the summer months of southerly winds laden with vapor from the Gulf, the great thermal fountain whence is drawn the bulk of the precipitation of the interior valleys. The following table gives, as a basis of comparison, the average rainfall for the four critical months of the year, viz: May, June, July and August, at a number of stations in the Atlantic states and in Iowa:

| EASTERN STATIONS. | INCHES. | IOWA STATIONS. | INCHES. |
|---|---|---|---|
| Albany, N. Y. | 15.24 | Des Moines | 17.20 |
| Rochester, N. Y. | 12.47 | Council Bluffs | 19.10 |
| Buffalo, N. Y. | 13.28 | Logan | 19.50 |
| Oswego, N. Y. | 11.66 | Dubuque | 17.35 |
| Cleveland, Ohio | 14.68 | Muscatine | 18.50 |
| Atlantic City, N. Y. | 13.88 | Keokuk | 18.30 |

It should be noted that these four months make the corn, as also the other staple crops of this region, excepting hay, and a glance at the figures of the above table will show the great advantage enjoyed by the Mississippi valley in the distribution of summer rainfall. The average rainfall of Iowa for the four months named is as follows: May 4.15 inches; June 4.95; July 4.30; August 3.60. Total for the four months 17.00 inches.

But let us take the six crop months, adding April and September to the four above named, and we have a total average rainfall of 23.25 inches, or an average of 3.87 inches per month. This amount of moisture in the soil, and a mean summer temperature of 71 degrees, give a hot-house development to the staple crops of this region.

Dr. Gustavus Hinrichs, who originated the Iowa Weather Service and served over twelve years as its director, said in his last annual report: "While Iowa has a continental climate in regard to temperature, it enjoys the fertilizing advantages of a high and well distributed rainfall usually restricted to the coasts only. In fact there is no region in the interior of any continent that has a climate like that of Iowa, in which the extremes of temperature are coupled with an abundance of fertilizing moisture. Right close to the south, the immense boiler of the Gulf is furnishing vapor; the heated continental expanse north causes the southerly current prevailing throughout the summer. These southerly winds carry the moisture of the Gulf all over the Mississippi valley, where it descends normally in great abundance, making it the best watered valley in the world."

In Hall's Geology of Iowa the following statement occurs in the opening chapter; "The most marked feature in the distribution of moisture precipitated in the form of rain and snow through the year is a relative increase in the quantity falling in the spring and summer, and a very considerable dimunition in winter; which condition becomes more and more marked as we advance westward from the Mississippi. The dimunition in the quantity of snow, as compared with the eastern States on the same parallel, is one of the features of the climate which is practically most felt by settlers in that region."

The climatic feature has a favorable effect upon the health and comfort of the inhabitants of this region, the relatively dry atmosphere enabling them to easily withstand the low temperature prevalent in the winter months. Those who have experienced the chilling atmosphere and "eternal drizzle" of the so-called milder climates of the sea coast region can appreciate the difference.

### CROPS IN DROUGHTY SEASONS.

While a high average of summer rainfall has been recorded for the past fifty years, this State like all other sections of the country is subject to fluctuations or variability in the seasonal precipitation, and occasional droughty seasons have been experienced. But as a compensation there is a peculiar quality of the Iowa soil which enables it to withstand droughts and produce abundantly with an average summer rainfall that would be totally insufficient in eastern and southern states. This fact was noted by Prof. T. S. Parvin some years ago, who in a contribution to the American Journal of Science, Vol. XXIII, said:

"In 1854 occurred the great drought in this and the western States generally; but owing to the porous nature of our soil the crops with us turned out much better than in the States east of the Mississippi."

"1856. This season was very dry; the total quantity of rain in the summer months was only 6.78 inches, or 10.20 below the summer mean. The crops were, notwithstanding, more than an average yield, both of corn and small grain; and the three or four dry seasons we have had abundantly prove that the soil and climate of Iowa are unsurpassed on the continent for farming purposes."

These facts so well stated by Prof. Parvin have been remarked in the occasional dry seasons that have occurred since the above was written, justifying the assertion that there has never been any very near approach to absolute failure of crops in Iowa since its settlement by civilized man. And the years of severe drought in the summer months have been very few in comparison to the number suffered in some of the States which have a larger average annual rainfall.

The severest drought in recent years, affecting the lower part of the State, occurred in the mid-summer of 1890. The average amount of rainfall in July was only 1.98 inches, and in August, 3.41 inches. And the severity of the drought was greatly increased by very high winds during the periods of high temperature. And yet in that year of untoward conditions, Iowa produced 239,000,000 bushels of corn, 71,368,000 bushels of oats, 2,979,081 bushels of flax, 8,332,000 bushels of potatoes, 4,991,000 tons of hay, and over $50,000,000 worth of poultry products. There is no danger of a famine in a country, which, in the worst seasons, can produce such vast amounts of food stuffs.

The same porous nature of the soil which causes it to withstand severe droughts, also gives it the requisite quality to take up a considerable surplus of rainfall, making it fairly productive in abnormally wet seasons. These extremes, however, are exceptional, by far the greater number of years being normal and abundantly productive. The State is favorably situated in the heart of the valley, escaping frequent liability to the extremes of wet and dry to which other sections are subject.

Prof. W. I. Chamberlain, of Ohio, who served about five years as president of the Iowa Agricultural College, gave the following unbiased testimony concerning the soil and climate of this state:

"One thing has surprised me each spring and summer, viz: that the spring is considerably earlier here than it is a hundred miles further south in Ohio, and the summer is much hotter and surer to mature the corn crop before frost. The proportion of clear sky and hot days and nights is far greater, and the power of the sun's rays upon the black soil is immense. I believe Iowa to be on the whole the best and surest corn State in the Union the surface is more rolling, the soil more porous and sandy and better drained by nature than most of the prairie soils in other States. Hence the corn is not so subject to damage from too much rain here as in Illinois and Missouri. It dries out for cultivation quicker."

## TABULATED PRECIPITATION DATA.

The following table gives the average monthly and annual precipitation (rain and melted snow) in inches, at a number of Iowa Stations, covering the records of years named in the last column. The United States Weather Bureau furnished the data from various official sources:

| STATIONS. | J'N'RY | FEB'RY | MARCH | APRIL | MAY | JUNE | JULY | AUGUST | SEPT'R | OCTOB'R | NOV'R | DEC'R | ANNUAL | NO. OF YEARS |
|---|---|---|---|---|---|---|---|---|---|---|---|---|---|---|
| Algona | .92 | 1.57 | 1.03 | 2.29 | 3.46 | 4.62 | 3.04 | 3.82 | 3.29 | 2.21 | 1.30 | .99 | 27.77 | 16 |
| Amana | 1.61 | 1.38 | 2.03 | 2.45 | 3.99 | 4.95 | 3.88 | 3.80 | 3.53 | 3.13 | 2.00 | 1.55 | 34.07 | 16 |
| Ames | 1.22 | 1.01 | 1.63 | 2.43 | 3.81 | 4.49 | 4.51 | 3.74 | 3.76 | 2.32 | 1.42 | 1.04 | 30.96 | 9 |
| Brookside | 1.43 | 1.07 | 2.43 | 2.99 | 4.62 | 5.78 | 5.97 | 5.29 | 4.60 | 3.02 | 2.14 | 1.36 | 40.98 | 10 |
| Brookville | 1.96 | 1.36 | 1.99 | 3.06 | 3.68 | 4.97 | 2.82 | 3.39 | 5.09 | 2.95 | 1.77 | 1.62 | 32.24 | 11 |
| Cedar Rapids | 1.70 | 1.73 | 2.45 | 2.90 | 4.78 | 3.80 | 4.29 | 3.30 | 2.68 | 3.30 | 1.64 | 1.69 | 33.83 | 8 |
| Cresco | 1.38 | 1.00 | 1.77 | 2.16 | 8.47 | 6.14 | 4.32 | 3.13 | 3.94 | 2.36 | 1.50 | 1.42 | 31.45 | 19 |
| Council Bluffs | .80 | 1.18 | 1.57 | 2.08 | 4.59 | 5.96 | 4.12 | 3.34 | 3.45 | 2.96 | 1.10 | .90 | 33.36 | 13 |
| Clinton | 1.92 | 2.32 | 2.97 | 8.12 | 4.47 | 4.63 | 3.53 | 3.63 | 3.33 | 2.95 | 1.98 | 2.11 | 37.45 | 17 |
| Davenport | 1.74 | 1.63 | 2.16 | 2.77 | 4.40 | 4.36 | 3.81 | 3.82 | 3.17 | 3.05 | 2.04 | 1.23 | 34.70 | 20 |
| Dubuque | 1.40 | 1.56 | 2.31 | 2.75 | 3.98 | 6.08 | 4.57 | 3.40 | 2.49 | 3.53 | 2.14 | 1.85 | 37.99 | 18 |
| Des Moines | 1.03 | 1.81 | 1.43 | 2.06 | 4.62 | 6.85 | 3.19 | 3.51 | 1.90 | 3.53 | 1.90 | 1.40 | 35.56 | 13 |
| Denmark | 1.24 | 2.22 | 2.46 | 2.11 | 4.42 | 5.76 | 3.81 | 3.82 | 3.60 | 3.42 | 1.81 | 1.95 | 34.90 | 12 |
| Dysart | 1.69 | 1.53 | 1.73 | 2.69 | 3.94 | 4.17 | 4.79 | 3.67 | 4.75 | 3.13 | 1.73 | 1.06 | 34.74 | 11 |
| Elkader | 1.70 | 1.66 | 2.88 | 3.11 | 3.80 | 3.77 | 3.65 | 4.02 | 3.47 | 3.03 | 2.77 | 2.37 | 41.31 | 12 |
| Fairfield | 3.90 | 2.09 | 2.77 | 2.83 | 5.13 | 4.47 | 4.62 | 3.82 | 3.65 | 3.17 | 2.71 | 2.98 | 37.96 | 12 |
| Ft. Madison | 2.14 | 1.17 | 1.86 | 1.86 | 4.30 | 5.77 | 3.90 | 3.88 | 2.39 | 2.96 | 2.39 | 1.98 | 34.18 | 37 |
| Glenwood | 1.06 | .98 | 1.46 | 1.60 | 3.55 | 5.17 | 4.62 | 3.62 | 4.24 | 2.82 | 2.01 | 1.69 | 31.73 | 4 |
| Guttenberg | 1.74 | 1.55 | 2.36 | 2.21 | 5.43 | 5.82 | 4.14 | 2.66 | 2.39 | 3.11 | 1.20 | .83 | 39.87 | 23 |
| Iowa City | 1.57 | 1.05 | 1.29 | 3.13 | 4.17 | 5.68 | 4.35 | 4.67 | 4.24 | 2.87 | 2.64 | 1.48 | 53.87 | 22 |
| Independence | 1.73 | 1.60 | 2.16 | 2.21 | 4.04 | 6.65 | 4.72 | 5.43 | 4.70 | 3.11 | 1.82 | 1.96 | 35.87 | 20 |
| Keokuk | 1.88 | 1.99 | 2.21 | 2.96 | 4.94 | 4.92 | 4.19 | 3.12 | 3.53 | 3.49 | 2.03 | 1.78 | 38.20 | 9 |
| Le Claire | 1.80 | 1.36 | 2.08 | 2.73 | 4.46 | 5.22 | 4.09 | 3.25 | 3.26 | 2.61 | 1.71 | 1.35 | 35.51 | 16 |
| Logan | 1.64 | 1.86 | 2.50 | 2.63 | 4.34 | 4.51 | 5.41 | 3.91 | 3.94 | 2.93 | 2.39 | 2.39 | 36.79 | 37 |
| Monticello | 1.81 | 2.06 | 2.79 | 3.41 | 3.84 | 4.86 | 4.23 | 4.38 | 3.72 | 3.04 | 2.28 | 2.11 | 39.22 | 43 |
| Muscatine | 1.59 | 1.21 | 1.93 | 2.39 | 3.66 | 4.95 | 3.68 | 3.57 | 4.04 | 3.16 | 1.79 | 1.75 | 34.97 | 16 |
| McGregor | 1.54 | 2.23 | 2.76 | 2.07 | 4.19 | 5.20 | 5.68 | 5.81 | 5.81 | 8.45 | 2.34 | 3.54 | 45.16 | 10 |
| Nashua | .98 | 3.11 | 2.09 | 2.65 | 3.43 | 4.41 | 3.59 | 3.12 | 3.43 | 8.44 | 1.82 | 1.29 | 31.99 | 9 |
| Omaha, Nebraska | .67 | .73 | 1.46 | 3.11 | 3.46 | 8.64 | 2.15 | 3.43 | 3.98 | 2.77 | 1.53 | 1.01 | 33.86 | 19 |
| Sac City | 1.29 | 1.13 | 1.56 | 2.91 | 4.36 | 5.34 | 4.11 | 3.37 | 3.46 | 2.95 | 1.27 | 1.28 | 30.82 | 15 |
| Waterloo | 1.18 | 1.24 | 1.49 | 2.09 | 3.83 | 3.36 | 4.05 | 3.71 | 4.01 | 3.27 | 1.40 | 1.40 | 30.76 | 12 |
| Waukon | 1.60 | 1.39 | 2.21 | 2.34 | 3.57 | 4.63 | 4.99 | 3.43 | 4.41 | 3.27 | 1.77 | 1.74 | 35.30 | — |
| Wesley | 1.14 | 1.03 | 1.62 | 2.30 | 3.90 | 4.74 | 3.50 | 2.29 | 3.64 | 2.17 | 1.13 | 2.16 | 29.60 | 10 |
| AVERAGES | 1.37 | 1.42 | 2.03 | 2.60 | 4.15 | 4.85 | 4.30 | 3.80 | 3.70 | 2.85 | 1.70 | 1.65 | 34.88 | |

Total for the six growing months, 23.25 inches.
Average per month of crop season, 3.90 inches.

## SUNSHINE, CLOUDINESS, ETC.

Notwithstanding its copious rainfall and the abundant humidity of the air in the growing season, Iowa has a large average percentage of sunshine, and a correspondingly small amount of cloudiness. A little over fifty per cent of the days are clear, or partially obscured by clouds, and the average annual cloudiness is not over 47 per cent. The rainfall comes largely in the form of evening showers, and it may be stated that nearly one-third of the summer storms occur between the hours of six and ten p. m., and more than 65 per cent of the precipitation falls at evening or during the night. The rising sun, increasing heat and expanding air of the morning hours, and throughout the larger part of each day, serve to dissipate the clouds and rapidly dry the surface of the fields moistened by evening showers. Fogs are of rare occurrence, and usually of short duration. At Des Moines the average number of days on which there is a fall of rain or snow amounting to .01 of an inch or more is 117 per year, and the average number of cloudless days is 126 per year. Prof. Parvin's thirty-two years records at Muscatine and Iowa City show an annual average of 116 clear days, 169 variable and 80 cloudy. The average for the State is 115 clear days, 144 partly cloudy, and 105 cloudy days per year. For the three summer months the average is 30 clear, 41 partly cloudy, and 21 cloudy days. That shows a very large average amount of sunshine during the season of crop production. The maximum of cloudiness is in March and December, and the minimum in July, August and September.

## TEMPERATURE.

In Iowa the summers are decidedly warmer, and the winters slightly colder than in the eastern States on the same parallels. The annual mean temperature is about 47 degrees, ranging from 42 at the more elevated northern points to 50 degrees near the southern line. The mean temperature of spring and autumn very nearly correspond to the yearly average. And the normals of April and October also approximate very closely to the spring, autumn and yearly means.

The temperature range of the State is quite high, averaging probably 120 degrees from the minimum of winter to the maximum of summer. But the winters are relatively of much shorter duration than on the same lines of latitude in the Atlantic states. And the transition from winter to summer temperature is usually very rapid, the average increase in April and May being a third of a degree per day. The average of the three summer months is as follows: June 69.2, July 74.1, August 71.0, giving a mean summer temperature of 71.4. The mean of the three winter months is 20.6; spring 46.5; autumn 48.5.

The charts issued by the Signal Service, showing the isothermal lines of the United States, furnish a basis of comparison of the temperature of Iowa and the eastern States. In January the State lies between the isotherms 15° and 25°. The lines of 20° passes diagonally through the northern half of the State from a point below Sioux City to the northeast corner, thence diagonally through Wisconsin to the northern part of Michigan; and eastward through Kingston, Canada; northern New York, Vermont and New Hampshire to Eastport, Maine. In February the 20° and 30° lines cut the northwestern and southeastern corners of the State, and the 25° isotherm crosses the State on a nearly direct line from Sioux City to Dubuque, curving slightly northward across Wisconsin through Milwaukee, thence eastward with slight curvatures through Michigan and Canada, and along the southern shore of Lake Ontario, through northern New York, ending in Portland, Maine. And for the three winter months the normal temperature of Iowa corresponds very nearly with that of the latitude of northern Michigan, northern New York, Vermont, New Hampshire and Maine. The Iowa winters, however, are much more endurable and enjoyable than the corresponding season in the regions above named, which have a much larger number of stormy days and heavier precipitation.

In March the isotherms touching Iowa follow more nearly the parallels of latitude, with sharp curvatures to the southward in crossing the Alleghanies. In April the temperature of Iowa corresponds nearly with that of central Ohio, southern Pennsylvania, Washington, Philadelphia and New York city. In May and through the summer months the isotherms curve sharply southward on nearing the Atlantic coast, and the temperature of Iowa is as high as that of central Ohio, southern Pennsylvania, West Virginia, Maryland and New Jersey.

These comparisons show the wide range between the winter and summer temperature of this portion of the Mississippi valley. In short, the winter temperature is like unto that of Montreal, and the summer heat is equal to that of Baltimore and Washington.

The marked extremes of temperature above noted give to this region its marvelous productiveness, the cold as well as the heat being an important factor in the growing of crops. The myriad plowshares of Jack Frost penetrate the earth to great depths, pulverizing the soil and preparing it to respond to the quickening influences of the gentle rains and almost tropical heat of the summer months. The winter campaign is usually short and sharp, and the clear, pure air tones up the systems of all who have the vitality to withstand extremes. It is not exactly an ideal climate for invalids who need an equable temperature, but the tables of vital statistics show that it is remarkably healthful.

## THE SEASONS IN IOWA.

The calendar year is divided into four seasons of equal length, but in matter of fact in this latitude the seasons are of variable duration. In Iowa, summer is the longest season, averaging about four months, during which the mean temperature ranges above 60 degrees. The average duration of winter, during which the mean temperature is below 30 degrees, is a little over three and a half months. The balance of the year is divided about equally between spring and autumn, the mean temperature ranging between 30 and 60 degrees. On this basis the average dates of beginning and ending of the seasons in this State may be tabulated as follows:

Winter—November 28th to March 17th.
Spring—March 18th to May 20th.
Summer—May 21st to September 23d.
Autumn—September 24th to November 27th.

Spring and summer usually open from one to two weeks earlier in the extreme southern part of the State than in the northern and more elevated localities. There is, however, less difference in the opening of the winter season.

## TEMPERATURE DATA.

The following table gives the average monthly and annual mean temperature in degrees, at a number of stations in Iowa from records covering the number of years in the last column.

| STATIONS. | JAN'RY | FEB'RY | MARCH | APRIL | MAY | JUNE | JULY | AUGUST | SEPT'R | OCT'R | NOV'R | DEC'R | ANNUAL | NO. OF YEARS. |
|---|---|---|---|---|---|---|---|---|---|---|---|---|---|---|
| Ames | 16.2 | 23.5 | 30.4 | 49.2 | 59.1 | 69.7 | 75.3 | 71.4 | 62.4 | 49.2 | 30.7 | 22.3 | 47.4 | 8 |
| Amana | 18.2 | 20.4 | 29.6 | 47.8 | 59.5 | 68.9 | 73.4 | 69.8 | 60.6 | 47.7 | 31.6 | 21.2 | 45.4 | 14 |
| Algona | 10.7 | 17.3 | 25.5 | 43.6 | 59.3 | 67.7 | 73.3 | 70.2 | 59.9 | 46.8 | 31.1 | 17.8 | 43.6 | 11 |
| Brookside | 12.7 | 19.9 | 29.1 | 45.1 | 60.0 | 68.6 | 73.4 | 69.9 | 61.0 | 46.6 | 31.4 | 17.5 | 44.3 | 9 |
| Cedar Rapids | 15.8 | 21.0 | 30.8 | 49.0 | 57.8 | 69.4 | 74.3 | 70.5 | 61.1 | 34.9 | 31.4 | 25.1 | 46.9 | 9 |
| Clinton | 19.1 | 22.7 | 32.2 | 47.8 | 59.8 | 69.2 | 73.4 | 70.5 | 62.5 | 48.7 | 32.5 | 25.0 | 47.0 | 20 |
| Cresco | 9.8 | 15.4 | 28.5 | 43.9 | 56.4 | 66.1 | 70.8 | 68.5 | 58.9 | 46.8 | 29.2 | 18.4 | 42.5 | 19 |
| Davenport | 20.8 | 26.1 | 34.5 | 49.8 | 61.0 | 70.4 | 75.0 | 72.5 | 64.2 | 52.1 | 37.8 | 25.0 | 49.3 | 20 |
| Dubuque | 18.1 | 23.1 | 34.1 | 45.6 | 60.2 | 68.9 | 73.8 | 72.1 | 63.5 | 50.8 | 35.4 | 26.1 | 47.7 | 18 |
| Des Moines | 17.9 | 24.0 | 34.2 | 50.6 | 60.9 | 69.3 | 74.4 | 70.0 | 63.6 | 51.3 | 36.9 | 21.2 | 45.3 | 11 |
| Elkader | 11.3 | 19.4 | 29.8 | 47.8 | 59.2 | 69.1 | 77.6 | 47.8 | 61.1 | 47.8 | 31.3 | 26.9 | 45.3 | 11 |
| Fort Madison | 22.4 | 27.5 | 37.1 | 51.1 | 63.0 | 73.1 | 77.6 | 70.0 | 66.7 | 52.7 | 38.2 | 26.9 | 50.8 | 89 |
| Glenwood | 15.2 | 22.3 | 31.7 | 46.9 | 57.9 | 67.4 | 70.8 | 74.6 | 59.1 | 46.8 | 33.9 | 19.8 | 46.1 | 16 |
| Guttenberg | 13.9 | 20.0 | 31.5 | 51.4 | 63.0 | 69.1 | 73.4 | 70.1 | 59.5 | 47.1 | 33.1 | 19.5 | 45.7 | 17 |
| Independence | 14.7 | 21.8 | 29.2 | 44.6 | 57.7 | 69.1 | 74.1 | 70.2 | 61.8 | 48.1 | 31.9 | 27.6 | 44.0 | 24 |
| Iowa City | 16.9 | 25.9 | 33.3 | 48.1 | 63.7 | 69.8 | 74.1 | 71.3 | 63.0 | 50.3 | 33.3 | 27.6 | 45.7 | 16 |
| Keokuk | 22.6 | 29.1 | 37.2 | 51.9 | 62.9 | 72.1 | 77.1 | 74.1 | 66.7 | 54.1 | 40.0 | 29.6 | 49.3 | 50 |
| Logan | 18.0 | 24.8 | 34.3 | 49.2 | 61.0 | 69.5 | 72.9 | 72.5 | 61.4 | 61.8 | 34.3 | 27.6 | 48.3 | 20 |
| Monticello | 15.4 | 21.6 | 31.9 | 48.3 | 59.4 | 68.4 | 74.1 | 69.9 | 61.4 | 48.9 | 33.5 | 22.1 | 46.0 | 37 |
| Mount Vernon | 17.1 | 21.8 | 31.5 | 48.7 | 60.0 | 70.4 | 74.1 | 71.1 | 63.0 | 49.1 | 33.1 | 24.3 | 45.6 | 12 |
| Muscatine | 20.2 | 24.7 | 35.0 | 46.2 | 59.8 | 69.8 | 73.0 | 70.5 | 62.4 | 49.3 | 27.6 | 24.3 | 43.9 | 82 |
| Na-i-na | 6.5 | 15.4 | 25.0 | 41.8 | 54.0 | 64.7 | 70.6 | 66.3 | 57.1 | 48.2 | 30.6 | 18.1 | 41.8 | 7 |
| Omaha | 18.8 | 25.6 | 35.4 | 49.6 | 61.3 | 71.1 | 76.3 | 74.0 | 63.9 | 48.2 | 30.5 | 25.4 | 49.4 | 19 |
| Oskaloosa | 16.0 | 25.7 | 32.6 | 50.9 | 59.6 | 72.1 | 76.3 | 70.9 | 62.9 | 49.4 | 36.4 | 17.2 | 49.0 | 7 |
| Washington | 16.8 | 23.7 | 32.2 | 50.9 | 61.1 | 72.5 | 77.9 | 73.6 | 62.8 | 51.4 | 35.4 | 15.1 | 46.5 | 10 |
| AVERAGES | 16.2 | 22.2 | 31.7 | 48.0 | 59.7 | 69.2 | 74.1 | 71.0 | 62.0 | 49.5 | 34.1 | 23.5 | 46.5 | |

Average for the six growing months of the year, 63.8

## LATE AND EARLY FROSTS.

On an average there are 140 to 150 days between the latest damaging frost of spring and the first killing frost of autumn. The latest of spring occurs on an average, about the last week in April or the first week in May; and the earliest damaging frost of the fall is about the 25th of September. Light and comparatively harmless frosts occasionally occur between those dates, but as a rule there is in every season ample time to produce a well-matured crop of the best varieties of western dent corn, which with favoring conditions may be grown in 100 to 110 days after germination. Prof. Parvin's very complete records, covering the years from 1839 to 1869, show the mean dates to have been for the latest frost May 4, and for the earliest September 24. This would give an average exemption from hurtful frosts of 142 days. Prof. Parvin, writing in 1870 said:

"It has happened but once or twice in the last thirty years that the frost has, over a great extent, seriously injured the corn crop. When the spring is late, the fall is either quite hot or lengthened, so as to afford time for the crop to mature."

This has been the result of observation in the years since this paragraph was written. A careful study of all available records leads to the conclusion that Iowa has, on an average, as long a period of exemption from killing frosts in the crop season as any State within the same parallels of latitude in the eastern part of the United States, except possibly within a few miles of the coast.

## DESTRUCTIVE STORMS.

In common with nearly all portions of the United States east of the Rocky Mountains, Iowa is subject to the occasional visitation of violent atmospheric disturbances, in form of wind-squalls, hail and thunder storms. The more destructive effects of these disturbances, however, are purely local, and limited to small areas compared with the extent of territory benefitted by the storm. Being well watered, it cannot escape these almost universal conditions.

The Gulf is the great thermal fountain of humidity, and the boreal regions send down the valley the titanic forces which wring fertilizing moisture from the vapor-laden winds of the south. The Gulf and the Arctic sea are the positive and negative poles of the battery which propels the alternating life currents through this favored region. And the earth is watered and made fruitful by this conflict of elements, which at times becomes so intense and violent at local points as to cause destruction to life and property. But the more violent storms which occasionally sweep over small areas of the State are the incidental ills resulting from conditions which promote the general good. Hail-storms, thunder storms, tornadoes and wind-squalls are the exceptional products of the benign elements, of heat and moisture which make this valley a paradise of abundance. If the course of this great valley had been east and west instead of north and south, with the mountain ranges at right angles with their present direction, the interior of the continent would be exempt from atmospheric disturbances of this character; but it would be an uninhabitable desert instead of the garden of the world. There are regions of wide extent which enjoy almost perfect immunity from the class of storms above referred to, but they are deserts or arid sections which must needs be irrigated to yield even a scanty support to their inhabitants. The climate of this State, with all its drawbacks and incidental disturbances is vastly to be preferred to the deserts or semi-arid regions, notwithstanding their exemption from destructive storms.

The reputation of Iowa's climate has been injured among people who are not well informed on the subject, by exaggerated descriptions of the occasional severe storms incident to this latitude; and the idea has prevailed to some extent that this section is alternately plowed by tornadoes and harrowed by blizzards. This has resulted from the fact that newspaper reports of wind-storms are often highly over-wrought, from indulgence in the American passion for sensationalism. And, unfortunately, some of these exaggerated reports have been embodied in official records to the detriment of the State. Using these highly colored newspaper reports as a basis, there was published a few years ago in the American Meteorological Journal, a so-called "Iowa Tornado Chart," giving the tracks of alleged tornadoes for the period of fifty-two years. The total number charged to the account of this State was 128, and the year of greatest frequency was 1886, which year was credited with a crop of twenty-six veritable tornadoes raised on Iowa soil! A careful investigation showed that the bulk of these disturbances were merely wind-squalls accompanying thunder-storms of some local severity. The aggregate of damage from storms that year was very light. The tendency to exaggerate the importance or violence of local phenomena causes certain newspaper reporters to apply the term "cyclone" to every wind gust which is powerful enough to demolish some of the frail structures which were very common in this State in the pioneer era, and which are yet quite numerous. But the people who have resided in Iowa through good and evil report have learned that it is as safe as any other section within the temperate zone.

And despite the exaggerated reports it may be positively affirmed that veritable tornadoes are quite infrequent in this State. Since its settlement by the whites, there have been in Iowa two notably destructive tornadoes which are entitled to rank with the great disturbances of like nature at Lawrence, Mass., Reading, Pa., and Louisville, Ky.

Dr. Gustavus Hinrichs, in his annual report of the Iowa Weather Service for the year 1888, published a very complete refutation of the exaggerated statements that had been given currency relative to Iowa tornadoes. Gen. Greely, Chief Signal Officer, in his book on American Weather, says that three thousand persons have been killed in the United States by this class of storms, and the loss of life has been greatest in relative order in States as follows: Missouri, Mississippi, Iowa, Illinois, Minnesota, Wisconsin and Ohio. The loss of property aggregates several millions, and has been fixed in round numbers, as follows: Ohio, over eight millions of dollars; Minnesota, six millions; Missouri, three millions; Mississippi, two millions; Iowa, one and a half millions; Wisconsin, over one million.

In his report for 1890, Gen. Greely gives a statement of the relation between the total area visited annually by violent storms of all classes to the area of the State, with the following result: In Alabama, one square mile of limited destruction to each 8,866 square miles; Arkansas, one to 14,418; Georgia, one to 6,696; Illinois, one to 8,162; Indiana, one to 6,210; Iowa, one to 7,164; Kansas, one to 9,720; Missouri, one to 5,336; Ohio, one to 4,554; Wisconsin, one to 12,042. Gen. Greely adds:

"It appears that in no State may a destructive tornado be expected oftener, on an average, than once in two years, and the area over which the total destruction can be expected is exceedingly small, even in the States most liable to these violent storms."

And he further concludes that, dangerous as are tornadoes, they are not so destructive to life as thunderstorms. This accords with observations in Iowa, as it is evident that, in the aggregate, very many more deaths have been caused by lightning strokes than by any class of wind-storms.

### WIND MOVEMENT.

The State is sufficiently well ventilated to make it healthful. On an average the wind movement is ample to secure immunity from malaria and the germs of disease which arise from decaying vegetation, and to furnish mechanical power for the pumping of stock water and the grinding of feed. The mean velocity of the wind over the State accords very closely with the average for the United States. The average hourly movement is 7 to 8 miles. At an early period, when the prairies were comparatively treeless, the effects of winds were more apparent than now, their force having been greatly modified in recent years by artificial groves, hedges and timber belts. The prevailing winds are southerly in summer and westerly at other seasons.

### IS THE CLIMATE PERMANENT?

All the recorded weather observations of the past fifty years answer affirmatively. In recent droughty seasons fears were expressed by certain writers that through tillage, ditching and tile drainage, and from the effects of clearing away extensive forests in the northwest, the climate of this portion of the Mississippi valley has been materially changed by decreasing the humidity and seasonal rainfall. But the records prove absolutely that there has been no diminution in the humidity and rainfall within the last decade as compared with any preceding decade, nor within the last twenty years as compared with any preceding score of years since the States was settled by civilized people. There have been seasons of excess and of deficiency all along the line of recorded observations, but the shortage has been no more serious in the eighties and nineties than in the fifties and sixties.

No, there has been no appreciable change in any essential feature of the climate. It is as stable as the everlasting hills, and as permanent as the inflow and outflow of the currents of the Gulf, by which it is so copiously watered.

In concluding this chapter the writer desires to acknowledge his indebtedness to the Chief of the Weather Bureau for voluminous records relating to the climate of this State, and to Dr. Geo. M. Chappel, Local Forecast Official and Assistant Director of the Iowa Weather and Crop Service, for very efficient aid in the arrangement and tabulation of meteorological data.

## NATURAL RESOURCES.

Nature gave to Iowa a better dowry than mines of diamonds or mountains stored with silver and gold. Its more valuable resources consist in water, sands, rocks, coal and timber, and above all its deep, porous wonderful soil. Gold, silver, nickle, zinc, iron, aluminum, and natural gas have been found; but whether they exist in remunerative quantities is to be determined by future efforts for their development.

### WATER.

We class water as one of the natural resources of this productive state. Go west—cross the continent to the Pacific—and you ask why those great deserts which you pass in your journey. They are desert because the rainfall, the natural irrigation essential to vegetable production, is withheld. Here fructifying showers nourish, invigorate and perpetuate vegetable life. In the three score years of our written history no pen has ever written of Iowa's fields being made barren by burning drouth, or of her people suffering the pangs of famine because the essential rainfall was withheld until crops were parched and starvation befell them. The beneficient Creator gave to Iowa a wealth of resources of more priceless value than mountains of the precious metals, in her ever duly recurring showers, and her numerous springs and perennial streams.

### MEDICINAL WATERS.

We have valuable healing waters in Iowa. Streams flow from unfailing fountains that give strength to the weak, ease to the pain-ridden, and healing to the sick. We can speak only of a few of such fountains.

The Lake View Mineral Spring—This is a natural spring near the western shore of Wall Lake, a body of water lying in Sac county and furnishing fine opportunities for boating, fishing and pleasure driving in its vicinity. Circumstances have led to the improvement of the surroundings of this healing fountain that has now wide reputation for the cure of many of the ills to which mortal nature is subject. We give the following analysis of its water made by Prof. Walter J. Haines, of Rush Medical College August, 1888.

Each gallon of 231 inches contains:

|  | GRAINS. |
|---|---|
| Chloride of Sodium | 1.124 |
| Sulphate of Potassium | .285 |
| Sulphate of Sodium | 1.566 |
| Bicarbonate of Calcium | 18.111 |
| Bicarbonate of Magnesium | 9.478 |
| Bicarbonate of Sodium | .336 |
| Bicarbonate of Iron | .032 |
| Phosphate of Sodium | Trace |
| Alumina | .150 |
| Silica | 1.180 |
| Organic Matter | Trace |
| Total | 32.284 |

### THE SARATOGA OF THE WEST.

Who has not heard of Colfax, the famous health resort of Iowa, and its waters that have won a fame that has crossed oceans? This now famous health and pleasure resort is in Jasper county, on the main line of the Chicago, Rock Island and Pacific railroad.

Some fifteen years ago an enterprising citizen surmising that a paying vein of coal lay hidden under the high wooded hill east of the village, procured a drilling apparatus and started the tools downward in quest of the desired treasure. By slow, laborious process he put his drill down about four hundred and fifteen feet when a sudden bursting forth of a fine stream of water caused a stoppage of his work. He was not pleased with what he then considered ill luck, but his complaints interposed no check to the gushing stream. It continued its bright and abundant flow. The workmen and spectators sipped thereof to investigate its quality. Its taste at first peculiar, after a little use was not unpleasant; those who drank freely, however, were soon admonished that it possessed unusual qualities, and a quantity of the sparkling fluid was sent to an educated physician at Davenport for examination. Acting on his recommendation a quantity was forwarded to Prof. Heinrichs of the State University, who reported the following analysis of the fluid:

| NAME OF COMPOUND. | GRAINS PER GALLON. | | Millogrammes per litre or parts per million |
|---|---|---|---|
| | American Gallon of 231 cubic inches. | Imperial Gallon of 70,000 Grains. | |
| Sodium chloride | 3.85 | 4.62 | 66 |
| Sodium sulphate | 78.86 | 94.57 | 1,351 |
| Potassium sulphate | .41 | .49 | 7 |
| Magnesian sulphate | 31.87 | 38.22 | 546 |
| Calcium sulphate | 13.07 | 15.68 | 224 |
| Calcium carbonate | 17.51 | 21.00 | 300 |
| Iron carbonate | .67 | .81 | 11.5 |
| Silica alumina | .29 | .35 | 5 |
| Lithia | Trace | Trace | Trace |
| Carbon dioxide | 7.18 | 8.61 | 123 |
| TOTAL | 153.71 | 184.35 | 2,633.5 |

Other borings have been made and similar fountains have been reached in that locality. Their analysis varies but slightly from that above given. The "Colfax Springs" running "abundant, free and clear" are already of great value. Their healing virtues have been tested by thousands of visitors from our own and other states who came to them enfeebled by disease, but went from them with radiant cheek and buoyant step to proclaim their health restoring power.

### DES MOINES MEDICINAL WELLS.

Several artesian flows of water have been struck in and near the city of Des Moines that are reputed to have medicinal value. The water from one in the central part of the city has been used quite extensively with great benefit to many persons.

At Cherokee, Lineville and other places in the state there are waters reported to be of considerable medicinal value.

### THE CLINTON WELLS.

The city of Clinton is finely supplied with pure health giving water, obtained from artesian wells, drilled into the Potsdam sandstone. Of the source and abundance of the supply, Superintendent Highlands of the city water works reports as follows:

"It might not be amiss in this connection to say something about the source of this magnificent water supply. In this locality the Potsdam sandstone is reached by the drill at 1,475 feet, or about 1,400 feet below low water line in the river and this is the source from which the water is derived. This stratum of sandstone is covered over with 1,100 feet of limestone and 300 to 500 feet of shale. The 400 to 500 feet of limestone immediately over the sandstone was broken up by some convulsion of nature and whenever the drill strikes one of these crevices the water will flow to the surface, with the same pressure, but with less volume, as if the drill had penetrated the sandstone. In drilling well No. 3 the drill penetrated three such crevices. The pressure of water from each of those crevices or apparent veins was carefully tested by packing off the water above them and it was found exactly the same as when tested at the depth of 1,600 feet. The fact that the water will only raise 68 feet above the river, shows conclusively that the water does not come from any point near the head waters of the Mississippi river, and it is also equally plain that it could not enter the ground on the line of the river where it is only 68 feet above us, for the reason that in so short a distance it could not have penetrated through the shale and limestone into the sandstone. The only alternative is that it must come from the Lake Superior region where the sandstone crops out." The difference in levels between this and Lake Superior would seem to bear out this opinion.

Speaking of the city wells he says: "The rise and flow of our wells now are as follows:

"No. 1, eight inch bore, 1,450 feet deep; daily flow 700,000 gallons.
"No. 2, five inch bore, 1,235 feet deep; daily flow 400,000 gallons.
"No. 3, eight inch bore, 1,675 feet deep; daily flow 900,000 gallons."

These three wells are drilled within a radius of 200 feet and the flow and pressure seem to remain constant.

The city mains are connected with three other wells, one owned by the city of Lyons and the other by private parties, and the total supply at command is thus stated: "Our mains are also connected with the pumping stations of the Lyons water works, W. J. Young & Co., and C. Lamb & Sons' Chancy mills. The total pumping capacity for fire protection is as follows:

|  | GALLONS PER DAY. |
|---|---|
| Clinton station | 9,000,000 |
| Lyons station | 3,000,000 |
| W. J. Young & Co | 6,000,000 |
| C. Lamb & Sons | 4,000,000 |
| Total | 22,000,000 |

"As our maximum daily consumption rarely reaches 2,500,000 gallons per day this would leave 19,500,000 gallons per day for fire protection, or water enough to supply eighty-one inch fire streams with 100 pounds of pressure through 400 feet of hose; or if any one of the stations were disabled it would be very easy for the other three to afford adequate fire protection."

The quality of this abundant supply is shown by the following analysis, made by E. G. Smith, Professor of Analytical Chemistry of Beloit College, Wisconsin:

SOLID RESIDUE IN PARTS PER 1,000 OF WATER.

| | |
|---|---|
| Silica | .0105 |
| Sulphuric acid | .0640 |
| Chlorine | .0692 |
| Alumina | .0003 |
| Ferric oxide | |
| Lime | .0663 |
| Magnesia | .0343 |
| Soda | .1499 |
| Carbonic acid, etc | .1182 |
| | .5129 |
| Less Oxygen equivalent to chlorine | .0156 |
| | .4973 |
| Total solids from 1,000 parts of water actually weighed after drying at 140c | .4980 |

Or to state it in another manner as showing grains per gallon it would show thus:

GRAINS PER GALLON 231 CUBIC INCHES.

| | |
|---|---|
| Sodium Sulphate | 6.6266 |
| Sodium Chloride | 6.6616 |
| Sodium bicarbonate | 6.2824 |
| Calcium Bicarbonate | 11.2291 |
| Magnesium Bicarbonate | 7.4267 |
| Alumina | .0174 |
| Ferric acid | |
| Silica | .6124 |
| | 38.8552 |

At the city of McGregor there are two artesian flows from the same source. The largest one flows a large volume, the bore being put down 1,008 feet. The Potsdam stone here lies many hundred feet higher than the stratum lies at Clinton, the stratum cropping out at the former place. The water in the McGregor wells appears to be more highly medicinal than the Clinton water. We cannot give any reported measurement of the flow at McGregor, but the facts that we have given indicate that abundant supplies of the purest water can be obtained in the cities along the Mississippi wherever the Potsdam sandstone can be reached.

SOIL.

Soil, sunlight and water are the great essentials to the production of the bread, meats and fruits that feed our race. Iowa has world-wide fame for the depth and richness, the mellowness and productive quality of her soil. Prof. White, in his report as State Geologist. speaking of the soil of Iowa said:

"After careful consideration of the results of my examinations, I do not hesitate to thus publicly announce my estimate that 95 per cent. of the surface of Iowa is tillable land. The state being without mountain ranges, hills or other barren surfaces and everywhere covered with a soil of such fertility and depth, its agricultural capabilities are almost beyond computation."

The theory of geologists that the soil of Iowa is formed largely of decomposed rocks floated over the portion of the State the drift covers, may be true or not. Its depth and productive qualities are the matters of our chief concern. There are but few places in this remarkably productive state where a plow can turn up barren subsoil; the fertile soil is found through the state ranging in depth from one to one hundred feet. This is more fully described in the chapter on the Geology of Iowa, by Prof. Keyes.

One great advantage of our soil is its porousness. It is easily pulverized, is light and warm and the roots of growing crops easily penetrate it. This characteristic not only makes farm labor inviting on account of the crop produced, but doubly so by the ease with which the cultivation is done. We hear nothing in Iowa of soil being worn out. It cannot be worn out with any proper farming, hence there is wealth for the ages in its fertility and productive power, and there is perpetual comfort in the ease with which agricultural operations are performed.

## CLAYS.

This species of earth is important in essential manufactures. The savage may build his wigwam frame of poles and cover it with grass or skins or barks. The pioneer will build his cabin of logs or sod, but by industry and economy he soon provides the means for better things. The brick maker and mason's services are soon needed and openings invite the pottery and the tile factory, and search is made for suitable clays for these manufactures.

In all parts of Iowa, clays suitable for the manufacture of excellent brick is easily obtained, hence the brick industry is obtaining large dimensions. The demand for building brick, paving brick and the finest quality of pressed brick is having yearly increase.

The day of building cheap, perishable shanties for residences, and structures of cheap combustible and perishable material for business uses is outgrown in this State. Three to eight story solid, stately business blocks now grace our cities, and solid brick and stone residences are found in our numerous thrifty villages. Our cities and towns now mostly have their "fire limits," and the indulgence of a false economy in the erection of cheap, unattractive, combustible structures in our business centers is largely prohibited. This wise provision encourages improved architecture and the use of building material of substantial quality, and so the brick makers art is encouraged and his business enlarged. No better clays can be found for the manufacture of the finest quality of pressed brick than are now obtained in numerous places in this state.

Superior clays for the manufacture of stoneware and finer forms of pottery are found in numerous places. During the year 1892 several hundred carloads of clay, for the manufacture of tableware were shipped from Hardin county to Sheboygan, Wisconsin, Milwaukee and elsewhere. Tests of this clay have been made at Liverpool, Paris, and Wellsville, Ohio, Terre Haute, Indiana, Perth Amboy, N. Y., and elsewhere with most satisfactory results in the manufacture of white ware. Large deposits of this quality of clay are found.

With the taking up of the wild lands and the consequent increased value of lands the demand for tile to drain springy, spouty places and waste sloughs is rapidly increasing, and the manufacture of tile for drainage purposes has already assumed large proportions. Excellent clays for this manufacture are found throughout the state.

The settlement of the country with its increasing population and wealth makes good roads more important and leads to road improvement. The growth of flourishing towns and cities, and care for their cleanliness and healthfulness provide enlarging markets for sewer pipe, and its manufacture is becoming an important and growing industry.

### SAND.

According to slang phrase, is a valuable quality in the mental constitution. It is an essential element in our industries. Many important mechanical and manufacturing operations demand its use. The people of Iowa have rich endowment of the mental element expressed by the term, and nature has provided numerous banks of this material in suitable qualities and quantities for mechanical operations. The builder readily finds suitable sand. The brick maker and iron moulder find sands suitable for their operations, while glass factories and smelting furnaces export sands in quantities from our state for their work.

### STONE.

Iowa is not a mountainous nor rocky State, but the exact reverse. Yet there is abundant supply of stone for building, the manufacture of lime and other uses. The general distribution of railroads throughout the state, makes these supplies, that the Creator liberally provided, everywhere available.

Census bulletin No. 78, Census of 1890, devoted to Mines and Mining, treating of limestone, gives important figures respecting this important natural commodity.

The whole number of limestone quarries reported in the country was 1,954. Of these 143 were in Iowa. These Iowa quarries had a reported value of $530,863.

The product of these 143 quarries in this state was reported as 6,280,727 cubic feet of stone for building purposes, valued at $236,792. Lime burned 365,394 barrels of 200 pounds each, of the value of $170,043. For street work 1,732,630 cubic feet of the value of $70,387 were produced. These products of the 143 limestone quarries of Iowa, having a reported value of $477,222. Relatively among the states of the Union Iowa has fair rank in the production of this useful and valuable stone. In the number of limestone quarries having fifth place; in the number of employees working such quarries seventh place; in amount of wages paid tenth place; in amount of stone produced, twelfth place; and in the aggregate value of the product of limestone quarries tenth place.

The limestone beds of Iowa are not found in one corner or in one locality of the State merely, but have quite general distribution over its area. A further description of the rocks of the State is given in his chapter by Prof. Keyes.

### GYPSUM.

Is found in large deposits in Webster county, along the Des Moines river. All the operators in its production in 1889 had their headquarters at Fort Dodge. All the deposits or beds of gypsum being found near that city.

To quite a large extent gypsum has been used in Fort Dodge for building purposes. When first quarried it is easily dressed with an axe or saw, hardens when in the wall and makes a solid structure. Prof. White, in his geographical report, wrote in 1870 of a residence built of this rock in 1861: "Its walls appear as unaffected by exposure and as beautiful as they were when first erected."

In the year named gypsum was produced in California, Colorado, Iowa, Kansas, Michigan, New York, Ohio, South Dakota, Utah, Virginia and Wyoming. Iowa ranking third in the quantity produced and third in the total value of the product. In that year the industry at Fort Dodge gave employment to 59 men.

Part of the product is sold and used as a fertilizer, 14,434 short tons of the Iowa product being sold in 1889 for that purpose 7,550 tons were calcined for stucco. The product of the mines and factories that year in Iowa was valued at $55,270.

The deposits are found in the bluffs of the Des Moines river, covering an extent of about seven miles along the river valley.

Prof. White gives the thickness of the deposit at Goss' Mill, then its known southern extremity, as ten feet. At the Cummins quarry, six miles northward from the Goss Mill, as twenty feet. The deposit is sufficiently large to be virtually inexhaustible, but is formed in somewhat irregular layers. Prof. White pronounces it of "as good quality as any in the country, even for the finest uses."

Iowa gypsum manufactured into stucco, was very largely used in the manufacture of "staff," the material used for the external covering of the exhibition buildings in Jackson Park.

## COAL.

The coal product of the country is of the utmost importance to the public prosperity. While this statement is true in regard to the whole country it is energized when we apply it particularly to a prairie State. Iowa may not be far known as a mining State, yet the productions of her mines are no mean interest. Few suppose that she has place in the list of States near to the top in any mining production. But she has high rank in the production of bituminous coal. The United States census of 1890 reports twenty-seven coal producing States and their entire production is 95,729,026 tons. It reports the following five States as producing for the year 1889, the amounts given below, they being the five leading States:

| STATES. | PRODUCTION. |
|---|---|
| Pennsylvania | 36,174,089 tons |
| Illinois | 12,104,272 " |
| Ohio | 9,976,787 " |
| West Virginia | 6,231,890 " |
| Iowa | 6,095,358 " |

Iowa ranges tenth in population but fifth in the production of bituminous coal, producing in 1890 one bushel in every twenty-two bushels of the product of the country.

The state mine inspectors in their last biennial report to the governor of the State, report production of coal in twenty-three counties. The State has three mining districts. We copy tables given by the several inspectors showing the number of mines, production and other interesting items relating to this business in each county named:

Showing number of mines, annual output, number of miners and other employes, value of product, etc., in District No. 1, for the year ending June 30, 1891.

| NAME OF COUNTY. | Number of mines. | Number of tons of coal produced. | Number of miners employed. | All other employes | Average price per ton paid for mining. | Total amount paid miners. | Total amount paid to all other employes. | Average selling price per ton at mine. | Total value of product at the mine. |
|---|---|---|---|---|---|---|---|---|---|
| Adams | 15 | 14,872 | 89 | 14 | $1.31 | $20,031.42 | $2,296.00 | $2.04 | $29,384.00 |
| Appanoose | 58 | 893,255 | 1,193 | 249 | .95 | 308,924.61 | 60,256.98 | 1.37 | 540,767.10 |
| Davis | 6 | 3,272 | 17 | 7 | .91 | 2,972.00 | 180.00 | 1.58 | 5,160.50 |
| Lucas | 6 | 136,722 | 187 | 20 | .76 | 103,400.00 | 6,600.00 | 1.26 | 172,190.00 |
| Monroe | 18 | 355,477 | 609 | 192 | .72 | 255,773.84 | 95,508.05 | 1.23 | 536,172.58 |
| Page | 3 | 2,700 | 26 | 3 | 1.63 | 4,400.00 | 500.00 | 2.41 | 6,550.00 |
| Taylor | 12 | 13,430 | 62 | 34 | 1.37 | 18,405.00 | 4,013.00 | 2.02 | 27,130.00 |
| Wapello | 21 | 169,290 | 358 | 123 | .75 | 120,376.27 | 44,404.11 | 1.30 | 217,737.23 |
| Wayne | 8 | 31,578 | 101 | 30 | .90 | 28,252.00 | 10,875.00 | 1.40 | 44,172.00 |
| Warren | 23 | 15,604 | 80 | 15 | 1.04 | 16,303.61 | 2,797.23 | 1.80 | 27,809.60 |
| Total | 170 | 1,136,190 | 2,721 | 687 | $.83 | $938,838.75 | $227,430.37 | $1.32 | $1,507,012.08 |

DISTRICT NO. 2.

| Jasper | 16 | 146,091 | 283 | 70 | $.85 | $125,134.25 | $30,328.67 | $1.43 | $208,587.96 |
|---|---|---|---|---|---|---|---|---|---|
| Jefferson | 7 | 2,932 | 18 | 8 | .93 | 2,714.49 | 556,36 | 1.80 | 5,247.20 |
| Keokuk | 20 | 363,517 | 665 | 240 | .74 | 269,102.04 | 87,269.95 | 1.40 | 509,230.03 |
| Mahaska | 40 | 963,558 | 1,105 | 415 | .75 | 719,976.14 | 214,440.06 | 1.25 | 1,207,099.08 |
| Scott | 7 | 10,534 | 47 | 4 | .97 | 10,195.32 | 1,180.00 | 3.75 | 18,411.50 |
| Van Buren | 7 | 46,764 | 93 | 18 | .65 | 39,596.00 | 6,940.00 | 1.31 | 61,258.00 |
| Total | 97 | 1,533,496 | 2,211 | 754 | $.76 | $1,166,718.24 | $290,715.04 | $1.32 | $2,009,916.77 |

DISTRICT NO. 3.

| Boone | 19 | 189,577 | 480 | 128 | $.94 | $177,003.75 | $60,364.41 | $1.86 | $351,826.31 |
|---|---|---|---|---|---|---|---|---|---|
| Dallas | 6 | 43,324 | 106 | 34 | .93 | 40,278.40 | 14,450.00 | 1.78 | 76,943.40 |
| Guthrie | 16 | 11,953 | 87 | 15 | 1.48 | 17,770.00 | 2,260.00 | 2.50 | 29,982.50 |
| Greene | 4 | 74,544 | 158 | 32 | .85 | 63,593.79 | 14,558.03 | 1.59 | 118,173.29 |
| Marion | 27 | 210,061 | 347 | 132 | .75 | 158,679.32 | 43,341.19 | 1.30 | 275,300.31 |
| Polk | 18 | 397,833 | 652 | 217 | .88 | 321,048.73 | 97,844.26 | 1.53 | 604,921.25 |
| Webster | 20 | 134,963 | 273 | 96 | .84 | 104,360.09 | 44,638.17 | 1.61 | 200,328.50 |
| Total | 110 | 1,052,295 | 2,103 | 654 | $.84 | $882,732.76 | $277,146.06 | 1.57 | $1,657,465.56 |

SUMMARY.

| NUMBER OF DISTRICT. | Number of mines. | Number of tons of coal produced. | Number of miners employed. | All other employes | Average price per ton paid for mining. | Total amount paid miners. | Total amount paid all other employes. | Average selling price per ton at mine. | Total value of product at mine. |
|---|---|---|---|---|---|---|---|---|---|
| District No. 1 | 170 | 1,136,190 | 2,721 | 687 | $.83 | $938,838.75 | $227,430.37 | $1.32 | $1,507,012.08 |
| District No. 2 | 97 | 1,533,496 | 2,211 | 754 | .76 | 1,165,718.24 | 290,715.04 | 1.32 | 2,009,916.77 |
| District No. 3 | 110 | 1,052,295 | 2,103 | 654 | .84 | 882,732.76 | 277,146.06 | 1.57 | 1,657,465.56 |
| Total | 377 | 3,721,981 | 7,035 | 2,095 | $.81 | $2,988,289.55 | $795,291.47 | $1.39 | $5,174,394.39 |

This summary of the three mining districts of the State includes reports from 377 mines. It reports the production of 3,721,981 tons of bituminous coal, being 1.94 tons *per capita* to the population of the State. It shows that this industry gave employment to 9,130 persons, paying to those employes the sum of $3,783,572.02. That the coal produced was valued at upwards of five million dollars. No further elucidation is necessary to prove that Iowa has highly important and valuable mining interests. Her producers of "Black Diamonds" add greatly to her prosperity. It may be remarked that many mines operated only in the winter months are not reported by the inspectors, and coal is mined in six counties not included in the above tables. Hence the discrepancy between the census and state mine inspectors' reports.

Iowa coal is not anthracite. It may not be a fine quality of coking coal. It may not be renowned for its excellence as a gas coal, but it is an excellent fuel coal, a fine steam producer and is of great value to her people for household use, for locomotive consumption and for all industries using steam power.

Coal is found and mined in the following counties not named in the above tables, namely, Cass, Adair, Fremont, Lee, Hardin and Hamilton counties. It will doubtless be found by deeper prospecting in counties where it is not now known to exist. The field now as developed, extends from Scott county on the Mississippi on the east, to Fremont county on the Missouri on the west, a distance of upwards of 200 miles. While in the opposite direction it extends from the Missouri line into Hamilton and Hardin counties, a distance of 140 miles. Nature has stored away in the deep and hidden chambers of this vast field, supplies of fuel to furnish heat and light for Iowa's millions.

## THE MINERAL RESOURCES OF ALLAMAKEE COUNTY, IOWA.

*Iron Ore* We know that it is not in accordance with the arrangement of geological strata as usually seen that a bed of iron ore should exist in this part of Iowa, and the imperfect surveys heretofore officially made of the State have either ignored, or unjustly misrepresented their existence. We know, also, from years of personal examination, the many test pits that have been dug, varying from a few to thirty-two feet deep, and the bottom of the ore not yet reached, all through an almost solid mass of iron ore, lying below one to four feet of surface soil, though cropping out above the ground in many places, and from the hundreds of tons of ore that have been mined, that it exists here in vast quantities. One bed about one and one-half miles northeast of Waukon, covers three hundred or more acres. It has been estimated that 500 tons daily could be taken out for 100 years. Its quality is a brown hematite, is quite porous, permitting heat to permeate the center of the mass, making its reduction easy. On the north and west sides it laps on Trenton limestone; on the south and east sides on St. Peter's sandstone. It lies on top of one of the highest points of land in the county, about 700 feet above the Mississippi, and about fourteen miles distant from that river. A railroad could be run right into its sides, and up a valley into its very center so that loading would be all down hill. Several analyses have been made ranging from 52 to 60 per cent. One analysis was as follows:

Sesquioxide of iron................................................52.751
Sesquioxide of magnese.............................................8.054
Sesquioxide of cobalt..............................................  .230
Alumina........................................................... 1.777
Lime.............................................................. 1.090
Magnesia..........................................................  .374
Sulphuric acid....................................................  .047
Phosphoric acid................................................... 4.092
Water and organic matter..........................................13.134
Silicious matter..................................................10.631
                                                                 ——————
                                                                100.000

Another test made by Prof. Fisher, analytical chemist, of Milwaukee Wis., from ore taken by himself from the mines, gave these results, as he reported to the writer:

|  | Black. | Yellow. | Constituents of average ore. |
|---|---|---|---|
| Metallic Iron | 58.59 | 54.79 | |
| Oxide of iron | | | 76.74 |
| Silica | 4.00 | 5.12 | 11.02 |
| Water | | 11.92 | 11.92 |
| Phosphorus (Phosphoric Acid) | | .131 | .30 |
| Sulphur | | | |
| Lime | | .70 | .70 |
| Total | | | 100.68 |

Magnesia, trace. Alumina Trace. Manganese, trace.

These deposits were first discovered by Mr. C. Barnard about fourteen years ago, who soon after called the attention of the writer to them, who with him made personal and extensive examination of the same, though neither one ever has had, nor has to-day, a dollar's worth of interest in the lands in any form. Our aim has been to develop the resources of this county. These lands have been leased at three different times to outside parties. The changes in the tariff in 1883 caused a suspension of their development at that time. Again they were being opened and on the point of successful development when the principal capitalist and promoter interested, died. And since they have been leased by parties who seem to hold them in abeyance while they are devoting immediate, personal attention to the Lake Superior newly developing iron regions. There is not local capital to open and work them. It is not desirable that they should fall into the hands of speculators, because we believe that we have the quantity and the quality here for the development of a great industry on a solid foundation. It advertises itself best by a personal examination by experts and competent judges.

Other extensive beds of iron ore exist in the county.

Lead also is profitably mined in large quantities five or six miles northwest of Lansing, and is also believed to exist in paying quantities near Dorchester in the northern part of the county.

### ZINC.

This metal is mined in the vicinity of Dubuque and quite extensive works are being erected in that city for the preparation of the metal for commerce.

While Iowa has mineral interests that are of great value, and give promise of enlarged development and commercial importance in the near future, the tools of the farm more than the mine have been the chief instruments used in her great wealth production. It may be conceded that this State will never lead some others as a mining State, but her mining and manufacturing interests are becoming important factors in her industrial enterprises, and will hereafter add largely to wealth acquisition.

## COMMERCIAL FACILITIES.

We have already intimated something of the commercial opportunities and facilities of Iowa. We find the state situated in a position to command

the advantages of 20,000 miles of inland water navigation. No transportation can be so cheap as that carried on the great water channels formed by the Creator.

Our great rivers are permanent fixtures; the lakes and springs pouring their flows into the Mississippi and the snows of the mountains sending their streams into the Missouri must ever maintain these great rivers as navigable thoroughfares. As the years roll on and population and wealth increase, public interest will demand still greater outlays to perfect those great channels of interior communication and transportation, and their benefit to this commonwealth will increase with each succeeding generation. Those divinely formed channels of trade and transportation are indispensible to Iowa. They will yet bear a large proportion of the products of her farms, orchards, dairies, mines and shops to distant markets, and bring in return immense supplies of commodities and material that her industries and her people will demand, and by their competitive position will keep the cost of transportation to the lowest figure possible. The vast development of wealth in the country will yet be interested in providing for the safety, enlarged capacity and consequently cheaper transportation on those channels that must ever be free as air to commercial interests. The country is moving in behalf of cheap transportation, and the people of Iowa are in position to gain great commercial advantages from the consummation of these movements.

We have spoken of the development of steam as a motive power on the rivers of the country. That success led to experimenting as to the application of steam as a motive power on land, and at the time of the commencement of the settlement of Iowa, the invention of railways and transportation thereon by steam power was, though yet in crude condition, proving successful. It was not until twenty years after the founding of the first permanent settlement in Iowa that a locomotive reached the Mississippi river.

## THE RAILROAD FACILITIES OF IOWA.

The first settlers of Iowa came from the east by teams. The first movement in the interest of railroad construction culminated in a convention at Iowa City in the winter of 1848. It projected two roads, one from Keokuk to Dubuque, the other to span the state from Davenport via Iowa City to some point on the Missouri at or near Council Bluffs. The first organization of a company to construct a railroad in this state was organized to build the proposed road from Davenport to Council Bluffs. Petitions were sent to Congress asking for grants of land to aid in the construction of the projected road, but soon there was heated contention respecting the lines on which the projected roads should be located. The petitioners of that day could not foresee the Iowa they were making, ribboned with tracks of steel as it is now. The road from Keokuk to Dubuque was never built.

In February. 1854, the Chicago & Rock Island reached the Mississippi and the enthusiasm for railroad building was intensified In May, 1856, the national Congress made its first grant of land in aid of railroad building in this State. That act was approved by President Pierce the fifteenth day of that month. It made grants to four roads as follows. We quote from the act:

"SEC. 1. Be it enacted by the Senate and House of Representatives of the United States in Congress assembled, that there be and is hereby granted to the State of Iowa for the purpose of aiding in the construction of railroads from Burlington on the Mississippi river to a point on the Missouri river near the mouth of the Platte river, from the city of Davenport via Iowa City and Ft. Des Moines to Council Bluffs, from Lyons City northwestwardly to a point of intersection with the main line of the Iowa Central Air Line Railroad near Maquoketa, thence on said main line of the Iowa Central Air Line as near as practicable to the 42d parallel across the State of Iowa to the Missouri river. From the city of Dubuque to a point on the Missouri river near Sioux City, with a branch from the Tete des Mortes to the nearest point on said main line, to be completed as soon as the main line is completed to that point, every alternate section of land designated by odd numbers for six sections in width on each side of said road."

This legislation further provided that when the lines of these roads should be definitely fixed, if it should appear that the United States had sold any section or part thereof, granted as aforesaid, or the right of preemption had attached to the same, then the roads, by agents duly appointed by the governor, might select, subject to the approval of the Secretary of the Interior, from the lands of the United States nearest to the tiers of sections above specified, so much land in alternate sections or parts of sections as shall be equal to such lands as the United States have sold or otherwise appropriated or to which the rights of pre-emption have attached as aforesaid. The lands so located to be in no case farther than fifteen miles from the line of said road.

Some other grants of land for internal improvements in Iowa followed this first grant. Under these land grant acts the several aided roads in Iowa received land as follows:

| | ACRES. |
|---|---|
| Burlington & Missouri River (now C. B. & Q.) | 287,095.24 |
| Mississippi & Missouri River (now the C., R. I. P.) | 550,193.57 |
| Iowa Central Air Line (now C. & N. W.) | 775,454.19 |
| Dubuque & Pacific (now Illinois Central) | 1,226,558.33 |
| McGregor & Missouri (now C., M. & St. Paul) | 372,293.27 |
| Sioux City & St. Paul | 407,879.31 |
| Des Moines River Improvement Company | 1,105,967.88 |

The grand total of land bestowed by these grants aggregated 4,674,744.88 acres. It is true the gift was princely but it is equally true that the benefits sought in return were commensurate. Iowa was then without railroads, its interior unsettled and unless railroad advantages were secured it would largely remain unsettled. The reader should remember that these grants were made forty years ago. Then much of the land entered or preempted in the interior of the State had been taken by speculators. The few settlers in those interior counties who were trying to improve homes were laboring in privation, difficulty and poverty. The surplus they raised had to be wagoned over unbridged sloughs and streams to far away markets. Millions of acres about them were in market to the first taker at $1.25 per acre, but were taken slowly at that price. There was no wealth in the State to provide the transportation facilities that every settler desired, and those pioneer settlers far out from market, in great breadths of sparsely settled prairie were willing that Congress should give out of its immense domain what seemed to them at that time a mere pittance, in order that they might secure facilities of transportation that were absolutely essential

HIGHWAY AND C. & N. W. RY. BRIDGES AT CLINTON, IA.

alike to their prosperity and happiness. They figured the value of the land, not as we figure it now, with daily railroad trains speeding through every neighborhood, but as they figured it when the nearest railroad yet lingered by the Mississippi, one or two hundred miles from them, and the millions of acres of this seemingly boundless west were awaiting purchasers at the government price. But though the land was granted and railroad surveys were made the railroads did not come. The financial crash of 1857, prostrating business all over the country, followed. Before the country fully recovered from that disaster the civil war broke out and its horrors engrossed the thoughts of the people. It was not possible to proceed with the building of these great lines of road until the pageant of the laurel crowning of the victors in that terrible conflict was made possible by the supremacy of the olive branch through the surrender at Appomattox. Soon thereafter work was begun to push the construction of railroads across Iowa.

The Chicago & Northwestern, first to cross the State, reached Council Bluffs in 1867. The Chicago, Rock Island & Pacific and the Chicago, Burlington & Quincy reached that city early in 1869, and connection was made to the Pacific coast. Then the commerce and travel of the Orient heard of a shorter route to Occidental Europe and the great highway of travel between the empires of the far away east and the Kingdoms of Europe turned a cross this grandeur of vale and hill the world soon learned to know as Iowa.

We will not ask what Iowa would be now had no railroads been built in her territory, we will rather endeavor to comprehend what she is today with her lacework of railroads that has brought to her every neighborhood commercial advantages unsurpassed, and now secure grace to her homes and wealth to her people.

The report of her railroad commissioners for 1892 publishes the fact that Iowa now has 8,513.76 miles of railroad within her boundaries or one mile of railroad to every 6.46 square miles of her area. There is not a county in Iowa without railroad facilities, and but one county seat of her 99 without a railroad, and yet that county—Pocahontas—has four lines of railroad within its borders and seven railroad towns. If we estimate these 8,513.76 miles of railroad with their rolling stock, side trackage, depots and other terminal facilities, to have cost but $25,000 per mile, then we have an expenditure of $212,844,000.00 for this great property interest. The expenditure of this sum of millions in Iowa in railroad construction with the general distribution of market facilities brought to every locality in the State, with the development of mines, quarries and other interests made possible by their construction and the encouragement thereby given to agriculture, has been a potent factor in the material development made in Iowa in the last two decades, and the wonderful advance in property values that have been effected.

The advantages of railroad transportation are equally distributed and farmers in all parts of the State have easy access to railroad markets. Five of Iowa's ninety-nine counties have within their area from 150 to 172 miles of railroad, twenty-six have from 100 to 150 miles, fifty-three have from 50 to 100 miles, while there are now only fifteen Iowa counties that have less than 50 miles of railroad and but six that have less than 40 miles of railroad line, and but two counties having fewer than five railroad stations, namely, Ida, four and Emmet, five.

There are 1,150 railroad stations in the State. The railroads are divided into three classes for taxation and charges for freightage and railroad fares. They are under the supervision of a board of three commissioners elected by the people and are being wisely controlled.

A glance at the State map found in this volume will reveal that all our farmers are within easy range of railroad markets. We doubt the possibility of a farm being now found in Iowa, the occcupant of which in fair weather and with fairly good roads, cannot start with his team from his home in the daylight hour of the morning and returning from his market reach his home ere the twilight of the evening has declined into the darkness of the night. While the majority of Iowa farmers are so situated that with their teams they can haul off at least two loads of produce in a day. We have heard it said "no farmer is so far from market as he who has nothing to sell." The farmers of Iowa do have produce to sell and have market places and good markets of easy access.

### TONNAGE CARRIED.

The total tonnage carried by the railroads of commodities moved from place to place in Iowa is difficult to obtain. Last year the two great roads, the Chicago, Rock Island & Pacific and the Chicago, Burlington & Quincy made no report in this matter. The roads reporting their business to the Board of R. R. Commissioners moved the following tonnage :     TONS.

| | |
|---|---|
| Grain | 3,457,688 |
| Flour | 369,064 |
| Live stock | 1,808,271 |
| Coal | 2,783,965 |
| Lumber | 1,476,902 |

For the two great roads failing to report, alike for their main line and numerous important branches, the mileage controlled by these two roads aggregating nearly one-fourth of the mileage of the State, the commissioners estimated an addition of one-fourth to the above tonnage in the five items named. This would make a total of upwards of eleven millions tons of those five commodities for the year, largely produced or consumed by the agricultural population of the state. Facilities furnished for the rapid and cheap movement of such a mass of commodities are a solid factor to our business prosperity.

### EARNINGS.

The total earnings of the roads of Iowa for passenger service in the state for the year ending June 30, 1892, was $10,387,247.89. The total freight earnings of Iowa business was $26,359,095.00. Total earnings on Iowa business $37,405,473.32. Total operating expenses $25,076,828.00, leaving as net earnings the sum of $12,328,645.22

### EMPLOYES AND SALARIES.

The whole number of employes in this service was 30,192, salaries paid, $17,807,915.89. Nature made it possible to bring those great aids to agricultural, mining, manufacturing and commercial pursuits into every locality and community in the State, and the enterprise and liberal spirit of our people has so encouraged the improvement of these favoring opportunities that in the grand threadwork of iron track-ways now flecking the state, every business pursuit and every community enjoys those facilities absolutely vital to its prosperity. No state of the Union can show these essential advantages more general and equably distributed than they are now in Iowa. But the work of railroad building is not complete. Some localities yet need better railroad facilities, and the work of railroad building will go on till the demands of all for the best possible railroad advantages are met.

## POSTAL FACILITIES.

In this age postal conveniences are important to the business interests and social life of every community. No agricultural state in the central portion of the country has more complete and convenient postal facilities than the people of Iowa enjoy.

We have shown that there are 1,150 railroad stations in Iowa. These places all have daily mail facilities. Many country postoffices have also daily mail. Postoffices in Iowa with only a weekly mail are obsolete.

Under date of January 17th, 1893, the First Assistant Postmaster General informed us that January 1st, 1893, there were 1835 postoffices in the state. That of this number 179 were presidential offices namely: 1st class 7; 2nd class 23; 3rd class 149; other postoffices 1,556.

The whole number of mail routes in the State was then 834. Their total length being 13,484 miles. Number of miles of travel required yearly to carry the mails 13,229,678.

The gross amount of postal receipts in this State for the year ending June 30, 1792, was $1,949,847.05.

These figures show that the people of Iowa are large patrons of the postal department. Her people read newspapers and write letters.

## TELEGRAPHS AND TELEPHONES.

These modern inventions for the speedy conveyance of intellegence are established throughout this State and are largely patronized by the people aiding business transactions and facilitating communication.

## BANKING.

The growth of wealth in Iowa has brought enlargement of business, has developed new lines of business pursuit and incited the founding of new and important business enterprises.

The banking business is an essential to commercial transaction and accommodation in this age of quickened activity and communication. The interests of commerce and security of the patrons of banking institutions incorporated under our State legislation demand a careful, legal supervision to secure their wise management. This is provided by our banking laws.

Provisions are made by our laws for the incorporation of two classes of banking institutions denominated severally, State banks and Savings banks, both classes being banks of exchange and deposit; National banks being the only banks of issue. Hon. J. A. Lyons, Auditor of State, in his annual bank report, June 30, 1892, returned 104 Savings banks, and 141 State banks. The Savings banks having a capital of $5,304,000.00, and holding deposits to the amount of $26,115,384.25. The 141 State banks were reported as having a capital of $7,430,000.00, holding on deposit $16,361.011.34. The total capital of these two classes of banks being $12,734,200. The total deposits held by them $42,476,395.79.

### PRIVATE INSTITUTIONS.

The Comptroller of the Treasury, Hon. A. B. Hepburn, reported June 30, 1892, eight incorporated loan and trust companies doing business in Iowa. These had a capital stock of $2,122,028 and held deposits amounting to $1,001,399.

At the same date the same officer reported 185 private banks in the State with a capital of $5,404,914.00. Individual deposits $10,928,893.

### NATIONAL BANKS.

In the same document that officer reported 154 National banks in this State, having a capital stock of $14,325,000, and holding on deposit $30,491,755.68.

That officer estimated the population of the State June 1, 1892, at 1,964,000 persons. He reported the total banking capital in the State at $44,586,152. Individual deposits held by the several classes of banks above named, $84,899,443.227.

The total sum of deposits in the several institutions enumerated averaged $43.22 *per capita*, to the estimated population. Surely a people with such an amount of cash *per capita* at command in banks if not rich are at least in that happy condition desired by Agur: "Give me neither poverty nor riches, feed me with convenient food for me, lest I be full and deny thee and say who is the Lord? Or lest I be poor and steal and take the name of my God in vain."

## INSURANCE.

The insurance business has assumed large dimensions and like the banking business it is placed under strict legal supervision. It is operated under two lines, namely, stock and mutual companies, all subjected to the same strict supervision.

There were in the State 141 Co-operative or Farmers' Insurance companies, carrying December 31, 1891, risks to the amount of $93,291,790. They paid for losses during the year 1890, $103,912.75, doing their business at an average cost of $1.57 per $1,000 of insurance. Insuring nothing but farm property or what are strictly detached dwellings in towns their losses are light, and doing business strictly on the mutual plan and without expensive agencies their expenses are very low and insurance is carried in them at the lowest possible rate.

There are nineteen other companies incorporated under the laws of Iowa, doing general fire insurance business. Of these eleven are joint stock companies holding a paid up capital of $875,000. Seven are mutual companies. The eighteen companies have a total of gross assets of $3,890,463. Their total income in 1891 was $1,883,461.25. They wrote risks during that year to the grand total of $97,785,403.87, and paid in losses $784,386.31.

### FOREIGN COMPANIES.

All foreign companies before they can do business in Iowa must make satisfactory showing of their condition to the Auditor of State. There were 108 of such companies doing business in Iowa in 1890, namely, 1 German company, 2 Scotch, 14 English, 2 Canadian, 7 Connecticut, 27 New York, 6 Massachusetts, 4 New Jersey, 1 Maryland, 1 Pennsylvania, 14 Wisconsin, 4 Colorado, 1 Michigan, 3 Rhode Island, 3 Illinois, 5 Tennessee, 1 New Hampshire and 2 Minnesota. Three foreign countries and fifteen other states are represented in the fire insurance business in this state. These do a large business.

### LIFE INSURANCE.

The life insurance business is carried on by home and foreign companies. Including both classes twenty-nine life insurance companies were authorized to do business in this State in 1892. Of these companies four were home incorporations and twenty-five were foreign, namely, five Connecticut, nine New York, one each Massachusetts, Michigan, New Jersey, Vermont, Wisconsin, California, Nebraska, Ohio and Maine and two Pennsylvania incorporations.

The total number of life policies in force December 31, 1892, was 38,302. The total amount of life insurance in force at that date was $78,356,022. The total premiums received during the year 1891 was $2,237,425.99. Amount of losses paid $659,922.69.

## DEVELOPMENT OF WEALTH.

Iowa, in regard to her rank in the accumulation of wealth, occupies a position of which her citizens may well be proud. In the census of 1850 thirty-two of the thirty-three states then forming the Union exceeded her in wealth, *per capita;* a fact that at once proves that her pioneers were men in very moderate circumstances. In the census returns of 1860 thirty of the thirty-six States of the Union exceeded Iowa in *per capita* wealth. In 1870 Iowa had reduced the gap between her place in 1860 and the head of the list by passing ten of the thirty states that had outranked her in this particular in 1860. In 1880 she had surpassed others until by the census of that year, but six states east of the Rocky Mountains exceeded her; and but five in the Union, namely, New York, Pennsylvania, Ohio, Illinois and Massachusetts outranked her in aggregate wealth. In this respect Iowa is still gaining, and in the past twelve years has outstripped others of her sister states in the development of wealth, *per capita.* That Iowa has enjoyed such material prosperity and that her people are in thriving condition are facts which we gladly record.

## A HISTORIC RESUME.

Sixty years ago, a space of time embraced in the life of men yet active in business, Iowa was devoid of the essentials of a civilized State. There was not a charitable institution, public building, postoffice, church, school, mill, bridge, orchard, farm, or scarcely a squatters cabin or barn within its boundaries. The whole region was then traversed only by Indians.

The only dwellings, save a few cabins in Lee county, being the tepee or wigwams. The means of interior transportation in aid of trade, were the shoulders of the squaw, the Indian pony or canoe, or the pack horse of an occasional venturesome hunter.

Consider further the greatness of the change made in these three score years, a mere hand-breadth of time in the life of a nation. Look at the 110,000 miles of broad, largely well constructed, open highways, with their innumerable culverts and thousands of substantial bridges which now carry those highways across our streams, furnishing ready means of communication and transportation to all. Look at the 215,000 grand farms in Iowa, with their barns and other outbuildings, many of them costly structures; the grand pastures flecked with feeding herds and flocks of noblest blood and finest form; the spacious orchards and gardens of fruit, the stately artificial groves which grace those fine farm homes. View the 370,000 family dwellings, the homes of comfort and elegance of our two millions of intelligent, Christian citizens, thousands of those homes being spacious dwelling places, palatial in architecture, luxurious in furniture, and royal in their surroundings. Then view the beautiful, prosperous towns and cities which have sprung up as though thrown forth by magic all over our broad prairies; and the shops, the mills, the mines, the manufacturing plants, the bazaars of trade, teeming with life and activity, the halls of art, the public schools, with their 13,275 fine school houses, the private and parochial schools, the academies, seminaries, normal schools, colleges, technical and professional schools and the universities which now give grace and culture to our social life. Extend your vision and take in the 4,500 church edifices, many of them majestic temples, standing everywhere with open doors, inviting all to enjoy their sanctifying associations. Then look further at the noble charitable and reformatory institutions, the great schools and asylums for our unfortunate classes, our homes for the maimed, the infirm and the poor. View these and consider that all have been constructed and are maintained either by means voluntarily donated or by taxation which has been generously and freely voted. Then consider that in addition to the outlays essential to the construction, maintenance and improvement of the institutions mentioned our people have made a large accumulation of private wealth. Surely such gains attest not only that Iowa has an industrious, economical citizenship, but also that her generous soil has great wealth producing power.

### THE DEMONSTRATION OF FIGURES.

We are not left merely to rhetorical statement to express the growth of wealth in this inland State. The rapid increase in valuation of taxable property in Iowa shows an almost incomprehensible growth of wealth. In 1850, 13,732,600 acres of land were assessed for taxation. Its average assessed value was but $3.54 per acre, and the aggregate valuation $48,611,280, the total valuation for the purpose of taxation that year being $58,007,121. This was only two score and three years.

In 1860, 24,386,217 acres were assessed for taxation, their aggregate value being $123,447,181, or $5.06 per acre. The valuation of personal property assessed that year was $30,147,858. The total aggregate assessed valuation in 1860 was $153,539,116.

In 1870, 33,018,604 acres of land were assessed for taxation. Of this amount only 9,369,467 were reported as improved land. The average assessed value per acre was $5.50, and the aggregate valuation $181,881,953, while the total taxable valuation that year had reached $294,532,250, the real wealth in the State had according to the United States census, grown to the sum of $717,644,750.

In 1880 the aggregate value of taxable property within the State had grown to the sum of $409,819,020, the area of assessed lands being 34,-569,858 acres. Only 19,860,514 acres, or little more than one-half the area of the State, were reported as improved lands, but the average taxable valuation of the lands that year was $7.11 per acre.

In 1890 the taxable lands had increased to 34,734.579 acres, and their valuation to $272,847,509, which was an average of $7.85 per acre, the total taxable valuation in the State that year being $523,862,858.

But these remarkable figures fall far short of showing the true growth of wealth in this prosperous State. The flight of time has not been more rapid than has been the advance in all lines of improvement, in labor saving machinery, modes of transportation, and business facilities. Railways, telegraphs and telephones have extended their conveniences and industrial inspiration through every county. Hamlets have grown into thriving towns and thrifty towns have developed into large and prosperous cities. Yet as wealth has grown the ratio of the taxable to the true value of property has been reduced. The assessments in 1850 and 1870 were nearer the true value of property than were the assessed values of 1890. We give a few instances in support of this statement.

In 1870 cattle were assessed at an average of $12.67 per head, in 1890 at only $7.11.

In 1870 horses were assessed at an average value of $42.67 per head, in 1890 at $25.64.

In 1870 swine were assessed at an average value of $3.09 per head, in 1890 at $1.64.

Nearly the same reduction in ratios of the assessed, to the true values, has obtained in all lines of property. As shown above, the average assessed value of lands throughout the State was $5.50 per acre in 1870. Then there were but 9,369,467 acres of land, or only one-fourth of the area of the State, reported as improved lands. In 1880 the improved land had more than doubled in area, being that year reported as 19,866,541 acres. The value of the improvements on the land had largely increased. In 1870 we had but 2,683 miles of railroad, in 1890 there were 8,436 miles, traversing every county in the State. While land has increased several times (a hundred per cent.) in value, its assessed valuation has only increased from an average of $5.50 to $7.85.

Well informed judges of property-value in this State believe that the present taxable valuation does not exceed twenty per cent. of the real value of the property of the people. Taking this figure as a factor in the calculation, it will be seen that the real value of property is now in excess of $2,700,000,000. In the brief period of sixty years property values have grown from nothing to the immense sum named.

It is worthy of mention in this place that this vast aggregate of wealth has been developed from the soil of Iowa. None of these thousands of millions have been washed from glittering river beds. Iowa has scores of "sunny fountains" but none of them

"Roll down their golden sands."

Nor have any of these millions been mined from argentiferous or auriferous rocks, in which hundreds of golden millions lie, awaiting the workman with his picks and drills; they have been won almost solely in agricultural pursuits. The tillers of the soil and herdsmen have been their chief producers, and the plow, the harrow and the corn cultivator, the mower and the reaper the chief implements used in their acquisition.

The healthfulness of Iowa for man and beast, through the earlier as well as the later years of its settlement has had important bearing on this gain of wealth. Iowa has ever been rightfully recognized as a healthy State.

#### COMPARATIVE GROWTH OF POPULATION AND WEALTH.

We take the following figures from the returns of the several enumerations of population and wealth made in Iowa by the National Census authorities, placing the same in concisely tabulated form, not only to present still more clearly, if posssble, the fact of the great development of wealth, but also to show how the growth of wealth has outran the growth of population in the history of the State.

The first national census in Iowa was the sixth of the country. It was taken in 1840. The population of the territory was then returned as 43,113 persons. Of the real wealth of the territory at the time of that census we are not informed.

#### COMPARATIVE GROWTH OF POPULATION AND WEALTH.

| YEARS. | POPULATION. | PER CT. INCREASE. | TRUE WEALTH. | WEALTH PER CAPITA |
| --- | --- | --- | --- | --- |
| 1850 | 192,214 | 288. | $ 23,714,638 | $ 123.39 |
| 1860 | 574,913 | 251. | 247,338,265 | 366.46 |
| 1870 | 1,194,752 | 96.91 | 717,644,750 | 640.89 |
| 1880 | 1,634,615 | 36. | 1,721,000,000 | 1,059.00 |
| 1890 | 1,911,896 | 17. | 2,700,000,000 | 1,412.00 |

The fact that this development of wealth has come from the areable fields, the pastures and meadows of Iowa, and that it has been developed while large areas of the State have been but sparsely settled, and while but little more than one-half of its area has been "tickled with the plow," unmistakably demonstrates the excellence of her soil, the richness and healthfulness of her sunshine, the fertilizing potency of the rains that fall upon her lands, and its pre-eminence as a field for successful agricultural industry. Such vast development of wealth in a State of the population, area and age of Iowa, having neither ocean commerce, nor great fisheries, nor forests, nor rich bonanzas of precious metals, will ever be one of the marvels of history.

## FINANCE AND TAXATION.

Iowa is in happy financial condition. The State has an elegant, commodious, solid Capitol of stately proportions, located in the city of Des Moines on a commanding site. It has numerous other public buildings providing accommodations and educational advantages for unfortunate classes, as the blind, deaf and dumb, the feeble minded; reformatory schools for the unruly of both sexes, insane asylums, orphans home, a home for aged and needy veterans, penitentiaries for the punishment of criminals, the Normal school, Agricultural college and State university. All these great properties have been built up and millions paid for their maintenance. All expenses for State government have been met, yet taxation has been low— the assessed valuation has ever been far below the cash value of property. Taxation for all purposes has been less than one per cent. on the true value of property; and yet Iowa occupies the proud position occupied by only three other States in the American Union, of having no State debt either bonded or floating. According to the figures given in Census Bulletin No. 64, its total debt, State and county, in 1890 was but $1.91 *per capita*. In 1880 it was $2.10; a pleasing reduction for the ten years. On the ninth page that bulletin shows that only three of the States of the Union have a less State and county indebtedness *per capita*, namely Vermont, $.46; Rhode Island, $1.22 and West Virginia $1.81, while the State and county indebtedness of the States adjoining Iowa range from $2.21 to $10.04 *per capita*. The average State and county indebtedness for the States of the Union is $5.83. Although the cry, that the farmers of Iowa are overwhelmed by mortgage indebtedness, is raised by uninformed persons, there are but few farmers in Iowa distressed on that account. It cannot be expected that in a new State, in which within the twenty years last past so great an area has been improved and such great improvements in farm homes, schools, roads, business structures and machinery have been made, that there would be no debt contracted, but that there has in the ten years last past, been a rapid reduction of the mortgage indebtedness against the people of Iowa, is a fact not only shown by the census of 1890, but one well known to all intelligent observers. The reduction in the three years that have elapsed since the taking of the last census has been very large. The prosperity of the people during those years has been unequaled in any previous period in the history of this, or any other State.

On page 7, Census Bulletin No. 16, census of 1890, the mortgage indebtedness on the farms of Iowa is given at $148,457,144. The total mortgage indebtedness on the entire reality within the State being $199,774,171. The whole number of mortgages on farms was 171,441. Considering each as a first mortgage, then the figures indicate the number of farms mortgaged. The average amount of these mortgages was $876. The records however do not show the fact that many of them were nearly paid, and that on others the debt secured was largely reduced by payment made thereon, but not shown on the record. Nor do they show the fact that the major part of these mortgages were given for purchase money on lands, or to raise money to buy more lands, to improve lands or to purchase stock where-by more money might be made on lands occupied. Estimating the farms covered by those 171,441 mortgages at eighty acres each, then we have 13,715,220 acres of mortgaged land. Further estimating their average value at $25 per acre, a moderate estimate, and we have for their total value the sum of $342,882,- 000,—certainly a good security for the sums owed; while there remains 22,000,000 acres of farm lands free from mortgage with upwards of $208,- 000,000 of live stock, the increase of which is applicable to the reduction of this indebtedness. It should not be forgotten that the dairy and poultry products alone would wipe out the mortgage indebtedness on Iowa farms within two years. The farmers of Iowa may not do all of their business on a cash basis but they certainly do it on a very safe one. The large sums held on deposit by the banks, as shown in the chapter on "Banks and Banking," much of which is money made on Iowa farms and subject to check by Iowa farmers, shows that very many of the farmers are money lenders rather than borrowers.

The assessments of real and personal property for purposes of taxation are made by local authorities, each civil township and incorporated town and the several wards in cities electing the assessors. Personal property is assessed each year and real property biennially. The township trustees and town and city councils, the county boards of supervisors and the Executive Council of the State constitute boards of equalization. The Executive Council assesses the railroads, telegraph and telephone lines.

Taxes are low when compared with the true value of property. The valuations of property for taxation as equalized by the several boards for the year 1890 were reported by Hon. J. A. Lyons, State Auditor, as follows:

Lands, 34,734,579 acres and town lots...........................$374,753,112
Personal property......................................................... 105,543,264
Railroad property.......................................................... 42,962,264
Telegraph companies.................................................... 502,874
Telephone companies................................................... 162,000

Total taxable valuation..................................................$523,862,858

The lands within the State were assessed at $8.18 per acre; cattle at $7.11 per head; horses $26.46; mules $28.80; sheep $1.18, and swine at $1.64. Cattle, horses and mules under one year old and sheep and swine under six months are not listed or valued for taxation.

The taxes levied for the year 1890 were reported by the State Auditor as follows:

For purposes of State government.............................$1,207,872.85
For county purposes.................................................... 5,107,000.27
For insane fund............................................................ 348,098.27
For support of common schools.................................. 6,021,758.68
For municipal government.......................................... 2,405,156.65
For special purposes................................................... 384,098.27

Total..............................................................................$15,563,974.04

Taking the estimate of the real value of property within the State at the moderate figure of $2,700,000,000, the taxes levied for the year for all purposes aggregated the small figure of .71 of one per cent. The interest on county and municipal indebtedness, and provisions for sinking funds are provided for in the taxes levied as above given. In no State in the Union are the people less burdened with taxation.

## AGRICULTURAL PRODUCTIVENESS.

Iowa has world wide fame for its agricultural productiveness. Its soil produces all the standard grains, grasses, vegetables and fruits, successfully grown north of the Ohio river. The figures required to express the vast production of grains, vegetables, meats and fruits within this region are of surprising-magnitude, but the capabilities of Iowa's thirty-five millions of acres to produce foods are yet uncomprehended. With the cultivation of her yet unimproved acres, better drainage of her wet lands and the more perfect cultivation of her arable fields, meadows and orchards the products of this superlatively fine farming region will have a wonderful increase.

Iowa does not owe the greatness of her food productiveness to the extent of her area. In this regard she has but 20th place in the list of the States of the Union. Michigan, Minnesota, the Dakotas, Nebraska, Kansas, Missouri and Illinois, her near kin in locality and climate, all outrank her in this particular. Compared with Texas and California, she ranks respect-

MAIN BUILDING IOWA AGRICULTURAL COLLEGE.

place in the rank of States. She also held the tenth place in 1880, in respect to persons engaged in agricultural occupation, so that her larger agricultural productiveness is to be found in other causes than the greater number of her agricultural laborers or her larger area. In the census just referred to, this State ranked fifth in the number of farms, sixth in the production of wheat, sixth in the production of potatoes, fourth in the production of barley, second in the production of Indian corn, second in the production of oats, second in the production of hay, second in the production of all grains, third in respect to the number of horses, second in respect to the number of cattle, and first in respect to the number of swine. Although this State then ranked second in the production of all grains, second in the production of beef animals, and first in the production of swine, only 19,866,541, or a trifle more than one-half of her thirty-five million acres were reported as being improved. Iowa, then largely unimproved, was outranked by only three other States in the total value of her agricultural productions The four leading States compared then as follows:

| STATES. | VALUE OF AGRICULTURAL PRODUCT. |
|---|---|
| Illinois | $263,980,137.90 |
| New York | 178,025,695.00 |
| Ohio | 156,737,152.00 |
| Iowa | 136,103,473.00 |

The above schedule clearly establishes the fact that an agricultural laborer in Iowa's climate and working Iowa soil effects larger production than an agricultural laborer in any other climate and any other State of the Union. This one fact accounts for its unequalled development of wealth.

In the annual report of the National Department of Agriculture for 1888, Iowa is placed second in the list of States in the production of potatoes, her production that year being over 16,000,000 bushels. New York alone led Iowa in this important crop; but the reported yield per acre in Iowa, largely exceeded that of New York.

The same high authority gave Iowa for the same year second place in the production of hay, her production being 5,972,783 tons. The crop of New York, the only State then leading Iowa was 5,462,667 tons, or only 143,984 tons more than the product of Iowa.

The National Department of Agriculture reported that 9,506,716 acres of Iowa farms in 1891 were cultivated in "corn," and reported their aggregate products at 350,878,000—an excess of 115,993,000 bushels over our neighboring state on the east, then the second in rank in the corn producing states. If corn is "king" then surely Iowa is the prime province of his kingdom.

Since 1886 Iowa has been the largest corn producing State in the Union. No region on this earth of the same area furnishes such vast production of this most important cereal. The production of corn in Iowa for the years 1888, 1889, 1890 and 1891, according to the report of the National Department of agriculture, aggregated 1,221,305,000 bushels on a total of 34,963,753 acres. This is an average production for the four years of 33.4 bushels per acre. A few special yields of this cereal in this famous corn State may properly be mentioned in this connection.

In the winter of 1890-1 Mr. Henry Wallace, editor of the Homestead, an agricultural paper published in Des Moines, offered three prizes for the best three acres of corn grown within the State in the season of 1891. It will be noticed that the competitors came from nine counties, these counties covering one-half of the State from south to north.

| | | | |
|---|---|---|---|
| Wm. M. Husted, Des Moines, Polk County | 364 bu., | and | 65 lbs |
| James Pemble, Wapello, Louisa " | 315 | " | 65 lbs |
| J. W. Rynearson, Yorktown, Page " | 300 | " | 5 lbs |
| A. F. White, DeWitt, Clinton " | 291 | " | |
| Frank Wright, Anamosa, Jones " | 285 | " | 34 lbs |
| A. D. Belknap, Amber, Jones " | 217 | " | 55 lbs |
| A. D. Zimmerman, Avoca, Pottawattamie County | 277 | " | 20 lbs |
| A. D. Irving, Madrid, Boone " | 270 | " | 3 lbs |
| J. H. DeFord, Mt. Sterling, Van Buren " | 269 | " | 30 lbs |
| J. C. Frazey, Shelby, Shelby " | 262 | " | 14 lbs |

The largest yield was 115 bushels and 45 pounds per acre, the smallest 67 bushels and 18 pounds per acre, for the three acres.

The immense importance of the corn crop in Iowa agriculture is evident to all. Secretary Shaffer of the State Agricultural Society in the report for 1891 said: "Iowa's single product of corn is worth more than the entire output of all the gold and silver mines of all the states combined."

President Harrison in returning from his journey to the Pacific coast, having seen the land of "the orange and the palm," and having reached on that return the great fields of "golden ears," in his address at Omaha, said:

"I have seen the orange groves and all the fruits which enrich and characterize the state of California. I have seen the summit cities whose mining camps are on the peaks where the men are delving into the earth to bring out the rich stores there; but I return again to the land of the corn stalk with an affection that I cannot describe. I am sure those friends who have delighted us with visions of loveliness and prosperity will excuse me if my birth and earlier training in Ohio and Indiana leads me to the conclusion that the states that grow corn are the greatest states in the world."

The directors of the Iowa State Agricultural Society in their report for 1891, by their Secretary, Hon. Jno. R. Shaffer, present the following table estimating the agricultural products for Iowa for that year and their values:

### AGRICULTURAL PRODUCT OF IOWA FOR 1891.

| KIND. | PRODUCT. | VALUE. |
|---|---|---|
| Corn, bushels | 335,031,598 | $ 100,509,479 |
| Wheat, bushels | 34,151,488 | 25,741,039 |
| Oats, bushels | 115,810,800 | 26,636,484 |
| Rye, bushels | 2,051,400 | 1,333,410 |
| Barley, bushels | 4,528,669 | 1,411,467 |
| Buckwheat, bushels | 414,000 | 276,900 |
| Potatoes, Irish, bushels | 25,620,350 | 5,586,271 |
| Potatoes, sweet, bushels | 207,900 | 207,900 |
| Grass seeds, estimated | | 1,750,000 |
| Flax seed, bushels | 3,154,016 | 2,523,212 |
| Hay, tame, tons | 5,582,800 | 31,497,340 |
| Hay, prairie, estimated | | 6,800,000 |
| Broom-corn, tons | 3,480 | 270,570 |
| Sorghum, gallons | 2,092,485 | 904,718 |
| Butter, pounds | 168,690,715 | 33,738,158 |
| Cheese, pounds | 5,000,000 | 450,000 |
| Wool | | 300,000 |
| Horses, number | 1,312,079 | 91,911,133 |
| Mules, number | 41,648 | 2,459,938 |
| Sheep, number | 452,000 | 1,430,750 |
| Hogs, number | 5,921,100 | 29,478,238 |
| Milch cows, number | 1,278,612 | 23,973,975 |
| Other cattle, number | 2,080,247 | 47,038,347 |
| Orchard and vine products | | 3,000,000 |
| Hive products | | 550,000 |
| Poultry products | | 5,600,000 |
| Small fruits | | 750,000 |
| Timber | | 3,000,000 |
| Miscellaneous | | 10,000,000 |
| Total | | $ 464,219,308 |

In Iowa in 1892 there were 565,031 head of sheep, 4,011,233 head of cattle, and 7,105,320 head of swine and flocks innumerable of turkeys, geese, ducks and other barn yard fowls. At least 5,000,000 head of finely fatted swine were supplied for slaughter, furnishing fifteen pounds, *per capita*, of the best pork to the whole country, while at least 400,000,000 pounds of finest beef was furnished to the markets of the world, These figures of moderate estimate, are given to convey some idea of the abundance that is found in this most fertile region. Iowa farmers not only feed well all of Iowa's people, but feed also millions in other states and countries. In grain and meat production Iowa, but sixty years removed from absolute wilderness state, now stands without an equal.

## THE OLDEST LEGENDS OF THE ORIGIN OF MAIZE.

Maize (zea mays—L) derives its name from a Greek word zea, meaning *spelt*. There are many varying opinions as to its first home. It never occurs naturally, but is a native of all tropical America, and probably indigenous there. Humboldt says it is an American Plant. Some older writers, however, claim that it originally came from Asia, going thence to America, from which country it was first brought into Europe. Gerard in the "Herbal" written in 1597, calls it "Turkey Corn," and says, "This kind of grain was first brought into Spain, and thence into other provinces of Europe out of Asia, which is in the Turke's Dominions, as also out of America." No corn is found in Egyptian tombs, but the plant is represented in an ancient Chinese Book in the French Library at Paris. There is a variety known in Chili, (Zea Curagua) which has small grains, some of which are often found in tombs. The Chilians are superstitious about these, as they split so as to image a cross on their inner surface. This corn is called *Caru* in Quichua, and it is to the kind suggestion of the great Americanist, Count de Charencey, that I owe the statement that many similar names are given to rice in various Asiatic tongues, probably referring to the small eared corn, (Cha-rang, among the Rodongs of Napaul, *Chasrak* in Chungthansia, *Sila* in Nachhereng, *Sera* in Chourasya, and *Seri* in Kolunyga.) These facts, heretofore unnoticed, so far as I know, would seem to indicate the Asiatic origin of the grain. Several tribes of the Nepaul hills call Sorghum, *Mazyi*.

But we may find a legend of Asiatic origin to account for maize, which, however foolish it may seem in its details, is significant, as indicating a knowledge of this plant at an early period. The legend is from the *Manck Maya*, a Javanese legendary poem of unknown date. It relates that the body of a certain maiden who died from the too ardent embrace of her pursuing lover, *Sang Yang Gurn*, (the personification of man) was buried in a wood; from the head, sprang the cocoanut; from the hands, the plantain tree; and from the teeth, Indian corn or Maize.

This legend, referring the origin of corn to the teeth of the buried woman, carries us back to the antique fable of the armed men springing from the dragon's teeth, and it is a curious fact that in central Illinois the sharp kernelled variety is popularly known as "Horse-tooth corn."

We may, however, find legends among the American Indians which bears a close resemblance to the old Javanese story of the origin of corn. Dr. Brinton relates an Iroquois myth of Ioskhea, the dawn-hero, one of the great American culture-heroes, which accounts for the appearance of Maize among the Indian tribes. The heavens are here said to have been peopled by a race of supernatural beings, and one of these a woman, *Atalensia*, fell through the sky. As a result of her fall, being pregnant, she died, after one of her twins Ioskhea, had burst from her arm pit into the world. Her body was buried, and from it sprung the vegetables; from the head, the pumpkin; from the breast, maize, (hence the milk;) and from the limbs, the bean.

We may also have a key to both of these myths, which seem to express the operations of nature in promoting the growth of so beneficial a plant. As Dr. Brinton says, plainly expressed, "The sense of the story is that the orb of light moves daily over the water (*Atalensia*, sea, water) preceeded by its child, Ioskhea, (light, dawn.)

Still another legend, from a different tribe, ascribes the origin of corn to the body of a woman. This Cherokee myth is reported by James Mooney. Two boys, one the child of a hunter living at Looking Glass Mountain (Tsuwakida) in North Carolina, the other issuing from the water, from the blood poured into it by the hunter, kill the hunter's wife because she was a witch, they having seen her rub corn out of her body. She tells them: "When you have killed me, clear a large piece of ground in front of the house, and drag my body seven times around the circle. Then drag me seven times over the ground inside of the circle, and stay up all night and watch, and in the morning you will have plenty of corn." They kill her with clubs, cut off her head, and set it on the tent-pole, then clear away the ground. Instead of all of it, they only clear seven little spots, and this is why corn only grows in certain parts of the world. Then they drag the body of Nela around the circle and where her blood falls, corn springs up. Instead of dragging it about seven times, they do so twice, and this is why the Indian only works his crop twice. In the morning the crop is ripe.

Instead of the body of a mortal, the body of an animal has been substituted in an Osage legend, reported by Rev. J. O. Dorsey. In this tradition, four Buffalo bulls came by, and as each rolls upon the ground he dropped from his left hind leg an ear of corn and a pumpkin: red corn came from the first, spotted from the second, black from the third, and white from the fourth. Therefore, when a child is named in the *Tsicu* Gens, the head man of that Gens takes a grain of each kind of corn, and a slice of each variety of pumpkin, which he puts into the mouth of the infant.

The early Spanish conquerers found the native tribes here in possession of this esculent vegetable, which sustains life among so many indigenous tribes of our Hemisphere. They endeavored to find the history of its origin. As might be expected, they found nothing but legends to account for this as well as other plants. One of them is given by Brasseur de Bourbourg, from a Caqciquel manuscript of Mexico. It is a legend of the creation. The primitive Gods of Mexico and the world becoming discouraged for lack of food Gueatzalcoatl, the Culture hero, decided to visit the interior of the Country and of distant lands, to find some alimentary food. The legend relates that he found some of the people of a distant country bearing stalks of maize, which he received from them, and brought back to the Mexican valley. The region was called "Paxil Calaya", the place of divided waters, to a hill known as "Tonacatapetl", "or the hill of our Subsistance." It has been named as a sort of Terrestrial paradise, says the Abbe, throughout all antique America.

Another Mexican myth reported by Sahagun, relates not to the origin, but to the mysterious connection of maize with the Gods. Tezcatlipoca, disguised as an old woman, parches maize, and the odor of the savory corn attracts the Toltecs, whom she then destroys. One of the names of Quetzalcoatl was Ce-acatl, "one reed", a corn stalk (possibly phallic also). A day in the Mexican calendar was named after him, and this day, Ce-acatl, was a most unlucky one, as he was the God of Storms. Persons born on this corn-stalk day would lose their possessions by having them blown away.

In Aztec, *elotl* is milky corn, *mumnehtl* ripe corn in the ear, *tlaxcaeli* corn cakes, and *atoeli* hasty-pudding. Centestl is the Mexican Maize Goddess, and sometimes bears a corn-stalk in her hand. A stalk of grain carried by a bird-headed Deity, signified the winds. South American Indians, and those of Central America, also know the value of maize. Many of them use it as food, but more ferment it as a sort of beer. Sometimes it is mixed with other substances, such as quinoa seeds, to make a fermented drink. D'Orbigny says the Guarany Indians of Brazil attribute the discovery of maize to Tamaui, a Culture hero.

A Quichua legend, according to Comara, relates that *Con*, son of the Sun and the Moon, gave maize to man.

One of the four Maya Gods (Bacubs) was *Hobnil*, the Belly. His habitat was the South, and he was of the color of ripe yellow corn, and was favorable and propitious to man. Stalks of maize-colored red were expressive of generative force. The spirit of the South brought maize to the Iriquois.

Mr. A. M. Stephens relates the following curious legend of the Snake order of the Moquis Indians. Many years ago, several bachelor brothers lived together in a house. Their names were, in the order of their ages, Red Corn, Blue Corn, Yellow Corn, Green Corn, Spotted Corn, and Black Corn. When the last attained his majority, the others told him to find a bride. He was dissatisfied at this, not knowing where to find a suitable one. He started out on a journey with four feather plume sticks and a bag of sand meal. He finally came to a stream by a lake, where he was told by Dawa, the sun-chief, to throw his plume sticks into the water. They immediately grew into a raft on which he embarked. He came to Napa Tcua (Big Rattlesnake) after a four days sail, his raft again becoming plume sticks, after wafting him ashore. A snake fiend approached him, and gave him a bag and stick. His name here changes suddenly to Kueteat-ri-yi (White Corn), without any assignable cause. Finally, after many miracles have been performed by the aid of the bag and stick, he arrived in the presence of the Snake King, where he obtained a beautiful bride, first obtaining a snake skin dress for himself. He then learned the many songs and ritual still practiced by this gens of the tribe. After this, he returned to the South, with his wife Tcua-wati.

Among all the Indian tribes of the Southwest, corn has a peculiar significance. Its connection with their religious ceremonials will be alluded to again.

Schoolcraft, who chronicled many Indian legends now unattainable, relates the following "Algic" story of the advent of maize.

Kitchimonedo (the Creator) first made men who looked like men, but were really worthless. He put them and the world into a great lake, and drowned them. From the water he then made a very handsome young man and afterwards he sent a sister to live with him, as he was lonesome. After some years, this young man had a dream, after which he told his sister "Five young men will come to your lodge door this night to visit you. The Great Spirit forbids you to answer or even look up and smile on the first four, but when the fifth comes, you may speak and laugh, and show that you are pleased." She acted accordingly. The first of the five strangers who called was *Itsaman*, meaning tobacco, and on being repulsed, he fell down and died. *Wapako*, or pumpkin, was next. *Eshkorsini*, the melon, third, and fourth *Kokseels*, the bean. All these perished, but when *Tamin*, or Montanin (Maize), presented himself he was admitted. From the union of the maiden and Montanin sprang the Indian race. This legend, however, is not so well known, as another related by Schoolcraft, which, through

its being utilized by Longfellow, in his poem "Hiawatha", has been widespread. The legend is here given, condensed from the diffuse story as published.

The son of a poor Indian hunter (in another version it is Massuamium, or Manalozho, the magician), on attaining the age of fifteen, built a fasting lodge in the forest, and set about his task of fasting for several days, as all young Indians did at that age. He was a serious young man, and got to thinking how he could be of service to his people. On the third day, he became too weak to walk, and kept his bed. He fancied as he lay there that he saw approaching a handsome young man dressed in green with green plumes on his head.

> "And he saw a youth approaching
> Dressed in garments green and yellow,
> Coming through the purple twilight,
> Through the splendor of the sun-set,
> Plumes of green bent o'er his forehead
> And his hair was soft and golden."

This young man bade him arise, weak as he was, and wrestle with him, telling him that he might benefit his whole race. After three trials, each resulting in failure, the seventh and last day of his fast came, and the stranger returned to a final struggle. He told the young man that he would prevail, and then instructed him what to do. Let the poet again speak:

> "Make a bed for me to lie in,
> Where the rain may fall upon me,
> Where the sun may shine and warm me;
> Strip the garments, green and yellow,
> Strip this nodding plumage from me;
> Lay me in the earth and make it
> Soft and loose and light above me,
> Let no hand disturb my slumber,
> Let no weed nor worm molest me,
> Let not Kahgahgee, the raven,
> Come to haunt me and molest me."

The young man, as the story goes, obeyed this injunction and carefully buried the young man after he had conquered him. He still kept the secret, partook sparingly of food, and tended the grave, keeping it inviolate:

> "Till at length a small green feather
> From the earth shot slowly upward,
> Then another and another,
> And, before the Summer ended,
> Stood the Maize in all its beauty,
> With its shining robes about it,
> And the long, soft yellow tresses,
> And in rapture Hiawatha
> Cried aloud, It is Mondamin,
> Yes, the friend of man, Mondamin."

Schoolcraft, who gives in this beautiful tale in prose-guise, almost as the poet has made it, says of Mon-da-min, "It is the spirit grain." I cannot forbear quoting the closing lines of the poem which appeals to every Western man from the Corn Belt:

> "And still later, when the Autumn
> Changed the long green leaves to yellow,
> And the soft and juicy kernels
> Grew like wampum hard and yellow,
> Then the ripened ears he gathered,
> Stripped the withered husks from off them
> As he once had stripped the wrestler,
> Gave the first feast of Modamin
> And made known unto the people
> This new gift of the Great Spirit."

Many of the Indian tribes had, and some still have, extended religious ceremonies connected with corn. Several have a Green Corn Dance, some a dance at corn planting, and others at the harvest time, while corn or its products is used in nearly all the ceremonies of some of the tribes of the Southwest.

The Chahta-Muscogees of Florida held their Busk or Green Corn Dance when the corn was just old enough to use. They then held a feast of several days.

Hawkins, an early traveler, describes it. Several purging plants were used, and an elaborate dance was held.

Among the Iroquois, the Green Corn Dance was preceeded by a four day's hunt, during which the corn was parched by the squaws. At the end of this time, a feast was held, and the especial feature was that of gambling, in which all indulged, as well as partaking of the pudding of corn, beans and bear's meat.

Seven days were given up to the corn planting feast, the first four were spent in council, all the chiefs making boastful speeches in turn. On the fifth day, the chiefs took hold of a belt of wampum, and made a sort of a lame confession of their sins. On the sixth day the other warriors did the same, and on the seventh, there was a feather dance—quite an elaborate ceremonial—and a feast of dog-meat.

At Corn gathering, the last public feast of the year, corn tassels, silks, and leaves were worn as ornaments by the dancers.

Among the Seminoles, and other Southern tribes, the Green Corn Dance was a great event.

The Omahas have a Hunting Feast in which, after a Buffalo hunt, they have a certain formula of songs, which reproduce in mimicry the growth of maize. These songs are called: 1. I clear the land. 2. I put in corn. 3. The corn comes up. 4. It has blades. 5. The ears appear. 6. The ears have hair on. 7. At length we try the corn to see if it is ripe. 8. At length it is ripe. 9. At length we pull the ear from the stalk. 10. At length we husk the ear. 11. At length we shell the corn. 12. At length we eat the corn. A feast follows these songs.

All the various colors and kinds of corn have different names among these and other Indian tribes. The Omaha names are, Wata-zi-ska, white corn; Wata-zi-sko, blue corn; Wata-zi-zi, yellow corn; Wata-zi yscije, spotted corn; Wata-zi-tsijde, reddish blue; Wata-zi-jiveghi, red; Wata-nyaan-figured yellow and red stripes; Wachstya, sweet corn.

The Hopi, or Moqui Indians of Arizona, in making certain rounds, required by their religious ceremonies, use corn-meal, which is sacred in the Southwest among many tribes, sprinkling it on the sand. Ears of corn are also placed at the extremities of lines drawn to the four points of the compass, with the tips pointing in. Meal is also sprinkled to these cardinal points. The corn is afterward washed by the priest.

Among the Tusayans, in the same neighborhood, corn is even more extensively used in religious observances. Corn husks fillets are worn on the heads of the novices and meal plentifully scattered on the shrines. The novices carry corn in their hands at certain times during a dance, and a quantity of corn is shelled, the kernels being stuck all over clay images. The standard of one of the clans has corn plumes at the top, and the helmets of two of these men are made of a mosaic of split corn ears. A magic altar was made and at its six corners and sides, corn, feathers, and pebbies were laid, always keeping the colors as here indicated for the corn:

1. Northwest, yellow corn.
2. North, black corn.
3. Northeast, white corn.
4. Southeast, red corn.
5. South, sweet corn.
6. Southwest, blue corn.

Among the Navajos, corn meal is also used in sacred ceremonies. It is sprinkled on the sand-pictures made in these ceremonies, carried in fawn skin bags by carriers of sacred heralds, and used by them in incantations. The priest who instructs them says, "Sprinkle meal across a little valley, across a big arroyo, across the roots of a tree sprinkle meal, and then you may step over. Sprinkle meal on a flat rock."

In the mythical journey taken by the ancestors of these Indians, they came to the first Corn Palace—a house built of corn pillars, with a door of daylight, a ceiling supported by four spruce trees, and rainbows over the house. Corn meal and pollen formed their food here. The account of this is given by Dr. Washington Matthews.

In the ceremony commemorative of this journey, some sick person is usually introduced, to be cured by the rites of the Hoshkamn dance. This sick person carries corn meal, and sits in a sand picture, where a corn stalk is drawn. This corn stalk is in the hands of a white bodied figure, representing the Southeast—the symbolism of color always being carefully preserved. A corn cake baked in a hole in the heated earth is given to the attendant priests during the ceremonies. The white bodied figure alluded to above is accompanied by three others typifying the bean, the pumpkin and the tobacco, the four sacred plants. Among the Zunies, meal is also sacred in many ceremonies. A pinch of it forms the heart of a dummy rabbit used in the Kok-ko Initiation, as described by Mrs. Stephenson.

The novices, as they come from the north, present yellow corn to the priests. Those from the West, blue corn. Those from the South, red, and those from the East, white.

In the Navajo prayer to the Gods, the priest says, "I give to you food of corn pollen, etc."

One of the Tusayun Gens is the corn Gens. The 4th Gens of the Moquis, the 7th of the Zunis, the 5th of the San Felipe Puebloes, the 6th of the Santana Pueblo, the 9th of the Cochiti, the 1st of the Isleta, the 3rd of the Jemez and the 4th of the Zia Pueblo, are all *Corn* Gentes, according to Capt. Bourke's list.

Tradition says that corn was planted by the Navajo Chiefs in the primitive migrations, and that it would grow by night of the same day. The stem, roots, leaves and ears are all used in the ceremonials of certain Gentes.

A line of meal is spread upon the floor of the house in the dance Hasjalia Daljis, also on the debris from it, while the soles of the feet, the hands the knees, the breast, the shoulders and the head of the officiating priest. A deer is smothered to death as a sacrifice, and in its mouth corn pollen is put and a line drawn from mouth to tail along the breast. Corn pollen is sprinkled on little balls, and on blankets used in other parts of the ceremony. Meal is sprinkled in the water used on the second day of these ceremonies. Corn husks containing beads are placed on blankets on the east side of the house on the third day. Medicine tubes of corn husks, sprinkled with meal and pollen are also used.

One of the mythical sand figures is composed of five grains of corn put on a sand bed, one white, one yellow, one blue, and two variegated ones arranged in quincunx order.

Corn pollen is put on the soap suds used in purification by the priests, and the waters are sprinkled with pollen. Dried and ground as gruel it is given as medicine. In the sand paintings, which are a part of these extended ceremonies, the stalk appears frequently. The red of the bodies means red corn. The goddess is clothed in corn husks, and ten ears of yellow corn wrapped in pinion leaves are placed at the girl's feet in certain ceremonies.

Superstitious usages with reference to planting or harvesting corn, or caring for the crop, among our farmers are not abundant. The old custom of corn huskings celebrated by Longfellow in Evangeline and Hiawatha, is almost entirely in abeyance. As these lines may not be in sight, it will not be amiss to quote them:

> " And whene'er some lucky maiden
> Found a red ear in the husking,
> Found a maize ear red as blood is,
> Nushka cried they altogether,
> Nushka, you shall have a sweetheart,
> You shall have a handsome husband."

> "And when e'er a youth or maiden
> Found a crooked ear in husking,
> Blighted, mildewed or mis-shapen,
> Then they laughed and sang together,
> Crept and limped about the corn fields,
> Mimiced in their gait and gestures.
> Some old man bent almost double,
> Singing singly or together;
> Wagemin, the thief of corn fields,
> Pancosaid, who steals the maize ear!"

These scenes are also borrowed from Schoolcraft who describes them in much the same terms. Wagemin means "crooked," and Pamosaid, "He who walks", both being taken as meaning a thief in the corn field. These words, he said, from the basis of the cereal song, which, however, is not repeated. In the same song is a description of blessing the corn field based on these lines of Schoolcraft. "It was the practice of the hunter's wife, when the field of corn had been planted, to choose the first dark or over-clouded evening to perform a secret circuit *sans habiliments* around the field. For this purpose, she slipped out of the lodge in the evening, unobserved, to some obscure nook where she completely disrobed, then taking her malchecota, or principal garment, in her hands she dragged it around the field. This was thought to insure a prolific crop and to prevent the assaults of insects and worms upon the grain."

Among Pennsylvania Germans, Dr. Hoffman tells us when corn and beans are reserved for the next year's planting, the cob, husks and stalk must be carried out into a field or highway and quickly destroyed. Should they be burned, the next crop would be attacked by the black fungus (Brant).

Contributed by Lieutenant Fletcher S. Bassett, U. S. Navy, Sec'y, Chicago Folk Lore Society, author of "Legends and Superstitions of the Sea" "Folk Lore Manual", etc., etc. A former resident of Burlington, Iowa.

## THE LIVE STOCK INDUSTRY.

To show the growth and present magnitude of the live stock industry in Iowa we present the following table which we compile from the United

States Census Reports and the report of the secretary of Agriculture, the figures for 1892 being given from the report last named:

| Year. | No. Horses | No. Mules. | No. Neat Cattle. | No. Swine. | No. Sheep. | Value. |
|---|---|---|---|---|---|---|
| 1850 | 38,563 | 754 | 136,621 | 323,247 | 149,960 | $ 3,689,275.00 |
| 1860 | 175,088 | 5,734 | 540,088 | 934,820 | 259,040 | 22,476,209.00 |
| 1870 | 433,642 | 25,425 | 1,006,235 | 1,353,908 | 855,493 | 82,987,133.00 |
| 1880 | 792,322 | 44,224 | 2,612,036 | 6,034,316 | 455,326 | 134,715,103.00 |
| 1892 | 1,314,300 | 41,029 | 4,011,233 | 7,165,330 | 565,031 | 208,768,191.02 |

In 1891, according to the report of Hon. J. M. Rusk, Secretary of Agriculture, the total value of the wheat, oats and corn products and the live stock of the six leading states of the Union were as follows:

### IOWA.
Grain products..................................................$154,269,430
Live stock...................................................... 181,967,670

Total.........................................................$336,236,100

### ILLINOIS.
Grain products..................................................$147,843,414
Live stock...................................................... 169,151,563

Total.........................................................$316,994,977

### MISSOURI.
Grain products..................................................$105,800,269
Live stock...................................................... 121,217,095

Total.........................................................$227,017,364

### OHIO.
Grain products..................................................$ 89,878,403
Live stock...................................................... 109,516,961

Total.........................................................$215,603,173

### KANSAS.
Grain products..................................................$ 98,321,629
Live stock...................................................... 109,516,961

Total.........................................................$207,838,590

### INDIANA.
Grain products..................................................$ 99,121,446
Live Stock...................................................... 103,255,029

Total.........................................................$202,376,475

These figures gleaned from the high authority named, establish the fact that these central prairie States are the great food producing States of the country, and in this respect Iowa, though but fourth in area—Illinois, Missouri and Kansas all being larger—leads all in the value of her grain production, and exceeds all in the value of her live stock. With such permanent agricultural productiveness, Iowa must ever be one of the wealthiest States of the Union.

In 1892 Illinois ranked first of the States in the number and value of its horses, and Iowa second. In the number and value of milch cows New York ranked first, and Iowa second. In the number and value of work oxen and other cattle Texas ranked first, and Iowa second. In the number and value of swine Iowa ranked first and Illinois second. In the total value of live stock Iowa stands at the head, leading Illinois, the next in rank, by the grand sum of $22,000,386.

But the superior quality of the live stock of Iowa may be seen by an examination of the values reported by Commissioner Rusk. Kentucky, with her famed blue grass and her generations of fleet horses, leads Iowa in the average value of her horse stock only in the ratio of 69 to 66, while Iowa leads Texas in this matter in the ratio of 66 to 41. Iowa farmers have not given so much attention to breeding fleet animals for sport on the track as they have given to the breeding of animals for service on the road and farm; yet Iowa's pastures, grain and atmosphere have produced Axtel and Allerton to win world-wide fame by their speed qualities, and thousands of massive Percherons, Clydesdales, Belgians, Shires or Cleveland Bays of noble form, fine stylish coach animals or fleet standard-breds are found in every locality. No country nor State need desire finer horses than are seen at our county fairs, or are shown in the great displays at Iowa's famous State fairs.

### CATTLE.

In this department of the live stock industry Iowa knows no superior. The best beef and milk breeds are all encouraged by the votaries of these different interests, so that all the improved breeds, as Shorthorns, Herefords, Galloways, Polled Angus, Polled Durhams, Dutch Belted, Swiss, Devons, Holsteins, and the butter producing Alderneys, Guernseys, and Jerseys are all bred in Iowa to perfection. In her pastures thousands of full-bloods thrive and add wealth to their fortunate owners, while herds of fine grades are seen on every farm. The longhorned rangers of the wilderness and the bony, coarse and scrawny "scrubs" no longer waste Iowa grass unless in some chance way such a bovine specimen is imported from some distant State.

### SHEEP.

By the table given above it is shown that the sheep husbandry in Iowa declined largely from 1870 to 1880. Formerly, for various reasons, sheep were found to be inconvenient stock. But Iowa farmers are now enclosing and subdividing their farms with good fences, and more attention is given to sheep raising and wool growing and flocks are rapidly increasing in numbers. Animals of the fine and long wooled breeds are being largely imported. Iowa's climate, soil, pure waters and nourishing pastures are finely suited to this industry, and the State in the near future will become as famous for her wool and mutton production as she is now for her corn, butter and pork.

### SWINE.

Iowa excels, not only in the number of swine yearly produced and marketed, but also has no superior in the quality of the blood and breeding of her herds. Swine production has been a potent factor in Iowa's development of wealth, and will long remain so. Iowa soil, from the richest spot in the flood-plain by the river's brink to the summit of her highest "divides," will grow corn; and corn fed to Poland Chinas, Chester Whites, Berkshires, Durocs and Victorias, is turned into pork of as superb a quality as ever graced the board of Norman or Saxon lord. The markets of the world are now open to pork and lard from this interior west, and the farms of Iowa can furnish supplies in quantities which the world will almost deem incredible.

### THE GRASSES.

Grass is a natural product of Iowa prairies. Kentucky's blue grass pastures have world-wide fame, but Iowa farmers now enjoy as rich, abundant, healthful, nourishing and beautiful blue grass pasturage as was ever found in Kentucky or any other State. Everywhere in Iowa blue grass has become a spontaneous product.

Timothy, the clovers, millet and other grasses thrive luxuriantly in Iowa sunshine and soil. In all parts of the State great clover fields are plentiful. Timothy meadows produce surprising crops, and large quantities of grass seeds are annually exported. The power of Iowa soil to produce grass will ever make stock raising a highly remunerative industry in Iowa husbandry.

### FLAX.

But little attention was devoted to this crop in the early years. It was ever found to be productive, but the absence of machinery or mills for working up and giving value to the fiber, precluded its being largely remunerative to its producers, yet its production has increased until Iowa has attained second place in the rank of States in the production of flax seed—her product aggregating in 1891, (according to the returns of the Department of Agriculture) 2,898,596 bushels.

Lately, considerable attention has been given to the fiber in Winnebago and other northern counties of the state, and it has been found that the fiber, there produced, is unexcelled in quality for linen fabric. There are inviting openings in Iowa for the manufacture of linen and other flax products.

## THE DAIRY INDUSTRY.

Butter and cheese are important items upon the table and also in the markets of the country. The reports of the Department of Agriculture for 1891, show that there are in the United States 16,416,351 milch cows, of the aggregate value of $351,378,132. In the following table we give the number of milch cows, their aggregate and average value in each of the five states leading in this respect:

| STATES. | NO. OF MILCH COWS. | AGGREGATE VALUE. | VALUE PER HEAD. |
| --- | --- | --- | --- |
| New York | 1,552,217 | $40,637,041 | $26.18 |
| Iowa | 1,304,184 | 24,479,534 | 18.76 |
| Illinois | 1,164,861 | 24,561,060 | 21.27 |
| Pennsylvania | 929,091 | 23,459,548 | 25.25 |
| Missouri | 869,726 | 15,220,305 | 17.50 |

The dairy industry, as a distinct business, is comparatively new in Iowa. Having no great cities or manufacturing centers within our area, we had to seek markets for our dairy products abroad. These products were without reputation in the East prior to the Centennial Exhibition of 1876. The awards received there opened markets in the east for Iowa creamery butter.

The plans for an Iowa exhibit in that exposition were made, and the work of providing exhibits therefor was largely done, and the expense therefor met by private organizations before any provision was made for State aid. In February, but three months before the opening of the

Exposition, the Iowa General Assemby passed an act providing for State supervision and the encouragement of an Iowa exhibit, and appropriated $20,000 therefor.

This was our first effort for an exhibition in a "World's Fair." Intelligent, patriotic citizens saw that it was a prime opportunity to promote the interests of Iowa and made earnest effort to improve it.

The managers of that Exposition made no reservation of space in the agricultural department for the dairy interest, and the dairymen of the country found their industry without place for display. The American Dairymen's Association arranged with the managers of the Exposition for the erection of a building at the expense of the dairymen of the country, to provide a place for the exhibition of dairy products. The dairymen of Iowa were assessed by the American Dairymen's Association $1,000 for this purpose.

On the 14th day of April, 1876, John Stewart, of the firm of John Stewart & Co., manufacturers of "fine creamery butter," Manchester, Iowa, addressed a letter to Governor Kirkwood in which he stated the facts outlined above, and urged him to favor the dairy interests and said:

"If we can exhibit our butter side by side with the eastern dairymen, we can succeed in breaking down the prejudice that has been so prevalent in the minds of eastern people; and if so, we will get one million dollars more, annually, for our dairy products than we do now. If it is not asking too much of you in your official position, we would ask you to urge the executive committee to appropriate this amount or so much of it as is possible out of the $20,000. We do not ask the State to transport our goods, but simply to give us a place to exhibit them."

But the State authorities did not appropriate $1,000 or any other sum out of the $20,000 or any other fund, for a dairy exhibit, but John Stewart & Co., and other creamery men exhibited twenty-nine packages of their butter, having a total weight of 9,150 pounds and won for Iowa butter the following award—gaining a first prize.

"Creamery 859. Stewart & Mellen, Manchester, Iowa, Creamery Butter. Commended for its clear sweet flavor, firm texture and superior excellence."

That award gave Iowa butter an entrance into eastern markets in which it soon won a reputation that has been worth scores of millions of dollars to the State. The dairy business has become of vast importance in Iowa agriculture.

State Dairy Commissioner Tupper, in his report to the Governor, December, 1892, said:

"The total shipments of butter billed out of the State for the year ending September 30, were 71,563,013 pounds. The best authorities estimate the home consumption of butter to be fifty pounds, *per capita*, or 100,000,000. This would bring the total product of the State up to 171,563,013 pounds. Estimating it at 20 cents per pound, the value of Iowa's product for the year would be $34,312,602."

As the amount shipped out of the State was ascertained by correspondence with the several railroad authorities and getting reports of their actual shipments to points in other States, the report of shipment is practically correct. The Commissioner reports the ninety-nine counties in detail. The amount consumed at home of course is estimated. Iowa people live well and the estimate is reasonable.

The butter production of the State is most largely in its northeastern portions. In Delaware county there are 38 creameries, in Linn 29, in Bremer 21, and Fayette 23. Mr. Tupper reports 729 creameries in ninety-seven counties.

The Dairy Commissioner's report for 1892 is the sixth annual report from that office. The dairy business, furnishing an export of 71,536,013 pounds of butter to go into the great markets of the country, and in addition furnishing 50 pounds, *per capita*, for 1,911,896 people, is an industry of large importance. Only 1.4 cents, per pound, on the amount exported, would raise John Stewart's $1,000,000 to the creamery men of Iowa. This business may appear to have immense proportions, but it may be said of the dairy industry of Iowa, "There yet is room,"—the dairy business is still growing.

Dairy Commissioner Tupper reported one hundred and eleven cheese factories in operation in Iowa in 1891, twenty new ones having been established that year. In 1892 he reported one hundred and fourteen cheese factories operated in fifty-one counties. He made no report of the production as he had been unable to collect full statistics.

## HORTICULTURE.

The culture of the garden is a higher form of agriculture than that of the common field. It is the tilling of the soil to produce things more delicate, beautiful and valuable than the common grains, grasses or coarser root crops. It includes the culture of garden vegetables, seeds, nursery stock, fruits and flowers. Floriculture, being a higher type of horticultural industry; may be classed as a lighter form of labor, requiring greater intelligence and care than common farm operations. Having no place nor part in a savage state, it is only when some degree of wealth is developed, taste incited, and culture takes the place of barbarous conditions that the nterests of horticulture prosper.

Common gardening is the first branch of horticultural industry pursued in the settlement of new countries, the nursery business being the next in order. The latter has now become of great importance. The number of established nurseries in the State was reported, in the census of 1890, as 183, employing 1,193 persons, and occupying 12,049 acres of land devoted to the growth of apple, crab, pear, quince. peach, apricot, plum and cherry trees for orchard planting; various nut bearing trees, evergreens and flowering shrubs. Thirteen and a half acres were devoted to the propagation of the rose; 427 acres to the propagation of the grape, and numerous acres to strawberries, raspberries, blackberries, currants, gooseberries and other fruit bearing plants. The total value of these 183 nurseries was reported at $1,276,379.

Of these 183 nurseries so far as information conld be gained, eight were established between 1850 and 1860; thirteen between 1860 and 1870, twenty-six between 1870 and 1880, and sixty-seven between 1880 and 1890. While these figures do not give full data in the matter, they show that this business has rapidly increased in the State as wealth and improvement have developed.

But twenty years ago large quantities of apples were imported into Iowa from States farther east. Then orchardists in Indiana, Ohio and

Michigan imagined that apples could not be successfully grown on Iowa's prairie soil, and that this State would ever afford a great market for the products of their orchards. The fine exhibits of Iowa-grown pears at the Centennial Exposition in 1876, by Messrs. C. B. Brackett, of Lee county and W. T. Smith of Mahaska, with the exhibit of forty varieties of Iowa-grown apples by W. S. Willett of Malcolm, of seventy-five by L. Hollingsworth, of Montrose, and 160 varieties by James Smith of Des Moines, dispelled that idea forever. Iowa won, by those exhibits, high encomiums for the superior size and quality of her fruit. At the New Orleans Exposition, ten years later, her apples again won high honors, and thereby opened the markets of all the great cities alike on the Atlantic, the Gulf and the Pacific coasts for the products of Iowa orchards. Under these inspirations pomological industry in Iowa has been greatly increased, immense orchards have been planted and great attention has been given to their culture, and the exportation of apples from Iowa is becoming a business of large volume. Our apples find profitable markets in both our own and foreign countries.

In the fall of 1891, the shipments of apples from Iowa reached large figures. The "Red Oak Sun" gathered the amounts shipped from a few counties in the southwestern part of the State. We copy its reported shipments from the five counties named below:

| COUNTIES. | BBLS. SHIPPED. |
|---|---|
| Freemont | 43,144 |
| Mills | 41,309 |
| Page | 26,115 |
| Montgomery | 17,384 |
| Adams | 14,574 |
| Total | 142,528 |

Peaches, plums, apricots, quinces, cherries, and pears are successfully grown. Many varieties of these fruits specially adapted to our climate and soil have been produced. The production of grapes is becoming immense. It is now known by all that Iowa produces fruits of finest size and appearance, abundant in variety and unexcelled in quality and flavor, in quantities not only to supply her own population, but also to meet the large demands that come from other States. Fifteen carloads of Iowa grapes were shipped from Council Bluffs in one month the past season. The small fruits, as raspberries, blackberries, gooseberries, currants and strawberries all grow in this State to superlative perfection in size, appearance and flavor. The tables of Iowa farmers throughout the season abound with those luxuries grown in their own gardens.

### VEGETABLES.

Iowa's soil, climate and rainfall all combine to promote the growth of vegetation. Its depth and mellowness make gardening a pleasure. In no country is the labor of the gardener more abundantly repaid. Every kind of vegetable grown in the country east of the Rocky Mountains and north of Mason and Dixon's line is cultivated with success in the gardens of Iowa.

### FLORICULTURE.

Iowa is a land of flowers. The Violet, the Crimson Phlox, the Lily, the Helianthus, the Rose, the Aster and the Golden Rod in many varieties are native to the prairies; and, in grand profusion in their season, waved their magnificent welcome to the pioneer who delighted in beautiful surroundings. Iowa homes, from the occupancy of the first cabin, have ever been adorned with Flora's magnificent handi-work. The early settlers brought in the cultivated annuals and perennials common to the home surroundings in the States from which they came; and no country produces flowers of richer hue or grander magnificence in form and fragrance than are grown about the homes of Iowa.

### COMMERCIAL FLORICULTURE.

The enumerators of the census of 1890 report for the whole country 4,659 floral establishments. Idaho, Nevada, Indian Territory and Oklahoma were the only portions of the country in which such establishments were not found. Three hundred and twelve were owned and conducted by women. These four thousand and more establishments, including fixtures and heating apparatus were of the value of $38,823,547, and gave employment to 16,847 men and 1,958 women.

Such an industry is an important one. Its most favorable field of operation is in the vicinity of the great cities, the centers of wealth and luxurious living. Iowa has a respected place in this esthetic industry. The number of florists establishments, reported for Iowa in that census, was sixty-nine. Of forty-four reporting the date of their establishment, twenty-four were started between 1880 and 1890. In this business that census reported for Iowa the employment of 166 men and 49 women, and $66,234 paid the male employees in wages and $13,818 were paid female employees. It further reported the propagation of 255,330 roses, 1,100,037 hardy plants and of 1,838,850 other plants. The value of the plants sold was $125,164.55; of cut flowers sold, $107,633.29; the total for sales reaching the sum of $232,808.34. There is not only pleasure but profit in the florist's occupation.

With the increase of wealth floriculture is encouraged as taste is gratified, and the love of the beautiful ever strengthens with the development of the finer elements of our nature. In this State this business receives great encouragment, not only in our large and prosperous growing cities, but in the scores of beautiful, thrifty and progressive towns which offer inviting openings to persons of taste and enterprise, who desire to engage in this pleasant industry. The people of Iowa, lovers of the beautiful in nature as well as in morals and social culture, have taste for floral decorations and are liberal patrons of floral production.

### SEED FARMS.

This branch of horticultural industry has been rapidly enlarged in the state during the last decade.

In the census of 1890 attention was given for the first time to gathering the statistics of this industry. The enumerators found that there were then in the country 596 farms with a total of 169,851 acres of land devoted exclusively to seed growing. This was an average of 284 acres to the farm. The total value of farms, implements and buildings reported was $18,325,935.86. Those farms employed in that census year 13,500 men and 1,541 women.

Of these 596 seed farms, eighteen were located in Iowa. Such farms are found in thirty-six of the forty-four States, and one of 120 acres in the District of Columbia. The eighteen seed farms in this state embrace 11,152 acres of land valued at $27.75 per acre. The total value of farms, implements and buildings being $633,823.67. The average acreage of such farms in Iowa is 620 acres. Of course considerable portions of these farms are devoted to meadow and pasturage. Ten of these were established in the last decade. Those eighteen farms gave employment to 354 men.

Of the seeds cultivated on Iowa seed farms we notice the following varities named in the census report: Asparagus, beans, beets, cabbage, carrot, corn (sweet), corn (field), cucumber (to which 472 acres of Iowa farms were devoted), egg plant, lettuce, melon (musk), melon (water), okra, onion (seed), onion (sets), parsnip, pease, potatoes, pumpkin, radish, rhubarb, salsify, spinach, squash, tomato turnip, and flower seeds, fourteen acres of land being devoted to the latter production. One man in Poweshiek county raised last year forty acres of sunflowers for their seed.

Prior to 1850 this industry was confined almost exclusively to the New England States.

The extensive and very rapid settlement of the northwest since 1870 created an immense demand for garden seeds, and led to the establishment of this industry on quite a large scale in the central western States.

### SORGHUM.

This saccharine plant is cultivated successfully in Iowa. Our light, deep prairie soil and moist, warm summer months are favorable to its development. In the table given elsewhere, from the report of the Secretary of the State Agricultural Society, the value of the sorghum product for 1892 was estimated at $1,000,000, the product being over 2,000,000 gallons of syrup. This plant is grown in all parts of the State and is an important adjunct to family supplies. But little effort has been made to grow this cane as a source from which to manufacture sugar, but its cultivation and the manufacture of syrup therefrom reduces sugar consumption in many households. Years of experience in its cultivation has proved that a cane very rich in saccharine matter can be grown almost as cheaply as corn.

### BEETS.

Experiments have proven that beets, very rich in saccharine substance, can be easily grown, and no soil produces a more vigorous growth of the beet. No plant has yet been erected for the manufacture of sugar in this State. With large coal fields, cheap fuel, cheap lands and suitable soil for beet culture; with our rapidly increasing population that each year furnishes a larger supply of labor for the better cultivation of our fields and the raising of crops that involve large labor, Iowa offers inviting opportunities for the profitable employment of capital in the beet sugar industry.

### STATE ENCOURAGEMENT.

State Legislation has extended wise encouragement to agricultural and horticultural interests.

### THE STATE AGRICULTURAL SOCIETY.

This is an efficient, well officered and ably managed State organization. It owns very fine, extensive and conveniently located grounds, lying immediately east of the city of Des Moines, and of easy access by railroad and electric car lines from the capital city. These grounds are now well improved and a State fair is held annually thereon. The Iowa State Fair is becoming widely known as one of the most successful Agricultural Fairs of the country. The grounds embrace several hundred acres, afford fine camping grounds, fine shade and are well supplied with pure water. No intoxicating drinks are sold on the grounds and all gambling schemes are excluded from them, and yet most interesting and successful fairs are annually held.

### COUNTY AND DISTRICT FAIRS.

These are provided for by law, and are encouraged by annual financial aid. There are now few counties in the State without a duly organized County Agricultural Society and its annual County Fair. Where no County Organization exists, there are District Fairs. These cover parts of two or more counties. Our County and District Fairs are excellent educators of our people in agricultural interests, presenting the newest features in agricultural progress and affording pleasant opportunities for enlarging acquaintance and mutual interchange of ideas, and the enlargement of agricultural knowledge.

### THE STATE HORTICULTURAL SOCIETY.

This is an important and highly serviceable organization to the people of the State. It is financially aided by the State and holds an annual meeting at the State Capital in which it has rooms. At its meetings horticultural matters are discussed, the leading horticulturalists of the State interchange thought and compare experiences. Its proceedings are published and freely circulated and so most useful horticultural information is thereby freely disseminated.

In addition to the parent State society there are several auxilliary district and county societies which hold frequent meetings, and render valuable service in the spread of horticultural knowledge.

### LIVE STOCK BREEDERS ASSOCIATIONS.

We have various organizations in the interest of breeders and farmers interested in the improvement of the live stock and poultry of the State. Almost each particular breed of live stock having an organization of its friends working earnestly to set forth its merits. They are doing successful work in improving the several varieties of domestic animals kept on farms.

### POULTRY.

The poultry interests of Iowa are worthy of consideration. Hon. J. R. Schaffer, Secretary of the State Agricultural Society in a late report estimated the poultry products of the State to have an annual value of $5,000,000. The flocks of "biddies," geese, ducks, turkeys, guineas, and pea fowls that grace our farm yards and furnish dainty luxuries for our daily meals and holiday feasts, add millions yearly to the profits of Iowa farms and by their valuable production the managing, industrious housewife multiplies the family comforts.

The traveler everywhere in the agricultural portions of Iowa sees numerous flocks of the purest fowls, all the improved breeds being found in every locality. Hundreds of men using large capital are engaged in the poultry and egg business. Could we gather the true figures representing the extent of this business they would present a startling sum. This business is a growing one because the production of poultry is found to be profitable on the farms of Iowa. The shipment of live fowls is becoming a large business and the exhibit of patent cars in the Transportation Building at the Columbian Exposition for their transportation shows that the inventors as well as the transportation companies of the country are awake to the fact that this to some seemingly trifling "chicken business" is one of such magnitude as to be worth caring for.

## NATIVE FLORA OF IOWA.

### By Prof. L. H. Pammel, Iowa Agricultural College.

The climate and physical features of the State have not favored a very large number of flowering plants compared with some of the States within our borders, and yet we have a good many species. We have few mountain forms as the conditions favoring the perpetuation of these species are absent. A few are maintained along our streams, especially in the eastern and northeastern parts of the State. The Red Berried Elder, with its bright red fruit, is a conspicuous object along the Mississippi above Dubuque. Here too may be found the Mountain Maple overhanging the rocks; an occasional Paper Birch stands in strong contrast to the southern Kentucky Coffee tree. An occasional Sycamore or Honey Locust in the bottoms indicate that we have here a commingling of northern and southern forms. Our Oaks in central, eastern and western Iowa are those common to the north. The White Oak and the tall, majestic Red Oak, large and handsome but less valuable than the White Oak are common. The swamp White Oak, a southern species, may be found in the southern part of the State. Another common Oak in this State is the Burr Oak with its sweet acorns, also a valuable tree for its wood. Common throughout Iowa is the Soft Maple, the Cottonwood, and the American Basswood. The Elms are familiar objects; the most graceful of the family is the American or White Elm. The Slippery or Red Elm is common and is a valuable tree.

### NUT BEARING TREES.

In this class the widely known Black Walnut is the most valuable; then there is the White Walnut or Butternut, a species growing on high grounds. The Black Walnut prefers lower grounds, and is a southern tree which gradually diminishes northward; the Butternut being a northern tree. The most valuable of the Hickory family is the Shag or Shell Bark. It is so by reason of its wide distribution as well as for the superior value of its wood. The Mocker-nut Hickory occurs in the southern part of the State bordering on Missouri. The Pecan is also a southern species extending northwardly along the Mississippi and Missouri rivers. The Bitternut is quite common in many parts of the State.

### CONIFEROUS TREES.

There are some coniferous trees found in Iowa, the White Pine and the more widely distributed Red Cedar.

## THE ASH.

There are several species of the Ash in this State. The White Ash, on account of its beauty strength and value should not be overlooked. It is a valuable tree for cultivation, being easily propagated and a rapid grower. It grows naturally along our streams and as an ornamental tree along fence rows, roads or lawns and in parks is worthy of attention. Its wood, especially the young growth, is of great value in many lines of manufacture.

## SHRUBS.

Of smaller trees and shrubs which lend beauty to our landscapes, there are many. Conspicuous among them is the Wild Crab. Its shape is symmetrical and when in flower the sweet perfume fills the air. Nothing excells it in beauty when in flower. The Wild Plum is found in all parts of the State. When in bloom the plum groves are masses of creamy beauty and the fruit is of great value, but was especially valuable to the early settlers. Many of our most valuable cultivated plums have been developed from a wild parentage. The Flat Topped Thorn, with its masses of flowers is especially striking in June. The Red Bud is limited in its distribution, yet its purple flowers coming out before the leaves, makes it an interesting object. It is found as far north as Muscatine. In the month of May, before the forests are clothed with their green leaves, a white flowering shrub dots the forests here and there; it is the Shad Bush, or Service Berry. It bears an inviting fruit. We should also mention the primitive form of the Snow Ball, commonly called High Bush Cranberry, which occurs in wet grounds in the northern part of the State. In this connection we may also speak of the Red Root, a common low shrub on the prairies, well known to prairie breakers for its hard, strong root. Its red stems, rich green leaves and cream colored tufts of flowers in June and July make it conspicuous.

## HERBACEOUS PLANTS.

Of these we have many striking forms. Our flora on the prairies partakes largely of the western type. We have also many species that are common in the eastern states. Some of these are introduced and some are woodland species that have kept in close contact with our forest trees. In early spring soon after the snow disappears, in shaded banks, the little (Hepatica L.) Liverwort makes its appearance, soon followed by the Spring Beauty, the Blue Violet, the Dutchman's Breeches with delicate white flowers, and the Dog Toothed Violet. These are early flowering woodland species and common further east. In the open prairies we find the Pasqueflower, its flowers are pale blue, coming out long before the fields are green. There are also several species of Crowsfoot. Several varieties of the Phlox family give beauty to our prairies by their brilliant colors. The common American Columbine should be remembered, a beautiful flower in different colors, easily transplanted and worthy of cultivation for the long season of its bloom and beauty. There is nothing common about it either in its color or form. Of the same family, but growing on the prairies the Azure Larkspur should be mentioned. In the southern part of the state another species occurs, a woodland species, but like the former its flowers show a tendency to vary in color.

In June, July and August the prairies are bright with various flowers of the Composite Family. Some of the species are coarse, yet many are very showy. There is the Cone-flower. The tall Compass-plant, Pilot Weed or Prairie Burdock, a resinous plant, and its near relative the Cup-plant. These bear showy yellow flowers. In July we have the purple Cone-flower or Comb-flower, the upright Lily and, later, two varieties of Lilies with pendant flowers. But few cultivated flowers are more beautiful than the Lilies of our prairies.

There are several pretty members of the Orchis family, the fringed Orchis, with its long spur containing nectar and fringes to its petals is an interesting plant. Several species of Ladies Tresses occur. I have not mentioned the Moccasin-flower, two species of which are not uncommon in Iowa. The Large White Moccasin-flower also occurs. The Larger Yellow Moccasin-flower, or Ladies' Slipper, is an early flowering species in our moist woods.

September is the month for Asters, Golden Rod, Sunflowers, Wild Artichoke, Boneset, and members of that family. The Lobelia (Greater Blue) and the Cardinal-flower, growing in moist places, the latter especially growing near streams where the alluvial deposits occur, some river bottoms being fairly red with them in their season. The writer remembers the first impression made on his mind when he first saw this species in flower. The Missouri river valley has some most striking plants. The Yuccas, so distinctively American, are represented by the Yucca angustifolia, to be appreciated this plant should be studied as it is a most remarkable plant as regards its pollination. The Wild Licorice is distinctively western. The Mint family is also represented on our prairies by a few western species.

The grasses are numerous. Blue Grass (*Poa pratensis*) has become naturalized everywhere in Iowa. The Wild Ryes are common. But more than any other grass the Blue Joint was found everywhere in Iowa on its rich dry prairie lands. The Beard Grass is also a native variety. These are typical prairie species and in the autumn add to the beauty of our extended prairie landscapes.

The Ferns are rare except in certain sheltered and isolated places. Muscatine county has, perhaps, more species than any other county. The Brake, Maidenhair Fern, Sensitive Fern, and one Spleenwort are widely distributed. The rocky hills of the east support several interesting species. The Walking Leaf Fern and other varieties are interesting plants.

The chief feature of our native flora is its diversity. It lacks species of trees which may truly be called grand, but our trees may be characterized as vigorous and sturdy.

I would call attention to several catalogues of the Flora of the State. One of the earliest accounts of plants in this State was by the late Dr. C. C. Parry, in David Dale Owens' Geological Survey. Prof. C. E. Bessey published an account in one of the early Bi-ennial Reports of the Iowa Agricultural College. Dr. J. C. Arthur published a list of Iowa plants for the Centennial Exposition which was nearly complete. Later Prof. A. S. Hitchcock published a catalogue of the Anthophyta and Pteridophyta of Ames. The writer also published a short list in Proceedings of Iowa Academy of Sciences for 1892.

## FORESTS AND ARTIFICAL GROVES.

Iowa is rightly classed as a prairie State. It has never had forest nor timber resources to give it fame as a lumbering state, yet its surface at the time of its discovery and settlement was flecked with groves of timber that were serviceable to its early settlers. In all parts of the State there were found groves that yielded supplies for fuel, building and fencing purposes in advance of railroad construction. In many localities there are yet extensive and valuable bodies of native timber.

In the valleys and along the acclivities bordering the Mississippi, Des Moines, Cedar, Iowa, and other rivers and many of the smaller streams in the eastern portions of the State, there were many considerable bodies of timber, some of which yet furnish large supplies for manufacturing purposes.

Along the Cedar, before the settlement of the country bordering it, there were valuable groves of Red Cedar. These attracted the forest pirate and ere immigration came. these groves were mostly cut off and rafted to St. Louis.

No county in Iowa was entirely destitute of timber. Many counties had comparatively small supplies, yet there were native groves which were central places in the early settlement, and and gave names to places and postoffices which are still retained. Some were important land marks to the traveler before the roads were distinctly marked. The changes resulting from settlement and the construction of railroads have rendered the names of many of these once widely known groves obsolete.

There were many valuable varieties of timber native to those groves: the black and white walnut, the white oak, burr oak, red oak, the maples, the white ash, the hickories, the elms, the honey locust, and many others. The hard maple in some localities was found in quantities to be of service to the pioneers in sugar production.

With the stoppage of the annual destructive prairie fires the acreage of young timber has been greatly enlarged. But the people are not dependent upon their native groves for supplies of lumber. Railroads now transport fencing and building lumber from the timbered states at reasonable rates, and a few acres of prairie cultivated in corn settles the fuel and lumber matter. It is easy to buy the lumber and coal needed for the farm and family with the money the corn brings. Timber lands are now of less value than corn growing lands.

### ARTIFICIAL GROVES.

The settlers on the prairies soon planted groves. Some on a liberal scale, which soon became, not only objects of convenience and beauty, but of usefulness and value for the shelter they afforded. In half a dozen years from such planting, with careful cultivation, the settler had a beautiful grove. For a few years the soft maple would make more rapid growth than the black walnut. After ten years the walnut would be the faster grower and make the stronger and more valuable timber tree. Many groves were planted of the white ash, the honey locust, and oak. Young elms could be had in almost every fringe of native timber. The law gave exemption from a certain amount of taxation for planting groves and orchards, and thus timber and fruit growing were encouraged. Pines, Cedars, Firs and Spruces have been numerously planted for wind breaks and ornamentation; and the broad prairies have been relieved of their wild magnificence by intelligent industry, and have been made more beautiful by these serviceable ornamentations—the handi-work of industrious settlers.

## IOWA AND MANUFACTURES.

People living in different portions of the country, generally regard Iowa as exclusively an agricultural state. Very few even of those who are resident here have just conceptions of the extent and value of our mineral resources or our possibilities for success in manufacturing industries. All know that in this famous wealth producing region we have unequalled advantages of soil and climate for great success in the industries common to the orchard, the garden and the field. It is equally true that we have here most inviting openings for the establishment of great and profitable manufacturing enterprises. Two millions of intelligent people possessing the wealth producing power for which this State has now wide fame will ever assure an immense and constant market for the vast supplies of manufactured commodities demanded in their industrial and social life.

This portion of the country having unequalled possibilities to produce foods, the laborer will ever find here, at reasonable pricees, the essential articles of human subsistence; the best social and moral surroundings, and clothing as cheap as it is obtainable in other markets. These desirable circumstances combined with our healthful climate, and excellent educational opportunities will invite the most intelligent and desirable class of citizens. Our ever-flowing rivers furnish valuable water powers that may be cheaply harnessed to drive manufacturing machinery. As we have shown elsewhere almost one:third of our ninety-nine counties produce coal, and excellent fuel to produce steam is cheaply obtained. The facts we present are worthy of consideration by all who are seeking opportunities for the investment of capital in manufacturing enterprises.

Supplies of raw material for important manufactures are readily obtainable. In convenient and readily accessible localities there are large deposits of metallic ores; as lead, zinc, and iron. Alluminous clays, rich in that valuable and now largely used metal, exist in many places. Clays of quality suited for the manufacture of the best qualities of stoneware and finer qualities of pottery are found in heavy deposits in the state, while clays for the manufacture of building, and the best qualities of paving brick, articles now in very large demand in Iowa towns and cities are common. Timber is found, in valuable varieties and abundant quantity in the eastern and southeastern counties, of large value in many lines of manufacture. Straw and flax fibre suitable for the manufacture of paper and other commodities is grown abundantly. The vegetable productions and summer fruits suitable for canning are easily produced. For starch and glucose manufacture, the raw material is produced throughout the State in larger quantities than in any other equal area on earth. For the packing house industry most finely fed cattle and swine everywhere await the buyer. The vast improvements being constantly made in the building of new bridges, large, fine, and solid buildings, the construction of waterworks, electric light plants, and other improvements in our growing towns and cities, create a large and constantly growing demand for the products of the foundry and machine shop. The common use of all lines of labor-saving machines, alike in the homes and shops, and on the farms throughout the State makes Iowa a most inviting field for the manufacture of such machines. The use of buggies and fine carriages will ever be large in this center of wealth and pleasure. Our citizens enjoy the good things possible in earthly state and live in a style of luxury not excelled in the life of any agricultural population anywhere. They enjoy the best of literature in their homes, and fine furniture in their parlors; they cultivate music in their families and are esthetic in their tastes. Such a people dwelling in such surroundings and possessing such ample means of enjoyment, will ever offer a vast home market for the products of the factory, and Iowa must ever be an inviting field for the operation of manufacturing capabilities and the employment of capital therein.

The pioneer settlers came not here to mine gold, to gain wealth by lumbering pursuits or to make their living by quest of game with the gun, or fish with rod or net. They came here for higher purpose; namely, to build homes, to turn our then barbarous wilds into a fruitful country and to found a Christian common-wealth that would secure to its every citizen equal privilege to work out the best and happiest conditions possible in their surroundings. Their first concern was to provide shelter, their second to provide for the cultivation of the soil. The first manufacturing plants for which they had concern were grist and saw mills. The streams flowing in their surroundings furnished them ample power to run the simple machinery their needs then required.

The national census of 1840 found in the Iowa territory only 1,629 persons engaged in what was then reported as manufacturing industries. When the census of 1850 was taken the count showed that the number of persons engaged in such industries had increased during the decade to but 1,707. Only 522 establishments were in the latter census reported as being engaged in manufacturing and mining pursuits, employing the nominal capital of $1,292,875. One woolen mill was then found in operation in the then new State. Three small iron foundries were reported that employed the trivial force of seventeen men. Four distilleries were then operated that employed sixteen hands, consumed 51,150 bushels of corn, and 7,200 bushels of rye, producing 67,600 gallons of high-wines and whisky. Such were the chief manufacturing industries found in Iowa forty-three years ago.

The census of 1860 showed that increased attention was being given to manufacturing interests in the State. It reported 1,939 establishments, employing a capital of $7,247,130 and 6,307 men, their products being valued at $13,971,325.

The census of 1870 revealed a very great increase in these important industrial interests, reporting 6,566 establishments in the State, in which 899 steam engines, and 726 water wheels were employed to furnish power. Those establishments employed 25,032 persons to whom were paid $6,892,-292 in wages. The value of their products aggregated $46,534,322. Our manufacturing interests were then becoming of consequence in our industrial system.

DUBUQUE AND THE HIGH BRIDGE FROM THE ILLINOIS SHORE.

These interests made still further material increase in the decade extending from 1870 to 1880. That advance would have been still greater but for the severe financial depression that existed throughout the country during a considerable part of the period. The census of 1880 enumerated 6,921 establishments, employing a capital of $33,987,886 and 28,364 persons. The wages paid during the year 1879 aggregated $9,725,962, the value of products aggregating $71,045,926. That enumeration reported 1,546 water wheels and 1,768 steam engines employed to furnish motive power.

The monufacturers reported for the latter period named, embraced agricultural implements, bakery products, brick and tile, bridges, carriages, wagons, butter and cheese, clothing, cooperage, flouring and grist mill products, foundry and machine shop products. (These being of the reported value of $1,594,349,) furniture, liquors, (distilled,) liquors, (malt,) lumber, marble and stone work, linseed oil, printing and publishing, saddlery and harness, sash, doors, and blinds, slaughtering and meat products, soap, candles, tinware. copperware, sheet-iron ware, tobacco, cigars, woolen goods, and miscellaneous productions.

We have been unable to obtain the census enumeration of Iowa manufactures for 1890, the figures not yet being in form to be given to the public.

The woolen industry may however be excepted from this statement as the returns for it have been made. The number of woolen mills in the State were reduced in the period, but production was increased. The number of establishments reported were twenty-four, sets of cards twenty-six, spindles 10,828, looms 158, knitting machines 19, capital employed in woolen manufacture, $901,900, value of lands and buildings, $500,150, number of hands employed 387, amount paid in wages, $135,790, value of production $700,981.- There is room in Iowa for a large increase in this important industry.

We have before us partial returns of the manufacturing interests in several cities of the State as made by the census of 1890. These, while far from complete, are sufficiently so to show a large increase in the manufacturing industries in those cities during the decade. Agents of the census authorities have recently been in the State collecting more complete returns of those interests.

From census bulletins numbered 224, 274, 315 and 317 we gather these facts regarding manufacturers in the cities of Des Moines, Davenport, Sioux City and Burlington, the enumeration published covering only the industries in which three or more establishments were engaged. These four cities in 1890 reported 1,176 of such establishments, employing $19,-359,547 of capital and 14,910 hands to whom were paid as wages $7,057,831. The value of their products reached the sum of 36,111,831, being about one-half of the reported value of the products of the manufacturing industries of the entire State in the preceding census. These facts although meager are sufficient to show an important increase of our manufacturing industries during the last census period. In the three subsequent years the increase has been proportionately much greater. The following lines of manufacture were reported in the cities named. Brick and tile, carriages and wagons, confectionery, druggists preparations not including prescriptions, flouring and gristmill products, marble and stone work, foundry and machine shop products, iron work (architectural and ornamental work), planing mill products, printing and publishing, saddlery and harness, lumber, clothing, cooperage, malt liquors, slaughtering meat and packing, tobacco, cigars and cigarettes ; of lumber the production was large in Clinton and other river cities.

The report of the Secretary of Agriculture shows that the beet sugar belt is located in the very heart of this State. All the requisites for growing the beets and manufacturing the sugar are here. The climate, the rainfall, the sunshine, the soil exactly suited to the cultivation of the sugar beet, are Iowa's proposed contribution to the people's sugar bowl, it only requires a little more education to give to capital the necessary confidence to establish factories and make it desirable for our farmers to engage in growing the beets.

In the manufacture of cotton this State offers inviting openings.

The rapid denudation of the forests of the country creates an extensive demand for metallic material for fencing purposes. Barbed wire is found to be the most efficient and enduring material for farm fences. With iron and steel easily procured, and with the advantages we have shown Iowa to possess, there is reason to believe that in the near future the manufacture of iron fencing material will become a great indusry in the State.

Start at the Mississippi river and extend the line of the southern boundary of Missouri to the Pacific Ocean, and all the territory north of

AN OLD TIME IOWA BUSINESS BLOCK.

that line and west of the Mississippi river belonging to the United States may be made contributory to a large extent to the prosperity of Iowa manufacturers. A grand empire is there traversed by railroads and inhabited by thrifty, prosperous people, numbering millions, who are consumers of articles that can be manufactured in Iowa in competition with the manufacturing communities of the east.

The territory thus bounded contains 53,376 miles of railroad, one-third of the railroad system of the country. It has an area of 1,429,185 square miles, or nearly one-third of the territory of the Union. It numbers in its popoulation 12,000,000 persons, nearly one-fifth of the population of the country. The growth of this great country for the next quarter of a century will be very largely confined to the area we have described. With public attention properly called to our advantages as a manufacturing State, capital will do the rest. Iowa manufacturers will in the near future enter this vast territory and find profitable market therein for the goods it is peculiarly within their province to provide

No State in the Union offers more complete transportation facilities than does ours. The two great rivers on its borders offer conveniences for moving heavy or bulky commodities over extended regions of the country at the cheapest possible rates. Steam navigation is still and will doubtless be for ages successfully prosecuted along their channels with great advantage to the river cities and communities. But Iowa is netted with railroads, great arteries of commerce, along which moves its throbbing currents, giving life and vital force to business and animating industry at every point reached by them. There is now scarcely a spot of Iowa soil but what the man who stirs it hears the inspiring sound of the locomotive's rumble as it hurries the commodities he needs almost to his door. These everywhere present transportation facilities in our State, secure incalculable advantages for the employment of capital in manufacturing enterprises within its bounds. With the superior advantages it possesses, Iowa must inevitably in the near future become as noted for its manufacturing production as it is now for its agricultural superiority.

We are indebted to Hon. E. H. Thayer, of Clinton, for very valuable aid in the preparation of this chapter.

## THE IOWA FISH COMMISSION AND ITS WORK.

### By T. J. Griggs, Fish Commissioner of Iowa.

In the early days of Fish Commissions the chief effort of those engaged in the work were directed toward the propagation and distribution of the brook trout, and the work was mainly in the interest of the angler. As the years wore on, the attention of the people generally was drawn to the subject by the gradual depletion of the public waters, and the necessity became apparent of taking active measures toward stocking the streams, and protecting their product. As the outgrowth of such public sentiment, nearly all the States established Fish Commissions, and through their legislatures enacted a code of laws for the protection of fish.

The waters of many of the western States were not adapted to the culture of brook trout, and some method of re-stocking the streams with fish indigenous to them was a necessity. Mr. Shaw, of Cedar Rapids, Iowa, conceived the idea of utilizing the fish that annually went to waste along the rivers, taking them from the ponds and sloughs where they were left by the spring overflow, and transporting them to inland streams and lakes. This plan was taken up by the Illinois Commission and carried into practical effect. Their work in this direction attracting the attention of the United States Fish Commission, they adopted the method, and inaugurated a system of work in the benefits of which all the western States were to share. Iowa, as well as other States, has been thus cared for, and during the last year I have induced them to distribute in our State about ten car loads of indigenous fish, which have been distributed as equally as possible throughout the State.

Iowa has great natural resources as a fish producing State. Filled as it is with beautiful lakes and streams, it presents a magnificent opportunity for becoming the first in the list of States engaged in this work. Aside from the food so produced, there is the advantage to be gained in adding to the attractions of our magnificent lakes and streams, so popular as summer resorts, by furnishing a plentiful supply of fish for the pleasure-seeking angler.

Some of these lakes are well worthy of special mention. Spirit Lake and its connections have a shore line of fifty miles. Clear Lake twenty miles; Wall Lake twelve miles; and Twin Lakes fifteen miles.

All of these lakes are especially adapted to native fish, and all have been carefully stocked the present season.

The work of the Commission has not been alone the stocking of the waters, but the enforcement of the laws for the protection of the fish, as well. This latter work has been, for the greater part, of a thankless nature, not only attended by personal risks but incurring, for those engaged in it, the enmity of the fisherman and citizen alike whenever the operation of the laws interfered with what they had come to consider their vested rights. It has been an uphill fight to try to bring public sentiment into line with the laws, but we feel that something at least has been accomplished.

Our output last season was as follows:

400,000 black bass fry; 300,000 crappie fry; 50,000 wall-eyed pike fry; 100,000 lake trout fry.

These have been distributed throughout the State as generally and equably as our limited appropriation would permit, and are exclusive of those mentioned before as distributed by the United States Fish Commission cars.

Our property consists of nearly four acres of land situated on the isthmus dividing the waters of Spirit Lake and Lake Okoboji, in Dickinson county, near the tracks of the Burlington, Cedar Rapids & Northern Railroad. The grounds of the plant are surrounded by a wide fence, and the improvements thereon consist of a barn and a frame building 20x40 feet, with a stone foundation, having a cemented floor. The apparatus consists of hatching troughs and screens sufficient to handle a half million trout eggs, and jars sufficient to handle from five to six million pike eggs, with all other necessary appliances, such as tools, nets, etc., to carry on the work.

There are six winter ponds, properly walled, for storage purposes. The ponds are properly connected with a supply pipe extending out into Spirit Lake about 200 feet.

Iowa should, from its natural advantages, become the home of thousands of pleasure seekers every season, and there could be no more effective means of securing this end than to make our waters teem with fish. Angling is the favorite sport of a large majority of those who seek an outing during the warm months. We have the water, beautifully located and fairly stocked, and its product should be carefully protected by a rigid enforcement of the law, and the supply frequently renewed. As our State fills up these same waters will furnish a supply of food at small cost.

## EDUCATION IN IOWA.

### EARLY HISTORY.

The time when Iowa was an almost uninhabited region is within the vivid memory of those surviving citizens who were among the earliest settlers. No longer ago than half a century the larger part of its area, so richly stored with Nature's gifts, was still untenanted by the white man. Over broad stretches of fertile prairie the bright flowers of each returning spring and summer blossomed unheeded. The dancing leaves of her woodlands and the rippling waters of hundreds of streamlets awaited patiently the coming of the industrious pioneer, ambitious to establish anew under more favorable opportunities, the advantages of a superior civilization.

The first school in what is now Iowa was held in the three closing months of 1830, at Nashville, Lee county, Berryman Jennings, teacher. On the present site of Keokuk, I. K. Robinson taught a school commencing in December, 1830. These two teachers and many of their scholars are living at this time. Geo. Cubbage taught a school in a log church in Dubuque, in the winter of 1833-4. The first woman to teach in Iowa was Mrs. Rebecca Palmer, at Fort Madison, in 1834. A school for young ladies was opened in Dubuque in 1837, by Louisa King, and conducted for several years. In 1839, Alonzo P. Phelps established in the same city a classical school for both sexes, afterwards continued by Thos. H. Benton, Jr.

The first building to be used chiefly as a public school-house, was erected at Burlington in 1833, of roughly hewed logs, while to Dubuque must be accorded the credit of erecting the first school-house by taxation under the law of January 1, 1839, which granted the voters of any school district the power to levy a tax, select a place, and build a school-house. This was in 1844.

The constitution under which Iowa entered the Union in 1836 declared: "The General Assembly shall encourage by all suitable means the promotion of intellectual, scientific, moral and agricultural improvement." This constitution also required that every school district support a school for at least three months in each year. The right and duty of the State to maintain a general system of popular education, and generously to support the same by a uniform levy of taxes, became thus clearly recognized and permanently established as the policy of the new State.

The school law of 1849 authorized the electors of any district to determine whether a school of higher grade should be maintained. Several of the more populous districts availed themselves of this favorable enactment, and very early began to classify and grade their schools.

During the fifties the increase in population was very rapid and there was a corresponding development of school facilities. Rural communities and hamlets multiplied as if by magic, towns and villages in many cases put on the air of cities, larger school-houses were demanded and supplied, and the need of graded and high schools became more keenly felt. A few cities made provision before 1860 for a complete system or organization and the selection of a city superintendent, notably Dubuque, Davenport, and Tipton.

The statistics collected in Iowa in 1857 gave Iowa 3,265 school districts 2,708 schools, 2,996 teachers, and 195,285 children and youth between five and twenty-one.

Up to this time the money raised by general taxation had been insufficient to maintain the schools for as long a period in each year as the people desired, and the term of school had been supplemented by subscription, usually assessed upon the scholars attending. An enlightened public sentiment was demanding that the schools be wholly free, and supported by general taxation.

## THE LAW OF 1858.

This comprehensive enactment, the first adopted by the General Assembly and afterwards with slight amendments, by the board of education, made a radical change for the better in our school system. Small districts were replaced by the civil township as the unit of organization, and adequate provision was made for sustaining the schools for at least six months in each year, and as much longer as the board of any district might desire, by public funds alone. The office of County Superintendent was created, and provision made for the thorough examination of teachers, the supervision of the schools, and the easier establishment and more generous support of graded and high schools. The management of the permanent school fund was removed from the school authorities. By the new law, the County Teachers' Institute was made a part of the school system. In many other ways the former laws were greatly simplified and improved upon. In its essential features the present school law differs but slightly from the Statute popularly known as The Law of 1858.

## THE SYSTEM DESCRIBED.—ORGANIZATION.

There are two districts provided for in the law, district townships and Independent districts. The district township usually agrees in boundaries with the civil township. Of independent districts there are two leading varieties, the village, town, or city district, and the rural independent district, the latter in size resembling the division in district townships known as the sub-district. All directors are chosen for a term of three years. Women are eligible to any school office. Boards determine the amount to be raised by tax for teachers' and contingent funds, fix the additional months of school over the legal requirement of six, establish graded schools and adopt courses of study, locate sites and build school houses, the money having been voted by the electors, and in general have full control over school matters.

Other school officers are the Superintendent of Public Instruction, and the several County Superintendents. These officers are elected for a term of two years. The Superintendent of Public Instruction has general supervision of the County Superintendents and the common schools. He may meet County Superintendents in convention, and as far as able must attend and lecture before teachers' institutes, must give written opinions in explanation of the school laws, decide appeals from decisions made by County Superintendents, and compile the school laws and decisions. He is president of the board of the State Normal School, president of the Board of Educational Examiners, and a regent of the State University. He makes a bi-ennial report of the condition and progress of the public schools, with plans for their more perfect organization and efficiency. Each County Superintendent has general control over schools and teachers in his county. He visits schools, holds a normal institute, examines teachers and issues certificates for a period of not more than one year, hears and decides appeals from orders made by boards of directors, and makes a complete annual report to the Superintendent of Public Instruction.

## SCHOOL HOUSES.

The pioneer log school house increased in numbers until 1861, when 893 were reported, out of a total of 3,479. As population and wealth increased, larger school houses were built, of better material, more inviting in appearance, and more frequently well supplied with the many facilities required in order that the highest success in school work might be attained.

In 1849, the average value of each of the 387 school houses was about $100; in 1860 the average of the 3,208 was $376; in 1874 of 9,228, $892; and in 1892 of 13,275, $1,040. The gradual and continued improvement in school houses and their surroundings is an index of the great advancement in all valuable and desirable particulars. Our state furnishes for the constant use of her people school houses of fine architecture, commodious and well furnished, having good sanitary provisions, thoroughly well equipped with the best apparatus, libraries, and other needed accessories. And these school houses are supplied in abundance, one for each 4.14 square miles of the State, including all river and lake surface in the distribution.

## TEACHERS.

In 1850 seventy teachers out of every hundred employed were men. This difference gradually diminished, until 1862, when the number of the gentler sex employed became the greater. The eminent fitness of women for the office of teacher has ever been favorably recognized in Iowa. As the number of women employed has increased in 1892 to 22,275 against 4,978 men, the relative difference in wages paid has decreased. And this apparent difference in monthly salary is really in most cases much less than shown, because of the higher salaries paid a larger number of men as superintendents and principals, which has the effect materially to increase the average paid men, while as a rule the larger number of the men receive only the same wages as the women teachers of the same grade doing the same work.

## SCHOOL FINANCES.

The constant and rapid increase in the amount of money expended for educational purposes is indisputable evidence that the public schools are appreciated by the people. In many communities, the amounts paid for the support of free instruction aggregate more than one-half of the total taxes. This condition could continue only because there is a settled conviction in the minds of those voting and paying such taxes, that the money given for popular education is after all the wisest expenditure possible.

The total amount paid in 1892 for school purposes was $7,490,191, all raised by voluntary taxation, excepting the semi-annual apportionment, $780,040, a part of which is derived from the interest on the permanent school fund.

## THE STATE BOARD OF EDUCATIONAL EXAMINERS

grants state certificates good for five years, and State diplomas valid for life. This official recognition of professional teachers of merit has become very popular, and many hold one of these credentials.

IOWA STATE NORMAL SCHOOL

## TEACHERS' INSTITUTES.

The development of the institute cannot well be considered apart from the grand services of the pioneers in education. The early fathers laid the foundations of our school system broad and deep. Early in the fifties associations of teachers for consultation and instruction were frequently held. Several volunteer county institutes were held prior to 1858. The law of 1858 required the institute to be in session at least one week and a donation of $50 to its support was made from State funds. From this time institutes multiplied, and their usefulness increased greatly. The normal institute law of 1874 extended the term, and enlarged the opportunities for instruction in methods of teaching and in the principles of education. In many counties the session is now three weeks, and as a rule the very ablest educators to be secured are selected as conductors and instructors. In 1892 an institute was held in every one of the ninety-nine counties, 18,955 teachers were in attendance for an average of 2.4 weeks, and $52,934 were disbursed for expenses.

## THE IOWA STATE TEACHERS' ASSOCIATION

has been in continuous existence since 1854. A general meeting of several days is held every year, in connection with which special sections or divisions apart from the others to discuss portions of the work more particularly related to themselves as engaged in a single line of school work. This yearly gathering of the prominent educators of the State is productive of great good to all attending.

## COUNTY TEACHERS' ASSOCIATIONS AND ROUND TABLES.

In 1892 eighty counties reported a live teachers' association. These meetings usually begin on Friday evening with a lecture or some entertainment likely to interest patrons and school officers, and are continued through Saturday. Frequently city superintendents and principals of high schools join the teachers of the ungraded schools, in a meeting which may include several counties, their deliberations being conducted under the name of a teachers' round table. In some cases only the teachers in graded and high schools in several counties meet in a round table for high school teachers. These informal gatherings are always entertaining and profitable.

## TEACHERS' READING CIRCLE.

Since 1889 a course of professional reading has been followed by a large number of teachers. A board chosen by the County Superintendents from their own number, selects books and gives advisory direction to the course of reading, and each County Superintendent is *ex-officio* manager of the circle in his county. More than nine-tenths of the counties are co-operating in this excellent work.

## PUPILS' READING CIRCLE.

This organization commends itself by helping to direct the children in the reading of good books. The very best works for those of different ages are recommended by the board of directors and arrangements are completed by which the books chosen may be secured at a low cost. Teachers find that the circle brings new interest into the school work. In 1893 about 22,000 school children are reading the books selected for them.

## COURSES OF STUDY.

The State University offers instruction in advanced subjects, and affords special preparation for the work of teaching, for the law, medicine, dentistry, and pharmacy. The courses of study for a very large number of the high schools connect directly with the course of study in the University, the Normal School, the Agricultural College, and many of the colleges of the State. For the ungraded schools of the rural districts a uniform course of study for country schools has received almost universal adoption, and is in very general use, with the most beneficial results. The value of a carefully outlined course of study in unifying and harmonizing the work and securing the wisest working plans for the schools, is conceded by all teachers and school officers who desire to avail themselves of the best means of advancing the interests of the schools.

## ARBOR DAY.

In general a school-house contains an acre of ground. If natural shade

COE COLLEGE, CEDAR RAPIDS.

does not already exits the law directs that trees for shade and ornament shall be planted and cared for. This enactment led the way for the State-wide observation of tree-planting, and since 1887 a day has been designated for this annual spring festival. An Arbor Day pamphlet containing suitable lessons on nature, with choice selections about trees, birds, and flowers has been sent out from the Department of Public Instruction each year in numbers sufficient to secure uniform exercises in all the schools. Emulation and a just pride in local surroundings have been stimulated by the naming of trees planted, and the floating of a school flag on Arbor Day, making this the children's own day of patriotic celebration. Thus it has come to pass that though not legally established, Arbor Day has found such favor with the people that its continuance is assured.

## STATE UNIVERSITY.

This grand institution stands at the head of the educational system. It is intended that the work of instruction shall commence where that of the best high schools ends. The ungraded rural schools are the large and massive base, the graded schools of the towns and villages and the high schools of the cities, the intermediate blocks, and the State University is the crown of an enduring monument, our system of free public schools.

Both sexes have been admitted to all departments of the University on an equal footing since 1859. The first class in the collegiate department graduated in 1863. The law department was established in 1868, the medical in 1870, and the homeopathic medical in 1876. A dental and a pharmaceutical department have since been added. Seventy-nine persons are employed in the work of instruction, and 950 students are in attendance.

### STATE NORMAL SCHOOL.

This important factor in the school work of Iowa was established in 1876. From the first the school has enjoyed the greatest prosperity. Enlarged several times by the addition of increased facilities, the school has always been patronized to the utmost limit of its capacity. Its students are everywhere sought for as teachers and their work in the schools has proven clearly the wisdom of the State in affording to those about to teach, an opportunity to fit themselves in a superior manner for this important work.

### THE AGRICULTURAL COLLEGE

offers six courses of study. It is designed that instruction shall be furnished in all the arts and sciences that have any bearing upon agriculture. Of the large income a goodly amount is expended each year directly upon investigations and experiments, and in practical instruction in agriculture and horticulture.

### CHARITABLE SCHOOLS.

Iowa provides bountifully for those prevented by infirmity from receiving instruction in schools for other children. The College for the blind, the School for the Deaf, and the Institution for the Feeble Minded, supply for these wards of the State the very best facilities that can be secured. The Soldiers' Orphans' Home and Home for Indigent Children furnishes care and instruction for many who otherwise would be homeless.

### CLOSING SUMMARY.

Attendance on the schools is voluntary. The school population, 5 to 21, in 1892 was 675,024. The enrollment in public schools was 509,830. It should be noted that this number does not include the many of school age in attendance upon private schools, colleges, and other institutions of learning than the public schools.

The average monthly salary paid males was $37.76, paid females, $30.78. The schools were continued for an average of 158 days during the year, at an average cost of tuition for each pupil of $1.81 per month.

The census of 1880 credited Iowa with a lower percentage of illiteracy than any other State of the Union. In the results of the census of 1890 no doubt this exalted position will be maintained easily. This is indeed a high honor and an enviable distinction.

The school facilities of Iowa are being improved every year, better buildings are erected, teachers are paid a higher monthly compensation and relatively the attendance upon the schools is higher than at any time in the previous history of the State. The public schools are open to all residents, the children of poor parentage equally with those born to affluence, to persons of color as well as those of lighter skin, the idea being free, universal education. From the humblest rural school to the highest

WASHINGTON HIGH SCHOOL BUILDING, CEDAR RAPIDS, IOWA.

class-room in the State University, equal freedom of access is offered and all are invited to the fullest enjoyment of the invaluable privileges so liberally provided for the fortunate youth of this noble State. The interest which the people of Iowa have always manifested in all that pertains to education furnishes abundant ground for confidence in the continued growth and development of their matchless system of free schools.

In 1876 at the Centennial Exhibition, the schools of Iowa made a very creditable showing. At the Exposition in New Orleans in 1884 and 1885, Iowa received a diploma of honor for her collective educational display, and certificates of special merit were given to individual schools. The enviable distinction conferred upon Iowa by the award of first honors at the Paris Exhibition of 1889, and the bestowal of a gold medal and a handsome diploma, gave our proud State added reasons for self-congratulation, and increased the zeal of its people in the cause of education.

It requires no gift of prophecy to trace out the future path of Iowa. An observing eye need but take the past for a precedent, the present for an earnest, to draw a vast panorama of prosperity, such as our Union has never witnessed, and yet one which Iowa will not fail herself to excel.

## PUBLIC LIBRARIES.

The people of Iowa are concerned to provide and disseminate sound reading and have given earnest attention to the establishment of public libraries; not only to their establishment in connection with State and city schools but also by generous contributions to establish such institutions in our chief cities and also in connection with secular and denominational schools and Universities. The State Library founded in 1840 contains now 42,637 volumes and has become one of the great Libraries of the country. The State Historical Library at Iowa City, founded in 1857, contains 15,000 volumes. The library of the State University embraces 28,344 volumes, the library of its law school 15,000 volumes. The Iowa State Agricultural College 9,500 volumes. The Library of the Grand Lodge of Free and Accepted Masons is the largest known collection of Masonic literature in the country, containing 12,000 volumes, gathered since its establishment in 1844. The Library of the Davenport Academy of Sciences contained at latest report 27,416 volumes. The Burlington Free Public Library catalogues 12,954 volumes. The Council Bluffs Free Library 14,894 volumes. The Iowa Official Register for 1893 reports one hundred and seven libraries in the State. Thirteen of the number belonging to State schools, or are State property; twenty-one belong to denominational schools; three to Young Mens' Christian Associations; and eight to secular colleges or academies. The whole number of volumes reported in the several libraries being 493,820 The report as published was not complete, there being many parochial and other school libraries not reported. There are in the State many large and valuable professional and other private libraries of which no enumeration is made.

## CHURCHES AND CHURCH WORK IN IOWA.

We have shown elsewhere that the people of Iowa spend upwards of seven million dollars yearly in support of their common or public schools; they spend other large sums each year in support of parochial and other private schools, secular and denominational colleges and professional and technical schools. They show large interest in securing for their young people the means of an intellectual culture essential to useful and honorable life. They recognize also the importance of the proper culture of the moral faculties and desiring the predominance of sobriety, piety and good order, they not only tax themselves to provide facilities for public education but they contribute voluntarily large gifts to promote religious instruction and moral culture. No tax is or can be levied in this State for the building of churches or the support of the institutions of religion.

Devoted Christian men and women came in with the first immigration in the permanent settlement of the territory. Loyal alike to their God, their Christian profession and the moral interests of the communities they were establishing, they soon invited the services of the ministers of religion, and in their humble circumstances generously planned and labored to secure this beautiful region to the dominion of their Lord. They endured privations, worshiped in lowly cabins, often in "Gods first Temples," the shading grove, and by their fidelity to Christian principles, made the religious freedom, privileges and moral excellence we now enjoy a gracious possibility.

Enthusiasm in religious work led to the discovery of Iowa. The settlement of the territory did not immediately follow its discovery. One hundred and sixty years passed before the first settlers came to found homes in the area now constituting this State. In that flight of time, through the leadings of Divine Providence, great intellectual, moral and political changes occurred. Inventive genius evolved new agencies of moral, as well as intellectual, mechanical and military power, that resulted in vast changes, not only in their geography, but also in the social condition and the religious ideas pervading Christian nations. Under divine guidance this fertile and divinely favored region was reserved for settlement until these forces were in effective operation and an intelligent, liberal, Christian citizenship, hating oppression and loving righteousness, should bring to this "beautiful land" the highest type of Christian civilization ever enjoyed by men.

When the permanent settlement of Iowa began in 1833, the first emigrants were attracted to the vicinity of Dubuque and that place was founded; Galena, on the east side of the river, by its lead mining had become an active frontier town, and ministers of religion soon crossed to the new settlement west of the river. On the 8th day of August of the year named, a Congregational minister visited the new place and held religious services at the dwelling of a Mrs. Willoughby, the first religious service, so far as now known, ever held within the boundaries of the State. Soon thereafter Father McMahon, a Catholic clergyman, celebrated mass at the house of Patrick Quigley, in the new village. On the 6th of November the same year the Rev. Barton Randle, a missionary of the M. E. Church visited it and held services in a private house. Early in the following summer he organized a class in the town, the first religious society, so far as history shows, formed in Iowa. During that season the Methodists built a small church of logs, 20x26 feet, it being the first religious structure erected in the State. From these small beginnings, then offering but dim prospect of rapid or great enlargement, have grown the great religious plants that now cover the State with richness of blessing and yield their rich fruitage of cultured, Christian beneficence now sent forth, to carry the tidings of grace from this to other peoples.

It will be noticed that in this brief period, of fifty-nine years, this great work of building up our Christian societies, with their conferences, associations, yearly meetings, synods, Presbyteries, elderships, and assemblies, with their beautiful Christian temples, parochial schools, seminaries, colleges and universities has been organized and accomplished, and the millions raised that were required for their support and endowment. In those fifty-nine years there were crosses borne and privations endured but,

A WESTERN IOWA PIONEER CHURCH

ITS LINEAL DESCENDANT

there were wonderful accomplishments. Thousands, of liberal devisers of liberal things in Christian work, "crossed the flood," but their godly devotion won increasing thousands to take their places, and so as the workmen fell the work progressed with the results we present.

### CHURCH STRENGTH IN 1850.

The census of 1850, taken but seventeen years after the settlement of the State began, presented many interesting facts regarding church work in the young State. It enumerated 207 church edifices, of the value of $177,425, an average value for each edifice of $809; they having a seating capacity of 43,529 persons, a small fraction less than one-fourth of the entire population. The total number of edifices then averaged seven to each of the twenty-nine settled counties. They were devided among thirteen denominations, as follows: Baptists 23, Christians 11, Congregationalists 14, Episcopalian 5, Friends 5, German Reformed 4, Lutheran 5, Methodist 76, Moravian 3, Presbyterian 38, Roman Catholic 18, Union 3, Universalist 1, Minor Sects 1. The total value of Church property reported in that census being $235,412.

### CHURCH STRENGTH IN 1870.

Passing over two decades we reach the census year of 1870. Though the rebellion of 1861, with its awful cost of life and treasure had involved Iowa as it had involved every other State, immense progress was made during that trying period in all lines of church work. This census, the fourth national enumeration made in the State, reported 1,446 church edifices with seating capacity for 431,709 persons, being 38 in each 100 of the population. The value of church property had increased during the period to $5,730,352, an increase during the twenty years of $5,484,841, a gain of more than twenty fold, a sum larger than the original amount being added for each year of the period. The Baptists then had 165 church edifices, a gain of 142; the Disciple body 48, a gain of 37; the Episcopalian church 36, a gain of 31; the Congregational church 125, a gain of 111; the Evangelical Association 11; the Friends 60, a gain of 55; the Lutheran body 45, a gain of 40; the Methodist Episcopal church 492, a gain of 416; the Presbyterian body 222, a gain of 184; the Reformed Church in the U. S. 13; the Reformed Church in America 4; the Roman Catholic church 165, a gain of 147; the Adventists 10; the Unitarian body 2, Universalist 15, United Brethren in Christ 28. The total increase of church edifices during the period being 1,239. Surely the devoted Christian men and women in those years of trial, made great sacrifices to promote religious interests in the State.

Religious work in all communities is a vital factor to their truest prosperity. The work done by those devoted godly men and women who worked out these grand results in Christian work in the formative years of our commonwealth did much to accomplish its permanent prosperity. The census of religious work here presented, reveals not only the religious devotion of our people but also the general diffusion of religious privileges throughout the State.

### DENOMINATIONAL ORGANIZATION.

In our researches regarding denominational organization in Iowa, we found in 1850 thirteen denominations existing and owning church edifices. The early settlers coming here to found homes brought with them their distinctive religious ideas, and sought to establish them. In 1870 a larger number of denominational organizations were reported. In the exercise of the freedom of religious opinion, secured to every citizen by our laws denominational organizations had multiplied.

The figures we herein present reveal a very great advance in this impotant interest since 1870, and yet great as they appear they fall far short of presenting the real accomplishment. The returns for many of the churches named being the statistics for 1889, they being the latest possible to obtain, we having to take their statistics from the last national census. Some denominations decline for "conscience sake" to furnish the information desired, others do not gather their statistics in such form as to enable them to furnish the information sought, respecting their work within this State. In a few cases the church officials addressed were not willing to take the time necessary to compile or gather the items we desired, the work requiring extensive correspondence. Our school statistics are gathered under legal authority. The reporting of church statistics is entirely voluntary. Many ministers and other church officials however aided us most kindly in the matter.

Only three denominations have organized existence in every county of the State, namely, Methodist Episcopal, Baptist and Roman Catholic. The Presbyterian church by a mutual arrangement with the Congregational churches has no organization in several counties, but in seven of the eight counties in which the Presbyterian church is unorganized the Congregationalists have organized churches, so that only Worth county is without a Congregational or Presbyterian church. In the counties of Davis, Decatur, Madison, Monroe, Ringgold, Taylor and Warren there are no Lutheran organizations reported by the United States Census. We have tabulated eighty distinct denominational organizations in the State. Many of these however are divisions of general bodies, as the Methodist, Presbyterian and Lutheran. In some cases difference in language or nationality is the cause of separate organization. In others differences in the construction of expressions in their articles of faith. Other divisions have grown out of matters relating to social state, as dress or secrecy. Some of the Plymouth brethren, and the body we have denominated Christ's Church' deny being a sect or separate denomination, yet they are bound together by such ties of affiliation as constitute them separate and distinct bodies. We have not given any figures in connection with the latter named body as there are no means of obtaining any statistics regarding it. They deny having any officiary or leadership. The editor of "The Tumbling Stone," Toledo, Ohio, who may be regarded as their chief minister informs us that he is acquainted with them in forty-four towns in this State.

| DENOMINATIONS. | No. of Counties in which Denomination exists. | No. of Church Edifices. | No. of Parsonages. | Value of Church Property. | No. of Church Members. | No. of Sunday Schools. | Amount raised during year for Church Work and Benevolences. |
|---|---|---|---|---|---|---|---|
| The New Church, (Swedenborgian) | 6 | 3 | | $ 6,000 | 138 | 4 | |
| The Salvation Army | 15 | | | | 387 | | |
| ADVENTIST CHURCHES— | | | | | | | |
| Life and Advent Christian Union | 1 | | | | 48 | | |
| Church of God (Adventist) | 4 | 1 | | 2,000 | 121 | | |
| Seventh Day Adventist Church | 51 | 48 | | 65,000 | 2,929 | 125 | |
| Advent Christian Church | 21 | 11 | | 17,300 | 1,372 | | |
| The Theosophical Society | 3 | | | | 20 | | |
| Brethren in Christ (River Brethren) | 2 | 2 | | | 40 | | |
| Moravian Church | 3 | 3 | | 4,500 | 100 | | |
| Plymouth Brethren | 9 | | | | 163 | | |
| Christ's Church (Come-outers) | | | | | | | |
| THE MENNONITE CHURCHES— | | | | | | | |
| The Mennonite Church | 3 | 10 | | 10,000 | 1,000 | 6 | |
| The Amish Mennonite Church | 4 | 5 | | 6,700 | 903 | | |
| General Conference Mennonite Church | 3 | 5 | | 5,950 | 509 | 4 | |
| Mennonite Brethren in Christ | 1 | 1 | | 500 | 14 | | |
| THE REFORMED CHURCHES— | | | | | | | |
| The Reformed Church in America | 11 | 28 | | 90,900 | 2,605 | | |
| The Reformed Church in the United States | 34 | 30 | | 68,350 | 2,513 | 19 | |
| The Christian Reformed Church | 3 | 6 | | 18,000 | 623 | | |
| THE BAPTIST CHURCHES— | | | | | | | |
| The German Baptist (Conservative) | 41 | 38 | | 49,605 | 2,769 | | |
| The German Baptist (Progressive) | 6 | 4 | | 6,850 | 601 | | |
| The German Baptist (Old Order) | 8 | 2 | | 2,000 | 100 | | |
| Old Two Seed Baptist | 1 | | | | 10 | | |
| Seventh Day Baptist Church | 3 | 2 | | 4,300 | 169 | | |
| Primitive Baptist Church | 25 | 16 | | 9,950 | 853 | | |
| Free Will Baptist Church | 24 | 36 | 7 | 65,830 | 2,029 | 42 | |
| Regular Baptist Church | 99 | 333 | 76 | 1,277,435 | 32,323 | 336 | $ 355,856 |
| German Evangelical Synod of N. America | 25 | 43 | | 110,300 | 6,902 | | |
| Roman Catholic Church | 90 | 439 | | 3,843,400 | 161,684 | | |
| JEWISH CONGREGATIONS— | | | | | | | |
| Orthodox Jewish Congregation | 1 | | | | 50 | | |
| Reformed Jewish Congregation | 4 | 4 | | 58,000 | 487 | | |
| SOCIETY OF FRIENDS— | | | | | | | |
| Friends (Orthodox) | 27 | 73 | | 102,682 | 9,760 | | |
| Friends (Hicksite) | 4 | 4 | | 3,800 | 440 | | |
| Friends (Wilburite) | 9 | 13 | | 12,350 | 1,539 | | |
| Re-Organized Church of Jesus Christ of Latter Day Saints | 32 | 30 | | 50,500 | 5,683 | 42 | |
| Independent Churches of Christ in Christian Union | 11 | 20 | | 21,500 | 1,259 | | |
| Church of God (Winebrennarian) | 16 | 21 | | 25,000 | 1,280 | 15 | 7,000 |
| Evangelical Association | 49 | 83 | | 178,135 | 5,699 | | |
| United Brethren in Christ | 73 | 173 | | 336,300 | 10,501 | 224 | 94,161 |
| United Brethren in Christ (Old Consti'tion) | 14 | 20 | | 19,250 | 272 | | |
| Spiritualists | 10 | | | 23,075 | 2,613 | | |
| Christadelphians | 5 | | | | 67 | | |
| Congregationalists | 87 | 244 | | 1,231,896 | 24,262 | 288 | $37,529 |
| Universalists | 19 | 25 | 20 | 218,300 | 987 | 18 | |
| Unitarian Churches | 10 | 9 | 1 | 78,500 | 1,575 | 11 | 20,780 |
| THE PRESBYTERIAN CHURCHES— | | | | | | | |
| The United Presbyterian Church of North America | 44 | 101 | 25 | 314,301 | 7,796 | 60 | 121,494 |
| The Cumberland Presbyterian Church in the United States of America | 17 | 25 | | 34,550 | 1,167 | | |
| Reformed Presbyterian Church in the United States of America | 7 | 9 | | 21,900 | 984 | | |
| General Synod of the Reformed Presbyterian Church | 2 | 1 | | 1,000 | 33 | | |
| Associate Presbyterian Church of N. A. | 4 | 5 | | 5,300 | 233 | | |
| Welsh Calvinistic Methodist Church | 5 | 7 | | 7,650 | 349 | | |
| Presbyterian Church of the U. S. of N. A. | 91 | 347 | | 1,552,860 | 30,170 | 387 | $84,899 |

| DENOMINATIONS. | No. of Counties in which Denomination exists. | No. of Church Edifices. | No. of Parsonages. | Value of Church Property. | No. of Church Members. | No. of Sunday Schools. | Amount raised during year for Church Work and Benevolences. |
|---|---|---|---|---|---|---|---|
| THE METHODIST CHURCHES— | | | | | | | |
| The Primitive Methodist Church | 3 | 3 | 3 | $ 5,000 | 100 | 5 | |
| The Wesleyan Methodist Church | 20 | 21 | 5 | 25,000 | 750 | | $ 6,567 |
| The Free Methodist Church | 44 | 62 | 17 | 56,153 | 2,230 | 63 | |
| The Methodist Protestant Church | 22 | 65 | 23 | 105,000 | 5,645 | 70 | 15,430 |
| The African Methodist-Episcopal Church | 24 | 29 | | 87,361 | 1,820 | | |
| The Methodist-Episcopal Church, South | 2 | 7 | | 9,200 | 730 | | |
| The Methodist-Episcopal Church | 99 | 965 | 486 | 3,669,306 | 111,389 | 1294 | 1,076,133 |
| THE LUTHERAN CHURCHES— | | | | | | | |
| General Synod Evangelical Lutheran Church | 19 | 28 | | 173,100 | 2,043 | 22 | |
| Synodical Conference Ev'ng'lic'l Lutheran Church | 61 | 82 | | 194,715 | 18,452 | | |
| General Council Evangelical Lutheran Church | 62 | 132 | | 420,680 | 20,000 | | |
| Joint Synod of Ohio and other States | 3 | 8 | | 10,500 | 650 | | |
| Hagues Synod Norwegian Luther'n Church | 10 | 14 | | 27,200 | 1,593 | | |
| Danish Evangelical Lutheran Church in America | 16 | 14 | | 24,800 | 2,211 | | |
| Norwegian Evangelical Lutheran Church in America | 19 | 26 | | 97,800 | 7,059 | | |
| German Augsburg Synod Evangelical Lutheran Church | 1 | 1 | | 1,000 | 70 | | |
| Danish Lutheran Church Association in America | 6 | 2 | | 3,800 | 413 | | |
| United Norwegian Lutheran Church of America | 36 | 85 | | 220,100 | 14,819 | 58 | |
| Independent Lutheran Congregations | 2 | 4 | | 11,400 | 694 | | |
| Protestant Episcopal Church | 68 | 77 | | 1,359,720 | 6,266 | | 146,879 |
| Reformed Episcopal Church | 1 | | | | 27 | 1 | 366 |
| Diciples of Christ or Christians | 82 | 309 | | 708,100 | 30,989 | | |
| The Christian Church or Bible Christians | 33 | 32 | | 92,755 | 2,555 | | |
| Independent Churches of Christ in Christian Union | 11 | 20 | | 21,500 | 1,253 | | |
| Christian Scientist | 20 | 1 | | 5,200 | 640 | | |
| Congregational Churches | 87 | 241 | | 1,231,886 | 23,733 | | 337,529 |
| Community of True Inspiration Society | 1 | 7 | | 20,000 | 1,700 | | |
| Icarian Community | 1 | | | | 21 | | |
| Plymouth Brethern II | 2 | | | | 48 | | |
| Plymouth Brethern III | 6 | | | | 166 | | |
| Independent Congregations | 1 | 1 | | 1,000 | 75 | | |
| TOTALS | | 4520 | | $ 18,485,639 | 579,960 | | |

J. D. Roth, of Catasaqua, Pennsylvania, a leading statistician of the Lutheran churches in this country, estimates the expenditures of the several divisions of that body for church support and benevolent work in 1892 at $586,944. Accepting this estimate then the twenty-four denominational bodies which we report on this item raised and expended in their work in 1892 the grand sum of $3,174,055. These twenty-four bodies raising this princely sum by generous donation, contributed voluntarily for the maintenance and propagation of their religous convictions the sum of $9.49 for each of their 323,728 members. Taking the above average for the 578,756 church members, we find that the people of Iowa voluntarily paid that year $5,492,394.44 for the support and advancement of religion. Not a very small sum to be annually voluntarily assumed and paid. Such liberality demonstrates, not only that the Christian people of Iowa are of a generous disposition, but also that they are in prosperous circumstances, and have high regard for their religious convictions and privileges.

The census for 1890 enumerated 4,482 church edifices in this State, of the reported value of $16,901,061, an average value of $3,771, furnishing seating room for 1,175,768 persons, or 60.9 per cent. of our population. It enumerated and named sixty-nine denominational organizations having existence within Iowa. Comparing these figures with the census enumeration of the churches for 1870, they show an increase that borders on the marvelous, the increase in the number of church edifices being 3,058 within the period of twenty years, equal to one new church edifice for each 2.39 days of the period. Surely, glorious things may truly be spoken of the lengthening of the "cords" and the strengthening of the stakes of "Zion" in this fair, beautiful and prosperous prairie State.

### SABBATH SCHOOL WORK.

Iowa has an active, working State Sabbath School Association which holds an annual convention. At its session held May, 1893, there was reported within the State 5,079 Sunday Schools, having 42,321 officers and teachers, and 342,511 scholars, a total membership of 384,932; one person in each five of the population of the State, according to this report, being connected with Sunday school work. Many Sabbath schools are not reported to the Association.

Its report for 1892 embraced 4,782 schools, Worth county reporting the smallest number, 12; Winnebago and Palo Alto each reported 15, Woodbury county reported 100, Clinton 105, Jasper 135, Linn 140, and Polk 158. The average to the ninety-nine counties, according to the report for 1893, is 51.3 schools, a number that shows that our people are generously and earnestly engaged in this work.

The amount expended for the year ending May, 1893, for the support of Sunday schools, according to the report to the State Association was $129,414, not a meager sum to be voluntarily given for the support of this enterprise, Mrs. Mattie M. Bailey, Secretary of the Association, reports that 75 per cent. of the Sunday schools within the State are continued throughout the year, and that at least one million copies of Sabbath school papers are taken and that the libraries of these Sabbath schools contain at least 100,000 volumes.

### PAROCHIAL SCHOOLS, DENOMINATIONAL AND NON-SECTARIAN COLLEGES AND UNIVERSITIES.

A census of church work in Iowa would not be complete nor would our educational work be fully shown, unless some report was made of the parochial schools and the denominational and secular universities and colleges maintained within the State.

Our laws make no provision for exempting persons of any denomination or sect from the payment of school taxes, it matters not how much they may have paid to support schools maintained by their own sect or church. Neither do our laws preclude any church or sect from maintaining schools for the education of its youth. The colleges and universities of the State are mostly built and maintained by religious denominations. No appropriation of any part of the school funds raised by taxation can be legally made for the support of denominational schools.

The three State schools, the Iowa State University, the Agricultural College, and the State Normal School are entirely non-sectarian. We have many other secular schools of high grade.

## STATE SCHOOLS.

| NAME OF SCHOOL. | NO. OF STUDENTS. | | | NO. OF INSTRUCTORS. | | | Volumes in Library. | Endowment. | Yearly Income. | Value of Grounds and B'ld'gs. |
|---|---|---|---|---|---|---|---|---|---|---|
| | Male. | F'male. | Total. | Male. | F'male. | Total. | | | | |
| Iowa State Normal | 191 | 515 | 706 | 9 | 9 | 18 | 5,000 | | $ 21,000 | $ 75,000 |
| Iowa State Agricultural College | 454 | 93 | 547 | 22 | 7 | 29 | 9,300 | $679,784 | 60,000 | 450,000 |
| Iowa State University | 752 | 152 | 904 | 69 | 6 | 75 | 28,000 | 231,964 | 150,000 | 300,000 |
| TOTALS | 1,397 | 760 | 2,157 | 100 | 22 | 122 | 42,300 | $911,748 | $ 231,000 | $ 825,000 |

## OTHER SECULAR SCHOOLS.

| NAME OF SCHOOL | NO. OF STUDENTS. | | | No. OF INSTRUCTORS. | | | Volumes in Library. | Endowment. | Yearly Income. | Value of Grounds and B'ld'gs. |
|---|---|---|---|---|---|---|---|---|---|---|
| | Male. | F'male. | Total. | Male. | F'male. | Total. | | | | |
| Audubon Normal College | | | 90 | 3 | 2 | 5 | 2,500 | | $ 4,000 | $ 40,000 |
| Amity College | 190 | 173 | 363 | 7 | 5 | 12 | | $ 40,000 | 8,000 | 40,000 |
| Decorah Institute | 261 | 211 | 472 | 4 | 2 | 6 | | | | 4,200 |
| Iowa City Academy | 200 | 110 | 319 | 5 | 4 | 9 | 300 | | 4,000 | 6,000 |
| Dexter Normal College | 165 | 168 | 313 | 7 | 5 | 12 | 2,736 | | 25,000 | 25,000 |
| Keokuk Medical College | 147 | 13 | 160 | 15 | | 15 | | | | 40,000 |
| Guthrie County High School | 98 | 105 | 203 | 1 | 4 | 5 | 632 | | | 10,000 |
| LeMars Normal School and Business College | 104 | 101 | 205 | 3 | 3 | 6 | 200 | | 4,000 | 30,000 |
| Afton Normal School and Business College | 98 | 174 | 272 | 4 | 6 | 10 | 1,000 | 10,000 | | 40,000 |
| National Normal School and Business College | | | 190 | 5 | 2 | 7 | 370 | | | 20,000 |
| Highland Park Normal College | 100 | 90 | 190 | 21 | 5 | 26 | 5,580 | | | 450,000 |
| TOTALS | 1,353 | 1,135 | 3,330 | 75 | 38 | 113 | 13,106 | $ 50,000 | $ 45,000 | $ 634,220 |

* Supported by tax on county, it being a county institution.

## DENOMINATIONAL UNIVERSITIES.

| NAME. | NO. OF STUDENTS. | | | NO. OF INSTRUCTORS. | | | Volumes in Library. | Endow-ment. | Yearly Income. | Value of Grounds and B'ld'g's. | Denomination. |
|---|---|---|---|---|---|---|---|---|---|---|---|
| | Male. | F'male. | Total. | Male. | F'male. | Total. | | | | | |
| Iowa Wesleyan University. | 84 | ...... | 397 | 14 | 4 | 18 | ...... | $ 62,600 | ...... | $ ...... | Methodist. |
| Central University of Iowa | ...... | 78 | 163 | 5 | 3 | 8 | 5,000 | 126,275 | $ 24,988 | 20,000 | Baptist. |
| Drake University | ...... | ...... | 662 | 34 | 6 | 40 | ...... | ...... | 24,988 | 107,067 | Disciple. |
| Upper Iowa University | 329 | 155 | 484 | 11 | 11 | 22 | 5,322 | 15,000 | 7,000 | 75,000 | Methodist. |

## DENOMINATIONAL COLLEGES.

| NAME. | NO. OF STUDENTS. | | | NO. OF INSTRUCTORS. | | | Volumes in Library. | Endow-ment. | Yearly Income. | Value of Grounds and B'ld'g's. | Denomination. |
|---|---|---|---|---|---|---|---|---|---|---|---|
| | Male. | F'male. | Total. | Male. | F'male. | Total. | | | | | |
| Elkhorn College | 100 | 80 | 180 | 5 | 2 | 7 | 500 | $ ...... | $ ...... | $ 10,000 | Lutheran. |
| The Norwegian College | 213 | ...... | 213 | 8 | ...... | 8 | 6,500 | 7,500 | 4,000 | 80,000 | Lutheran. |
| Lenox College | 57 | 58 | 115 | 4 | 4 | 8 | 1,460 | 11,000 | 12,000 | 20,000 | Presbyterian. |
| Parsons College | 69 | 80 | 149 | 5 | 3 | 8 | 2,500 | 150,000 | 10,000 | 100,000 | Presbyterian. |
| Coe College | 95 | 127 | 222 | 7 | 6 | 13 | 5,300 | 100,000 | 10,000 | 250,000 | Presbyterian. |
| Tabor College | 250 | 329 | 650 | 17 | 11 | 28 | 11,000 | 60,000 | 28,000 | 50,000 | Congregational. |
| Cornell College | 228 | 188 | 416 | 6 | 6 | 12 | 2,500 | 110,000 | 75,000 | 175,000 | Methodist. |
| Simpson College | 223 | 200 | 423 | 19 | 4 | 23 | 18,000 | 60,000 | 5,387 | 100,000 | Methodist. |
| Iowa College | 87 | 71 | 158 | 6 | 6 | 12 | 3,000 | 200,000 | 30,000 | 150,000 | Congregational. |
| Des Moines College | ...... | ...... | 298 | 8 | 5 | 13 | 3,000 | 100,000 | ...... | 13,000 | Baptist. |
| Penn College | ...... | ...... | 419 | 15 | 4 | 19 | 3,000 | 30,000 | ...... | 75,000 | Friends. |
| Western College | 220 | 189 | ...... | 6 | ...... | 6 | 3,500 | 25,000 | 10,000 | 105,000 | United Brethren. |
| St. Ambrose College | 80 | ...... | 80 | ...... | ...... | ...... | ...... | ...... | 10,000 | 80,000 | Roman Catholic. |

## SEMINARIES.

| NAME. | NO. OF STUDENTS. | | | NO. OF INSTRUCTORS. | | | Volumes in Library. | Endow-ment. | Yearly Income. | Value of Grounds and B'ld'g's. | Denomination. |
|---|---|---|---|---|---|---|---|---|---|---|---|
| | Male. | F'male. | Total. | Male. | F'male. | Total. | | | | | |
| Epworth Seminary | 125 | 100 | 225 | 4 | 8 | 12 | 1,500 | $ ...... | $ 5,000 | $ 20,000 | Methodist. |
| Cedar Valley Seminary | 157 | 110 | 267 | 4 | 4 | 8 | 1,500 | 30,000 | 5,000 | 30,000 | Baptist. |
| Burlington Institute | 80 | 124 | 204 | 5 | 7 | 12 | 2,500 | 30,000 | 1,500 | 40,000 | Baptist. |
| Albion Seminary | 41 | 39 | 80 | 3 | 2 | 5 | 400 | ...... | 1,500 | 5,000 | ...... |
| St. Katherena Hall | ...... | 110 | 110 | 1 | 11 | 12 | 1,000 | 10,000 | 25,000 | 60,000 | Protestant-Episcopal |

## PAROCHIAL SCHOOLS.

The Roman Catholic, several branches of the Lutheran body, and some other churches maintain denominational schools. Desiring as a part of their education, the instruction of their youth in their religious doctrines and usages, they spend large sums for the maintainance of their parochial or church schools. In the Diocese of Davenport there are 145 Catholic churches, six academies instructing 1,100 students, and 37 parochial schools with 4,510 pupils. The church also maintains hospitals and orphan asylums at large expense. In the Diocese of Dubuque there are 250 churches 1 seminary, 1 college, 8 academies and 100 parochial schools with 12,500 pupils. We addressed circular letters to upwards of 100 of these schools and received replies from twenty-two. They reported 2,755 pupils, namely, 1,305 males and 1,405 females, they having six male and sixty-five female instructors, with 2,415 volumes in their libraries. Ten of the twenty-two schools reported an aggregate yearly income of $4,750, and eighteen reported an endowment of $142,200.

We have been unable to obtain the statistics of the Luthern schools, as the several Lutheran Synods are not bounded by State lines and do not gather their statistics with reference to such lines, some Synods embracing several States. Rev. Geo. H. Schnurr of Nevada, Iowa, a gentleman who very kindly aided us in collecting facts regarding the Lutheran body, wrote us under date of July 7, 1893: "I am not able to give you the figures desired. The fact is that parochial school statistics have never been gathered or arranged by States. From incomplete statistics that I have seen, a safe estimate could be made at 15,000 pupils."

It is an encouraging fact that the several religious denominations within this State are earnestly interested in securing for their youth most liberal educational advantages. These parochial schools and denominational seminaries Colleges and universities, furnishing educational advantages, many of them in the higher grades require large sums, which are generously given for their support.

We recognize fully the incompleteness of this report of church and school work within the State. Our attempt has revealed to us the difficulty of gathering complete statistics on these lines. We trust, however, that the facts we present will interest intelligent readers. They have cost us great labor—having involved extensive correspondence and research. A proper effort in the coming State census might present a complete enumeration of those interesting matters.

## IOWA'S PALACES.

Some seven years ago the palace idea for exhibiting agricultural, horticultural, mechanical and mineral productions and other resources originated in this State, the citizens of Sioux City being the first to attempt its development, they adopting corn as the principal material for the decoration of their structure which was worthily named the "Corn Palace." It was made a thing of beauty and its unique decorations won large favor and drew to the city thousands of visitors.

A number of counties in Southeastern Dakota, Northeastern Nebraska, and Northwestern Iowa combined with the people of Sioux City to make exhibits of their resources and productions in the Palace Exposition, special booths or space being assigned to each county for its special exhibit. These exhibits at once demonstrated that Sioux City was central in a fine agricultural and fruit growing region, while the fine artistic and truly beautiful decorations of the spacious palace wrought out of corn and other grains and grasses at once won extended fame and favor.

The exterior as well as the interior of the Corn Palace was decorated with corn, all varieties of that cereal in size, color and tint being used in happy combination of form and shade which made the Corn Palace to the beholder, when the rich autumn sun light shone upon it, a thing of surprising grandeur. The decorations, while they were of Nature's perfect painting and so most pleasing to the eye, were not durable for external adornment and when the annual exposition closed the Corn Palace structure was removed and reconstructed the following year in entirely new architectural and decorative designs. This gave the artists drawing the designs for and superintending the decorations of the structure fine opportunity for studying the blending of the rich tints and many rich colors found in the numerous varieties of this kingly cereal so as to produce in its use the most marvelous, yet pleasing artistic effects. The use of corn as decorative material reaching a happy climax in the decoration of the Iowa Pavillion in the Agricultural Building and the Exhibition Hall in the Iowa Building at the Columbian Exposition, where the visiting thousands of intelligent people from foreign countries as well as from the eastern and southern states of our country are enraptured with the beauty of these Iowa structures. Their charming decorations accomplished by the intelligent artist's use of the simple products of Iowa's fertile farms and fields commanding their admiration. The Corn Palace was a grand advertisement of the energy, culture and enterprise of the people of the city giving it being.

### THE FLAX PALACE.

Forest City, the county seat of Winnebago County, is central in the leading flax producing region west of the Mississippi river. Its stirring business men united their energies and capital for the erection of a Flax Palace. That important farm product being susceptible of use in beautiful ornamentation in the hands of persons of suitable taste. The city named and the people of the region surrounding it may not equal in wealth the larger and older palace cities of Iowa, but they energetically took hold of the project and the Flax Palace with an exhibit of the superior farm products of northern Iowa favorably advertised through the medium of visiting thousands the superior advantages of that beautiful region, abounding in natural advantages, and won thereto a large immigration and rapid development. The "Palaces" of Iowa by their unique structure, attractive adornment, novel and superbly fine exhibits of the resources of their surroundings attracting visitors from other states rendered valuable service in spreading knowledge of our excellencies and inviting desirable immigration with capital to assist in the further improvement and progress of the country surrounding them.

## THE BLUE GRASS PALACE.

The enterprising citizens of Creston inspired by the success of Sioux City with its Corn Palace, conceived the idea of a "Blue Grass Palace," and a number of counties in the southwestern portion of the State were organized in what was named the Blue Grass League, to make an annual exhibit of their productions and resources in a structure in the erection and decoration of which the grasses, especially Blue Grass should predominate. A very commodious structure was erected and attractively decorated with the materials named. Space was assigned to the several counties forming the

league. Each county decorating its booth and making exhibits therein The varied productions of that wonderfully fertile portion of this queenly State were placed on exhibition and thousands were attracted from distant parts by the beauty of the unique structure and the rich and varied exhibit it contained. The Blue Grass Palace and its attractive ornamentation and industrial exhibits attracted scores of emigrants to the beautiful Blue Grass region.

## THE COAL PALACE.

The citizens of the busy manufacturing city of Ottumwa, originated the idea of a Coal Palace. That city lies in a great coal producing region, has extensive water power and has developed important manufacturing industries. It planned for an annual exhibit of its productions in its Coal Palace. It may be thought by some that there could be no beauty developed from the dark, smutty black diamonds, but cultured architectural and decorative skill works out new forms of beauty often from very crude materials. The Coal Palace was made winsome in architectural design, and while it may not have been so richly or gorgeously beautiful as the Corn Palace it was made serviceable by its fine exhibits of the products of the fields, the orchards, gardens. mills, shops, and mines of the growing city and the region surrounding it, and Ottumwa is deservedly known as one of the Palace Cities of the State.

## IOWA BOOKS AND AUTHORS.

### By Mrs. Sara B. Maxwell.

It has been said that Iowa is too young and has no time nor opportunity to write "great" books. Iowa is young and has of necessity heretofore devoted her time and energy to developing her material resources. She therefore deserves the more credit for the literary progress she has made and for the many good books she has written; books which compare favorably with those, in the same line, of any other place.

Theorists claim that we have not the environment necessary to the inspiration of the grandest themes. This may be so; but the imagination of the Rev. Samuel McClurg Osmond needed not the aid of lofty mountain peak, or rapidly rolling river, when he penned the beautiful story of "Sulamith." A prairie flower called forth the sweet and tender "Golden Rod," from the heart of Rev. G. W. Crofts. No battle array, nor sound of clashing arms inspired the production of the "Siege of Calias," by Rev. A. L. Frisbie. We have no mountains; no ruined castles; no ancient history; no ghostly inheritance to project themselves through our fancy; but we have broad rolling prairies and an invigorating atmosphere which gives us broad views, humane hearts, and a common sense capable of grasping and analyzing the problems of life.

Book-making in Iowa began at an early day and we now have over seven hundred authors of books and pamphlets. The limits of this chapter allow the mention of only a few of the best known.

To Prof. James Pierson belongs the honor of having published the first poem of any length, viz: "The Judaid," a book of 267 pages, published in 1842.

Many Iowa books have attained national reputation and influence, and some are known beyond the seas, several having been translated into other languages; notably, the ethical works of W. McIntosh Salter; the scientific works of Prof. W. J. McGee, and of Charles Wachsmuth, who has been recognized by the Russian government as authority in his specialty.

Bishop W. Stevens Perry is known on both sides of the Atlantic as a scholarly writer on the annals of his church and other subjects of permanent interest. Two continents recognize Major S. H. M. Byers as a polished writer of both prose and poetry. "Sherman's March to the Sea" has immortalized him. The novel and stories of Miss Alice French (*Octave*

*Thanet*) and of Hamlin Garland are read and quoted everywhere. As a writer of field sports, W. Bruce Leffingwell has the reputation of being the best in the world. "The Medical and Moral Care of Female Patients in Hospital for the Insane," a paper read before the National Conference of Charities in Chicago, 1879. by Dr. Margaret A. Cleaves, molded public opinion and had a far reaching influence. It was published by the government of New South Wales and has been quoted in English and American papers.

One of Iowa's most interesting and instructive books is Hon. D. N. Richardson's "Girdle Round the Earth," full of valuable information so charmingly given one wishes to read it again and again. "The History of the Amana Society," by Prof. W. R. Perkins, is said by competent critics to be the finest historical monologue ever written; critical, analytical, scholarly, in every way a most valuable contribution to the literature of social science as well as history.

Our law writers stand with the best in the country.

May Rogers in her "Waverley Dictionary" has done for Scott's Waverley Novels, what G. A. Pierce did for the novels of Dickens in his "Dickens Dictionary."

Our good books embrace every class in the field of knowledge, but our greatest book is undoubtedly "The Evolution of Love," by Rev. Dr. Emory Miller. This has been called an "epoch making book." That it marks a distinct advance in the history of philosophy is acknowledged by many of the ablest philosophic minds and best informed scholars (in the history of philosophy) of the United States, who hail with profound delight the results of the Doctor's "hard years of thinking," recognizing that he has taken up the grand quest of philosophy—the finding "an ultimate unit of thought and thing" that will account for all variety, where Hegel, having like all his predecessors failed—left it, and that *he* has succeeded.

For convenience of reference, we will, according to the latest approved classification, group the books into nine classes without subdivision, except in 3 and 8, as follows: 1, Philosophy; 2, Religion; 3, Sociology; 4, Philology; 5, Natural Science; 6, Useful Arts; 7, Fine Arts; 8, Literature; 9, History, including Biography, Geography and Travels.

### I. PHILOSOPHY, MENTAL AND MORAL.

In philosophy there are, as far as we know, twenty books. We mention the following:

Miller, Emory, D. D., LL. D., The Evolution of Love. 346 p. 12° Chic., 1892.
Patrick, *Prof.* G. T. W. Fragments of the Work of Heraclitus of Ephesus, on Nature. Translated from the Greek text of Bywater, with an introduction, historical and critical. 131 p., 8° Balto., 1889.
Salter, W. Macintosh. Ethical Religion. Phila., 1892.
    First Steps in Philosophy. Phila. 1889.
    Die Religion der Moral. Tr. into German by Prof. Dr.] George Von Gyzicki of the University of Berlin. 358 p., Leipzig, 1885.
    Moralische Reder. Tr. same as above, 93 p., Leipz., 1889.
    Zedelyke, Relige. Tr. into Dutch by Rev. P. H. Huganholtz, Trs. of Amsterdam. 277 p., Amsterdam, 1888.

NOTE. Many of Mr. Salter's lectures are translated into French.
Welch, *Dr.* A. S. Talks on Psychology. N. Y., 1889.
Wood, *Rev.* Stephen. Physics and Metaphysics, in the Light of the New Philosophy. 67 p., 8°, Chic. 1884.

II. RELIGION.

NOTE. In this class there are so many good books which have been widely circulated in the denominations to which the authors belong that it is difficult to select the few to fill the allotted space; therefore popular books may be omitted, from necessity. There are about two hundred religious books of Iowa authorship.

Adams, *Rev.* Ephraim The Iowa Band. A History of Early Congregationalism in Iowa. 184 p., 12°, Bost., 1870.
Archibald, *Rev.* Andrew The Bible Verified. New ed., 252 p., 16° Phila., 1892.
  Same in Spanish.
Blair, *Eld.* W. W. Joseph the Seer. 208 p., 16°, Lamoni, 1889.
Carpenter, *Rev.* G. T. The Bible vs. Spiritualism. 107 p., 16°, Oskaloosa, 1870.
Dunn, *Rev.* L. A. Foot-prints of the Redeemer in the Holy Land. 308 p., 12°, D. M., 1880.
Ells, Eliza Truth Made Manifest. 391 p., 12°, Lamoni, 1891.
Fox, *Mrs.* Nettie Pease. Mysteries of the Border Land. 536 p., 12°, Ottumwa, 1883.
Hallock, *Mrs.* M. A. The Story of Moses il., 246 p., Phila., 1889.
Hattlestadt, *Rev.* O. S. Historiske Meddelelser om den Norske Augustana Synode i America. 264 p., 16°, Decorah, 1887.
Herron, *Rev.* G. D. A Plea for the Gospel. 108 p., 16°, N. Y., 1892.
  The Larger Christ. il., 122 p., 16°, Chic., 1891.
Hofer, Andrea. The Christ Child. 12°, Chic., 1892.
Johnson, *Rev.* B. A. Vision of the Age, or Lectures on the Apocalypse. 360 p., 12°, St. Louis.
Kempker, J. F. History of the Catholic Church in Iowa. 64 p., 16°, unb., I. C., 1886.
Lambert, *Eld.* J. R. What is Man? 249 p., 24°, Lamoni. 1891.
Magoun, H. W. The Asuri—Kalpa. A Witchcraft Practice of the Atharva-Veda. 33 p., 8°, Balto., 1889.
"Manuscript Found," or Manuscript Story of the Late Rev. Solomon Spaulding. 144 p., 16°, Lamoni, 1885.
Mikkelsen, *Rev.* A. Nogle af en Prests Erfaringer. 347 p., 12°, Decorah, 1893.
Mitchell, *Rev.* S. H. Historical Sketches of Iowa Baptists. 504 p., 8°, Burl., 1886.
Perkins, *Prof.* W. R. Trappists of Melleray.
Perry, *Rt. Rev.* W: Stevens. Historical Collections of the American Colonial Church. (And some seventy other books.)
Taylor, *Rev.* Landon The Battlefield Reviewed. 375 p., 12°, Chic., 1881.
Wulfsberg, *Rev.* E. Praedikener over Kirke-Aarets Evangelier. 728 p., 9°, Decorah, 1888.

A HOME ON THE CREST OF IOWA—RESIDENCE OF S. H. MALLORY, NEAR CHARITON.

### III. SOCIOLOGY.

NOTE. Under this head the sub-divisions Education and Law are given. There are about sixty-five books in this class and sixty in education, while the law claims about seventy titles, exclusive of supreme court reports, etc.

Ashby, N. B. Riddle of the Sphinx. 474 p., 8°, D. M., 1890.
    Wealth and Civilization. 293 p., 12°, Chic., 1891.
Baker, E. P. The Money Monopoly. 189 p., 16°, D. M., 1892.
Baylies, Nicholas. Political Controversy Between the United States and Great Britain. 196 p., 12°, D. M., 1885.
Brown, Leonard. Pending Conflict. 144 p., 8°, D. M., 1890.
    Rights of Labor. 68 p, D. M., 1875.
Cloud, D. C. Monopolies and the People. 462 p., 8°, Davenport, 1873.
Dean, H. Clay. Crimes of the Civil War, and Curse of the Funding System. 512 p., 8°, Balto., 1868.
Duryea, J. B. Business of Banking and Commercial Credits. Ed. 2, 423, p., 8°, D. M., 1892.
Gibbons, J. Tenure and Toil. 316 p., 16°, Phila., 1888.
Macy, *Prof.* Jesse Our Government; How It Grew, What It Does, and How It Does It. Rev. Ed. 296 p., 16°, Bost., 1890.
Miller, *Dr.* Ign. Communism. 24 p., *pam.*
Price, Hiram. Speeches and Letters. 399 p., 8°. Wash., 1889.
Van Valkenberg, J. Knights of Pythias Manual and Text Book. 502 p., 12°, Canton, O. 1889.

### III. SOCIOLOGY. EDUCATION.

Bell, Hill M. Rhetoric Book for the Use of Students. sq. 8°, 1891.
Blakeslee, *Prof.* T. M. Academic Trigonometry, Plane and Spherical Chart. 35 p., 16°, Bost., 1888.
Ensign *Prof.* Laura Outlines, Tables and Sketches in United States History. 82 p., 16°, Chic., 1885.
Gates, *Pres.* G. A. Iowa College—Baccalaureate Sermons, 1887, '89 '91.
Kratz, *Prof.* H. Naturalism in Pedagogy, *pam.*
King, *Rev.* W. F. Cornell College—Baccalaureate Sermons, 1883, '88.
Macy, *Prof.* Sherman R. Outline Course of Theoretical Pharmacy. 127 p., 24°, D. M., 1891.
Morris, R. Anna Physical Education, 192 p., 11°, Chic., 1892.
Parish, *Prof.* L. W. Analysis of Compayres Pedagogy. 105 p., 16°, C. F. 1892.
Scott, *Dr.* C. Etymological Outlines of the Elements of Physiology and Anatomy. 92 p., 24°, 1890.
Shoup, *Prof.* W. J. Graded Didactics, 2v. 12°, Chic., 1889.
    History and Science of Education. 303 p., 12°, Chic., 1891.
Thompson, Albert H. Examiner's Companion. 380 p., 12°, Chic., 1890.
Throndsen, K. Norske Laesebog. 2v. Decorah, 1892.
Warman, *Prof.* E. B. How to Read, Recite and Impersonate.
    Gestures and Attitudes; An Exposition of the Delsarte Philosophy. 416 p., 8°, Chic., 1892.
    Physical Training; or the Care of the Body. 190 p., 12°, 1890.

Welch, W. N. How to Organize, Classify and Teach a Country School. 107 p., 12°, Chic., 1886.
Ylvisaker, *Rev.* Joh. Norwegian Luther College, Decorah, Iowa. History from 1861 to 1890. 68 p., ob. 12°, Decorah, 1890.
*Same* in Norwegian.

### III. SOCIOLOGY. LAW.

Baker, Andrew J. Annotated Constitution of the United States. Chic., 1892.
Brown, Timothy Commentaries on the Jurisdiction of Courts. 8°, Chic., 1891.
Dillon, *Judge* J: F. Law of Municipal Bonds. 8°, St. L., 1876.
　Removal of Causes from State to Federal Courts. Ed. 1, 2, 3, 4 and 5, St. L., 1876, '79.
　Treatise on the Law of Municipal Corporations. Ed. 1, 2, 3 and 4, 1872 '90.
Field, G. W. Doctrine of Ultra Vires. 8°, D. M. 1881.
　Lawyers' Briefs. 6v., 8°, Phila., 1884, '86.
　Treatise on the Law of Damages. 8°, D. M. 1876.
Kinne, *Judge*, G. L. Pleading, Practice and Forms. 8°' Chic., 1888.
Lacey, J. F. Digest of Railway decisions. 2v., 8°, Chic., 1875.
McClain, *Prof.* Emlin Annotated Code and Statutes of Iowa. 2v., 8°, Chic., 1888.
McCrary, G. W. American Law of Elections. Ed. 2 and 3, 1880-1887.
Miller, *Justice* Samuel F. Constitution of the United States; Three Lectures before the University Law School of Washington. 8°, Wash., 1880.
　Biographies of the Judges of the United States Supreme Court. Rev. ed. D. M., 1875.
Miller, *Judge* W. E. Probate, Law and Practice in Iowa. 8°, D. M., 1890.
　Revised Annotated Code of Iowa. 2 v, 8°, D. M., 1890.
　Treatise on Pleading and Practice in the Courts of Iowa Under the Code. Rev. ed. 8°, D. M., 1875.
Rorer, *Judge* David American Inter-State Law. Ed. 2, 8°, Chic., 1878.
　Law of Railways. 2v. 8°, Chic., 1884.
Shiras, *Judge* O. P. Equity Practice in the United States Courts. 12°, Chic., 1889.
Withrow, T. F. *Ed.* American Corporation Cases. 4v. N. Y.

### IV. PHILOLOGY.

NOTE. So far as ascertained, thirty titles comprise the books in Philology.

Bell, *Prof.* Hill M. Orthoepy and Orthography. D. M., 1892.
Currier, *Prof.* Amos N. Table of Latin Suffixes and a Table of Prefixes. 1889.
Ely, *Prof.* E. H. Latin in the Public Schools. pam.
Pollard, *Mrs.* Rebecca S. Manual of Synthetic Reading. 217 p., 8°, Chic., 1892.
Shoup, *Prof.* W. J. Graded Speller. St. Paul, 1888.

Warman, *Prof.* E. B. Practical Orthoepy. Chic., 1889.
Wright, *Prof.* D. Sands Drill Book in English Grammar. 16°, Chic., 1887.

### V. NATURAL SCIENCE.

NOTE. Our catalogue contains seventy-five titles: there are probably one hundred.

Bennett, *Prof.* A. A. Inorganic Chemistry. Pt. 1, 357 p., 16°, B., N. Y. and Chic., 1892.
Bessey, *Prof.* C. E. The Essentials of Botany. N. Y., 1889.
Call, *Prof.* R. Ellsworth Annual Report of the Geological Survey of Arkansas. 1889. v2, 283 p., 8°, L. R. 1891.
    Artesian Wells in Iowa, Sketch of the Physical Geography of Iowa (and many other valuable papers).
McGee, *Prof.* W. J. Pleistocene History of Northeastern Iowa. From the 11th Report of the United States Geo. Survey, 1889-90. 568 p., f°, Wash., 1791. (And a great many valuable monographs).
McLennan, Evan. Cosmical Evolution. 12°, Chic., 1891.
Macomber, S. K. Matter and Force. 93 p., 16°, Ames, 1876.
Matthews, *Dr.* Washington On Composite Photography as Applied to Craniology. pls. 4°, Wash.
    Ethnography and Philology of the Hidatsa Indians. 239 p., 8°, Wash., 1877.
Wacksmuth, C: and Frank Springer. Revision of the Palaeocrinoidea. pts. 1 and 2, and pt. 3 of Sections 1 and 2. 8°, Phila., 1879-1886.
White, C. A. Report of the Geological Survey of Iowa. 1870. 2v., 8°, D. M., 1870.

### VI. USEFUL ARTS.

Sixty books and pamphlets.
Anderson, Nellie Van The Right Knock. 316 p., 16°, Chic., 1889.
Carpenter, C. C. Instructions to Surveyors. 129 p., 12°, D. M., 1870.
Cleaves, *Dr.* Margaret A. Colony of the Insane at Gheel, Belgium, 1891.
    Medical and Moral Care of Female Patients in Hospitals for the Insane. 1879.
Clute, Oscar (*John Allen*) The Blessed Bees. 172 p., 16°, N. Y., 1878.
Davis, *Prof.* Floyd Potable Water. 118 p., 12°, B., N. Y. and Chic., 1891.
Dodge, *Gen.* G. M. Union Pacific Railroad; Reports of the Chief Engineer for 1867, '68, '80.
Eaton, *Dr.* C. W. Things Young Men Should Know. 584, 187 p., D. M., 1884.
Goodyear, S. H. Theory of Accounts. 228 p., 8°, C, R. 1890.
Hutchinson, *Dr.* Woods *Ed.* Vis Medicatrix. D. M., 1891.
Scott, *Mrs.* Mary Indian Corn as Human Food. 16°, Nevada, 1891.

### VII. FINE ARTS.

Twenty titles, not including sheet music.
Bartlett, *Prof.* M. L. Class and Chorus. 176 p., 8°, Chic., 1890.
Dinsmore, G. A. Old Violins.
Dunham, *Prof.* J. R. The Banner. 160 p., ob. 16°, Chic., 1886.
Forscutt, Mark *Ed.* Saints Harmony. 565 p., 4°, Lamoni, 1889.

Leffingwell, W. Bruce  Shooting on Upland, Marsh and Stream. 437 p., 8°, Chic. and N. Y., 1890.
  Wild Fowl Shooting. 373 p., 8°, Chic., 1890.
Parker, Rev. H. W.  The Spirit of Beauty.  Essays, Scientific and Esthetic. Ed 2, 252 p., 12°, N. Y., 1891.
Psalmabog for den Norske Evangelisk Luteriske Kirke i Amerike. 292 p., 16°, Decorah, 1877.
Randall, R. H.  Bethel Chimes.  144 p., 12°, Marion, Iowa, 1891.
Taylor, Virgil C.  The Enchanter.  176 p., N. Y., 1864.
Woolett. J.  Songs.  The Autumn Time; Bring Sweet Flowers; Home of Our Fathers; and My Maude.

### VIII. LITERATURE.

Thirty books.

NOTE. This class is divided into general and miscellaneous, poetry and fiction.

Anderson, L. J. and Nellie V.  Every Day Helps.  24°, Chic., 1890.
Burdett, Robert J.  Rise and Fall of the Mustache.  (humorous).
Davidson, C.  Studies in the English Mystery Plays.  173 p., 8°, unb., 1892.
Folsom, Moses  Treasures of Science, History and Literature.  8°, 1876.
Jones, Prof. R.  Literature as a Means of Culture.  65 p., 16°, unb.
Rogers, May.  The Waverley Dictionary.  12°, Chic., 1885.
Springer, J:  The Caxton Reproductions, with the Early Press of Iowa. C. 1880.
Throndsen, R.  Skolelaereren og hans Son.  112 p., 12°, Decorah, 1886.
Wilkie, Frank B.  Davenport, Past and Present.
Wynn, Rev. W. H.  Addresses and Reviews.  12°, n. t. p., n. d.

### VIII. LITERATURE. POETRY.

Sixty-five books.

Boylan, Will M.  Life's Purest Gold.  8°, Eldora, 1889.
Butz, Caspar.  Gedichte eines Deutch-Amerikaners.  8°, 312 p., Chic., 1879.
Byers, S. H. M.  Happy Isles and other poems.  162 p., Ed. 2, N. Y. 1891.
Collier, Mrs. Ada L.  Lilith, The legend of the First Woman.  104 p., 16°, Bost., 1885.
Crofts, Rev. G. W.  Golden Rod.  207 p., 12°, Omaha, 1889.
Fearing, Lilian Blanch.  City by the Lake.  192 p., Chic., 1892.
Frisbie, Rev. A. L.  The Siege of Calais and other poems.  166 p., 16°, D. M., 1880.
Gonner, NS.  Prairieblummen.  166 p., 8°, Dubuque, 1883.
Judd, Rev. T. E.  The Owls.  143 p., 8°, Marshalltown, 1889.
McCreery, J. L.  Songs of Toil and Triumph.  143 p., 16°, N. Y., 1883
Manning, Jessie Wilson.  Passion of Life.  75 p., 16°, Cin., 1837.
Osmund, Rev. S. McClurg.  Sulamith.  211 p., 12°, Phila., 1892.
Parkhurst, Clint.  Poems.  153 p., 16°, Chic., 1874.
Percival, Rev. C. S.  Poetic Parallels and Simile in Song.  162 p., 13° Cleve., 1892.
Pierson, Johnson.  The Judaid.  267 p., 12°, 1842.
Richman, DeWitt C.  The Talisman and other poems.  152 p., 12°, Muscatine, 1867.

Smith, *Mrs.* D. (*Maude Meredith.*) The Rivulet and Clover Blooms. 75 p., 24°, N. Y. and Chic., 1881.
Throndsen, K. Orkenblomster. 240 p., 24°, Decorah, 1890.

### VIII. LITERATURE. FICTION-

One hundred books.

Anderson, Nellie Van. It is possible. Chic., 1891.
Baldwin, *Mrs.* Mary R. Along the Anataw. N. Y., 1891.
    Around Bronton. N. Y., 1891.
Claggett, Sue Harry. Her Lovers. Phila., 1877.
French, *Miss* Alice, (*Octave Thanet.*) Expiation. N. Y., 1892.
    Knitters in the Sun. B. and N. Y., 1892.
    Otto the Knight, and other trans-Missippi Stories. B. and N. Y., 1891.
    We All. N. Y. 1891.
Garland, Hamlin. Jason Edwards. B., 1892.
    Main Travelled Roads. B., 1892. ;
Harbet, Lizzie Boynton. Amore. Chic., 1892.
    Out of Her Sphere. D. M., 1871.
Leffingwell, W. Bruce. Manulito; or a Strange Friendship. Phila., 1892.
Smith, *Mrs.* D. (*Maude Meredith.*) The Parson's Sin. Chic., 1892.
Vittum, *Rev.* Edw. M. Head of the Firm. Bost., 1891.
Wetmore, *Mrs.* Mai M. (*Oaks.*) Wee Folks in No-Man's Land. Chic., 1893.

### IX. HISTORY.

Including Biography, Geography and Travels. One hundred books exclusive of County histories.

Aldrich, C., *Ed.* Life and Times of A. B. F. Hildreth. 556 p., 12°, D. M., 1891.
Baylies, Nicholas. Life of General Eleazer Wheelock Ripley of the War of 1812. 12°, D. M., 1890.
Burrows, J. M. D. Fifty Years in Iowa. 16°, Dav., 1888.
Byers, S. H. M. Iowa in War Times. 615 p., 8°, D. M., 1888.
Chapin, *Mrs.* Nettie S. American Court Gossip; or Life at the National Capitol. 269 p., 13°, Marshalltown, 1877.
Clark, *Capt.* J. S. Thirty-Fourth Iowa Regiment. Breif history.
Crooke, *Adj.* G. Twenty-First Regiment of Iowa Volunteer Infantry. 282 p., 8°, Milwaukee, 1892.
Fuller, C. E. Reminisences of James A. Garfield. 441 p., 8°, Cin., 1886.
Fulton, A. R. Notes of the Northwest. 255 p., 8°, D. M., 1878.
    Red Men of Iowa. Il. 559 p., 8° D. M., 1882.
Grinnell, Josiah B. Men and Events of Forty Years. 426 p., 8°, Chic., 1891.
Ingersoll, L. D. History of the War Department. 613 p., 8°, Wash., 1880.
Landers, Frank E. Historical Geographical Atlas of the U. S. A., from the Earliest Colonial Days to the present time. F°, 1889.
Lathrop, *Dr.* C. H. History of the First Iowa Volunteer Cavalry. 231 p., Milwaukee, 1891.
Nourse, C. C. Iowa and the Centennial. 42 p., 12°, D. M., 1876.
Perkins, *Prof.* W. R. History of the Amana Society. 94 p., 8°, 1891. *Pam.*
Reid, Harvey. Biographical Sketch of Enoch Long. 184 p., 8°, Chic., 1884.
Richardson, D. N. Girdle Round the Earth. 451 p., 8°, Chic., 1890.

Rouse, *Mrs.* Clara B. Iowa Leaves. Six chapters. 451 p., 12°, Chic., 1891.
Salter, *Rev.* W. Life of James W. Grimes, Governor of Iowa, 1854-58. A Senator of the U. S. 398 p., 8°, N. Y., 1876.
Augustus C. Dodge, Senator of the U. S. from Iowa. 88 p., 8°, I. C., 1887.
Columbian Calendar, the Voyage of Christopher Columbus from the third day of August to the Discovery of America, A. D. 1492. Burl., 1892.
Sharp, Abbie Gardner. History of the Spirit Lake Massacre. 316 p., 12°, D. M., 1885.

## IOWA AND PATRIOTISM.

When the permanent settlement of Iowa opened, after the Indian war of 1832, the contentions regarding negro slavery, that finally culminated in the civil war which overthrew that institution, had began to agitate the country. The Missouri Compromise, adopted as a settlement of the slavery question in 1821, was, when the pioneers crossed the river in 1833 to found a permanent settlement at Dubuque, in its most vital force. By its provisions the area forming this State was consecrated to freedom. Yet under its territorial government a few slaves were held in Iowa, sixteen according to the National Census of 1840, being held within its borders. Ultimate freedom from slavery was however fully assured to this region. Immigrants from the New England states flocked to this new field bringing with them as one of their chief possessions, an intelligent patriotism, a legacy of patriotic sires, who stood bravely for freedom at Lexington, Bennington, and Bunker Hill. Other settlers coming from the central and eastern states to this free western country to establish a new commonwealth, brought with them a hearty affinity with that spirit. Others coming from the then slave-cursed south, came to enjoy a deliverance from the scenes and associations of that oppression. They believed that all men were endowed equally by the Creator, with the right to their own muscle, bone and mental powers, and with equal rights to free volition and action in the pursuit of happiness. When a National Administration, to maintain its party dominancy, consented to aid in the extension of the institution of slavery by the repeal of the Compromise that had, from its enactment, been regarded as a perpetual guaranty of freedom, to the great Northwestern portion of the country, the people of Iowa cast a decisive majority vote on the platform declaring, "We most unqualifiedly and emphatically disapprove of the efforts now being made in Congress to legislate slavery into the territory of Nebraska." The next year they declared by the largest majority the State had ever cast, down to that time, "That under the constitution and by right, freedom alone is national." They then believed that the broadest possible individual freedom was essential to the true happiness of the people, and the real prosperity of the State. They claimed civic freedom for themselves and their posterity, and patriotically gave voice and vote, that others, settling new territories throughout this broad west, should enjoy these same heaven-bequeathed advantages. Inspirations of the noblest patriotism determined the lines of development that have made Iowa, in its brief history, not only one of the freest and progressive but also one of the most orderly States of the Union.

When in April, 1861, the stirring message that rebel hosts assailing Fort Sumpter, had compelled the striking of the National banner to the Palmetto flag, and the proclamation of Mr. Lincoln summoned the states to send armed men to maintain the national authority and repossess the national government of its property, the citizens of no one of the twenty-four loyal states were more earnest in patriotic determination and deed than were the people of this state. The sturdy, patriotic, Kirkwood, Marylander by birth, was then governor. With the hearty approval of the people he at once proceeded to fill the quota of troops then called for from the young state. No one of the loyal states responded more earnestly. The uprisings on the Patapsco and Potomac, cut him off for some days from communication with the national authorities, but the patriotism of the people precluded any dallying with doubtful questions. Governor Kirkwood, with their hearty approval, proceeded at once to raise the quota of troops, which telegrams, flashing through the country, announced that the general government was calling into the field, without waiting to receive the official notice sent out by the Secretary of War.

Governor Kirkwood took early steps to call the General Assembly to meet in Extraordinary Session. Responding to his call that body convened May 16, 1861,—but one month after the surrender of Ft. Sumpter. In his message to that body he said:

"In this emergency Iowa must not and does not occupy a doubtful position. For the Union as our fathers formed it, and for the Government founded so wisely and so well, the people of Iowa are ready to pledge every fighting man in the State, and every dollar of her money and credit, and I have called you together in Extraordinary Session for the purpose of enabling them to make that pledge formal and effective."

In that message Governor Kirkwood further informed the people that he was met at the outset by two difficulties. First. The State treasury was empty, there were no funds under his control to meet the necessary expenses of transportation and providing uniforms and other requisites for the troops volunteering to meet the call. Second. "There was no efficient military law under which to operate."

The first difficulty was obviated by the patriotic action of chartered banks and wealthy citizens of the State, who placed at his disposal, all the money the State authorities might need. Governor Kirkwood informed the General Assembly that he "determined although without authority of law, to accept their offer," trusting that that body would legalize his acts. He did not trust its patriotism in vain.

The Secretary of War asked that the troops be in readiness to proceed to the field by the 20th of May. The wise and patriotic action of the people, Governor Kirkwood informed the General Assembly enabled him "to place them in uniform on the eighth instant, twelve days in advance of the time named by the national authorities." He also stated "that they would have been there a week sooner had not the mob at Baltimore cut off all communications with the government and left him without instructions for two weeks."

The patriotism of the people brought out more people than the call required and a second regiment was placed in camp in anticipation of a second call. Gov. Kirkwood stated in his message that he had received a "tender of troops to form five full regiments when only one had been called for by the national authorities."

The people of no State were more patriotic or truly loyal or devoted to maintenance of the Union of the States than were the people of Iowa in that terrible conflict. Her citizen soldiery toiled in almost every march, fought in almost every battle, and bravely fell everywhere at the front. Her generals from her shops and corn fields made honorable history and won renown on many fields. No spot nor stain tarnished the honor of Iowa in that terrible trial. With Lyon at Wilson Creek; Curtis in the Ozarks; with Banks on the Red River; with Steele in Arkansas; Thomas at Chickamauga, on the Chattanooga; in Sherman's march to the sea; the struggle through the swamps of the Carolinas; with Sheridan at Cedar Creek; Sherman and Grant at Vicksburg; Rosecrans at Murfreesboro, and Sherman at Bentonville, the courage and patriotism of the soldiers of Iowa were nobly attested, and none had better right to share in the pageant of the grand review. Forty-nine regiments of infantry (forty-eight of white troops and one colored), nine regiments and two extra companies of cavalry and four batteries of artillery were enrolled in the patriotic force,—a total of 56,364 men in duly organized and reported Iowa troops, while there were 19,155 enlistments of Iowa men in regiments in other states, making a grand army of 75,519 men enrolled, being one for each ten persons of her population at the close of the grim struggle. Of the troops reported in Iowa organizations 3,360 were killed or died of wounds received in battle, while 8,810 died of disease or fell by accident. Iowa's part in the conflict for perpetual, national unity in a redeemed country was costly in precious lives. Her homes were made sad by the sorrows of war, but her people faltered not when called to its stern duty; her sons freely going to their country's summons. The draft wheel made but few turns to secure her quotas.

When the rebellion terminated by the surrenders of Appomattox and Durham Station, Iowa citizen soldiery were too patriotic to be resentful and too intelligent to refrain from peaceful industry. Recognizing those who, but the preceding day they fought in the war as rebels, in that day of proclaimed peace as friends, they recognized them then as citizens of one country, having mutual interests to be promoted by perpetual unity in its perfected freedom, the highest devolopment of which was to be achieved by the united intelligence of a citizenship having mutual and equal rights to freedom and happiness. Under such patriotic inspirations Iowa has made her unexampled progress.

Situated in the central region of the grand constellation of States, Iowa favors their perpetual union. Her intelligent citizens regard each star with equal respect. In the national parliamentary halls her citizens have won honor; in the highest judicial chambers her citizens have gained honored name; in the high duties of cabinet councils and diplomatic offices her sons have rendered distinguished service. Exalting the fatherhood of God and the brotherhood of man, she recognizes each of her citizens as having equal rights to life, liberty, the advantages of her schools and the protection of her government.

## IOWA AND ART.

In the difficulties and privations inevitable in the formation of a new state, the improvement of a new country and the accomplishment of the work necessary to be done in the construction of homes, roads, churches, schools and all the other public and private institutions necessary in the construction of a new commonwealth, so large in area as Iowa, and in the brief period of only sixty-three years in which this vast work has been done, it should not be a source of serious alarm if the attention of its people should be directed more to matters merely material than to such things as have only relation to taste, or the study of the beautiful.

The people of Iowa, however, in the pressure of the material matters which have directly and necessarily concerned them, have not been unconcerned about the arts. Nature filled the surroundings of their homes with bloom and beauty, and esthetical tastes were incited by the loveliness and grandeur of these broad landscapes that Natures artists painted in gold and pearl.

Our people have been liberal patrons of the liberal and fine arts. We may not in our brief history have produced great masters, but that our accomplishments and creations have been respectable is well known. In music our bands have won respectful recognition in distant states and cities. In sculpture, architecture, and painting we have furnished names that are well known. The name of Mrs. Ketchum will by her works in sculpture and architecture be long perpetuated. The country that gave to the world the "Swedish Nightingale" had gained world-wide fame by its deeds of military heroism before Iowa was discovered, but in its longer history it has produced but one Jennie Lind. The names of England's great military heroes, statesmen, navigators and scientists are multitudinous, the list of her names great in architecture, sculpture and painting is brief.

The history of the pioneer days in Iowa is made. Her public schools, her colleges and her universities are now planted on enduring foundations. Her schools of art are passing from infantile condition, their patronage is respectable, and the "science of the beautiful" receives respectful attention. The work of Iowa artists has place in the Columbian Exposition. In the Woman's building their beautiful creations have place. In the Iowa building there is a very inviting exhibition.

During the past year a State Art Association was formed with a membership respectable in numbers and accomplishments. Its annual meetings will inspire an honorable enthusiasm in esthetical study.

## IOWA AND WORLD'S FAIRS.

### THE CENTENNIAL.

The first effort made by this state to present its resources in a world's Exposition was made in the Philadelphia Exposition, the Centennial of 1876. The Fifteenth General Assembly met in January, 1874, and adjourned in March following, but took no action looking toward an exhibit of the resources of the state in the then pending Exposition. In the summer of 1875 fuller information regarding that Exposition having been disseminated, the people became interested in the improvement of that opportunity to present their resources, accomplishments and possibilities to the knowledge of the nations: To effect this purpose a voluntary organization of citizens was effected, which gave time and means to raise the necessary material and money to secure a creditable presentation of the industries, agricultural, and mineral resources and educational advantages and facilities of Iowa therein. The Sixteenth General Assembly, convening in January preceding the opening of the Exposition in May, appropriated $20,000 for an exhibit, and provided for a commission to take the matter in charge. The citizens' organization then turned the means it had raised and the material it had gathered over to the state commission, and an exhibit of the resources, soils, products and educational work of the state was made that won it great favor. The display of the soils of Iowa made in glass tubes six inches in diameter and showing the soil as it was taken from the ground to the depth of six feet, was unique and being true to the natural condition attracted great attention. The exhibits of Iowa fruits, which won high awards, and the exhibit of dairy products taking the highest prizes won, honors that proved of great financial advantage to Iowa, opening a wide and ready market for her fruit and dairy products that had previously been unknown in distant markets. The efforts in that exposition resulted in great advantage to the state,

### THE WORLD'S INDUSTRIAL AND COTTON CENTENNIAL.

In February, 1893, the Congress of the United States took action to constitute an International Exposition of the resources, industries, productions, arts and accomplishments, especially of the north, Central and South American States; they each being especially invited to unite therein. This Exposition was opened in the City of New Orleans, in December, 1884. The exhibit that Iowa there made was gathered, installed and managed solely by private enterprise, the state authorities making no appropriation to assist in the work. On the recommendation of Governor Sherman, the President appointed Mr. H. S. Fairall, of Iowa City, Commissioner for the state. An Iowa Commission was also formed by voluntary organization, Governor Sherman being President.

In the Horticultural department of this Exposition Iowa made a most commendable display. Her fine show of pomaceous fruits won a gold medal and the first prize of $200 for the largest and best display of apples, not exceeding two hundred varieties, and gaining twelve other valuable premiums. This state also won twenty-two first premiums in its agricultural display. In the Dairy department Iowa carried off the honors, making the largest display of butter ever exhibited up to that time by any state at any dairy fair or exposition, and winning the highest premiums.

In the department of Education an exhibit was made under the supervision of Hon. J. W. Akers, State Superintendent of Public Instruction, presenting the work of our public school system. It was representative, comprehensive and complete, and placed Iowa in the foremost rank; thirty-nine honorable awards being won by her educational exhibit in that exposition.

The plans of the Commission were greatly frustrated by a railroad wreck which occurred on the Burlington, Cedar Rapids and Northern railway, in which a large portion of the material intended for the exhibit was totally destroyed, many articles being utterly ruined, the principal portion being damaged beyond use. The accident was costly to the state in the results of the Exposition, as the lateness of the season at which it occurred, to a large degree, precluded replacing the articles damaged or destroyed; the wreck occurred December 1st, 1884.

At the Exposition of 1889, at Paris, Iowa was represented by a few exhibits, a full report of which was made to Governor Larrabee by Commissioner James O. Crosby. Two gold medals were awarded. One to the state of Iowa for an exhibit of its school system made by Hon. Henry Sabin, State Superintendent of Public Instruction. The other was for Hall's Report of the Geological Survey of Iowa, exhibited by a son of the author.

## IOWA IN THE COLUMBIAN EXPOSITION.

In April, 1890, the Twenty-third General Assembly of this state took action to provide for an exhibit of its agricultural, mineral, mechanical, industrial, educational, and other resources in the World's Columbian Exposition. Iowa was the first of the states of the Union to take action providing for an exhibition therein.

Its Legislative Assembly, meeting only biennialy, was in session when the National Congress was considering the matter of providing for the Exposition. When the lower house in that body passed its measure for making provision for the great Fair, our General Assembly was on the eve of closing its session. It was evident that the National Senate would enact the House bill into law. If Iowa should make an exhibit of her resources in the contemplated Exposition, under the auspices of state authority, it was necessary that immediate action should be taken, as that body would not again convene until January, 1892, a short time before the opening of the Fair if it should be held, as was then proposed, in 1892. Under these circumstances the Legislature, taking hasty action in the premises, enacted the following measure which was approved by the Governor ten days before the National enactment was approved by the President:

AN ACT to Provide for a Creditable Exhibit of the Resources of the State of Iowa in the "Columbian Exposition" or the World's Fair, to be held in Chicago.

WHEREAS, Congress is now considering, and the House of Representatives has already passed a bill, providing for a World's Fair, to be known as the "Columbian Exposition," and held at Chicago during the year 1892 or 1893; and

WHEREAS, It is highly desirable that the agricultural, mineral, mechanical, industrial, educational and other resources and advantages of the State of Iowa shall be creditably represented in such exposition, therefore

*Be it Enacted by the General Assembly of the State of Iowa:*

SECTION 1. That the Executive Council be and is hereby authorized and directed to appoint an exhibition committee to be known as the "Iowa Columbian Commission." Such commission shall consist of eleven members, to be selected one from each congressional district in the State, not more than six of whom shall be from the same political party, and shall have full power to devise and execute plans for the State Exhibit herein contemplated, take charge of the same and disburse the appropriations. It may appoint such officers as in its judgment may be necessary for carrying out this act, including the right to delegate to an Executive Committee the duty and power to execute all or any plans that may be devised or ordered by such Commission. One member thereof shall be chosen to act as Treasurer, and he shall be (*ex-officio*) custodian of the moneys herein appropriated; but before entering upon the duties of such position he shall furnish a bond, subject to the approval of the Executive Council, and running to State of Iowa in the penal sum equaling amount herein appropriated. If the said "Columbian Exposition" is held during the year 1892, the Commission created by this section shall be appointed at some time prior to January 1st, 1892. Any vacancy occurring in said Commission shall be filled by the Executive Council by the choice of some citizen residing in the congressional district wherein such vacancy occurs. The Commission herein created shall receive as compensation for the service of its members not to exceed five dollars for each day actually and necessarily engaged in the work of the Commission, and actual railroad fare paid.

SECTION 2. The sum of Fifty Thousand Dollars is hereby appropriated out of any money in the State Treasury not otherwise appropriated, for the purpose of carrying into execution the intent of this act; Provided that, if said Fair or Exposition be not held before 1893, not more than ten per cent. of the sum hereinbefore named shall be drawn from the State Treasury before the convening of the Twenty-fourth General Assembly and the remainder shall be covered back into the Treasury, and the subject of further appropriation shall be referred to the said Twenty-fourth General Assembly; but no part of any such appropriation shall be drawn from the State Treasury until the commission through its duly chosen officers, shall certify to the Auditor of State that the same is actually necessary for disbursement, and shall then be drawn only in portions, not exceeding one-fourth the amount appropriated, as may from time to time become requisite. All payments of money by the Treasurer must be under complete vouchers and under conditions to be fixed by said commission. At the close of its services the commission shall make to the Governor a statement of its proceedings, which shall include a list of all disbursements, with complete vouchers therefor attached. Provided further, no appointments under this act shall be made, nor shall any money herein appropriated be drawn or any charge or expense made until it is definitely known when the exposition is to be held. Provided further, that said commission shall be restricted in expenditures to the amount herein appropriated.

Approved, April 15th, 1890.

In pursuance of this enactment, the Executive Council appointed the following persons to constitute the commission provided by the law:

    First District, Edward Johnstone, of Keokuk.
    Second   "    H. W. Seaman, of Clinton.

Third       "   F. N. Chase, of Cedar Falls.
Fourth      "   James O. Crosby, of Garnavillo.
Fifth       "   James Wilson, of Traer.
Sixth       "   J. W. Jarnagin, of Montezuma.
Seventh     "   Henry Stivers, of Des Moines.
Eighth      "   S. H. Mallory, of Chariton.
Ninth       "   Charles Ashton, of Guthrie Center.
Tenth       "   John F. Duncombe, of Fort Dodge.
Eleventh    "   Wm. H. Dent, of Le Mars.

On the call of the Governor the several appointees met in the capitol, at Des Moines, and having duly qualified, on the second day of September 1890, organized the Commission, elected the following officers, appointed the following committees, and entered upon its work.

*President.*
Edward Johnstone, Keokuk.

*Vice President.*
James Wilson, Traer.

*Secretary.*
F. N. Chase, Cedar Falls.

*Treasurer.*
Wm. H. Dent, Le Mars

*Executive Committee.*
S. H. Mallory, Chariton.
J. W. Jarnagin, Montezuma
J. F. Duncombe, Fort Dodge.

*Auditing Committee.*
James Wilson, Traer.
Henry Stivers, Des Moines.
James O. Crosby, Garnavillo.

*Committee on Rules.*
H. W. Seaman.
Chas. Ashton.
Jas. O. Crosby.

This was one of the first State Commissions organized. It took early action to secure a site for an Iowa State building in the park selected for the Exposition. The act of Congress deciding that the Fair should be held in 1893, left the Commission with only $5,000 at its command prior to an appropriation by the ensuing General Assembly. It proceeded however to form plans and take the necessary preliminary steps to secure such an exhibition of the resources of the State as was contemplated by the act constituting it.

The Twenty-fourth General Assembly enacted the following law, making a final appropriation for the work of the Commission, which was approved by the Governor April 8th, 1892.

AN ACT making appropriation for an exhibit of the resources of the State of Iowa at the World's Columbian Exposition of 1893, to be held in the city of Chicago.

*Be it Enacted by the General Assembly of the State of Iowa:*

SECTION 1. That the sum of One Hundred and Twenty-five Thousand Dollars ($125,000) is hereby appropriated out of any money in the State Treasury, not otherwise appropriated, for the purpose of carrying out the intent of chapter 126 of the acts of the Twenty-third General Assembly, an act entitled, "An act to provide for a creditable exhibit of the resources of the State of Iowa in the Columbian Exposition or World's Fair to be held in Chicago." Said sum hereinbefore named is the whole amount to be used and expended by said Columbian Commission; the unexpended appropriation by the Twenty-third General Assembly being considered as covered into the State Treasury and no longer available for the uses of said Commission.

SECTION 2. No part of the moneys appropriated by this act shall be drawn from the State Treasury until the Commission, through its duly chosen officers, shall certify to the Auditor of State that the same is actually necessary for disbursement at the time requisition is made, *provided*, that not more than sixty (60) per cent of the amount herein appropriated shall be drawn from the State Treasury in the year 1892. *Provided further* that not more than twelve and one-half per cent. of the moneys hereby appropriated shall be expended for salaries and other expenses of employes.

SECTION 3. This act being of immediate importance shall take effect and be in force from and after its publication in the *Iowa State Register* and *Des Moines Leader*, newspapers published in Des Moines, Iowa.

In February, 1891, a vacancy occurred in the Commission by the resignation of Hon. James Wilson, who having been elected to a professorship in the Iowa Agricultural College, found it necessary to resign his place in the body. Hon. S. B. Packard, of Marshalltown, was appointed to fill the vacancy.

In May, 1891, a second vacancy occurred in the body by the death of the Hon. Edward Johnstone, its able and honored President, who departed this life in his seventy-sixth year. He came to Iowa in 1837, and for upward of half a century had occupied high position in social, business and political relations. Hon. Theodore Guelich, of Burlington, was appointed to succeed him.

A third vacancy occurred through the death of Mr. Guelich, January 27th, 1893. This gentleman had proved himself a most useful and respected member of the body. He was succeeded by Dr. A. C. Roberts, of Fort Madison.

The two enactments appropriated a total of $130,000 for the work of the Commission. This body knew the sum to be meager, considering the magnitude of the work in its hands. To secure the best exhibit possible of the resources and accomplishments of the State by the most economical use of the funds appropriated, it reorganized the Commission, elected the following officers, constituted the following committees, and arranged its work in the following departments, which were placed in charge of members of the Commission as follows:

President—James O. Crosby.

Vice-President—John F. Duncombe.

Treasurer—Wm. Hamilton Dent.
Secretary—Frank N. Chase.
Executive Committee—S. H. Mallory, S. B. Packard, H. W. Seaman.
Auditing Committee—Theodore Guelich, S. B. Packard, Henry Stivers.
Archaeological, Historical and Statistical Committee—Charles Ashton, James O. Crosby, J. W. Jarnagin.

### DEPARTMENTS.

A  Live Stock ................................................. S. B. Packard
B  Agricultural and Dairy ................................... F. N. Chase
C  Horticulture .............................................. W. H. Dent
D  Mineral and Geological ............................. John F. Duncombe
E  Press ...................................................... Henry Stivers
F  Woman's Work ........................................ James O. Crosby
G  Manufacturing and Machinery ...................... H. W. Seaman
H  Education and Fine Arts ............................. J. W. Jarnagin
I  Forestry .................................................. Theo. Guelich

After the death of Commissioner Guelich, his successor, Dr. A. C. Roberts, was appointed to fill his place in the department of Forestry.

## POPULATION.

We give the population by counties for each national census taken since the settlement of Iowa:

| COUNTIES. | 1840. | 1850. | 1860. | 1870. | 1880. | 1890. |
|---|---|---|---|---|---|---|
| Adair | | | 984 | 3,982 | 11,667 | 14,534 |
| Adams | | | 1,533 | 4,614 | 11,888 | 12,292 |
| Allamakee | | 777 | 12,237 | 17,868 | 19,791 | 17,907 |
| Appanoose | | 3,131 | 11,931 | 16,456 | 16,636 | 18,961 |
| Audubon | | | 454 | 1,212 | 7,448 | 12,412 |
| Benton | | 672 | 8,496 | 22,454 | 24,888 | 24,178 |
| Black Hawk | | 135 | 8,244 | 21,706 | 23,913 | 24,219 |
| Boone | | 735 | 4,232 | 14,584 | 20,538 | 23,772 |
| Bremer | | | 4,915 | 12,528 | 14,081 | 14,630 |
| Buchanan | | 517 | 7,906 | 17,034 | 18,546 | 18,997 |
| Buena Vista | | | 57 | 1,585 | 7,537 | 18,548 |
| Butler | | | 5,724 | 9,951 | 14,291 | 15,463 |
| Calhoun | | | 147 | 1,602 | 5,595 | 13,107 |
| Carroll | | | 281 | 2,451 | 12,351 | 18,828 |
| Cass | | | 1,612 | 5,464 | 16,943 | 19,645 |
| Cedar | 1,253 | 3,941 | 12,949 | 19,731 | 18,936 | 18,253 |
| Cerro Gordo | | | 940 | 4,722 | 11,461 | 14,864 |
| Cherokee | | | 58 | 1,967 | 8,240 | 15,659 |
| Chickasaw | | | 4,336 | 10,180 | 14,534 | 15,019 |
| Clark | | 79 | 5,427 | 8,735 | 11,513 | 11,332 |
| Clay | | | 52 | 1,523 | 4,248 | 9,309 |
| Clayton | 1,101 | 3,873 | 20,728 | 27,771 | 28,829 | 26,733 |
| Clinton | 821 | 2,822 | 18,938 | 35,357 | 36,763 | 41,199 |
| Crawford | | | 383 | 2,530 | 12,418 | 18,804 |
| Dallas | | 854 | 5,244 | 12,019 | 18,764 | 20,479 |
| Davis | | 7,264 | 13,764 | 15,565 | 16,468 | 15,258 |
| Decatur | | 965 | 8,677 | 12,018 | 15,336 | 15,642 |
| Delaware | 168 | 1,759 | 11,024 | 17,432 | 17,950 | 17,349 |
| Des Moines | 5,577 | 12,988 | 19,611 | 27,256 | 33,099 | 35,894 |
| Dickinson | | | 180 | 1,389 | 1,901 | 4,328 |
| Dubuque | 3,059 | 10,841 | 31,164 | 38,969 | 42,996 | 49,848 |
| Emmet | | | 105 | 1,392 | 1,550 | 4,274 |
| Fayette | | 825 | 12,073 | 16,973 | 22,258 | 23,141 |
| Floyd | | | 3,744 | 10,768 | 14,677 | 15,424 |
| Franklin | | | 1,309 | 4,738 | 10,249 | 12,871 |
| Fremont | | 1,244 | 5,074 | 11,174 | 17,652 | 16,482 |
| Greene | | | 1,374 | 4,627 | 12,727 | 15,797 |
| Grundy | | | 793 | 6,399 | 12,639 | 13,215 |
| Guthrie | | | 3,058 | 7,061 | 14,394 | 17,380 |
| Hamilton | | | 1,699 | 6,055 | 11,252 | 15,319 |
| Hancock | | | 179 | 999 | 8,453 | 7,621 |
| Hardin | | | 5,440 | 13,684 | 17,807 | 19,003 |
| Harrison | | | 3,621 | 8,931 | 16,649 | 21,356 |
| Henry | 3,772 | 8,707 | 18,701 | 21,463 | 20,986 | 18,895 |
| Howard | | | 3,168 | 6,282 | 10,837 | 11,182 |
| Humboldt | | | 332 | 2,596 | 5,341 | 9,836 |
| Ida | | | 43 | 226 | 4,382 | 10,705 |
| Iowa | | 822 | 8,029 | 16,644 | 19,221 | 18,270 |
| Jackson | 1,411 | 7,210 | 18,493 | 22,619 | 23,771 | 22,771 |
| Jasper | | 1,280 | 9,883 | 22,116 | 25,968 | 24,943 |
| Jefferson | 2,773 | 9,904 | 15,038 | 17,839 | 17,463 | 15,184 |
| Johnson | 1,491 | 4,472 | 17,573 | 24,898 | 25,429 | 23,082 |
| Jones | 471 | 2,007 | 13,306 | 19,731 | 21,052 | 20,233 |
| Keokuk | | 4,822 | 13,271 | 19,434 | 21,258 | 18,863 |
| Kossuth | | | 416 | 3,351 | 6,178 | 13,120 |
| Lee | 6,093 | 18,861 | 29,232 | 37,210 | 34,859 | 37,715 |
| Linn | 1,373 | 5,444 | 18,947 | 31,080 | 37,237 | 45,303 |
| Louisa | 1,927 | 4,939 | 10,370 | 12,877 | 13,142 | 11,873 |
| Lucas | | 471 | 5,776 | 10,388 | 14,530 | 14,563 |
| Lyon | | | | 221 | 1,968 | 8,680 |
| Madison | | 1,179 | 7,339 | 13,884 | 17,224 | 15,977 |
| Mahaska | | 5,989 | 14,816 | 22,508 | 25,302 | 28,805 |
| Marion | | 5,482 | 16,813 | 24,436 | 25,111 | 23,058 |
| Marshall | | 338 | 6,015 | 17,576 | 23,752 | 25,842 |
| Mills | | | 4,481 | 8,718 | 14,137 | 14,584 |
| Mitchell | | | 3,409 | 9,582 | 14,363 | 13,299 |
| Monona | | | 832 | 3,654 | 9,055 | 14,515 |
| Monroe | | 2,884 | 8,612 | 12,724 | 13,719 | 13,666 |
| Montgomery | | | 1,256 | 5,934 | 15,859 | 15,848 |
| Muscatine | 1,942 | 5,731 | 16,444 | 21,688 | 23,170 | 24,504 |
| O'Brien | | | 8 | 715 | 4,155 | 13,060 |
| Osceola | | | | | 2,219 | 5,574 |

POPULATION.—CONTINUED.

| COUNTIES. | 1840. | 1850. | 1860. | 1870. | 1880. | 1890. |
|---|---|---|---|---|---|---|
| Page | | 551 | 4,419 | 9,975 | 19,667 | 21,341 |
| Palo Alto | | | 132 | 1,336 | 4,131 | 9,318 |
| Plymouth | | | 148 | 2,199 | 8,566 | 19,568 |
| Pocahontas | | | 103 | 1,446 | 3,713 | 9,553 |
| Polk | | 4,513 | 11,625 | 27,857 | 42,395 | 65,410 |
| Pottawattamie | | 7,828 | 4,968 | 16,893 | 39,850 | 47,430 |
| Poweshelk | | 615 | 5,668 | 15,581 | 18,936 | 18,394 |
| Ringgold | | | 2,923 | 5,691 | 12,085 | 13,556 |
| Sac | | | 246 | 1,411 | 8,774 | 14,521 |
| Scott | 2,140 | 5,968 | 24,959 | 38,599 | 41,266 | 43,164 |
| Shelby | | | 818 | 2,540 | 12,696 | 17,611 |
| Sioux | | | 10 | 576 | 5,426 | 18,370 |
| Story | | | 4,051 | 11,651 | 16,906 | 18,127 |
| Tama | | 8 | 5,285 | 16,131 | 21,585 | 21,651 |
| Taylor | | 204 | 3,590 | 6,989 | 15,635 | 16,384 |
| Union | | | 2,012 | 5,986 | 14,980 | 16,900 |
| Van Buren | 6,146 | 12,270 | 17,081 | 17,672 | 17,043 | 16,253 |
| Wapello | | 8,471 | 14,518 | 22,346 | 25,285 | 30,426 |
| Warren | | 961 | 10,281 | 17,980 | 19,578 | 18,269 |
| Washington | 1,594 | 4,957 | 14,235 | 18,952 | 20,374 | 18,468 |
| Wayne | | 340 | 6,409 | 11,287 | 16,127 | 15,670 |
| Webster | | | 2,504 | 10,484 | 15,951 | 21,582 |
| Winnebago | | | 168 | 1,562 | 4,917 | 7,325 |
| Winneshiek | | 546 | 13,942 | 23,579 | 23,938 | 22,528 |
| Woodbury | | | 1,119 | 6,172 | 14,996 | 55,632 |
| Worth | | | 756 | 2,892 | 7,593 | 9,247 |
| Wright | | | 653 | 2,392 | 5,062 | 12,057 |
| TOTALS | 43,112 | 192,214 | 674,913 | 1,194,020 | 1,624,615 | 1,911,896 |

POPULATION OF IOWA—NATIVITY AND SEX.

As shown by the above table the population of the State in 1890 was 1,911,896. Of this population 324,069, but 17 per cent were persons of foreign birth, while 1,587,827 were born in this country. 994,453 persons in the State were males and 917,343 were females.

## STATE GOVERNMENT AND INSTITUTIONS.

The Iowa territory was separated from the territory of Wisconsin and given a separate territorial organization by act of congress, approved by Martin Van Buren, President, June 12, 1839, who appointed Robert Lucas, a well known democratic statesman of his day, who had served through two terms as Governor of Ohio, Governor of the new territory. The first legislative assembly of the territory convened at Burlington, November 12th, of that year. Two sessions of the territorial legislature of Wisconsin had previously met at Burlington and provided for the organization of sixteen counties west of the Mississippi.

In the political changes resulting from the famous campaign of 1840, John Chambers, whig, of Kentucky, was appointed by President William Henry Harrison. to succeed Governor Lucas. After the presidential election of 1844, President Polk appointed Hon. James Clark to succeed Governor Chambers. Mr. Clark was a Pennsylvanian by birth, learned the printing trade in boyhood, came to Iowa in 1836, and established the second newspaper published in the territory. He was appointed Secretary of the Territory by Martin Van Buren in 1839. By act of congress, approved December 28th, 1846, Iowa was admitted as a State. It had at that time twenty-seven organized counties with a population of nearly 160,000, and the frontier settlements were well advanced toward the Missouri River. Hon. Ansel Briggs was elected Governor of the new State.

The Missouri River being fixed as its western boundary, Iowa City was far east of its center and it was deemed wise to establish the State capital at a point more nearly central in its territory, and the first session of its General Assembly enacted a law providing for the re-location of the seat of government, the capitol building and its site, ten acres of land at Iowa City, being appropriated for the State University. This action ultimately led to the location of the State Capital at Des Moines. The beautiful site of the present fine capitol structure was selected in 1856. The three constitutional conventions in the State were held in Iowa City. The city of Des Moines was declared to be the capital of the State by the proclamation of Governor Grimes, issued October 19, 1857. The old capitol at Iowa City then became the property of the State University. In 1870 the General Assembly made an appropriation and provided for the appointment of a board of commissioners to commence the construction of the present capitol edifice. This board embraced honored names. Governor Samuel Merrill being *ex-officio* its President, Granville M. Dodge of Councill Bluffs, James F. Wilson of Fairfield, James Dawson of Washington, Simon G. Stein of Muscatine, James O. Crosby of Garnavillo, Charles Dudley of Agency City, John N. Dewey of Polk county, and William M. Joy of Woodbury county were its members, with Alexander R. Fulton of Des Moines Secretary. The first Board of Capitol Commissioners was appointed for a term of two years. In making its report to the General Assembly it recommended the reorganization of the board and a reduction of its number to five. The General Assembly enacted a law April 10th, 1872, embodying its suggestions, and Messrs John G. Foote of Burlington, Martin L. Fisher of Farmersburg, Peter A. Dey and R. S. Finkbine of Iowa City, were appointed thereon, the Governor being *ex-officio* its President. The new board elected A. H. Piquenard, of Springfield, Illinois, Architect, General Ed. Wright its Secretary, Robert Finkbine Superintendent of Construction, and John G. Foote, Superintendent of Finance. This organization continued until the completion of the structure, except as changes resulted from deaths. In November, 1876, Mr. Piquenard died, and Messrs. Bell and Hackney, both young men who had assisted him, were elected to succeed him as architect. In February, 1879, Mr. Fisher died, and Mr. Cyrus Foreman of Osage was appointed his successor. The gentlemen composing these boards discharged their important trust with eminent fidelity and ability, giving to the State one of the finest State capitols of the country.

The following gentlemen have filled the executive chair of the State in the line of succession from Governor Briggs:

Hon. Stephen Hempstead, of Dubuque county.
Hon. James W. Grimes, of Des Moines county.
Hon. Ralph P. Lowe, of Lee county.
Hon. Samuel J. Kirkwood, of Johnson county.
Hon. Wm. M. Stone, of Marion county.
Hon. Samuel Merrill, of Clayton county.
Hon. Cyrus C. Carpenter, of Webster county.
Hon. Joshua G. Newbold, of Henry county.
Hon. John H. Gear, of Des Moines county.
Hon. Buren R. Sherman, of Benton county.
Hon. Wm. Larrabee, of Fayette county.
Hon. Horace Boies, of Black Hawk county.

Hon. Joshua G. Newbold was elected Lieutenant-Governor, but became Governor on the resignation of Hon. Samuel J. Kirkwood upon his election as United States Senator.

### THE JUDICIAL SYSTEM.

In our country townships we have magistrates called Justices of the Peace, who are elected by the people and hold their office for two years. In our incorporated towns and cities we have Mayor's and Police Courts.

For the higher courts the State is divided into eighteen districts. Of these, two districts, the eighth and seventeenth, elect one Judge each; the first, third, twelfth, thirteenth, fourteenth, sixteenth, and eighteenth each elect two Judges; the fifth, sixth, ninth, tenth and eleventh each elect three; and the second, fourth, seventh and fifteenth each elect four. The several Judges are elected for terms of four years. There are courts in four cities of the State called Superior Courts, namely: in Cedar Rapids, Creston, Council Bluffs and Keokuk. These have each one Judge. From these District and Superior Courts appeals may be taken to the Supreme Court.

### THE SUPREME COURT.

The supreme judicial body of the State is composed of five Judges, elected by the people for a term of six years, one Judge being elected yearly, the sixth year there being no election. As prosecutor an Attorney General, elected by the people, appears in behalf of the people. The court is now constituted as follows, the position of Chief Justice comes to the several Judges by rotation in the last year of their term.

Chief Justice: Gifford S. Robinson, Storm Lake.

Justices: Charles T. Granger, Waukon; Josiah Given, Des Moines; Jas. H. Rothrock, Cedar Rapids; L. G. Kinne, Toledo.

Attorney General: John Y. Stone, Glenwood.

The Supreme Judges are elected by the voters of the whole State. The District Judges by the voters of their several districts. The Judges of the Superior Courts by the voters of the city in which the court is located.

## CONGRESSIONAL.

The State has eleven representatives in the National Congress. For their election the State is divided into eleven Districts.

The First District, composed of Lee, Van Buren, Jefferson, Henry, Des Moines, Louisa and Washington counties, is represented by Hon. John H. Gear, of Burlington.

The Second District, composed of the counties of Iowa, Johnson, Muscatine, Scott, Clinton and Jackson, is represented by Hon. Walter I. Hayes of Clinton.

The Third District, composed of the counties of Wright, Franklin, Hardin, Butler, Bremer, Black Hawk, Buchanan, Delaware and Dubuque, is represented by Hon. D. B. Henderson, of Dubuque.

The Fourth District, composed of the counties of Worth, Cerro Gordo, Floyd, Mitchell, Howard, Chickasaw, Fayette, Winneshiek, Allamakee and Clayton, is represented by Hon. Thomas Updegraff, of McGregor.

The Fifth District, composed of the counties of Grundy, Marshall, Tama, Benton, Linn, Jones and Cedar, Hon. Robert G. Cousins, is its Representative.

The Sixth District, composed of the counties of Jasper, Poweshiek, Keokuk, Mahaska, Monroe, Wapello and Davis, Hon. John F. Lacey, Representative.

The Seventh District, composed of the counties of Story, Polk, Dallas, Madison, Warren and Marion, Hon. J. A. T. Hull, Representative.

The Eighth District, composed of the counties of Appanoose, Wayne, Lucas, Clark, Decatur, Ringgold, Union Adams, Taylor, Page and Fremont, Hon. W. P. Hepburn, Representative.

The Ninth District, composed of the counties of Adair, Guthrie, Audubon, Cass, Montgomery, Mills, Pottawattamie, Shelby and Harrison, Hon. A. L. Hagar, Representative.

The Tenth District, composed of the counties of Boone, Greene, Carroll, Crawford, Calhoun, Webster, Hamilton, Humboldt, Pocahontas, Palo Alto, Emmet, Kossuth, Hancock and Winnebago, Hon. J. P. Dolliver, Representative.

The Eleventh District, composed of the counties of Monona, Woodbury, Ida, Sac, Buena Vista, Cherokee, Plymouth, Sioux, O'Brien, Clay, Dickinson, Osceola and Lyon, Hon. George D. Perkins, Representative.

## CABINET OFFICERS.

Five citizens of Iowa have held Cabinet positions. Hon. James Harlan was Secretary of the Interior in the second administration of Abraham Lincoln. Hon. W. W. Belknap was Secretary of War in Gen. Grant's administration, and Hon. S. J. Kirkwood was Secretary of the Department of the Interior under Presidents Garfield and Arthur. Hon. Geo. W. McCrary was Secretary of War under President Hayes, and Hon. Frank Hatton was Postmaster-General during part of President Arthur's administration.

In the United States Judiciary several of her citizens have won honorable reputation.

The following gentlemen have represented Iowa in the United States Senate:

Geo. W. Jones, Dubuque, 1848 to 1859.
Augustus C. Dodge, Burlington, 1848 to 1855.
James Harlan, Mt. Pleasant, 1855 to 1865.
James W. Grimes, Burlington, 1858 to 1870.
Samuel J. Kirkwood, Iowa City, 1866 to 1867.
James Harlan, Mount Pleasant, 1867 to 1873.
James B. Howell, Keokuk, Jan. 20, 1871, to March 4, 1871. (To fill vacancy caused by the death of James W. Grimes.)
George G. Wright, Des Moines, 1871 to 1877.
William B. Allison, Dubuque, 1873 to the present time.
Samuel J. Kirkwood, 1877 to 1881.
James W. McDill, 1881 to 1883.
James F. Wilson, Fairfield, 1883 to the present time.

The following gentlemen now constitute the Executive Council of the State:

Hon. Horace Boies, Black Hawk county, Governor.
Hon. Wm. McFarland, Emmet county, Secretary of State.
Hon. C. G. McCarthy, Story county, Auditor of State.
Hon. Byron A. Beason, Marshall County, Treasurer of State.

The other elective Executive State officials are:

Hon. J. B. Knoepfler, Allamakee county, Superintendent of Public Instruction.

Railroad Commissioners:
Hon. John W. Luke, Franklin county.
Hon. Peter A. Dey, Johnson county.
Hon. Geo. W. Perkins, Fremont county.

## THE GENERAL ASSEMBLY.

The Legislative Department of the State government is composed of two houses. The Senate or Upper House consists of fifty members so divided that about one-half of its members are elected bi-ennially, the official term being four years. The Lower House or House of Representatives has one hundred members, elected bi-ennially. The Constitution provides that the sessions of the General Assembly shall be bi-ennial. In cases of emergency extra sessions may be called.

The first extra session convened at Iowa City on the second day of July, 1856, for the purpose of accepting the grant of lands by Congress in aid of railway construction, and to carry into execution the trust conferred upon the State. Grants were made to the Burlington & Missouri, the Mississipi & Missouri, the Air Line, and the Dubuque & Pacific railroad companies.

An extra session was held in May, 1861, for the purpose of placing the State on a war footing to maintain the Union of the States.

A third extra session convened on the third day of September, 1862, and was occupied principally with military matters.

An adjourned session of the Fourteenth General Assembly was begun on the third Wednesday of January, 1873, for the purpose of considering and passing upon the report of the Codifying Commission. The revision of the laws at that adjourned session was designated as the "Code," though by way of distinction it is called the "Code of 1873."

### STATE INSTITUTIONS· STATE UNIVERSITY.

This great school was established early in the history of the State. In July, 1840, Congress passed an act providing for the setting apart of 45,928 acres of land within the territory of Iowa for the use and support of a state university, whenever the territory should become a state. By the adoption of the constitution of 1846, the people of the State accepted the grant. At the first session of the General Assembly, February 25, 1847, an act was passed locating and establishing the State University at Iowa City. That act set apart the public buildings with the ten acres of land on which

STATE UNIVERSITY, IOWA CITY.

the same were situated for the use of the university, provided the capitol should be used for state purposes until otherwise provided by law. The first session of the university opened in March, 1855.

The Collegiate Department embraces four courses of study: Classical, Philosophical, Scientific and Engineering. Four years are required to graduate in any of the courses. In the Law Department the course of study covers two years. The Medical Department requires three terms of six months each. The Dental and Pharmacy Departments cover two years each.

The General Assembly at each session makes liberal appropriations for its support. The Twenty-third General Assembly appropriated $125,000, the twenty-fourth $78,000.

During the past school year a total of 904 students were enrolled in its classes, namely: females 152, males 752. Seventy five persons were employed as instructors. There are 28,000 volumes in its library. Its yearly income is reported at $120,000. Value of grounds and buildings, $300,000.

### THE STATE AGRICULTURAL COLLEGE.

This state school was established in 1858. The legislature of that year appropriated $10,000 to purchase a farm for the location of the college buildings and for experiments in agriculture.

In 1859 a farm of 640 acres, near Ames, Story county, was purchased. In 1862 Congress passed a bill granting to each state public lands to the amount of 30,000 acres for each senator and representative to which the states were then entitled. The conditions of that act and the grant thereunder was accepted by the General Assembly of the State in September, 1862.

In 1887 Congress passed a bill establishing Agricultural Experiment stations in connection with the Agricultural College and appropriated $15,000 annually for the support of each.

In August, 1890, a bill for the more complete endowment and support of Agricultural Colleges was approved by President Harrison. This bill provided for increased appropriations for their support. The annual income of the Iowa college from the several appropriations of the General Government is now $78,000. The State erects and keeps in repair all buildings, and for this purpose it has appropriated about $355,000 for the exclusive use of the several departments of the college. The main college building is five stories high. The college domain now embraces 900 acres. The school has courses in agriculture and dairying, veterinary science, mechanical engineering, civil engineering, electrical engineering, science, and a special course for lady students.

The Twenty-fourth General Assembly appropriated $56,500 for this school. It reported last year an enrollment of 547 students, namely: 454 males and 93 females. Instructors, 29. Its library contains 9,300 volumes. The value of its endowments are reported at $679,784, its yearly income $80,000, and value of grounds and building at $450,000.

### STATE NORMAL SCHOOL.

This important school was established by the Sixteenth General Assembly for the special training of teachers for the common schools of the State. It was organized by the board of directors June 7th, 1876, and was opened for the reception of students September 6th, 1876. The first year 155 students were enrolled in its classes. The last year it had an enrollment of 746, namely: 191 male and 515 female students.

The province of this school is in no respect a duplicate of other educational institutions of the State. It adheres strictly to the object assigned at its founding—that of preparing professional teachers for public schools. For its support and improvement the General Assembly makes liberal appropriations.

This important school has 5,000 volumes in its library. The value of its grounds and buildings is reported at $75,000.

These three important State schools are doing good work in securing to the State in professional life men and women of cultured intellect and special qualifications.

### OTHER STATE SCHOOLS.

The Iowa College for the Blind was first opened in Iowa City in 1853 and removed to its present location at Vinton in 1862. During the forty years of its existence it has received from the State for improvements, repairs, clothing for pupils, support and current expenses upward of $870,-000.

The design of this institution is to furnish to the blind children of the State equal educational advantages with children who enjoy the boon of sight. The branches taught are raised print, point system, arithmetic, spelling, geography, history, grammar, natural philosophy, algebra, rhetoric, physiology, zoology, chemistry, moral philosophy, civil government, political economy, geometry, and English and American literature. The department of music is supplied with twenty-three pianos, one pipe organ, three cabinet organs and a sufficient number of violins, guitars, bass viols and brass instruments. Every student capable of receiving it, is given a complete course in this branch.

In the industrial department the girls are required to learn knitting, crocheting, fancy work, hand and machine sewing. The boys, netting, mattress-making and cane seating. Those of either sex who so desire may learn carpet weaving and broom making. The advantages of the school are free to every person either blind or of defective vision, and of suitable age and capacity in the State. The pupils are treated free of charge by skilled oculists.

### INSTITUTION FOR THE DEAF AND DUMB.

This institution is located in Pottawattamie county near the city of Council Bluffs. The education it offers is free. Pupils are received from the age of nine to twenty-five who are sound of mind and free from offensive or contagious diseases. A competent corps of instructors of long and successful experience is employed in every department. The trades taught in the institution are printing, shoe-making, carpentering, dressmaking, farming and gardening, drawing and painting, light house work, plain sewing and knitting are also taught.

The last General Assembly appropriated $26,050 for this school.

### INSTITUTION FOR THE FEEBLE MINDED.

This worthy institution is located at Glenwood, Mills county. The first child was admitted September 1876. For a time there was an unwillingness on the part of parents of this class of children to turn them over to its care. That diffidence is now largely outgrown. The object of the institution is to provide special means for this unfortunate class. The course embraces not only the course of the common schools where that is practicable, but a course of training in the practical matters of every day life, the cultivation of proper personal habits, and the fitting of the pupil for useful occupation.

The value of the lands and buildings pertaining to this worthy institution is now about $100,000.

### INDUSTRIAL HOME FOR ADULT BLIND.

The object of this worthy institution is to provide a working home and means for the blind to earn their own subsistence. The institution was established by an act of the twenty-third General Assembly which appropriated $40,000 for the purchase of grounds and erection of buildings. It was located by the Commission at Knoxville, Marion county. Accommodations were designed for two hundred inmates. The institution was opened for the reception of eligible persons in 1862.

### THE SOLDIERS' ORPHANS' HOME.

This institution was opened for the reception of children July 13th, 1864. The eleventh General Assembly assuming control, providing a special fund for its maintenance, and providing for its management and its permanent location at Davenport.

There is in connection with this worthy charity a well lighted, pleasant and commodious school building. It is the purpose of the Board of Management to have the course of instruction reach a high standard of practical usefulness.

In 1880 the General Assembly widened the sphere of usefulness of this institution by opening its doors to other dependent children. There were on the thirtieth of June, 1893, —— soldiers' orphans and other dependent children enjoying its advantages. Great attention is given to the moral instruction of children placed in its care.

The library of the institution contains about 800 volumes of carefully selected juvenile literature.

### THE SOLDIERS' HOME.

This institution was created by the twenty-first General Assembly. The main building being completed was opened with proper ceremonies November 30th, 1887. Since that time enlargements and improvements have been made by authority of the succeeding sessions of the body creating it.

The hospital is 131 feet in length, 60 feet in width, two stories in height above basement, with spacious verandas and balconies. Great care was taken to secure good ventilation. The home is a worthy monument of the grateful patriotism of the people of the State towards its defenders who, broken in health, or suffering from wounds received in their country's dangerous service, now need its care. Down to June 30, 1891, 743 persons had been admitted to its care and comforts.

Since the adjournment of the twenty-fourth General Assembly, a number of cottages have been erected for the accommodation of married veterans needing the advantages of this home.

### INSANE ASYLUMS.

Liberal provision has been made by the people of the State for the care of this unfortunate class.

The hospital at Mt. Pleasant is the oldest of the three institutions established by the State for the care and treatment of insane persons. It was established by the act of the Fifth General Assembly, approved January 24, 1855. It was formally opened March 6, 1861.

The hospital at Independence, Buchanan county, was opened on the first day of May, 1873.

The hospital at Clarinda, Page county, was opened for the reception of patients December, 15, 1888. The original plans for this institution, not yet fully carried out, contemplated accommodations for one thousand patients. The appropriation by the twenty-third General Assembly for the three institutions reached in the aggregate $237,500. The special appropriations made by the twenty-fourth General Assembly for repairs and improvements were $91,300.

These institutions are each controlled by a board of trustees elected by the General Assembly, composed of men of different political parties. Full staffs of eminent medical service are secured. The treatment of the unfortunate inmates is humane and wise, and care is given to promote their restoration to reason.

### INDUSTRIAL OR REFORMATORY SCHOOLS.

Of these the State supports two; one for boys at Eldora, Hardin county. The persons eligible for commitment to its instructions and care are boys from eight to sixteen years of age, whose natures are yet susceptible to good impressions and who may be influenced to a better life by kindness, moral training and a proper discipline. This school was opened September 1st, 1868. In the almost twenty-three years elapsing from its opening to June 30, 1891, there were admitted 1,655 boys; of these 1,254 had been discharged and otherwise released, 401 still remaining under its care.

Care is taken to give its inmates useful instruction and correct moral training. The work of the institution has been most valuable to its inmates and honorable and serviceable to the State.

### THE GIRL'S INDUSTRIAL SCHOOL.

Is located at Mitchellville, Polk county. This is virtually a branch of the Eldora school, designed for the moral training of wayward girls. The buildings and grounds of the Universalist Seminary at Mitchellville were purchased in 1879 and this school was established at that time. "The discipline is gentle and home like," and it has been estimated that seventy per cent. of those committed to the institution leave it reformed in character and conduct.

### THE PENITENTIARIES.

Iowa has two such institutions, and may boast of the small percentage of its population classed as criminals.

The oldest of its penal institutions was located at Ft. Madison, Lee county, and was established by act of the Legislature of Iowa territory, January 25, 1839.

By an act of the fourteenth General Assembly of the State, commissioners were appointed to "locate and provide for the erection of an additional penitentiary." That commission located the additional institution at Anamosa, Jones county.

The number of convicts in the Anamosa penitentiary, March 23 last were males 293, females 12. Total 305. The prison has accommodations for 800, 495 more than are confined therein. In the Ft. Madison institution there were 420 prisoners in confinement, all males. Making a total for the two prisons of 725 persons, only twelve being females. This is one prisoner to each 2,413 of the State's population. We notice that according to census bulletin number ninety-five, the number of prisoners in the county jails were 327, being 171 prisoners in jail for one million of population. Although Iowa was tenth in rank of population, twenty-three of the States of the

Union exceeded Iowa in the number of prisoners in their jails. The ratio of prisoners in jail to population was 171 prisoners to one million population, and forty-three of the States and Territories exceeded this ratio. There is crime in Iowa but there are few States in the Union that have so little crime in proportion to population. We gladly acknowledge valuable assistance from the Iowa Register in the preparation of this chapter.

## PAUPERISM.

The great Master, when on earth, said to the murmuring Judas: "The poor ye have always with you." The saying is ever true in earthly conditions. The physically and mentally infirm—the unfortunates are present in all countries. For her poor Iowa makes comfortable provision of shelter, food, clothing and medical attendance. Her alms houses may not be palaces, but they are not prisons nor places of cruelty. There were in 1890, as shown by the national census, in the alms houses of the country 73,045 persons, or 1,166 to each million of population. Iowa had but 848 to the million of her population in her alms houses. The sobriety of her people diminishes extreme poverty. And crime and pauperism alike are reduced to a minimum by the prevalence of sobriety, intelligence and piety, virtues that when observed in practical life alike preclude criminal action and pauperized condition.

## THE NEWSPAPER PRESS.

The people of this State are known to be generous patrons of literature. They are liberal supporters of the press. The State, though comparatively young, was settled before the telephone or telegraph was invented. Yet when Iowa was opened for settlement, the newspaper had won recognition as an instrument of power in political and social affairs, and soon after its settlement had its own newspaper establishment. In 1836, but three years after its permanent settlement was commenced, John King started "The Visitor" in Dubuque, issuing the first number on the 11th day of May of that year. The press on which that paper was printed was of the Smith pattern, and was purchased in Cincinnatti. It did worthy pioneer service. After being used some six years in Dubuque it was sold and removed to Lancaster, Wisconsin. After being used there some time it was removed to St. Paul, Minnesota, and in another mutation of its ownership was taken to Sioux Falls, Dakota, where in March, 1862, on the raiding of that place by the Sioux Indians, it was destroyed in the conflagration of the building in which it was located. In its somewhat brief history it served in printing the first newspapers ever issued in Iowa, Western Wisconsin, Minnesota and Dakota. In 1837 James Clark, afterwards Governor of the Iowa territory, established a newspaper at Burlington, naming it "The Gazette." It has survived the mutations of political administrations, commercial struggles and business changes, and is now one of the influential journals of the State, publishing daily and weekly editions.

There are now published in Iowa 951 periodical journals, but four of the forty-four States exceeding us in the number of such publications, namely, New York with 2,131, Illinois 1,560, Pennsylvania 1,478, and Ohio with 1,190.

Newspapers are published in each of our ninety-nine counties, there being but one of the ninety-nine county seats without a newspaper, namely, Concord, the county seat of Hancock county. Two papers are published, however, in the town of Garner, but a mile distant from Concord. Newspapers are published in 446 of the cities, towns or villages of the State. Of our "ninety and nine" counties five, in 1892, each had three papers, namely, Adair, Clark, Winnebago, Emmet and Worth. Eleven counties had four papers each, namely, Adams, Audubon, Dickinson, Franklin, Grundy, Hancock, Lucas, Monroe, Palo Alto and Ringgold. Eight other counties each had five journals, while Dubuque had 20, Scott 23, Woodbury 26, Linn 29 and Polk 45.

Of these 951 publications in this State fifty-eight are daily issues, five are tri-weekly, twelve are semi-weekly, 769 weekly, three semi-monthly, one bi-monthly, eighty-five are monthly journals and two are published quarterly. One is published in the Bohemian, nine in the German, three in the Hollandist, seven in the Norwegian and Danish, and one in the Swedish languages. Thirteen of the whole number represent collegiate interests, twenty are published in the interests of agriculture and live stock, thirteen in advocacy of the interests of fraternities, seven are educational journals, two medical, two are devoted to the advancement of science, eight specially advocate temperance and prohibition, one is published in the advocacy of Woman's Suffrage, one in the interests of people of color, ten specially represent various industrial and commercial interests, several are published in aid of Sabbath school work, and one is a juvenile journal. There are also a number representing denominational and religious interests, while 563 of the whole number are classed as political journals, 330 advocating the principals of the Republican party, 194 the principles of the Democratic party, thirteen are styled Independent-Republican, twelve are classed as Independent Democrat, and fourteen are assorted as Greenback, Union Labor, Peoples Party and Anti-Monopoly journals.

The people of Iowa not only liberally patronize the larger city journals but they liberally support their county and village press. All business and moral interests and lines of thought are represented by the press of Iowa. Our newspaper writers have won fame throughout the country, and have borne able part not only in the discussion of matters of national interest but also in the dissemination of intelligence respecting our resources, progress and possibilities and by their work have given valuable aid in promoting the prosperity and happiness of our people, thereby promoting the settlement of our wild lands, and the wondrous development of this fair and noble Iowa. Here the largest possible liberty has ever been allowed the press in the discussion of all public questions. This happy privilege has led to the multiplication of newspapers but it has resulted in energizing thought, quickening activities, inspiring worthy ambitions and noble purposes, and giving to our honored State the world wide fame it enjoys for the superior excellence of its commercial, social and domestic conditions.

# Report of Auditing Committee.

### BY S. B. PACKARD, CHAIRMAN.

In compliance with a resolution adopted Nov. 1, 1893, the Auditing Committee beg to submit a full financial and itemized statement of the receipts and disbursements of the Commission from its organization to April 1, 1894.

The funds for the preliminary work of this Commission were appropriated by the 23d General Assembly, and a resolution of this Board adopted October 15, 1890, authorized the proper officers to make requisition upon the Auditor of State for the sum appropriated, amounting to...... $ 5,000 00

An additional appropriation of $125,000 was made by the 24th General Assembly for the practical work of the Commission, and was drawn upon requisition of the Board made upon the State Auditor, on the following dates:

| | |
|---|---|
| April 7, 1892 | $ 5,000 00 |
| June 8, 1892 | 10,000 00 |
| Sept. 1, 1892 | 25,000 00 |
| Oct. 14, 1892 | 25,000 00 |
| Jan. 13, 1893 | 20,000 00 |
| Mach 2, 1893 | 25,000 00 |
| Aug. 2, 1893 | 10,000 00 |
| Feb. 4, 1894 | 5,000 00 — $125,000 00 |

$130,000 00

The Executive Council, under an Act of the 23d General Assembly, was enabled to aid the Commission in the support, in part, of the Iowa State Band at the Iowa Building, and but for this assistance one of the most attractive features, the music, could not have been maintained during the Exposition. Recognizing this fact the Executive Council appropriated in the month of March six thousand five hundred dollars to be paid to the Band through the Executive Committee of the Commission as follows:

| | | |
|---|---|---|
| For the month of May | $ 2,250 00 | |
| June | 2,000 00 | |
| July | 2,250 00 — $ 6,500 00 |

Later in the summer the Council voted the sum of two thousand dollars for each of the months of August, September and October... $ 6,000 00

Inasmuch as the money was received monthly from the Council to be disbursed to the Band, as needed, through the Chairman of the Executive Committee, none of it was deposited with the Treasurer of the Commission and this fund will not appear in his account.

The Commission was able to further add to its resources by a concession granted to C. S. Young & Co. for an exhibit of seeds and grain collected throughout the State, under a contract requiring Messrs. Young & Co. to supply the center piece of the Collective Exhibit in the State Building, it being a model of the State Capitol, where the best of the grain and seeds could be exhibited. The concession mentioned allowed Messrs. Young & Co. to appropriate to their use the surplus grain and seeds collected, for which the Commission was to receive without charge, mounted in the place assigned in the center of the pavilion, the model Capitol constructed of metal and glass with exhibits of grain and seeds in place, which cost the contractors $6,000, besides a cash bonus paid into the Treasury of the Commission Dec. 10, 1892, of............ $ 5,000 00

$147,500 00

By the generous and patriotic action of the women of the State, through their organization known as the Iowa Board of Lady Managers, a handsome sum of money was collected and expended by that organization in promoting the interest of the Iowa exhibit. In addition to the sum so used by that organization, under its rules there was turned over by it, to this Commission, the sum of 515 30

The grand total of the resources of the Commission, though less than half of the estimated requirements, for such an exhibit as the Commission wished to make, amounted to the sum of............ $148,015 30

The Commission at its meeting June 22, 1892, adopted as a basis for the expenditure of the appropriation of $125,000 made by the 24th General Assembly, certain estimates which

REPORT OF AUDITING COMMITTEE 379

set apart for the preparation of exhibits and their installation $45,000; for the general cost of a State Building, furnishing, and the administration and maintenance during the six months of the Exposition $80,000.

No estimate for music was made at that time, as the funds were not then in sight to warrant any expenditure in that direction.

These estimates were subdivided to the use of Departmental and various branches of the work as follows:

| | |
|---|---|
| Pavilion, alteration and restoration | $ 5,500 |
| New building, structure complete | 27,000 |
| Decorations | 3,000 |
| Furniture, chairs, desks, awnings and carpets | 5,000 |
| Attendants, helpers during six months of Fair | 15,500 |
| Administration, Commissioners per diem and R'y | 12,500 |
| Expressage, postage and stationery | 4,000 |
| Contingent | 7,500 |
| | $ 80,000 |
| Collective Exhibit | $ 8,000 |
| Literary Bureau | 5,000 |
| Live Stock | 5,000 |
| Agriculture and Dairy | 8,000 |
| Horticulture | 2,000 |
| Mineral and Geology | 2,000 |
| Press | 1,500 |
| Woman's Work | 1,500 |
| M'f'rs. and Machinery | 2,000 |
| Education and Liberal Arts | 5,000 |
| Forestry and Sanitary Work | 2,000—$ 45,000 |
| | $125,000 |

These estimates were formed before any considerable expenditures had been made, and were designed only as an approximation of what might be necessary in the prosecution of the work. The actual expenses by departments, as evidenced by the following table, will show how nearly these estimates were borne out in the amounts actually required.

The additional funds outside of those supplied by the direct appropriation of the General Assembly, as before explained, enabled the Commission to add the musical features to the other attractions; under general heads the expenditures have been as follows:

| | |
|---|---|
| Publicity and Promotion | $ 5,000 00 |
| Construction—Iowa State Building | 30,501 21 |
| Furniture and Fixtures | 3,881 21 |
| Administration | 16,881 86 |
| Salaries and Expenses of Employees | 13,844 43 |
| Archaeological, Historical and Statistical | 5,504 15 |
| Ceremonies { Dedication, Opening Day, State Days } | 6,592 34 |
| Music—Iowa State Band, 6 months | 16,500 00 |
| Printing, Postage, Stationery and Telegrams | 1,918 88 |
| Electric Lights, Fuel and Insurance | 1,859 94 |
| Contingent Expenses | 2,195 23 |
| Collective Exhibit, including Decorations | 11,180 46 |
| Live Stock | 7,241 92 |
| Agriculture and Dairy | 8,015 05 |
| Horticulture | 1,844 75 |
| Mineral and Geology | 2,292 94 |
| Press | 759 78 |
| Woman's Work | 1,291 41 |
| M'f'r's and Machinery | 11 39 |
| Education and Liberal Arts | 5,322 64 |
| Forestry | 146 50 |
| | $141,039 12 |

The items of expenditure which follow were incurred by the officers and members of the Commission under the authority of the Board, and each item is supported by a receipted bill which constitutes a voucher upon which the Auditing Committee has acted. Having examined and fully verified them, we hereby return them to the Commission as being sufficient and correct, and recommend that they be transmitted with this report to the Governor of the State, as directed by the law creating this Commission.

1890.

| | | | |
|---|---|---|---|
| Nov. | 1. | N. H. Defoe, P. M., postage stamps | $ 4 32 |
| Dec. | 1. | " " " | 6 30 |
| | 3. | Geo. H. Benedict & Co., drawing and plate | 18 00 |
| | 12. | American Express Co | 1 68 |
| Jan. | 1, 1891. | N. H. Defoe, P. M., postage | 11 80 |
| | 27. | U. S. Express Co | 2 50 |
| Feb. | 1. | F. N. Chase, secretary, per diem Oct. 20, 1890, to Feb 1, 1891 | $150 00 |
| | | R R fare | 8 64—$ 158 64 |
| | 1. | N. H. Defoe, P. M., postage | 15 00 |

| | | | |
|---|---|---|---|
| Jan. 30. | Snyder & Hurd, printing | 59 50 | |
| Nov. 1, 1890, | F. N. Chase, Sec'y, stationery | 1 25—$ | 275 99 |
| Nov. 10, 1890, | F. N. Chase, per diem, Sept., 1 day | 5 00 | |
| | " Oct., 14, 15, 16, 3 days | 15 00 | |
| | R. R. fare | 6 40—$ | 26 40 |
| | Edward Johnston, per diem, Sept., 3 days....$ | 15 00 | |
| | " Oct., " | 15 00—$ | 30 00 |
| | S. H. Mallory, per diem, Sept., 2 days | $ | 10 00 |
| | Wm. F. King, expense attending Com'rs meeting | | 19 80 |
| | J. F. Duncombe, per diem, Sept., days 3........$ | 15 00 | |
| | " Oct., " 3 | 15 00—$ | 30 00 |
| | Jas. O. Crosby, per diem, Sept., 4 days........$ | 20 00 | |
| | " Oct., 4 " | 20 00 | |
| | " Nov., 1 " | 5 60 | |
| | R. R. fare | 35 63—$ | 80 63 |
| | J. W. Jarnagin, per diem, Sept., 3 days........$ | 15 00 | |
| | " Oct., 3 " | 15 00 | |
| | R. R. fare | 9 12—$ | 39 12 |
| | H. W. Seaman, per diem, Sept., 6 days.........$ | 30 00 | |
| | " Oct., 4 " | 20 00 | |
| | R. R. fare | 43 01—$ | 93 01 |
| | Wm. H. Dent, per diem, Sept., 3 days..........$ | 15 00 | |
| | " Oct., 3 " | 15 00 | |
| | R. R. fare | 22 56—$ | 52 56 |
| | Chas. Ashton, per diem, Sept., 3 days.........$ | 15 00 | |
| | " Oct., 3 " | 15 00 | |
| | R. R. fare | 5 60—$ | 35 60 |

1891.

| | | | |
|---|---|---|---|
| Feb. 10. | N. H. Defoe, P. M., postage | 15 00 | |
| 17. | U. S. Express Co | 1 00 | |
| Mch. 7. | " " | 35 | |
| 2. | " " | 15 | |
| 5. | S. B. Humbert, P. M., postage | 6 00 | |
| 21. | Ill. Cent. R. R. | 1 70 | |
| 20. | Wyckoff, Seamans and Benedict one No. 5 typewriter and cabinet | 135 00 | |
| 25. | Packard and Fabrick stationery | 16 25 | |
| 27. | Snyder & Hurd, stationery | 12 50 | |
| 28. | F. A. Hotchkis, letter press | 4 00 | |
| 30. | W. U. Telegraph Co | 1 00 | |
| Apr. 1. | F. N. Chase, Sec'y, per diem, Mch..........$ 120 00 | | |
| | R. R. fare 9 14 | | |
| | per diem, Feb., 120 00 | | |
| | R. R. fare 13 22—$ | 262 36—$ | 457 31 |
| | Henry Stivers, per diem, Sept., 1 day, Oct., 1 day, Feb., '91, 2 days | $ | 25 00 |
| | J. F. Duncombe, per diem, Feb., 3 days | | 15 00 |
| | Wm. H. Dent, " " 4 " | 20 00 | |
| | R. R. fare | 11 28—$ | 31 28 |
| | H. W. Seaman, Com. work Jan., 1 day, Feb. meeting, 5 days | 30 00 | |
| | R. R. fare | 16 50—$ | 46 50 |
| | Chas. Ashton, per diem, Jan., 5 days..........$ | 25 00 | |
| | R. R. fare | 3 60—$ | 28 60 |
| | J. W. Jarnagin, Com. work, Dec. 2 days, Feb. meeting, 4 days.....$ | 30 00 | |
| | R. R. fare | 9 12—$ | 39 12 |
| | Edward Johnston, per diem, Feb., 4 days | $ | 20 00 |
| | Jas. O. Crosby, " " 5 " .........$ | 25 00 | |
| | R. R. fare | 17 31—$ | 42 31 |
| | H. W. Seaman, Committeee work Feb., 6 days...$ | 30 00 | |
| | R. R. fare | 12 75—$ | 42 75 |
| | Wm. H. Dent, Committee work, Feb., 5 days....$ | 25 00 | |
| | R. R. fare | 36 50—$ | 61 50 |

## REPORT OF AUDITING COMMITTEE 381

| | | | |
|---|---|---|---|
| | Wm. H. Dent, per diem, Mch., 1 day, Apr., 2 days..........$ | 15 00 | |
| | R. R. fare........................................... | 11 28—$ | 26 28 |
| | Henry Stivers, per diem, April, 1 day................... | $ | 5 00 |
| | Jas. O. Crosby, per diem, Mch., Com. w'rk, 5 days........ $ | 25 00 | |
| | " " April, 4 days...................... | 20 00 | |
| | R. R. fare............................. | 22 92—$ | 67 92 |
| | J. F. Duncombe, per diem, Mch., 1 day, April, 2 days, | $ | 15 00 |
| | J. W. Jarnagin, " March, 3 days, April, 2 days..$ | 25 00 | |
| | R. R. fare................................ | 4 56—$ | 29 56 |
| | H. W. Seaman, per diem, April, 5 days...................$ | 25 00 | |
| | R. R. fare.................................. | 16 50—$ | 41 50 |
| | S. B. Packard, per diem, Mch., 1 day, Apr., 2 days.......$ | 15 00 | |
| | R. R. fare................................. | 3 50—$ | 18 50 |
| | Chas. Ashton, per diem, Feb., 2 days, March, 1 day....... | | |
| | April 2 days............................................$ | 25 00 | |
| | R. R. fare............................................. | 11 32—$ | 36 32 |
| | S. H. Mallory, per diem, April, 2 days..................$ | 10 00 | |
| | R. R. fare.................................. | 1 34—$ | 11 34 |
| | Jas. Wilson, per diem, Sept., '90, 3 days, Oct., '90,..... | | |
| | 3 days...............................................$ | 30 00 | |
| | R. R. fare............................................ | 11 80—$ | 41 80 |
| May 29. | Packard & Fabrick, printing ...........................$ | 13 00 | |
| 21. | Snyder & Hurd, letter heads............................ | 16 50 | |
| 30. | B. F. White, envelopes................................ | 2 15 | |
| Apr. 24. | Wyckoff Seamans & Benedict, carbon paper............... | 1 00 | |
| May 28. | Wise & Bryant, stationery............................. | 9 60 | |
| June 1. | Am. Express Co........................................ | 1 40 | |
| | U. S. Express Co ...................................... | 1 45 | |
| May 30. | W. U. Telegraph Co., 10 messages...................... | 3 40 | |
| June 1. | H. W. Seaman, paid telegrams.......................... | 2 85 | |
| 3. | J. W. Jarnagin, paid typewriter....................... | 1 00 | |
| Apr. 22. | S. B. Humbert, postage............................... | 4 00 | |
| May 21. | " " ................................. | 2 00 | |
| Apr. 20. | " " ................................. | 5 00 | |
| 17. | " " ................................. | 5 00 | |
| 9. | " " ................................. | 20 00 | |
| | F. N. Chase, Sec'y., per diem, April...............$ 130 00 | | |
| | " May............... 130 00 | | |
| | R. R. fare............... 26 88—$ | 286 88—$ | 375 23 |
| | S. H. Mallory, per diem, June, 3 days................... | $ | 15 00 |
| | Jas. O. Crosby, " " 5 " ........................$ | 25 00 | |
| | R. R. fare............................ | 17 20—$ | 42 20 |
| | J. W. Jarnagin, Com. work, May, 2 days .................$ | 10 00 | |
| | per diem, June, 4 days................ | 20 00 | |
| | R. R. fare............................ | 8 16—$ | 38 16 |
| | Chas. Ashton, per diem, June, 4 days...................$ | 20 00 | |
| | R. R. fare............... | 3 60—$ | 23 60 |
| | S. B. Packard, Com. work, May, 2 days..................$ | 10 00 | |
| | per diem, June, 3 days ......... | 15 00 | |
| | R. R. fare................... | 10 94—$ | 35 94 |
| | Wm. H. Dent, per diem, June, 3 days....................$ | 15 00 | |
| | R. R. fare...................... | 11 18—$ | 26 18 |
| | H. W. Seaman, Com. work, May, 1 day...................$ | 5 00 | |
| | per diem, June, 5 days................ | 25 00 | |
| | R. R. fare........................... | 16 50—$ | 46 50 |
| | Henry Stivers, per diem, June, 2 days................... | $ | 10 00 |
| | Wm. H. Dent, Com. work, July, 3 days..................$ | 15 00 | |
| | R. R. fare............................ | 31 50—$ | 46 50 |
| | H. W. Seaman, Com. work, July, 3 days .................$ | 15 00 | |
| | R. R. fare. ............................ | 10 28—$ | 25 28 |
| Apr. | The Gazette Co., advertising...........................$ | 1 90 | |
| June 6. | S. B. Humbert, P. M., postage.......................... | 14 00 | |

382   REPORT OF IOWA COLUMBIAN COMMISSION

|  |  |  |  |
|---|---|---:|---:|
| July 10. | " " " | 4 00 | |
| | F. N. Chase, Sec'y., per diem, June ............ $130 00 | | |
| | R. R. fare ..................... 20 28 | | |
| | per diem, July ............... 135 00 | | |
| | R. R. fare .................... 14 67 | | |
| | per diem, Aug ................ 120 00 | | |
| | R. R. fare .................... 7 90—$ | 427 85 | |
| Aug. 4. | S. B. Humbert, P. M., postage .......................$ | 7 00 | |
| July 17. | " " " ......................... | 5 00 | |
| Aug. 6. | W. H. Shaw & Co., 1 seal............................. | 3 50 | |
| 24. | W. U. Telegraph Co., 5 telegrams .................... | 2 07 | |
| 24. | U. S Express Co..................................... | 1 38 | |
| | Am. Express Co...................................... | 40 | |
| | F. N. Chase, filing case for papers .................. | 2 50—$ | 169 60 |
| | H. W. Seaman, Com. work, June, 1 day.............$ | 5 00 | |
| | " July, 3 days................... | 15 00 | |
| | " Aug., 2 days.................. | 10 00 | |
| | R. R. fare...................................... | 5 08 | |
| | Telegrams....................................... | 3 07—$ | 38 15 |
| Aug. 26. | Jarnagin & McKee, printing .........................$ | 30 00 | |
| Sept. 5. | A. J. Doll, cloth signs............................... | 3 00 | |
| Aug. 26. | Chase & West, chairs and table ...................... | 7 00 | |
| 27. | Walters Talbot Printing Co., book .................... | 75 | |
| Sept.11. | W. A. Winchester, signs ............................. | 1 00 | |
| 30. | S. B. Humbert, P. M., postage ....................... | 8 00 | |
| 5. | F. W. Bigelow, labor ................................ | 15 00 | |
| 17. | Snyder & Hurd, printing ............................. | 57 75 | |
| Oct. 10. | H. E. Machlan, cottage on Iowa State Fair Grounds. | 196 60 | |
| Oct. 1. | F. N. Chase, Sec'y., per diem, September ........ $105 00 | | |
| | R. R. fare.................... 18 31—$ | 123 31 | |
| Sept. 8. | M. J. Bronson, drayage..............................$ | 50 | |
| 9. | Minn. and St Louis R'y.............................. | 1 17 | |
| Oct. 1. | L. J. Wells, drayage................................ | 2 00 | |
| Sept. 8. | Chicago, St. Paul & K. C. R. R..................... | 2 04 | |
| Aug. 26. | " " " ..................... | 1 54 | |
| Sept. 5. | Frank Wilson, drayage .............................. | 1 50 | |
| Oct. 3. | U. S. Express Co ................................... | 1 35 | |
| Sept.23. | " " " .................................. | 1 25 | |
| Aug. 25. | " " " .................................. | 2 35 | |
| 31. | " " " .................................. | 2 40 | |
| Sept.22. | " " " .................................. | 75 | |
| 5. | " " " .................................. | 50 | |
| 9. | Geo. W. Richards, paid express ..................... | 40 | |
| 14. | Am. Express Co..................................... | 30 | |
| Oct. 1. | " " .................................... | 50—$ | 462 96 |
| Oct. 8. | S. B. Packard, per diem, Oct., 3 days ..............$ | 15 00 | |
| | R. R. fare .................................... | 4 48—$ | 19 48 |
| | H. W. Seaman, Com. work, 2 days..................$ | 10 00 | |
| | per diem, Oct., 4 days................. | 20 00 | |
| | R. R. fare............................. | 15 50—$ | 45 50 |
| | Wm. H. Dent, per diem, Oct., 3 days..............$ | 15 00 | |
| | R. R. fare .................................. | 11 22—$ | 26 22 |
| | Chas. Ashton, Com. work, Aug., 6 days.............$ | 30 00 | |
| | " Sept., 3 days................. | 15 00 | |
| | per diem, Oct., 4 days ................. | 20 00 | |
| | R. R. fare.................................... | 18 10—$ | 83 10 |
| | Theo. Guelich, per diem, Oct., 3 days..............$ | 15 00 | |
| | R. R. fare................................... | 6 40—$ | 21 40 |
| | J. W. Jarnagin, Com. work, June, 2 days...........$ | 10 00 | |
| | " Aug., 1 day................ | 5 00 | |
| | " Sep., 6 days............... | 30 00 | |
| | per diem, Oct., 4 days ................ | 20 00 | |
| | R. R. fare .................................. | 17 76—$ | 82 76 |
| | Jas. O. Crosby, Com. work, Sept., 3 days.......... $ | 15 00 | |
| | per diem, Oct., 5 days..................... | 25 00 | |
| | R. R. fare.................................. | 18 84—$ | 58 84 |
| | J. F. Duncombe, per diem, Oct., 3 days............. | $ | 15 00 |

## REPORT OF AUDITING COMMITTEE 383

```
         Henry Stivers, Com. work, July, 2 days..................$   10 00
                        "       Aug., 1 day.....................    5 00
                        per diem, Oct., 2 days..................   10 00
                        R. R. fare..............................   24 00–$   49 00

Nov.  2. W. U. Telegraph Co...................................$    89
      24. U. S. Express Co.....................................    45
Oct.  5.   "        "                                              25
      13. Am.       "                                            1 95
       7.  "        "                                            1 15
Oct.  8. H. W. Seaman, paid express...........................   1 35
Nov.  5. W. H. Shaw & Co., rubber stamps......................   1 25
Dec.  9. S. B. Humbert, P. M., stamps.........................  15 00
Nov.  7.   "        "        "                                   5 00
      20. Wyckoff, Seamans & Benedict, paper..................   3 00
         B. F. Chase Co., envelopes...........................     85
Dec. 11. Snyder & Hurd, letter heads..........................  10 50
   1. F. N. Chase, Sec'y., per diem, Oct............$ 135 00
                        R. R. fare..............    12 72
                        per diem, Nov..............  120 00
                        R. R. fare.......... ,.....   20 96–$ 288 68–$    330 32

Dec. 18. H. W. Seaman, Com. work, Nov., 7 days..............$  35 00
                         "       Dec., 2 days...............  10 00
                        per diem, Dec., 4 days...............  20 00
                        R. R. fare...........................  70 84
                        Telegrams............................    82 $   136 66

         Jas. O. Crosby, Com. work, Dec., 4 days............$  20 00
                         per diem,  "  5 "  ................  25 00
                         R. R. fare..........................  25 84–$   70 84

         S. H. Mallory, per diem, Dec., 3 days..............$  15 00
                         R. R. fare..........................     66–$   15 66

         S. B. Packard, per diem, Dec., 3 days..............$  15 00
                         R. R. fare..........................   4 48–$   19 48

         Chas. Ashton, Com. work, Oct., 1 day...............$   5 00
                        "      Nov., 1 "  ................    5 00
                        per diem, Dec., 4 "  ................  20 00
                        R. R. fare..........................   3 20–$   33 20

         J. W. Jarnagin, Com. work, Nov., 1 day............$    5 00
                         per diem, Dec., 5 days...............  25 00
                         R. R. fare..........................   4 56–$   34 56

         Theo. Guelich, per diem, Dec., 2 days...............$  10 00
                         R. R. fare..........................  10 00–$   20 00

         Wm. H. Dent, Com. work, Nov., 4 days...............$  20 00
                         R. R. fare..........................  31 30–$   51 30

Dec.  1. W. U. Telegraph Co....................................$   31
     29. U. S. Express Co., 5 packages.........................  2 17
     15. Guthrian Printing Co., printing.......................  4 25
     18. Ida M. Canfield, stenographer.........................  3 60
     14. Jarnagin & McKee, printing minutes................... 21 70
Jan. 1, 1892. W. U. Telegraph Co...............................    45
         S. B. Humbert, P. M., postage.........................  13 60
         Packard & Fabrick, stationery.........................   6 75
      9. Wise & Bryant, envelopes..............................   2 50
      1. F. N. Chase, Sec'y., per diem, Dec.........$ 130 00
                         R. R. fare............... 10 24–$ 140 24–$  194 98

Jan. 17. Chas. Ashton, Com. work, Jan., 5 days.............$  25 00
                         R. R. fare..........................   3 60–$   28 60

Feb.  4. Chas. Ashton, Com. work, Jan., 6 days.............$  30 00
                         R. R. fare..........................   6 40–$   36 40

         Theo. Guelich, per diem, Jan., 4 days...............$  20 00
                         R. R. fare..........................  10 10–$   30 10

         S. B. Packard, Com. work, Jan., 7 days.............$  35 00
                         R. R. fare..........................   8 48–$   43 48

         J. W. Jarnagin, Com. work, Jan., 5 days............$  25 00
                         R. R. fare..........................   4 56–$   29 56
```

|         |                                                                 |          |          |
|---------|-----------------------------------------------------------------|----------|----------|
|         | F. N. Chase, Sec'y., per diem, Jan., 10 days............$       | 50 00    |          |
|         | R. R. fare............................                         | 19 54—$  | 69 54    |
| Apr. 20.| F. N. Chase, Sec'y, paid following bills—                        |          |          |
|         | S. B. Humbert, P. M., postage..................$                | 10 00    |          |
|         | U. S. Express Co...............................                | 1 65     |          |
|         | American Express Co.,.........................                 | 45       |          |
|         | Express and supplies...........................                | 1 80     |          |
|         | Watters-Talbot Printing Co., placards............               | 75       |          |
|         | circulars......................                                | 2 00     |          |
|         | J. Kuhec & Co., typewriter ribbon................               | 1 75     |          |
|         | F. N. Chase, per diem from Jan. 12 to Feb. 1, 16 days           | 80 00—$  | 98 40    |
|         | Jas. O. Crosby, per diem, Feb., 6 days..............$           | 30 00    |          |
|         | R. R. fare................................                     | 16 66—$  | 46 66    |
|         | Theo. Guelich, per diem, Feb., 3 days...............$           | 15 00    |          |
|         | R. R. fare................................                     | 10 10—$  | 25 10    |
|         | S. B. Packard, per diem, Feb., 4 days...............$           | 20 00    |          |
|         | R. R. fare................................                     | 4 48—$   | 24 48    |
|         | J. W. Jarnagin, per diem, Feb., 5 days..............$           | 25 00    |          |
|         | R. R. fare................................                     | 4 56—$   | 29 56    |
|         | Chas. Ashton, per diem, Feb., 5 days...............$            | 25 00    |          |
|         | R. R. fare................................                     | 3 60—$   | 28 60    |
|         | H. W. Seaman, Com. work, Jan., 1 day...............$            | 5 00     |          |
|         | per diem, Feb., 4 days..............                            | 20 00    |          |
|         | R. R. fare................................                     | 17 50—$  | 42 50    |
| Mch 31. | S. B. Humbert, P. M., postage.....................$             | 7 50     |          |
| Apr. 2. | Am. Express Co................................                 | 2 60     |          |
| Mch. 1. | W. U Telegraph Co.............................                 | 66       |          |
| 10.     | Cora Wagner, services.........................                 | 6 00     |          |
| 18.     | Des Moines Rubber Stamp Co., stamp..............                | 35       |          |
| 11.     | World's Fair Art Lithograph Co. 185 art portfolios.........     | 37 00    |          |
| 31.     | F. N. Chase, Secy. telegrams and exchange..............         | 4 72     |          |
|         | per diem March..................  $130 00                       |          |          |
|         | R. R. fare...................... 33 82—$                        | 163 82—$ | 222 65   |
| Apr. 20.| H. W. Seaman, Com. work Feb., 4 days................$           | 20 00    |          |
|         | Com. work March, 3 days..............                           | 15 00    |          |
|         | R. R. fare...........                                           | 35 00    |          |
|         | per diem, April, 4 days..............                           | 20 00    |          |
|         | R. R. fare................................                     | 17 50—$  | 107 50   |
|         | S. B. Packard, Com. work, Feb., 2 days..............$           | 10 00    |          |
|         | "         Mch., 2 days..............                            | 10 00    |          |
|         | per diem, April, 4 days..............                           | 20 00    |          |
|         | R. R. fare................................                     | 12 95—$  | 52 95    |
|         | Jas. O. Crosby, per diem, April, 5 days..............$          | 25 00    |          |
|         | R. R. fare................................                     | 13 12—$  | 38 12    |
|         | Chas. Ashton, per diem, April, 5 days..............$            | 25 00    |          |
|         | R. R. fare................................                     | 3 60—$   | 28 60    |
|         | S. H. Mallory, per diem, April, 3 days..............$           | 15 00    |          |
|         | R. R. fare................................                     | 67—$     | 15 67    |
| Feb. 29.| S. B. Humbert, P. M., postage.....................$             | 5 00     |          |
| 2.      | U. S. Express Co..............................                 | 45       |          |
| 29.     | Cora D. Wagner, services......................                 | 6 00     |          |
| 20.     | "          "                                                    | 6 00     |          |
| 13.     | "          "                                                    | 12 00    |          |
| Jan. 23.| "          "                                                    | 3 00     |          |
| 20.     | Times-Republican, papers......................                 | 7 50     |          |
| Feb. 18.| Savery Hotel, W. I. Buchanan, expense.............             | 6 50     |          |
| 29.     | F. N. Chase, Sec'y., telegrams..................                | 2 21     |          |
|         | "         "   per diem, Feb.............$ 125 00                |          |          |
|         | R. R. fare................... 15 02—$                           | 140 02—$ | 188 68   |
| Apr. 20.| J. W. Jarnagin, per diem, April, 5 days..............$          | 25 00    |          |
|         | R. R. fare................................                     | 4 56—$   | 29 56    |
| Apr. 1. | W. U. Telegraph Co............................$                | 00 25    |          |
| 30.     | "          "    4 messages..................                    | 1 54     |          |
| 29.     | S. B. Humbert, P. M., stamps....................                | 15 00    |          |

## REPORT OF AUDITING COMMITTEE 385

|  |  |  |  |  |
|---|---|---|---|---|
| | 30. | U. S. Express Co., 7 packages | 3 95 | |
| | 30. | Am. " 2 " | 4 95 | |
| | 20. | Adams " " | 35 | |
| | | " " | 50 | |
| | | " " | 60 | |
| | 8. | H. W. Seaman, paid telegrams | 65 | |
| | 9. | Redhead, Norton, L. & Co., record book | 5 00 | |
| May | 12. | T. W. Mears, services | 11 00 | |
| | 13. | World's Columbian Exposition folders and portfolios | 47 50 | |
| Apr. | 30. | F. N. Chase, Sec'y, per diem, April $130 00 | | |
| | | R. R. fare 25 90 — $ | 155 90 | |
| Mch. | 31. | World's Fair Art Lithograph Co., art portfolios | 10 00 — $ | 290 19 |
| May | 5. | H. W. Seaman, Ex. Com. work, Chicago, April, 5 days $ | 25 00 | |
| | | R. R. fare | 12 56 — $ | 37 56 |
| | | H. W. Seaman, Com. work, April, 4 days $ | 20 00 | |
| | | R. R. fare | 4 80 | |
| | | per diem, May, 3 days | 15 00 | |
| | | R. R. fare | 12 50 — $ | 52 30 |
| | | S. B. Packard, Com. work, April, 3 days $ | 15 00 | |
| | | per diem, May, 3 days | 15 00 | |
| | | R. R. fare | 43 26 — $ | 73 26 |
| | | Jas. O. Crosby, per diem, May, 6 days $ | 30 00 | |
| | | R. R. fare | 11 65 — $ | 41 65 |
| | | Theo. Guelich, per diem, May, 4 days $ | 20 00 | |
| | | R. R. fare | 12 20 — $ | 32 20 |
| | | Chas. Ashton, Com. work, April, 2 days $ | 10 00 | |
| | | per diem, May, 5 days | 25 00 | |
| | | R. R. fare | 23 50 — $ | 58 50 |
| | | J. W. Jarnagin, Com. work, April, 4 days $ | 20 00 | |
| | | per diem, May, 6 days | 30 00 | |
| | | R. R. fare | 18 00 — $ | 68 00 |
| | | S. H. Mallory, Com. work, April, 4 days $ | 20 00 | |
| | | per diem, May, 3 days | 15 00 | |
| | | R. R. fare | 9 00 — $ | 44 00 |
| | | J. F. Duncombe, per diem, Jan., 6 days $ | 30 00 | |
| | | Com. work, April, 1 day | 5 00 | |
| | | per diem, April, 3 days | 15 00 — $ | 50 00 |
| June | 10. | Jas. O. Crosby, per diem, June, 5 days $ | 25 00 | |
| | | R. R. fare | 13 18 — $ | 38 18 |
| | | S. B. Packard, Com. work, May, 3 days $ | 15 00 | |
| | | " June, 2 days | 10 00 | |
| | | per diem, June, 3 days | 15 00 | |
| | | R. R. fare | 30 76 — $ | 70 76 |
| | | Theo. Guelich, per diem, June, 4 days $ | 20 00 | |
| | | R. R. fare | 10 10 — $ | 30 10 |
| | | Wm. H. Dent, per diem, Feb., 3 days $ | 15 00 | |
| | | " June, 4 days | 20 00 | |
| | | R. R. fare | 11 25 — $ | 46 25 |
| | | H. W. Seaman, Com. work, May, 3 days $ | 15 00 | |
| | | " June, 1 day | 5 00 | |
| | | R. R. fare | 4 95 — $ | 24 95 |
| | | H. W. Seaman, per diem, June, 5 days $ | 25 00 | |
| | | R. R. fare | 17 50 — $ | 42 50 |
| | | J. W. Jarnagin, Com. work, May, 5 days $ | 25 00 | |
| | | per diem, June, 4 days | 20 00 | |
| | | R. R. fare | 4 36 — $ | 49 36 |
| | | Chas. Ashton, per diem, June, 4 days $ | 20 00 | |
| | | R. R. fare | 3 60 — $ | 23 60 |
| | | Henry Stivers, per diem, Dec., 2 days $ | 10 00 | |
| | | " April, 3 " | 15 00 | |
| | | " June, 2 " | 10 00 — $ | 35 00 |

|  | |  | |  |
|---|---|---|---|---|
| Apr. | 4. | Lancaster & Corey, 51 plates and prints | | 59 80 |
| May | 31. | S. B. Humbert, P. M., postage | $ 15 00 | |
| June | 6. | U. S. Express Co., 4 packages | 2 55 | |
| | 2. | Am. " " " | 2 80 | |
| | 1. | W. U. Telegraph Co., 5 messages | 2 64 | |
| May | 28. | Florence Albright, stenographer | 36 00 | |
| | 19. | E. L. Andrews, office supplies | 2 50 | |
| | 11. | Ill. Central R. R. | 85 | |
| | 26. | J. Kubec & Co., paper | 1 30 | |
| | 17. | Thayer & Jackson Stationery Co., one neostyle and paper | 21 44 | |
| | 24. | B. F. White & Son, stationery | 1 05 | |
| June | 1. | Iowa State Register, printing notices to contractors | 12 42 | |
| | 1. | Chicago Herald. " " " | 7 50 | |
| May | 7. | S. D. Childs & Co., letter files | 2 50 | |
| | | " " stationery and books | 24 50 | |
| June | 1. | Snyder & Hurd, letter heads | 20 50 | |
| May | 31. | F. N. Chase, Sec'y., exchange on drafts | 40 | |
| | | " " per diem, May $ 130 00 | | |
| | | R. R. fare 26 49—$ 156 49—$ | | 312 74 |
| May | 13. | C. M. Aitken, hauling trees | $ 2 50 | |
| June | 4. | Jarnagin & McKee, printing minutes and circulars | 70 35 | |
| | 4. | J. W. Jarnagin, paid postage | 8 75 | |
| | | " " for addressing circulars | 3 00—$ | 84 60 |
| June | 24. | J. Manz & Co., 2 zinc plates and drawing building with 150 electros | $ | 40 00 |
| | 23. | Jas. O. Crosby, per diem, June, 5 days | $ 25 00 | |
| | | R. R. fare | 9 74—$ | 34 74 |
| | | J. W. Jarnagin, per diem, June, 6 days | $ 30 00 | |
| | | R. R. fare | 8 00—$ | 38 00 |
| | | H. W. Seaman, per diem, June, 4 days | $ 20 00 | |
| | | Com. work, June, 4 days | 20 00 | |
| | | R. R. fare | 24 00—$ | 64 00 |
| | | Wm. H. Dent, per diem, June, 3 days | $ 15 00 | |
| | | R. R. fare | 12 65—$ | 27 65 |
| June | 23. | Chas. Ashton, Com. work, June, 3 days | $ 15 00 | |
| | | per diem, June, 3 days | 15 00 | |
| | | R. R. fare | 10 60—$ | 40 60 |
| | | Theo. Guelich, per diem, June, 2 days | $ 10 00 | |
| | | R. R. fare | 12 40—$ | 22 40 |
| | | S. B. Packard, Com. work, June, 2 days | $ 10 00 | |
| | | per diem, June, 2 days | 10 00 | |
| | | R. R. fare | 12 70—$ | 32 70 |
| June | 20. | S. B. Humbert, P. M., postage | $ 20 00 | |
| | 21. | Thos. W. Mears, services | 20 00 | |
| July | 2. | Chicago Tribune, printing proposals | 26 10 | |
| June | 20. | Florence Albright, stenographer | 24 00—$ | 90 10 |
| June | 24. | C., R. I. & P. R. R., freight on trees | $ | 28 00 |
| | 17. | Wash Butt, hauling trees | $ 45 00 | |
| | 20. | E. M. Anderson, wrapping trees | 4 50 | |
| | 25. | W. G. McKee, selecting trees | 9 00 | |
| | | Elizabeth Rives, 1 tree | 3 00 | |
| | 17. | Jas. W. Lynn, wrapping trees | 4 50 | |
| | 20. | D. Kiser, 1 tree | 5 00 | |
| | | L. A. Johnson, three trees | 3 00 | |
| | | J. W. Jarnagin, procuring trees | 6 50 | |
| | | " twine and rope | 1 30—$ | 81 80 |
| June | 23. | Josselyn & Taylor, architect services | $ | 61 25 |
| July | 23. | Jas. O. Crosby, Com. work, 6 days | $ 30 00 | |
| | | R. R. fare | 7 08—$ | 37 08 |
| | | Mrs. E. G. Rhodes, expenses June meeting Woman's Board | $ | 8 60 |
| | | Mrs. E. K. Cook, " " " | | 6 00 |
| | | Miss Mary B. Hancock, " " " | | 5 30 |
| | | Mrs. N. C. Deering, " " " | | 9 00 |
| | | Mrs. F. J. McAchran, " " " | | 12 00 |
| | | Mrs. W. S. Clark, " " " | | 10 14 |
| | | Miss Jennie F. Rogers, " " " | | 22 90 |
| | | Miss Ora E. Miller, " " " | | 8 25 |
| July | 8. | Josselyn & Taylor Co., to apply on contract | | 600 00 |
| Aug. | 5. | John G. Coder, to apply on contract | | 1,970 15 |

## REPORT OF AUDITING COMMITTEE

| | | | | |
|---|---|---|---|---|
| Aug. 23. | Jacobs, Coles & Co., stationery | | | 34 50 |
| Aug. 31. | J. F. Duncombe, expenses incurred in securing collections for Mines Department | | | 146 52 |
| Aug. 24. | S. B. Humbert, P. M., postage | $ 21 00 | | |
| 22. | U. S. Express Co., 5 packages | 1 75 | | |
| 23. | Am " | 35 | | |
| | Wise & Bryant, stationery | 2 00 | | |
| 22. | Snyder & Hurd, stationery | 50 00 | | |
| 23 | Packard & Fabrick, stationery | 10 75 | | |
| 31. | Albert Allen, services | 52 00 | | |
| | Florence Albright, services | 40 00 | | |
| 18. | H. Dahl, chairs and table | 10 75 | | |
| 31. | F. N. Chase, Sec'y., supplies and telegrams | 2 22 | | |
| | " " per diem, Aug | $ 135 00 | | |
| | R. R. fare | 10 12—$ | 145 12—$ | 344 94 |
| June 30. | U. S. Express Co., June bills | $ 2 60 | | |
| 30. | Am " | 3 20 | | |
| July 1. | W. U. Telegraph Co., 4 messages | 1 33 | | |
| June 9. | H. W. Seaman, paid telegrams and express | 1 25 | | |
| 15. | Frank Kilborn, photographs Fair building | 1 75 | | |
| 30. | Packard & Fabrick, stationery | 10 75 | | |
| 11. | Florence Albright, expense attending meeting of Com's | 13 15 | | |
| 30. | F. N. Chase, Sec'y, telegrams and exchange | 1 10 | | |
| | " " per diem, June | $ 130 00 | | |
| | R. R. fare | 17 17—$ | 147 17—$ | 182 30 |
| Aug. 30. | H. E. Machlin, material and painting cottage on State Fair grounds | | $ | 13 65 |
| Aug. 31. | Mrs. S. B. Maxwell, stationery | 14 25 | | |
| | salary, June 15 to Aug. 31 | 125 00—$ | | 139 25 |
| Aug. 29. | The Guthrian Printing Co., printing | | | 18 75 |
| July 21. | J. F. Widman, printing | $ 18 00 | | |
| Aug. 18. | " " | 25 00 | | |
| | Jas. O. Crosby, telegrams | 1 50—$ | | 44 50 |
| Mch. 12. | Marshall Printing Co., circulars | $ 1 75 | | |
| June | W. U. Telegraph Co | 2 96 | | |
| July 6. | Marshall Printing Co | 2 50 | | |
| | S. B. Packard, express | 55—$ | | 7 76 |
| Aug 31. | Des Moines Leader, adv. for bids | | $ | 9 63 |
| July 1. | Chicago Herald, adv. for bids | $ 37 50 | | |
| | T. W. Mears, services | 16 00 | | |
| 30. | U. S. Express Co., July, packages | 3 15 | | |
| | Am | 1 10 | | |
| | Florence Albright, stenographer | 32 00 | | |
| June 24. | S. D. Childs & Co., stationery | 15 50 | | |
| Aug. 1. | S. B. Humbert, P. M., stamps | 23 00 | | |
| July 30. | F. N. Chase, Sec'y., per diem, July | $ 130 00 | | |
| | R. R. fare | 15 32—$ | 145 32—$ | 273 57 |
| Sept. 2. | Chas. Ashton, Com. work, July, 7 days | $ 35 00 | | |
| | " Aug., 2 days | 10 00 | | |
| | per diem, Sept., 4 days | 20 00 | | |
| | R. R. fare | 2 00—$ | | 67 00 |
| | Jas. O. Crosby, per diem, Sept., 6 days | $ 30 00 | | |
| | R. R. fare | 11 40—$ | | 41 40 |
| | Theo. Guelich, per diem, Sept., 4 days | $ 20 00 | | |
| | R. R. fare | 10 10—$ | | 30 10 |
| | J. W. Jarnagin, Com. work, July, 8 days | $ 40 00 | | |
| | " Aug., 8 days | 40 00 | | |
| | per diem, Sept., 4 days | 20 00 | | |
| | R. R. fare | 38 22—$ | | 138 22 |
| | J. F. Duncombe, per diem, Sept., 3 days | | $ | 15 00 |
| | Henry Stivers, " " 3 days | | | 15 00 |
| Sept. 2. | Mrs. L. O. Ferson, expense, meeting of Woman's Board | | | 17 40 |
| | Miss J. E. Rogers, " " " | | | 16 85 |
| | Mrs. Cook, " " " | | | 7 50 |
| | Miss O. E. Miller, " " " | | | 16 85 |
| | Miss Mary B. Hancock " " " | | | 24 55 |
| | Mrs. E. G. Rhodes " " " | | | 12 22 |
| | Mrs. McAchran, " " " | | | 9 00 |
| | Mrs. N. C. Deering, " " " | | | 14 90 |
| | Mrs. J. F. Duncombe, " " " | | | 8 00 |

|  |  |  |  |  |
|---|---|---|---|---|
|  | Miss Mary B. Hancock, additional expense |  |  | 75 |
|  | Mrs. N. C. Deering, " " |  |  | 5 25 |
|  | Mrs. L. O. Ferson, " " |  |  | 4 40 |
| Sept. 2. | H. W. Seaman, Com. work, June, 3 days | $ | 15 00 |  |
|  | " July, 9 days |  | 45 00 |  |
|  | " Aug., 11 days |  | 55 00 |  |
|  | " Sept., 2 days |  | 10 00 |  |
|  | per diem, Sept., 4 days |  | 20 00 |  |
|  | R. R. fare |  | 61 60—$ | 206 60 |
| 7. | S. B. Packard, Com. work, July, 4 days | $ | 20 00 |  |
|  | " Aug., 1 day |  | 5 00 |  |
|  | per diem, Sept., 5 days |  | 25 00 |  |
|  | R. R. fare |  | 26 30—$ | 76 30 |
| Aug. 31. | Josselyn & Taylor, to apply on contract |  | $ | 118 50 |
| Sept. 3. | J. G. Coder, to apply on contract |  |  | 2,738 35 |
| Sept. 16. | Harden Hand Grenade Co., grenades |  |  | 39 00 |
| Oct. 3. | John G. Coder, to apply on contract |  |  | 4,905 75 |
| Sept. 23. | World's Columbian Exposition, to apply on electric lighting |  |  | 560 00 |
| Oct. 26. | Thos. W. Mears, expense and per diem for September |  |  | 144 15 |
| Oct. 1. | Milward & Clark, to apply on contract | $ | 150 00 |  |
|  | R. R. fare |  | 21 75—$ | 171 75 |
| Sept. 12. | Iowa Tribune Publishing Co., printing |  | $ | 19 70 |
| Sept. 2. | John Price, grass and grain | $ | 1 25 |  |
|  | F. H. Wilson, expense attending fairs |  | 10 35 |  |
| 17. | Albert Allen, " " " |  | 7 70 |  |
| Oct. 17. | U. S. Express Co. |  | 10 15 |  |
|  | Am. Express Co. |  | 1 60 |  |
| Sept. 3. | W. U. Telegraph Co., 4 messages |  | 1 27 |  |
| Oct. 1. | " 4 " |  | 1 92 |  |
|  | Chicago, Great Western R. R. |  | 65 |  |
| Sept. 8. | H. W. Seaman, express and telegrams |  | 1 95 |  |
| Oct. 17. | S. B. Humbert, P. M., postage |  | 101 00 |  |
| Sept. 2. | F. H. Wilson, services |  | 8 00 |  |
| Oct. 1. | Florence Albright, stenographer |  | 32 00 |  |
| Sept. 17. | Albert Allen, services |  | 32 00 |  |
| Oct. 1. | F. N. Chase, Sec'y., per diem, Sept. | $ 130 00 |  |  |
|  | R. R. fare | 45 26—$ | 175 26 |  |
| 1. | F. N. Chase, Sec'y., frt. exchange and expense |  | 15 30—$ | 400 40 |
| Oct. 22 | H. W. Seaman, Com. work, Sept., 12 days | $ | 60 00 |  |
|  | " Oct., 7 days |  | 35 00 |  |
|  | per diem, Oct., 6 days |  | 30 00 |  |
|  | R. R. fare |  | 76 17—$ | 201 17 |
|  | Theo. Guelich, Com. work, Sept., 1 day | $ | 5 00 |  |
|  | per diem, Oct., 6 days |  | 30 00 |  |
|  | R. R. fare |  | 25 90—$ | 60 90 |
|  | J. W. Jarnagin, per diem, Oct., 8 days | $ | 40 00 |  |
|  | R. R. fare |  | 18 20—$ | 58 20 |
|  | S. B. Packard, Com. work, Oct., 5 days | $ | 25 00 |  |
|  | per diem, Oct., 7 days |  | 35 00 |  |
|  | R. R. fare |  | 50 35—$ | 110 35 |
|  | Chas. Ashton, Com. work, Sept., 1 day | $ | 5 00 |  |
|  | " Oct., 4 days |  | 20 00 |  |
|  | per diem, Oct., 8 days |  | 40 00 |  |
|  | R. R. fare |  | 16 00—$ | 81 00 |
|  | Wm. H. Dent, per diem, Oct., 8 days | $ | 40 00 |  |
|  | R. R. fare |  | 30 50—$ | 70 50 |
|  | Jas. O. Crosby, Com. work, Sept., 10 days | $ | 50 00 |  |
|  | " Oct., 5 days |  | 25 00 |  |
|  | per diem, Oct., 7 days |  | 35 00 |  |
|  | R. R. fare |  | 28 42—$ | 138 42 |
| Oct. 22. | E. P. Seeds, expense, account dedicating Iowa Building |  | $ | 24 35 |
| Oct. 22. | J. W. Jarnagin, Com. work, Sept., 11 days | $ | 55 00 |  |
|  | " Oct., 9 days |  | 45 00 |  |
|  | R. R. fare |  | 23 76—$ | 123 76 |
| Oct. 22. | Milward & Clark, paid for labor |  | $ | 14 00 |
| Aug. 27. | Jarnagin & McKee, printing |  |  | 48 30 |
| Sept. 24. | North Iowa Times, printing | $ | 20 00 |  |
| 23. | Am. Express Co. |  | 80 |  |
|  | Jas. O. Crosby, telephone |  | 30—$ | 21 10 |

## REPORT OF AUDITING COMMITTEE 389

|  |  | |  |
|---|---|---|---|
| Oct. 12. | Iowa Printing Co., printing | $ 55 00 | |
| " " | " " " | 136 50—$ | 191 50 |
| Sept. 30. | Miss Mary B. Hancock, stationery | $ | 11 59 |
| Oct. 17. | Siegel, Cooper & Co., cloth | | 37 66 |
| Oct. 31. | J. F. Duncombe, per diem, Oct., 6 days | | 30 00 |
| Nov. 2. | John G. Coder, to apply on contract | | 5,910 75 |
| Nov. 2. | Milward & Clark, to apply on contract | | 150 00 |
| Oct. 10. | B. F. Chase Co., bunting flags | | 52 30 |
| 18. | J. S. Ford Johnson Co., chairs | | 175 30 |
| 22. | Virginia Hotel, carriages to depot acc't, dedicating services | | 28 00 |
| 19. | G. F. Foster, Son & Co., badges | | 50 00 |
| Oct. 31. | Thos. W. Meers, expense and per diem for October | | 83 67 |
| Nov. 1. | S. B. Humbert, P. M., postage | $ 9 00 | |
| Oct. 1. | U. S. Express Co., 18 packages | 9 30 | |
| Nov. 1. | Am. " 12 " | 4 30 | |
| Oct. 18. | Jesse Hamilton, services | 1 00 | |
| 29. | Florence Albright, stenographer | 32 00 | |
| 22. | H. W. Seaman, telegram | 40 | |
| 20. | John J. Kelley, drayage | 2 50 | |
| Nov. 1. | F. N. Chase, Sec'y., telegrams | 11 58 | |
| 1. | " " " per diem, Oct | $ 135 00 | |
| | " " " R. R. fare | 65 01—$ | 200 01—$ 270 12 |
| Nov. 2. | W. U Telegraph Co., Oct., messages | $ 8 22 | |
| Dec. 9. | Chas. Frendenberg, envelopes | 1 75 | |
| Nov. 11. | F. C May, labor | 3 00 | |
| Dec. 2. | Peterson Bros., wheat | $ 21 90 | |
| Nov. 29. | L. G. Clute, per diem and expense gathering grain | 47 55—$ | 69 45 |
| 23. | L. G. Clute, per diem and expense gathering grains | 42 43 | |
| | paid for lumber | 11 50—$ | 53 93 |
| 28. | B. F. White & Son, stationery | $ 17 80 | |
| | Florence Albright, stenographer | 32 00 | |
| 30. | Geo H. Boehmler, services | 39 25 | |
| Nov. 1. | Packard & Fabrick, stationery | 23 70 | |
| 29. | Ill. Cent. R. R | 35 | |
| 2. | Am. Express Co. | 1 80 | |
| 24. | B., C. R. & N. R. R. | 65 | |
| 30. | J. W. Camper, rent of storage room | 25 00 | |
| | S. B. Humbert, P. M., postage | 21 00 | |
| 29. | Wilson & Chase, cloth and making sacks | 14 90 | |
| | Boehmler & Sheerer, soil tubes | 31 83 | |
| 30. | F. N. Chase, Sec'y., telegrams, oil | 2 30 | |
| | " " per diem. Nov | $ 130 00 | |
| | " " R. R. fare | 45 62—$ | 175 62 |
| | U. S. Express Co. | $ 3 75 | |
| Dec. 1. | Am. Express Co., Nov., packages | 4 35—$ | 130 65 |
| Dec. 2. | John G. Coder, to apply on contract | $ | 1,500 00 |
| 1. | Milward & Clark, to apply on contract | | 150 00 |
| 14. | S. B. Packard, Com. work, Nov., 9 days | $ 45 00 | |
| | " " Dec., 6 days | 30 00 | |
| | R. R. fare | 106 17—$ | 181 17 |
| Dec. 1. | John G. Coder, to apply on contract, pavilion | $ | 971 25 |
| Nov. 30. | Thos. W. Mears, per diem and expense for November | | 161 11 |
| Dec. 20. | Josselyn & Taylor Co., to apply on contract | | 474 00 |
| Dec. 31. | H. L. Chase, stove and pipe | $ 14 75 | |
| | A. Mathesen, services | 30 00 | |
| | J. W. Camper, rent of room | 8 35 | |
| 22. | A. J. Stevens, expenses | 6 30 | |
| 24. | Andrew Preston, labor | 2 00 | |
| 20. | F. N. Chase, oil and twine | 55 | |
| Jan. 3, 1893. | S. B. Humbert, P. M., stamps | 26 00 | |
| Dec. 1, 1892. | B., C. R. & N. R. R | 50 | |
| 16. | Chicago, Great Western R. R. | 1 20 | |
| 19. | B., C. R. & N. R. R. | 85 | |
| 30. | " " | 2 05 | |
| 31. | Am. Express Co., Dec., packages | 2 00 | |
| Jan. 3, 1893. | U. S. " " " | 3 60 | |
| Dec. 20, 1892. | W, U, Telegraph Co. | 40 | |
| 21. | " " " | 50 | |
| 1. | " " 2 messages | 1 23 | |
| Jan. 21, 1893. | " " Dec., messages | 6 96 | |
| Dec. 24, 1892. | Florence Albright, stenographer | 32 00 | |
| 9. | Denison M'f'g Co., shipping tags | 12 65 | |
| 2. | " " " | 4 00 | |
| 12. | Ill. Cent. R. R., frt on car exhibits from Manchester, Ia. | 56 30 | |

390    REPORT OF IOWA COLUMBIAN COMMISSION

| | | | | |
|---|---|---|---|---|
| Nov. 11. | S. D. Childs & Co., envelopes | | 3 50 | |
| Dec. 31. | F. N. Chase, Sec'y., per diem, Dec .... $ 135 00 | | | |
| | R. R. fare .... 62 63—$ | 197 63—$ | | 412 72 |
| Dec. 30. | John G. Coder, to apply on contract | | $ 5,000 00 | |
| Feb. 23, 1893. | Iowa State Band | | 200 00 | |
| Jan. 12, 1893. | Mrs. S. B. Maxwell, salary, Sept., Oct., Nov., Dec. and Jan .... $ | 250 00 | | |
| | postage and express | 31 95—$ | | 281 95 |
| Dec. 30, 1892. | Thos. W. Mears, salary, Dec | 60 00 | | |
| | copy book and postage | 3 95—$ | | 63 95 |
| Nov. 2, 1892. | S. H. Mallory, paid transportation of guests, band and Governor's escort from Chicago to Fair Grounds at dedication of Iowa Building | | $ | 64 72 |

1893.

| | | | | |
|---|---|---|---|---|
| Jan. 13. | Jas. O. Crosby, Com. work, Dec., 4 days .... $ | 20 00 | | |
| | per diem, jan., 4 days | 20 00 | | |
| | R. R fare | 15 55—$ | | 55 55 |
| | Henry Stivers, Com. work, Oct., 1 day .... $ | 5 00 | | |
| | per diem, Oct., 1 day | 5 00 | | |
| | " Jan., 2 days | 10 00—$ | | 20 00 |
| | Wm. H. Dent, per diem, 4 days .... $ | 20 00 | | |
| | R. R. fare | 11 52—$ | | 31 52 |
| | H. W. Seaman, Com. work, Oct., 1 day .... $ | 5 00 | | |
| | " Nov., 12 days | 60 00 | | |
| | " Dec., 13 days | 65 00 | | |
| | " Jan., 4 days | 20 00 | | |
| | per diem, Jan., 6 days | 30 00 | | |
| | R. R. fare | 96 65—$ | | 276 65 |
| | S. H. Mallory, Com. work, July, 11 days .... $ | 55 00 | | |
| | " Aug., 7 " | 35 00 | | |
| | " Sept., 7 " | 35 00 | | |
| | " Oct., 6 " | 30 00 | | |
| | " Nov., 9 " | 45 00 | | |
| | " Dec., 6 " | 30 00 | | |
| | per diem, Sept., 5 " | 25 00 | | |
| | " Oct., 7 " | 35 00 | | |
| | R. R. fare | 10 00—$ | | 300 00 |
| | S. B. Packard, Com. work, Jan., 2 days .... $ | 10 00 | | |
| | per diem, Jan., 3 days | 15 00 | | |
| | R. R. fare | 2 66—$ | | 27 66 |
| | Theo. Guelich, per diem, Jan., 4 days .... $ | 20 00 | | |
| | R. R. fare | 10 10—$ | | 30 10 |
| | Chas. Ashton, per diem, Jan., 4 days .... $ | 20 00 | | |
| | R. R. fare | 3 60—$ | | 23 60 |
| Jan. 13. | Chas. Ashton, Com. work, Nov., 13 days .... $ | 65 00 | | |
| | " Dec., 19 " | 95 00 | | |
| | " Jan., 7 " | 35 00 | | |
| | R. R. fare | 10 00 | | |
| | Postage stamps | 3 00—$ | | 208 00 |
| Jan. 9. | Mrs. E. G. Rhodes, Sec'y. of Board of Lady Managers, stationery and printing | | $ | 27 35 |
| Jan. 25. | John G. Coder, to apply on contract | | | 1,225 00 |
| Jan. 25. | N. W. McIvor, Acting Adj't. Gen'l, part of expense account dedication of Iowa Building | | | 500 00 |
| Jan. 27. | John G. Coder, to apply on contract statement as follows | | | 1,456 25 |

To original contract ................$ 23,700 00
Contract for changes in the pavilion ... 1,850 00
Extra ... 317 50
Fixing pavilion for decorators.......... 250 00
Five urinals............................ 87 80
Platform for dedication ....... 15 00
                                    $26,220 30

CR.

By Cash ...............$24,221 25
Painting ............. 450 00
Less on platform...... 5 00
Less on water closet ........ 87 80—$24,764 05

Balance due............ $ 1,456 25

## REPORT OF AUDITING COMMITTEE 391

Jan. 31. Committee on Live Stock expense incurred, paid on order
of Commission Jan. 12th ..........................................
| | |
|---|---|
| D. P. Stubbs..................................$ | 11 05 |
| C. W. Norton.................................... | 12 50 |
| W. A. McHenry.................................. | 10 40 |
| J. J. Richardson................................. | 17 95 |
| W. B. Barney.................................... | 9 18 |
| W. W. McClung.................................. | 13 90 |
| C. S. Barclay..................................... | 11 95 |
| Daniel Sheehan.................................. | 13 50 |
| C. L. Gabrilson................................... | 13 75—$ 114 18 |

Jan. 30. Premiums awarded on Winter exhibits as follows:
| | |
|---|---|
| B. B. Clark......................................$ | 5 00 |
| E. H. Smith...................................... | 40 00 |
| Jas. Hethershaw................................ | 20 00 |
| L. Hudler........................................ | 15 00 |
| F. S. White...................................... | 25 00—$ 105 00 |

| | | | |
|---|---|---|---|
| Feb. 11. | The Yale and Towne M'fg Co., hardware for Iowa B'ld'g... | $ | 118 16 |
| Jan. 31. | Thos. W. Mears, per diem and expense for January........ | $ | 115 21 |
| Feb. 3. | Premiums awarded on Corn Exhibit to L. Hudler............ | | 15 00 |
| Jan. 13. | H. W. Seaman, telegrams and express.........................$ | 1 90 | |
| Jan. 14, 1892. | Ia. Union Telephone Co.......................$ 00 50 | | |
| | W. U. Telegraph Co.  "  ......................... 84 | | |
| Nov. | "  "  ......................... 51 | | |
| Oct. | "  "  ......................... 1 40 | | |
| Oct. | "  "  ......................... 35 | | |
| | $ 3 60 | | |
| | Vouchers attached to S. B. Packard's bill.................? | 3 60 | |
| Jan. 12, 1893. | I. M. Canfield, typewriting................................ | 1 50 | |
| 15. | Florence Albright, expense attending meeting Jan., 11-15... | 15 65 | |
| 1. | Bryant-Neely Lumber Co., coal............................. | 8 25 | |
| Dec. 30, 1892. | Snyder & Hurd, stationery................................ | 11 50 | |
| Jan. 25, 1893. | Wyckoff, S. & Benedict, ribbon and paper for typewriter | 5 65 | |
| Dec. 28, 1892. | Veatch & Bull, prints of plans............................ | 1 25 | |
| 21. | John G. Coder, paid freight.............................. | 2 35 | |
| Jan. 26, 1893. | B., C. R. & N. R. R. | 60 | |
| 19. | "  " ......................... | 35 | |
| | "  " ......................... | 9 95 | |
| 16. | "  " ......................... | 70 | |
| 12. | "  " ......................... | 2 65 | |
| 13. | Chicago & Great Western R. R........................... | 7 00 | |
| 11. | B., C. R. & N. R. R........................................ | 25 | |
| 13. | "  "  freight and drayage............... | 70 | |
| Feb. 3. | Florence Albright, stenographer.......................... | 40 00 | |
| 4. | S. B. Humbert, P. M., stamps............................ | 48 00 | |
| | U. S. Express Co........................................... | 2 50 | |
| | Am. Express Co............................................ | 2 10 | |
| | G. H. Boehmler, services.................................. | 17 50 | |
| 1. | J. W. Camper, rent of room.............................. | 8 35 | |
| | Andrew Mathesen, services............................... | 15 00 | |
| 1. | F. N. Chase, Sec'y., per diem, Jan.....................$ 130 00 | | |
| | R. R. fare..................... 69 33—$ | 190 33 | |
| 1. | W. U. Telegraph Co., Jan., messages.................$ | 8 23 | |
| 3. | F. N. Chase, Sec'y., telegrams and drayage.............. | 7 73—$ 118 59 | |
| Feb. 20. | Keokuk & Western R. R., frt. on car from Centerville...... | $ 60 20 | |

EDUCATIONAL EXHIBIT AT CEDAR RAPIDS, IOWA.

| | | |
|---|---|---|
| Nov. 29, 1892. | O. J. Laylander, services ..............................$ | 3 75 |
| Sept. 10. | Rand, McNally & Co., 6 maps.............................. | 5 50 |
| Oct. 5. | J. B. Knoepfler, expense incurred......................... | 21 45 |
| Dec. 24. | Saturday Chat, printing.................................... | 1 50 |
| 22. | Stein Bros., drayage...................................... | 50 |
| | Victor Stritesky, labor................................... | 7 20 |
| 29. | T. J. Lowell, hardware.................................... | 5 76 |
| | T. S. Metcalf, printing.................................... | 5 50 |
| | "  "  ......................................... | 2 00 |
| 30. | Republican Printing Co., stationery....................... | 17 75 |
| 29. | Cedar Rapids Electric L. and P. Co. for lights............ | 6 46 |
| 31. | T. S. Metcalf, printing.................................... | 1 00 |
| | Chicago & Northwestern R. R........................... | 35 |
| | Am. Express Co........................................... | 85 |
| | "  "  ......................................... | 85 |
| 30. | "  "  ......................................... | 85 |
| 31. | "  "  ......................................... | 1 50 |
| Jan. 2, '93. | Adams  "  ......................................... | 45 |

| | | | |
|---|---|---|---|
| Jan. 2, '93. Adams Express Co. | | 25 | |
| " " | | 1 00 | |
| " " | | 1 50 | |
| Dec. 31, '92. U. S. " 26 packages | | 27 60 | |
| " " | | 1 75 | |
| Jan. 5, '93. " " | | 50 | |
| Oct. 10, '92. Mrs. A. B Billington, services. | | 45 00 | |
| Nov. 11, '92. " " | | 20 00 | |
| Dec. 23. J. O. Jefferies, services | | 10 00 | |
| 29. A. Charles, Agt., insurance. | | 9 40 | |
| 23. J. A. Bishop, expenses | | 10 50 | |
| 29. J. J. McConnell, expenses. | | 8 50 | |
| 29. Geo. W. Carver, labor | | 9 50 | |
| 31. Theo. D. Merrill, labor. | | 4 50 | |
| Victor Stritesky, labor | | 7 80 | |
| C. A. McLuen, labor | | 27 00 | |
| R. J. Allison, labor. | | 4 15 | |
| Lillie Aiken, labor. | | 18 50 | |
| Feb. 16, '93. C. C. Dudley, Supt., premium | | 20 00 | |
| J. E. Williamson, premium. | | 10 00 | |
| S. W. Heath, premium | | 25 00 | |
| Clara E. Burston, teacher, premium | | 15 00 | |
| O. P. Bostwick, premium | | 15 00 | |
| L. E. A Ling, premium. | | 5 00 | |
| O. J. Laylander, premium | | 70 00 | |
| S. H. Sheakley, premium. | | 25 00 | |
| 17. Fay Bros. & Co., material | | 23 22 | |
| 18. G. W. Bryan, premium. | | 10 00 | |
| 21. E. A. Higley & Co., rent of room | | 122 00 | |
| 16. Wm. Wilcox, Supt., premium | | 40 00 | |
| J. B. Young, premium | | 15 00 | |
| J. W. Jarnagin, telegrams and sundry expenses in connection with Educational Exhibit at Cedar Rapids, Dec., '92 | | 19 62—$ | 765 49 |
| Mch. 30. Jas. O. Crosby, per diem, March, 6 days | $ 30 00 | | |
| R. R. fare | 11 68—$ | | 41 68 |
| S. B. Packard, Com. work, Feb., 3 days | $ 15 00 | | |
| per diem, March, 5 days | 25 00 | | |
| R. R. fare | 13 80—$ | | 53 80 |
| S. B. Packard, Com work, Dec., 2 days | $ 10 00 | | |
| " Jan., 4 " | 20 00 | | |
| " Feb., 7 " | 35 00 | | |
| R. R. fare | 87 93—$ | | 152 93 |
| Wm. H. Dent, per diem, March, 8 days | $ 40 00 | | |
| R. R. fare | 32 00—$ | | 72 00 |
| Chas. Ashton, Com. work, Jan., 12 days | $ 60 00 | | |
| " Feb., 17 days | 85 00 | | |
| per diem, March, 5 days | 25 00 | | |
| R. R. fare | 40 14—$ | | 210 14 |
| A. C. Roberts, per diem, March, 6 days | $ 30 00 | | |
| R. R. fare | 15 80—$ | | 45 80 |
| J. W. Jarnagin, Com. work, Nov., 14 days | $ 70 00 | | |
| " Dec., 26 " | 130 00 | | |
| " Jan., 26 " | 130 00 | | |
| " Feb., 22 " | 110 00 | | |
| R. R. fare | 60 60 $ | | 500 60 |
| H. W. Seaman, Com. work, Jan., 9 days | $ 45 00 | | |
| " Feb., 16 " | 80 00 | | |
| per diem, Mach, 5 days | 25 00 | | |
| R. R. fare | 63 75—$ | | 213 75 |
| Feb. 20. Ill. Cent. R. R | $ 00 15 | | |
| 18. Chicago & Great Western R. R | 65 | | |
| 20. Wilson & Chase, muslin and making sacks | 7 82 | | |
| 21. A. J. Bonfield, drayage. | 2 25 | | |
| M. Israel, box | 50 | | |
| F. Matthias, screw driver. | 35 | | |
| Boehmler & Sheerer, nails. | 20 | | |
| 25. S. D. Childs & Co., stationery | 2 65 | | |
| Florence Albright, stenographer | 32 00 | | |
| 25. S. B. Humbert, P. M., postage | 65 00 | | |
| A. Mathesen, labor | 15 00 | | |
| 22. B. F. White & Son, stationery | 9 06 | | |
| 27. G. H. Boehmler, services | 22 50 | | |

## REPORT OF AUDITING COMMITTEE

|  |  |  |  |  |
|---|---|---|---|---|
| 21. | J. H. Cox, services | 5 00 | | |
|  | Belt Line Transfer Co., services | 4 00 | | |
| 17. | Chicago & Great Western R. R., freight on car from Des Moines to Chicago | 48 00 | | |
| 28. | F. N. Chase, Sec'y., telegrams, Feb. | 3 96 | | |
|  | " " per diem, Feb. .........$ 120 00 | | | |
|  | " " R. R. fare............. 46 37—$ | 165 37—$ | 385 46 | |
| Feb. 27. | Jarnagin & McKee, printing and stamps | | $ | 43 26 |
| Mch. 1. | Mrs. S. B. Maxwell, postage and express | 19 25 | | |
|  | " salary, Feb. and Mch. | 100 00 | $ | 119 25 |
| Apr 27. | Iowa State Band | | $ | 200 00 |
| Jan. 11. | Josselyn & Taylor Co., preparing drawings for Agricultural pavilion..........................$ | 47 75 | | |
| Oct. 1, 1892. | Wilson & Chase, muslin and making sacks | 6 96 | | |
| Sept.30. | J. S. Fairgrave, labor and material | 8 90 | | |

PAID PREMIUMS SPECIAL CLASS 312:

|  |  |  |  |  |
|---|---|---|---|---|
|  | J. B. Rutherford | 5 00 | | |
|  | D. B. Nims | 35 00 | | |
|  | L. Hudler | 20 00 | | |
|  | Jas. Hethershaw | 40 00 | | |
|  | E. H. Smith | 55 00 | | |
|  | L. G. Clute | 125 00 | | |
| Oct. 12. | L. G. Clute, per diem, Sept., 5 days........$ 10 00 | | | |
|  | Expense and paid for grain......... 108 99—$ | 118 99 | | |
| Jan. 1, 1893. | D. B. Nims, collecting grasses ...................$ | 17 35 | | |
|  | Nims Bros., " | 30 35 | | |
|  | " " | 6 25 | | |
|  | " premium on Exhibit Corn, class 311 | 10 00 | | |
|  | " " " " 312 | 50 00 | | |
| Dec.13, 1892. | Ill. Cent. R. R. | 14 30 | | |
| Feb. 1, 1893. | Whitall, Tatum & Co., glass labels | 2 40 | | |
| 9. | " " " glass show bottles | 286 35 | | |
| Jan. 14. | J. W. Wadsworth, expense as judge | 6 00 | | |
|  | J. H. Cox, labor | 15 00 | | |
| 13. | W. H. McCannon, labor | 2 00 | | |
| 16. | E. H. Smith, labor | 8 00 | | |
|  | Jas. Pemble, labor | 2 00 | | |
| 17. | L. G. Clute, per diem, Jan., 5 days.........$ 10 00 | | | |
|  | Expense gathering exhibits........ 11 82—$ | 21 82 | | |
| Feb. 1. | L. Porter, labor................................$ | 4 00—$ | 937 15 | |
|  | J. S. McNair, express and stationery................$ | 4 35 | | |
| May 10, 1892. | Peter Larson, table, desk and chairs | 48 00 | | |
| 11. | Jacobs, Coles & Co., letter press and stand | 10 00 | | |
| 7. | Lakeside Sign Works, lettering | 1 75 | | |
| Aug. 1. | L. Lodge, stenographer | 1 68 | | |
| Oct. 1. | " " | 90 | | |
|  | S. H. Mallory paid Chicago office rent, May 10, '92, to Jan. 1, '93 | 243 79—$ | 310 92 | |

**1893.**

|  |  |  |  |  |
|---|---|---|---|---|
|  | Pay roll Dec. 27, to June 7, 1893 .................$ | 145 65 | | |
| Jan. 17. | Machinist's Supply Co., belt | 50 | | |
| 11. | Standard Oil Co., oil | 52 | | |
| 19. | Albert Allen, paid for ink and pens | 38 | | |
| 16. | C. H. Rice, oil | 1 00 | | |
| 10. | " pails and pokers | 1 60 | | |
|  | " pails | 95 | | |
|  | John J. Magee, oil, etc | 1 25 | | |
|  | The Fair, hasp and lock | 75 | | |
|  | Jones Stationery and Printing Co., stationery | 50 | | |
| 11. | F. C. Wilson & Co., zinc filler | 45 | | |
|  | Rob't. Prayer, iron | 60 | | |
|  | O. F. Schmidt, oil | 35 | | |
|  | Abbott & Co., ink | 50—$ | 155 00 | |
|  | Pay roll, Jan. 9 to 21 ...............................$ | 398 42 | | |
| Jan. 31. | Albert Allen, car fare, telegrams, etc | 10 05 | | |
|  | John J. Magee, cobalt blue | 3 00 | | |
|  | C. H. Rice, hinges, lock and staple | 50 | | |
| 30. | " sand paper | 15 | | |
|  | Hibbard, Spencer, B. & Co., tacks, etc | 1 17 | | |
|  | Geo. E. Watson & Co., paper | 1 80 | | |
| 27. | L. M. Brown, files | 65 | | |
| 28. | Marshall Field & Co., cloth | 4 70 | | |

|  |  |  |  |  |
|---|---|---|---|---|
| 27. | Carson, Pirie, Scott & Co., cloth | | 21 81 | |
| | L. M. Brown, rope | | 1 06 | |
| 26. | Carson, Pirie, Scott & Co., cloth | | 42 87 | |
| 11. | Merchant's Parcel Delivery Co., drayage | | 75 | |
| | Decorators Supply Co. | | 3 00 | |
| 24. | Marshall Field & Co., cloth | | 9 55 | |
| 24. | Hibbard, Spencer, B. & Co., hardware | | 50 | |
| | H. F. Barndt, coal | | 21 75 | |
| 18. | J. J. Magee, paints | | 12 91 | |
| 25. | A. R. Porter, muslin | | 8 33 | |
| 30. | Pearson Lumber Co., lumber | | 98 17—$ | 641 14 |

| | | | | |
|---|---|---|---|---|
| Jan. 14. | John Price, corn and boxing | $ | 5 00 | |
| 3. | L. G. Clute, per diem, Dec., 6 days | $ 12 00 | | |
| | Expense gathering exhibits | 53 20—$ | 65 20 | |
| | L. G. Clute, per diem, Jan., 2 days | $ 4 00 | | |
| | Expense gathering exhibits | 19 70—$ | 23 70 | |
| Dec.,'92. | E. A. Conway, car corn | $ 214 13 | | |
| | freight on same to Chicago | 97 37—$ | 311 50 | |
| Jan. 24, '93. | Ill. Cent. R. R., freight on car from Manchester to Chi. | $ | 42 00 | |
| 10. | J. T. Fairgraves, grain and boxing | | 4 90—$ | 452 30 |

| | | | | |
|---|---|---|---|---|
| Feb. 16. | Pearson Lumber Co., lumber | $ | 46 50 | |
| 15. | C. H. Rice, stove and fixtures | | 7 20 | |
| | H. F. Barndt, coal | | 1 00 | |
| | Cheattle & Bawley, oil and can | | 35 | |
| | M. D. Rider, stationery | | 80 | |
| | Rollo Frank, express | | 7 55 | |
| | Rukgaber & Crane, crayons | | 1 00 | |
| 17. | L. M. Brown, hardware | | 4 90 | |
| 20. | Pearson Lumber Co., lumber | | 1 35 | |
| | H. F. Barndt, coal | | 21 75 | |
| | John Cole, clay | | 5 00 | |
| 21. | J. J. Magee, plaster | | 2 70 | |
| | Standard Express Co., drayage | | 6 75 | |
| | Pay roll, Feb. 8-14 | | 415 25—$ | 522 10 |

| | | | | |
|---|---|---|---|---|
| Feb. 1. | D. E. Milward, tracing paper | $ | 1 40 | |
| | Jas. Wadsworth, nails | | 90 | |
| | Pearson Lumber Co., lumber | | 3 60 | |
| 2. | J. J. Magee, ink and pad | | 30 | |
| 10. | " plaster of Paris | | 3 30 | |
| 7. | Standard Express Co., drayage | | 50 | |
| 1. | Al. S. Miller, repairs | | 75 | |
| 8. | S. J. Stebbins, hardware | | 50 | |
| 6. | Am. Express Co. | | 2 65 | |
| 9. | L. M. Brown, files and twine | | 75 | |
| 10. | " nails | | 13 25 | |
| | Hibbard, Spencer, B. & Co., pick and handle | | 52 | |
| 1. | Parker Bros., teams | | 28 00 | |
| 13. | H. F. Barndt, coal | | 21 75 | |
| | A. Allen, car fare | | 5 10 | |
| | L. M. Brown, tacks | | 1 25 | |
| Mch. 1. | Milward & Clark, to apply on contract | | 150 00 | |
| | Pay roll, Feb. 15-21 | | 450 05—$ | 684 67 |

| | | | | |
|---|---|---|---|---|
| Dec. 24, 1892. | W. W. DeLong, labor | $ | 48 00 | |
| | J. W. Kibler, labor | | 33 60 | |
| 31. | Milward & Clark, to apply on contract | | 150 00 | |
| Jan. 4, 1893. | Western Rubber and Belting Co., belt | | 1 72 | |
| | Samuel Harris & Co., files, wrench, etc | | 1 98 | |
| 6. | Chicago Skein and Axle Co., labor | | 3 00 | |
| 4. | J. A. Fay & Co., saw blades | | 3 60 | |
| 6. | C. H. Rice, saw clamp | | 1 20 | |
| 5. | " oil and latch | | 35 | |
| 6. | A. F. Bock, gas fittings | | 10 26 | |
| Feb. 1. | J. S. McNair, paid drayage, etc | | 3 76 | |
| Jan. 7. | Albert Dickinson Co., grass seed | | 7 69—$ | 265 25 |

| | | | | |
|---|---|---|---|---|
| Dec. 8, 1892. | Sawyer Goodman Co., lumber | $ | 98 20 | |
| 9. | " " " | | 187 67 | |
| Jan. 10, 1893. | " " " | | 14 00 | |
| Dec. 7, 1892. | S. D. Kimbark, nails | | 27 95 | |
| 15. | W. McGregor & Co., portable engine | | 160 00 | |
| 22. | " " band saw | | 62 50 | |
| Jan. 2, 1893. | Milward & Clark, paper and card-board | | 1 10 | |

| | | | | | |
|---|---|---|---|---|---|
|Dec. 17, 1892.| |Morrison, Plummer & Co., plaster| |10 00| |
|Jan. 3, 1893.| |"   "   " paints| |33 09| |
| | |"   "   "| |3 01| |
| |5.|H. F. Barndt, coal| |21 75| |
| |28.|Office Toilet Co., towel supply, Jan| |1 00| |
| | |L. Lodge, typewriting| |1 10| |
| | |The Fair, cloth| |2 25| |
| | |"   "| |3 00| |
|Dec. 15, 1892.| |Standart & Co., Agents, stove| $ 20 00 | | |
| | |                   hardware| 21 14—$ |41 14| |
| |30.|C. H. Rice, tar, felt, brooms, etc| $ |3 80| |
| |19.|Bour Bros., barrels| |4 70| |
| | |Robert Finley, barrels| |3 00| |
| |14.|L. Gould, binding twine| |18 64—$ |697 96|
|Dec. 10.| |Wm. Kibler, labor| $ |11 20| |
| | |W. W. DeLong, labor| |60 00—$|71 20|
|Nov. 14, 1892.| |Peter Ryan, stove and fixtures| $ |21 00| |
| |15.|C. H. Rice, pails and wire| |2 08| |
| |14.|Morrison, Plummer & Co., plaster, etc| |11 16| |
| |15.|C. P. Van Inwegen, coal| |15 00| |
| |12.|Orr & Lockett, hardware| |3 58| |
| | |J. B. Lukanitsch, files, etc| |4 30| |
| |18.|C. H. Rice, paper| |1 65| |
| |21.|John Jones, labor| |70| |
| |30.|Geo. E. Watson & Co., paints| |6 23| |
|Dec. 7.| |Chicago Tribune, advertisement| |45| |
| | |Chicago News,    "| |38| |
| | |J. S. McNair, drayage| |1 15—$|67 68|
| | |Pay Rolls, Jan. 21-31| $ |311 25| |
| | |              Feb. 1-7| |360 40| |
|Feb. 22.| |Hibbard, Spencer, B. & Co., tacks| |50| |
| |23.|J. V. Farwell & Co., cloth| |5 27| |
| | |Pearson Lumber Co., lumber| |16 50| |
| | |Am. Express Co| |2 50| |
| | |"   "| |2 75| |
| | |Adams  "| |95| |
| | |"   "| |1 60| |
| | |U. S.  "| |4 30| |
| |24.|Am.    "| |1 80| |
| | |Adams  "| |1 00| |
| | |U. S.  "| |5 05| |
| | |J. J. Magee, white lead, etc| |8 45| |
| | |L. M. Brown, tacks and twine| |1 78| |
| | |Boston Store, cloth| |2 00| |
| |25.|John J. Zoller, paint| |1 75| |
| | |H. May, barrels| |80| |
| | |Backus & Sisley, barrels| |2 00| |
| | |U. S. Express Co| |2 30| |
| |27.|Am. Express Co| |80| |
| |28.|A. Allen, car fare and ink| |4 70| |
| | |Adams Express Co| |1 50| |
| | |R. A. Wells, lumber| |11 95| |
| | |C. Jevne & Co., express| |70| |
| |31.|Geo. G. Standart & Co., nails| |18 10| |
| |20.|Chicago Edison Co., light| |1 00| |
|Jan. 23.| |"   "   "| |1 00—$|773 69|
| | |Pay Roll, March 22-31| $ |563 85| |
|Mch. 22.| |Wells Fargo & Co., express| |1 40| |
| | |Adams Express Co| |3 55| |
| |20.|John Doyle & Co., castings and plaster| |16 00| |
| |25.|C. H. Rice, oil| |4 00| |
| |27.|L. M. Brown, nails| |8 10| |
| |29.|U. S. Express Co| |7 90| |
| |30.|Wells Fargo & Co| |1 25| |
|Apr. 3.| |Adams Express Co| |1 75| |
| | |Am.    "| |80| |
| | |Adams  "| |3 75| |
| | |Wells Fargo & Co| |80| |
| | |Am. Express Co| |8 35| |
| |1.|World's Columbian Exposition, storage| |1 60| |
| | |"   "   " charges on grain| |2 15| |
| |4.|L. M. Brown, nails| |9 00| |
|Mch. 30.| |G. W. Straight, lumber| |1 40| |
| - 23.| |Standard Express Co., drayage| |21 25| |
|Apr. 6.| |Adams Express Co| |1 30| |
| | |H. F. Barndt, coal| |7 25| |

|  |  |  |  |  |
|---|---|---|---|---|
| 7. | E. Harrold, drayage | 9 00 | | |
|  | L. M. Brown, nails | 3 05 | | |
|  | C. H. Rice, tacks | 60 | | |
| 8. | B. McCartney, plaster | 2 00 | | |
|  | C. H. Rice, hardware | 1 40 | | |
|  | J. V. Farwell Co., cloth | 7 22 | | |
| 10. | Am Express Co | 1 20 | | |
|  | A. Allen, drayage and car fare | 10 15 | | |
|  | C. H. Rice, nails | 6 15 | $ | 706 32 |
| Mch. 1. | J. W. Camper, rent of storage room | $ 8 35 | | |
| 10. | E. Kretchmer, expense in Apiary Department | 14 92 | | |
| 4. | A. J. Doll, cloth sign | 4 70 | | |
| 6. | Iowa State Ag'l Society, part expense of corn exhibit at Winter Exhibit | 13 35 | | |
| 2. | J. T. Knapp, services | 45 00 | | |
| 11. | W. O. Mitchell, boxing and drayage | 9 80 | | |
|  | freight on grain Corning to Chicago | 16 15 | | |
| 15. | Whitall, Tatum & Co., glass cylinders | 118 02 | $ | 260 29 |
| Mch.11. | Geo. A. Mullin, stationery | $ 10 38 | | |
|  | Wm. Jewell, 2 model school houses | 21 10 | | |
| 21. | Laura George, express | 80 | | |
| 14. | Iowa Iron and Brass Works, part payment on revolving stand | 70 00 | | |
| 15. | C. E. Baldwin, services | 9 00 | | |
| 21. | Ella Lyon, services | 2 56 | | |
| 25. | E. C. Lee, calico and brass rings | 47 95 | | |
| Feb. 16. | C. L. Suksdorf, Co. Supt., premium | 10 00 | | |
|  | J. W. Kitch, premium | 5 00 | | |
| Mch.31. | Moler & Clark, lumber | 85 97 | | |
| Apr. 4. | U. S. Express Co | 53 40 | | |
|  | " " | 25 | | |
|  | " " | 60 | | |
| 5. | Ira C. Kling, services | 50 00 | | |
| 7. | Jos. Schell, labor | 50 00 | | |
| 8. | Jas. McDonald, labor | 100 00 | | |
|  | Iowa Cottage for Blind, expense of exhibit | 100 00 | | |
|  | Institution for Feeble Minded, expense of exhibit | 100 00 | | |
|  | Iowa School for Deaf, expense of exhibit | 100 00 | | |
|  | Iowa State Normal School, expenses of exhibit | 125 00 | | |
| 12. | Pearson Lumber Co., lumber | 1 75 | | |
|  | J. W. Jarnagin, expense | 4 90 | $ | 898 96 |
| Mch.29 | Geo. T. Gunn, honey | $ 13 35 | | |
| 31. | Wm. Mavor, cases for wool exhibit | 84 60 | | |
|  | cases for honey exhibit | 213 75 | $ | 311 70 |
| Mch.11. | Mrs. Whiting S. Clark, expense | $ 20 15 | | |
|  | Mrs. Flora J. McAchran, expense | 20 00 | $ | 40 15 |
| Mch. 6. | Thos. W. Meers, salary, Feb | $ 60 00 | | |
|  | expense, Feb | 54 05 | $ | 114 05 |
| Mch.27. | East Sioux Falls Granite Quarries, cutting stone and frt | | $ | 35 79 |
| Dec.27, 1892. | Marshall Field & Co., cloth | $ 168 40 | | |
|  | " " " | 52 85 | | |
|  | " " " | 3 18 | | |
| Feb. 1, 1893. | Milward & Clark, to apply on contract | 150 00 | | |
| 4. | Garver & Maish, insurance | 200 00 | | |
| Jan. 2. | S. H. Mallory, paid for telegrams | 4 06 | $ | 578 49 |
| Mch. 1. | Pearson Lumber Co., lumber | $ 26 76 | | |
| 2. | " " " | 4 00 | | |
| 3. | C. H. Rice, tacks, etc | 1 70 | | |
|  | Backus & Sisley, brooms | 1 50 | | |
| 2. | J. J. Zoller, Japan | 1 20 | | |
| 6. | L. M. Brown, nails | 2 90 | | |
| 2. | U. S. Express Co | 1 50 | | |
| 6. | Adams " | 2 50 | | |
| 1. | " " | 60 | | |
|  | U. S. " | 3 45 | | |
| 6. | Marshall Field & Co., cloth | 18 92 | | |
|  | Pay Roll, Feb. 22-28 | 452 15 | $ | 541 18 |
| Feb. 24. | Pettibone, Wells & Co., souvenirs | $ 368 00 | | |
|  | J. O. Crosby, paid for 2,500 frontis half tones | 25 00 | $ | 393 00 |
| Apr. 14. | Mrs. S. B. Maxwell, salary, April | $ 50 00 | | |
|  | Freight paid C., R. I. & P. R. R | 8 45 | | |
|  | Paid for stamps | 20 25 | $ | 78 70 |

## REPORT OF AUDITING COMMITTEE 397

| | | | | | |
|---|---|---|---|---|---|
| Mch. 8 | S. J. Stebbins, tacks | | $ 00 69 | | |
| 10. | A. R. Porter, muslin | | 3 20 | | |
| 11. | Carson, Pirie, Scott & Co., cloth | | 1 95 | | |
| | Marshall Field & Co., cloth | | 9 31 | | |
| 9. | J. J. Magee, paint | | 3 75 | | |
| | C. H. Rice, nails | | 3 15 | | |
| 13. | E. A. Young, nails | | 2 95 | | |
| 10. | J. J. Magee, plaster | | 2 25 | | |
| 15. | L. M. Brown, nails | | 5 30 | | |
| Feb. 23. | L. Lodge, typewriting | | 95 | | |
| Mch. 10. | H. F. Barndt, coal | | 18 11 | | |
| 15. | Pearson Lumber Co., lumber | | 5 90 | | |
| 13. | " " " | | 16 50 | | |
| 4. | Jacobs, Coles & Co., stationery | | 3 05 | | |
| Feb. 4. | Sawyer, Goodman & Co., lumber | | 73 86 | | |
| 1. | " " " | | 42 99 | | |
| 2. | " " " | | 40 72 | | |
| 1. | " " " | | 37 62 | | |
| Jan. 5. | " " " | | 59 54 | | |
| Feb. 2. | " " " | | 40 39 | | |
| | Pay Roll, March 1-7 | | 412 10 | $ 817 78 | |
| Apr. 8. | Packard & Fabrick, envelopes | | | $ 15 25 | |
| 19. | A. C. Roberts, expense incurred gathering Forestry and Photograph exhibits | | $ 15 05 | $ 15 05 | |
| | Pay Roll, March 15-21 | | $ 347 40 | | |
| Feb. 27. | E. A. Conway, car of corn | | 404 63 | | |
| | freight, car of corn | | 78 26 | $ 830 29 | |
| | Pay Roll, March 8-14 | $ | 390 90 | | |
| Mch. 21. | A. Allen, car fare and drayage | | 5 85 | | |
| 15. | Jones Stationery and Printing Co., stationery | | 1 15 | | |
| 21. | H. F. Barndt, coal | | 14 50 | | |
| 16. | L. M. Brown, tacks | | 75 | | |
| 17. | " nails | | 3 25 | | |
| 20. | " " | | 2 60 | | |
| 17. | Hibbard, S., Bartlett & Co., hardware | | 7 82 | | |
| Feb. 4. | Marshall Field & Co., cloth | | 50 50 | | |
| Mch. 18. | Vilas Bros., alabastine | | 45 | | |
| | J. S. McNair, services | | 75 00 | | |
| Feb. 28. | Garver & Maish, insurance | | 200 00 | $ 752 77 | |
| Apr. 3. | Milward & Clark, to apply on contract | | | $ 150 00 | |
| Mch. 13. | S. B. Humbert, P. M., stamps | | $ 10 00 | | |
| 1. | F. N. Chase, Sec'y., telegrams and express | | 7 85 | | |
| 15. | " " " | | 10 68 | | |
| 3. | " " per diem, March | $ 135 00 | | | |
| | R. R. fare | 43 67 | 198 67 | $ 257 20 | |
| Mch 28. | Thos. W. Meers, paid freight | | $ 19 11 | | |
| | March salary | | 60 00 | | |
| | March expenses | | 22 36 | $ 101 17 | |
| Mch. 30. | L. G. Clute, five days time | $ 7 50 | | | |
| | boxing and drayage, per voucher | 8 50 | | | |
| | baskets, per voucher | 3 20 | | | |
| | grotto, per voucher | 22 65 | | | |
| | crates, per voucher | 7 00 | | | |
| | freight, per voucher | 2 62 | | | |
| | " " | 8 09 | | | |
| | frt., Dubuque to Chicago, per voucher | 48 53 | | | |
| | drayage | 5 50 | | | |
| | telegrams | 1 30 | | | |
| | car fare and expenses | 19 40 | $ 134 29 | | |
| Feb. 16. | Chas. Ashton, postage | | $ 1 50 | | |
| | Wise & Bryan, stationery | | 5 25 | | |
| 22. | Wyckoff, Seamans & B., chair | | 5 00 | | |
| | cabinet for typewriter | | 25 00 | | |
| Mch. 27. | B., C. R. & N. R. R. | | 7 80 | | |
| | Chicago Fine Art Co., pictures | | 3 00 | | |
| Apr. 1. | Snyder & Hurd, printing | | 12 10 | | |
| Mch. 1. | W. U. Telegraph Co., Feb. messages | | 8 61 | | |
| | B., C. R. & N. R. R. | | 7 71 | | |
| 15. | H. L. Chase & Co., telegrams and freight | | 11 30 | | |
| 16. | Am. Express Co. | | 25 | | |
| | U. S. Express Co. | | 60 | | |
| | W. U. Telegraph Co. | | 77 | | |
| Apr. 3. | H. L. Chase & Co., freight, express and drayage | | 11 85 | | |
| Mch. 29. | John McLane, 6 book cases | | 48 60 | | |

| | | | | |
|---|---|---|---|---|
| Apr. 1. | I. T. Knapp services, March | | 65 00 | |
| | Florence Albright, services, March | | 75 00 | |
| | S. D. Childs & Co., stationery | | 4 45 | |
| 8. | G. O. Higham, paid freight | | 7 76 | |
| Mch. 1. | U. S. Express Co | | 15 25 | |
| 1. | F. N. Chase, Sec'y., express | | 1 80 | |
| Apr. 1. | W. U. Telegraph Co | | 76 | |
| | J. W. Camper, rent of storage rooms | | 8 35—$ | 462 00 |
| Apr. 20. | S. B. Packard, Com. work, March, 17 days | $ 85 00 | | |
| | per diem, April, 5 days | 25 00 | | |
| | R. R. fare | 68 15—$ | | 178 15 |
| | Chas. Ashton, per diem, April, 6 days | $ 30 00 | | |
| | R. R. fare | 27 50—$ | | 57 50 |
| | Jas. O. Crosby, Com. work, March, 2 days | $ 10 00 | | |
| | " April, 12 days | 60 00 | | |
| | per diem, April, 6 days | 30 00 | | |
| | R. R. fare | 4 78—$ | | 104 78 |
| | H. W. Seaman, Com. work, March, 18 days | $ 90 00 | | |
| | " April, 5 days | 25 00 | | |
| | per diem, April, 5 days | 25 00 | | |
| | R. R. fare | 50 00 | | |
| | telegrams | 1 70 | | |
| | express and telegrams | 50—$ | | 192 20 |
| | A. C. Roberts, Com. work, March, 15½ days | $ 77 50 | | |
| | R. R. fare | 25 30—$ | | 102 80 |
| | J. W. Jarnagin, Com. work, March, 21 days | $ 105 00 | | |
| | " April, 13 days | 65 00 | | |
| | per diem, March, 3 days | 15 00 | | |
| | per diem, March, 5 days | 25 00 | | |
| | R. R. fare | 70 96—$ | | 280 96 |
| May 3. | H. W. Seaman, Com. work, April, 4 days | 20 00 | | |
| | per diem, May, 5 days | 25 00 | | |
| | R. R. fare | 25 00—$ | | 70 00 |
| Apr. 6. | The Guthrian Printing Co., printing | $ | | 15 45 |
| May 2. | Florence Albright, salary, April | $ 60 00 | | |
| | Joe T. Knapp, salary, April | 65 00 | | |
| | H. W. Seaman, telegrams and express | 8 05 | | |
| Apr. 29. | W. H. Lewis, drayage | 4 00 | | |
| | M. Walrath, drayage | 4 00 | | |
| 20. | J. W. Camper, rent of room | 5 56 | | |
| May 1. | J. C. Grass, laying carpet | 10 95 | | |
| Apr. 29. | Empire Carpet Cleaning Co., laying carpet | 22 27 | | |
| 30. | F. N. Chase, Sec'y., per diem, April | $ 150 00 | | |
| | R. R. fare | 30 17—$ | 180 17—$ | 360 00 |
| May 5. | Jas. O. Crosby, per diem, May, 9 days | $ 45 00 | | |
| | R. R. fare | 5 10—$ | | 50 10 |
| | J. W. Jarnagin, Com. work, April, 9 days | $ 45 00 | | |
| | per diem, May, 5 days | 25 00 | | |
| | R. R. fare | 2 50—$ | | 72 50 |
| | Wm. H. Dent, per diem, May, 8 days | $ 40 00 | | |
| | R. R. fare | 27 50—$ | | 67 50 |
| | Chas. Ashton, per diem, May, 8 days | $ 40 00 | | |
| | R. R. fare | 23 60—$ | | 63 60 |
| | Henry Stivers, per diem, March meeting, 3 days | $ 15 00 | | |
| | Com. work, March, 2 days | 10 00 | | |
| | per diem, April, 5 days | 25 00 | | |
| | R. R. fare | 48 60—$ | | 98 60 |
| May 1. | Thos. W. Meers, salary, April | $ 60 00 | | |
| | R. R. fare and expenses | 56 95—$ | | 116 95 |
| Apr. 12. | Marshall Field & Co., cloth | $ 31 80 | | |
| 21. | " " | 14 70 | | |
| May 1. | Milward & Clark, to apply on contract | 150 00 | | |
| | H. J. Straight & Co., Agents, insurance | 125 00 | | |
| 8. | John C. Ure, sodding and filling | 158 00 | | |
| 1. | D. R. Armstrong & Co., paints | 18 75 | | |

|  |  |  |  |
|---|---|---|---|
| 29. | Robert Stevenson & Co., glass jars | 17 07 | |
| 17. | " " " | 21 28 | |
| 13. | A. H. Treat, freight on exhibit | 60 00 | |
| Apr. 28. | A. J. Press M'f'g Co., mirrors | 51 50 | |
| 27. | T. W. Wilmarth Co., to apply on electric light fixtures | 200 00 | |
| May 13. | H. L. Clark, labor | 17 00 | |
| Apr. 1. | Marshall Field & Co., oak grilles | 89 24 | |
| 24. | " " express | 75 | |
| 3. | " " matting | 110 11 | |
| 15. | " " beds, springs and cots | 57 02 | |
| 18. | " " rugs and wire mat | 49 32 | |
| 5. | " " lace curtains | 42 00 | |
| 27. | " " carpets and making | 239 05 | |
| 28. | " " brushes and combs | 5 72 | |
| " | " " soap | 1 24 | |
| " | " " soap | 3 67 | |
| " | " " blankets | 16 85 | |
| " | " " pole and brackets | 2 60 | |
| " | " " towels | 24 98 | |
| " | " " bed clothing | 10 90 | |
| " | " " matting | 15 00 | |
| " | " " matting, $35.20, less $27.17 disct on bills | 8 03 | |
| May 13. | J. M. Raymond, labor | 1 50 | |
| 10. | John G. Coder, balance of contract | 350 00 | 1,923 01 |
| | deposit | $ 50 00 | |
| Apr. 29. | Hyde Park Gas Co., service for gas | 12 90 | |
| | gas permit | 3 00 | $ 65 90 |
| Apr. 27. | Andrews & Noel, to apply on contract | | $ 1,000 00 |
| Apr. 17. | C. H. Rice, tacks and hardware | $ 2 36 | |
| 15. | C. H. Rice, tacks and wire | 1 60 | |
| | Geo. E. Watson & Co., oil | 4 15 | |
| | Orr & Lackett, bolts | 1 95 | |
| 17. | H. F. Barndt, coal | 7 25 | |
| Aug 14. | Adams Express Co | 65 | |
| 14. | " " " | 1 00 | |
| | Backus Grocery, dusters | 75 | |
| Apr. 13. | World's Fair D. & E. Co., corn stalks | 1 00 | |
| 14. | U. S. Express Co | 1 20 | |
| 12. | Jas. H. Walker Co., cloth | 10 06 | |
| 12. | Siegel Cooper Co., cloth | 5 00 | |
| | L. M. Brown, hardware | $ 40 | $ 42 37 |
| | Pay Roll, April 1-7 | $ | 421 10 |
| | " " 8-14 | | 424 70 |
| | " additional, April 1-17 | | 178 55 |
| | " May 1-5 | | 185 60 |
| | " May 1 13 | | 346 65 |
| | " May 15-20, also | | |
| | " Attendants, May 1-20 | | 758 31 |
| June 5. | A. L. Deane & Co., safe | $ 100 00 | |
| May 3. | F. N. Chase, Sec'y., paid Wellington Catering Co | 16 85 | |
| Mch.10. | J. H. Cox, labor | 3 50 | |
| Apr. 28. | C., R. I. & P. R. R. | 3 90 | |
| Apr. 26. | U. S. Express Co | 3 90 | |
| June 1. | Iowa Printing Co., printing | 71 75 | |
| Apr. 20. | Chas. Frendenberg & Co., printing | 4 75 | |
| May 29. | Max Schachner, printing | 1 15 | |
| 27. | C. H. Rice, hose, reel and attachments | 5 75 | |
| 29. | Siegel, Cooper & Co., two dozen cuspidors | 17 00 | |
| Apr. 11. | The Fair, ice chest | 6 35 | |
| 13. | " " " | 3 85 | |
| May 5. | Garden City Awning and Tent Co., 2 flags | 6 00 | |
| May 5. | The Fair, scissors and thread | 79 | |
| 25. | Raisor Door Check Co., 2 door checks | 2 00 | |
| Apr. 26. | Jas. Colon, 2 days hauling | 27 60 | |
| May 10. | Backus M'f'g Co., express on heaters | 18 00 | |
| 22. | W. S. Loomis, services | 30 85 | |
| Apr. 24. | Am. Express Co | 4 85 | |
| 27. | J. Murphy, drayage | 4 50 | |
| 28. | " " | 4 00 | |
| 23. | L. M. Brown, hardware | 30 | |
| 25. | " pail | 30 | |
| Apr. 8. | S. D. Childs & Co., paper | 2 90 | |
| 17. | " " " | 1 80 | |
| 26. | " " stationery | 5 05 | |
| May 5. | " " pen holders and pens | 1 80 | |
| Apr. 10. | Hortense Crosby, services | 5 00 | |
| Feb. 9. | " " | 5 00 | |
| May 15. | Am. Express Co | 25 | |
| | | 40 | |

| | | | | |
|---|---|---|---|---|
| Apr. 27. | C. B. & Q. R. R. | | 75 | |
| May 26. | L. M. Brown, bolts | | 1 00 | |
| | Wyckoff, S. & Benedict, shelf | | 55 | |
| 5. | Morrison, Plummer & Co., corks | | 6 80 | |
| 13. | Adams Express Co | | 2 05 | |
| 23. | B. F. Simons, sack for papers | | 1 00 | |
| 27. | Sam'l R. Hull, drayage | | 7 75 | |
| 2. | Mrs. F. N. Chase, services April 13 to May 1 | | 60 00 | |
| 20. | H. S. Towle, services April 19 to May | | 21 00 | |
| 1. | L. G. Hill, guard work | | 2 00 | |
| Apr. 5. | Inter-Ocean, papers | | 3 00 | |
| 22. | Chicago News, papers | | 1 00 | |
| 27. | S. B. Humbert, P. M., postage | | 20 00 | |
| June 1. | | | 30 20 | |
| Apr. 27. | World's Columbian Commission, grain | | 21 75 | |
| 28. | The Fair, crockery | | 25 02—$ | 366 94 |
| May 26. | Jas. King Seed Co., corn hooks | $ | 3 25 | |
| | Am. Express Co. | | 1 00 | |
| 12. | Crane Co., copper finished rail | | 305 00 | |
| 22. | M. Larson, desk and chairs | | 36 00 | |
| 27. | Creamery Package M'f'g Co— | | | |
| | butter tubs and express | | 5 69 | |
| | " " " | | 70 50 | |
| | " " " | | 23 87 | |
| Apr. 22. | E. Kretchmer, paid express | $ 1 25 | | |
| | paid for broken can | 50 | | |
| | paid C., B. & Q. R. R. | 65 | | |
| | paid for honey and express | 12 30 | | |
| | paid for supplies | 39 86 | | |
| | paid R. R. fare | 25 00—$ | 79 56 | |
| 30. | Ben Packard, services, April | $ | 55 00 | |
| | car fare | | 2 20 | |
| May 8. | Am. Express Co. | | 1 55 | |
| 1. | C. L. Gabrilson, premium on wool | | 30 00 | |
| | telegram | | 50 | |
| 15. | State Ag'l Society pd. freight and expenses sending exhibit | | 68 45 | |
| Apr. 29. | Chas. W. Dahlgreen, 10 banners | | 55 00 | |
| May 8. | E. Kretchmer, 15 days labor | $ 45 00 | | |
| | expenses | 30 15 | | |
| | paid for supplies | 8 55—$ | 83 70 | |
| May 1. | C. L. Gabrilson, salary 2½ months | $ 150 00 | | |
| | R. R. fare and expenses from Feb. 22 to May 1 | 121 84 | | |
| | paid for printing and postage | 34 05—$ | 305 89—$ | 1,125 16 |
| | Pay Roll, April 22-30 | $ | 575 93 | |
| | April 22-30, additional | | 172 30 | |
| | April 15-22 | | 460 65 | |
| | April 15-22, additional | | 94 50—$ | 1,303 30 |
| | Pay Roll, May 20-27 | | $ | 399 17 |
| Apr. 20. | B. F. Chase Co., 2 glass charts framed | | | 80 00 |
| Apr. 20. | Mrs. E. G. Rhodes, 8 months services (half time) as Sec'y Iowa Board of Lady Managers | | | 160 00 |
| June 1. | J. F. Duncombe, January and May meetings, 9 days | | | 45 00 |
| | Com. work, 4 days | $ | 20 00 | |
| 9. | J. F. Duncombe, per diem, June, 6 days | | 30 00—$ | 50 00 |
| | J. W. Jarnagin, Com. work, May, 16 days | $ | 80 00 | |
| | per diem, June, 7 days | | 35 00 | |
| | R. R. fare | | 51 00—$ | 166 00 |
| | A. C. Roberts, per diem, June, 5 days | $ | 25 00 | |
| | R. R. fare | | 17 60—$ | 42 60 |
| | Wm. H. Dent, per diem, June, 6 days | $ | 30 00 | |
| | R. R. fare | | 26 50—$ | 56 50 |
| | H. W. Seaman, Com. work, May, 1 day | $ | 5 00 | |
| | " June, 3 days | | 15 00 | |
| | per diem, May, 2 days | | 10 00 | |
| | " June, 5 days | | 25 00 | |
| | R. R. fare | | 25 00—$ | 80 00 |
| | Chas. Ashton, per diem, June, 6 days | $ | 30 00 | |
| | R. R. fare | | 21 10—$ | 51 10 |
| | Chas. Ashton, Com. work, March, 18 days | $ | 90 00 | |
| | " April, 14 days | | 70 00 | |

# REPORT OF AUDITING COMMITTEE

|  |  |  |  |  |
|---|---|---|---|---|
|  | Chas. Ashton, Com. work, May, 14 days | 70 00 |  |  |
|  | " June, 2 days | 10 00 |  |  |
|  | R. R. fare | 9 85—$ |  | 249 85 |
| June 9. | Jas. O. Crosby, Com. work, May, 6 days $ | 30 00 |  |  |
|  | per diem, June, 11 " | 55 00 |  |  |
|  | R. R. fare | 5 00—$ |  | 90 00 |
|  | A. C. Roberts, Com. work, April, 14 days $ | 70 00 |  |  |
|  | R. R. fare | 13 10—$ |  | 83 10 |
| May 4. | Drake, Parker & Co., livery $ | 49 50 |  |  |
|  | " " hotel | 106 00 |  |  |
|  | S. H. Mallory paid for tickets above in connection with dedication of State Building | 48 00—$ |  | 203 50 |
| May 30. | Jarnagin & McKee, printing minutes | $ |  | 74 20 |
| Apr. 29. | Library Bureau— |  |  |  |
|  | card index outfit | 15 00 |  |  |
|  | 5 L. B. file boxes | 1 00 |  |  |
|  | 10 C. C. pamphlet cases | 2 40 |  |  |
| May 27. | 5 newspaper racks | 56 25 |  |  |
|  | 100 Athenaeum files | 15 00—$ |  | 119 65 |
| May 1. | F. N. Chase, Sec'y., Telegrams and R. R. fare, April $ | 23 66 |  |  |
|  | per diem, May | 155 00 |  |  |
| June 7. | telegrams, express and R. R. fare, May | 17 16—$ |  | 195 82 |
| May 31. | Milward & Clark, decorating and installation in excess of contract | $ |  | 150 00 |
| June 14. | J. O. Crosby-paid share of entertaining Foreign Commissioners joining with other states |  |  | 30 00 |
| May 24. | Pettibone, Wells & Co., envelopes $ | 10 00 |  |  |
|  | copyright fee | 1 00—$ |  | 11 00 |
| Mch. 29. | Ora E. Miller, salary and expenses $ | 100 00 |  |  |
| 31. | Nonpariel Printing and Publishing Co., printing | 11 50 |  |  |
| Apr. 6. | Press and E. D. Forcum, labor | 20 00 |  |  |
| 10. | C. R. I. & P. R. R. | 3 21 |  |  |
| 12. | U. S. Express Co | 1 20 |  |  |
|  | " " | 2 80 |  |  |
|  | " " | 3 15 |  |  |
| 17. | Smith Bros., 5 stands | 75 00 |  |  |
| 26. | Hibbard, Spencer, B. & Co., Hardware | 75 |  |  |
| 27. | J. M. Stonestreet, photographs | 75 00 |  |  |
|  | J. O. Briner, labor | 6 80 |  |  |
|  | Gilbert Temple, photographs | 76 30 |  |  |
|  | Jas. McDonald, balance on frames | 71 00 |  |  |
|  | Jos. Schell, balance on frames | 25 00 |  |  |
|  | S. W. Heath, Co. Supt., glass school house | 17 20 |  |  |
| 28. | Frank B. Cooper, expenses | 40 70 |  |  |
| 29. | Iowa Iron and Brass Works, balance on stand | 15 00 |  |  |
| May 1. | Cravath & Ray, printing | 110 15 |  |  |
| 3. | Ira C. Kling | 44 75 |  |  |
| 4. | W. C. McKee, paid for supplies | 35 90 |  |  |
| 9. | W. J. Johnston, burlap | 4 80 |  |  |
|  | C. A. Frederick, labor | 53 00 |  |  |
|  | Thos. Sedgwick, labor | 3 00 |  |  |
| 11. | J. H. Rice & Co., glass | 1 20 |  |  |
| 12. | S. D. Childs & Co., stationery | 1 40 |  |  |
|  | Thos. Sedgwick, labor | 4 50 |  |  |
|  | Chas, E. Simmons, labor | 7 50 |  |  |
|  | Leslie G. Hill, labor | 6 00 |  |  |
| 16. | Am. Express Co | 1 60 |  |  |
|  | Ira C. Kling, labor | 50 00 |  |  |
| 17. | T. A. Kellett, labor | 20 15 |  |  |
| 9. | Rand, McNally & Co., sphere and stand | 81 50 |  |  |
| May 20. | Callie Silvers, labor | 20 00 |  |  |
| 21. | E. D. Forcum | 5 00 |  |  |
| 22. | Rayburn & Porter, frames | 203 35 |  |  |
| 30. | W. C. McKee, labor | 41 00 |  |  |
| 31. | Robert McCay, labor | 4 30 |  |  |
| Apr. 1 | U. S. Express Co | 8 55 |  |  |
| 4. | " " | 9 05 |  |  |
| June 3. | C. B. & Q. R. R. | 11 60 |  |  |
| 5. | Emma Munson, labor | 60 00 |  |  |
| May 27. | H. E. Kratz, paid express | 11 49 |  |  |
| 30. | Jarnagin & McKee, printing | 33 00 |  |  |
| Apr. 28. | Veatch & Bull, photographs | 58 60 |  |  |
| May 1. | Gilbert Temple, photographs | 11 25 |  |  |
| 27. | Platt Bros., paper | 10 60 |  |  |
|  | J. W. Jarnagin | 216 87—$ |  | 1,674 75 |

| | | |
|---|---|---|
| July 7. | H. W. Fairchild paid following bills— | |
| | N. Zoller, stone..........$ | 4 00 |
| | Giles B. Lumbard, lumber.. | 20 |
| | J. S. Flannagan, boxes...... | 80 |
| | B. T. Holmes, labor......... | 15 00 |
| May 6. | World's Col. Ex., hauling....... | 1 10 |
| 19. | Backus & Sisley, brooms ................. | 3 80 |
| 20. | C. L. Hanson & Co., glass ................ | 2 05 |
| | The Fair, 2 chairs................. | 2 10 |
| 31. | Backus & Sisley, matches .................. | 25 |
| June 1. | Bullard & Gormley Co., padlocks ........... | 55 |
| | The Fair, crockery............. | 7 90 |
| | A. C. Waters, disinfectant machines......... | 30 00 |
| 4. | The Fair, towels ............ | 50 |
| 6. | E. Harrold, teaming ............ | 2 10 |
| | Marshall Field & Co., carpet sweeper........ | 2 96 |
| 7. | McClelland & Taylor, drugs........... | 1 25 |
| 10. | Hercules Iron Works, ice.............. | 1 05 |
| 11. | Albert Allen, carfare........ | 5 35 |
| 12. | World's Col. Expo., removing garbage........ | 7 50 |
| | Siegel Cooper & Co., cloth........... | 95 |
| 13. | J. C. Johnston, painting .............. | 27 00 |
| | Cheatle & Bowley, mops ............ | 70 |
| 15. | John Hyland, oil and chimneys......... | 1 20 |
| 17. | Hercules Iron Works, ice............... | 2 33 |
| 18. | Adams Express Co .............. | 1 40 |
| 19. | Pettibone, Wells & Co., envelopes........... | 10 00 |
| 20. | Adams Express Co.............. | 40 |
| 22. | World's Col. Expo., removing garbage........ | 2 50 |
| | W. B. Conkey Co., Fair Directory........... | 2 50 |
| 23. | Marshall Field & Co , towels............... | 4 80 |
| | Geo. C. Mages & Co , frame ............... | 2 00 |
| | Marshall Field & Co., soap ............... | 1 80 |
| | Mrs. L. W. Deering, expenses............... | 17 70 |
| 24. | Iowa Printing Co., printing............... | 30 00 |
| | Hercules Iron Works, ice ............... | 2 45 |
| | Walker & Dietz, alcohol ............... | 1 50 |
| | Associated Express Co ............... | 3 75 |
| 26. | Am. Express Co............... | 75 |
| | "  "  " ............... | 1 00 |
| | "  "  " ............... | 1 00 |
| | "  "  " ............... | 1 00 |
| | J. M. T. Myers, expense on exhibits............... | 50 00 |
| 29. | Mrs. E. G. Rhodes, expenses ............... | 11 20 |
| | Mrs. Flora J. McAchran, expenses ............... | 13 90 |
| | Adams Express Co ............... | 1 75 |
| | Hyde Park Gas Co............... | 3 36 |
| May 5. | B. F. Chase Co., 6 signs............... | 9 00 |
| 31. | "  "  5 signs ............... | 4 50 |
| 24. | "  "  1 sign ............... | 1 50 |
| June 16. | "  "  1 sign............... | 75 |
| July 1. | Hercules Iron Works, ice ............... | 2 40 |
| May 5. | Mrs. L. P. Barnard, expenses in connection with mines— | |
| | Grotto by Dubuque ladies ............... | 39 65 |
| Apr 15. | World's Col. Expo., hauling............... | 14 63 |
| Mch. 8. | Chi., St. Paul & K. C. R. R............... | 7 20 |
| July 13. | J. S. Ford, Johnson & Co., benches............... | 17 00 |
| | "  "  "  settees............... | 11 10 |
| Aug. 1. | F. Newhall & Sons, apples ............... | 62 00 |
| July 18. | J. J. Richardson, expense live stock dept ............... | 21 94 |
| June 28. | S. B. Humbert, P. M., stamps............... | 21 00—$ 498 37 |
| May 7. | S. D. Childs & Co., pens............... | 35 |
| June 26. | Yale & Towne Mfg. Co., keys and labor............... | 3 25 |
| 28. | World's Col. Expo., labor ............... | 1 85 |
| Dec. 20, 1892. | Yale & Towne Mfg. Co., sash lifts............... | 6 48 |
| June 28, 1893. | Jos. Fahndrick & Sons, saw dust ............... | 4 45 |
| July 4. | Backus & Sisley, brooms............... | 1 85 |
| 6. | Bryant-Neely Lumber Co , lumber ............... | 9 14 |
| June 6. | Am. Express Co ............... | 40 |
| July 6. | C. H. Rice, mops ............... | 1 05 |
| 7. | McClelland & Taylor, drugs............... | 3 10 |
| 8. | Hercules Iron Works, ice............... | 2 70 |
| | W. S. Loomis, services ............... | 15 65 |
| | Marshall Field & Co., soap ............... | 2 49 |
| | "  "  " ............... | 50 |
| | "  "  rugs ............... | 1 25 |
| | "  "  towel rollers............... | 40 |
| | C. H. Rice, dusters ............... | 1 95 |
| | Ben Packard, paid for cleaning floor............... | 2 00 |
| 10. | L. M. Brown, ladders and hardware ............... | 29 80 |

## REPORT OF AUDITING COMMITTEE

|  |  |  |  |  |
|---|---|---|---|---|
|  | Am. Express Co............... |  | 25 |  |
|  | "        "   ................. |  | 30 |  |
| 11. | Adams Express Co............. |  | 65 |  |
| 12. | Bullard & Gormley Co., bolts....... |  | 55 |  |
|  | Dennison Mfg. C., tags........... |  | 10 85 |  |
| 8. | S. D. Childs & Co., stationery....... |  | 17 60 |  |
| 12. | "        "   twine............ |  | 40 |  |
|  | Geo. E. Watson & Co., paper....... |  | 50 |  |
| 13. | A. Allen, car fare.............. |  | 2 90 |  |
|  | G. F. Foster, Son & Co., caps for helpers..... |  | 20 30 |  |
|  | S. D. Childs & Co., stationery...... |  | 8 75 |  |
| 11. | Am. Express Co.,.............. |  | 75 |  |
| 13. | Atlas Laundry Co.............. |  | 18 19 |  |
| 14. | Am. Express Co............... |  | 25 |  |
| 15. | Geo. W. Reed & Co., washing....... |  | 7 75 |  |
|  | John C. Ure, supplies and labor...... |  | 13 85 |  |
| July 1. | F. N. Chase, Sec'y., per diem, June........ $ 150 00 |  |  |  |
|  |           R. R. fare............ 29 23 |  |  |  |
|  |           telegrams........... 3 46—$ | 182 69—$ | 375 39 |  |
| June 30. | World's Col. Expo., removing garbage........$ | 1 80 |  |  |
| July 12. | St. Louis, K. & N. W. R. R............. | 5 11 |  |  |
| 13. | Standard Express Co., drayage........ | 2 75 |  |  |
| 14. | Am. Express Co.............. | 55 |  |  |
| 15. | W. N. Donaldson, ice........... | 1 80 |  |  |
|  | Am. Express Co.............. | 55 |  |  |
| 18. | L. M. Brown, brackets.......... | 1 40 |  |  |
| July 19. | S. B. Packard, telegrams........ | 2 43 |  |  |
| 20. | Mrs. L. O. Ferson, expenses....... | 17 50 |  |  |
| 19. | Garden City Flag Mfg. Co., 4 banners..... | 26 00 |  |  |
| 21. | World's Col. Expo., drayage....... | 25 |  |  |
|  | Sam'l G. Derbam, to apply on filters..... | 10 00 |  |  |
| 1. | Associated Express Co........... | 55 |  |  |
| 21. | Garden City Flag Mfg. Co., 3 awnings..... | 12 00 |  |  |
|  | Marshall Field & Co., soap........ | 2 52 |  |  |
| 22. | Adams Express Co............. | 45 |  |  |
| 22. | Am.       "   .............. | 25 |  |  |
| July 7. | F. Newhall & Sons, apples........ | 62 00 |  |  |
| 12. | "        "   ................. | 15 50 |  |  |
| 23. | Am. Express Co.............. | 2 00 |  |  |
| 25. | "        "   ................. | 1 05 |  |  |
| 26. | S. D. Childs & Co., ink.......... | 50 |  |  |
| 27. | Carqueville Litho. Co., lithographs Iowa bld.... | 7 20 |  |  |
|  | Am. Express Co............... | 1 20 |  |  |
| May 24. | Estate of C. Schotte, window shades..... | 88 00 |  |  |
| July 29. | Adams Express Co............ | 25 |  |  |
| 31. | Atlas Laundry Co............. | 10 31 |  |  |
|  | E. H. Exelby, removing garbage....... | 4 70 |  |  |
| 22. | E. Baggot, to apply on plumbing...... | 100 00 |  |  |
| 31. | F. N. Chase, Sec'y, per diem, July........ $ 155 00 |  |  |  |
|  |           R. R. fare............ 3 10—$ | 158 10 |  |  |
|  |           telegrams and express............ | 2 80—$ | 539 82 |  |
| 20. | S. B. Packard, com. work, Apr., 6 days...... | 30 00 |  |  |
|  |           per diem, May, 3 days.......... | 15 00 |  |  |
|  |           Com. work, June, 1 day......... | 5 00 |  |  |
|  |           per diem, July, 4 days.......... | 20 00 |  |  |
|  |           R. R. fare............... | 57 64—$ | 127 64 |  |
|  | Henry Stivers, per diem, May, 2 days...... | 10 00 |  |  |
|  |           "       July, 6 days....... | 30 00 |  |  |
|  |           R. R. fare............... | 21 50—$ | 61 50 |  |
|  | Chas. Ashton, Com. work, June, 1 day.........$ | 5 00 |  |  |
|  |           attendance at Iowa bld., July 10 days..... | 50 00 |  |  |
|  |           R. R. fare............... | 10 55—$ | 65 55 |  |
|  | Jas. O. Crosby, attendance at Iowa bld., June 10 to July 21— |  |  |  |
|  |           30 days................ | 150 00 |  |  |
|  |           R. R. fare............... | 3 00—$ | 153 00 |  |
|  | A. C. Roberts, per diem, July, 5 days........$ | 25 00 |  |  |
|  |           R. R. fare............... | 17 60—$ | 42 60 |  |
|  | J. W. Jarnagin, attendance at Iowa bld., June 17 days.....$ | 85 00 |  |  |
|  |           per diem, July 5 days......... | 25 00 |  |  |
|  |           R. R. fare............... | 27 65—$ | 137 65 |  |
| 19. | Henry Stivers, paid postage and freight..... |  | 11 35 |  |
| 13. | W. C. McKee, services........... | 75 00 |  |  |
|  | Lilly I. Aiken, services.......... | 60 00—$ | 135 00 |  |

|   |   |   |   |   |
|---|---|---|---|---|
| 17. | Jarnagin & McKee, printing | | $ | 32 20 |
| Aug. 3. | J. F. Duncombe, per diem, July, 5 days | $ 25 00 | | |
| | Aug., 4 days | 20 00 | $ | 45 00 |
| | Henry Stivers, per diem, Aug., 4 days | $ 20 00 | | |
| | R. R. fare | 16 15 | —$ | 36 15 |
| | H. W. Seaman, per diem, Aug., 4 days | $ 20 00 | | |
| | R. R. fare | 12 50 | —$ | 32 50 |
| June 6. | A. G. Colpoys, services | | $ | 25 00 |
| Aug. 1. | S. B. Packard, per diem, Aug., 3 days | $ 15 00 | | |
| | R. R. fare | 17 22 | $ | 32 22 |
| | J. W. Jarnagin, per diem, Aug., 4 days | $ 20 00 | | |
| | R. R. fare | 13 70 | —$ | 33 70 |
| | Wm. H. Dent, per diem, Aug., 6 days | $ 30 00 | | |
| | R. R. fare | 21 00 | —$ | 51 00 |
| | Chas. Ashton, attendance Iowa bld., July, 21 days | $ 105 00 | | |
| | Aug., 5 days | 25 00 | | |
| | R. R. fare | 10 63 | | |
| | telegrams | 1 15 | —$ | 141 78 |
| Aug. 7. | S. H. Mallory, Com. work, Jan., 6 days | $ 30 00 | | |
| | " Feb., 14 " | 70 00 | | |
| | " Mch., 10 " | 50 00 | | |
| | " April, 4 " | 20 00 | | |
| | " May, 20 " | 100 00 | | |
| | " June, 13 " | 65 00 | | |
| | per diem, Jan., 2 days | 10 00 | | |
| | " Mch., 4 " | 20 00 | | |
| | " April, 4 " | 20 00 | | |
| | " May, 5 " | 75 00 | | |
| | " June, 4 " | 20 00 | —$ | 430 0 |
| Aug. 29. | A. C. Roberts, attendance at Iowa Building, Aug. and Sept., 35 days | $ 165 00 | | |
| | R. R. fare | 17 66 | —$ | 182 6 |
| July 29 | E. Kretchmer paid following bills— | | | |
| | May 27, E. Kretchmer, postage | $ 7 71 | | |
| | May 25, Boll & Clark, printing | 3 50 | | |
| | July 15, E. Kretchmer, postage | 8 25 | | |
| | July 27, Boll & Clark, printing | 10 25 | | |
| | July 24, shipping cases | 21 00 | | |
| | July 27, " " | 3 00 | | |
| | July 29, express and freight | 15 75 | | |
| | July 27, labels | 2 00 | | |
| | July 25, Thos. G. Newman, glass pails | 28 32 | | |
| | July 28, postage | 2 52 | | |
| | July 19, Muth & Son, glass jars | 19 77 | | |
| | July 29, exhibition cases | 58 45 | | |
| | July 26 C., B. & Q. R. R. | 25 | | |
| | July 29, boxes and labor | 10 00 | —$ | 190 77 |
| Aug. 26. | L. G. Clute, 24 days labor, Aug | $ 48 00 | | |
| | expenses, Aug | 35 95 | —$ | 83 95 |
| July 15. | C. L. Gabrilson, paid for butter and expenses from June 27 to July 15 | | $ | 131 36 |
| Aug. 31. | E. Kretchmer paid following bills— | | | |
| | Aug. 23, Dean, Foster & Co., glass jars | $ 20 85 | | |
| | 24. Am. Express Co | 50 | | |
| | Schlesinger & Mayer, ribbon | 55 | | |
| | Aug. 13. Shipping cases | 3 70 | | |
| | 26. C. Kretchmer, labor | 8 75 | | |
| | 18. C., B. & Q. R. R | 1 52 | | |
| | E. Kretchmer, labor, Aug., 18 days | 54 00 | | |
| | expenses | 38 50 | | |
| | R. R. fare | 14 50 | | |
| | tickets | 1 50 | | |
| | washing compound | 10 | —$ | 144 47 |
| July 25. | L. G. Clute, 2 days, June | 4 00 | | |
| | expenses | 1 80 | | |
| | 2 days | 4 00 | | |
| | per diem, July, 20 days | 40 00 | | |
| | expense, July | 25 40 | —$ | 75 20 |

REPORT OF AUDITING COMMITTEE   405

| | | | | |
|---|---|---|---|---|
| June 30 | L. G. Clute, salary and expenses April, May and June | | $ 174 80 | |
| | | paid for help | 4 00 | |
| | | paid for grain | 20 00 | |
| | | paid for honey | 19 57 | |
| | | paid express and freight | 29 13 | |
| | | paid R. R. fare | 26 05—$ | 273 55 |
| June 1. | C. L. Gabrilson, services, May | | $ 100 00 | |
| July 1. | " " June | | 100 00 | |
| Aug. 1. | " " July | | 100 00 | |
| June 1. | McArthur Bros., butter cases | | 395 39 | |
| Aug. 8. | Jas. H. Rice & Co., glass | | 3 00 | |
| June 21. | Garden City Awning and Tent Co., 1 banner | | 21 00 | |
| Aug. 5. | Ben Packard, paid for cleaning floor | $ 75 | | |
| | paid for painting cards | 1 00—$ | 1 75 | |
| 23. | Adams Express Co | | $ 4 90 | |
| 25. | Robert Stevenson Co., glass jars | | 23 25 | |
| June 9. | C. L. Gabrilson, expense gathering butter | $ 128 52 | | |
| | freight on car butter | 98 00—$ | 226 52 | |
| July 31. | C. L. Gabrilson paid bill of A. H. Barber, freight | $ 26 87 | | |
| | " cartage | 28 40—$ | 55 27 | |
| Aug. 10. | E. Kretchmer, paid express and freight | $ 50 34 | | |
| | paid labor | 26 60—$ | 76 94 | |
| May 26. | Creamery Package Manufacturing Co— | | | |
| | buttertubs and express | | $ 13 01 | |
| June 28. | brass figures | | 1 98 | |
| July 3. | buttertubs and express | | 17 29 | |
| May 31. | butter boxes | | 2 10 | |
| June 5. | buttertubs | | 58 | |
| | labor and paraffine | | 1 58 | |
| | buttertub | | 29 | |
| | labor and paraffine | | 10 80 | |
| 16. | buttertubs and express | | 5 80 $ | 2,063 75 |
| July 26. | S. B. Humbert, P. M., stamps | | $ 26 18 | |
| 29. | Hercules Iron Works, ice | | 2 40 | |
| 31. | G. F. Foster, Son & Co., badges | | 80 | |
| 30. | B. F. Chase Co., signs and lettering | | 29 75 | |
| 31. | C. H. Rice, brooms | | 2 00 | |
| Aug. 1. | Marshall Field & Co., cloth | | 2 53 | |
| 2. | W. N. Donaldson, ice | | 2 70 | |
| 5. | " " | | 2 25 | |
| | W. U. Telegraph Co | | 50 | |
| | The Fair, 3 dozen glasses | | 2 88 | |
| | bowls | | 90 | |
| | strainer | | 22 | |
| | trays | | 46 | |
| | squeezer | | 20 | |
| 1. | Marshall Field & Co., brush | | 1 75 | |
| | S. D. Childs & Co., carbon paper | | 3 50 | |
| Sept. 1. | Atlas Laundry Co., laundry, Aug. 14-19 | | 1 72 | |
| | " 1-5 | | 2 92 | |
| | " 21-26 | | 4 92 | |
| Aug. 11. | E. H. Exelby, removing garbage, July 21-31 | | 4 50 | |
| 18. | " Aug. 1-10 | | 5 30 | |
| 25. | " 11-21 | | 4 50 | |
| 5. | Albert Allen, carfare | | 3 75 | |
| 17. | Atlas Laundry Co., Aug 8-12 | | 4 23 | |
| 16. | S. D. Childs & Co., paper and pencils | | 7 95 | |
| 23. | Marshall Field & Co., soap | | 3 00 | |
| 24. | S. D. Childs & Co., ink | | 50 | |
| 25. | C. H. Rice, brooms | | 1 75 | |
| 12. | W. N. Donaldson, ice | | 2 10 | |
| 19. | " " | | 2 25 | |
| 26. | " " " | | 3 15 | |
| 5. | Am. Express Co | | 1 25 | |
| 4. | Mrs. A. M. Ainsworth, expense | | 15 50 | |
| July 31. | Mary B. Hancock, expense | | 8 75 | |
| Aug. 7. | A. Levi, setting glass | | 75 | |
| July 29. | Jas. H. Rice Co., glass | | 65 | |
| Aug. 14. | World's Col. Expo., drayage | | 38 | |
| | " " | | 1 50 | |
| Meb.25. | C. & N. W. R. R | | 2 00 | |
| Aug. 31. | Adams Express Co | | 2 30 | |
| 2. | Am. Express Co | | 25 | |
| 14. | " " | | 1 55 | |

| Date | Description | Amount | Subtotal | Total |
|---|---|---:|---:|---:|
| Apr. 16. | C., R. I. & P. R. R. | 15 40 | | |
| Aug. 9. | J. Murphy, teaming | 2 50 | | |
| 24. | A. H. Revell & Co., chairs and tables | 8 50 | | |
| 23. | Marshall Field & Co., tacks | 19 | | |
| " | "   "  cloth | 1 80 | | |
| 25. | "   "  cloth | 5 45 | | |
| " | "   "  tacks | 19 | | |
| 26. | "   "  cloth | 7 94 | | |
| 23. | "   "  " | 4 22 | | |
| 26. | B. F. Chase Co., 2 signs | 15 00 | | |
| 31. | Carson, Pirie, Scott & Co., bunting | 2 69 | | |
| 3. | Schraps & Kahn, catering for press reception | 67 00 | | |
| July 3. | T. C. Rogers, flowers | 3 00 | | |
| Aug. 23. | S. D. Childs & Co., stationery | 50 | | |
| July 31. | Jacobs, Coles & Co., envelopes | 17 00 | | |
| Aug. 24. | S. D. Childs & Co., letter tabs | 1 75 | | |
| 18. | Snyder & Hurd, stationery | 2 50 | | |
| 26. | Iowa Printing Co., letter heads | 45 20 | | |
| 17. | Henry Dahl, tables and chairs | 8 15 | | |
| Aug. 24. | McClelland & Taylor, drugs | 1 60 | | |
| Sept. 11. | Mrs. Orry Salts, expense | 17 50 | | |
| Aug. 12. | Wendell & Co., 11 badges for Commissioners | 90 00 | | |
| 31. | F. N. Chase, Sec'y., freight and express | 6 90 | | |
| | telegrams and express, Aug | 16 92 | | |
| | per diem, Aug ........$ 155 00 | | | |
| | R. R. fare ........ 26 96—$ | | 181 96—$ | 851 30 |
| Sept. 13. | H. W. Seaman, Com. work, Aug., 4 days ........$ | 20 00 | | |
| | per diem, Aug., 1 day | 5 00 | | |
| | R. R. fare | 30 00 | | |
| | Com. work, Sept., 1 day | 5 00 | | |
| | per diem, Sept., 5 days | 25 00—$ | 85 00 | |
| | Wm. H. Dent, per diem, Sept., 6 days ........$ | 30 00 | | |
| | R. R. fare | 21 50—$ | 51 50 | |
| | S. B. Packard, attendance account Live Stock— | | | |
| | Aug., 7 days ........$ | 35 00 | | |
| | Sept., 6 days | 30 00 | | |
| | per diem, Sept., 6 days | 30 00 | | |
| | R. R. fare | 74 38—$ | 169 38 | |
| Sept. 5. | Geo. F. Ferris, charging phonograph battery | 2 35 | | |
| Aug. 31. | Hyde Park Gas Co., gas, June 30-Aug. 31 | 3 36 | | |
| Sept. 15. | J. F. Duncombe, telegrams | 1 29 | | |
| 11. | Geo. W. Reed & Co., washing | 6 50 | | |
| | W. U. Telegraph Co | 37 | | |
| Aug. 14. | U. S. Express Co | 25 | | |
| Sept. 5. | Associated Press Co | 1 25 | | |
| 2. | C. H. Rice, mops and dust pans | 1 00 | | |
| Aug. 30. | L. M. Brown, bellows | 1 00 | | |
| Sept. 12. | A. Allen, R. R. fare | 8 25 | | |
| 16. | Geo. E. Watson & Co., paper | 1 50 | | |
| | Marshall Field & Co., cloth | 18 51 | | |
| | "   "   "   " | 1 14 | | |
| | Chicago Bank Note Co., invitations for Iowa days | 60 00 | | |
| 6. | Pearson Lumber Co., lumber | 9 50 | | |
| 19. | Roundy Regalia Co., badges, Iowa Days | 135 00 | | |
| 20. | Art Floral Co., flowers, Iowa Days | 9 00 | | |
| 21. | Harmon Male Quartette, music, Iowa Days | 100 00 | | |
| 22. | Adams express Co | 1 25 | | |
| | Portable chair, concession chairs, Iowa Days | 10 00 | | |
| | Fish, Joseph & Co., ribbon | 2 85 | | |
| 19. | 1 font type | 1 50 | | |
| 22. | H. W. Seaman, telegrams | 1 20 | | |
| 20. | Regan Printing House, printing | 35 20 | | |
| 21. | Pettibone, Wells & Co., badges, Iowa Days | 220 00 | | |
| 20. | "   "   "   " | 40 00 | | |
| Sept. 11. | B. F. Chase Co., silk banner for Band | 75 00 | | |
| 22. | F. N. Chase, Sec'y, telegrams, Sept. 2-18 | 10 18—$ | 757 45 | |
| Sept. 22. | Henry Stivers, attendance at Iowa Bldg., Sept., 13 days ....$ | 65 00 | | |
| | R. R. fare | 14 15—$ | 79 15 | |
| | S. B. Packard, Com. work, Sept., 7 days ........$ | 35 00 | | |
| | R. R. fare | 17 22—$ | 52 22 | |
| | J. W. Jarnagin, Com. work, Aug., 1 day ........$ | 5 00 | | |
| | attendance at Iowa Bldg., Sept., 15 days | 75 00 | | |
| | R. R. fare | 13 70—$ | 93 70 | |

## REPORT OF AUDITING COMMITTEE 407

|  |  |  |  |
|---|---|---:|---:|
|  | H. W. Seaman, per diem, Sept., 6 days ......$ | 30 00 |  |
|  | R. R. fare ...... | 12 50—$ | 42 50 |
| June 23. | Merle & Heaney Mfg. Co., stools ......$ | 10 00 |  |
| 28. | Regan Printing House, cards ...... | 19 00 |  |
| May 6. | U. S. Express Co ...... | 80 |  |
| June 22. | " " ...... | 1 75 |  |
| Apr. 6. | " " ...... | 1 40 |  |
| June 27. | Am. Express Co ...... | 60 |  |
|  | D. S. Clark, carpenter work ...... | 50 00 |  |
| May 13. | Crane Co., Cop, Fin. rail ...... | 38 50 |  |
|  | Iowa Fire Insurance Co., insurance ...... | 90 00 |  |
| June 14. | Regan Printing House, cards ...... | 3 00 |  |
| 10. | W. B. Ketcham, expense on exhibit ...... | 26 15 |  |
|  | A. H. Andrews & Co., settees, desk and chair ...... | 37 00 |  |
| 22. | B. F. Chase Co., signs for Educational Department ...... | 441 40 |  |
| 33. | Chas. Bodach, show case and stand ...... | 16 50 |  |
| 10. | Regan Printing House, cards ...... | 7 75 |  |
| 3. | U. S. Express Co ...... | 1 00 |  |
| May 30. | " " ...... | 80 |  |
| June 30. | E. P. Fogg, Co. Supt., photographs ...... | 40 00 |  |
| 24. | W. W. Steward, 5 show cases ...... | 225 00 |  |
| July 10. | Jas. Mortland, labor ...... | 20 00 |  |
| June 27. | J. Fred Smith, express ...... | 11 10 |  |
| 24. | W. F. Cramer, express ...... | 3 95 |  |
| May 31. | Emma Munson, labor ...... | 15 00 |  |
| June 23. | J. W. Butler Paper Co., cardboard ...... | 32 75 |  |
| 25. | J. W. Jarnagin, paid drayage, flags, etc ...... | 26 10—$ | 1,119 55 |
| Mch. 29. | C., B. & Q. R. R. ......$ | 75 |  |
| Apr. 25. | U. S. Express Co ...... | 1 25 |  |
| 27. | Rand & Leopold Desk Co., paid freight ...... | 98 |  |
| May 18. | Garden City Awning and Tent Co., flags ...... | 15 85 |  |
|  | The Fair, pen racks ...... | 50 |  |
| 31. | Siegel, Cooper & Co., 4 book cases ...... | 58 00 |  |
|  | " " " rose bowl ...... | 48 |  |
|  | " " " towels ...... | 70 |  |
| June 3. | E. Harrold, teaming ...... | 7 50 |  |
|  | Wells, Fargo & Co., express ...... | 25 |  |
| July 12. | Backus & Sisley, brooms ...... | 2 80 |  |
| June 7. | Atlas Laundry Co., May 15-June 1 ...... | 3 12 |  |
| Oct. 15. | Jas. Fahndrick & Son, saw dust ...... | 4 45 |  |
| June 9. | J. Paulsen, labor ...... | 20 00—$ | 116 63 |
| June 30. | Thos. W. Meers, salary, May ......$ | 60 00 |  |
|  | expenses, May ...... | 67 40 |  |
|  | salary, June ...... | 69 31 |  |
|  | expenses, June ...... | 50 35 | 247 06 |
| Oct. 2. | A. C. Roberts, attendance at Iowa Building, Sept., 13 days $ | 65 00 |  |
|  | R. R. fare ...... | 14 40—$ | 79 40 |
|  | J. F. Duncombe, attendance at Iowa Bldg., Aug., 6 days ....$ | 30 00 |  |
|  | per diem, Sept., 5 days ...... | 25 00—$ | 55 00 |
| Oct. 10. | S. B. Packard, attendance at swine exhibit, Sept., 4 days..$ | 20 00 |  |
|  | Oct., 6 days ...... | 30 00 |  |
|  | R. R. fare ...... | 36 24—$ | 86 24 |
|  | Jas. O. Crosby, per diem, Aug., 5 days ......$ | 25 00 |  |
|  | " Sept., 13 days ...... | 65 00 |  |
|  | R. R. fare ...... | 6 00—$ | 96 00 |
|  | Chas. Ashton, attendance at Iowa Bldg., Sept., 15 days ......$ | 75 00 |  |
|  | Oct., 11 days ...... | 55 00 |  |
|  | R. R. fare ...... | 17 94—$ | 147 94 |
| June 10. | S. H. Mallory, paid office rent in Chicago, Jan. 1-May 1, '93 |  | 127 00 |
| June 5. | J. C. Johnston, finishing and setting glass in show case ...... |  | 58 00 |
|  | Pay Roll, Oct. 1-7 ......$ | 358 12 |  |
| Oct. 7. | Genevieve Shaffer, expense as soloist, Iowa Days ...... | 31 00 |  |
| Sept. 30. | Hyde Park Gas Co., gas, Aug. 31 to Sept. 30 ...... | 16 32 |  |
| Oct. 11. | Carr Bros., crockery ...... | 1 35 |  |
| 10. | C. H. Rice, oil ...... | 1 25 |  |
|  | Backus and Sisley, groceries ...... | 3 05 |  |
| 7. | Adams Express Co ...... | 2 35 |  |
| 9. | Associated Express Co ...... | 60 |  |
| 10. | Wells Fargo " ...... | 1 60 |  |
| 4. | Northern " ...... | 1 15 |  |
|  | American " ...... | 1 25 |  |
| 6. | " " ...... | 1 00 |  |
| 9. | " " ...... | 1 20—$ | 122 94 |

| | | | |
|---|---|---|---|
| Sep. 23. | W. M. McFarland, expense Iowa days | $ 27 50 | |
| 25. | Jennie M. Sugg, " " " | 12 90 | |
| 23. | Marie Chambers, " " " | 32 85 | |
| Oct. 2. | Lucia Gale Barber, " " " | 23 25 | |
| | J. H. Barber, " " " | 15 80 | |
| Sep. 25. | Florence Castle, " " " | 6 00 | |
| 23. | Frederick A. Self, " " " | 2 00 | |
| 22. | Wellington Catering Co., catering Iowa days | 8 75 | |
| | Parker Bros., livery, Iowa days | 479 00 | |
| 5. | Albertype Co., souvenir programs | 55 00 | |
| 7. | " " " | 517 02 | |
| 25. | Jas. Pain & Sons, fire works, Iowa days | 150 00 | |
| 18. | C. H. Rice, tacks, etc | 1 25 | |
| 29. | " brooms | 1 80 | |
| 18. | Backus & Sisley, brooms | 1 00 | |
| 5. | E. H. Exelby, removing garbage Aug. 21-31 | 5 90 | |
| 25. | " " " Sept. 1-15 | 6 70 | |
| 16. | Jas. Wadsworth, tacks and twine | 1 40 | |
| 30. | Marshall Field & Co., soap | 1 59 | |
| | | 1 50 | |
| 26. | Thayer & Jackson Stationery Co., ink | 1 60 | |
| June 20. | C. H. Rice, oil | 25 | |
| Sep. 13. | " hardware | 10 | |
| 16. | O. J. Wocher, fly paper | 25 | |
| Aug. 7. | Rosalie Drug Co., borax | 25 | |
| Sep. 26. | G. A. Larson, labor | 25 | |
| 15. | Backus & Sisley, matches | 30 | |
| | I. C. Seifert, labor | 25 | |
| 30. | H. F. Barndt, coal | 11 75 | |
| 19. | U. S. Express Co., | 85 | |
| 18. | Am. " " | 1 35 | |
| 30. | " " " | 1 10 | |
| Oct. 2. | " " " | 1 25 | |
| Sep. 21. | Nat'l " " | 90 | |
| 30. | Adams " " | 40 | |
| 26. | " " " | 1 60 | |
| Aug. 31. | C. & N. W. R. R | 1 25 | |
| Sep. 18. | Telephone Co | 25 | |
| Oct. 2. | Sam'l G. Derham, balance of filters | 90 00 | |
| Sep. 30. | Herman Stirisi, plumbing | 5 00 | |
| 16. | E. Haggot, balance of plumbing | 83 45 | |
| 30. | W. S. Loomis, services | 35 60 | |
| 13. | Fred W. Gute, labor | 3 00 | |
| 18. | Marshall Field & Co., cloth | 2 42 | |
| | " " " | 23 16 | |
| | " " " brushes | 2 21 | |
| | E. H. Hunt, moss | 1 00 | |
| 13. | " " | 1 00 | |
| 26. | A. J. Brockway, labor | 1 25 | |
| 23. | W. M. McFarland, paid for printing | 6 00 | |
| 1. | Geo. Ashton, labor | 5 50 | |
| | Standard Express Co., drayage | 7 75 | |
| Aug. 1. | " " " | 228 50 | |
| Oct. 3. | Atlas Laundry Co., Aug. 28 to Sep. 29 | 20 46 | |
| Sep. 27. | C. R. Schraps, catering | 415 50 | |
| 19. | Garden City Awning and Tent Co., flags | 108 82 | |
| 29. | S. D. Childs & Co., blanks | 3 50 | |
| 26. | " " pens and ink | 1 40 | |
| Oct. 3. | F. N. Chase, Sec'y, paid for postage | 40 00 | |
| | " telegrams | 1 11 | |
| | " per diem, Sept | 150 00 | |
| | " R. R. fare | 31 63 —$ | 2,949 42 |
| Sep. 27. | Stadler & Torgerson, photographs | $ | 15 00 |
| 23. | J. Rush Lincoln, Commandant, portion of expense of 300 cadets | | 1,500 00 |
| July 29. | Board of Lady Managers, 1 show case | | 56 00 |
| June 12. | Andrews & Noel, painting | 167 80 | |
| May 31. | " " balance on decorating | 500 00 —$ | 667 80 |
| Apr. 10. | John McLane, post office furniture | $ 590 40 | |
| | " curtains | 8 00 | |
| | " lumber | 4 50 | |
| May 26. | Marshall Field & Co., ribbon | 4 11 | |
| 9. | " " " rope portieres | 19 50 | |
| 10. | " " " floor broom | 2 82 | |
| 11. | " " " mat | 6 00 | |
| | " " " 2 brushes | 4 21 | |
| | " " " sweeper | 2 00 | |
| 10. | " " " mattresses | 13 04 | |
| 31. | Hyde Park Gas Co., gas, May 4-31 | 21 72 | |

1895

| | | | |
|---|---|---|---|
| | 24. | Office Toilet Co., towels, April | 1 00 |
| | 8. | Hyde Park Gas Co., service | 23 75 |
| Mch. 31. | | Jerome Paper Co., toilet paper | 47 50 |
| Apr. 28. | | Tobey Furniture Co., furniture | 71 50 |
| May | 4. | "       "       "       " | 42 00 |
| | 19. | International Steel Post Co., iron fencing | 42 24 |
| Sep. 23. | | World's Col. Expo., teaming | 2 20 |
| May | 10. | Western Rubber and Belting Co., hose | 24 50 |
| | 13. | J. S. Ford, Johnson & Co., chairs | 54 00 |
| | 31. | Heywood & Morrill Rattan Co., chairs | 7 00 |
| | 12. | "       "       "       " furniture | 31 30 |
| | 18. | "       "       "       " chairs | 23 25 |
| Apr. 29. | | "       "       "       " tables | 11 20 |
| | 29. | "       "       "       " chairs | 98 25 |
| | 27. | "       "       "       " furniture . . . . . . . $320 35 | |
| | | discount . . . . . . . 18 15—$ | 302 20 |

| | | | | |
|---|---|---|---|---|
| Sep. 20. | | F. E. Green, labor | $ | 20 50 |
| | | T. Histe,      " | | 19 00 |
| | | H. Proesser,   " | | 6 00 |
| | | G. W. Copeland, labor | | 19 00 |
| | | F. S. Hale,    " | | 12 00 |
| | | F. E. Green, paints | | 29 92 |
| Oct. 10. | | S. H. Mallory, telegrams | | 85 |
| May | 22. | Dennison Mfg. Co., tags | | 14 30 |
| June 19. | | P. F. Pettibone & Co., book | | 1 50 |
| May 16, | | Chicago Edison Co., light, Mch. 16 to Apr. 18 | | 1 00 |
| Feb. 9. | | Floyd Davis, analysis of water | | 20 00 |
| June 1. | | Jacobs, Coles & Co., envelopes | | 9 00 |
| | 13. | J. C. Johnston, finishing stairs | | 15 00—$ 1,632 32 |

| | | | |
|---|---|---|---|
| | | Pay roll of employees in Iowa building and at exhibits in exposition buildings— | |
| | | May 28-June 3 | $ 316 63 |
| | | June 4-10 | 363 63 |
| | | June 10-17 | 327 63 |
| | | June 17-24 | 320 13 |
| | | June 25-July 1 | 365 34 |
| | | July 2-8 | 359 13 |
| | | July 9-15 | 355 80 |
| | | July 15-22 | 355 80 |
| | | July 23-29 | 355 80 |
| | | Pay roll, educational department, July | 120 00 |
| | | July 30-Aug. 5 | 365 80 |
| | | Aug 5-12 | 373 80 |
| | | Aug. 13-19 | 387 80 |
| | | Aug. 20-26 | 338 30 |
| | | Aug. 26-Sept. 2 | 402 30 |
| | | Sept. 3-9 | 378 30 |
| | | Sept. 10-16 | 374 80 |
| | | Sept. 17-23 | 469 13 |
| | | Sept. 24-30 | 409 13 |
| Apr. 28. | | Hollis & Duncan, paper | 1 40 |
| | 27. | Anderson & Hanson, paint | 11 18 |
| | | Geo. E. Watson & Co., paint | 5 30 |
| | | S. J. Stebbins, hardware | 1 76 |
| | 24. | Fuller & Fuller Co., asphaltum | 1 20 |
| | 22. | Sprague, Smith & Co., mirrors | 13 00 |
| | 30. | J. M. Kelly, cartage | 75 |
| | 26. | L. M. Brown, tacks, hammer, etc. | 6 15 |
| | 29. | "       nails and paper | 3 90 |
| | | J. J. Magee, soda | 25 |
| May | 8. | Marshall Field & Co., cloth | 10 15 |
| | | Pitkin & Brooks, glass jars | 8 28 |
| | 6. | J. J. Zoller, glass | 75 |
| Apr. | 6. | Heath & Milligan Mfg. Co., paint | 80 |
| May | 3. | "       "       paint | 3 00 |
| Apr. | 30. | "       "       duster | 50 |
| May | 9. | "       "       hard oil | 90 |
| | 11. | "       "       " | 90 |
| | 10. | Eureka Show Case Co., show case | 9 50 |
| | 9. | Hiram J. Thompson, moulding | 95 |
| Apr. | 25. | "       "       " | 3 50 |
| | 29. | C. H. Rice, hardware | 2 40 |
| May | 5. | H. L. Clark, paint and labor | 3 50 |
| | 11. | Carson, Pirie, Scott & Co., ribbon | 2 54 |
| | 9. | Adam Zeska & Co., wire rings | 10 00 |
| | 8. | S. J. Stebbins, hooks | 50 |
| | 4. | L. M. Brown, tacks | 1 10 |
| Apr. | 21. | "       nails | 6 40 |
| | 19. | W. L. Dow, Agt., cement | 5 50 |

27

|  |  |  |  |  |
|---|---|---|---|---|
| 27. | Marshall Field & Co., ribbon | 32 90 | | |
| " | " " cloth | 9 41 | | |
| 26. | James King Seed Co., grass seed | 3 50 | | |
| 25. | " " corn screws | 8 10 | | |
| 28. | " " green moss | 2 00 | | |
| May 4. | " " | 2 00 | | |
| 2. | " " | 2 50 | | |
| Apr. 18. | Henry Fowler, cement | 3 75 | | |
| May 2. | Heath & Milligan Mfg. Co., lampblack | 30 | | |
| Apr. 29. | Jas. H. Walker Co., ribbon | 11 25 | | |
| | Marshall Field & Co., cloth | 10 53 | | |
| 24. | " " " | 15 81 | | |
| May 7. | Martin Johnson, teaming | 2 00 | | |
| Apr. 29. | E. Harrold, teaming | 5 00 | | |
| 24. | Adams Express Co | 27 85 | | |
| 22. | American " | 80 | | |
| 20. | Associated " | 50 | | |
| 21. | " " | 5 65 | | |
| Apr. 24. | F. N. Chase, Sec'y., telegrams, express and R. R. | 4 85 | | |
| 19. | Backus & Sisley, tubs and soap | 1 90 | | |
| | A. Allen, dusters | 1 50 | | |
| May 13. | H. F. Barndt, coal | 7 25 | | |
| Apr. 27. | " " | 7 25 | | |
| 25. | C. H. Rice, tacks | 1 15 | | |
| 21. | Siegel, Cooper & Co., cloth | 92 | | |
| 22. | C. H. Rice, pails | 1 35 | | |
| 19. | Bridgeport Wood Finishing Co., paint | 1 80 | | |
| | C. French, cloth | 50 | | |
| May 10. | A. Allen, R. R. fare, Apr. 10-May 10. | 9 20 | | |
| 12. | Bullard & Ormley Co., brackets | 1 98 | | |
| Apr. 25. | John Doyle & Co., casting | 5 00 | | |
| 26. | Marshall Field & Co., ribbon | 5 17 | | |
| 25. | " " " cloth | 9 55 | | |
| 24. | Jas. King Seed Co., Lycopdium | 3 50 | | |
| | Anderson & Hanson, hard oil | 4 50 | | |
| | A. R. Porter, ribbon | 4 82 | | |
| 20. | J. J. Magee, turpentine | 1 20 | | |
| 24. | T. W. Wilmarth Co. to apply on fixtures | 200 00 | | |
| Aug. 24. | " balance on light fixtures | 20 00—$ | 7,296 35 | |
| Oct. 13. | J. W. Jarnagin, per diem, Oct., 9 days | $ 45 00 | | |
| | R. R. fare | 18 20—$ | 63 20 | |
| Oct. 23. | J. Greenhill, express | $ 00 20 | | |
| 24. | American Express Co | 1 10 | | |
| 25. | Wells Fargo Express Co | 50 | | |
| 14. | J. Greenhill, express | 2 00 | | |
| 20. | Adams Express Co | 1 00 | | |
| 24. | Backus & Sisley, groceries | 13 21 | | |
| 26. | " " " | 1 00 | | |
| 23. | " " " | 1 80 | | |
| 21. | " " " | 1 85 | | |
| 16. | " " " | 1 98 | | |
| 10. | " " " | 94 | | |
| 14. | " " oil | 50 | | |
| 26. | " " oil | 60 | | |
| 23. | L. M. Brown, pails | 45 | | |
| | The Fair, cups | 1 92 | | |
| 24. | " " glasses | 1 65 | | |
| 23. | C. H. Rice, hardware | 2 75 | | |
| 12. | " " | 1 75 | | |
| 14. | " " | 1 47 | | |
| 24. | Art Floral Co., flowers | 4 25 | | |
| 20. | Pettibone, Wells & Co., printing | 5 50 | | |
| 23. | Chas. E. Marble Printing Co., printing | 9 28 | | |
| 7. | E. Baggot, gas fittings | 64 05 | | |
| 27. | Mary S. Scott, expenses | 89 72 | | |
| 26. | Emma P. Ewing, paid for assistants | 25 00 | | |
| | " supplies | 15 50—$ | 250 00 | |
| Nov. 1. | S. B. Packard, attendance Oct. 27 to Nov. 2, account of Live Stock, including Nov. meeting, 7 days | $ 35 00 | | |
| | R. R. fare | 14 50—$ | 49 50 | |
| | A. C. Roberts, attendance at Iowa Bldg., Sept. 27 to Oct. 31, 35 days | $ 175 00 | | |
| | R. R. fare | 18 00—$ | 193 00 | |
| | Chas. Ashton, attendance at Iowa Bldg., Oct. 20 to Nov. 2, 13 days | $ 65 00 | | |
| | R. R. fare | 13 55—$ | 78 55 | |

## REPORT OF AUDITING COMMITTEE

|  |  |  |  |
|---|---|---|---|
|  | Jas. O. Crosby, attendance Ia. Bldg., Oct. 3-Nov. 2, 31 days.$ | 155 00 |  |
|  | R. R. fare | 3 00—$ | 158 00 |
|  | H. W. Seaman, attendance at Iowa Bldg., Oct. 21 to Nov. 2, 12 days....$ | 60 00 |  |
|  | R. R. fare | 12 50—$ | 72 50 |
|  | Wm. H. Dent, attendance at Iowa Bldg., Sept. 28 to Nov. 3, 7 days....$ | 35 00 |  |
|  | R. R. fare | 16 00—$ | 51 00 |
| Aug. 25. | O. C. Scott, paid express....$ | 2 20 |  |
| Oct. 2. | Lizzie Fleming, services | 15 00 |  |
| Apr. 10. | H. H. Seerley, Prest., expense | 100 00 |  |
| Sept. 28. | U. S. Express Co. | 1 25 |  |
| Aug. 30. | " " | 2 40 |  |
| 12. | Craver & Steele Mfg. Co., iron and labor | 7 38 |  |
| Apr. 15. | Snider, McConnell & Co., paper | 11 50 |  |
| Sept. 16. | J. W. Jarnagin, express | 4 60—$ | 144 33 |
| Oct. 12. | Baltimore & Ohio R. R.....$ | 00 25 |  |
| Sept. 9. | " " | 75 |  |
| Oct. 3. | L. G Clute, per diem, Sept. 13-Oct. 3.....$ | 32 00 |  |
|  | " " 9 | 1 00 |  |
|  | expenses | 29 05 |  |
|  | paid freight and help | 1 65—$ | 63 70 |
| Aug. 22. | A. H. Barber, tubs and express, Sept. exhibit......$ | 19 67 |  |
| Oct. 3. | " 2 tubs......$ | 00 24 |  |
|  | " freight paid on Sept. exhibit | 25 62—$ | 25 86 |
| Oct. 1. | C. L. Gabrilson, salary, Aug. and Sept......$ | 200 00 |  |
|  | expenses, Aug. 12 to Sept. 12 | 82 18 |  |
|  | paid for wood and labor | 51 22 |  |
|  | salary, Oct.....$ | 100 00 |  |
|  | R. R. fare | 9 70—$ | 109 70 |
| Oct. 28. | C. L. Gabrilson, expense, Oct. exhibit......$ | 5 59 |  |
|  | paid J. G. Steiger, labor | 8 00 |  |
|  | paid John Kolthoff, butter | 16 52 |  |
|  | paid American Express Co. | 5 20—$ | 35 31 |
| 21. | A. H. Barber, freight and storage Oct. exhibit......$ | 45 64 |  |
| Sept. 30. | " cartage " Sept. exhibit | 26 60 |  |
| 29. | " tubs, express, etc. | 18 17 |  |
| Oct. 14. | " express | 2 95 |  |
| Nov. 6. | E. Kretchmer, paid C., B. & Q. R. R.....$ | 00 97 |  |
|  | per diem, Sept. 1-6 | 10 00 |  |
|  | expenses, Sept. | 10 10 |  |
|  | per diem, Oct. 8-26 | 22 50 |  |
|  | R. R. fare | 14 50 |  |
|  | expenses | 18 00 |  |
|  | per diem, Oct. 27 to Nov. 7 | 25 00 |  |
|  | expenses, " " | 22 80 |  |
|  | paid for nails, signs, etc. | 3 00 |  |
|  | " J. C. Kretchmer, labor | 20 00 |  |
|  | " freight | 6 67—$ | 153 54 |
| 15. | W. I. Buchanan, refrigeration in dairy dept | 100 00 |  |
| Oct. 21. | Jas. Hethershaw, potato exhibit crops 1892-93 | 20 00 |  |
|  | F. N. Chase, Sec'y, paid for vegetables | 22 95 |  |
| Sep. 9. | C., R. I. & P. R. R | 21 31—$ | 999 80 |
| 8. | D. M. Moniger, services supt. of cattle......$ | 63 60 |  |
| 27. | " " " horses | 19 60 |  |
|  | W. W. McClung, " swine | 73 85 |  |
| Nov. 29. | S. B. Packard, per diem from June, 1892, to Nov., 1893, promoting and preparing live stock exhibit | 395 00 |  |
|  | express and expense | 3 80—$ | 555 85 |
|  | Wm. G. Marshall, expense of swine exhibit......$ | 66 40 |  |
|  | A. J. Lytle, " " " | 67 90 |  |
|  | Stone & Stone, " " " | 56 40 |  |
|  | Jno. Johnston & Sons " " " | 42 40 |  |
|  | M. Dunn, " " " | 42 40 |  |
|  | Wm. Roberts & Son, " " " | 207 60 |  |
|  | Peter Mouw, " " " | 161 05 |  |
|  | Taft & Co., " " " | 187 00 |  |
|  | J. F. Bonner, " " " | 61 20 |  |
|  | T. R. Wilson, " " " | 52 90 |  |
|  | J. H. Lathrop, " " " | 80 10—$ | 1,025 35 |

412  REPORT OF IOWA COLUMBIAN COMMISSION

|  |  |  |  |  |
|---|---|---|---|---|
| | John Jacobs, expense of horse exhibit | $ 73 05 | | |
| | E. Knott & Co., " " " | 373 00 | | |
| | Lefebure & Son, " " " | 99 75 | | |
| | J. Murray Hoag, " " " | 419 80 | | |
| | Peter Hopley, " " " | 554 70 | | |
| | E. F. Kleinmeyer, " " " | 321 10 | | |
| | A. B. Holbert, " " " | 125 17 | | |
| | L. B Goodrich, " " " | 131 58 | $ 2,697 15 | |
| | J. H. Gilfillan, expense of cattle exhibit | $ 310 70 | | |
| | Wm. McTurk, " " " | 232 30 | | |
| | W. A. McHenry, " " " | 252 45 | | |
| | Geo. S. Redhead, " " " | 181 60 | 986 05 | |
| 3. | Iowa State Band | | $ 1,000 00 | |
| Oct. 7. | " " | 100 00 | | |
| 12. | " " | 250 00 | | |
| 17. | " " | 250 00 | 600 00 | |
| Sep. 3. | J. J. Magee, chloride lime | $ 45 | | |
| June 14. | Chicago Telephone Co., service from May 16 Sept. 1 | 56 00 | | |
| Sep. 30. | World's Col. Expo., labor | 3 75 | | |
| Nov. 7. | " " " bal. of bill for wiring and service of electric lights | 545 70 | | |
| June 20. | Andrews & Noel, decorating | 16 00 | | |
| Oct. 28. | J. H. Harvey, ribbon | 6 00 | | |
| 10. | Milward & Clark, making costumes (Chicago day) for Iowa parade | 60 00 | 687 90 | |
| | Pay roll Oct. 8-14 | | $ 132 46 | |
| | Oct. 15-21 | | 367 46 | |
| | Oct. 22-28 | | 367 46 | |
| | Oct. 29-Nov. 4 | | 383 47 | |
| | Nov. 5-11 | | 251 10 | |
| | Nov. 13-20 | | 167 93 | |
| Oct. 23. | C. T. Rush, premium on photo exhibit | 50 00 | | |
| | Wm. H. Morhiser, " | 30 00 | | |
| | A. Grossheim, " | 20 00 | | |
| July 21. | Orry H. Salts, expense | 21 13 | | |
| Oct. 7. | Iowa Ptg. Co., letter heads | 11 00 | | |
| Sep. 4. | " " envelopes | 10 20 | | |
| 11. | Jarnagin & McKee, printing minutes | 38 10 | | |
| 23. | The Hampden Co, hotel expenses of governor's party—Iowa days | 354 00 | | |
| 23. | A. B. Davis, team to haul Gatling gun | 8 00 | | |
| | S B Packard, expense account Iowa days | 4 20 | | |
| 24. | Milward & Clark, decorating, Iowa days | 225 00 | | |
| Oct. 11. | Associated Express Co | 4 00 | | |
| Sep. 20. | Boone Mill and Elevator Co., corn meal | 44 | | |
| Oct. 7. | Regan Printing House, printing | 3 50 | | |
| 28. | Jarnagin & McKee, " | 31 15 | | |
| 25. | C. R. Schraps, serving corn dinner | 91 00 | | |
| 28. | C. L. Garrilson, butter | 7 00 | | |
| Mch. 2. | W. U. Telegraph Co | 35 | | |
| 28. | J. H. Buhlman, freight prepaid on exhibit | 95 | | |
| 27. | W. S. Porter, " " " | 2 38 | | |
| Apr. 18. | M. W. Moir, " " " | 75 | | |
| Mch. 23. | Muscatine P. Brick Co., " | 1 00 | | |
| | McGregor Imp. Co., " | 3 60 | | |
| | Muscatine Terra Cotta L. Co. " | 4 10 | | |
| | Frank H. Sowden, signs and express | 7 25 | | |
| 17. | Am. Express Co | 65 | | |
| 15. | " " | 1 25 | | |
| 16. | " " 11 pkgs | 7 10 | | |
| Sep. 14. | Standard Express Co., drayage | 7 00 | | |
| 27. | Globe Savings Bank, exchange | 2 25 | | |
| 30. | E. H. Exelby, removing garbage, Sept. 16-30 | 7 50 | | |
| Oct. 16. | " " " Oct. 1-16 | 9 00 | | |
| 30. | Jos. Falundrey & Sons, saw dust | 5 75 | | |
| 31. | Atlas Laundry Co., Oct. 7-28 | 15 49 | | |
| 27. | C. H. Rice, screw driver and tacks | 50 | | |
| 25. | W. U. Telegraph Co | 50 | | |
| | A. Allen, car fare | 4 25 | | |
| 31. | F. N. Chase, Sec'y, per diem, Oct | $ 155 00 | | |
| | R. R. fare | 7 35 | 162 35 | |
| | postage | $ 31 00 | | |
| | telegrams | 3 33 | 34 33 | |
| Nov. 1. | C. W. Heafford, supt. storage of cases | $ 9 77 | $ 1,200 09 | |

## REPORT OF AUDITING COMMITTEE

|  |  | | | |
|---|---|---|---|---|
| Mch. 30. | Sawyer, Goodman & Co., lumber | $ 119 24 | | |
| " | " " " " | 63 63—$ | 182 87 | |
| Nov. 4. | Chas. Stadler, photographs | | $ 100 00 | |
| | Pay roll, Nov. 20-25 | | 92 15 | |
| | " Nov. 26-Dec. 2 | | 66 75 | |
| Dec. 12. | Jarnagin & McKee, cut of educational exhibit, express, etc. | 14 40 | | |
| 14. | J. W. Jarnagin, postage, telegrams, etc | 20 48 $ | 34 88 | |
| 15. | Chas. Ashton, telegrams and postage | | $ 1 30 | |
| Nov. 17 | B., C. R. & N. R. R | $ 4 13 | | |
| Oct. 21. | Northern Pacific Express Co | 50 | | |
| Nov. 17. | Adams Express Co | 5 60 | | |
| | " | 75 | | |
| 15. | " " | 2 65 | | |
| | " " | 50 | | |
| 23. | " " | 2 00 | | |
| 21. | " " | 1 30 | | |
| 11. | " " | 90 | | |
| 25. | Am. " " | 25 | | |
| 16. | " " | 1 90 | | |
| 14. | " " | 4 35 | | |
| 21. | " " | 3 00 | | |
| 9. | " " | 1 00 | | |
| 13. | " " | 80 | | |
| | Associated Express Co | 1 15 | | |
| 20. | " " | 4 40 | | |
| 7. | " " | 5 15 | | |
| 10 | " " | 5 10 | | |
| | " " | 114 15 | | |
| 3 | Backus Mfg. Co., freight | 3 20 | | |
| Nov. 25. | G. D. Gammon, drayage | 38 00 | | |
| 17. | " | 15 00 | | |
| 9 | Col. Transfer and Teaming Co., drayage | 1 00 | | |
| 8. | Jas. Henderson, drayage | 5 00 | | |
| 23. | W. B. Ketcham, return expense on exhibit | 23 70 | | |
| 6. | John Hayes, drayage | 1 50 | | |
| 18. | Sam'l Hull, " | 17 50 | | |
| 25. | " " | 8 75 | | |
| 9. | Jas. Henderson, drayage | 1 00 | | |
| 23. | H. S. Blanchard, services | 2 05 | | |
| 10. | Register Press Clipping Bureau, Iowa clippings | 5 00 | | |
| Oct. 9. | Parker Bros., team | 6 00 | | |
| Nov. 20. | Col. C. L. Root, expense of troops, Iowa Days | 60 00 | | |
| 10. | Chas. Stadler, photographs | 35 00 | | |
| Sept. 29. | F. N. Chase, Sec'y., admissions Iowa Days | 7 50 | | |
| Oct. 25. | Iowa State Agl. Society, loan of flags | 10 00 | | |
| 10. | Milward & Clark, decorating, Chicago Days | 15 00 | | |
| 7. | General Geo. Greene, expense Iowa Days | 14 50 | | |
| | Fred'k H. Little, " " | 17 81 | | |
| | J. T. Davidson, " " | 18 45 | | |
| | Thos. F. Cooke, " " | 14 03 | | |
| | H. H. Canfield, " " | 12 70 | | |
| | J. S. Wylie, " " | 2 50 | | |
| | T. S. Wand, " " | 11 90 | | |
| | J. M. Alexander, " " | 25 50 | | |
| | Patrick Brennan, " " | 19 90 | | |
| | B. H. O'Meara, " " | 5 50 | | |
| | J. W. Breckler, " " | 17 75 | | |
| | F. C. Goedecke, " " | 8 42 | | |
| Dec. 4. | H. F. Barndt, coal | 7 00 | | |
| Nov. 29. | C. H. Rice, nails, oil, etc | 4 10 | | |
| 15. | Chicago Telephone Co., service, Sept. 1-Nov. 15 | 39 63 | | |
| 24. | E. Baggot, plumbing | 4 50 | | |
| 25. | B. F. Chase Co., labor and express paid | 6 70 | | |
| Dec. 2. | E. H. Downing, laundry | 1 57 | | |
| Nov. 30. | F. N. Chase, Sec'y., per diem, Nov | $ 150 00 | | |
| | R. R. fare | 42 55—$ | 192 55—$ | 846 48 |
| Oct. 2. | Republican Printing Co., Columbian Visitors Register | | $ 75 00 | |
| Dec. 15. | A. F. Collman, Supt., ½ expense of Horticultural Exhibit | | 1,009 20 | |
| Nov. 21. | G. F. Ferris, charging phonograph battery | $ 00 50 | | |
| Oct. 13. | S. D. Childs & Co., paper and dusters | 2 25 | | |
| 14. | " " letter files | 1 25 | | |
| 18. | " " twine and glue | 95 | | |
| 20. | " " paper | 1 75 | | |
| 30. | " " ink | 1 20 | | |
| 21. | Jacobs, Coles & Co., stationery | 5 50 | | |
| Nov. 27. | Geo. S. Mornin, ink | 1 00 | | |
| 21. | Snyder & Hurd, printing | 1 75 | | |
| Oct. 23. | Jos. Spies, grapes | 1 00 | | |

| | | | |
|---|---|---|---|
| 23. | Barnard, Edwards & Co., grapes | 1 60 | |
| | H. P. Stanley & Co., apples | 4 00 | |
| 24. | L. M. Brown, pails | 50 | |
| Nov. 2. | Wendell & Co., 2 medals | 20 00 | |
| June 20. | F. N. Chase, Sec'y., p'd Treasurer of American and Foreign Agl. Exhibitors Association for Iowa membership | 10 00 | |
| Dec. 7. | A. J. W. Copelin, photographs | 5 00 | |
| Oct. 30. | Kincerbocker Ice Co., ice, Oct. 2-30 | 14 55 | |
| | " " ice, Sept. 2-30 | 18 30 | |
| 31. | Hyde Park Gas Co., gas, Sept. 30-Oct. 31 | 37 92 | |
| Nov. 20. | " " gas, Oct. 31-Nov. 20 | 4 56 | |
| | Geo. E. Watson & Co., paper | 2 40 | |
| 18. | E. H. Downing, laundry | 1 23 | |
| 10. | " | 91 | |
| 18. | Mrs. W. M. Stephens, expense | 1 75 | |
| 11. | L. M. Brown, twine | 60 | |
| Oct. 28. | Backus & Sisley, oil | 2 50 | |
| Nov. 16. | " " | 50 | |
| | C. H. Rice, twine and nails | 1 35 | |
| 1. | " hardware | 2 15 | |
| 6. | " hammers | 1 00 | |
| 10. | " nails and twine | 3 20 | |
| 9. | " nails | 50 | |
| 6. | S. B. Humbert, P. M., stamps | 22 00 | |
| Nov. 4. | H. F. Barndt, coal | 7 00 | |
| 23. | " " | 7 00 | |
| Oct. 31. | World's Col. Expo., removing garbage | 50 | |
| Nov. 2. | " " " " | 16 40 | |
| 8. | Wausau Excelsior Co., excelsior | 2 00 | |
| 13. | " " " twine and excelsior | 2 30 | |
| 1. | " " " boxes, barrels and excelsior | 9 40 | |
| 20. | Peter Wallin, packing furniture | 19 00 | |
| 16. | John R. Mitchell, excelsior | 5 00 | |
| Oct. 31. | W. S. Loomis, services | 91 90 | |
| Nov. 20. | Mattie Bowell, box for exhibit | 1 50 | |
| Oct. 1. | F. N. Chase, sign | 75 00 | |
| 6. | E. Baggot, oil heaters | 26 00 | |
| Sept.23. | " plumbing | 12 50 | |
| Nov. 29. | Adams Express Co | 5 07 | |
| Dec. 7. | Am. Express Co | 40 | |
| | " " | 8 55 | |
| | " " | 1 25 | |
| | " " | 1 10 | |
| Apr. 19. | Rand & Leopold Desk Co., freight paid | 15 43 | |
| Nov. 28. | B., C. R. & N. R. R | 2 56 | |
| 16. | C., R. I. & P. R. R | 1 50 | |
| 24. | " " | 1 56 | |
| 25. | " " | 1 21 | |
| | C., B. & Q. R. R | 1 60 | |
| 28. | St. Louis, K. & Western R. R. | 1 00 | |
| 25. | Ill. Cent. R. R. | 45 | |
| | " " | 4 65 | |
| Apr. 29. | " " | 5 85 | |
| Dec. 1. | F. N. Chase, Sec'y., telegrams | 7 53 | |
| | W. S. Loomis, services | 124 00 | |
| | C. H. Rice, hardware | 75—$ | 633 66 |
| 14. | J. F. Duncombe, per diem, Oct., 3 days | $ 15 00 | |
| | " per diem, Dec., 3 days | 15 00 | |
| | S. H. Mallory, attendance at Iowa Bldg., Aug., 2 days $ 10 00 | | |
| | Sept., 21 days 105 00 | | |
| | Oct., 31 days 155 00 | | |
| | Nov., 17 days 85 00 | | |
| | per diem, Dec., 2 days 10 00 | | |
| | R. R. fare 2 01—$ | 367 01 | |
| | A. C. Roberts, per diem, Dec., 4 days $ 20 00 | | |
| | R. R. fare 11 76—$ | 31 76 | |
| | Chas. Ashton, Com. work, Aug., 19 days $ 95 00 | | |
| | per diem, Nov., 1 day 5 00 | | |
| | " Dec., 3 days 15 00 | | |
| | R. R. fare 3 60—$ | 23 60 | |
| | J. W. Jarnagin, attendance at Iowa Bldg., Oct., 2 days $ 10 00 | | |
| | Nov., 13 days 65 00 | | |
| | per diem, Dec., 5 days 25 00 | | |
| | R. R. fare 45 36—$ | 145 36 | |
| | S. B. Packard, per diem and Com. work, Dec., 5 days $ 25 00 | | |
| | R. R. fare 4 50—$ | 29 50 | |

REPORT OF AUDITING COMMITTEE                                    415

|  |  |  |  |  |
|---|---|---|---|---|
|  | Jas. O. Crosby, per diem, Dec., 6 days | $ 30 00 |  |  |
|  | R. R. fare | 8 55 — $ | 38 55 |  |
| 20. | S. B. Packard, Com. work, Dec., 12 days | 60 00 |  |  |
|  | "    Jan., 12 days | 60 00 |  |  |
|  | R. R. fare | 18 00 — $ | 138 00 |  |
| Feb. 7, 1894. | E. A. Higley & Co. balance room rent | | $ | 2 00 |
| Jan. 4, 1894. | B. P. Holst, supplies | $ 15 50 | | |
| June 1, '93. | Ira C. Kling, services | 25 00 — $ | 40 50 |
| Dec. 20, '93. | L. G. Clute, services, Oct 16 to Dec. 12 | $ 150 00 | | |
|  | paid Ill. Cent. R. R. freight | 4 08 | | |
|  | "    "    " | 2 88 | | |
|  | " drayage and expense | 90 — $ | 157 96 |
| Dec. 11, '93. | C. L. Gabrilson, services, Nov | $ 86 68 | | |
|  | postage | 2 00 — $ | 88 68 |
| Dec. 26, '93. | E. Kretchmer, services | $ 6 00 | | |
|  | paid for honey | 18 87 | | |
|  | paid drayage and postage | 1 54 | | |
|  | paid C., B. & Q. R. R. | 3 00 | | |
|  | paid Adams Express Co. | 3 25 — $ | 32 66 $ | 279 30 |
| Mch. 24. | H. K. Ashton, services | $ 7 50 | | |
| Apr. 10. | J. C. Ashton, " | 37 25 | | |
| May 6. | Mrs. S. B. Maxwell. services | 15 00 | | |
| 29. | Rand, McNally & Co. 20,000 maps | 250 00 | | |
| June | Mrs. Hortense Crosby, services | 25 00 | | |
| July 1. | Emory Miller, | 10 00 | | |
| June 8. | Geo. H. Benedict & Co., 1 view | 25 00 | | |
| July 19. | Geo. W. Melville, engraving | 52 00 | | |
|  | "    "    " | 37 00 | | |
|  | "    "    " | 26 00 | | |
|  | "    "    " | 15 00 | | |
|  | "    "    " | 36 00 | | |
| 28. | "    "    " | 13 00 | | |
| Aug. 23. | Am. Express Co. | 1 40 | | |
| Sep. 4. | Chi., Gt. Western R. R. | 5 00 | | |
|  | Standard Express Co., drayage | 7 50 | | |
| 21. | S. D. Childs & Co., envelopes | 37 50 | | |
| 19. | Ill. Central R. R. | 3 20 | | |
| 20. | "    " | 11 66 | | |
| 28. | Standard Express Co., drayage | 5 50 | | |
|  | J. A. Sexton, P. M, stamps | 18 00 | | |
| 30. | H. S. Towle, P. M., " | 12 00 | | |
| Oct 3. | J. A. Sexton, P. M., " | 18 00 | | |
| 11. | "    "    " | 24 00 | | |
| 30. | "    "    " | 12 00 | | |
| 31. | Rand, McNally & Co., 5,000 maps | 62 50 | | |
| 25. | C. T. Peick, photographs | 6 50 | | |
| Nov. 13. | Dubuque Telegraph, account hand books | 1,925 00 | | |
| 1894. |  | | | |
| Jan. 9. | "    "    " | 100 00 | | |
| Feb. 1. | Chas. Ashton, postage and express | 18 95 — $ | 2,547 46 |
|  | Dubuque Telegraph Co., bal. account | | $ | 433 24 |
| Dec. 14, 1893. | Iowa State Band, bal. account | | | 2,000 00 |
|  | John Wilson, expense poultry dept | 4 25 | | |
|  | G. W. Stout, "    " | 3 50 | | |
|  | E. H. Strohmeier, "    " | 1 85 | | |
|  | W. H. Garland, "    " | 1 25 — $ | 10 85 |
| Nov. 14. | W. W. Wyant, postage | $ 3 02 | | |
| Dec. 1. | C. L. Gabrilson, R. R. fare and postage | 29 28 — $ | 32 30 |
| Feb. 1, 1894. | A. B. Holbert, expense horse dept | | $ | 42 63 |
|  | W. S. Niles,    " cattle " | $ 106 93 | | |
|  | Richardson Bros.. "    "    " | 217 50 — $ | 324 43 |
|  | John M. Sterr,   dairy test award | $ 50 00 | | |
|  | Wm. Miller, "    "    " | 100 00 | | |
|  | D. L. Heinsheimer, "    "    " | 250 00 | | |
|  | Dan'l Sheehan & Son, "    "    " | 300 00 | | |
|  | Richardson Bros., "    "    " | 600 00 — $ | 1,300 00 |
| Feb. 8. | D. W. Lotspeach, apples | | $ | 3 00 |
|  | R. W. Carson, fruit | | | 4 75 |
|  | Iowa State Horticultural Society | | | 626 02 |
|  | A. F. Collman, expense | | | 14 80 |

| | | | |
|---|---|---|---|
| Jan. 16, | A. J. W. Copelin, photographs............................... | | 18 60 |
| Feb. 7. | A. B Holbert, agt., expense horse dept ...................... | | 121 44 |
| 5. | Jarnagin & McKee, 300 lists of awards ..................$ | 1 00 | |
| | printing minutes.......................... | 37 10—$ | 38 10 |

| | | | |
|---|---|---|---|
| Feb. 25, 1893. | Mrs. J. D. Ainsworth, expenses........................ | $ | 30 00 |
| June 1. | Ora E. Miller, expenses........................... | | 331 15 |
| Jan. 29, 1894. | Albert Allen, services............................. | | 60 00 |
| Oct. 26, 1893. | Josselyn & Taylor Co., bal. of account . ............... | | 218 30 |
| Dec. 13. | A. G. Colpoys, services. ........................... | | 10 00 |
| | Pay roll, Dec. 10-16 ........................... | | 50 25 |
| | Dec. 17-31 ..................... | | 51 00 |
| | Jan. 1-7, 1894 ..................... | | 17 50 |
| | Dec. 3-9 ..................... | | 53 95 |
| Dec. 15, 1893. | Eunice E. G. Allen, water color ...................$ | 28 00 | |
| Jan. 2, 1894. | S. B. Humbert, P. M., postage..................... | 21 00 | |
| June 9, 1893. | Backus & Sisley, mdse ........................... | 1 75 | |
| Dec. 28. | C. Jevne & Co., mdse............................ | 12 90 | |
| Nov. 2. | Atlas Laundry Co ............................... | 2 11 | |
| Dec. 16. | Carter & Hussey, paper and pencils..................... | 2 70 | |
| 26. | J. C. Preston, rubber stamps...................... | 70 | |
| Nov. 21, 1892. | Wilson & Chase, thread ........................... | 25 | |
| Dec. 23, 1893. | W. L. Scott, services ........................... | 2 75 | |
| | H. M. Robers, services ........................... | 2 75 | |
| Nov. 1. | C. H. Rice, chimneys............................ | 20 | |
| Dec. 5. | " nails............................. | 1 80 | |
| 28. | Sam'l R. Hull, drayage ........................... | 2 00 | |
| | A. Allen, postage and R. R, fare ..................... | 1 20 | |
| | " R. R. fare....................... | 1 25 | |
| Jan. 1, 1894. | W. L. Robinson Coal Co., coal...................... | 3 75 | |
| Dec. 19, 1893. | " " " ...................... | 3 75 | |
| 22. | E. H. Downing, laundry... ........................ | 60 | |
| 16. | " " ........................ | 84 | |
| 22. | S. R. Hull, drayage ........................... | 75 | |
| 8. | G. D. Gammon, " ........................... | 4 00 | |
| 11. | " " ........................... | 2 50 | |
| 19. | U. S. Express Co.... ............................ | 55 | |
| 28. | White Line Transfer Co., drayage ..................... | 14 25 | |
| 8. | Thos. Collins, agt., terminal chgs..................... | 13 29 | |
| | " " " ..................... | 7 86 | |
| 21. | Chi. Gt. Western R. R ........................... | 27 02 | |
| 8. | Thos. Collins, agt., terminal chgs...................... | 12 00 | |
| 11. | C. R. I. & P. R. R............................. | 25 | |
| 1. | Chi., Mil. & St. Paul R. R......................... | 12 63 | |
| 27. | Adams Express Co............................ | 65 | |
| | Are. " " .......................... | 1 30 | |
| | " " " .......................... | 60 | |
| | " " " .......................... | 1 00 | |
| 8 & 11. | " " " .......................... | 42 40 | |
| Apr. 26. | Chi., Mil. & St Paul R. R......................... | 93 | |
| Dec. 31. | W. S. Loomis, services and expense... .................... | 166 20 | |
| | F. N. Chase, Sec'y, telegrams and R. R. fare ............ | 14 11 | |
| | per diem, Dec ..................$ 130 00 | | |
| | R. R. fare.................. 76 08—$ | 206 08—$ | 618 87 |

| | | | |
|---|---|---|---|
| Meb. 17, 1893. | B., C. R & N. R. R., car Cedar Falls to Chicago.......$ | 40 00 | |
| Apr. 7. | Balt. & O. R, R............................. | 75 | |
| 27. | World's Col. Expo., terminal chgs ..................... | 50 | |
| May 13. | " " " ..................... | 1 15 | |
| Sep. 9. | Adolph Witteman, express paid ..... .................. | 2 25 | |
| Jan. 2, 1894. | U. S. Express Co............................ | 30 | |
| 6. | " " ............................ | 30 | |
| 8. | " " ............................ | 12 10 | |
| 4. | S. R. Hull, drayage ..... ........................ | 75 | |
| 22. | Am. Express Co. ............................ | 1 00 | |
| 6. | C., R. I. & P. R. R............................. | 5 85 | |
| 10. | White Line Transfer Co., drayage ..................... | 3 25 | |
| Feb. 1. | " " " ..................... | 2 25 | |
| Jan. 12. | Thos. W. Mears, freight and drayage. ..................... | 8 60 | |
| 1. | Rukgaber & Crane, clock........................... | 1 25 | |
| 17. | C. J. Holman & Bro., exhibits broken ..................... | 7 50 | |
| 25. | W. B. Conkey Co., catalogues ........................ | 38 40 | |
| 30. | L. B. Abdill, picture frames ........................ | 35 39 | |
| 24. | Wendell & Co., gold medal ......................... | 55 00 | |
| 5. | W. U. Telegraph Co .... .......................... | 50 | |
| 6. | Carter & Hussey, book and pens ..................... | 35 | |
| 13. | Florence Albright, services ........................ | 118 50 | |
| Feb. 3. | " " " ........................ | 52 50 | |
| Jan. 24. | S. B. Humbert, P. M., postage......................... | 17 00 | |
| 25. | W. L. Robinson Coal Co., coal ...................... | 3 50 | |

# REPORT OF AUDITING COMMITTEE 417

|  |  |  |  |  |
|---|---|---|---|---|
| 28. | Joe T. Knapp, services | | 52 50 | |
| 31. | W. S. Loomis, " | | 160 00 | |
|  | F. N. Chase, Sec'y, express and telegrams | | 4 29 | |
| Feb. 1. | "    "   per diem, Jan | $ 135 00 | | |
|  |          R. R. fare | 33 80—$ | 168 80—$ | 791 53 |
| Feb. 8. | Chas. Ashton, com. work, Dec., 4 days | $ | 20 00 | |
|  |          Jan., 2 days | | 10 00 | |
|  |          Feb., 3 days | | 15 00 | |
|  |          per diem, Feb., 4 days | | 20 00 | |
|  |          R. R. fare | | 21 10—$ | 86 10 |
|  | S. B. Packard, com. work, Jan., 15 days | $ | 75 00 | |
|  |          Feb., 3 days | | 15 00 | |
|  |          per diem, Feb., 4 days | | 20 00 | |
|  |          R. R. fare | | 22 00 $ | 132 00 |
|  | A. C. Roberts, per diem, Feb., 4 days | $ | 20 00 | |
|  |          R. R. fare | | 13 21 $ | 33 21 |
|  | Henry Stivers, com. work, 2 days | $ | 10 00 | |
|  |          per diem, Feb., 2 days | | 10 00 | |
|  |          Dec., 2 days | | 10 00—$ | 30 00 |
|  | J. W. Jarnagin, per diem, Feb., 4 days | $ | 20 00 | |
|  |          R. R. fare | | 4 56 $ | 24 56 |
|  | H. W. Seaman, per diem, Feb., 5 days | $ | 25 00 | |
|  |          R. R. fare | | 17 50—$ | 42 50 |
|  | W. H. Dent, per diem, Feb., 1 day | | $ | 5 00 |
|  | Jas. O. Crosby, com. work, Dec., 2 days | $ | 10 00 | |
|  |          per diem, Feb., 5 days | | 25 00 | |
|  |          R. R. fare | | 5 10—$ | 40 10 |
|  | Chas. Ashton, com. work, June, 8 days | $ | 40 00 | |
|  |          Aug. 6 days | | 30 00 | |
|  |          Sept., 9 days | | 40 00 | |
|  |          R. R. fare | | 14 80—$ | 124 80 |
|  | Wm. H. Dent, per diem, Feb., 1 day | | $ | 5 00 |
| Sep. 29, 1892. | T. R. Rosier Co., fire extinguishers | | | 96 00 |
| Feb. 19, 1894. | Rand & Leopold Desk Co., desk | $ | 30 00 | |
| Feb. 10. | Am. Express Co | | 25 | |
| 13. | Adams    "    " | | 30 | |
| 28. | Am.    "    "    5 pkgs | | 2 74 | |
| 20, | F. Furst, honey, Apr. 1893 | | 8 00 | |
| 15. | John Anderson, coal | | 3 50 | |
| 28. | S. B. Humbert, P. M., stamps | | 11 56 | |
| 10. | Chas. Ashton, telegrams | | 1 10 | |
| 24. | 43d Street Laundry | | 1 03 | |
| 15. | Carter & Hussey, typewriter ribbons | | 1 00 | |
| 20, |     "       "    letter book | | 1 50 | |
| 16. | Joe T. Knapp, services | | 35 00 | |
| Mch. 3. |     "       " | | 52 50 | |
| Feb. 28. | Florence Albright, " | | 61 25 | |
| Mch. 1. | W. S. Loomis,    " | | 150 00 | |
| Feb. 28. | F. N. Chase, Sec'y, per diem, Feb | $ 120 00 | | |
|  |          R. R. fare and telegrams | 31 63—$ | 151 63—$ | 511 36 |
| Mch. 27. | S. B. Packard, com. work, Feb., 17 days | $ | 85 00 | |
|  |          Mch., 15 days | | 75 00 | |
|  |          R. R. fare | | 27 50—$ | 187 50 |
| Mch. 10. | Iowa State Register, advertisement | $ | 85 | |
|  | Des Moines Leader,     " | | 1 95 | |
| 8. | Chicago Tribune,       " | | 4 80 | |
| 24. |    "         "          " | | 4 00 | |
| 19. |    "    Record,         " | | 2 40 | |
| 8. |    "    Herald,         " | | 3 00 | |
| 19. |    "         "          " | | 3 40 | |
|  | Iowa State Register     " | | 7 20 | |
|  | Dubuque Herald,        " | | 5 00 | |
| 22. | Council Bluffs Nonpareil " | | 1 90 | |
| 19. | Burlington Hawkeye     " | | 4 44 | |
| 14. | Lansing M. and Smelting Co., ret. frt. | | 1 95 | |
| 9. | Chas. Barnard, ret. frt | | 2 54 | |
| 4. | Am. Express Co. | | 1 25 | |
| 7. | U. S.      " | | 35 | |
| Feb. 12. |    "      " | | 35 | |
| Mch 12. | Adams    " | | 25 | |

|  |  |  |  |  |
|---|---|---|---|---|
| 13. | White Line Transfer Co., storage and drayage | | 5 50 | |

1893.
|  |  |  |  |  |
|---|---|---|---|---|
| July 12. | World's Col. Expo., hauling | | 1 00 | |
| Apr. 10. | " " | | 16 05 | |
| Sept. 1. | " " water bill, Aug. 9-13 | | 10 84 | |
| Aug. 31. | " " water meter and bill to Aug. 9 | | 39 77 | |
| Oct. 4. | " " water bill Aug. 31 to Oct. 3 | | 32 64 | |

1894.
|  |  |  |  |  |
|---|---|---|---|---|
| Mch. 19. | Carter & Hussey, book | | 20 | |
| Apr. 2. | " " paper | | 1 05 | |
| Mch. 23. | S. B. Humbert, P. M., postage | | 6 00 | |
| 15. | Mrs. D. J. Thayer, stenographer | | 10 00 | |
| | E. Waller, labor | | 1 75 | |
| 28. | T. D. Hastie, services | | 2 00 | |
| 31. | Joe T. Knapp, " | | 71 00 | |
| | W. S. Loomis, " | | 150 50 | |
| | F. N. Chase, Sec'y., per diem, March | $ 135 00 | | |
| | telegrams and R. R. fare | 62 26—$ | 217 26—$ | 611 19 |

1893.
|  |  |  |  |
|---|---|---|---|
| Apr. 22. | Iowa State Band | $ | 100 00 |
| 25. | " " | | 100 00 |
| May 2. | " " | | 100 00 |
| 4. | " " | | 250 00 |
| 8. | " " | | 100 00 |
| 9. | " " | | 100 00 |
| 12. | " " | | 100 00 |
| 15. | " " | | 200 00 |
| 19. | " " | | 200 00 |
| 24. | " " | | 200 00 |
| 26. | " " | | 200 00 |
| June 5. | " " | | 600 00 |
| 12. | " " | | 400 00 |
| 19. | " " | | 400 00 |
| 26. | " " | | 200 00 |
| July 3. | " " | | 200 00 |
| 8. | " " | | 100 00 |
| 10. | " " | | 200 00 |
| 14. | " " | | 500 00 |
| 21. | " " | | 200 00 |
| 22. | " " | | 200 00 |
| Aug. 1. | " " | | 400 00 |
| 5. | " " | | 400 00 |
| 14. | " " | | 600 00 |
| 16. | " " | | 500 00 |
| 25. | " " | | 500 00 |
| 29. | " " | | 50 00 |
| Sept. 1. | " " | | 450 00 |
| 2. | " " | | 100 00 |
| 9. | " " | | 200 00 |
| 11. | " " | | 500 00 |
| 16. | " " | | 200 00 |
| 18. | " " | | 300 00 |
| 23. | " " | | 100 00 |
| 26. | " " | | 100 00 |
| Sept.27. | " " | | 250 00 |
| Oct. 24. | " " | | 150 00 |
| 12. | " " | | 250 00 |
| Nov. 4. | " " | | 250 00 |
| 10. | " " | | 750 00 |
| Mch. 31. | Chandler & Co., rent of room for Band | | 300 00 |
| June 12. | " " " " | | 300 00 |
| July 10. | " " " " | | 300 00 |
| Aug. 16. | " " " " | | 300 00 |
| Sept. 9. | " " " " | | 300 00 |
| Oct. | " " " " | | 300 00—$ 12,500 00 |

$ 141,039 12

Total amount received .................. $148,045 30
" expended ........................... 141,039 12

Balance on hand April 1, 1894 ................. $ 7,006 18

*To the President and Members of the Iowa Columbian Commission:*

We herewith submit statement of Disbursements of this Commission since date of last report, April 1st, 1894, (showing balance on hand of $7,006.18, after payment of Warrant No. 429,) as follows:

1893.
Oct. 1. American Express Co., express ....................... $ 00 70

## REPORT OF AUDITING COMMITTEE

**1894.**

|  |  |  | |  | |
|---|---|---|---|---|---|
| Mch. 21. | C. E. John, carpenter | | 6 00 | | |
| 31. | Perkins Bros. Co., advertising | | 1 81 | | |
| Apr. 1. | Iowa Printing Co., stationery | | 11 50 | | |
| 1. | S. H. Hall, hauling | | 3 50 | | |
| 2. | A. L. Reid & Co., laundry | | 1 76 | | |
| 3. | C. H. Rice, hardware | | 50 | | |
| 7. | U. S. Express Co., expressage | | 35 | | |
| 7. | American Express Co., expressage | | 30 | | |
| 8. | W. U. Telegraph Co., telegraphing | | 2 21 | | |
| 9. | Des Moines Leader, advertising | | 10 15 | | |
| 13. | Carter & Hussey, paper | | 1 00 | | |
| 17. | Davenport Democrat, advertising | | 2 50 | | |
| 19. | Joe T. Knapp, watchman | | 35 00 | | |
| 21. | W. S. Loomis, clerk | | 124 25 | | |
| 27. | B., C, R. & N. R. R.; freight | | 16 35 | | |
| 28. | S. B. Humbert, P. M., postage | | 7 00 | | |
| May 1. | O. E. Pearson, photographing | | 6 00 | | |
| 1. | F. N. Chase, Sec'y., per diem, April | $ 125 00 | | | |
| 1. | "    "    "    disbursements | 75 98 | —$ 200 98 | | |
| | Warrant No. 430 | | | $ | 434 19 |
| Apr. 20. | American Express Co., expressage | $ | 75 | | |
| 20. | "    "    "    " | | 65 | | |
| May 3. | Joe McDonald, teaming | | 6 00 | | |
| 3 | C. B. & Q. R. R., freight | | 1 00 | | |
| 8. | E. Harrold, teaming | | 4 00 | | |
| 9. | Smith & Hughes, teaming and labor | | 39 10 | | |
| 17. | White Line Transfer Co., drayage | | 2 00 | | |
| 26. | L. Emma Jones, typewriting | | 2 75 | | |
| 31. | Helen Bevens, typewriting | | 1 50 | | |
| 31. | S. B. Humbert, P. M., postage | | 12 00 | | |
| | W. U. Telegraph Co., telegraphing | | 71 | | |
| | P. Johnson, refund | | 12 50 | | |
| | F. N. Chase, Sec'y., per diem, May | $ 110 00 | | | |
| | disbursements | 42 23 | —$ 152 23 | | |
| | Warrant No. 431 | | | $ | 235 19 |
| July 1. | C. W. Bronson, drayage | $ | 2 10 | | |
| | American Express Co., expressage | | 3 20 | | |
| | Mrs. Townsend, cleaning | | 2 25 | | |
| | Lillie A. Pearce, stenographer | | 7 50 | | |
| | Joe T. Knapp, watchman | | 65 00 | | |
| | S. B. Humbert, P. M., postage | | 8 00 | | |
| 2. | J. G. Wyeth, storage | | 8 00 | | |
| 23. | U. S. Express Co., expressage | | 4 30 | | |
| 31. | F. N. Chase Sec'y., per diem, June | $ 90 00 | | | |
| | disbursements | 14 51 | —$ 104 51 | | |
| | Warrant No. 432 | | | $ | 204 86 |
| July 19. | W. U. Telegraph Co., telegraphing | $ | 00 25 | | |
| Aug. 1. | S. B. Humbert, P. M., postage | | 6 00 | | |
| | F. N. Chase, Sec'y., per diem, July | $ 100 00 | | | |
| | disbursements | 18 56 | —$ 118 56 | | |
| | Warrant No. 441 | | | $ | 124 81 |
| May 21. | J. W. Jarnagin, printing minutes | | | | |
| | Warrant No. 442 | | | $ | 11 90 |
| May 21. | Central Union Telephone Co., telephoning | $ | 00 40 | | |
| Sept. 1. | S. B. Humbert, P. M., postage | | 5 00 | | |
| | F. N. Chase, Sec'y., per diem, Aug | $ 65 00 | | | |
| | disbursements | 13 30 | —$ 78 30 | | |
| | Warrant No. 445 | | | $ | 83 20 |
| May 30. | W. S. Loomis, clerk | $ | 7 50 | | |
| June 9. | American Express Co., express | | 1 65 | | |
| 30. | Mrs. L. P. Barnum, Dubuque exhibit | | 11 70 | | |
| | J. K. P. Thompson, freight | | 2 45 | | |
| Sept. 15. | Snyder & Hurd, advertising | | 1 40 | | |
| 29. | U. S. Express, expressage | | 3 90 | | |
| Oct. 1. | Denia Severin, stenographer | | 22 50 | | |
| | S. B. Humbert, P. M., postage | | 5 00 | | |
| | F. N. Chase, Sec'y., per diem, Sept. | $ 80 00 | | | |
| | disbursements | 6 40 | —$ 86 40 | | |
| 4. | C. L. Dahlberg & Co., typewriting | | 12 00 | | |
| | White Line Trans. Co., storage | | 5 00 | | |
| | Warrant No. 446 | | | $ | 159 50 |
| Oct. 4. | C. W. Norton, Live Stock Dept | | | | |
| | Warrant No. 440 | | | | 61 75 |

|  |  |  |  |  |
|---|---|---|---|---|
|  | Peter Mouw, terminal charges |  |  | $ |
|  | Warrant No. 438 |  |  | 5 50 |
|  | Wm. Roberts & Sons, terminal charges |  |  |  |
|  | Warrant No. 439 |  |  | 5 00 |
| July 20. | Age Publishing Co., Clinton, adv. postoffice fixtures | $ 2 20 |  |  |
| June 8. | C. G. W. Ry. Co., freight | 80 |  |  |
| Nov. 1. | S. B. Humbert, P. M., postage stamps | 11 00 |  |  |
| Oct 16. | Adams Express Co., expressage | 1 15 |  |  |
| 15. | American " " " | 1 25 |  |  |
| 5. | Chas. Ashton, U. S. Exp. freight, exp | 85 |  |  |
| 30. | F. N. Chase, Sec'y., per diem, Oct | $ 85 00 |  |  |
|  | disbursements | 14 35 —$ 59 35 |  |  |
|  | Warrant No. 453 to F. N. Chase |  | $ | 116 60 |

1894.
| Nov. 26. | W. U. Telegraph Co., tel. to Chicago | $ 56 |
| Dec. 31. | Miss Denia Severin, stenographic work | 19 50 |
| Nov. 30. | F. N. Chase, per diem, Nov | $ 70 00 |
|  | disbursements | 23 22 — 93 22 |
| Oct. 17. | Am. Express Co., expressage | 1 65 |
| 18. | " " " | 70 |
|  | U. S. " " " | 75 |
| 17. | " " " | 1 85 |
| Nov. 30. | S. B. Humbert, P. M., postage stamps | 5 00 |
|  | Bryant-Neely Lumber Co., half ton coal | 4 50 |
| Dec. 31. | F. N. Chase, per diem, Dec | $ 40 00 |
|  | disbursements | 6 96 —$ 46 96 |

Warrant No. 455 to F. N. Chase ...... $ 174 69

1895.
| Jan. 25. | C. G. W. R. R. Co., frgt | $ 85 |
| 4. | S. B. Humbert, P. M., postage stamps | 7 00 |
| Apr. 3. | U. S. Express Co., expressage | 2 10 |
| Mch. 16. | " " " | 50 |
| 7. | H. H. Markley, P. M., postage stamps | 4 00 |
| Apr. 6. | F. N. Chase, per diem, Jan., Feb. & Mch | $ 70 00 |
|  | disbursements | 12 80 —$ 82 80 |

Warrant No. 456 to F. N. Chase... $ 97 25

1894.
Nov. 15. Anna M. Cooper, sten., typewriting and com. rep. ...... $ 10 00

1895.
Apr. 6. Warrant No. 458 to Anna M. Cooper ...... $ 10 00
9. A. H. Treat, on settlement claim for frgt. and terminal charges mineral exhibit ...... $ 25 00

Warrant No. 459 ...... $ 25 00
| 10. | H. H. Markley, P. M., postage | $ 2 00 |
| 15. | Wm. L. Veatch, photograph | 1 25 |
| May 13. | H. H. Markley, P. M., postage | 4 00 |
| June 7. | " " " | 2 00 |
| 29. | Denia Severin, stenographic work | 18 00 |
| Aug. 6. | H. H. Markley, P. M., postage | 4 00 |
| Apr. 10. | B. F. White & Son, stationery | 2 80 |
| Sep. 1. | Julia W. Pearce, recording minutes | 6 00 |
| Oct. 19. | A. J. Colpoys, type writing for Tr | 25 00 |
| 26. | H. H. Markley, P. M., postage | 2 00 |
| Nov. 7. | F. N. Chase, per diem, Apr., $15; May, 30; June, 25; July, 10; Aug., 20; Sept., 10; Oct., 10 | $ 150 00 |
|  | disbursements | 13 51 —$ 163 51 |

19. Warrant No. 464 to F. N. Chase ...... $ 230 56
15. J. W. Jarnagin, printing minutes ...... $ 13 30

25. Warrant No. 465 to J. W. Jarnagin ...... $ 13 30
19. S. H. Mallory—postage, $10; tel., $1 85 ...... $ 11 85

30. Warrant No. 466 to S. H. Mallory ...... $ 11 85

1894.
Oct. 5. F. N. Chase, Knapp bk loss ...... $ 354 17

Warrant No. 450 to F. N. Chase ...... $ 354 17
Miss Albright, stenographer ...... $ 15 00

Warrant No. 451 to her ...... $ 15 00
Nov. 1. State Treasurer, refund to state ...... 3,000 00
Warrant No. 452 to B. A. Beeson ...... $ 3,000 00

$ 5,374 32

REPORT OF AUDITING COMMITTEE                                      421

The following warrants were issued to Commissioners for per diem and R. R. fare after No. 429.

1894.
July 26.   No. 433, H. Stivers, 11 days and com. work .............. $    55 00
           434, S. B. Packard, 21 days and R. R. fare, $24 25......    129 25
Oct.  3.   435, J. F. Duncombe, 3 days ..............................    15 00
           436, H. W. Seaman, 5 days and R. R. fare, $17 50......      42 50
      4.   437,    "       "      4     "       "       "           37 50
           441, J. W. Jarnagin, 7    "    "    "    4 32 ......       39 32
           443, J. O. Crosby,    8   "    "    "   12 50......        17 50
      5.   447, A. C. Roberts,  10   "    "    "   14 70......        64 70
           448, S. B. Packard, per diem  "    "    ...........       125 25
           449, Chas. Ashton,        "    "    "   ...........        88 60
1895.
Apr.  6.   454, H. W. Seaman, 7 days  "    "    30 00 ......          65 00
           457, S B. Packard,  6   "    "    "   26 40......          56 40
July 26.   460, Chas. Ashton,  5   "   ..........................     25 00
Aug. 12.   461, J. O Crosby, appropriated for publishing report..  2,000 00
      26.  462, J. W. Jarnagin, com. work and R. R. fare..........    41 44
Nov. 18.   463, S. H. Mallory,    "    "    "    ...........         157 00
1896.
Feb. 19.   467 J. O. Crosby,      "    "    "    ...........         313 65 — $  3,303 11
                                                                           $  8,677 43

SUMMARY—RECEIPTS.

Appropriation by 22nd General Assembly ........................................$    5,000 00
        "         24th       "           "       ..............................   125,000 00
From Board of Lady Managers ..................................................       545 30
Concession for model of capitol ..............................................      5,000 00
Net salvage ..................................................................      2,576 54
Refund of cash on warrants to departments, unexpended ........................      4,248 81
Knapp & Co., bank assignee's dividends........................................         59 39
Increment in hands of Treasurer ..............................................             46
                                                                                $ 142,430 53
Total amount of 467 warrants..................................................   141,465 39

    Balance in Treasurer's hands .........................................$        965 14

There are some outstanding unpaid bills and expenses yet to be incurred in the distribution of the 5,000 printed copies of the Commission's report to the Governor. The above summary does not include the $12,500 appropriated by the executive council for the Iowa State Band, as that was disbursed by the executive committee and was not paid into the treasury of the commission.

Appropriations were made by the commission from time to time for the different departments, and warrants were drawn therefor on the requisition of the commissioner in charge for the sums so appropriated, and vouchers were returned by them as expenditures were made.

The first report of the auditing committee included the $12,500 appropriated by the executive council which had been expended and vouchers filed therefor. With that sum deducted the—

Total amount received by the treasurer was.................................... $ 135,545 30
Total warrants drawn and paid.................................................   132,787 96

    Leaving in treasury April 1, 1894 ......................................$      2,757 34
In hands of commissioners unexpended .........................................      4,248 84

    Total balance as per report .........................................$         7,006 18
Net salvage ..................................................................      2,576 54
Two dividends from assignee of Knapp & Co. bank ..............................         59 39
Increment in treasury.........................................................             46
                                                                                $   9,642 57
Amount of warrants—430-467 inclusive .........................................      8,677 43

    Balance in treasury ...................................................$         965 14

for which vouchers will be returned accompanied by a supplemental report.

ROSTER OF EMPLOYEES AT THE IOWA STATE BUILDING.

Mrs. F. N. Chase, hostess, Cedar Falls.
Albert Allen, superintendent, Dubuque.
Gen. Ed. Wright, Department of Information, Des Moines.
Henry Towle, postmaster, Clinton.
Miss Delia S. Hutchinson, registry clerk, Iowa City.
Miss Elizabeth Gardner, registry clerk, Clinton.
Mrs. Sara B. Maxwell, librarian, Des Moines.
Miss Blanche Maxwell, assistant librarian, Des Moines.
Master George Stivers, assistant Press Department, Burlington.
Miss Florence Albright, stenographer, Shell Rock.
Mrs. D. J. Thayer, commercial stenographer, Chariton.
J. T. Knapp, assistant, Cedar Falls.
J. C. Ashton, assistant, Guthrie Center.
Otto Hanson, assistant, Council Bluffs.
John Hyland, night-watch, Davenport.
Fred Branch, night-watch, Elkader.
Preston Erwin, janitor, Chariton.
W. J. Barnett, janitor, Muchakinock.
Henry Carter, assistant janitor, Chariton.
Louis Perkins, assistant janitor, Chariton.
Rebecca Brown, servant, Chicago.
Tillie Osten, servant, Chicago.
Anna Almason, servant, Chicago.
Ned B. Rehkopf, assistant in Iowa Building, Des Moines.
W. H. Patrich, bookkeeper, Des Moines.
W. S. Loomis, accountant, Red Oak.

### OTHER DEPARTMENTS.

C. L. Gabrilson, in charge of Dairy Department, New Hampton.
Ben S. Packard, Agricultural Department, Marshalltown.
L. S. Clute, Agricultural Department, Greeley.
E. Kretchmer, Apiary Department, Red Oak.
Wm. Duncombe, Mines and Mining, Ft. Dodge.
T. W. Mears, Mines and Mining, Centerville.

www.ingramcontent.com/pod-product-compliance
Lightning Source LLC
Chambersburg PA
CBHW022106290426
44112CB00008B/565